DATE DUE			

J. A. FABRICIUS.

From an engraving in Schröck's *Abbildungen berühmter Gelehrten*
(Leipzig, 1766), i pl. 30.

[*Frontispiece to Vol. III.*]

CAMBRIDGE UNIVERSITY PRESS WAREHOUSE
C. F. CLAY, Manager.
London: FETTER LANE, E.C.
Edinburgh: 100, PRINCES STREET.

Leipzig: F. A. BROCKHAUS.
Berlin: A. ASHER AND CO.
New York: G. P. PUTNAM'S SONS.
Bombay and Calcutta: MACMILLAN AND CO., Ltd.

A HISTORY

OF

CLASSICAL SCHOLARSHIP

A HISTORY

OF

CLASSICAL SCHOLARSHIP

VOL. III

THE EIGHTEENTH CENTURY IN GERMANY,
AND THE NINETEENTH CENTURY IN EUROPE
AND THE UNITED STATES OF AMERICA

BY

JOHN EDWIN SANDYS, Litt.D.,

FELLOW OF ST JOHN'S COLLEGE,
AND PUBLIC ORATOR IN THE UNIVERSITY OF CAMBRIDGE,
HON. LITT.D. DUBLIN

CAMBRIDGE
AT THE UNIVERSITY PRESS
1908

Die Bahn ist breit genug, um vielen Bewerbern um den Preis neben einander Raum zu geben; darum wollen wir nicht nur neidlos, sondern auch mit dankbarer Anerkennung den Leistungen unserer auswärtigen Mitkämpfer gerecht werden.

BURSIAN, *Cl. Philologie in Deutschland*, p. 1248, 1883.

Une renaissance des études classiques s'est manifestée chez nous. Elle se distingue par l'alliance des qualités françaises de clarté et de méthode avec la solidité de l'érudition et la connaissance des travaux étrangers.

S. REINACH, *Manuel de Philologie Classique*, i 13, 1883.

This century is the first since the revival of learning in which a serious challenge has been thrown down to the defenders of the humanistic tradition. But I think it will be found that the position of humanism in this country at the close of the century is much stronger than it was at the beginning.

JEBB, *Humanism in Education*, p. 30, Oxford, 1899.

European scholars...find that they have to count with a new factor and have to recognize in our philological work a national stamp.

GILDERSLEEVE, *Oscillations and Nutations of Philological Studies*, p. 11, Philadelphia, 1900.

CONTENTS.

CHRONOLOGICAL TABLES.

LIST OF ILLUSTRATIONS

continued from Vol. II p. xiv.

OUTLINE OF PRINCIPAL CONTENTS.

CORRIGENDA.

p. 143 l. 21; for Leignitz, read Liegnitz.

p. 167 l. 7; for poems of Theognis, read *Theogonia* of Hesiod.

p. 240 l. 30; Von Hartel has since died (1907); see *Addenda*, p. 479.

p. 265 l. 8; for 1794—1860 read 1802—1871.

p. 368 n. 2 l. 5; for Athanasios, read Anastasios.

Italy	France	Netherlands	England	Germany
	Montfaucon 1655—1741	Le Clerc 1657—1736	Bentley 1662—1742	Leibnitz 1646—1716
Ficoroni 1664—1747	Burette 1665—1747	P. Burman I 1668—1741	Maittaire 1668—1747	J. A. Fabricius 1668—1736
Muratori 1672—1750	Banduri 1671—1743	Küster 1670—1716	Wasse 1672—1738	
Maffei 1675—1755	C. Capperonnier 1671—1744	Bos 1670—1717	Ruddiman 1674—1757	
	Bouhier 1673—1746	Duker 1670—1752	S. Clarke 1675—1729	
	Sanadon 1676—1733		Davies 1679—1732	Hederich 1675—1748
Facciolati 1682—1769			Middleton 1683—1750	C. G. Schwarz 1675—1751
Forcellini 1688—1768	Olivetus 1682—1768	Havercamp 1684—1742	Pearce 1690—1774	Bergler 1680—1746
Gori 1691—1757	Pellerin 1684—1782	Drakenborch 1684—1748	Markland 1693—1776	Heinecke 1681—1741
Lami 1697—1770	Fréret 1688—1749	Hemsterhuys 1685—1766	Spence. Martyn 1699—1768	Heumann 1681—1794
Lagomarsini 1698—1773	Fourmont 1690—1745	Wesseling 1692—1764	J. Taylor 1704—1766	Heusinger 1690—1751
Corsini 1702—1765	De Caylus 1692—1765	J. F. Reitz 1695—1778	Heath 1704—1766	J. M. Gesner 1691—1761
Piranesi 1707—1778	Mariette 1694—1775	D'Orville 1696—1751	Dawes 1709—1766	Walch 1693—1775
Rezzonico 1709—1785	D'Anville 1697—1782	Oudendorp 1696—1761	Toup 1713—1785	Funck 1693—1777
Paciaudi 1710—1785	J. Capperonnier 1716—1775	J. Alberti 1698—1762	Stuart 1713—1788	Brucker 1696—1770
Foggini 1713—1783	Barthélemy 1716—1795	Abresch 1699—1782	R. Wood 1717—1771	Kortte 1698—1731
Mingarelli 1722—1793	Brotier 1723—1789	P. Burman II 1714—1778	Revett 1720—1804	Damm 1699—1778
Bandini 1726—1803	Larcher 1726—1812	Valckenaer 1715—1785	Tyrwhitt 1730—1786	J. F. Christ 1700—1756
Ignarra 1728—1808	Brunck* 1729—1803	Schrader 1722—1783	W. Hamilton 1730—1803	J. A. Ernesti 1707—1781
Lanzi 1732—1810	D'Agincourt 1730—1814	Ruhnken 1723—1798	Musgrave 1732—1780	Reiske 1716—1774
	Oberlin* 1735—1806	Pierson 1731—1759	Twining 1735—1804	Winckelmann 1717—1768
	Levesque 1736—1812	Koen 1736—1767	Horne Tooke 1736—1812	Lessing 1729—1781
Morcelli 1737—1821			Gibbon 1737—1794	Heyne 1729—1812
			Townley 1737—1805	F. W. Reiz 1733—1790
			R. Chandler 1738—1810	Rasche 1733—1805
Amaduzzi 1742—1792	Schweighäuser* 1742—1830		Adam 1741—1809	Wieland 1733—1813
Marini 1742—1815	J. A. Capperonnier 1745—1820		Mitford 1744—1827	Scheller 1735—1803
Garatoni 1743—1817	Sainte-Croix 1746—1806	Santen 1746—1798	W. Jones 1746—1794	Eckhel 1737—1798
Morelli 1745—1819		Luzac 1746—1807	Parr 1747—1825	Herder 1744—1803
E. Q. Visconti 1751—1818	Choiseul-Gouffier 1752—1817	Sluiter 1782—1815	Payne Knight 1750—1824	W. Heinse 1746—1803
Fea 1753—1836	Villoison 1753—1805	Wyttenbach 1746—1820	H. Homer 1753—1791	Schütz 1747—1832
	Gail 1755—1829		Wakefield 1756—1801	J. G. Schneider 1750—1822
	Millin 1759—1818		T. Burgess 1756—1837	
	Bast* 1771—1811		Porson 1759—1808	F. A. Wolf 1759—1824

* Alsace.

CHAPTER XXVI.

GERMANY IN THE EIGHTEENTH CENTURY.

(i) Fabricius, Gesner, Ernesti, Reiske.

In the year 1700 the earliest of German Academies was founded in Berlin. The intellectual originator of that Academy was the many-sided man of genius, Gottfried Wilhelm Leibnitz (1646—1716), whose scholarly tastes are represented by his Latin poems[1], by his speculations on the origin of language[2], and by his prompting the empress Catharine of Russia to collect the vocabularies of many nations[3]. At the age of eight, he had taught himself Latin with the aid of an illustrated edition of Livy and the *Opus Chronologicum* (1605) of Calvisius. Before he was twelve, he wrote Latin verses and had begun Greek. At Jena, in 1663, he attacked the imitators of the harsh and obscure Latinity of Lipsius[4], and published a treatise in which he proposed to prove the spuriousness of the ‘Epistles of Phalaris’ on the ground of their being written in the Attic dialect and in the style of Lucian[5]. In 1670 he wrote an essay on philosophic style as an introduction to an edition of the *Antibarbarus* of Nizolius[6]; and in Paris, three years later, during his correspondence with Huet on a proposed edition of Martianus Capella, he protested against the contempt for Plato and Aristotle

Leibnitz

---

[1] Roenickius, *Carmina Latina Selectiora* (1748), 3 f.

[2] Benfey, *Gesch. der Sprachwissenschaft*, 243 f; Haupt, *Opusc.* III i 215—222 (Bursian, i 358 n).

[3] Max Müller's *Lectures*, i 144 n. 28[5].

[4] Julian Schmidt, *Gesch. des geistigen Lebens in Deutschland von Leibnitz bis Lessings Tod* (1681—1781), i 101.

[5] Haupt, *Opusc.* III i 219.

[6] Sorley on Leibnitz, in *Enc. Brit.*; ii 146 n. 2 *supra*.

expressed by certain students of the natural sciences[1]. To the end of his life he could still recite long passages from Virgil.

A celebrated theologian of Augsburg, J. J. Brucker (1696—1770), author of the *Historia Critica Philosophiae*, was elected a member of the Berlin Academy in 1731, but, in the first half of the century, the interests of classical learning were far less promoted by the Academy than by masters of German schools, who studied the Classics in connexion with the general history of literature.

Foremost among these was Johann Albert Fabricius (1668—1736), a student in the university of his native town

J. A. Fabricius   of Leipzig, who, from 1699 to 1711, was successively an assistant-master and a head-master at Hamburg. He had already produced, in the three small volumes of his *Bibliotheca Latina*, a comprehensive biographical and bibliographical work on the Latin literature of the classical period (1697)[2]. He was still holding a scholastic appointment, when he began his far more extensive *Bibliotheca Graeca*, a work that, in the course of fourteen quarto volumes, traverses the whole range of Greek literature down to the fall of Constantinople (1705–28)[3]. It is founded, so far as possible, on a first-hand knowledge of every edition quoted, and it has supplied the basis for all subsequent histories of Greek Literature. The 350 quarto pages, assigned to Homer alone, include *indices* to all the authors cited in the *scholia* and in Eustathius. The earlier work on Latin literature was subsequently continued in the five volumes of the *Bibliotheca Latina mediae et infimae aetatis* (1734)[4], while the modern literature of Classical Antiquities was surveyed in the *Bibliotheca Antiquaria* (1713–6), and that of Numismatics in a new edition of Banduri's *Bibliotheca Nummaria* (1719). The varied learning and indomitable industry displayed in these four and twenty volumes may fairly entitle their author to be regarded as the modern Didymus. But the list of his published works is not yet

---

[1] Haupt, *l. c.*, 221 f; cp. Pattison, *Essays*, i 278.

[2] Finally revised ed. 1721; also in two vols. quarto, Venice, 1728 (better than Ernesti's ed. of 1773 f), and in six vols. Florence, 1858.

[3] Ed. Harless in 12 vols. 1790—1809 (incomplete); index, 1838.

[4] Suppl. by Schöttgen, 1746; also ed. Mansi, Padua, 1754.

exhausted. He edited Sextus Empiricus, the life of Proclus by Marinus, and the commentary of Chalcidius on Plato's *Timaeus*[1], while his valuable edition of Dion Cassius, including a full commentary, was completed after his death by his son-in-law and biographer, Reimar[2].

Fabricius counted among his correspondents the leading scholars of his age. He was assisted in the compilation of the *Bibliotheca Latina* by the Danish scholar, Christian Falster[3]; and, in that of the *Bibliotheca Graeca*, by Küster[4]. He was also largely aided in the latter by Stephan Bergler (*c.* 1680—*c.* 1746), who, by his knowledge of Greek, might have attained a place among the foremost scholars of his time, but was reduced to the level of a literary hack by an insatiable craving for drink. Early in the century he was a corrector of proofs at Leipzig; in 1705 he left for Amsterdam, where he produced *indices* to the edition of Pollux begun by Lederlin and continued by Hemsterhuys, and himself completed Lederlin's edition of Homer (1707). We next find him helping Fabricius at Hamburg and elsewhere. During his second stay at Leipzig, he produced an excellent edition of Alciphron (1715); his edition of Aristophanes was published after his death by the younger Burman (1760); his work on Herodotus is represented only by some critical notes in the edition of Jacob Gronovius (1715); while his Latin translation of Herodian was not published until 1789. His rendering of a modern Greek work on moral obligations[5] led to his being invited to undertake the tuition of the author's sons at Bucharest, a position for which his intemperate habits made him peculiarly unfit. However, he was thus enabled to send Fabricius a few notes on the Greek MSS in his patron's library. After this he disappears from view. On his patron's death in 1730, he is said to have left for Constantinople, and to have adopted the religion of Islam. If so, he probably ended his days in perfect sobriety[6].

Antiquarian and legal lore was the domain of Fabricius' contemporary, Christian Gottlieb Schwarz (1675—1751), who by his wide and varied learning raised the reputation of the university of Altdorf. A large part of that learning lies buried in a vast number of programs, and in the exegetical and critical notes to an edition of the *Panegyric* of the younger Pliny (1746)[7].

Bergler

Schwarz

---

[1] Printed with the ed. of Hippolytus.

[2] H. S. Reimar, *De Vita et Scriptis J. A. F. Commentarius*, Hamburg, 1737; Bursian i 360–2; for portrait see *Frontispiece* to this volume.

[3] Cp. chap. xxxviii *init.*

[4] ii 445 *supra.*

[5] Nic. Mavrokordatos, περὶ τῶν καθηκόντων, 1722.

[6] Cp. Burman's *Aristophanes*, i 2–14; Reimar, *De Vita Fabricii*, 169 f, 222 f; Saxe, *Onom.* vi 78—81; Bursian, i 362–4.

[7] Bursian, i 371 f.

The study of Roman Law is well represented by Johann Gottlieb Heinecke,
Heinecke *Heineccius* (1681—1741), professor at Halle, where he produced a celebrated *Syntagma*, which owes its abiding popularity
to its excellent Latin style[1]. His own treatise on style was more than once
reprinted[2].

An intelligent knowledge of the subject-matter of the Classics was promoted
Hederich by the lexicons of the Saxon schoolmaster, Benjamin Hederich
(1675—1748), and especially by his oft-reprinted Lexicon of
Mythology. His Latin and German Dictionary was long in use, and his Greek
and Latin Lexicon (1722) attained the honour of a new edition more than
a century later[3].

Among the numerous elementary editions of the Classics which appeared in
Walch this century, a place of honour is due to those produced in
1712–5 by Johann Georg Walch of Meiningen (1693—1775),
the well-known author of the *Historia Critica Latinae Linguae*[4]. In this work
he traces the history of the language from the earliest times to the Revival of
Learning, adding a survey of the principal works in each age[5]. The history of
Funck Latin was far more minutely treated by Johann Nicolaus Funck,
or *Funccius* (1693—1777), the author of a series of ten considerable treatises on the fortunes of the language, the titles of which are taken
from the successive stages of human life[6]. The last two remained unpublished.
Their place is inadequately taken by the work of Jacob Burckhard (1681—
1753) on the fortunes of the language in Germany (1713–21)[7].

Among scholars who were natives of Thuringia, mention may here be made
Heumann of Christoph August Heumann (1681—1764), for many years
a professor at Göttingen. Besides producing a considerable
amount of miscellaneous literature on classical subjects, he edited many of the
speeches of Cicero, and the 'Dialogue on the causes of the corruption of
eloquence', which he ascribed to Quintilian and not to Tacitus (1719)[8]. His
Heusinger countryman, Johann Michael Heusinger (1690—1751), who
ended his days as head of the *gymnasium* at Eisenach, is best
known as the editor of Cicero, *De Officiis*, posthumously published in 1783[9].
Latin usage was studied, and Latin MSS diligently collated, by Gottlieb Kortte,
Kortte *Cortius* (1698—1731), who in his short life distinguished himself as an able editor of Sallust (1724). His edition of the
Letters of the younger Pliny was completed and published by his pupil, Paul

---

[1] *Antiquitatum Romanorum jurisprudentiam illustrantium Syntagma
secundum ordinem institutionum Justiniani digestum* (1719); republished in
1841.

[2] Ed. Gesner, 1748, and Niclas, 1766. Cp. Bursian, i 372 f.

[3] Bursian, i 374.   [4] 1716; ed. 3, 1761.

[5] Bursian, i 377 f.

[6] *De origine, pueritia, adolescentia*, etc. *Latinae linguae* (1720–50).

[7] Bursian, i 380–2.   [8] Bursian, i 393–6.

[9] Bursian, i 396 f.

Daniel Longolius (1744), while his work on Lucan was first given to the world by K. F. Weber (1828)[1].

One of the greatest scholars in the eighteenth century was Johann Matthias Gesner (1691—1761), who, by his published works and by his influence as a teacher, did much towards raising the standard of classical studies in Northern and Central Germany. He was still a student at Jena, when he produced a striking treatise on the *Philopatris* ascribed to Lucian, as well as a work on Education giving proof of wide knowledge and remarkable maturity of judgement[2]. For the next twenty years he was a school-master at Weimar, Ansbach, and Leipzig, where the *Thomas-Schule* flourished under his sway. In 1734 he was called to the university of Göttingen, then in course of being founded by George II; and, for the remaining twenty-seven years of his life, he there remained as professor of Poetry and Oratory, as head of the classical and educational *Seminar*, as university librarian, as chief inspector of the schools of the Hanoverian kingdom, and as an active member of the Academy founded in 1751 as the second of the learned societies of Germany[3].

As a Greek scholar, he contributed an admirable Latin translation, and many excellent notes and emendations, to the great edition of Lucian, which bears the names of Hemsterhuys and Reitz (1743 f); and towards the end of his life he was engaged on an edition of the 'Orphic' poems (1764)[4]. As a head-master at Leipzig, he published a *Chrestomathia Graeca* (1731), which promoted the introduction of the best Greek Classics into the schools of Germany. In the province of Latin literature, he did similar service by his selections from Cicero and the elder Pliny, and by an important preface on the proper method of reading classical authors, originally prefixed to an edition of Livy (1735)[5]. In the same year he edited the *Scriptores Rei Rusticae*, which were soon followed by the *Institutio Oratoria* of Quintilian, and the *Letters*

J. M. Gesner

---

[1] Bursian, i 397 f.
[2] *Institutiones rei scholasticae*, 1715. Cp. Paulsen, ii 16[2] n.
[3] *Societas Regia Scientiarum Gottingensis.*
[4] Posthumously published at the above date.
[5] *Opuscula Minora*, vii 289 f.

and *Panegyric* of the younger Pliny, and ultimately by Horace, and
Claudian (1759). In the preface to the latter he candidly states
that his aim had been, not to make a display of learning, but
simply to explain his author; that he had frankly noticed anything he had failed to understand; and that, with a view to forming
the students' taste, he had drawn attention, not only to passages
that were beautiful and poetical, but also to those that were at
variance with nature and the best literary models. It will thus
be seen that Gesner anticipated Heyne in introducing the principles of taste into the interpretation of the Classics[1]. In all
these works the textual criticism is inadequate, but the explanatory
notes are models of their kind. All, except the Horace (founded
on Baxter's edition), are equipped with excellent *indices*. The
whole range of classical Latin literature is traversed in the four
folio volumes of his greatest work, the *Novus Linguae et Erudi-
tionis Romanae Thesaurus* (1749).

He had already produced, in 1726–35, his two revisions of the *Thesaurus*
of Faber (1571), the best edition of which appeared in the same year as his
own *Thesaurus*. Gesner's work, which was founded on Faber, and on the
recent London reprint of the *Thesaurus* of Robert Stephanus, was the result of
ten years of strenuous labour. We here find a marked improvement in the
correction of many errors; words and names unconnected with classical Latin
are removed; phraseology is treated more fully than before; and difficult
passages are explained. On the other hand, less is done for the writers of
prose than for the poets, and there is a certain unevenness in the execution,
while the historical developement of the use of individual words and phrases is
neglected. Nevertheless, it marks the most important advance in Latin
lexicography since the time of Stephanus[2].

While Gesner breaks new ground in many of his works, he
represents the traditions of the typical *Polyhistor* of the seventeenth century in the outlines of an encyclopaedia of philology,
history, and philosophy, which he produced as the syllabus of a
course of lectures given at the request of the authorities of the

[1] J. Schmidt, i 480.
[2] Cp. J. E. B. Mayor in *Journal of Cl. and Sacred Philology*, ii 279 (1855),
'By rejection of encyclopaedic articles and of barbarisms, by many insertions,
and particularly by interpretations of vexed passages, ⟨Gesner's *Thesaurus*⟩
did very much towards simplifying and enlarging the science: indeed for
fulness, neat arrangement, and exactness without pedantic minuteness of
explanation, it has strong claims to be regarded as the best that has appeared'.

university of Göttingen. These lectures, which consisted of observations on almost all the 1543 items of the syllabus, were afterwards published by one of his pupils[1].

Gesner was one of the foremost leaders of the movement known as the New Humanism. The Old Humanism had aimed at the verbal imitation of the style of the Latin Classics, and at the artificial prolongation of the modern life of the ancient Latin literature. This aim was gradually found to be impracticable, and, about 1650, it was abandoned. Latin was still taught in schools; it also survived as the medium of university instruction and as the language of the learned world. But the ancient literature came to be considered as a superfluity; neglected at school, it was regarded simply as a waste and barren field, where the learned might burrow in quest of the facts required for building up the fabric of an encyclopaedic erudition. Such was practically the view of the School of Halle.

The School of Göttingen, as represented by Gesner, found a new use for the old literature. The study of that literature was soon attended with a fresh interest. Thenceforth, in learning Greek (as well as Latin) the aim was not to imitate the style, but to assimilate the substance, to form the mind and to cultivate the taste, and to lead up to the production of a modern literature that was not to be a mere echo of a bygone age, but was to have a voice of its own whether in philosophy, or in learning, or in art and poetry. The age of Winckelmann, Lessing and Goethe, was approaching, and Gesner was its prophet and precursor[2].

Latin, in Gesner's view, should be learnt, not by committing to memory the rules of Grammar that make the language hateful to the learner, but, in the first place, by reading a Latin rendering of the New Testament. It was also to be learnt by practice. The master should converse with his pupils in Latin, ringing the changes on the shortest and simplest phrases ; and the pupil should be encouraged to speak Latin, even if he made mistakes at first. Gesner frankly records his earliest attempt, when, on meeting his master in the street after sunset, he gaily accosted him with the ungrammatical sentence : — *Domine praeceptor, precor te bona nox*[3]. At a later stage he recommends

---

[1] *Primae Lineae Isagoges in Eruditionem Universalem*, ed. J. N. Niclas, 1774.

[2] Cp. Paulsen (ed. 1896–7), ii 15, 21.

[3] *Isagoge* § 106 p. 111.

the cursory reading of large masses of the best Latin with a view to the appreciation of the Latin Classics as literature[1].

As a school-master at Leipzig, Gesner abolished the use of the old Latin *compendium*, and introduced the Latin Classics in its place, carrying his pupils in a few months through the whole of Terence, and insisting on the literary and educational value of the continuous study of a single author. For a quarter of a century, in his *Seminar* at Göttingen, he was constantly training a chosen band of the future preceptors of Germany, his aim being to produce intelligent teachers rather than erudite scholars. He set a high value on the study of Greek literature :—Latin itself (he held) could not be thoroughly understood without Greek. Boys at school (he added) should not be allowed to give up Greek. After learning the elements of the Grammar, they should go on to easy reading, such as Aesop, Lucian and the Greek Testament, and afterwards take up Homer. When he lectured on Homer (in and after 1739) he always had a good class[2].

The interest in Homer is a note of the New Humanism. Thus far the *Odyssey* and the *Iliad* had only once been rendered in German, in 1537 and 1610 respectively. But the middle of the eighteenth century was marked by two translations of the early books of the *Iliad*, followed in 1754 by the illustrated translation that was Goethe's first introduction to Homer. The text was edited by Ernesti in 1759–64. This was followed by five new translations, culminating in that completed by Voss in 1793, which was immediately succeeded by the edition of Wolf, with its memorable *Prolegomena* (1794–5), and by the edition of Heyne (1802 f)[3].

Gesner's life and works are well portrayed in Latin prose by Ernesti, his successor as the head of the school in Leipzig[4]. He assures us that the Cambridge scholar, Dr Askew, on coming to Leipzig, said of Gesner, whom he had just left at Göttingen, *talem virum nunquam vidi*[5]. The biographer also notices Gesner's learning and his social gifts, his refinement and courtesy, his services as an educational reformer, his disapproval of 'conjectures'

---

[1] Preface to Livy.

[2] *Isagoge* § 154, p. 171.

[3] Paulsen, ii 7² f.

[4] *Narratio…ad Ruhnkenium* in *Opuscula Oratoria*, 307—342, reprinted in *Biogr. acad. Gotting.* i 309 f.

[5] *Opusc. Or.* p. 308.

in his useful editions of the Greek and Latin Classics[1], his merits as a Latin lexicographer, his interest in Oriental and European languages[2], and his skill in literary portraiture.   He adds that the satirical touch was the only flaw in the excellent portrait of Gesner, which forms the frontispiece of the Latin *Thesaurus*[3].

In connexion with Gesner we may here notice some of the other lexicographers of the same century.   Christian Tobias Damm (1699—1778), the head of the oldest *gymnasium* of Berlin, besides producing a work on the elements of Greek and an annotated edition of the *Battle of the Frogs and Mice* (1732-5), made his mark, thirty years later, with his great lexicon to Homer and Pindar[4].   In the same year he translated into German the text of the Gospel according to St John, and, in the following year, was required, on theological grounds, to resign his head-mastership.   But he remained true to his two favourite Greek authors.   His prose translation of both was completed in 1771.   In his translation of Homer he unhappily endeavoured to represent the simplicity of a primitive age by constantly resorting to the language of the lower classes, but his renderings served to make both poets better known among the German people.   In his work in general he was prompted by a conviction that the Greek language and literature were superior to the Latin.   He held that the imitation of Greek models was necessary to raise the level of German culture, and, in the increasing interest in Greek literature, he saw the sign of a new Renaissance[5].   A very few years later, the 'imitation of Greek

Damm

[1] p. 331. *Conjecturas ingeniosas laudabat magis quam probabat ; et nihil magis quam dulces illas ingenii illecebras in judicando cavendum monebat.*

[2] p. 325, *nec ita admirabatur veteres, ut contemneret recentiores.*

[3] p. 341.   Other biographical notices by J. D. Michaelis in *Biogr. acad. Gotting.* i 245—276, and by Niclas, *ib.* iii 1—180, 287—496.   Cp. Gesner's *Epp.* (1768 f), Sauppe's *Vortrag* (1856) and 'Göttingen Professoren' in Göttingen *Abhandl.* (1872) p. 59 f; Julian Schmidt, i 475—481; and Eckstein's *Rede* (1869); Jahn, *Populäre Aufsätze*, 25; also Bursian, i 387—393, and Paulsen, ii 15—28[2].

[4] 1765; ed. 2, 1774.   The arrangement is etymological, all the words being placed under 300 roots.   Its contents were republished in alphabetical order by J. M. Duncan (1821), whose edition was improved by V. C. F. Rost (1831-3).

[5] 'Videor jam saeculum renascentis apud nos Graecitatis cernere animo:

models' in the world of Art was to be the theme of the earliest work of his most famous pupil, Winckelmann, who was an enthusiastic student of Homer. Winckelmann was under his tuition for a single year (1735–6), the year of the publication of the edition of the *Battle of the Frogs and Mice*, but the master's appreciation of Homer did not prevent the pupil from placing him in the class of pedants[1]. Damm appears in fact to have taken more interest in the vocabulary than in the poetry of Homer. That poetry was better appreciated by Moses Mendelssohn, who, with Friedrich Nicolai, resorted to him for instruction in the language that was now exciting a new interest in Germany. Nicolai complains that the master's delivery was monotonous, but adds that he had an admiration for exceptionally euphonious lines, and even smacked his lips over the finely sounding phrase πολυφλοίσβοιο θαλάσσης[2]. His interest was not confined to Greek literature. He produced an edition of Namatianus, translated the *Panegyric* of Pliny, with two of the Speeches and all the Letters of Cicero. His small hand-book of Greek and Roman Mythology long remained a standard work[3].

As a Latin lexicographer, Gesner had in the next generation a worthy successor in Immanuel Johann Gerhard

Scheller

Scheller (1735—1803), successively Rector of the school at Lübben, S.E. of Berlin, and of that at Brieg, S.E. of Breslau. His Latin-German Dictionary[4] was founded on an independent study of the authors, and on a careful and intelligent use of the best commentaries and lexicons. It was enlarged and improved in two later editions, and subsequently abridged by the lexicographer himself, who added a German-Latin Dictionary in 1792. He has been charged with borrowing from Forcellini (1771) without mentioning his name[5]. It is also alleged that

---

illustres viri, imo et foeminae, adamare incipiunt has literas et in pretio habere', Programm of 1752 (Justi's *Winckelmann*, i 34 n).

[1] 'praecep'ores ἀμούσους' (Justi, i 34).

[2] Justi, i 36.

[3] Bursian, i 385–7; cp. Justi's *Winckelmann*, i 30—36.

[4] *Ausführliches u. möglichst vollständiges lateinisch-deutsches Lexicon oder Wörterbuch zum Behufe der Erklärung der Alten u. Uebung in der lateinischen Sprache*, 2 vols. 1783; ed. 2, in 3 vols. 1788; ed. 3, in 5 vols. 1804–5.

[5] 'Censor Germanus', quoted in Furnaletto's ed. of Forcellini.

'if he studies a more scientific arrangement, if he displays considerable reading, and if he has not neglected new discoveries in criticism, his arrangement is still defective, his criticism is uncritical, and his reading mainly limited to Caesar, Cicero, and other classical authors'[1]. But his independence has been amply vindicated, and his appreciation of the importance of the authors of the Silver Age and his other merits have been fully set forth by Professor Mayor[2].

Scheller's counterpart among Greek Lexicographers is Johann Gottlob Schneider (1750—1822), who was born in Saxony, and died as professor and university libra- J. G. Schneider rian at Breslau.   His Greek lexicon[3] marked a great advance on the manuals of Schrevelius, Hederich and others, in fulness of material, and in critical skill and method.   It was also the first comprehensive and independent work that had appeared in this department since the lexicon of H. Stephanus (1572)[4].   Schneider did much in the way of collecting and explaining technical and scientific terms.   His knowledge of natural science, in combination with classical literature, is exemplified in his *Eclogae Physicae*, and in his editions of the zoological works of Aelian and Aristotle. He also edited the *Politics* and the second book of the *Oeconomics*, and the whole of Theophrastus, Nicander, and Oppian, as well as the *Scriptores Rei Rusticae*, and Vitruvius.

Gesner's efforts as an educational reformer were ably seconded by Johann August Ernesti (1707—1781).   Born in Thuringia and educated at Schulpforta[5], and at J. A. Ernesti

---

[1] Otto on *Lat. Lexicographie* in *Allg. Monatschrift*, Braunschweig, 1853, p. 990 ff.

[2] *Journal of Cl. and Sacred Philology*, ii 283—290 (1855).—Scheller also produced in two volumes the *Praecepta stili bene Latini* (1779), a longer and a shorter Latin Grammar (1779 f and 1780 f), an Introduction to the exposition of the Latin Classics and to the proper imitation of Cicero (1770), with Observations on Cicero and the first six books of Livy (1785).   Cp. Bursian, i 507–9.

[3] *Kritisches griechisches Wörterbuch*, in two vols. 1797 f; ed. 2, 1805–6; ed. 3, 1819; *Suppl.* 1821; abridged by F. W. Riemer, 1802–4.

[4] It has supplied the basis for the lexicons of Passow (1819–24 etc.), and Passow's for that of Rost and Palm (1841–57) and that of Liddell and Scott (1843 etc.).

[5] Far in advance of his fellow-pupils in a knowledge of Greek, he was

Wittenberg and Leipzig, he lived at the last of those seats of
learning for half a century.   He was for three years the colleague,
and, for a quarter of a century, the successor of Gesner as head of
the great local school.   For the last seventeen of those years he
was also professor of Eloquence in the university, and, on resigning both of those positions, in 1759, became professor of Theology
for the last twenty-two years of his life.   His reputation as a
scholar depends mainly on the edition of the whole of Cicero,
completed in six volumes in 1739, and supplemented in its third

already reading to himself in class the last book of Herodian, while the master
was slowly expounding the first.   Cp. *Opuscula Oratoria*, 311 f.

J. A. ERNESTI.

*Vir clarisſimus, ſæculi huius Cicero, qui et docendo et ſcribendo rebus
diuinis humanisque plurimum luminis attulit.*

From an engraving by J. Elias Haid (Augsburg, 1776) of a portrait
by Anton Graff.

edition by historical introductions and critical notes (1777). The most permanently valuable part of the original work is the *Clavis Ciceroniana*[1], an excellent dictionary of Cicero's vocabulary and phraseology, together with a conspectus of the Roman laws mentioned in the orator's pages. The explanatory and critical notes are kept within reasonable limits, and the choice between conflicting readings is generally determined by a fine taste for Ciceronian usage. But the standard of Cicero's style was injudiciously applied in his editions of Suetonius (1748) and Tacitus (1752). He was still a school-master, when he edited the *Memorabilia* of Xenophon and the *Clouds* of Aristophanes. On resigning that position he produced an edition of Homer (1759–64), founded on that of Samuel Clarke; he also edited Callimachus (1761), and (in 1764) re-edited Casaubon's *Polybius*. The orations and dissertations collected in his *Opuscula*[2], as well as the prefaces to his Latin texts, are written in an excellent style, and the same is true of the small encyclopaedic text-book of Mathematics, Philosophy and Rhetoric, the *Initia Doctrinae Solidioris*.

Superficial as a writer, but intelligent as an expositor, Ernesti has long been over-rated. Even his explanatory notes are meagre. What the Dutch commentators had carried to the excess of an inordinate prolixity, he carried to the opposite extreme. His pious horror of conjectural criticism did not prevent him, as an editor of Cicero, from accepting his own guesses, while he rejected the emendations proposed by his predecessors. But he deserves the credit of having contributed much towards the wider diffusion of classical education in Germany[3].

Of the three other scholars, who bear the same name, the best known is his favourite nephew, Johann Christian Gottlieb Ernesti (1756—1802), who was professor of Eloquence in Leipzig for the twenty years that succeeded his uncle's death, and produced, among other works, a ' technological lexicon' to

---

[1] Ed. Rein, 1831.

[2] *Opuscula Oratoria* (1762) and *Opuscula Philologica* (1764), both published at Leyden; also a *Novum Volumen* of the former (1791), and *Opusc. Varii Argumenti* (1794), both published at Leipzig.

[3] Urlichs, 105[2]. Cp. Bursian, i 400—404. Ernesti's opinions on classical education may be studied in his rectorial speeches (in the *Opuscula Varii Arg.*), especially those of 1736 and 1738, and also in his official scheme for the schools of Saxony, 1773 (ably analysed by Paulsen, ii 29—32[2]).

Greek and Latin rhetoric (1795–7). An elder nephew, August Wilhelm (1733—1801), the son of an elder brother, edited Livy in 1769 etc. For other pupils of Ernesti the briefest mention must suffice. Among these are Johann Tobias Krebs (1718–82), Rector of Grimma, and editor of Hesiod (1746); J. F. Fischer (1726–99), who, for the last thirty-two years of his life, was one of Ernesti's successors as head-master in Leipzig, and, besides producing several volumes of Animadversions on Weller's 'Greek Grammar', edited Anacreon and Palaephatus, and many dialogues of Plato, while he published no less than fourteen dissertations on the *Cratylus*; and lastly, K. L. Bauer (1730–90), who completed Gottleber's edition of Thucydides and produced a German-Latin Dictionary. All of them have been characterised as 'learned and industrious and dull scholars'[1]. Besides these there was C. A. Klotz (1738–71), professor in Göttingen and Halle, best known for his controversies with Burman and Lessing[2], and S. F. N. Morus (1736–92), professor in Leipzig, and editor of Isocrates' *Panegyricus*, 'Longinus', and Xenophon's *Cyropaedeia*, *Anabasis* and *Hellenica*. A pupil of Morus, C. D. Beck (1757—1832), joined him in an extensive edition of Musgrave's *Euripides* (1778–88), to which he contributed an excellent *Index Verborum*. His numerous editions include a diffuse Commentary on Demosthenes, *De Pace* (1799). He also wrote *De Philologia Saeculi Ptolemaeorum* (1818), and reviewed the progress of philological and historical studies during the fifty years ending in 1829[3].

When Gesner died at Göttingen in 1761, his vacant Chair was offered first to Ernesti, who, twenty-seven years before, had succeeded Gesner as a head-master in Leipzig. Ernesti declined the offer and suggested the name of Ruhnken, who, eighteen years previously, had been advised by Ernesti to learn Greek, not at Göttingen under Gesner, but at Leyden under Hemsterhuys. Ruhnken also declined, and suggested Ernesti's former pupil, Heyne, whose distinguished career at Göttingen will be noticed in the sequel[4]. Ernesti appears to have deliberately ignored the claims of Reiske, who had been living for the last fifteen years in Leipzig and had already given proof of being among the foremost Greek scholars of the day.

Johann Jacob Reiske (1716—1774), who had been well grounded in Latin at Halle, entered the university of Leipzig in 1732. He attended no lectures whatsoever; indeed, on Greek, there were none to attend. He worked

Reiske

---

[1] Urlichs, 105[2].

[2] Harless, *Vitae Philol.* i 168—211; p. 28 f *infra*.

[3] Cp. Bursian, i 417—426.

[4] p. 36 *infra*.

by himself at a few Greek authors, but found Demosthenes and
Theocritus too difficult at that stage of his reading.   He also
studied Arabic until 1738, when, notwithstanding his poverty, he
left for Leyden to attend the lectures of Schultens, whom he
ultimately surpassed in his knowledge of the language[1].   At
Leyden he supported himself by helping D'Orville in his edition
of Chariton, and by correcting the proofs of Alberti's *Hesychius*[2].
Under the stress of want, he was driven to the study of medicine
and took the degree of M.D. in 1746, though he never practised.
Shortly after his return to Germany, he settled once more in
Leipzig, supporting himself for twelve years by hack-work, while
Ernesti and other influential persons, who had it in their power
to help him, looked with suspicion on his frankness and independence of character[3].   Ernesti even warned visitors to Leipzig
'not to call on that strange man'[4].   It is fair, however, to remember, that, in Reiske's darkest days, it was Ernesti who invited
him daily to dinner[5].   Notwithstanding all his difficulties, he
never lost courage, his eager enthusiasm in the cause of scholarship never abated.   In 1748 he attained the barren honour
of being appointed 'extraordinary professor of Arabic' at an
almost nominal stipend, and even this was irregularly paid.   But,
early in 1756, his knowledge of the language led to his being
invited to Dresden to catalogue the Arabic coins in the Elector's
cabinet.   During the six months that he thus spent amid many
hardships, the keeper of the cabinet brought him a gem engraved
with minute characters, which no one had been able to decipher.
Reiske solved the riddle and was permitted to take the gem to
Leipzig, where he wrote and printed a description for the owner,
the Graf von Wackerbart, who at once presented Reiske with
100 thalers and, two years later, at a critical point of Reiske's
career, when he was a candidate for the office of Rector of the
Nicolai-Schule in Leipzig, intervened in his favour, secured him
the appointment, and placed the poverty-stricken scholar in a
position of dignity and emolument for the remaining sixteen years
of his life (1758)[6].   He thus obtained some of the leisure needed

---

[1] On Reiske's Arabic scholarship cp. *Enc. Brit.*
[2] *Lebensbeschreibung*, 22, 37 f.
[3] *ib.* 67.   [4] *ib.* 147.   [5] *ib.* 77.   [6] *ib.* 74—79.

for the completion of a number of important editions of Greek authors. In 1764 he married a lady of high spirit and noble temper, who, for her husband's sake, learnt Greek and Latin, pledged her jewels to enable him to pay for the printing of his Demosthenes[1], helped him in the collation of MSS[2], and completed and published the works that he left unfinished at his death.

The earliest proof of Reiske's profound knowledge of Greek was his *editio princeps* of the work of Constantine Porphyrogenitus on

[1] *Lebensbeschreibung*, 94 note.   [2] *ib.* 93.

REISKE.

From the portrait by J. D. Philippin geb. Sysangin, frontispiece to
Oratores Graeci (1770).

the customs of the Byzantine court (1751–4). His edition of three
books of the Palatine Anthology contains much that is valuable in
the departments of criticism, exegesis and literary history (1754).
He had meanwhile printed at his own expense his 'Animadversions' on Sophocles, Euripides and Aristophanes, including some
excellent emendations (1753–4). In the five volumes of his
further 'Animadversions' on Greek authors (1757–66), he proposed many corrections in the texts of the *Characters* of Theophrastus, Diodorus, Dion Chrysostom and Dion Cassius, as
well as the *Moralia* of Plutarch, with Thucydides, Herodotus,
Aristides, Polybius, Libanius, Artemidorus, and Callimachus.
He set a high value on this work[1]. As a school-master, he
devoted some years to the study of Cicero. He edited the
Tusculan Disputations with notes and various readings on the
first two books, but he soon abandoned Cicero for Demosthenes
and the other Greek Orators. The first-fruits of his study appeared
in the form of a vigorous German translation of the Speeches of
Demosthenes and Aeschines, with explanatory notes (1764). He
began this translation on the day on which the Prussians evacuated
Leipzig (15 Feb. 1763)[2]. His edition of the Orators involved ten
years of arduous labour. For the text of Demosthenes he used a
MS from Munich, and four from Augsburg; for that of Aeschines,
a MS from Helmstadt, obtained with the aid of Lessing; while
Askew, whom he had met at Leyden in 1746, sent him materials
collected by John Taylor[3]. His work on the Orators extended to
eight volumes (1770–3), followed by the 'Apparatus Criticus' and
'Indices' to Demosthenes, in four. The last three of these were
edited by his widow.

Before translating Demosthenes, he had prepared a rendering
of all the Speeches of Thucydides, but had generously kept it
back for a year, in the interest of a translation of the whole of
Thucydides produced in 1760 by his friend, the Göttingen professor, J. D. Heilmann (1727–64). At the request of a publisher,
he subsequently completed, in the short space of three months,
a hasty edition of Theocritus, which includes many acute sugges-

---

[1] *ib.* 70, 'Sie sind *flos ingenii mei*, wenn man anders meinem *ingenio* nicht
omnem florem abspricht'.

[2] *ib.* 87.   [3] Cp. Nichols, *Lit. Anecd.* iv 664.

tions for the improvement of the text (1765–6). Shortly before
his death he revised the text of Maximus Tyrius. He lived to
see the publication of the first two of the six volumes of his
Dionysius of Halicarnassus, and the first of the twelve of his
Plutarch. His important edition of Libanius was published by
his widow, who also produced his Dion Chrysostom.

The story of his life is unfolded in the pathetic pages of his autobiography.
He there tells us of all his weary struggles and his days of deep depression,
and also of his gratitude to those who had at last enabled him to obtain the
leisure needed for his further labours. He says of himself:—

God has given me gifts, not the best (perhaps), and yet, not the worst; He
has also endued me with the impulse and desire to use them for His glory and
for the common good...Doubtless I might have done much more, if the age in
which I lived had been more favourably disposed towards my line of study,
and if I had received more help and encouragement from my contemporaries;
yet I have done more than a thousand others would have done in my position.
Having made good use of my 'one talent', I can meet my Lord with a cheerful
courage, to render an account of my stewardship.

His devoted wife adds to the autobiography a brief sketch of his character,
dwelling on his transparent honesty, his enthusiasm in the cause of learning,
and his generosity even to those who had served him ill. Only those who
could not (or would not) know him, called him a misanthrope. Apart from
his wide reading in Greek and Latin and Arabic, he was familiar with the best
poets of Germany, France, Italy, and England, and among his favourite works
were the Sermons of Tillotson and Barrow[1].

In the latter part of Reiske's life, and for some years after his
death, a professorship of Greek and Latin was held at Leipzig
from 1768 to 1782 by Morus[2], one of the best of the pupils of
Ernesti. Morus was succeeded by Friedrich Wolfgang
   Reiz   Reiz (1733—1790). His eminence as a teacher is
attested by his famous pupil, Hermann[3]. He concentrated his

---

[1] pp. 146–9. The volume includes the letters he received from Abresch,
Askew, Gesner, Heilmann, Klotz, D'Orville, Reimar, and Wesseling, and
one from Winckelmann. Cp. Morus, *De vita Reiskii*, 1777; S. G. Eck, in
Frotscher's *Narrationes* (1826), i 3—77; Wyttenbach, *Bibl. Crit.* iii (1) 34, and
Opusc. i 413 f; *Mnemosyne*, i 57 and viii 297—351; Mommsen, *Inscr. Confoed.
Helv.* (1854) p. xii; Haupt, *Opusc.* iii 137 f; Jahn, *Populäre Aufsätze*, 26;
L. Müller, *Kl. Philol. in den Niederlanden*, 76 n.; Bursian, i 407—416; and
Förster in *A. D. B.*; *Briefe*, ed. Förster, 1897; Kämmel, *Neue Jahrb.* 1908,
200 f.   [2] p. 14 *supra*.

[3] *Opusc.* viii 453 f. He is also highly praised by F. A. Wolf, *Kl. Schr.*
ii 1155.

powers on the thorough exploration of the limited field of grammar, metre, and textual criticism.   His works include a treatise on the Greek and Latin moods and tenses (1786), and on accentuation (1791).   In the province of metre he was the first to introduce into Germany the opinions of Bentley, whom he was in the habit of describing as 'the most perfect pattern of a critic'.   These opinions he set forth in a brief treatise[1], and applied in an edition of the *Rudens*[2].   Specially interested in Aristotle, he anonymously contributed to the criticism of the *Rhetoric* and the seventh and eighth books of the *Politics*, besides publishing a text of the treatise on Poetry (1786).   He also edited the first four books of Herodotus.   Finally, he prepared a full description of De France's cabinet of antiques at Vienna, and a series of lectures on Roman Antiquities, published after his death.   His greatest glory lies in the fact that he was the preceptor of Hermann and that he was highly praised by Wolf[3].

[1] 'Burmannum de Bentleii doctrina metrorum Terentianorum judicare non potuisse' (1787).

[2] Described by a reviewer as 'the beginning of the true criticism of Plautus'.

[3] Bursian, i 419—422.

CHAPTER XXVII.

GERMANY IN THE EIGHTEENTH CENTURY.

(ii) WINCKELMANN, LESSING, HERDER, HEYNE, ECKHEL.

IN the eighteenth century the study of Classical Archaeology received an important impulse from the teaching of Johann Friedrich Christ (1700—1756). Born of a good family in Coburg, he was a man of many accomplishments as an artist, a linguist, and a poet; he studied law at Jena, and professed history and poetry at Leipzig (1734). As a specialist in Latin literature, he was a constant student of Plautus, knew Horace by heart, had a high admiration for Juvenal, read Tacitus through once a year, and keenly appreciated and frequently imitated Aulus Gellius. By travelling in Italy he became an expert in ancient and modern art ; and he gathered round him a large library and a considerable collection of engravings, coins, and gems. In a memorable course of lectures he urged his audience to become familiar, not only with the literature, the inscriptions, and the coins of the ancients, but also with their architecture and sculpture, their gems and their vases. These lectures, which were published long afterwards, mark the beginning of archaeological teaching in Germany[1]. In studying the monuments of antiquity from the artistic and aesthetic, and not merely from the antiquarian, point of view, he resembled his French contemporary, the Count de Caylus, while, in his appreciation of the distinctive style of Greek sculpture, he was a precursor of Winckel-

J. F. Christ

---

[1] Ed. Zeune, *Abhandlungen über die Litteratur und Kunstwerke, vornehmlich des Alterthums*, 1776.

mann.   He made a special study of gems, publishing a catalogue
of the Richter collection at Leipzig, and a revised Latin version
of the descriptive letter-press to the first 2000 casts in Lippert's
Dactyliotheca, a work subsequently completed by Heyne.   His
varied interests are attested in the thirty-two papers on Roman
law and antiquities, on textual criticism, and on the history of
literature and of scholarship, collected in his *Noctes Academicae*
(1727–9).   He also dealt with the monograms of artists, the *vasa
myrrhina* of the ancients, and the various representations of the
Muses.   In support of his fantastic opinion that the fables of
Phaedrus were composed by the Italian humanist, Perotti[1], he
himself translated two books of Aesop into Latin verse.   On his
death in 1756 a Latin oration in his memory was delivered by
Ernesti[2], who, with the aid of manuscript copies of his predecessor's lectures, continued the tradition of his teaching.   But
the abiding influence of the original lectures themselves is better
exemplified by the fact that it was from this source that Lessing
and Heyne derived their earliest interest in ancient art[3].

While an interest in the artistic side of ancient life had been
thus awakened by J. F. Christ, the permanent
recognition of its importance was due to the genius **Winckelmann**
of Johann Joachim Winckelmann (1717—1768).   The son of a
cobbler at Stendal (about sixty miles W. of Berlin), he succeeded
in learning Latin at the local school, and in acquiring a certain
knowledge of books in his master's library, while the prehistoric
tombs in the neighbourhood awakened his interest in ancient
monuments, and led to his even dreaming of a pilgrimage to the
Pyramids.   In 1735 he went to Berlin, to spend a year in learning
Greek under Damm, who was undoubtedly familiar with the
vocabulary of Homer[4].   Three years later he left Stendal to

---

[1] ii 71 *supra*.   [2] *Opusc. Orat.*, 171—182.

[3] Cp. Justi's *Winckelmann*, i 374—381; Stark, 159 f; Dörffel, *J. F. Christ,
sein Leben u. seine Schriften* (1878); and Bursian, i 404-6.—The year of his
death was also that of the death of the pupil of Christ and Ernesti, Johann
August Bach (1721–56), who vindicated the character of the Eleusinian Mysteries (1745), discussed the legislation of Trajan, edited the *Oeconomicus* of Xenophon (1747) and wrote an oft-reprinted history of Roman Jurisprudence (1754).
Cp. Bursian i 406 f.

[4] p. 10 *supra*.

complete his schooling at a place still further west, Salzwedel. In the same year Fabricius died, and, two years afterwards, when his books were to be sold by auction in Hamburg, the young student walked all the way, a distance of more than eighty miles, simply to purchase a few copies of the Greek and Latin Classics[1]. He soon entered the university of Halle, where he attended the lectures of J. H. Schulze, a collector of coins, who discoursed on Greek and Roman antiquities[2], and of A. G. Baumgarten, who, a few years later, was the first to apply the term 'Aesthetics' to the science of the beautiful[3]. He continued his studies at Jena, where, with a view to the medical profession, he worked at comparative anatomy. His early interest in miscellaneous learning was, however, soon afterwards merged in a keen admiration for Greek literature, and, during five years of hardship as a school-master at Seehausen, N. of his native place, he devoted the greater part of his nights to the study of Homer and Sophocles, and Herodotus, Xenophon, and Plato[4]. The six years that he subsequently spent in the library of the Count von Bünau, near Dresden, enlarged his interest in history and politics, and in the literature of France, England, and Italy (1748–54). At that time the finest collection of works of sculpture and painting in all Germany was to be found in Dresden; and it soon became clear to Winckelmann that the study of art was henceforth to be the main purpose of his life. It was also clear that he could not continue that study, to any serious purpose, without living in Italy, and, as the only means for carrying out this design, he finally resolved on joining the Church of Rome[5]. But it was not until a year later that the grant of an annual pension from the Elector of Saxony enabled him to start for the South. He employed the interval in studying gems and other examples of ancient art, and in composing his earliest work, 'Thoughts on the Imitation of Greek works in Painting and Sculpture' (1755). In words that soon became memorable he here describes Greek art as characterised by 'a noble simplicity and a calm grandeur'[6]. The first two years of his residence in

---

[1] Justi, i 42. [2] ib. i 54–6. [3] ib. i 75—80.
[4] 1743–8; ib. i 136—160. [5] 11 July, 1754.
[6] p. 21 (p. 314 of 'Selected Works', ed. J. Lessing) *eine edle Einfalt und eine stille Grösse*, a phrase probably inspired by Oeser (Justi, i 349, 410).

Rome were devoted to studying the great galleries of Sculpture and describing some of the finest works of ancient art in the Vatican Museum.   He afterwards spent three months in Naples, examining the results of the recent excavation of Herculaneum and Pompeii.   He also visited the great Greek temples at Paestum and Girgenti.   In 1760 he produced a descriptive Catalogue of the Stosch Collection of gems in Florence, dedicating his work to the Cardinal Albani, who had already received him into his house and had made him his librarian and supervisor of his fine collection of ancient sculptures.   Meanwhile, he had been studying the descriptions of works of Greek art in Pausanias, and the Greek conception of the Beautiful in Plato.   All these studies culminated in the two quarto volumes of his classic ' History of Ancient Art' (1764), the earliest book in which the developement of the art of Egypt, of Phoenicia and Persia, of Etruria, and of Greece and Rome, is set forth in connexion with the general developement of political life and civilisation.   The work was received with enthusiasm, and a second edition appeared in 1776. Meanwhile, in 1767–8, he had produced the two volumes of his *Monumenti Antichi Inediti*, describing more than two hundred works of ancient art, mainly reliefs from Roman sarcophagi, in the explanation of which he had shown for the first time that the designs were derived, not from the scenes of ordinary life, but from the legends of Greek mythology.   In the following April, he left Rome for the North.   The mountains of Tirol, which had inspired him with wonder on his journey into Italy, now awoke in him a sense of the profoundest melancholy.   He was bound for Berlin, where he proposed to see through the press a French edition of his great History.   During his stay in Augsburg, Munich and Vienna, he strove in vain to throw off the intense depression by which he was haunted; from Vienna he returned alone to Triest, and arranged to cross the water to Venice.   While he was preparing for his voyage, he lived incognito for several days at a hotel, where he became imprudently familiar with an Italian adventurer, indiscreetly showed him some of the large gold medals he had recently received at Vienna, and was treacherously murdered on the 8th of June, 1768.   The date of his birth, the 9th of December, has since been repeatedly commemorated by

the publication of papers on classical art and archaeology in
Rome, as well as in Berlin and in many other homes of learning
in Germany. Of his portraits the best is that painted by Angelica
Kauffmann[1]. The bust, once placed by Cardinal Albani beside
the tomb of Raphael in the Pantheon, has been removed to the
Capitoline Museum; a statue has been erected in his memory at
the village where he was born, and a monument in one of the
churches of the town where he died. As the votary of all that
was beautiful in the art of the ancient world, he has been im-
mortalised by an able and eloquent biographer, who bids farewell
to his hero in the impressive words :—*Er lebt in Gott, dem Urquell
des Schönen, dessen Abglanz er hier gesucht und geahnt hat*[2].

    The services rendered by Winckelmann, in bringing the old
Greek world into connexion with modern life, were
Lessing   continued in a still larger measure by Gotthold
Ephraim Lessing (1729—1781). His father was curate of Ka-
menz, a small town N.E. of Dresden. At the age of five, when
it was proposed to paint his portrait with a bird-cage beside him,
the future scholar vehemently protested :—'you must paint me
with a great, great heap of *books*, or I won't be painted at all'.[3] At
thirteen, he was sent to the famous school of St Afra at Meissen,
N.W. of Dresden. The education there given was mainly classical,
and the boy's private reading included Anacreon and the *Characters*
of Theophrastus, as well as Plautus and Terence. He was only
seventeen when he entered the university of Leipzig, where
J. F. Christ was already lecturing on ancient art, and on Plautus

---

    [1] Justi, ii (2) 440; *ib.* Frontispiece, and Könnecke's *Bilderatlas*, ed. 2
(1905) 230.

    [2] Complete ed. of his works in 12 vols., published at Donaueschingen
(1825-9) and Prato (1830-4). *Die Geschichte der Kunst des Alterthums*
(1764), and *Gedanken über die Nachahmung der griechischen Werke* (1755), and
some minor works, reprinted with Life and Introduction by Julius Lessing
(ed. 2, Heidelberg, 1882). Cp. Heyne's *Lobschrift*, and Herder's *Denkmal*
(1778, vol. viii 437 f, ed. Suphan); Goethe's *Winckelmann und sein Jahr-
hundert*, 1805 (vol. xxiv of ed. in xxx vols.); F. A. Wolf, *Kleine Schriften*,
ii 730-743; O. Jahn, *Biogr. Aufsätze*, 1—88; Julian Schmidt, ii 123—132;
Justi, *Winckelmann, sein Leben, seine Werke und seine Zeitgenossen*, in
3 vols., 1866-72; Stark, 193—206; and Bursian, i 426—436.

    [3] Picture reproduced in Düntzer's *Lessings Leben*, 17, and in Könnecke's
Bilderatlas, 231.

and Horace[1], and Ernesti was 'extraordinary professor of Eloquence', while Kästner, the young professor of mathematics, was soon to give proof of his special interest in literature, and—in Lessing. At Leipzig the young student became convinced that 'books might make him learned, but could never make him a man'[2], and it was there that he produced his earliest play, a satire on the conceited self-complacency of a youthful pedant[3]. The author had just become conscious of his own pedantry, his horizon had been widened, and the spirit of modern 'enlightenment' had breathed life into the dry bones of scholarship[4]. Early in 1749 he went to Berlin, and, besides making his mark as a dramatic critic, produced three plays, one of them founded on the *Trinummus*[5]. Late in 1751 he left for Wittenberg, where he stayed for less than a year, spending most of his time in the university library, every volume of which (he afterwards declared) had passed through his hands. At Wittenberg he studied the Roman poets, especially Horace and Martial, whose manner is reflected in his own terse and epigrammatic style, and especially in his Latin and German epigrams[6]. In his Letters, and in a separate treatise, he satirically attacked an inadequate translation of Horace, and vindicated the poet's character[7]. On returning to Berlin, he won the friendship of Nicolai and of Moses Mendelssohn, both of whom were interested, like himself, in English literature ; and he chose England as the scene of his first important tragedy, a 'household play', which was part of his protest against the servile imitation of antiquity then prevalent in France[8]. His interest in the drama led to his writing a treatise on the life and works of Plautus, a translation and examination of the *Captivi*[9], and an essay on the tragedies of Seneca[10]. A still more important influence on his career as a critic may be traced

---

[1] Julian Schmidt, i 618.   [2] Letter to his mother, *ib*. i 620.

[3] *Der junge Gelehrte*.   [4] Sherer, ii 49, E. T.

[5] *Der Schatz*.   [6] i 27—67 Göring.

[7] *Brief* 24 in 1753 (vi 300, ed. Göring) ; *Vademecum*..., and *Rettungen des Horaz*, 1754 (xv 11—72). Cp. Sime's *Lessing*, i 123.

[8] *Miss Sara Sampson*.   [9] vi 21—144.

[10] vii 162—236. Cp. Dietsch in *Philologen-Versammlung* xxii (Meissen) 18 f.

to his study of Aristotle's *Ethics*, *Politics*, *Rhetoric*, and *Poetic*[1],
and of the masterpieces of Greek tragedy, especially the plays of
Sophocles[2].　After nearly three years at Leipzig, he published at
Berlin his 'Prose Fables' and his 'Treatises on the Fable', the
latter being among the best of his essays in criticism (1759)[3].　It
was during his five years at Breslau (1760–5), that he began the
best known of his critical works, his *Laokoon*, or, 'on the limits of
Poetry and Painting', completed and published at Berlin in 1766[4].

Simonides had vividly described ' Poetry as a speaking Picture and Painting
as a silent Poem ', but Plutarch himself, in quoting this epigram, had observed
that Poetry and Painting '*differ* in their matter, and in their means of
imitation'[5].　Nevertheless, the limits of the two arts had been left undefined,
and Luigi Dolce, in his dialogue on Painting (1557), had even maintained
that a good poet must be a good painter[6].　Addison, again, in his *Dialogues
on Medals* (1702), had illustrated the designs on Roman coins by means of
passages from the Latin poets, and *vice versa*; Spence, in his *Polymetis* (1747),
had aimed at explaining the poets of Greece and Rome by the aid of monuments of ancient art; and, in France, Count Caylus had urged artists to find
their inspiration in Homer (1757).　Thomson's *Seasons* had meanwhile
awakened a passion for word-painting among the poets of Germany and
Switzerland.　Winckelmann himself 'saw no reason why Painting should not have
as wide boundaries as Poetry', and inferred that 'it ought to be possible for
the painter to imitate the poet'[7].　He had previously spoken of 'poetic pictures',
and had described Rubens as a 'sublime poet'[8].　He had also illustrated the
' noble simplicity and calm grandeur '[9] of Greek art by the subdued expression

---

[1] Letter to Nikolai, 2 Apr. 1757, and to Mendelssohn, 5 Nov. 1768;
Hamb. Dram. nos. 37—39, 75, 81-3, 89, 90, 101-4; cp. Gotschlich, *Lessing's
Aristotelische Studien* (Berlin, 1876).

[2] *Leben des Soph.* (1760), xi 13—96.　　　　　[3] i 194—292.

[4] x 1—167; *Fragments*, 168—224, Göring: ed. Blümner, 1876; Hamann,
1878; E. T., Sir R. J. Phillimore (1875) and E. C. Beasley (1879 etc.); cp.
Sherer, ii 65 f; Justi's *Winckelmann*, i 450—477; Sime, i 247—308;
Zimmern, 175—194; E. A. Gardner, *Gk Sculpture*, ii 468—472; *facsimile*
of p. 1 in Düntzer's *Lessings Leben*, 323.

[5] Plutarch, *De Gloria Ath.* 3, p. 346 F (and 347 A), echoed in *Ad Herenn.*
iv 39, 'poëma loquens pictura, pictura tacitum poëma debet esse', and in
Horace, *A. P.* 361, 'ut pictura poësis', where the reference is only to the
external aspects of the two kinds of art (Orelli); cp. Dryden's *Parallel of
Poetry and Painting* (1695).

[6] *Laokoon*, xx p. 237 Blümner.

[7] *Erläuterung der Gedanken u.s.w.* (1756), p. 347, ed. 1882.

[8] *Gedanken u.s.w.* p. 325.　　　　　　[9] p. 22, n. 6 *supra*.

of pain in the sculptured form of Laocoon, who, in contrast to the Laocoon of Virgil, bravely endures his pain, 'like the Philoctetes of Sophocles'.

Lessing, however, at the very outset of his Essay, shows that Philoctetes in the play, so far from suppressing his groans, fills the stage with loud laments, and, instead of supplying a *contrast* to Virgil's Laocoon, really *resembles* him. Winckelmann (he continues) had overlooked the essential difference between Sculpture and Poetry. The poet and the artist were equally right, both followed the principles of their respective arts. The sculptor did not 'aim at expressing a higher moral character in making his Laocoon suppress the cry of agony; he only obeyed the highest law of ancient art,—the law of beauty'. The artist is limited to a *moment* of time; the poet is not. 'The artist represents *coexistence in space*, the poet *succession in time*'. This point is illustrated from Homer, and in particular from his vivid story of the making of the Shield of Achilles, which is far more life-like, far more truly poetic than Virgil's dead description of the Shield of Aeneas. In Homer the great work grows under our very eyes; scene after scene starts into life; while Virgil toils in vain by tediously drawing our attention to a series of coexistent images. Thus Lessing condemns dead description in poetry, as contrasted with life-like action and movement....He ends by criticising some minor points in Winckelmann's 'History of Art', which had meanwhile been published.

While Winckelmann had a first-hand knowledge of works of ancient sculpture, and was also well versed in ancient literature, Lessing had approached the subject almost wholly from the *literary* side; he had read all that had been written on his theme; he had, in fact, been partly anticipated by the Abbé Dubos[1] in France, and by James Harris[2] in England; but this does not detract from the merits of his treatise as a lucid and masterly piece of convincing criticism. It is the most perfect specimen of his terse and transparent style, and it owes part of its perspicuity to the avoidance of parenthesis. It was hailed on all sides with enthusiasm. Herder read it through three times between noon and midnight. Goethe, then a student at Leipzig, afterwards said:—' One must be a youth to realise the effect produced upon us by Lessing's *Laokoon*...The phrase *ut pictura poësis*, which had so long been misunderstood, was at once set aside; the difference between art and poetry was now made clear'[3]. When the work reached Winckelmann in Rome, his *first* impulse prompted him to say:—' Lessing writes as oneself would wish to have written. ...As it is glorious to be praised by competent persons, so also it may be glorious to be held worthy of their criticism'[4]. Long afterwards, Macaulay read the *Laokoon*, 'sometimes dissenting, but always admiring and learning'; it was one of the books that filled him 'with wonder and despair'[5]. Lessing's

---

[1] *Réflexions critiques sur la poésie et la peinture* (1719).

[2] *On Music, Painting, and Poetry*, c. v § 2 (1744). Cp. Blümner on *Laokoon*, 173 f.

[3] *Dichtung und Wahrheit*, I c. viii; cp. Sime, i 304.

[4] Justi, ii (2) 234—246; Zimmern, 165.   [5] *Life*, ii 8 (ed. 1878).

opinions have, however, been corrected, or enlarged, by later authors. It is now agreed that the Laocoon-group does not belong to the time of Titus, but to the beginning of the rule of Augustus[1]. Again, in discussing the difference between *painting* and poetry, Lessing starts by examining a master-piece of *sculpture*, and adds that, 'whenever he speaks of *painting*, he means *sculpture* as well',—a point for which he has justly been criticised by Herder[2]. Lessing's belief, that the 'Borghese gladiator' was a statue of Chabrias, was afterwards abandoned at the prompting of Heyne[3]; and the use of the aorist instead of the imperfect in the signatures of Greek sculptors is no longer accepted as an indication of a late date[4].

The *Laokoon* remained a torso. Instead of completing it, the author left Berlin for Hamburg, where, as 'critic of the plays and actors', he produced more than a hundred chapters of brilliant dramatic criticism (1767–9)[5]. That criticism is mainly founded on Aristotle's treatise on Poetry, a German translation of which (with notes and essays) he had himself reviewed in 1753[6]. He repeatedly comments on Aristotle's opinions[7], finding in Aristotle's definition of tragedy, or rather, in his own interpretation of that definition, the true essence of the drama[8].

He was at the same time involved in a controversy with C. A. Klotz, a professor of Rhetoric and editor of three literary journals at Halle. Lessing had expressed his regret that 'a scholar of otherwise just and refined taste' had disapproved of the Homeric episode of Thersites[9]. Lessing himself had declared that there was no great number of pictures for which ancient artists were indebted to Homer[10], had rejected Pope's suggestion that Homer was 'not a stranger to aerial perspective'[11], and had observed that, while modern artists had represented Death as a skeleton[12], the ancients had represented him as the twin-brother of Sleep. All these opinions were attacked by Klotz in an

---

[1] Two of the three sculptors were priests of Athena Lindia in B.C. 22—21 (Blinkenberg and Kinch, in *Danske Videnskab. Selsk. Forhandl.* 1905, 29; cp. Michaelis, *Arch. Entd.* 169; and E. A. Gardner, in *The Year's Work* (1907), 34 f).

[2] p. 35 *infra*.　　　　　　　　[3] *Ant. Briefe*, no. 37 (xiii 98 Göring).

[4] c. xxvii, p. 307 Blümner; cp. Stark, 210.

[5] *Hamburgische Dramaturgie*, vol. xii Göring; E. T. in *Prose Works* (1879).

[6] xix 31 Göring.　　　　　　　　[7] p. 26 n. 1 *supra*.

[8] Lessing attributes to tragedy 'a direct moral purpose' and also holds that 'fear is always an ingredient in pity', E. T. 435 f (see Bernays, Breslau *Abhandl.* (1857) *init.*, and index to Butcher's ed. of Ar. *Poët.*).

[9] *Laokoon*, c. xxiv *ult.*　　　　[10] c. xxii.

[11] c. xix.　　　　　　　　　　[12] c. xi note 1.

'Essay on Gems' (1768), and defended by Lessing in his 'Antiquarian Letters' (1768–9), and in his admirable Essay 'on the Ancient Representations of Death'[1] where he shows that the ancients personified Death, not as a ghastly skeleton but as a beautiful 'Genius' with an inverted torch. The essay was greeted with a transport of delight by the youthful Goethe at Leipzig[2], and the gladness of Goethe found an echo in Schiller's 'Gods of Greece'[3]. It is in the same Essay that we find the memorable distinction between the mere 'antiquarian' and the 'archaeologist'. 'The former has inherited the *fragments*, the latter the *spirit* of antiquity; the former scarcely thinks with his *eyes*, the latter sees even with his *thoughts*; before the former can say *thus it was*, the latter already knows whether it *could* be so'[4]. The extant portraits of Klotz give us the impression of his having been a weak and conceited person[5]. Unfortunately his life was cut short at the early age of thirty-three, and few would now remember him, unless he had been embalmed forever in the translucent amber of his great opponent's style.

As librarian at Wolfenbüttel for the last eleven years of his life, Lessing published *inter alia* a few short papers on the Epigram, and on some of the principal Epigrammatists[6], also on Paulus Silentiarius and on the arithmetical problems of the Greek Anthology[7], while his abiding interest in the Classics is attested by his 'Notes on Ancient Writing'[8], and by his 'Collectanea'[9]. It was during this period that, in 1775, he spent nine months in Italy with a prince of Brunswick. On a day in Rome he was missed by the prince's attendants, who at last found him in the Vatican Museum gazing with rapture on the group of Laocoon.

Lessing was the most versatile of men, a writer on theology and on aesthetics, as well as a poet, a critic, and a scholar. As a theological controversialist, and as the author of *Nathan der Weise*, he was a champion of religious toleration,—but we are

---

[1] Vol. xiii Göring (the essay is translated by Miss Zimmern in *Select Prose Works*, 1879; cp. her *Life of Lessing*, 234—251).

[2] *Dichtung und Wahrheit*, I c. viii.

[3] Stanza 9 of Second Version, *Seine Fackel senkt' ein Genius*.

[4] E. T. p. 209.

[5] Düntzer's *Lessings Leben*, 337, and Könnecke's *Bilderatlas* 233. Ruhnken, writing to Heyne (*Epp. ad Div.* p. 25), calls him *hominem vanissimum et vix mediocriter eruditum*. Cf. Heeren's *Heyne*, 73, 82 f; Sime's *Lessing*, ii 63—81; Bursian, i 444—451.

[6] xv 73—154 Göring.　　　　　　[7] xv 199 f, 236 f.

[8] xv 256—278.　　　　　　[9] xx.

here concerned with him as a scholar and a critic alone. By his influence on his contemporaries he undoubtedly opened a new era in the appreciation of Homer and Sophocles; he also promoted the intelligent study of Aristotle's treatise on Poetry, and threw a clearer light on the aims of Plautus and Terence, and on the merits of Horace and Martial. His writings have a never-failing charm that is mainly due to their clearness and precision, and to their classic purity of style.

Action is, with him, not only the highest theme of poetry; it is also the true end of man. He has an eager delight in conversation, a perfect passion for controversy. He prefers the unceasing and untiring *quest* of Truth, even to its immediate possession and fruition[1]. He is an ardent patriot, a resolute hater of tyrants; amid the strain of poverty, he retains his frank independence of character, and his cheerful devotion to a literary life. He is ever the keenest of critics; ever the many-sided man of letters and of learning, who declines to degenerate into a pedant.

Von Gebler, writing to Nicolai, describes Lessing as 'that rare combination, a truly great and *amiable* scholar'[2]. It is also said that, in the uniform neatness of his dress, he was distinguished from the typical man of letters of his day. In his manner, he was firm without arrogance; and every variety of feeling, whether radiant gladness, or frank independence, or keen indignation, found expression in his deep blue eyes. The best of all his portraits[3] is that painted at the age of thirty-seven,—the age at which he wrote his *Laokoon*[4].

---

[1] *Duplik*, c. 1 *ad finem* (xviii 42 Göring).

[2] Zimmern, *Lessing*, 321.

[3] Könnecke's *Bilderatlas*, p. 232 f.

[4] *Works* in 13 vols. ed. Lachmann (1838 f) and Maltzahn (1853 f); also in 20 vols. (Hempel, 1868 f); 8 vols. illustrated (Grote, 1875 f); and 20 vols. ed. Göring (Cotta, 1882 f). *Lives*, in German, by K. G. Lessing, 1793; Danzel-Guhrauer, 1850–4; Stahr, 1859; Düntzer, 1882; and Göring; and, in English, by J. Sime, 1877 (and in *Enc. Brit.*), and H. Zimmern, 1878. Cp. Julian Schmidt, *Von Leibnitz bis auf Lessings Tod, passim*, esp. i 617—626, ii 6, 294—306; Justi's *Winckelmann*; Stark, 208—212; Bursian, i 436—454; also Sherer, ii 47—82 E. T., and the other current histories of German literature, and lastly, Kont's *Lessing et l'antiquité*, 1894–9.

One of Lessing's most important allies in promoting an interest in Greek literature in Germany, and in waging war against Klotz and his adherents, was Johann Gottfried Herder (1744—1803).   Humbly born at Mohrungen, amid the marshes near Königsberg, he was grounded in Latin by an awe-inspiring master named Grimm. He regarded the Grammar of Donatus as a 'book of martyrdom', and Cornelius Nepos as the 'author of torment'; but he rejoiced in wandering in solitude beside the local lake and through the 'Wood of Paradise', where, on a day in autumn, he burst into tears over the lines in which Homer compares the passing generations of man to the fading and falling leaves of the forest[1].   A Russian officer helped him to enter the university of Königsberg, where he attended the lectures of Kant, and was thereby stimulated to critical inquiry without becoming an adherent of that teacher's opinions.   As a student he was specially interested in Hebrew poetry, and in Pindar and Plato.   In his maturer years we note three main periods:—first, the time at Riga (1765-9); next, the tour in France (1769), the visit to Strassburg (where he made a profound impression on the youthful Goethe[2]), and the years spent as court preacher at Bückeberg (1771-6); and lastly, his residence in a similar position at Weimar (1776—1803).

It was at Riga that he published his three collections of *Fragments* on modern German literature (1766-7).   The first of these deals with the developement of language; the second in- cludes a discourse on the study of Greek literature in Germany, emphasising the connexion between the taste of each people and its material environment in successive ages.   In answer to the question, 'how far do we *understand* the Greeks?', he sketches the outline of a future History of Greek Poetry and Philosophy ; and, in connexion with the further inquiry, 'how far have we *imitated* the Greeks?', he characterises the several branches of Greek poetry, and the foremost poets of Greece, and similarly in the case of Roman poetry, with a marked appreciation of Lucretius and the *Heroides* of Ovid.   In the third, he touches on the German imitations of Latin poets, on the baneful influence of

[1] *Il.* vi 146 f; Nevinson, *Herder and his Times*, 10 f.
[2] *Dichtung und Wahrheit*, Part ii, book 10.

Herder

the Latin spirit in modern Germany, and on the proper use of ancient mythology in modern poetry. The following is the purport of a few passages :—

The history of a language is as the history of man from the lisping of child-hood, through the passion and music of youth, to the calm wisdom of age.... We see the remains of the childhood of man in the poems of Homer. The first authors in every nation are poets, and these poets are inimitable....With the introduction of writing, and the growth of political life, prose became possible, singing ceased, and poetry became a thing of art; instead of Homer, we have Tyrtaeus and the great tragedians, closely followed by the historians; for prose was the living language, till finally it reached its perfection in Plato[1].

How far can the Germans be said really to *understand* the Greeks, whom they imitate?...Our imitations are merely failures. It is absurd to mention Bodmer and Homer in the same breath....Klopstock, again, is really more akin to Virgil than to Homer. Still less can we hope to imitate the dithy-rambic poets....Our Anacreons do not succeed much better. Gessner with his *Idylls* falls far below Theocritus....Even more absurd is the comparison between Sappho and Anna Karschin. We might say to her, as Sappho said to her maid;—'Thou hast no part in the roses of Pieria', where the Muses and Graces have their haunt[2].

Latin was from the first the enemy of German, which might have resisted it, had not Charlemagne and the monks let loose upon us the barbarous deluge of *Latin* literature, *Latin* religion, and *Latin* speculation. O that we had been an island, like England!...*Latin*, being considered an end in itself, is ruining our education....What would the *real* Horace say, if he were compelled to read such poets as Klotz, or the work of any of our Latin pedants? We sacrifice everything to that accursed word, 'classical'. We must begin our reform by giving up Latin,—not as a learned language, but as a means of artistic ex-pression and as a test of culture[3]. In the second fragment he urges that Homer should be *translated*[4], Homer the true poet of Nature, whose song has a very different ring from that of Virgil and the artificial poets of modern times[5].

In his second great work he imagines himself roaming through the 'woodlands of criticism'[6]. He has a high appreciation of Lessing's *Laokoon*, but he does still more justice to Winckelmann[7].

Opposing Lessing's theory as to the Greek expression of the emotions, he maintains that Philoctetes does not shriek without restraint[8], while he demurs

---

[1] *Fragmente*, i (1768[2]) 151—224 (= *Werke*, i 151—155 + ii 60—88 Suphan); Nevinson, 106.

[2] *Fragm.* ii (i 285—352 S) ; Nevinson, 108.

[3] *Fragm.* iii (i 362—414 S) ; Nevinson, 108 f.   [4] i 289 S.

[5] Cp. Julian Schmidt, ii 325.   [6] *Kritische Wälder*, 1769.

[7] Cp. Herder to Scheffner, 4 Oct. 1766 ; Julian Schmidt, ii 324, 352.

[8] *Wäldchen*, i § 2 (iii 12 f S).

to the dogma that all poetry must represent *action*, a dogma limiting poetry to the epic and dramatic, to the exclusion of the lyric and the song[1]. At a later point he criticises the *Epistolae Homericae* and other works of Klotz, justifies the comic element in epic poetry, discusses the proper method of studying Horace, and insists that every work of Art or Poetry must be interpreted in the light of the people and the period, in which it came into being. He particularly objects to the Homeric poems being criticised by the standard of modern taste[2].

It was on the deck at night, during his voyage from Riga, that he first formed his theory of the genesis of primitive poetry and of the gradual evolution of humanity. In France he drew up a scheme of educational reform, beginning by overthrowing the predominance of his old enemy, the Latin grammar, and insisting that, in education, variety was absolutely essential.

As to languages, the mother-tongue must be thoroughly studied, French must be taught in conversation, Latin should be learnt for the sake of its literature, but even Latin is best taught by conversation. Greek and Hebrew follow in their turn, and the course is complete[3].

At Strassburg in 1770 he wrote the Essay on the Origin of Language that was crowned by the Berlin Academy[4]. The Academy had proposed the question:—'Was man capable of inventing language, if left to his own resources, and, if so, by what means could he have invented it?' Herder answers the first part of this question in the affirmative; and, in reply to the second, lays down four 'natural laws' governing the invention and developement of language, and its division into various tongues. The essay was written in less than a month, but the subject had been long in his mind, and, fortunately (perhaps) for himself, he had no books to hamper him. The result has been recognised as an important part of the first foundations of Comparative Philology[5].

He was still at Bückeburg when he published 'A New

---

[1] *Wäldchen*, i § 16 (iii 133 f S); cp. Nevinson, 113–5.

[2] *Wäldchen*, ii caps. i and iii (vol. iii 133 f, 320 f, S).

[3] *Reise-journal* (vol. iv *ad finem*, ed. Suphan); Nevinson, 128 f; cp. Paulsen, ii 42—44, 193–8.

[4] *Ueber den Ürsprung der Sprache*, 1771; ed. 2, 1789; *Werke*, ed. 1805 f, *Philosophie und Geschichte*, ii 1—183 (vol. v *init.* ed. Suphan); cp. Goethe, *u. s.*

[5] Benfey's *Geschichte der Sprachwissenschaft*, 293 f; cp. Julian Schmidt, ii 493; and Nevinson, 162 f.

Philosophy of History'[1], beginning with a sketch of the progress
of man from his childhood in the East, through his boyhood in
Egypt and Phoenicia and his youth in Greece, till in Rome he
reached man's estate, and attained his still maturer years in the
Middle Ages and in modern times.

Here, as elsewhere, he touches on the question of the originality of
Greece:—'That Greece received from some other quarter the *seeds* of
civilisation, language, arts and sciences, is, to my mind, undeniable, and
it can be clearly proved in the case of some of them,—Sculpture, Architecture,
Mythology, and Literature. But that the Greeks, practically, did *not* receive
all this; that, on the contrary, they gave it an entirely new nature, that, in each
kind, the Beautiful, in the proper sense of that term, is certainly their work;—
this, I think, is obvious[2].

Similar opinions recur in his 'Thoughts on the Philosophy
of the History of Mankind' (1784–91), a vast work, only partially
completed during his latest days at Weimar. Near the middle
he dwells on the 'Education of the Human Race'[3], and, in the
latter half, surveys the growth of civilisation in ancient times and
in the Middle Ages, devoting two most suggestive books[4] to
Greece and Italy. *'With Greece the morning breaks'*,—such are
the opening words of the enthusiastic passage on Greek life and
history that was specially admired by Heyne and Goethe[5]. In
other works connected with classical antiquity[6] he shows an
interest in the *historical* treatment of the growth of Greek civilisation and especially of Greek poetry and art, regarding both of
them as a 'School of Humanity'.

He is peculiarly interested in Homer. He was in fact one of
the first to elucidate the general character of the Homeric poems.
He finds in them the fullest illustration of the idiosyncrasy of
national poetry[7].

[1] *Auch eine Philosophie der Geschichte*, 1774 (v 475 f S).

[2] v 498 f S; cp. Nevinson, 212–5.   [3] *Ideen*, books viii—ix (vol. xiii S).

[4] xiii and xiv (Bursian, i 461 f), reserved for vol. xiv S.

[5] *Ideen*, book xiii *init*.; Nevinson, 366.

[6] *Ursachen des gesunkenen Geschmacks*, 1775 (v 595 S); *Ueber die Wirkung
der Dichtkunst*, 1781 (viii 334 f); *Briefen zur Beförderung der Humanität*,
series 3—8, 1794–6 (vols. xvii, xviii); cp. Bursian, i 463.

[7] *Ueber Ossian und die Lieder alter Völker*, 1773 (v 322). His later
writings include *Homer ein Günstling der Zeit*, 1795 (xviii 420), and *Homer
und das Epos*, 1803 (xxiv 229, cp. 233); cp. Bursian, i 464 f.

Homer is unique. When Homer had sung, we could expect no second Homer in his particular type of poetry; he had plucked the flower of the epic crown, and his successors were fain to rest content with the leaves alone. Hence the tragic poets took another line; they ate, indeed, as Aeschylus says, from the table of Homer, but they also prepared for the age, in which they lived, another kind of banquet[1].

In the context he contrasts Epic poetry with History, and with Tragedy[2], and elsewhere he enters on a full discussion of Aristotle's definition of the latter[3]. He produced metrical renderings of nine of the Olympian Odes of Pindar[4], and wrote an enthusiastic description of his characteristics as a poet[5]. He also discriminated between the several periods and types of Greek lyric poetry in his Essay on 'Alcaeus and Sappho'[6]. He is specially interested in Horace[7]. In his essay on the critical efforts of the past century, he duly recognises the importance of Bentley[8], and even notices the lesser lights, William Baxter and Thomas Creech[9].

His interest in ancient art is specially displayed in two treatises. In his work on Sculpture[10] he observes with surprise that Lessing had not cared to distinguish between Sculpture and Painting. Herder accordingly endeavours to establish the laws of this distinction. His short treatise 'on the Representation of Death by the Ancients'[11] suggests that the 'Genius with the inverted torch' on Greek tombs is not (as Lessing held) Death, the brother of Sleep, but Sleep, the brother of Death, or possibly a mourning Cupid. This last thought finds an echo in Herder's pathetic poem on the death of Lessing[12]. Finally, he insists on the importance, and indeed the necessity, of the study of ancient Art for the study of classical literature[13].

[1] xxiv 244 Suphan.
[2] xxiv 241 f, 244 f, S.
[3] *Das Drama*, xxiii 346—369 S.
[4] xxvi 188 f S.
[5] *Pindar ein Bote der Götter*, xxiv 335 S.
[6] xxvii 182—198 S.
[7] xxvi 213 f S.
[8] xxiv 183 f S.
[9] xxiv 198 f, 223 f, S; also Samuel Clarke, *ib.* 225 f.
[10] *Plastik*, 1778 (vol. viii Suphan); Nevinson, 310–4.
[11] *Zerstreute Blätter*, 1786 (iv 656 f S), 1796².
[12] *Der Tod, ein Gespräch an Lessings Grabe*, in *Zerstreute Blätter*, i (1785, 1791²), xxviii 135 S.
[13] xx 283 f Suphan.—First edition of Herder's *Works* in 45 vols. in three series, Tübingen, 1805–20; best ed. in 32 vols. ed. Suphan, 1877–99——. Cp.

In the latter part of a long literary career, Christian Martin Wieland
(1733—1813) did much for the diffusion of an interest in the
old classical world, although the influence of French literature
is apparent in his classical romances, the best known of which is *Agathon*,
while the modern element is also prominent in his poem, *Musarion*. He had
a far higher appreciation of Euripides than of Aristophanes, and one of his
favourite authors was Xenophon. He produced a rather free translation of
nearly the whole of Lucian, with notes on points of textual, historical, or
aesthetic criticism (1788–9). He had already translated the *Epistles* and *Satires*
of Horace (1782–6), and, in his 75th year, he began a rendering of Cicero's
Letters in chronological order, a work completed by Gräter (1808–21). The
Attisches Museum, which he founded, and edited in 1796—1811, included
translations of Attic writers of the ages of Pericles and Alexander[1]. Among
Wieland's pupils at Erfurt was Wilhelm Heinse (1746—1803),
the translator of Petronius, and the author of the romance of
Ardinghello (1787), the scene of which is laid in Italy in the sixteenth century.
Like his *Letters*, it gives abundant proof of the familiarity with ancient and
modern art, which he had acquired during a residence of three years in that
classic land[2].

Wieland

Heinse

Among professional scholars, Christian Gottlob Heyne (1729—
1812) has been justly praised for the new interest
in ancient literature and ancient art, which he
awakened both by his teaching and by his published works. He
was the eldest son of a poor weaver in Upper Saxony, and, as a
boy at school, when he first heard of a tyrannicide, he burned to
be a Brutus and thus to avenge the wrongs inflicted on his parents
by the tyranny of middle-men. Having no text-books of his own,
he was compelled to borrow those of his school-fellows, and to

Heyne

Julian Schmidt, ii 316—326, 352–5; 415—423; 446—450; 463–8; 490–4,
596—601; 686—690; H. Nevinson's *Herder and his Times*, 1884, and the
earlier literature there quoted; later *Lives* in German by Haym (1880–5),
Kuehnemann (1895) and Buerkner (1904), also Suphan in Goedeke's *Grundrisz*,
IV i 274—282, with bibliography, *ib*. 282—299 (1891[2]); cp. Herder's *Ansichten
des kl. Alterthums*, ed. Danz, 1805–6; G. A. Schöll, *Herder's Verdienst um
Würdigung der Antike und der bildenden Kunst*, and A. G. Gernhard, *Herder
als Humanist*, pp. 193 f and 255 f of *Weimarisches Herder-Album* (Jena,
1845); L. Keller, *Herder und die Kultgesellschaften des Humanismus* (Berlin,
1904[2]); and Bursian, i 454—469. Portrait in Nevinson, and several in
Könnecke, 248 f.

[1] Bursian, i 470–5. Portraits in Könnecke, 242 f. Cp. Goethe's farce
Götter, Helden und Wieland.

[2] Bursian, i 475 f; portrait in Könnecke, 256; Ziegler in Baumeister's
Handbuch, i (1) 257.

CHRISTIAN GOTTLIEB HEYNE.

I. H. Tischbein pinx.   C. G. Geyser sc.

HEYNE.

From C. G. Geyser's engraving of the early portrait by Tischbein.

copy out the portion required for each lesson. He complains that (like others since his time) he was compelled to make Latin verses before he had read any authors, or acquired any store of words. His master himself had only 'an Owen'[1], 'a Fabricius'[2], a couple of 'Collections of Epigrams', and a few sacred poets, from whose pages he used to dictate verses for his pupils to paraphrase[3]. To learn Greek he had to borrow Weller's Grammar, and his god-father's copy of 'Pasor'[4]. In his last year at school a new master came, by whom he was happily introduced to the *Ajax* of Sophocles. At the age of nineteen he went to Leipzig, there to endure all the miseries of a poor student's life. But he succeeded in gaining admission to the lectures of Ernesti, and it was thus that he first learnt what was meant by 'the inter-pretation' of the Classics[5]. Professor Christ, whose lectures were 'a tissue of endless digressions', took some interest in him, and recommended the poor youth, who was almost destitute of books, to follow the example of Scaliger and read all the Classics in chronological order. Heyne had to borrow the necessary books, and for half-a-year slept for only two nights in each week, and consequently fell into a fever. At the end of four years he graduated, and in the following year some Latin verses of his attracted the attention of Count Brühl, who made him an under-clerk in his library at Dresden, where Heyne shared a garret with a young divine, and was content to sleep on the floor, with a few folios for his pillow. In the library he made the acquaintance of Winckelmann, who was then preparing for his journey to Italy[6]. During this period Heyne produced an edition of Ti-bullus and of Epictetus (1755–6). In the latter year Dresden was attacked by Frederic the Great, and Brühl's library was destroyed[7]. Heyne thereupon promptly obtained a tutorship in the Schönberg family, where he met his future wife ; accompanied young Schönberg to Wittenberg, where he continued his own

[1] John Owen, *Epigrammata*, 1624 etc.

[2] Georg von Goldschmied (of Chemnitz), *Elegantiae Poeticae*, 1554, *Poemata Sacra*, 1560, *De re poëtica*, 1565 etc.

[3] Heeren, *Heyne*, 13.

[4] Georg Pasor, *Manuale graecarum vocum N. T.* 1640 (Leipzig, 1735); *Gramm. gr. sacra N. T.* 1655.

[5] Heeren, 30.   [6] Heeren, 44.   [7] Heeren, 62.

studies till he was driven out by the Prussian artillery; and
returned to Dresden, only to be expelled by another bombard-
ment, in which all his books and papers were burnt (1760)[1].
His future wife had already suffered a similar fate, but they
were happily united in the following year.   On the death of
Gesner at Göttingen, Ernesti at Leipzig was consulted as to the
choice of a successor.   Ernesti (as we have seen)[2] suggested
Ruhnken, and Ruhnken suggested Heyne, who had shown how
much he knew of Latin literature by his Tibullus; of Greek, by
his Epictetus.   Ruhnken added that Hemsterhuys agreed that
Heyne was the only one who could replace Gesner, and ended
with the assurance that such was Heyne's genius and learning,
that ere long all Europe would ring with his praise[3].   In June,
1763, Heyne settled at Göttingen, where he lived for forty-nine
years, loyally devoting himself to his duties as professor of
Eloquence, as director of the philological *Seminar*, as university
librarian, as secretary of the local Academy, as editor of the local
Review, and as an active administrator in business affairs connected with the University and with education in general.

He had a weak voice, an unimpressive presence, and a certain
lack of form and method, but his lectures were largely attended.
They owed their main attraction to the lecturer's undoubted
learning and to his lively interest in his subject.   They ranged
over a wide field, including the exposition of Greek and Latin
authors, especially the poets, the history of Greek and Latin
literature and antiquities, and the technology of ancient art.
During a brief journey to Hanover, he perused Lessing's *Laokoon*
(which had just been published), admiring the author's taste, which
he considered superior even to that of Winckelmann, and agreeing
with Lessing in his depreciation of Virgil in comparison with
Homer[4].   The immediate influence of Winckelmann and Lessing
is manifest in the fact that, in the very next year, Heyne announced
for the first time a course of lectures on archaeology (1767)[5].

[1] Heeren, 61, 87.   [2] p. 14 *supra.*

[3] *Ep.* 18 Oct. 1762 (Heeren, 74).

[4] Letter of 21 July 1766 (Heeren, 154 f).

[5] Heeren, 91.   Heyne afterwards published a syllabus of this course
(*Einleitung,* 1772), expanded by J. P. Siebenkees (1758–96), ed. 1799 f.
Heyne's later lectures of 1792 were published in 1822 (Bursian, i 478 n).

Much of his reputation rested on the excellent manner in which he trained the future school-masters of Germany in his small and select *Seminar*.

Heyne was not an original genius. He was a many-sided scholar, who studied and expounded ancient life in all its successive phases, and became the founder of that branch of classical teaching that deals with the study of *Realien*, the science of 'things' as contrasted with that of 'words', archaeology (in its widest sense) as contrasted with language and literature[1]. He was 'the first who with any decisiveness attempted '...'to read in the writings of the Ancients, not their language alone, or even their detached opinions and records, but their spirit and character, their way of life and thought'[2].

The criticism and exposition of ancient poetry is represented in his editions of Tibullus[3], Virgil[4], Pindar[5], and the *Iliad*[6]. Like Gesner, he is comparatively weak in textual criticism; his choice among different readings is guided more by personal preference than by an impartial weighing of the evidence. In his explanatory notes he assigns a subordinate place to points of grammar and metre. The preparation of the metrical part of his Pindar was entirely entrusted to Hermann, then twenty-five years of age. Heyne's own interest lay, not in the metre, but in the subject-matter of the *Odes*. His commentary supplied all that was immediately necessary for the understanding of the text, everything else being reserved for an *Excursus*. In his explanations (as in his textual criticism) there is a certain lack of decision. He has the merit, however, of being interested in the aesthetic interpretation of his author. Of the above editions the most important, as a whole, is the Virgil, the least successful part being the treatment of the subject-matter of the *Georgics*. His edition of the *Iliad*, which cost him fifteen years of labour, has far less permanent value. His interest in the subject was mainly

---

[1] Herbst, *Voss' Leben*, i 70 ; Paulsen, ii 35[2].

[2] Carlyle, *Heyne*, in *Misc. Essays*, ii 111 (ed. 1869). Cp. Ziegler in Baumeister's *Handbuch*, i (1) 255 f; Paulsen, i 602–5[2], ii 35—42[2].

[3] 1755; ed. 3, 1798.

[4] 1767–75. The best ed. is the German *Prachtausgabe* of 1800.

[5] 5 vols., 1798; cp. Heeren, 163–6.   [6] 8 vols., 1802.

aroused by the publication of Robert Wood's *Essay on the original Genius of Homer* (1769)[1]. The treatment of grammatical questions, in the course of the fifty-three appendices, is full, without being sufficiently exhaustive, or sufficiently precise. The work, as a whole, was practically a compilation, and the date of its appearance (1802) inevitably suggested a comparison with Wolf's *Prolegomena* (1795), a comparison which was bound to be to the disadvantage of Heyne.

Heyne failed to appreciate the importance of the *Codex Venetus* A, and the accompanying *scholia*, published by Villoison in 1788. He found himself unable to break loose from the text of Samuel Clarke and Ernesti. The questions as to the origin of the Homeric poems, which Wolf had handled in a masterly and methodical manner, were discussed in an uncertain and tentative way by Heyne, first in a paper presented to the Göttingen Academy later in the same year[2], and subsequently in two excursuses to the last book of the *Iliad*[3]. Heyne emphasises the fact that we have no trustworthy historical tradition, either as to Homer's personality, or as to the origin and the early fortunes of the Homeric poems. We must therefore rest content with conjectures, which cannot go beyond the bounds of mere probability. Such are the suggestions that Homer is not a historic person, that his name may be derived from the collecting of his poems, that certain parts of the *Iliad* were composed at different times by different poets, that these parts were recited separately for a long period of time by various rhapsodes, and were, at a comparatively late date, collected into a comprehensive whole (possibly by Peisistratus and his sons), and made generally known by being reduced to writing. These suggestions are practically those of Wolf, and it is deemed impossible to determine how far this identity of opinions was independently attained by Heyne. Yet some points are clear. In 1777 Heyne had no doubt as to the historic personality of Homer[4]. In 1790 he wrote to Zoëga :—'As to the age of the Homeric poems, how could it occur to me to go beyond the existing data? All the rest is a dream. To myself it seems *probable* that at first there were separate songs, which were subsequently combined. This, however, is only a *possibility*...'[5].

---

[1] Heeren, 210 f; cp. vol. ii, p. 432 *supra*.

[2] 1 Aug. 1795, *De antiqua Homeri lectione indaganda, dijudicanda et restituenda*, in *Commentationes Societatis...Gottingensis*, xiii 159—182.

[3] *De Iliade universe et de eius partibus rhapsodiarumque compage*, and *De Homero Iliadis auctore*.

[4] *De origine et caussis fabularum Homericarum* in *Novi Commentarii Soc. Gotting.* viii 34—58.

[5] Welcker, *Zoega's Leben*, ii 60 f (Bursian, i 482 n.). On the controversy raised by Heyne's statement that he had held these views for 30 years, and had expressed them orally, and in writing, cp. Wolf, *Briefe an Heyne*, 1797, and (in Heyne's favour) *Bibl. der red. Künste*, vols. iv, v, and Heeren's *Heyne*, 210—219.

But, *after* the publication of Wolf's *Prolegomena*, Heyne's references to the points in controversy become *more full and more definite*. Some of the questions had doubtless been in the air, ever since the publication of Wood's *Essay* in 1769. Wolf stated all these questions with greater precision and established them on a scientific basis. As his work on Homer begins a new era, its further consideration is reserved for the next chapter.

The only writers of Greek prose edited by Heyne were Epictetus and Apollodorus. His edition of the latter is a repertory of the mythological literature of the ancients, followed by genealogical tables and an index of all the authors cited.

Heyne is the founder of the scientific treatment of Greek mythology. He regards the old Greek myths as the summing up of the stories and the opinions of a primitive people prior to the introduction of writing, and he emphasises the difference between the religious conceptions of that early age and those prevailing in later times[1]. He also wrote much on ancient history. Among the most important of his numerous historical dissertations are those on Castor's chronology of the successive epochs of sea-power, on the Greek colonies, on the institutions of Sparta, on the treaties between Rome and Carthage, on the civilisation of the Ptolemies, and on the authorities followed by Diodorus.

In the domain of art he followed the lines laid down by Winckelmann. He had neither the enthusiasm and the artistic penetration of Winckelmann, nor the critical and philosophical acumen of Lessing ; but he surpassed both, in a full and accurate knowledge of antiquarian details, and in a trained aptitude for methodical historical investigation. In points of chronology and history he is able to correct Winckelmann[2]. He discusses many of the ancient masterpieces, from the Chest of Cypselus[3] down to the group of Laocoon[4], and discourses on the Philostrati and Callistratus, and on the ideal types of Greek divinities. He edits excerpts on ancient art from the elder Pliny[5]. He also gives proof of his knowledge of numismatics and welcomes the new impulse given to that study in his own life-time[6].

As inspector of the school at Ilfeld, he used his influence in 1770 in favour of the revival of a liberal education. The school had fallen into decay, but all,

[1] Bursian, i 484—490.   [2] *Opusc.* v 338—391.
[3] *Vorlesung*, 1770.   [4] *Antiquarische Aufsätze*, 1778-9, ii 1.
[5] 1790, 1811; cp. *Ant. Aufs.* i 3, ii 3—5.   [6] Bursian, i 493-6.

he felt sure, would be well, if a little Greek were introduced ; he would then feel no anxiety about Latin and all the other subjects known as *humaniora*, while, wherever Greek was neglected, everything else would remain 'mere patch-work and perpetual botching'[1]. His report of 1780 also proves him to have been an enlightened promoter of the New Humanism[2].

In 1803, during the French war, his intercession with Napoleon led to the university of Göttingen being protected from peril, and to the surrounding district being exempt from hostile invasion. In 1809 his 80th birthday was celebrated with a procession of professors and students, and with gifts of garlands of flowers. He delighted in roses, and always kept a bunch of them in water on his desk. His house was embowered among rose-bushes, and he was fond of the fields and skies, and could lie for hours on the grass reading a book[3]. His son-in-law and biographer supplies us with a detailed time-table of his well-spent day from five in the morning to eleven or twelve at night[4]. His shortness of sight led to his sometimes making odd mistakes about strangers from a distance who came to pay him their respects. It also disqualified him from being a good judge of the larger varieties of ancient sculpture. In 1798 he was much interested in helping to prepare the illustrations to Homer collected by Tischbein, who more than once painted his portrait[5]. His reputation spread to other lands, and he was once surprised to find in an English newspaper 'an extract of a letter from a Gentleman at Gottingen to his friend in Cambridge':—'A Mr HEYNE, to whom I was lately introduced, ought to be mentioned as the first genius of Gottingen'[6]. On the eve of his eightieth year, his second wife showed him a passage in which Gibbon had referred to Heyne's 'usual good taste'[7].

---

[1] *Nur Stückwerk und ewig Stümperei.*   [2] Paulsen, ii 38[2] f.

[3] Heeren, 412 f; Carlyle, 109, 113.   [4] Heeren, 325–8.

[5] Heeren, frontispiece, and p. 412. The earlier portrait has been engraved by C. G. Geyser (p. 37 *supra*); the later, by Riepenhausen. There is also an engraving by F. Müller.

[6] *Morning Post*, 20 April, 1775 (Heeren, 331 f).

[7] Heeren, 333. In iv 419, 509 Bury, Gibbon calls Heyne 'the excellent editor of Virgil', and 'the best of his editors'. In 1770 Heyne 'the last and best editor of Virgil' had called the unknown author of Gibbon's anonymous Observations on the Sixth Aeneid a *doctus...et eloquentissimus Britannus* (*Autob.* 85).

'On the whole' (says Carlyle), 'the Germans have some reason to be proud of Heyne: who shall deny that they have here once more produced a scholar of the right old stock; a man to be ranked, for honesty of study and of life, with the Scaligers, the Bentleys, and old illustrious men, who...fought like giants...for the good cause?' Pointing to the example of the 'son of the Chemnitz weaver', he adds:—'Let no lonely unfriended son of genius despair!'[1]

While the study of coins was one of the many departments of learning that attracted the notice of Heyne, it was the life-work of his contemporary, Joseph Eckhel (1737—1798), the founder of the scientific study of Numismatics. Early in life he had begun that study as a teacher at various schools in Vienna. To extend his knowledge, he left in 1772 for Italy, where he was invited to rearrange the collection of coins belonging to Leopold, Grand Duke of Tuscany, the second son of the Empress Maria Theresa. On his return, the Empress appointed him professor of Antiquities in the university of Vienna, and director of the Imperial Cabinet of Coins and Antiques (1775-6). He arranged the coins according to his own system and published in two folio volumes a complete catalogue, which is a model of its kind (1779). In his system (which had been only partially anticipated by the French numismatist, Joseph Pellerin) ancient coins were divided into two great classes. The first of these consists mainly of *Greek* coins of States, Peoples and Kings, together with colonial and imperial coins, all arranged in geographical order, passing from the West to the East of Europe, and, after traversing Asia, coming round again to the West through Egypt and North Africa. The second class was reserved for *Roman* coins alone, beginning with the consular and gentile coins in the alphabetical order of the *gentes*, and ending with the Roman imperial coins in chronological order. This

Eckhel

---

[1] *Misc. Essays*, ii 113. On Heyne, see the 'biographical portrait' by Heeren (522 pp., Göttingen, 1813), and its 'miniature copy' in Carlyle's *Miscellaneous Essays*, ii 75—114, ed. 1869. Cp. Paulsen, i 602-5, ii 34—42[2]; Stark, 212-5; and esp. Bursian, i 476—496, with the literature quoted by him, 477 n., and by Stark, 215, who considers Hettner (*Lit. Gesch. des xviii Jahrh.* iii 3, 2, p. 339 f) fairer to Heyne than Justi, who calls Heyne a typical German *Universitäts-philister* (Winckelmann, ii (2) 230-2). See also F. Leo, in Göttingen *Festschrift* (Berlin, 1901), 155—234.

system was applied to all the extant ancient coins in the eight
volumes of his classic work, the *Doctrina Numorum Veterum*[1].
The general Introduction deals with the history of Greek coinage,
the technique, weight, value and size of coins, the right of mintage,
the officials of the mint, inscriptions, types of coins, etc., etc.
The fourth volume closes with general observations. The remaining four begin similarly with an Introduction and end with
general observations on Roman coinage[2]. A modern expert, who
dedicates his work to the memory of Eckhel, characterises the
Historia Numorum Veterum as 'a marvellous compendium of
wide research and profound erudition, a work which can never
be altogether superseded'. But he also points out that its author
was imperfectly acquainted with the history of Greek art and with
metrology, both of which fields of study have been thoroughly
explored in later times, and that the absence of extant specimens
of certain coins (such as the electrum staters of Cyzicus, now
represented by as many as 150 varieties) led him to doubt the
literary evidence for their existence[3]. It may be added that a
comprehensive lexicon of ancient coinage was produced by J. C. Rasche (1733—1805), who was born   Rasche
near Eisenach and was the pastor of a place near Meiningen.
His lexicon extended to fourteen volumes (1785—1805). It was
begun before the beginning but not finished until after the completion of Eckhel's *Historia*[4].

Our survey of the eighteenth century in Germany must close
with the name of Christian Gottfried Schütz, who
lived far into the nineteenth (1747—1832). He was   Schütz
professor at Jena for the twenty-five years that elapsed between
the six years of his first and the twenty-eight of his second tenure
of office at Halle, where he died at the great age of 85. A man
of wide attainments, and remarkable freshness and force of intellect, he is well known as an editor of Aeschylus[5]. In the text
of that author many passages are arbitrarily altered, but we find

---

[1] Vienna, 1792–8; also Addenda and portrait, 1826; ed. 4, 1841.

[2] F. Kenner, *Vortrag* (Wien, 1871); Stark, 222 f; Bursian, i 496–9.

[3] B. V. Head, *Doctrina Numorum*, 1887, Preface.

[4] Bursian, i 499 f.

[5] 1782–94; ed. 2, 1799—1807; ed. 3, 1809—1822.

frequent proof of critical acumen and of poetic taste[1]. He had
already edited the *Phoenissae* and the *Clouds*; he afterwards
began a more extensive edition of Aristophanes, but the first
three plays alone were published. He is perhaps best known as
an editor of Cicero. After commenting on the Rhetorical works[2],
and on all the Letters in chronological order[3], he produced a
complete edition in twenty volumes, ending with a lexicon and
with various indices[4]. The substance of the twenty-four programs
of his time at Jena was published in 1830; and he is remembered
as the founder, and for nearly fifty years the editor, of the
Allgemeine Litteraturzeitung, which, for the first twenty years of
its existence, was the foremost critical Review in Germany, and,
for the next forty, found a rival in the Review started at Jena in
1804 under the influence of Goethe[5], whose relation to the
Classics will engage our attention for a brief portion of the
following chapter.

Early in the eighteenth century the whole range of Greek and Latin literature was traversed by the erudite Fabricius. The Latin scholars, Gesner
(1731) and Ernesti (1773), promoted the study of the Greek Classics in the
schools of Germany. Reiske taught himself Greek at Halle (1732), while, in
1743 and 1770, Ruhnken and Wyttenbach learnt their Greek at Leyden. But,
between those dates, the land which they deserted was awakened by Winckelmann to a new sense of the beauty of Greek art (1755), and learnt from
Lessing the principles of literary and artistic criticism (1766). Winckelmann
and Lessing had an immediate influence on Heyne's teaching at Göttingen
(1767). Germany was next impelled by Herder to appreciate Homer as the
national poet of a primitive people (1773); the popular ear was won for Homer
by the poetic version of Voss (1781-93); and the close of the century saw the
triumph of the New Humanism with Homer for its hero. In and after 1790
we find its foremost representatives in the literary circle of Weimar and Jena,
in Herder, in Goethe and Schiller, and in Wilhelm von Humboldt. The last
of these was the earliest link between that circle and F. A. Wolf, who, in the
time of transition from the eighteenth to the nineteenth century, was destined,
by his published work and by his professorial teaching at Halle, to do two
eventful things:—to raise the Homeric question by the publication of his
Prolegomena (1795), and to map out the vast province of classical learning, and
find in a perfect knowledge of the many-sided life of the ancient Greeks and
Romans the final goal of the modern study of the ancient world.

---

[1] *e.g.* in *Eum.* 268 f (Wecklein), ἀντιποίνους τείνης is corrected into ἀντίποιν᾽
ὡς τίνῃς, and ὄψει δ᾽ ἐκεῖ, τίς into ὄψει δὲ κεῖ᾽ τις.

[2] 1804-8.   [3] 1809-13.   [4] 1814-21.   [5] Bursian, i 514-6.

BOOK V.

THE NINETEENTH CENTURY.

Alle bisherigen Ansichten laufen zu diesem vornehmsten Ziele wie zu einem Mittelpunkte zusammen. Es ist aber dieses Ziel kein anderes als die Kenntniss der alterthümlichen Menschheit selbst, welche Kenntniss aus der durch das Studium der alten Ueberreste bedingten Beobachtung einer organisch entwickelten bedeutungsvollen National-Bildung hervorgeht. Kein niedrigerer Standpunkt als dieser kann allgemeine und wissenschaftliche Forschungen über das Alterthum begründen.

F. A. WOLF, *Darstellung der Alterthums-Wissenschaft*,
p. 124, 1807.

Excolere animum et mentem doctrina, rerum utilium observatione et cognitione ingenii dotes omnes acuere, intelligendi facultatem in dies augere, vetera nosse et cognita emendare et amplificare, nova excogitando reperire, inquirere in rerum causas, perscrutari rerum originem et progressum, ex veteribus praesentia explicare, obscura et intricata expedire, ubique vera a falsis discernere, prava et vitiosa corrigere, futilia et absurda confutare, labefactare, tollere, et, ut uno verbo absolvam, verum videre, hoc demum est humano ingenio ac ratione dignum, hoc pabulum est animi, hoc demum est vivere.

C. G. COBET, *Protrepticus ad Studia Humanitatis*,
p. 6, 1854.

The humanistic studies have, during this century, become wider and more real. They have gradually been drawn out of a scholastic isolation, and have been brought more and more into the general current of intellectual and literary interests. So far from losing strength or efficacy by ceasing to hold that more exclusive position which they occupied two or three generations ago, they have acquired a fresh vigour, a larger sphere of genuine activity, and a place in the higher education which is more secure, because the acceptance on which it rests is more intelligent.

R. C. JEBB, *Humanism in Education*, p. 34, 1899.

History of Scholarship in the Nineteenth Century.
Germany, Austria*, and German Switzerland†.

Latin

- Spalding 1762—1811
- Heinrich 1774—1838
- Hand 1786—1851
- †Orelli[l] 1787—1849
- Doederlein 1791—1863
- K. G. Zumpt 1792—1849
- Lachmann 1793—1851
- †Baiter[l] 1801—1873
- Weissenborn 1803—1878
- Naegelsbach[g] 1806—1859
- Ritschl[g] 1806—1876
- Georges 1806—1895
- R. Klotz[g] 1807—1870
- Haase[g] 1808—1867
- K. L. Kayser[g] 1808—1872
- Haupt 1808—1874
- M. Seyffert 1809—1872
- Halm[g] 1809—1882
- Merkel[g] 1811—1885
- Hertz 1818—1895
- Teuffel[g] 1820—1878
- Fleckeisen 1820—1899
- Nipperdey 1821—1875
- H. Keil 1822—1894
- O. Ribbeck 1827—1898
- Umpfenbach 1835—1885
- Reifferscheid 1835—1887
- L. Müller 1836—1898
- A. Kiessling[g] 1837—1893
- O. Seyffert 1841—1906
- Studemund 1843—1889
- Hiller 1844—1891
- Baehrens 1848—1888
- Mendelssohn[g] 1852—1896
- Traube 1861—1907

Greek

- F. A. Wolf[l] 1759—1824
- Ilgen 1763—1834
- Buttmann 1764—1829
- G. H. Schaefer[l] 1764—1840
- F. Jacobs 1764—1847
- Schleiermacher 1768—1834
- A. H. Matthiae 1769—1835
- G. Hermann[l] 1772—1848
- Heindorf[l] 1774—1816
- Ast 1778—1841
- Lobeck 1781—1860
- Dissen[l] 1784—1837
- F. W. Thiersch 1784—1860
- Bekker[l] 1785—1871
- F. Passow[l] 1786—1833
- G. W. Nitzsch 1790—1861
- V. C. F. Rost 1790—1862
- C. A. Brandis 1790—1867
- Meineke[l] 1790—1870
- Voemel 1791—1868
- Reisig[l] 1792—1829
- Stallbaum 1793—1861
- Goettling 1793—1869
- Zell[le] 1793—1873
- Poppo 1794—1866
- Krueger 1796—1874
- Baehr 1798—1873
- †Rauchenstein 1798—1879
- Wunder[l] 1800—1869
- Bernhardy[l] 1800—1875
- Hartung 1802—1867
- Trendelenburg 1802—1872
- Kuehner[l] 1802—1878
- Lehrs[l] 1802—1878
- K. W. Dindorf 1802—1883

Greek contd.

- L. Spengel[l] 1803—1880
- Benseler 1806—1868
- Westermann 1806—1869
- Classen 1806—1891
- Ahrens 1809—1881
- Sauppe 1809—1893
- Schneidewin[l] 1810—1856
- Bergk[l] 1812—81
- Bonitz 1814—68
- Koechly 1815—1876
- O. Schneider 1815—1880
- A.T.H.Fritzsche[l] 1818—1878
- Tycho Mommsen 1819—1900
- Prantl 1820—88
- Hercher 1821—1878
- A. Nauck 1822—1892
- M. Schmidt 1823—1888
- Rossbach 1823—1898
- Bernays 1824—1881
- Westphal 1826—1892
- Susemihl 1826—1901
- *K. Schenkl 1827—1900
- W. Christ 1831—1906
- Usener 1834—1905
- Blass 1843—1907
- Kaibel 1849—1901
- †Meisterhans 1858—1894

Science of Language

- W. v. Humboldt 1767—1835
- Bopp 1791—1867
- Pott 1802—1887
- Benfey 1809—1881
- Corssen 1820—1875
- G. Curtius 1820—1885
- Schleicher 1821—1868
- Steinthal 1823—1899

History and Antiquities

- Heeren 1760—1842

Roman

- Niebuhr[l] 1776—1831
- Drumann 1786—1861
- W. A. Becker 1796—1846
- K. L. Peter 1808—1893
- Marquardt 1812—1882
- Henzen 1816—1887
- Mommsen[le] 1817—1903
- K. W. Nitzsch 1818—1880
- Schwegler 1819—1857
- Gregorovius 1821—1891
- Ihne 1821—1902
- L. Lange 1825—1885
- Huebner 1834—1901
- G. Wilmanns[e] 1845—1878

Greek

- W. Wachsmuth 1784—1866
- Dahlmann 1785—1860
- Boeckh[ge] 1785—1867
- Schoemann[gl] 1793—1879
- M. H. E. Meier 1796—1855
- Franz[e] 1804—1851
- K. F. Hermann[gl] 1804—1855
- J. G. Droysen 1808—1884
- Duncker 1811—1886
- E. Curtius 1814—1896
- A. Schaefer 1819—1883
- Holm 1830—1900
- †Hug 1832—95
- Koehler[e] 1838—1903
- G. Gilbert 1843—1899
- R. Schoell 1844—1893
- G. Hirschfeld[e] 1847—1895

Geography etc.

- Ross 1806—1859
- H. N. Ulrichs 1807—1843
- Kiepert 1818—1899
- Bursian[l] 1830—1883
- Jordan[l] 1833—1886

Mythology etc.

- Creuzer[gl] 1771—1858
- Forchhammer 1801—1894
- Preller[g] 1809—1861
- A. Kuhn 1812—1881
- Mannhardt 1831—1880
- Rohde[g] 1845—1898

Archaeology

- Hirt 1759—1837
- K. A. Boettiger 1760—1835
- Welcker[g] 1784—1868
- Gerhard 1795—1867
- K. O. Mueller[gl] 1797—1840
- Panofka 1801—1858
- K. Boetticher 1806—1889
- Braun 1809—1856
- Wieseler 1811—1892
- Jahn[gl] 1813—1869
- K. L. Urlichs[l] 1813—1889
- Stephani 1816—1887
- Schliemann 1822—1890
- Brunn 1822—94
- Stark 1824—79
- Overbeck 1826—1895
- Friederichs 1831—1871
- *Benndorf 1838—1907
- Humann 1839—1896
- Heydemann 1842—1889
- Matz 1843—74
- Bohn 1849—98

---

[g] also Greek   [l] also Latin   [e] epigraphy

Italy	France *contd.*	Holland	England	England *ctd.*
Borghesi 1781—1860	Cousin 1792—1867	Peerlkamp 1786—1865	Elmsley 1773—1825	Babington 1821—1889
Mai 1782—1854	J. G. Patin 1792—1876	Bake 1787-1864	S. Butler 1774—1839	Maine 1822—1888
V. A. Peyron 1785—1870	Le Bas 1794—1860	Geel 1789—1862	Leake 1777—1860	H. A. Holden 1822—1896
Avellino 1788—1850	Alexandre 1797—1870	Karsten 1802—1864	Gaisford 1779—1855	Riddell 1823—1866
Canina 1795—1856	Thierry 1797—1873	Boot 1811—1901	Fynes Clinton 1781—1852	Conington 1825—1869
Cavedoni 1795—1865	Quicherat 1799—1884	Cobet 1813—89	Dobree 1782—1825	Sellar 1825—1890
Vallauri 1805—1897	Littré 1801—1881	**Belgium**	Monk 1784-1856	Grant 1826—84
Cavallari 1809—1898	Texier 1802—1871	Roulez 1806—1878	C. J. Blomfield 1786—1857	Chandler 1828—1889
De-Vit 1810—1892	(Dübner) 1802—1867	De Witte 1808—1889	Grote 1794—1871	Geddes 1828—1900
Bruzza 1812—1883	Duc de Luynes 1803—1867	Thonissen 1816—1891	Veitch 1794—1885	Burn 1829-1904
Garucci 1812—1885	Mérimée 1803—1870	Roersch 1831—1891	Arnold 1795—1842	Monro 1836—1905
A. Fabretti 1816—1894	B. St Hilaire 1805—1895	Willems 1840—1898	Key 1795—1875	Nettleship 1839—1893
Corradini 1820—1888	D. Nisard 1806—1888	**Scandinavia**	Henry 1796—1876	A. Palmer 1841—1897
De Rossi 1822—1894	C. Nisard 1808—1889	Zoëga 1755—1809	Thirlwall 1797—1875	Jebb 1841—1905
Fiorelli 1824—1896	De Presle 1809—1875	Bröndsted 1780—1842	Long 1800-79	A. S. Wilkins 1843—1905
Gandino 1827—1905	Renier 1809—1885	Madvig 1804—1886	B. H. Kennedy 1804—1889	Pelham 1846—1907
Bonghi 1828—1895	Duruy 1811—1894	Ussing 1820—1905	G. C. Lewis 1806—1863	Rutherford 1853—1907
Ascoli 1829—1907	Miller 1812—1886	Linder 1825—1882	W. Ramsay 1806—1865	J. Adam 1860—1907
Pezzi 1844—1906	Wallon 1812—1905	Bugge 1833—1907	T. W. Peile 1806—1882	
	Martin 1813—1884	**Greece**	C. Wordsworth 1807—1885	**United States of America**
France	Egger 1813—85	Koraës 1748—1833	H. E. Allen 1808—1874	Woolsey 1801—1889
Gail 1755—1829	C. Lenormant 1816—1881	Mustoxydes 1785—1860	Merivale 1808—1894	Felton 1807—1862
Quatremère de Quincy 1755—1849	Longpérier 1816—1881	Rangabes 1810—1892	Shilleto 1809—1876	(E. A. Sophocles) 1807—1883
Millin 1759—1818	Daremberg 1817—1872	Oeconomides 1812—1884	Blackie 1809—1895	Frieze 1817—89
Mionnet 1770—1842	Cougny 1818—1889	Kumanudes 1818—1899	Thompson 1810—1886	Drisler 1818—97
Walckenaer 1771—1852	Thurot 1823—1882	Semitelos 1828—1898	Donaldson 1811—1861	Hadley 1821-72
Boissonade 1774—1857	Desjardins 1823—1886	**Russia**	Scott 1811—87	A. Harkness 1822—1907
J. L. Burnouf 1775—1844	Beulé 1826—1875	Graefe 1780—1851	Lushington 1811—1893	Lane 1823—97
Clarac 1777—1847	W. H. Wadding-ton 1826—94	Kröneberg 1788—1838	Liddell 1811-98	W. D. Whitney 1827—1894
(K. B. Hase) 1780—1864	Tissot 1828—1884	Lugebil 1830—1888	Badham 1813—1884	Kellogg 1828—1903
Raoul Rochette 1783—1854	De Coulanges 1830—1889	Iernstedt 1854—1902	G. Rawlinson 1815—1902	Greenough 1833—1901
Naudet 1786—1878	Benoist 1831—1887	**Hungary**	Paley 1816—1888	C. T. Lewis 1834—1904
Letronne 1787—1848	F. Lenormant 1837—1883	Telfy 1816—98	Newton 1816—1894	Packard 1836—1884
Villemain 1790—1870	Rayet 1847—1887	Abel 1858—1889	Linwood 1817—1878	Merriam 1843—1895
Didot 1790—1876	V. Henry 1850—1907		Jowett 1817—1894	F. D. Allen 1844—1897
	Graux 1852—82		Cope 1818—69	Seymour 1848—1907
	Riemann 1853—1891		Munro 1819—1885	M. Warren 1850—1907
			Gifford 1820—1905	Earle 1864—1905
			W. G. Clark 1821—1878	

F. A. WOLF.

From Wagner's engraving of the portrait by Jo. Wolff (1823). Frontispiece
to S. F. W. Hoffmann's ed. of Wolf's *Alterthums-Wissenschaft*, 1833.

CHAPTER XXVIII.

F. A. WOLF AND HIS CONTEMPORARIES.

A NEW era begins with the name of Friedrich August Wolf (1759—1824). His father was the schoolmaster and organist of the little village of Hainrode near Nordhausen, south of the Harz, and it was to his mother that he owed the awakening of his intellectual life. Before he had attained the age of two, he knew a large number of Latin words, and, before he was eight, had acquired the rudiments of Greek and French, and could read an easy Latin author. His memory was as remarkable as that of Porson, who was born in the same year. His parents soon removed to Nordhausen, where, by the age of twelve, he had learned all that his instructors could teach him. At his new home, the first of his three head-masters was Johann Andreas Fabricius (1696—1769), the author of a History of Learning[1]. Towards the end of his school-days he became his own teacher. Starting once more with the declensions, he 'read with new eyes the Latin and Greek Classics, some carefully, others more cursorily; learnt by heart several books of Homer, and large portions of the Tragedians and Cicero, and went through Scapula's *Lexicon* and Faber's *Thesaurus*'. During this time of strenuous study, 'he would sit up the whole night in a room without a stove, his feet in a pan of cold water, and one of his eyes bound up to rest the other'[2]. Happily this severe ordeal ended with his removal to the university of Göttingen.

On the 8th of April, 1777, he entered his name in the matriculation-book as *Studiosus Philologiae*. The Pro-Rector, a professor of Medicine, protested:—" Philology was not one of

F. A. Wolf

---

[1] *Abriss einer allgemeinen Historie der Gelehrsamkeit*, 3 vols., 1752–4.
[2] W. Körte, i 21 f; Pattison's *Essays*, i 342 f.

the four *Faculties*; if he wanted to become a school-master, he ought to enter himself as a 'student of *Theology*'". Wolf insisted that he proposed to study, not Theology, but Philology. He carried his point, and was the first student who was so entered in that university[1]. The date of his matriculation has been deemed an epoch in the History of German Education, and also in the History of Scholarship. He next waited on the Rector, Heyne, to whom he had presented a letter of introduction a year before. Hastily glancing at this letter, Heyne had then asked him, who had been stupid enough to advise him to study 'what he called philology'. Wolf replied that he preferred 'the greater intellectual freedom' of that study. Heyne assured him that 'freedom' could nowhere be found, that the study of the Classics was 'the straight road to starvation', and that there were hardly six good chairs of philology in all Germany. Wolf modestly suggested that he aspired to fill one of the six; Heyne could only laugh and bid farewell to the future 'professor of philology', adding that, when he entered at Göttingen, he would be welcome to attend Heyne's lectures gratis. When he actually entered, Heyne, who was a busy man, treated him with a strange indifference. However, Wolf put down his name for Heyne's private course on the *Iliad*, noted all the books cited in the introductory lecture, gathered all these books around him, and carefully prepared the subject of each lecture, but was so disappointed with the vague and superficial treatment of the subject, that, as soon as the professor had finished the first book, he ceased to attend. In the next *semester*, he found himself excluded from the course on Pindar. However, he went on working by himself; to save time, he spent only three minutes in dressing, and cut off every form of recreation. At the end of the first year, he had nearly killed himself, and, after a brief change of air, resolved never to work beyond midnight. By the end of the second, he had begun to give lectures on his own account, and, half a year later, was appointed, on Heyne's recommendation, to a mastership at Ilfeld. There he remained for two years and a half, married, and, for little more than a year, was head-master of Osterode. At both

[1] There had been isolated entries of *philologiae studiosi* at Erlangen in 1749-74 (Gudeman's *Grundriss*, 193).

places he made his mark.   At Ilfeld he began to brood over the
Homeric question, and also to work at Plato.   In 1782 he produced an edition of the *Symposium*, in which he followed a recent
innovation by writing the notes in German.   His aim throughout
was to interest young students in the study of Plato.   In the
preface he introduced an adroit reference to Frederick the Great,
'the philosopher on the throne', and to his 'enlightened minister',
von Zedlitz, to whom Frederick had addressed his memorable
letter on education only three years before[1]; he also paid a
compliment to Gedike, who then had great influence with the
minister[2].   This preface, and the proof of his success as a school-
master, led to his being invited by the minister to fill a chair of
'Philosophy and *Pädagogik*' at the university of Halle.   The
stipend was only £45 a year, with no house, but the offer was
accepted, and thus Wolf, at the age of twenty-four, found himself
in a position rich in ample opportunities.   He had been commissioned to remove from Halle the only reproach to which it
was then open,—that of not being a 'school of philology'.   In a
few years he entirely changed the spirit of the university, and,
'through it, of all the higher education in Germany, waking in
schools and universities an enthusiasm for ancient literature
second only to that of the Revival in the sixteenth century'[3].
One of the means whereby he raised the level of classical studies
was the institution in 1786 of a philological *Seminarium* for the
training of classical teachers[4].   The other was his work as a
public lecturer.   During his twenty-three years at Halle, lecturing
on the average for rather more than two hours a day, he gave at
least fifty courses on classical authors.

His lectures on the *Iliad*, begun in 1785, were resumed in alternate years;
he lectured thrice on the *Odyssey*, while his other courses dealt with the
Homeric Hymns, Hesiod, Pindar, Theognis, the Dramatists, and Callimachus,
and, in prose, Herodotus, Demosthenes, Aeschines, Plato, Xenophon, Lucian,
Aristotle's treatise on Poetry, and 'Longinus', as well as the usual Latin
authors, together with the elder Pliny's outline of the history of ancient art.
He also gave fifteen courses of original lectures, including an introduction to

[1] Paulsen, ii 72[2].

[2] pp. 133 f of reprint in *Kleine Schriften*, i 131—157; abstract of *Symposium, ib.* ii 593.

[3] Pattison, i 359 f.   [4] Details in Pattison, i 367–9.

Homer and Plato, Latin Composition, History of Greek and Latin Literature, Greek and Roman Antiquities, Ancient Geography, Principles of History and Survey of Ancient History, Ancient Painting and Numismatics, History of Philology, and, as a general introduction, a course on the 'Encyclopaedia of Philology'[1]. This last course, which was first announced in 1785, assumed its final form when it was printed at Berlin in 1807 as a survey of the whole field of classical learning and a conspectus of all its component parts[2].

His lectures were fully prepared beforehand, but were delivered with the aid of only a few notes. Goethe, who, in 1805, more than once prevailed on one of the professor's daughters to conceal him behind a curtain in the lecture-room, tells us that the language impressed him as 'the spontaneous utterance of a full mind, a revelation springing from thorough knowledge, and diffusing itself over the audience'[3]. His aim was, not to communicate knowledge, but to stimulate and suggest. The spirit of critical inquiry that breathed through all his lectures was symbolised by the fact that the sole ornament of his lecture-room was a bust of Lessing.

When Wolf went to Halle, the 'philanthropists' serving under the banner of Basedow in the school of Dessau[1] had, for the first time since the Revival of Learning, succeeded in discrediting the study of the ancient languages in North Germany. Wolf 'represents the reaction against the new realism'[5], and his conflict with the modern school of useful knowledge brought into clear relief his ideal of a culture founded on Greek traditions. In 1807 he defines this ideal as a 'purely human education', an 'elevation of all the powers of the mind and soul to a beautiful harmony of the inner and outer man'[6].

Everything that he wrote arose out of his public teaching. Early in his career he had produced an edition of Hesiod's *Theogonia* (1783), of all the Homeric poems (1784–5), and of four Greek plays (1787)[7]. His reading of Demosthenes in connexion with Attic Law bore fruit in his edition of the *Leptines*

---

[1] Cp. Körte, ii 214–8; Arnoldt, i 119 f; Bursian, i 521.

[2] *Kleine Schriften*, ii 808—895, *Darstellung der Alterthums-Wissenschaft*.

[3] *Tag- und Jahres-Hefte* 1805, xxx 155 Cotta's Jubil. ed. (xxiv 195 ed. Düntzer); Pattison, i 371.

[4] Paulsen, ii 51[2].   [5] Pattison, i 373.

[6] Pattison, i 374.

[7] Aesch. *Ag.*, Soph. *O.T.*, Eur. *Phoen.*, Arist. *Eccl.*

(1789), which was intended for advanced students, and not for schools. It was welcomed by scholars, not excluding Heyne; and the way in which Greek Antiquities were treated in the *Prolegomena* inspired one of Wolf's greatest pupils, Boeckh, with the design of writing his 'Public Economy of Athens'. The corrected edition, announced twenty-seven years later, never appeared; of his 'Select Dialogues of Lucian', only one volume was published (1786); and his Herodian (1792) remained un-revised. He was fond of lecturing on the *Tusculan Disputations*, and printed a text for the use of his class; for the purport of his own exposition, which has been described as 'rich in keen remark on the force of words and phrases', we have to turn to the end of Orelli's edition of 1829[1].

Even his famous *Prolegomena to Homer* (1795) had a purely casual origin. His text of 1784–5 being out of print, he was asked to prepare a new edition, and, as there were to be no notes whatsoever, he proposed to write a preface explaining the principles on which he had dealt with the text. He did far more than this, for he roused into life the great controversy known as the Homeric question. Some of the points connected with the earlier stages of this controversy may here be noticed.

Josephus[2], writing about 90 A.D., had held that the art of writing 'could not have been known to the Greeks of the Trojan war', and 'they say' (he added) 'that even Homer did not leave his poetry in writing, but that it was transmitted by memory, and afterwards put together from the separate songs; hence the number of discrepancies'. This passage had been noticed in 1583 by Casaubon[3], who remarked that 'we could hardly hope for a sound text of Homer, however old our MSS might be'. Bentley, in 1713, had supposed that a poet named Homer lived about 1050 B.C. and '*wrote* a sequel of songs and rhapsodies...These loose songs were not collected together in the form of an epic poem till Pisistratus' time, above 500 years after'[4]. In 1730, the Italian scholar, Vico, had maintained that 'Homer' was a collective name for the work of many successive poets; but Vico's views were at this time unknown to Wolf. He was, however, familiar with Robert Wood's *Essay on the Original Genius of Homer* (1769)[5]. Only seven copies had then been printed, but one of them had been sent to Göttingen, and was reviewed by Heyne[6]. It was soon translated into German[7]. In the course of some pages on the learning

---

[1] Pattison, i 377.
[2] *Contra Apionem*, i 2.
[3] On Diog. Laërt. ix 12.
[4] Vol. ii 408 *supra*.
[5] Vol. ii 432 *supra*.
[6] *Gött. Gel. Anz.* 1770, 32.
[7] By J. D. Michaelis of Göttingen (1773; 1778[2]); 2nd English ed. 1775.

of Homer, Wood had argued that the art of writing was unknown to the poet.
Wolf refers to this passage, and builds his theory upon it[1]. The *scholia* of the
codex Venetus of the *Iliad*, published by Villoison in 1788, supplied evidence
as to divergencies between the ancient texts. Wolf maintained that these
divergencies were due to the Homeric poems having long been transmitted by
memory alone. He contended that it was impossible to arrive at the original
text, and that an editor could aim at nothing more than a reconstruction of the
text of the Alexandrian age.

The *Prolegomena*, written in great haste, formed a narrow octavo volume of
280 pages. The author begins by discussing the defects in the existing editions,
due to an imperfect use of Eustathius and the *scholia*. He next reviews the
history of the poems from about 950 to 550 B.C., and endeavours to prove the
four following points:—

'(1) The Homeric poems were composed without the aid of writing, which
in 950 B.C. was either wholly unknown to the Greeks, or not yet employed
by them for literary purposes. The poems were handed down by oral recitation, and in the course of that process suffered many alterations, deliberate or
accidental, by the rhapsodes. (2) After the poems had been written down
circa 550 B.C., they suffered still further changes. These were deliberately
made by 'revisers' (διασκευασταί), or by learned critics who aimed at polishing
the work, and bringing it into harmony with certain forms of idiom or canons
of art. (3) The *Iliad* has artistic unity; so, in a still higher degree, has the
Odyssey. But this unity is not mainly due to the original poems; rather it has
been superinduced by their artificial treatment in a later age. (4) The original
poems, from which our *Iliad* and our *Odyssey* have been put together, were
not all by the same author'[2].

In the *Prolegomena* Wolf supposes that Homer 'began the weaving of the
web' and 'carried it down to a certain point'[3], and, further, that Homer wrote
the *greater part* of the songs afterwards united in the *Iliad* and *Odyssey*. In
the preface to the text, dated March 1795, he adds, 'it is certain that, alike in
the *Iliad* and in the *Odyssey*, the web was begun, and the threads were carried
to a certain point, by the poet who had first taken up the theme...Perhaps it
will never be possible to show, even with probability, the precise points at
which new filaments or dependencies of the texture begin: but...we must assign
to Homer *only the greater part* of the songs, and the remainder to the Homeridae, who were following out the lines traced by him'[4].

'He has himself told us, in memorable words, how he felt on turning from
his own theory to a renewed perusal of the poems. As he steeps himself in that
stream of epic story which glides like a clear river, his own arguments vanish
from his mind; the pervading harmony and consistency of the poems assert

[1] *Proleg.* c. 12, n. 8.

[2] Jebb's *Homer*, 108 f; cp. Volkmann's *Geschichte und Kritik der Wolfschen
Prolegomena*, 1874, 48—67; and Bursian, i 526 f.

[3] c. 28 *ad finem*, and c. 31.

[4] *Praefat.* p. xxviii (Jebb, 109), *Kl. Schr.* 211 f.

themselves with irresistible power; and he is angry with the scepticism which
has robbed him of belief in one Homer'[1].

The book was dedicated to Ruhnken[2]. In the following year,
on Ruhnken's proposal, Wolf was invited to fill a professorship
then vacant at Leyden; the invitation was declined, but Wolf
visited Holland, and thus made the personal acquaintance of
Ruhnken and Wyttenbach. For the present, not a single authoritative voice was raised in favour of Wolf's views in Holland,
England, or France. The publication of the *Prolegomena* was
regarded as a 'literary impiety' by Villoison, who regretted that
his edition of the *scholia* had helped to forge the weapons of the
German critic[3]. A favourable review in a French periodical[4]
aroused Sainte-Croix to attempt the refutation of the literary
paradox[5]. Fauriel in France, and Elmsley in England, were only
twenty-two when the *Prolegomena* appeared; the former 'trans-
planted the Wolfian idea to French soil' at a later date[6]; the
latter showed little interest in the question in his review of
Heyne's *Homer*[7]. In Germany Wolf's views were welcomed by
Wilhelm von Humboldt, and by the brothers Schlegel[8]; but they
were disapproved by the poets, by Klopstock and Schiller and
Wieland, and by Voss, the translator of Homer[9]. Goethe was at
first in favour of Wolf[10], but, writing to Schiller in 1798, he was
more than ever convinced of the unity of the *Iliad*[11]. Meanwhile, Herder had published an anonymous paper headed 'Homer,
Time's Favourite'[12], in the course of which he incidentally
remarked that the rhapsodic origin of the Homeric poems had
long been known to himself; that as a boy he had discovered
the distinct authorship of the *Iliad* and *Odyssey*, and that the

[1] *ib.* xxi f (Jebb, 110).

[2] Vol. ii 460 *supra*; on Wolf and Ruhnken, see S. Reiter in *Neue Jahrb.
f. kl. Alt.* xviii (1906) 1—16, 83—101.

[3] Vol. ii 398 *supra*.   [4] Caillard in *Millin's Magazin Encycl.* iii 10.

[5] *Réfutation d'un paradoxe littéraire de M. Wolf* (1798); Volkmann, 106 f.

[6] Pattison, i 383.

[7] *Edin. Rev.* July, 1803. In 1804 Flaxman, writing as an artist, said:
'the *Prolegomena* strongly enforces' the truth, 'that human excellence in art
and science is the accumulated labour of ages' (Körte, ii 224 f).

[8] Volkmann, 74, 77 f.   [9] Bursian, i 529.

[10] Körte, i 277 f.   [11] Körte, i 280; Volkmann, 75 f.

[12] *Horen*, Sept. 1795; xviii 420—446, ed. Suphan.

suspicions of his boyhood had been confirmed by the newly-published Venetian *scholia*, which he had seen during his recent visit to Italy[1]. Wolf, who regarded Herder's article as a kind of plagiarism, wrote to Heyne complaining of Herder's behaviour, and begging Heyne to review the *Prolegomena*. Heyne had already written his review, and had treated the work as 'the first-fruits of the unexampled labours of Villoison', adding that he had always held the same views himself, and even intimating that Wolf had originally derived them from Heyne's lectures[2]. Wolf reminded Heyne of the Essay on Homer which he had sent him in 1779; Heyne replied that he had forgotten the Essay, but remembered conversing with Herder on Homer as early as 1770. Heyne's charge of plagiarism was not repeated, but it was not withdrawn[3]. In 1797 Wolf replied by publishing, in the form of a pamphlet, his 'Letters to Heyne'[4]. Heyne's *Homer* appeared in 1802, and was reviewed in an exceedingly bitter spirit by Voss and Eichstädt, who were aided by Wolf[5]. It was not until the next generation that the *Prolegomena* bore fruit in the continued study of the Homeric question. Meanwhile, the author's only subsequent Homeric publication was the singularly beautiful and correct edition of the text printed by Göschen at Leipzig, with Flaxman's illustrations (1804–7).

Wolf was still at Halle when he edited Cicero's four orations *post reditum* (1801). Their spuriousness had been suspected by Markland (1745)[6]; their genuineness had been maintained by Gesner (1753)[7]. Markland's suspicions were approved by Wolf[8], who in the following year even denied the genuineness of the *pro Marcello*[9]. Not a few of the faults criticised by Wolf have since been removed with the aid of better MSS. . Wolf's opinion was approved at the time by Boissonade in France, but the in-

[1] Pattison, i 386 f; Volkmann, 79—82 ; Bursian, i 464 f.
[2] *Gött. Gel. Anz.* 21 Nov. (and 19 Dec.) 1795.
[3] Heyne's letter of 28 Feb. 1796 (Pattison, i 388).
[4] Reprinted at the end of Peppmüller's ed. of the *Prolegomena* (1884).
[5] Jena *Litteraturzeitung*, Mai 1803, in 16 of the numbers 123—141; Bursian, i 531 ; Volkmann, 116—119.
[6] Vol. ii 413 *supra*. [7] *Comm. Gott.* iii 223—284, *Cicero restitutus*.
[8] *Kl. Schr.*, i 369—389; Körte, i 321-8.
[9] *Kl. Schr.* i 389—409; Körte, i 328 f.

vestigations have been characterised by Madvig as 'superficial and misleading'[1]. Wolf produced a comprehensive edition of Suetonius in 1802, while his interest in the best modern Latin led him to reprint Ruhnken's eulogy of Hemsterhuys, with Ernesti's oration on Gesner[2].

The twenty-three years of Wolf's memorable career at Halle were brought to a sudden end in 1806 by the catastrophe of Jena. On the 17th of October the French troops took possession of Halle, and, three days later, the French general closed the university and sent the students to their homes. Under the advice of Goethe, Wolf spent part of his enforced leisure in revising his survey of the domain of classical learning, which was to be the opening article of the ' Museum ' of *Alterthums-Wissenschaft* founded by Wolf and his pupil Buttmann in 1807. From the spring of that year he lived at Berlin for the remaining seventeen years of his life, but it proved impossible for the State to utilise his abilities either at the Board of Education or in the newly-founded University (1810). Thenceforth he produced little, and that little not of the best quality. In 1816 he published his *Analecta*, in which he gave proof of his interest in the careers of the leading scholars of England[3].

At Halle, Wolf had invited his pupil Heindorf to join him in preparing a complete edition of Plato. As Wolf's plan made no progress, Heindorf, who had meanwhile left for Berlin, produced in 1802 the first of the four volumes of his twelve select dialogues (1802–10). It was dedicated to Wolf, but Wolf was dissatisfied, and, with the aid of Bekker, produced in 1812 a text of three dialogues[4], in the preface of which he announced his intention to publish the whole. In April, 1816, Wolf, in the preface to his *Analecta*, referred to Heindorf in ungenerous terms[5], which aroused a protest ascribed to the joint authorship of some of the foremost scholars of the day[6]. Heindorf died at Halle two months later, and, not long afterwards, Wolf's health began to fail. He pro-

---

[1] Madvig's pref. to Nutzhorn's ed. (1869); *Opusc. Acad.* (1841), ii 339, and *Adv. Crit.* (1873), ii 211.

[2] 1788; cp. *Jena Litt. Zeitung*, 1791.   [3] *Kl. Schr.* ii 1030—1116.

[4] *Euthyphro, Apol., Crito*; Praef. in *Kl. Schr.* i 418 f.

[5] *Kl. Schr.* ii 1022.

[6] Buttmann, Schleiermacher, Schneider, Niebuhr, Boeckh (Körte, ii 106 f).

duced nothing after 1820. A serious illness in 1822 was followed
two years later by his being ordered to Nice ; on his way, he died
at Marseilles, where a Latin epitaph marks the approximate site
of his grave. A bust, copied by Heidel from that of Tieck,
commemorates him amid the scenes of his greatest success as a
teacher, in the *aula* of the university of Halle. A portrait, painted
by an artist bearing the same surname as himself, represents him
in the year before his death[1]. ' In personal appearance Wolf had
an imposing, dignified, somewhat imperious air. He was slightly
above the middle size, broad-shouldered, deep-chested ; hands and
feet well-proportioned. A capacious forehead, prominent eye-
brow, searching blue eye, combined to express keenness and
force of mind '[2]. His greatest work is to be found, not in the
books that he produced but in the pupils that he stimulated to be
the future leaders of classical learning in Germany during the first
half of the nineteenth century. He himself claimed to be a
teacher rather than a writer, and his published works were only
parerga[3]. But in the broad survey of the whole range of classical
learning, which formed part of his teaching, he was the first to
present a systematic description of the vast fabric that he called
by the name of *Alterthums-Wissenschaft*, to arrange and review
its component parts, and to point to a perfect knowledge of the
many-sided life of the ancient Greeks and Romans as the final
goal of the modern study of the ancient world. He raised that
study to the rank of a single comprehensive and independent
science, and thus deserved to be reverently regarded by posterity
as the eponymous hero of all the long line of later scholars[4].
Like Bentley, to whom he was drawn by the admiring sympathy
of a kindred genius, he was one of the founders of a right method
in the historic criticism of ancient literature. Like Herder, he
regarded the *Iliad* and the *Odyssey* as part of the popular poetry of
a primitive age, but it was not until the next generation that his
theory as to the origin of those poems was widely discussed by
scholars[5].

[1] Reproduced on p. 50.

[2] Pattison, i 412.   [3] *Kl. Schr.* ii 1019.

[4] Cp. Niebuhr, *Kl. Schr.* ii 227 (ap. Bursian, i 548).

[5] *Prolegomena ad Homerum*, 1795 (1859²; *cum Bekkeri notis*, 1872);

While Wolf, with his views as to the divided authorship of the
songs composing the Homeric poems, appealed to
scholars alone, and received little recognition even
from scholars in his own age, the ear of the German people had
happily been won for Homer by a poet, who doubtless found a new
reason for resisting the Wolfian theories in the fact that he had
himself succeeded in preserving in his German version 'that
uniform tone of simplicity and nature, which distinguishes the
Homeric poetry from all artificial writing'[1]. The famous translator of Homer, Johann Heinrich Voss (1751—1826), was born
at Sommersdorf in the district of Mecklenburg in North Germany.
Entering the university of Göttingen in 1772, he began by
attending Heyne's lectures on Homer, but was soon estranged by
the influence of some of the youthful poets of the day[2]. He was
mainly self-taught. Homer was the centre of his early studies,
and, before leaving Göttingen, he had begun to translate parts of
the Homeric poems into German hexameters. He published the
first specimens of these translations in 1776, in his rendering of
Blackwell's *Enquiries into the life and writings of Homer*. He
soon afterwards formed the design of translating the whole of the

Voss

Briefe an Heyne, 1797; both reprinted by Peppmüller, 1884. *Kleine Schriften*,
1200 pp., ed. Bernhardy, 2 vols., 1869, including Wolf's *Darstellung der
Alterthums-Wissenschaft. Encyclopaedie der Philologie*, ed. Stockmann, 1831,
1845; *Vorlesungen über die Enc. der Alterthumswissenschaft*, ed. Gürtler and
Hoffmann, 5 vols. 1831–5; *Vorlesungen über die ersten vier Gesänge der Ilias*,
ed. Usteri, 1830–1. Bibliography in Goedeke's *Grundriss*, vii[2] 807–11.

Life by his son-in-law, W. Körte, 2 vols. (1833), and by Arnoldt in part i of
F. A. W. in seinem Verhältnisse zum Schulwesen (1861–2); cp. A. Baumstark,
F. A. W. und die Gelehrtenschule (1864). Pattison's *Essays*, i 337—414;
Bursian, i 517—548; Paulsen, ii 208—227[2]; W. Schrader, *Gesch. der Univ.
Halle*, i (1894) 434—462; A. Harnack, *Gesch. der preuss. Akad.* ii 565 f, 660 f;
M. Bernays, *Goethes Briefe an W.* 1868; S. Reiter, *Wolfs Briefe an Goethe*, in
Goethe-Jahrb. xxvii (1906) 3—96; on Wolf, *id.* in *Neue Jahrb. f. kl. Alt.* xiii
(1904) 89—111, and on Wolf and Ruhnken, *id.* p. 57, note 2 *supra*.

[1] Pattison, i 384 f.

[2] Herbst, i 67. Voss' notes of Heyne's lectures, apparently copied from
those of a fellow-student, show that Heyne drew special attention to the works
of Blackwell (1736) and Robert Wood (1769), and that he held that the *Iliad*
and *Odyssey* could not have been reduced to writing, while he expressed no
doubt as to the personality of the author or the unity of each of the two poems.

Odyssey. He began by attacking the episode of Polyphemus and
the eight lines on Sisyphus[1], brooding over the latter during his
lonely walks for a whole fortnight. His earliest rendering of this
passage, approved by Klopstock in 1777, was subsequently submitted to no less than four successive revisions. In the final
version the toilsome effort to heave the stone up to the crest of
the hill is effectively rendered:—*Eines Marmors Schwere mit
grosser Gewalt fortheben*; and the swift rebound to the valley is
no less effective:—*Hurtig mit Donnergepolter entrollte der tück-
ische Marmor*[2]. Meanwhile, Voss had settled near Hamburg
(1775–82), being for the last four of those years master of the
school at Ottendorf on the estuary of the Elbe. His *Odyssey*
(1781) surpassed all previous attempts to render the original in
German verse[3]. In the same year he translated into Latin the
Homeric Hymn to Demeter[4], and his abiding interest in that poem
is attested by the improved text, translated into German verse and
accompanied with a comprehensive commentary, which was posthumously published in 1826. His *Odyssey* was followed twelve
years later by his *Iliad* (1793), and by a closer rendering of the
Odyssey, which, in the opinion of competent critics, is not an
improvement on his earlier version[5]. He applied the same principles of rigidly literal translation to his subsequent rendering of
the whole of Virgil, and the *Metamorphoses* of Ovid, as well as
Tibullus, Propertius, and Aristophanes; but his method had by
that time become unduly mechanical, and he failed to represent
either the variety of Aristophanes or the charm of Ovid. As
master of the school at Eutin, amid the lakes of Holstein (1782—
1802), he began his work on Virgil with an edition of the *Georgics*
including a translation in German verse, and a German commentary, mainly on the subject-matter (1789). Its publication
led to a feud with Heyne, who, in his own edition, had neglected
that part of the commentator's duty[6]. Eight years afterwards,

---

[1] xi 593 f.   [2] Herbst, i 30, 303.
[3] Herbst, ii (1) 78 f.   [4] *ib.* i 238.
[5] So Wieland, A. W. Schlegel, Goethe, Herder, Schiller, W. v. Humboldt,
and Hermann (*ib.* ii (1) 207, 315); cp. M. Bernays, *Introd.* to reprint (1881) of
first ed. of *Odyssey*.
[6] Bursian, i 553 n.

Voss published a similar edition of the *Eclogues* (1797)[1]. On resigning his mastership, he lived for three years at Jena (1802–5), and, for the last twenty-one years of his life, enjoyed the status and stipend of a professor at Heidelberg (1805–26). It was there that he produced his translation of Tibullus, in the preface to which he showed, on chronological grounds, that the third book of the Elegies was the work of another poet. He added a critical edition of the text. He also translated and expounded Aratus (1824). To the vast review of Heyne's *Iliad*, already mentioned[2], he contributed by far the largest share[3]. His own commentary on the first *Iliad* and on part of the second was posthumously published[4]. Of his prolix exposition of the *Odyssey* only two specimens were printed, an essay on the Ocean of the Ancients[5], and a paper on the site of Ortygia[6]. While he was rash and injudicious as a textual critic, he was too cautiously conservative to appreciate the value either of Wolf's *Prolegomena*[7], or of K. O. Müller's investigation of the old Greek legends. Apart from his translation of Homer, his best work was in the field of ancient Geography[8], a work continued by his pupil, F. A. Ukert (1780—1851)[9]. In his mythological studies there were two periods, marked by his opposition (1) to Heyne and his school, and (2) to Creuzer. The evidence for the former is contained in his *Mythologische Briefe* (1794); that for the latter, in his *Anti-Symbolik* (1824–6)[10].

The *Homeric Hymns*, with the *Batrachomyomachia* and its later imitations, were edited in 1796 by Karl Ilgen (1763— 1834), who inspired his private pupil, Hermann, with his earliest interest in the Classics (1784–6), and when the

Ilgen

---

[1] *Ecl.* and *Georg.* republished in four vols., 1800, with a plate in iii 100 giving 17 illustrations of Virgil's 'plough', 1, 2, 3 derived from the Virgil published by Knapton and Sandby (London, 1750).

[2] p. 58, n. 5 *supra*.   [3] Reprinted in his *Kritische Blätter*, i 1—168.

[4] *ib.* i 169—254.   [5] *Antisymbolik*, ii 145—155.

[6] Boie's *Deutsches Museum* (1780), 302 f.

[7] Volkmann, on Wolf, 71 f, and Voss' *Briefe*, ii 213—254 (Bursian, i 529 n).

[8] *Kritische Blätter*, ii 127—451.

[9] *Geographie der Griechen und Römer*, 1816–46.

[10] Bursian, i 559—562. On Voss in general, see the admirable work of W. Herbst, 1872–6; and Bursian, i 548—562; 583 f.

important position of head-master of Schulpforta was declined by
Hermann, was appointed at Hermann's instance to an office
which he long continued to fill with the highest distinction
(1802–31)[1].

The *Greek Anthology* is permanently associated with the name
of Christian Friedrich Wilhelm Jacobs (1764—
Jacobs   1847), who was born and bred at Gotha, studied
at Jena and Göttingen, and, with the exception of a few years at
Munich (1807–10), spent the rest of his life in his native place,
first as a master in the local school, and afterwards as Librarian
and Director of the Cabinet of Coins and the Museum of Art. In
connexion with the *Anthology*, he produced (**1**) an edition in
thirteen volumes (1794—1814), in which the text of the epigrams
in Brunck's *Analecta* is followed by a learned and judicious commentary[2]; (**2**) a text in three volumes (1813–7), printed from a
transcript of the Palatine MS made by Spaletti, the Secretary of
the Vatican Library ; (**3**) a selection for the use of schools (1826);
and (**4**) a translation of 700 epigrams in German verse (1803–23)[3].
He published the first complete edition of the *Antehomerica*,
Homerica, and *Posthomerica* of Tzetzes (1793). He also edited
Achilles Tatius (1821), the Philostrati and Callistratus, with notes
by Welcker (1825), and Aelian's *Historia Animalium* (1832), and
produced Animadversions on Athenaeus (1809) and on Stobaeus[4].
He contributed to the emendation of the text of Euripides[5] and
the Bucolic poets[6]; executed an admirable rendering of the
Philippics and *De Corona* of Demosthenes, and discussed the
text of Horace[7] and the *Dirae* of Valerius Cato[8]. He also wrote
many papers on the history of Greek literature and civilisation[9],
besides promoting the improvement of elementary text-books by
his Greek and Latin Readers (1805–9). He showed a special

---

[1] Köchly's *Hermann*, 4, 18, 114, 128 ; Bursian, ii 666.

[2] Vols. 1—4 (text), 5 (indices), 6—13 (animadversiones).

[3] On Jacobs' friend, I. G. Huschke (1761—1828), author of *Analecta
Critica*, and *Literaria*, cp. Bursian, i 641 f.

[4] *Lectiones Stobenses*, 1827.   [5] *Animadv.* 1790.

[6] *Exercitationes Criticae*, 1796.

[7] *Vermischte Schriften* (in nine vols., 1823–62), v 1—404.

[8] *ib.* 637 f.

[9] *ib.* iii 1 f, 375 f, 415 f; iv 157—554; v 517 f; viii 72 f.

aptitude for conjectural criticism, a sound judgement, and a wide knowledge of classical literature, while, in personal character, he was one of the most attractive and amiable of men.   Among his literary interests was the higher education of women.   His portrait represents him in a smoking-cap, seated at his desk and busily engaged in writing, while his left hand rests on a large open volume[1].

The circle of scholars at Gotha included F. Wilhelm Döring (1756—1837), for forty-seven years head of the local school, who, in his editions of Latin Classics, **Döring** such as Catullus (1788–92), and Horace (1803–24), and in his continuation (1816–24) of Stroth's Livy (1780-4), is as apt as Heyne to be vague in his textual criticism and evasive in his exegesis[2]. It also included Valentin Christian Friedrich Rost (1790—1862), best known in connexion with his **Rost** Greek Grammar (1816, 1856[7]), his German-Greek and Greek-German Lexicons (1818–20), his improved edition of Damm's lexicon to Homer and Pindar, and his contributions to the Greek Lexicon of Passow[3].   It was at Gotha also that Ernst Friedrich Wüstemann (1799—1856) edited Theocritus, revised Heindorf's *Satires* of Horace and Monk's *Alcestis*, **E. F. Wüste-mann** besides writing on the Gardens of the Ancients, and publishing in a tasteful form a well-arranged collection of select sentences from the Latin Classics[4].

Mythology and Neo-Platonism were the main interests of Georg Friedrich Creuzer (1771—1858), who studied at his native place, Marburg, and at Jena, and, after **Creuzer** holding a professorship for four years at the former university, spent the remaining fifty-four years of his life at Heidelberg, with the exception of a single *semester* at Leyden.   His earliest work dealt with Herodotus and Thucydides, in connexion with Lucian's treatise on the proper method of writing History; he also dis-

---

[1] Frontispiece of *Personalien*, ed. 1840.   On his life and works, see *ib. Verm. Schr.* vii; E. F. Wuestemann's *laudatio* (1848); and Bursian, i 634—640.

[2] Jacobs, *ib.* vii 591 f; Eckstein in *A. D. B.*; Bursian, i 640 f.

[3] Bursian, i 636 f.

[4] *Promptuarium Sententiarum* (1856, 1864); Bursian, i 640.

cussed the historical works of Xenophon, and the origin and developement of the historical art of the Greeks. This early interest in History was continued at Heidelberg, where he formed a plan for collecting all the fragments of the Greek Historians,—a plan that was only partially executed. He began an edition of Herodotus but left its completion to his industrious pupil, Christian Felix Bähr (1798—1872), who produced an erudite work in four volumes[1]. While Creuzer was still at Marburg, he had been stimulated to the study of ancient Law by his colleague, Savigny (1779—1861), afterwards eminent as a jurist in Berlin. Creuzer's continued interest in that study was represented by an Outline of Roman Antiquities, a treatise on Slavery in Ancient Rome, and editions of Cicero, *De Legibus, De Republica,* and the second of the Verrine Orations[2]. He also edited the *De Natura Deorum, De Divinatione,* and *De Fato,* in conjunction with his pupil Georg Heinrich Moser (1780—1858), who himself produced editions of the *Tusculan Disputations* and the *Paradoxes,* and of six books of Nonnus.

Creuzer's main interest, however, lay in Mythology. In his autobiography he confesses to an innate vein of mysticism[3], which was further developed by his attending the highly imaginative lectures on Philosophy and Mythology delivered at Heidelberg in 1801–8 by Joseph Görres. He was specially attracted to the study of the indications of Egyptian and Oriental influence on the Greek legends of Dionysus[4]. This study culminated in the four volumes of his *Symbolik*[5].

He here aims at representing the religious life of the ancient world, not only in its outward aspects, its various cults, and the poetic versions of its mythology, but also in its inner essence, beginning with the origin of religious

---

[1] 1830–5; new ed. 1855–7. Bähr also edited some of Plutarch's *Lives,* and produced several useful books of reference,—a History of Roman Literature (1828, etc.), with supplementary volumes on the Christian Poets and Historians (1836) and Theologians (1837), and on the Latin Literature of the Age of Charles the Great (1840).

[2] *Act.* ii, *Or.* 2. In all these edd. he was associated with Moser.

[3] *Deutsche Schriften,* v (i) 12.

[4] *Studien,* ii 224—324 (1806); *Dionysus* (1808).

[5] 1810–2; new ed. 1819–21; ed. 3, 1837–43; French transl. by Guigniaut in 10 vols., 1825–41.

ideas and ending with the downfall of paganism.   The work is in fact a natural history of Gentile religions, especially those of the Greek and the Italian world[1].   It assigns a large space to the Eleusinian Mysteries.

Creuzer's mystical views on Greek mythology were attacked, with pleasantry[2] and with learning[3], by Lobeck; with perfect courtesy and good-temper, by Hermann[4], and, in a violent and polemical spirit, by Voss[5].

The death of that persistent critic permitted Creuzer to spend the evening of his days in the undisturbed study of Neo-Platonism and Archaeology.   He had already published a critical and ex-planatory edition of Plotinus, *De Pulchritudine* (1814), with contributions from Wyttenbach.   It was at the suggestion of the latter that Creuzer was asked by the Clarendon Press to prepare a complete edition, published in three quarto volumes in 1835[6]. Creuzer's interest in Classical Archaeology is represented by papers on the Greek vases in the collection at Carlsruhe (1839), and on Varro's book of portraits (1843).   One of his latest works was a sketch of the History of Classical Philology (1854)[7].

One of the allies of Voss in his controversy with Creuzer was Wilhelm Adolf Becker[8] (1796—1846), who had already produced an edition of some of the minor works of Aristotle[9], and was after-

W. A. Becker

wards to present Roman and Greek life in a popular form in his *Gallus* and *Charicles*, to write on Roman topography, and to begin (in 1843) the publication of a well known hand-book of Roman Antiquities, which was continued by Marquardt and Mommsen.

Among the contemporaries of Wolf there were several men of mark, who, without being professional scholars, had, in different

---

[1] Bursian, i 570–2; cp. Otto Gruppe, *Gr. Culte u. Mythen*, i (1887) 34—43.

[2] *Jena Litteratur-Zeitung*, 1810, 137 f.

[3] *Aglaophamus, sive de theologiae mysticae Graecorum causis*, 2 vols., 1829.

[4] *Briefe über Homer u. Hesiodus*, 1818 ; cp. *Opusc.* ii 167—216; also his *Brief* of 1819.

[5] *Jena Litt. Zeitung*, May, 1821, and *Anti-Symbolik*, 1824–6.

[6] Moser helped in this work, and in the new ed. of the *Enneades* (Didot, 1855).

[7] *Deutsche Schriften*, v vol. ii, *Zur Geschichte der cl. Philologie*, 238 pp. Autobiography in *Deutsche Schriften*, v vol. i (1848), with portrait, and iii (1858); cp. L. Preller in *Halle Jahrbücher*, i (1838) n. 101—6, and B. Stark in *Vorträge* etc. (1880) 390—408, 480—507, and in *Handbuch*, 262 f; and Bursian, i 562—587.

[8] *Der Symbolik Triumph*, Zerbst, 1825.   [9] *De somno* etc., 1823.

degrees, a close connexion with the scholarship of that age.
Wolf had a loyal friend in Wilhelm von Humboldt
W. v. Hum-   (1767—1835), then a leading Prussian statesman,
boldt   the elder brother of Alexander, the celebrated
naturalist and traveller.   At the age of 19, he wrote an essay on
the opinions of Socrates and Plato on the Godhead and on
Providence and Immortality[1].   A pupil of Heyne at Göttingen in
1788, he produced a poetic version of several odes of Pindar
(1792 f), and, in the same year, the friendship formed with Wolf
in Halle led to his studying the Greek Classics as an essential
element in a completely humane education.   His correspondence
with Wolf has left some interesting traces in that scholar's survey
of classical learning[2].   During the year and a half (1809–10), in
which Humboldt was at the head of the educational section of the
Prussian Home Office, the university of Berlin was founded (1810),
and the general system of education received the direction which
it followed (with slight exceptions) throughout the whole century[3].
In 1816 he produced a highly finished rendering of the *Agamemnon*.
A visit to Spain, in 1799 f, during the four years of his residence
in Paris, had meanwhile led to his taking an interest in the general
history of language.   In this connexion he studied Basque, as well
as the languages of North America, of Malacca and of Polynesia,
together with Sanskrit and Chinese.   The results of these studies
appeared from time to time in the *Transactions* of the Berlin
Academy.   His greatest work in this department, that on the
ancient Kawi language of Java, posthumously published in 1836–9,
begins with a remarkable introduction on 'Diversity of Language,
and its Influence on the Intellectual Developement of Mankind'.
The latter, which was criticised by Steinthal, and edited and
defended by Pott (1876), has been described as 'the text-book of
the philosophy of speech'.   It may be added that, after all his
linguistic studies, he came to the conclusion that the Greek
language and the old Greek culture still remained the finest
product of the human intellect[4].

---

[1] *Gesammelte Schriften*, i (1903) 1—44.

[2] Notes in *Kl. Schr.* ii 884–6, 888—890.

[3] Paulsen, ii[2] 200 f, 248 f, 280 f.

[4] *Letters to Welcker*, ed. Haym, 102, 134.   On W. v. Humbolt in general,

As a student at Leipzig, Goethe (1749—1832) had been profoundly impressed by Lessing's *Laokoon*, and by the writings of Winckelmann; at Strassburg, he had been prompted by Herder to study Homer[1]. In 1772 he translated Pindar's *Fifth Olympian*[2], and in 1780 produced a free imitation of the first part of the *Birds* of Aristophanes[3]. In his 'first period' he also wrote his *Prometheus*. During his tour in Italy (1786-8), he rejoiced in living amid the memories of the old classical world; it was on the Bay of Naples and in Sicily that he first realised the beauty of the scenery of the *Odyssey*. At Palermo he translated the description of the Gardens of Alcinoüs, but did not commit his rendering to writing until many years later (*c.* 1795)[4]. Under the influence of the Homeric translations of Voss, he meditated the composition of an *Achilleis*; and, at the suggestion of Wilhelm von Humboldt, studied Wolf's *Prolegomena*, and once more read the *Iliad*[5]. 'The theory of a *collective Homer*' (he writes) 'is favourable to my present scheme, as lending a modern bard a title to claim for himself a place among the *Homeridae*'[6]. In the spring of 1796, he thanks Wolf for that theory[7]; in December, he 'drinks to the health' of the scholar, 'who at last has boldly freed us from the name of Homer, and is even bidding us enter on a broader road'[8]; and he writes in the same spirit on sending Wolf a copy of *Wilhelm Meister*[9]. But, after abandoning his proposed *Achilleis*, he returns to the old faith, and sings his palinode in *Homer wieder Homer*[10]. He had already translated the Hymn to the Delian Apollo[11], and, in later years, he endeavoured to restore the plot of the *Phaëthon* of Euripides[12] with the aid of the fragments published by Hermann. The *Eumenides* of Aeschylus has left

Goethe

---

cp. *Ges. Schriften*, in 12 vols., 1903-4; Benfey, *Sprachwissenschaft in Deutschland*, 515 f; *Einleitung* to Pott's ed. of the treatise *Ueber die Verschiedenheit des menschlichen Sprachbaues*, 1876; *Sechs...Aufsätze*, ed. Leitzmann, 1896; Delbrück's *Einleitung in das Sprachstudium*, c. ii p. 26 f, ed. 1893; Bursian, i 587—592; and Sayce, in *Enc. Brit.*

[1] Herder etc., *Briefe an Merck*, 43 f, ed. K. Wagner.

[2] *Briefe an F. A. Wolf*, ed. M. Bernays (Berlin, 1868), 122 f.

[3] *Werke*, vii 279 f (Cotta's Jubilee ed.).

[4] Published by Suphan in *Goethe-Jahrbuch*, 1901.

[5] G. Lotholz, *Das Verhältnis Wolfs und W. v. Humboldts zu Goethe und Schiller*, 1863.

[6] Pattison, i 385.   [7] *Briefe u.s.*, 26 f.

[8] *Elegie, Hermann und Dorothea*, l. 27 f.

[9] 26 Dec. 1796 (Körte, i 278).

[10] ii 181, 329, *c.* 1821; cp. Letter to Schiller, 16 May 1798, no. 463, *Ich bin mehr als jemals von der Einheit und Untheilbarkeit des Gedichts* (sc. *der Ilias*) *überzeugt u.s.w.* (Körte, i 280; Volkmann, 75; cp. *Briefe*, 82 f; xxix 557 f Hempel; Pattison, i 385); F. Thalmayr, *Goethe und das classische Alterthum*, 128—137.

[11] Schiller's *Horen* (1795), ix 30.   [12] xxix 500—516 Hempel.

its impress on the second part of *Faust*[1], and on some fine passages in the *Iphigenie auf Tauris*[2].

Goethe's familiarity with the scientific literature of the ancients is apparent in the first part of his *Farbenlehre*. Late in life he is prompted by a program of Hermann's to examine the tragic tetralogies of the Greeks[3]; he discusses the meaning of *katharsis* in Aristotle's Treatise on Poetry[4]; he reviews the similes of the *Iliad*[5], and introduces a classical *Walpurgisnacht* into the second part of *Faust*.

His interest in ancient art, first awakened in the gallery at Mannheim in 1771, had been enhanced by his tour in Italy and his residence in Rome. It was in Rome that he first met the Swiss painter, Heinrich Meyer (1710—1832), a diligent student of the writings of Winckelmann and an admirer of the Roman masterpieces of ancient sculpture and modern painting. At Goethe's suggestion, Meyer was appointed instructor, and afterwards director, of the Academy of Art at Weimar. Meyer was the first link between Goethe and Schiller. Under the inspiration of Winckelmann, Goethe contributed papers on ancient art to the pages of Schiller's *Horen*[6], and wrote on the group of the Laocoon[7] and on other themes of ancient art, in the short-lived *Propyläen*, besides discussing the paintings of Polygnotus in the *Lesche* at Delphi[8]. In 'Winckelmann and his Century', while Wolf reviews the early studies of the future historian of ancient art, Goethe himself portrays the man and the author, and urges the publication of a complete edition of his works. Goethe's friend, Meyer, joined Böttiger in preparing a monograph on the celebrated painting in the Vatican, known as the 'Aldobrandini marriage' (1810), and himself produced, as his latest and maturest work, a history of Greek Art (1824-6).

Goethe was also under the influence of the accomplished architect, Aloys Hirt (1759—1837), according to whom it was the 'characteristic' and the 'individual', and not the 'beautiful' (as held by Winckelmann), that was the true aim of the best Greek sculpture. Hirt elucidated his views in his *Bilderbuch* (1805-16), in his important works on Ancient Architecture[9], and in his History of Ancient Art (1833), which, however, could hardly compete with the excellent Handbook recently published by K. O. Müller (1830). In 1816 Goethe

---

[1] ii 3, 8647-96.

[2] 1052-70; 1129-38; 1341-64 (Breul in *Camb. Rev.* 6 Dec. 1906). Cp. Otto Jahn, *Populäre Aufsätze*, 353—402; F. Thümen, *Iphigeniensage*, 1895[2].

[3] xxix 493 f, Hempel.

[4] xxix 490 f, Hempel; *Ausgleichung, aussöhnende Abrundung*; cp. Letter to Schiller, 28 April, 1797, no. 304.

[5] *Ueber Kunst und Alterthum*, iii (2) 1 f and (3) 1 f.

[6] i (2) 29—50, 1795.

[7] *Aufsätze zur Kunst*, (1798) xxxiii 124 f, Cotta.

[8] *ib.* 231 f, 862 f, Hempel.

[9] *Die Baukunst nach den Grundsätzen der Alten* (1809); *Die Geschichte der Baukunst bei den Alten* (1821-7).

founded a review, in which he published his paper on 'Myron's Cow'[1], while he also attempted to reconstruct for artistic reproduction the supposed originals of the pictures described by the Philostrati[2].

Schiller (1759—1805) had been well grounded in Latin, but, in the study of the Greek masterpieces, he had to rely on translations; even his own poetic rendering of the *Iphigeneia at Aulis* and the *Phoenissae* was founded on the Latin version by Joshua Barnes.   The first period of his poems opens with the 'Parting of Hector', while the second comprises 'Troy', and 'Dido', and the two versions of his memorable 'Gods of Greece'; and the third, the 'Lament of Ceres', the 'Festival of Eleusis', the 'Ring of Polycrates', 'Hero and Leander', 'Cassandra', and the 'Cranes of Ibycus'.   This last was not published until it had been examined and approved by Böttiger[3].   It includes a free rendering of the song of the Furies which Schiller had studied in Wilhelm von Humboldt's fine translation of the *Eumenides*, and the influence of that play is also apparent in his 'Bride of Messina'[4], which was directly inspired by the *Oedipus Tyrannus*, and is prefaced by a suggestive Essay on the Chorus in Greek Tragedy.   His interest in Greek literature is no less manifest in his paper on the Tragic Art[5].   His conception of the old classical world and of the difference between the ancient and the modern spirit had a great effect on his countrymen.   In his Essay 'On naive and sentimental poetry' he is peculiarly felicitous in comparing the merits of several of the ancient poets[6].

It was under the influence of Schiller that the characteristics of the ancient drama were fruitfully studied by A. W. von Schlegel (1767—1845), who had attended Heyne's lectures at Göttingen, and in 1796 was appointed professor at Jena, where he made the acquaintance of Goethe and Schiller, and began the excellent translation of Shakespeare, which he continued after his appointment as professor in Berlin (1801).   In 1805 he accompanied Madame de Staël, the future author of *Corinne*, on a tour in Italy, France,

Schiller

August Wilhelm von Schlegel

---

[1] *Aufsätze zur Kunst*, xxxv 145, Cotta.

[2] *ib.* 69—139.   On Goethe and the Classics, cp. J. Classen in *Philologen-Versammlung* xx (Frankfurt) 13—26 (1863); Urlichs, *Goethe und die Antike* in 'Goethe-Jahrbuch' ii (1882) 3—26; Bursian, i 592—607; Carl Olbrich, *Goethe's Sprache und die Antike* (1891); F. Thalmayr, *Goethe und das classische Alterthum*, 1897; and Otto Kern, *Goethe, Böcklin, Mommsen*, 29—52 (1906).   On Goethe and ancient Art, cp. Stark's *Handbuch*, 223—230.

[3] K. A. Böttiger, *Eine biogr. Skizze von Dr K. W. Böttiger* (1837), 136.

[4] 1986 f.   [5] iv 527 f, ed. 1874; p. 1019 ed. 1869.

[6] iv 653 f; p. 1070.   Cp. L. Hirzel, *Ueber Schiller's Beziehungen zum Alterthume* (Aarau, 1872; 1906[2]), and Bursian, i 607—611; also E. Wilisch, in *Neue Jahrb. f. kl. Alt.* xiii (1904), 39—51.

Germany, and Sweden; in 1813 he became Secretary to Berna-
dotte, the future king of Sweden, and, having studied Sanskrit
in Paris, first under the Indian civilian, Alexander Hamilton
(1762—1824)[1], and next under Bopp, he became professor at
Bonn in 1818 and held that position for the remaining twenty-
seven years of his life.

As the fruit of his Sanskrit studies, he published at Bonn his
Indische Bibliothek (1820–6), and established a press for the
printing of the *Râmâyana* (1825) and the *Bhagavad-Gita* (1829).

Schlegel, who was specially skilful in his translations from
Greek poets, and wrote a drama on the same theme as the *Ion*
(1803), is best known as the author of the 'Lectures on Dramatic
Art and Literature,' delivered in 1808 before a brilliant audience
in Vienna[2]. Nearly half of the thirty Lectures deal with the
Ancient Drama, and of these few, if any, are more familiar than
the Lecture comparing Aeschylus, Sophocles, and Euripides in
their treatment of the theme of Electra. Schlegel, who here
censures the *Electra* of Euripides, had not succeeded in improving upon the *Ion*, but he shares with Goethe the honour
of having been among the first of modern critics to appreciate
the *Bacchae*[3].

While the Greek Drama was reviewed in a critical spirit by
A. W. von Schlegel, the Epic poetry of Greece
attracted the attention of his younger brother,

Friedrich
von Schlegel

Friedrich (1772—1829), who studied law in Göt-
tingen and Leipzig and, after living in Dresden, Jena, Berlin,
Paris and Vienna, was appointed Austrian counsellor of legation
at the Germanic Diet (1814–8). He afterwards returned to
Vienna, resumed his literary work, and died at Dresden in 1829.
Early in life, in 1797, he had produced the first volume of his

[1] Helmina von Chezy, *Unvergessenes*, i 250, 268 (Benfey, *Gesch. der
Sprachwissenschaft*, 358, 379–82).

[2] Ed. 2 (1817), reviewed by K. W. F. Solger (1780—1819), the author of
an excellent translation of Sophocles (1808). This review, reprinted in
Solger's Works, ii 493—628, and regarded by Süvern as the profoundest work
that had ever been written on the subject of Tragedy, represents Irony as the
very centre of the Dramatic Art and also deals with the conception of Fate
and the significance of the Chorus (Bursian, i 614 f).

[3] p. lxxxvi, ed. Sandys.

historical and critical inquiries on the Greeks and Romans, including an extensive treatise on the study of Greek poetry. Instead of completing the work, he began another, on the History of Greek and Roman Poetry[1]. Among his later works the most important is the short treatise 'On the Language and Wisdom of the Indians' (1808)[2], the fruit of his study of Sanskrit under Alexander Hamilton[3]. An important impulse was thus given to the comparative study of language in Europe. The elder brother's example, as a lecturer in Vienna, was ably followed by Friedrich in 1812, in a course of Lectures on the History of Literature, Ancient and Modern (1815)[4].

The Greek Drama was critically studied by Johann Wilhelm Süvern (1775—1829), who, after residing at Jena and Halle, prepared himself for an educational career in Berlin, and, after seven years' experience as Director of the Schools at Thorn and Elbing, and two years' tenure of a professorship at Königsberg, passed the remaining twenty years of his life as a prominent official in the Educational Department in Berlin[5]. While he was still at Halle, he was prompted by C. G. Schütz to study the Greek Tragic poets, and Aeschylus in particular. His earliest work was a German translation of the *Septem* (1799), followed by an essay on Schiller's *Wallenstein* in relation to Greek Tragedy (1800). Later in life, he wrote on the tragic element in the historical works of Tacitus[6], and on the historical character of the Greek Drama[7]. He also discussed the date and aim of the *Oedipus Coloneüs*[8], and the historic purpose of the *Clouds* and the *Birds* of Aristophanes[9].

Süvern

---

[1] Vol. I, part i, 1798.

[2] Trans. by Millington (1849) in *Aesthetic and Miscellaneous Works* (Bohn), 425—465; Max Müller's *Lectures*, i 182[5]; Benfey, 357-69.

[3] 1802-7. Cp. p. 72 *supra*.

[4] Trans. in Bohn's *Standard Library*; Lectures i—iv on Greek and Roman Literature.

[5] Paulsen, ii 281[2].

[6] *Ueber den Kunstcharacter des Tacitus*, Berlin Acad. 1822–3 (1825), 73 f.

[7] *ib.* 1825 (1828), 75 f.

[8] *ib.* 1828 (1831), 1 f.

[9] 1826-7. Translated by W. R. Hamilton (1835-6). On Süvern, cp. Passow (Thorn, 1860), and Bursian, i 617—623.

The same department of study is represented by the early
work of H. T. Rötscher (1803—1871), the author
Rötscher
of 'Aristophanes and his Age' (1827), a work de-
fending the poet's treatment of Socrates, and representing that
philosopher as the enemy of the Greek world of his own day.
A similar view was afterwards held by Forchhammer (1837); but
both of these writers were reviewed and refuted by Zeller[1].

The literary and artistic circle of Weimar and Jena included
Karl August Böttiger (1760—1835), who was edu-
Böttiger
cated at Schulpforta and Leipzig, and, under the
influence of Herder, held for thirteen years a head-mastership at
Weimar (1790—1804). For the remaining thirty-one years of his
life, he resided at Dresden as Director of the Museum of Antiques,
and was singularly active as a journalist and a public lecturer.
As a schoolmaster, he had published a considerable number of
pedagogic and philological programs[2]. His archaeological works,
mainly produced at Dresden, fall into three groups: (1) Private
Antiquities, (2) the Greek Theatre, and (3) Ancient Art and
Mythology. (1) is best represented by his 'Sabina, or morning-
scenes in the dressing-room of a wealthy Roman lady', which
was promptly translated into French and served as a model for
Becker's *Gallus* and *Charicles*. It was continued in the fragment
called 'Sabina on the Bay of Naples'[3]. (2) His interest in the
theatre dated from the time when he was a dramatic critic at
Weimar; his unfavourable critique on A. W. von Schlegel's *Ion* was
withdrawn at the request of Goethe. It was mainly as a school-
master at Weimar that he wrote his papers on the distribution of
the parts, on the masks and dresses, and on the machinery of the
ancient stage[4], as well as a dissertation on the masks of the
Furies (1801)[5]. (3) His work in the province of ancient art[6]
and mythology[7] was popular and superficial. It may be added

---

[1] c. x of *Socrates and the Socratic Schools*, E.T.—Bursian, i 623 f.

[2] *Opuscula*, ed. Sillig, 1837; bibliography in *Kleine Schriften*, ed. Sillig,
1837 f, I xiii—cxviii.

[3] *Kl. Schr.* iii 243 f.

[4] *Opuscula*, 220—234, 285—398.

[5] *Kl. Schr.* i 189—276.   [6] *Kl. Schr.* ii 3—341.

[7] *Kl. Schr.* i 3—180, and (his latest independent work) *Ideen zur Kunst-
Mythologie* (a term invented by Böttiger).

that he supplied the descriptive letter-press to the German edition (1797 f) of Tischbein's reproductions from Sir William Hamilton's second collection of Greek vases, and thus introduced the study of Greek vase-painting into Germany. He published lectures on the History of Ancient Sculpture (1806) and Painting (1811), and edited the three volumes of an archaeological periodical entitled *Amalthea* (1820–5), including contributions from the best of the classical archaeologists of the day[1].

Böttiger's example was followed by his pupil, Karl Julius Sillig (1801—1855), who edited many of his master's works. Born at Dresden, he studied at Leipzig and Göttingen, and was a schoolmaster at Dresden for the last thirty years of his life. His *Catalogus Artificum* (1827) was a useful work in its time. His edition of Catullus is far less important than his edition of the elder Pliny[2]. As an editor he is too much given to the accumulation of details, and is deficient in judgement and in critical method[3].

Among the pupils of Heyne at Göttingen was August Matthiae (1769—1835), a son of the *custos* of the University Library, who had adopted the Latinised name of Matthiae instead of the German name of Matthiesen. After leaving the university, the son spent four years as a private tutor at Amsterdam, and, for the last thirty-three years of his life, was Director of the *gymnasium* at Altenburg. The most important of his works was his larger Greek Grammar[4]. He also published an extensive edition of Euripides in nine volumes, with the Fragments and the *scholia* (1813–29); a tenth volume includes *addenda* to the *scholia*, and *Indices* by Kampmann (1837). Lastly, he collected the Fragments of Alcaeus, and published 'animadversions' on the Homeric Hymns, as well as scholastic works on Greek and Roman Literature, and on Latin Prose Composition[5].

---

[1] *Biographische Skizze*, by K. W. Böttiger (1837); Eichstaedt, *Opusc. Orat.* 665—672; Stark, 52, 71; Bursian, i 628—634.

[2] 1831–6 in 5 vols; larger ed. in 6 vols., with two vols. of *Indices* by Otto Schneider.

[3] Bursian, i 634.   [4] 1807; ed. 3, 1835.

[5] Life by his son Konstantin (1845), including an account of August's elder brother Friedrich Christian (1763—1822), editor of Aratus, etc. (1817); Bursian, i 642 f.

NIEBUHR.

From Sichling's engraving of the portrait by F. Schnorr von Carolsfeld.

The study of History was well represented at Göttingen by Heyne's pupil, son-in-law, and biographer, Arnold Hermann Ludwig Heeren (1760—1842). After writing on the Chorus in Greek Tragedy, and editing the rhetorician Menander's treatise on *Encomia*, he went abroad for nearly two years to collate the MSS of the *Eclogae* of Stobaeus, his publication of which extended over a considerable period (1792—1801). Meanwhile, he had already begun to devote himself to those historical studies with which his name is mainly associated. He produced, in 1793, the first volume of his well-known work on the Politics and Trade of the foremost peoples of the ancient world[1]; and, in 1799, his Handbook of the History of Ancient States, with special reference to their constitution, their commerce, and their colonies[2]. He also wrote several monographs on the commerce of Palmyra and India. The criticism of the authorities for Ancient History, a field of research first opened out by Heyne, was the theme of several papers by his pupil[3]. Heeren published, in 1797—1801, a History of the Study of Classical Literature from the Revival of Learning, with an Introduction on the History of the works of the Classical authors in the Middle Ages. In the second edition of 1822 this work is entitled a History of Classical Literature in the Middle Ages, the first part going down to the end of the fourteenth century, and the second including the Humanists of the fifteenth[4].

A shorter life was the lot of another historian, the historian of ancient Rome, Barthold Georg Niebuhr (1776—1831). His father had been famous as a traveller in Arabia and Persia. Born at Copenhagen, and educated at Meldorf and at Hamburg, he studied at Kiel and Edinburgh. After holding civil appointments at Copenhagen, he entered the service of Prussia, and in 1810 was appointed professor in the

[margin note: Heeren]

[margin note: Niebuhr]

---

[1] Ed. 4 in 6 vols.; vols. 10—15 of 'Historical Works', 1824–6; E.T. 1833.

[2] Ed. 5, 1828; E. T. 1829.

[3] Trogus Pompeius, Plutarch's *Lives*, Strabo, and Ptolemy are discussed in vols. i, iii, iv, v, xv, of the *Commentationes* of the Royal Society of Göttingen.

[4] Characterised by Bursian (p. 5) as 'superficial and sketchy'; it deserves credit, however, for its lucid arrangement, and its breadth of view. On Heeren's life, cp. his 'Hist. Works', I xi f: Karl Hoeck's *Gedächtnissrede* in 'Neuer Nekrolog der Deutschen', xx 217 f; and Bursian, i 645–7.

newly-founded university of Berlin. His lectures on Roman history were attended by a distinguished audience, and thenceforth he regarded the history of Rome as the main interest of his life. He completed the first two volumes of his History in 1812. He was Prussian ambassador at Rome in 1816–23, but was discontented with Rome and with Italy, and made little progress with his literary work. For the rest of his life he settled at Bonn, where he delivered lectures on ancient history, ethnography and geography, and on the French Revolution. The revolution of July, 1830, filled him with apprehensions for the future of Europe. In the following winter he caught a chill during his return from a news-room, where he had been eagerly studying the account of the trial of the ministers of Charles X; and early in 1831 he died.

Voss, the translator of Homer, was a frequent visitor in the house of Niebuhr's childhood, and the German *Odyssey* was the delight of the future historian's early years[1]. At the age of fourteen he was absorbed in the study of a MS of Varro, which his father had borrowed from the library at Copenhagen. The boy discovered for himself that the difficulty of many passages was really due to *lacunae*, which had not been indicated in the printed editions[2]. During a visit to Scotland he acquired a new appreciation of the beauties of nature, and he afterwards admitted that his 'early residence in England' gave him 'one important key to Roman history':—'it is necessary to know civil life by personal observation in order to understand such States as those of antiquity; I never could have understood a number of things in the history of Rome without having observed England'[3]. In Berlin, his friends were Spalding, Savigny, Buttmann, and Heindorf. He stood in no such relation to Wolf[4]. In his *History of Rome* he describes 'the poems, out of which' (in his view) 'the history of the Roman kings was resolved into a prose narrative'[5], as 'knowing nothing of *the unity which characterizes the most perfect of Greek poems*'[6], thus ignoring the

---

[1] Herbst, *Voss*, i 227.   [2] *ib*. ii 136.

[3] *Enc. Brit.*

[4] Eyssenhardt, 47—53.

[5] End of Pref. to *Hist. of Rome*, ed. 1.   [6] i 258 f, E.T., ed. 1837.

results of Wolf's *Prolegomena*. But the critical spirit, which inspired Wolf, was in the air, and its influence affected Niebuhr. His theory that the early legends of Rome had been transmitted from generation to generation in the form of poetic lays was not new. It had been anticipated by the Dutch scholar, Perizonius[1], but Niebuhr was not aware of this fact until a later date[2]. Similarly, a French scholar, Louis de Beaufort, had published in Holland (1738–50) a work on the uncertainty of the first five centuries of Roman history, but this was purely negative in its results. Niebuhr's work marks an epoch in the study of the subject. His main results, 'such as his views of the ancient population of Rome, the origin of the *plebs*, the relation between the patricians and the plebeians, the real nature of the *ager publicus*, and many other points of interest, have been acknowledged by all his successors'[3]. He was the first to deal with the history of Rome in a critical and scientific spirit[4]. His *History of Rome* grew out of his lectures at Berlin. The same theme was predominant in certain courses of lectures delivered at Bonn, which were not published until after his death[5].

Niebuhr's work as a scholar was far from being confined to the domain of History. The two volumes of his 'minor historical and philological writings' (1828–43) include much that is connected with the history of classical literature and the criticism of classical texts. In 1816, with the aid of Buttmann and Heindorf, he published in Berlin an improved edition of the remains of Fronto (which had been printed for the first time in the previous year from the Bobbio MS found by Angelo Mai at Milan). Late in the summer of 1816, on his way to Rome,

[1] *Animadversiones Historicae* (1685), c. 6; vol. ii 331 *supra*.

[2] i 254 E.T., and *Pref*. vii. His discovery led him to propose Perizonius as the theme for a prize-essay; the result was Gustav Kramer's *Elogium* (1828).

[3] Schmitz, quoted in *Enc. Brit*.

[4] *Römische Geschichte*, vol. i, 1811 (ed. 2, 1827, ed. 3, 1828); vol. ii, 1812 (ed. 2, 1830); vol. iii, ed. Classen, 1832. Complete ed. in one vol. 1853; new ed. 1873–4. Engl. Transl. 1828–42, by Thirlwall and Julius Hare; last ed. 1847–51.

[5] Lectures on Ethnography, 1851; on Ancient History, 1847–51; on Roman History, from the earliest times to the fall of the Western Empire, 1846–8 (E.T. 1853); and on Roman Antiquities, 1858 (=*Hist. und philol. Vorträge an der Univ. Bonn gehalten*, ed. Isler and M. Niebuhr, Berlin, 1846–58).

he discovered, in a palimpsest of the Capitular Library at Verona, the 'Institutions' of the Roman jurist, Gaius; he immediately informed Savigny, and an edition of the work was accordingly published by the Berlin Academy[1]. In Rome he discovered in a Vatican MS certain fragments of Cicero's Speeches *pro M. Fonteio* and *pro C. Rabirio*[2]. In the course of his edition of Fronto, he had criticised Mai's arrangement of the fragments of Cicero, *pro Scauro*, and his own arrangement had been confirmed by a MS discovered by Peyron at Milan[3]. Mai, on his appointment as librarian of the Vatican, was somewhat jealous of Niebuhr's acumen as an editor, and Niebuhr was not disposed, as the representative of Prussia, to ask the Vatican for favours which he might readily have sought as an ordinary scholar. However, he generously contributed to Mai's edition of the Vatican palimpsest of Cicero, *De Republica*, several learned notes, together with a historical and a verbal index (1822). Niebuhr was the first to make use of Lagomarsini's vast collection of various readings preserved in the Collegio Romano; he also identified the MSS collated by that scholar[4].

In 1822 he addressed, to a young friend, a memorable letter, in which he sets forth a high ideal of a scholar's life. The authors specially recommended for study are Homer, Aeschylus, Sophocles and Pindar, with Herodotus, Thucydides, Demosthenes and Plutarch, and Cicero, Livy, Caesar, Sallust and Tacitus[5]. All these were to be read with reverence, not with a view to making them the themes of aesthetic criticism, but with a resolve to assimilate their spirit. This (he declares) is the true 'Philology' that brings health to the soul, while learned investigations (in the case of such as attain to them) belong to a lower level[6].

---

[1] Ed. Göschen and Bethmann-Hollweg, 1821; ed. 2, 1824; cp. K. G. Jacob's *Abhandlung*, 61 f.

[2] Ed. 1820, with a fragment of Livy, xci, and fragments of Seneca.

[3] K. G. Jacob, 82 f.   [4] K. G. Jacob, 89.

[5] Horace's *Satires* are recommended (less strongly than his *Odes*), with only a few of Juvenal's. No other poets are named. Virgil and Horace are depreciated in his *Lectures on Roman History*, no. 107, iii 135—142 E.T.

[6] *Brief an einen jungen Philologen*, printed in *Lebensnachrichten*, ii 200 f; and by K. G. Jacob, p. 142; translated by Julius Hare, *On a Young Man's Studies*, in the *Educational Magazine*, 1840.

Niebuhr also wrote a historical outline, and several topographical articles, for the Description of the City of Rome
undertaken by the artist, Ernst Platner, who had resided in
Rome since 1800, and by Bunsen, who arrived in 1818, as
Niebuhr's Secretary of Embassy. At Naples Niebuhr collated
a MS of the *Dialogus de Oratoribus*, and a MS of Charisius
(formerly at Bobbio), and afterwards handed over these collations
to Bekker and Lindemann. On his way back to Germany in
1823, his attention was drawn in the library of St Gallen to
a palimpsest including considerable fragments of poems, and a
panegyrical oration, which he identified as the work of the
Spanish poet and rhetorician, Merobaudes. He immediately
produced an edition at St Gallen, followed by an improved
edition after his arrival at Bonn.

At Bonn he organised a plan for publishing a series of critical
texts of the Byzantine historians, with Latin introductions, translations and notes. His principal contribution to the *Corpus
Scriptorum Historiae Byzantinae* was an edition of Agathias
(1829). After his death, the series was continued under the
auspices of the Berlin Academy, and, by the end of 1855, forty-
eight volumes had been published. He must also be remembered
as the founder (in 1827) of the *Rheinisches Museum*, in which he
was associated with Brandis and Boeckh.

His early connexion with Denmark did not prevent his being
perfectly loyal to Prussia, but neither in England nor in Italy
did he succeed in assimilating himself to his surroundings. It
is said that a certain excitability of temper kept him from feeling
at perfect ease either in public or in private life; but he was
undoubtedly inspired with the loftiest aims, and had a warm
heart, and a magnanimous and noble spirit. The main interest
of his greatest work, the *History of Rome*, has been found in
its 'freshness, its elation of real or supposed discovery, the
impression it conveys of actual contact with a great body of
new and unsuspected truths'[1]. He may perhaps have been
justified in saying :—'the discovery of no ancient historian could
have taught the world so much as my work'; but his prediction,
that new discoveries would 'only tend to confirm or develope'

[1] Garnett in *Enc. Brit.*

his principles, has not been entirely fulfilled. His theory of the derivation of ancient Roman history from popular lays was refuted by Sir George Cornewall Lewis, in his *Essay on the Credibility of Early Roman History*; and archaeological discoveries have corrected his attitude of general scepticism as to early traditions[1]; but 'the main pillars of his grand structure are still unshaken'[2].

Among Niebuhr's friends at Berlin was Georg Ludwig Spalding
Spalding   (1762—1811), a scholar of Pomeranian birth, who
          had been educated in Berlin, and who, after studying at Göttingen and Halle, became in 1787 a professor at a *gymnasium* in Berlin. Besides writing on the Megarian School of Philosophers, and preparing an edition of the Speech of Demosthenes against Meidias, he produced in 1798 f the first three volumes of a memorable edition of the *Institutio Oratoria* of Quintilian[3]. On his visit to Rome in quest of materials for his Quintilian, he unfortunately gave W. von Humboldt the impression of being a trifler and a pedant[4].

The popularisation of Plato was an important part of the work of Schleiermacher (1768—1834). His translation (1804-10) included all the dialogues except the *Laws, Epinomis, Timaeus*

---

[1] Niebuhr himself 'repeatedly expresses the conviction that the various vicissitudes by which learning has been promoted are under the control of an overruling Providence: and he has more than once spoken of the recent discoveries, by which so many remains of Antiquity have been brought to light, as Providential dispensations for the increase of our knowledge of God's works, and of His creatures'. Julius Hare, in *Guesses at Truth*, 61 f, ed. 1866.

[2] Dr Schmitz, *Preface* to first ed. of the Engl. transl. of Mommsen's *History*, quoted by R. Garnett in *Enc. Brit.* ed. 9. The chief authority for his Life is the *Lebensnachrichten*, consisting mainly of letters, linked by a brief biographical narrative by his friend, Frau Hensler (3 vols., 1838 f). The letters are reduced and the biography expanded (with selections from the *Kleine Schriften*) in Miss Winkworth's ed. (1852[2]). Cp. Julius Hare's *Vindication of Niebuhr*, 1829; Francis Lieber's *Reminiscences* (1835); introduction to K. G. Jacob's reprint of the *Brief an einen jungen Philologen* (1839); Classen's *Gedächtnisschrift* (1876); Eyssenhardt's *Biographischer Versuch* (1886); Bursian, i 647—654; and R. Garnett in *Enc. Brit.*; also A. Harnack, *Gesch. der preuss. Akad.* i 624 f, 670 f, ii 379—409.

[3] Vol. iv was seen through the press by Buttmann; and new materials for the criticism of the text were supplied in vol. v by K. G. Zumpt (1829). Vol. vi contained an admirable *Lexicon Quintilianeum* by Bonnel (1834).

[4] Varnhagen, *Verm. Schriften*, ii 242[3], in Eyssenhardt's *Niebuhr*, 48.

and *Critias*.   As a professor, and as a university-preacher at
Halle in 1804, he had been familiar with Wolf, and
had been stimulated by that scholar in his Platonic   Schleier-
                                                        macher
studies.   When Halle became part of the new
Napoleonic kingdom of Westphalia, both of them fled to Berlin,
where their friendship was, for a time, unimpaired.   Schleiermacher's translation was the earliest successful attempt to render
a great writer of Greek prose in German of an artistic and literary
type.   His Introduction presented a complete survey of Plato's
works in their relation to one another.   The dialogues were
there divided into three groups :—(1) preparatory or elementary
dialogues ; (2) dialogues of indirect investigation ; (3) expository
or constructive dialogues,—a division taking inadequate account
of chronological sequence[1].   Schleiermacher also broke new
ground in his researches on some of Plato's precursors.   Among
the most important of these was his treatise on Heraclitus[2] and
his paper on Socrates[3].

Julius Hare describes him as 'gifted with the keenest wit', and as 'the
greatest master of irony since Plato'.   'Yet...the basis of his character, the key-
note of his whole being, was...a love which delighted in pouring out the
boundless riches of his spirit for the edifying of such as came near him, and
strove with unweariable zeal to make them partakers of all that he had.
Hereby was his heart kept fresh through the unceasing and often turbulent
activity of his life, so that the subtilty of his understanding had no power to
corrode it ; but when he died, he was still, as one of his friends said of him,
ein fünfundsechzigjähriger Jüngling'[4].

The circle of scholars at Berlin included Ludwig Friedrich
Heindorf (1774—1816).   Born in Berlin, he was an
                                                        Heindorf
eager and enthusiastic pupil of Wolf at Halle.   After
teaching for a time in the city of his birth, he was appointed to a
professorship at Breslau (1811–6), and died soon after his acceptance of a call to Halle.   Heindorf, who was ignobly disowned by
his master, Wolf, is well known in connexion with the edition of
twelve dialogues of Plato (1802–10), which (as we have seen) led

[1] Zeller's *Plato*, etc. E.T. 100; Grote's *Plato*, i 172.

[2] *Sämmt. Werke*, III, ii 1 f.

[3] *ib*. ii 147 f.   Cp., in general, Schleiermacher's *Leben in Briefen*, 1858–
63; Zeller's *Vorträge*, 1865; Lives by Dilthey (1867) and Schenkl (1868);
Bursian, i 663 f.

[4] *Guesses at Truth*, 254, ed. 1866.

to a breach between himself and his master[1].   His editions of
Cicero, *De Natura Deorum*, and of the *Satires* of Horace, both
published in 1815, are specially useful for their explanatory
notes[2].

Berlin was the scene of the active life of the distinguished
grammarian, Philipp Karl Buttmann (1764—1829),
Buttmann   a member of a family of French Protestant refugees,
whose original name was Boudemont.   Born at Frankfurt and
educated at the local school and under Heyne at Göttingen, after
spending eight months with Schweighäuser at Strassburg, he
became a master for eight years at a *gymnasium* in Berlin (1800–8).
In 1806 he was elected a member of the Academy and, in 1811,
keeper of the Royal Library.   Without belonging to the cor-
poration of the newly-founded university, he took part in the
superintendence of the 'philological seminary'.   His best-known
work was his Greek Grammar, first published as a brief outline in
1792, and constantly expanded and rearranged and improved in
many subsequent editions.   In its expanded form, it was known
as the 'intermediate Grammar'[3], to distinguish it from the new
School Grammar of 1812; and from the 'Complete Grammar' of
1819–27, to which additions were made by Lobeck.   The success
of his 'Intermediate Grammar' was due to its remarkable clearness.
The rules deduced from the observation of grammatical facts are
here laid down in a lucid form, but without any attempt to trace
the linguistic laws on which those rules depend.   The introduction
of this Grammar led to a marked improvement in the Greek
scholarship of the schools of Germany[4].

In his *Lexilogus*[5] he proves himself an acute investigator of
the meanings of Homeric words, and displays a keen sense of the
historic developement of language, but is obviously unconscious of
the importance of the principles of comparative philology[6].   We
can hardly, however, be surprised at his ignoring Bopp's work on

---

[1] p. 59 *supra*.   [2] Bursian, i 544, 654.

[3] E. T. 1840; ed. 3, 1848.

[4] Bursian, i 655 f; Eckstein, *Lat. und Gr. Unterricht*, 394 f; Wilamowitz
in *Reform des .. Schulwesens*, ed. Lexis, 1902, 164.

[5] 1818–25 ; ed. 4, 1865; also E.T.

[6] G. Curtius, *Principles of Gk Etym.*, i 17 E.T.

the Conjugations (1816) and Jacob Grimm's German Grammar (1819 f), when we remember that even Hermann and Lobeck regarded the new science with suspicion. Buttmann's editions of Greek Classics have no claim to being considered as independent works. His edition of four Platonic dialogues is founded on that of Biester; that of the *Meidias*, on Spalding; that of the *Philoctetes*, on Gedike, and his *scholia* to the *Odyssey*, on Mai. He also edited Aratus. His study of Latin literature is represented by a few papers on Horace, one of which was the precursor of many less judicious attempts to discover interpolations in the pages of that poet[1]. But his main strength lay in Greek Grammar and Homeric Lexicography. His keen interest in Homer even led to his giving his children the Homeric names of Helen and Hector, Achilles and Alexander[2].

The textual criticism of the Greek Classics was ably represented by Immanuel Bekker (1785—1871), who was born and died in Berlin. Educated under Spalding, he studied at Halle under Wolf, who made him inspector of his 'philological seminary'. He gave early proof of his familiarity with the Homeric poems in his reviews of Heyne's *Iliad* and of Wolf's *Homer*[3]. On the foundation of the university of Berlin, he was appointed to an extraordinary, and, in the following year, to an ordinary, professorship,—a position which he held for sixty-one years without making any considerable mark as an academic teacher. The few courses of lectures that he announced on the speeches of Thucydides, or on selections from Isocrates and Aeschines, were either not delivered at all, or were attended by a very small audience, before whom he scattered a few of the golden grains of his learning with every appearance of a certain reluctance in parting with his treasures. On the other hand, he set a brilliant example to all the younger generations of scholars by the industry and the ability that he lavished on the collation of MSS and the preparation of improved texts of important authors. The number of MSS that he collated, either in whole or in part, exceeded four hundred. In 1810–12 he was sent by the Berlin Academy to

Bekker

---

[1] *Horaz und Nicht-Horaz*, appendix to his *Mythologus* (1828–9).
[2] D. Boileau in E.T. of *Gk Gr.* p. xiii. Cp., in general, Bursian, i 655–8.
[3] *Homerische Blätter*, 29 f.

work in the Paris Library. The firstfruits of his labours in France appeared in the *editio princeps* of Apollonius Dyscolus, *On the Pronoun* (1811). In 1815 he transcribed (for discussion in the future *Corpus*) the Greek inscriptions collected by the Abbé Fourmont in 1728–30[1]. In 1817–19 he was collating the MSS of Aristotle in the libraries of Italy. On his return he revisited Paris. Part of 1820 was spent in Oxford, and, after a few further visits to England, he returned to Italy in 1839. With the exception of the lyric and the tragic poets, there is hardly any class of Greek authors whose text has not been definitely improved by his labours. He produced two editions of Homer; the first, published in Berlin in 1843, was founded on the principles of Wolf, and aimed at restoring (so far as practicable) the recension of Aristarchus; the second, published at Bonn in 1858, was an attempt to attain an earlier text than that of the Alexandrian critics. The principles, on which this edition was founded, were mainly set forth in a series of papers, which were presented to the Berlin Academy and afterwards published in a collected form[2]. He also produced an edition of the *scholia* to the *Iliad* (1825–27), which, without being exhaustive, or perfect in all points of detail, has the advantage of presenting the *scholia* of the *Codex Venetus* in their proper order and in a trustworthy form[3]. Of the later epic poets, he edited Aratus, Coluthus and Tzetzes, and the 'Helen and Alexander' of Demetrius Moschus. For his editions of Theognis, he was the first to use the important MS at Modena. For the two volumes of the text of Aristophanes, published in London with the ancient *scholia* in 1828, he collated afresh the Venice MS, and the Ravenna MS, the importance of which had, after 250 years of neglect, been brought to light by the Roman lawyer, Invernizi (1794). On the basis of a careful collation of MSS, Bekker edited Thucydides with the *scholia*, as well as Pausanias and Herodian. He also prepared new editions of Herodotus, Polybius, Dion Cassius, Diodorus, Appian, Josephus, and the *Lives* of Plutarch, as well as the 'Bibliotheca' of Apollodorus, together with Heliodorus and Lucian. There is less

---

[1] Cp. R. C. Christie's *Selected Essays*, 86; p. 99 *infra*.

[2] *Homerische Blätter*, 1863–72.

[3] Cp. La Roche, *Text, Zeichen und Scholien des .. Codex Venetus* (1862), 17 f.

originality in his work on the twenty-five volumes which he contributed to the *Corpus* of the Byzantine Historians.   A marked
advance is, however, shown in his editions of the whole of Plato
(with the *scholia* and a full critical commentary)[1], and the whole of
Aristotle[2].   He prepared a new recension of Sextus Empiricus.
His edition of all the Attic Orators was published first at Oxford
(1822), and in the following year at Berlin.   New materials for
the history of Greek Grammar and Rhetoric were provided in the
three volumes of his *Anecdota Graeca*, and new texts of grammatical works in his editions of the *Syntax* of Apollonius, the
Bibliotheca of Photius, the lexicons of Harpocration and Moeris
and Suïdas, the Homeric lexicon of Apollonius, and the *Onomasticon* of Pollux.   As a contribution to Greek lexicography, he
produced a new edition of the small Greek lexicon of Niz, in
which the words are arranged according to their etymology.   The
only Latin texts which he edited (apart from a few items in the
Byzantine series) were Livy, with short notes by Raschig, and
Tacitus, with the commentaries of earlier scholars.   His extraordinary activity as an editor seems to have left him little energy
for anything else; he was held in the highest esteem by scholars,
but he did not shine in ordinary conversation.   It was said of the
editor of some sixty volumes of Greek texts, and the collator of
more than four hundred MSS, that he could be silent in seven
languages[3].

---

[1] 8 vols., 1816–23.   [2] 4 vols., 1831–36.
[3] E. J. Bekker, *Zur Erinnerung an meinen Vater* in *Preuss. Jahrb.* (1872),
xxix 553 f, 641 f; H. Sauppe, Göttingen, 1872; Haupt, *Opusc.* iii 228 f;
Halm, in *A.D.B.*; and Bursian, i 658—663; also M. Hertz, in *Deutsche
Rundschau*, Nov. 1885 (on Boeckh and Bekker); Leutsch, in *Philol. Anz.*
xvi 224 f; Harnack, *Gesch. der preuss. Akad.* i 857 f; and Gildersleeve, in
A. J. P. xxviii (1907) 113.

GOTTFRIED HERMANN.

From Weger's engraving of the portrait by C. Vogel (1841); frontispiece to
Köchly's *Gottfried Hermann* (1874).

CHAPTER XXIX.

HERMANN AND BOECKH.

In the generation next to that of Wolf, the two great scholars, Gottfried Hermann and August Boeckh, were conspicuous as the heads of two rival schools of classical learning. The first was the *grammatical and critical* school, which made the text of the Classics, with questions of grammar and metre and style, the main object of study. The second (already represented by Niebuhr) was the *historical and antiquarian* school, which investigated all the manifestations of the spirit of the old classical world. The precursors of the first school were to be mainly found among the scholars of England and Holland; those of the second, among the scholars of France. The first was concerned with words, the second with things; the first with language and literature; the second with institutions, and with art and archaeology. The adherents of the first were twitted by their opponents with a narrow devotion to notes on classical texts; those of the second were denounced as *dilettanti*. It is now, however, generally agreed that, while, in theory, the comprehensive conception of the wide field of classical learning formed by Boeckh is undoubtedly correct, in practice a thorough knowledge of the languages is the indispensable foundation for the superstructure. That knowledge is in fact (to change the metaphor) the master-key to all the departments of the intellectual life of the ancient classical world[1].

Hermann (1772—1848) was born at Leipzig, where his father was the senior member of the local court of Sheriffs; his mother, a very vivacious and interesting person, of French descent, retained her marvellous memory

Gottfried Hermann

---

[1] Bursian, ii 665 f.

to the age of ninety. A boy of delicate frame, high spirits, and unruly temper, the young Hermann was fortunate in being entrusted, at the age of twelve, to the strict discipline and the stimulating teaching of Ilgen, the future Rector of Schulpforta[1]. Matriculating at Leipzig at the early age of fourteen, he attended the lectures of F. W. Reiz, who pointed out the importance of the study of metre, and set before him the example of Bentley. From Reiz, whom he always remembered with gratitude, he learnt three things in particular, (1) never to study more than one writer, or one subject, at a time, (2) never to take any statement on trust, and (3) always to be able to give a good reason for holding any opinion which he deemed to be true[2]. He joined the university of Jena for a single *semester*, with a view to attending Reinhold's lectures on Kant (1793–4), which were not without their influence on the logical precision which subsequently marked his own teaching of metre and grammar[3]. Passing rapidly through the preliminary stages at Leipzig, he became professor of Eloquence in 1803 and of Poetry in 1809. His mastery of Latin prose was manifest in all the speeches and letters that he composed on behalf of the university, while a long line of enthusiastic pupils first learnt from his eloquent lips the true meaning of the old Greek poets. As a teacher, he had a singularly attractive and engaging personality, combined with a primitive simplicity of character and an unswerving love of truth. His lectures, which were usually delivered in Latin, were simple and clear in style, and free from all striving for rhetorical effect; but they were inspired with a keen enthusiasm for the old classical world. His talent as a teacher was most conspicuous in his lectures on the Greek tragic poets, and on Pindar and Homer; but he also lectured on Hesiod and Theocritus, on Thucydides, and on Aristotle's Treatise on Poetry, and on Plautus and Terence. Of his other courses the most important were those on metre and grammar, and on criticism and hermeneutics, while he occasionally lectured on Greek literature, on the Greek festivals, and on the antiquities of the Greek

---

[1] Otto Jahn, *Biogr. Aufsätze*, 92 f; p. 63 *supra*.

[2] *Opusc.* viii 453 f; Jahn, 96 f; Köchly's *Hermann*, 5 f, 115 f.

[3] Jahn, 99. Cp. p. 91, n. 8 *infra*.

theatre[1]. But his main interest was in the study of the ancient *languages*[2], and he always insisted on the supreme importance of a first-hand acquaintance with the *writings* of the ancients[3]. In an early work he urged that a strictly logical and rational method should be applied to the study of Greek Grammar (1801)[4], and in the following year dealt with a number of points of Syntax in his additions to the German version of Viger's work on Greek idioms[5]. Of his later discussions on Syntax the most notable were his papers on 'Ellipse and Pleonasm'[6], his dissertation on αὐτός[7], and his 'four books on the particle ἄν'[8]. He was opposed to the comparative philologists of his day[9].

In his writings on ancient metre he had no important modern precursors except Bentley and Porson. Bentley's only separate treatise on the subject was his brief *Schediasma* on the metres of Terence, while Porson had been led by a careful observation of facts to formulate rules for the ordinary iambic and trochaic metres of the Greek drama. Brunck and Reisig had also paid some attention to the subject. Hermann's work, however, was more systematic; he began by studying the ancient authorities, above all Hephaestion, expounding and correcting them by the light of his own study of the Greek poets[10]. He elucidated the rhythms of Greek poetry by the effective recitation of passages from the poets, and for this purpose he abandoned the customary Reuch-

---

[1] Cp. Thiersch, *Ueber gelehrte Schulen*, ii 115 (Bursian, ii 669 n.).

[2] Jahn, 104, 108 f.   [3] *Opusc.* vii 98 f.

[4] *De emendanda ratione Graecae Grammaticae*, pars prima.

[5] *De praecipuis Graecae dictionis idiotismis* (1627), ed. 1802 etc., and, finally, 1834. Cp. Jahn, 106 f.

[6] *Opusc.* i 148—244.

[7] *ib.* i 308—342.

[8] *ib.* iv 1—204. Cp. Koechly, 30 f. For protests against the metaphysical treatment of Syntax by Hermann and others, see Gildersleeve, in *A. J. P.* ii 480; and W. G. Hale, in *Cornell Studies*, i (*Cum-Constructions*, 1887–9) 7, 98, 247, and in *A Century of Metaphysical Syntax* (*Proc. St Louis Congress*, 1904, vol. iii).

[9] Pref. to *Acta Soc. Graecae*, xii, quoted in vol. i 12 n. 5 *supra*.

[10] His earliest treatise, *De Metris Poëtarum Graecorum et Romanorum* (1791), is enlarged in his German 'Handbook of Metrik' (1799), and is further developed in his *Elementa Doctrinae Metricae* (1816) with the corresponding *Epitome* (1818). Goethe was much interested in his 'Handbook' (Koechly, 27).

linian method of pronunciation for one which was closely akin to that of Erasmus[1].

In textual criticism his conjectures rest on a fine sense of Greek idiom. When the text is clearly corrupt, he relies mainly on his own sense of what the original author *ought* to have written. But he does not resort to conjecture for its own sake ; his aim is strictly to make his author say what he really meant to say[2]. Textual criticism, he maintained, must go hand in hand with *exegesis*. The exponent of the Classics must explain the individual words, elucidate the historical references, set forth the author's aim, and the general scheme of his work, with its merits and its defects[3]. But he must always be conscious of the limits to our knowledge of the ancient world:—*est quaedam etiam nesciendi ars et scientia*[4].

Among his published works a foremost place must be assigned to his editions of the Greek tragic poets. As a specimen of his Aeschylus, he put forth the *Eumenides* in 1799, but more than fifty years elapsed before the appearance of his posthumous edition of the whole (1852)[5]. His work on Sophocles was connected with that of his pupil, Erfurdt (1780—1813), who had produced in 1802–11 a critical edition, which was completed by the publication of the *Oedipus Coloneüs* by Heller and Doederlein in 1825, while Erfurdt's proposed lexicon was ultimately produced by Ellendt (1834). Erfurdt had also begun a smaller edition for the use of students; his *Antigone* appeared in 1809, and the series was completed by Hermann in 1811–25. Between 1810 and 1841 Hermann produced separate editions of thirteen plays of Euripides[6]. In place of an edition of the *Medea*, we have his notes on that of Elmsley[7]. The only play of Aristophanes that he edited was the *Clouds*.

The different kinds of interpolations in the *Homeric Hymns*

---

[1] Koechly, 24.   [2] Jahn, 116.

[3] *De officio interpretis*, in *Opusc.* vii 97 f.

[4] *Opusc.* ii 288. Cp. vol. ii 319 n. 3 *supra*.

[5] Jahn, 117.

[6] *Herc.* 1810, *Suppl.* 1811, *Bacchae* (mainly supplementary to Elmsley's ed.) 1823 ; *Ion*, and *Alc.* (with notes from Monk), 1827; *Hec.*, *Iph. Aul.*, *Iph.T.*, *Hel.*, *Andr.*, *Cycl.*, *Phoen.*, *Or.* (1831–41).

[7] *Opusc.* iii 143—261.

and in Hesiod's *Theogonia* are distinguished in the Letter to Ilgen prefixed to Hermann's early edition of the former (1806). His mature opinions on the Homeric question are presented in his papers of 1831–2 [1].

He here defends the hypothesis of Wolf against the opinion of the most important and most scholarly of its opponents, Nitzsch, who held that Homer composed the *Iliad* with the aid of older poems, and that he probably also composed the *Odyssey*, in which he was more original and less indebted to his predecessors. Wolf had held that the weaving of the Homeric web had been *carried down to a certain point* by the first and chief author of the poem, and had been continued by others. Hermann, improving on this opinion, suggested that the original sketch of our *Iliad* and our *Odyssey* had been produced by the first poet, and that the later poets did not *carry on the texture*, but completed the design *within* the outline that was already drawn [2].

Hermann made many valuable contributions to the criticism and exposition of Hesiod [3]. His edition of the *Orphica* (1805) supplies a much improved text, with an appendix showing, on metrical and linguistic grounds, that the date of these poems lies between that of Quintus Smyrnaeus and Nonnus [4]. It is of this appendix that Lehrs remarked that nothing had appeared in modern times more worthy of the genius of Bentley [5].

Pindar was the theme of his life-long study. As early as 1798 he had contributed to Heyne's *Pindar* a treatise on the poet's metres. In a later paper he showed that the language of the different odes had an Aeolic or a Doric colouring which varied with the rhythm in which they were composed [6]. His text of Bion and Moschus was published in 1849.

His work was mainly limited to the Greek poets, the only

---

[1] *Opusc.* v 52—77 (1832), vi (1) 70 f (1831), and viii 11 f (1840). He had printed a Tauchnitz text of Homer in 1825 (Praef. in *Opusc.* iii 74—82).

[2] *Opusc.* vi (1) 86 f; Jahn, 109; Koechly, 36—40; Jebb's *Homer*, 119 f. In connexion with the method of reciting the Homeric poems enjoined by Solon, Hermann opposed the views of Boeckh in two papers on the meaning of the term ὑποβολή (*Opusc.* v 300, vii 65); cp. vol. i 19 n. *supra*.

[3] Review of Goettling's ed. 1831 in *Opusc.* vi (1) 142 f. In vii 47 he suggests that the *Theogonia* originally consisted of 156 stanzas of 5 lines each.

[4] Cp. *Opusc.* ii 1—17 (1811).

[5] Lehrs, *Quaestiones Epicae*, 255; Koechly, 37, 169.

[6] *Opusc.* i 245 f; see also iii 22 f (on *Nem.* vii), v 182 f (θρῆνος), vi (1) 3 f (review of Dissen); also emendations etc. in vii 129 f, viii 68—128; cp. Jahn, 111 f.

Greek prose text[1] which he edited being Aristotle's *Poetic* (1802) with a dissertation on tragic and epic poetry[2]. The early interest in Plautus, which he owed to Reisig, bore fruit in editions of the *Trinummus*[3], and the *Bacchides*, the former of which was highly praised by Ritschl[4]. His attention was drawn to Greek Mythology by Creuzer, whose views he elaborately examined in 1819. In his papers on Greek Inscriptions (mainly on those in metre), he severely criticises the way in which they had been handled by archaeologists such as Boeckh and Welcker[5].

His lectures, no less than his dissertations, gave proof of his command of an excellent style in Latin prose. For 23 years he hardly ever failed to send on New Year's Eve a set of Latin verses in remembrance of the birthday of his friend Carl Einert[6], and in 1817 he celebrated the tercentenary of the Reformation in 120 lines of Latin Elegiacs. He exemplified the difference between the stately style of Greek tragedy, and the spasmodic movement of modern drama, by some thoroughly idiomatic renderings from Schiller's *Wallenstein*, which he executed amid the distractions of his drawing-room[7]. His life-long practice in riding lends a special value to his brief papers on the various phrases used in Greek to denote the different paces of a horse[8]. An officer of dragoons was so struck by the excellence of his horsemanship that he asked the professor whether he had ever served in the cavalry; and a scholar, who had learnt much from one of his reviews, described him, in the words of Horace, as *grammaticorum equitum doctissimus*[9]. Even at his professorial lectures he was wont to appear in his blue riding-coat, and in high boots and spurs[10], and his pupils were

---

[1] Except his text of Photius (1808).

[2] Koechly, 32, 152.

[3] 1800; ed. 2, 1853.

[4] *Kl. Philol. Schr.* ii 190. Cp. Jahn 116 f; Koechly, 46 f, 185—191.

[5] *Ueber Herrn Professor Boeckh's Behandlung der griechischen Inschriften* (1826); also *Opusc.* iv 303—332, v 164—181, vii 174—189.

[6] Koechly, 61 f, 265—286.

[7] *Opusc.* v 355—361; Koechly, 197 f.

[8] On Xen. *De Re Eq.* c. 7, in *Opusc.* i 63 f.

[9] Göttling's *Hesiod*, Proleg. xxxii; Koechly, 223; p. 117 n. 2 *infra*.

[10] Koechly, 7, 70, 223 f; Jahn, 101; Donaldson, *Scholarship and Learning*, 156—9.

vividly impressed by the brightness of his eyes and the breadth of
his lofty brow, by the singular transparency of his character, and
by the simple eloquence of his language.   The Greek Society,
which he founded at Leipzig, numbered nearly 200 members
during the half-century of its existence.   It is these who in a
special sense founded the school of Hermann, and they included
scholars of such note as Passow, Thiersch, Meineke, K. F.
Hermann, Trendelenburg, Spengel, Classen, Ritschl, Sauppe,
Haupt, Bergk, Koechly, Bonitz, and Arnold Schaefer[1].

While Hermann, the representative of pure scholarship, concentrated his attention on the language, and especially on the
poetry, of the old Greek Classics, it was the historic interest that
predominated in the case of his great contemporary,
August Boeckh (1785—1867).   At the school of   Boeckh
his birth-place, Carlsruhe, he attained that proficiency in mathematics which lends distinction to several of his maturer works.
At Halle he studied theology, philosophy, and philology, with a
view to a clerical or a scholastic career; but the influence of Wolf
led to his concentrating himself on the Greek Classics, while the
lectures of Schleiermacher guided him to the special study of
Plato.   His earliest work dealt with the pseudo-Platonic *Minos*
(1806).   He next spent a year in Bellermann's *Seminar* at Berlin,
where he enjoyed the friendship of Heindorf and Buttmann.   In
1807 he returned to his native land of Baden, and became a full
professor at Heidelberg only two years later.   His lectures at that
university covered a wide range of authors and of subjects[2].   His
continued interest in Plato was proved by his four papers on the
Timaeus[3], and by his edition of six pseudo-Platonic dialogues
(1810)[4].   At the same time, his study of Aeschylus, Sophocles,

---

[1] Koechly, 89, 257.   Cp. in general Otto Jahn's *Gedächtnissrede* (1849),
reprinted in *Biogr. Aufsätze*, 91—132, ed. 1866 ; K. F. Ameis, *G. Hermann's
pädagogischer Einfluss* (1850) ; H. Köchly, *G. Hermann* (1874), 330 pp. ;
Paulsen, ii 404-8[2]; Urlichs, 125-8[2]; Bursian, ii 666—687, and in *A. D. B.*;
Wilamowitz, *Eur. Her.* i 235-9[1].   *Opuscula* in eight vols., i—vii (1827–39),
viii (1876).

[2] Bursian, ii 688 n. 2.

[3] *Kl. Schr.* iii 109 f, 181 f, 229 f, 266 f.

[4] Bratuscheck, *A. Boeckh als Platoniker*, in Bergmann's *Philos. Monats-
heften*, i 272 f.

Γηράσκω αἰεὶ πολλὰ διδασκόμενος.

Αὐτόγς.

Aug. Böckh.

Boeckh.

From the frontispiece to Max Hoffmann's *August Boeckh* (1901).

and Euripides bore fruit in a treatise on those poets, in which verbal criticism is very subordinate to questions of wider literary interest, such as the extent of the changes early introduced into the original texts by actors, etc.[1] This treatise was dedicated in eulogistic terms to his future critic, Hermann, to whom he was then unknown. At Heidelberg he also gave early proof of his study of Pindar in three papers, the longest of which deals with the poet's metres, proving that words must never be broken in two at the end of the lines[2]. The greater part of his Pindar must have been practically finished while he was still at Heidelberg, at a time when he was more interested in the literary than the historical and antiquarian aspects of classical learning. The first volume was published in 1811, and it was completed in 1821 with the aid of his friend, Ludolph Dissen, who wrote the commentary on the Nemean and Isthmian Odes. In this edition the text is founded on the collation of numerous MSS, and the *exegesis* on a renewed study of the *scholia* printed in the first part of the second volume. It is still more important for the light that it throws on the poet's metres, and on the principles of his composition.

In the spring of 1811 he left Heidelberg for the position of professor of Eloquence and of Classical Literature in the newly-founded university of Berlin, and for 56 years he continued to be one of the chief ornaments of that seat of learning. The wide range of his earlier lectures was gradually narrowed into a course extending over two years, and including a general survey of classical learning, with special courses on *Metrik*, Greek Antiquities and Greek Literature, and lectures on Pindar, on a play of Euripides or Sophocles (generally the *Antigone*), a dialogue of Plato (usually the *Republic*), and a speech of Demosthenes. His delivery was not so animated as that of Wolf or Hermann, but his maturer students could not fail to appreciate the depth and solidity of his attainments and his perfect mastery of his subject. In Berlin the publication of his Pindar was delayed for several years by the Napoleonic war, but some important papers on that poet

---

[1] *Graecae tragoediae principum...num...genuina omnia sint...* (1808).

[2] This had been asserted (without proof) by C. W. Ahlwardt (1760—1830), in 1798 f, and had been noticed, as an almost invariable rule, by J. H. Voss in his *Zeitmessung*, 243 (Herbst, ii (2) 164, 320 f).

were laid before the Berlin Academy[1]. His papers on the *Antigone* (1824) were printed in his edition of the text together with a free translation, the publication of which, in 1843, was prompted by the first performance of the play with Mendelssohn's music in Berlin in 1841[2]. The date of the *Oedipus Coloneüs* was discussed in 1825–6[3], and the distribution of the first choral ode among the members of the chorus in 1843[4]. A paper on a corrupt passage of Euripides supplies an exceptional example of his success as a conjectural critic[5]. Meanwhile, his continued interest in Plato had led to his writing a valuable paper on Philolaus (1819).

In the historical and antiquarian province of classical learning Boeckh is represented by two important works, which have laid the foundation for all later research in the departments with which they are concerned. The first of these is the *Public Economy of Athens*, originally published in two volumes[6] with an Appendix of Inscriptions on the Athenian Navy (1840). The second is the *Corpus Inscriptionum Graecarum*. The former was partly inspired by Wolf's *Prolegomena* to the 'Leptines', and it is dedicated to Niebuhr. It supplies us with a full and systematic statement of the economic side of the Athenian constitution in its actual working. The treatise on the Silver Mines of Laurium arises out of the same subject and is included in the English translation of 1828[7].

The second and third German editions have an appendix of inscriptions relating to the finances of Athens. In the course of the preparation of the original work, the author formed a plan for a complete collection of such documents. The proposal was supported by Buttmann and Niebuhr, and accepted by the Berlin Academy. The first two folio volumes of the *Corpus* (1825–43) were edited by Boeckh, the third (1845–53) by Franz, the fourth was begun by Ernst Curtius and continued by Kirchhoff, and the whole was completed when Roehl's *Indices* were published in 1877,

---

[1] *Kl. Schr.* v 248, vii 369.

[2] Cp. Jebb's ed. xli; Max Hoffmann's *Boeckh*, 96 f.

[3] *Kl. Schr.* iv 228.   [4] *ib.* 527.

[5] *Iph. Aul.* 188, οὐδὲ κατατενῶ λίαν (for καταινῶ λίαν σ') ἐγώ.

[6] 1817 (E. T. 1828 and 1842); ed. 2, 1851 (E. T. Boston, 1857); ed. 3, 1886.

[7] Ed. 2, 1842.

more than fifty years after the work had been begun by Boeckh.
The first part of the first volume was severely reviewed by Hermann in 1825[1], and this severity was largely justified. Boeckh,
who had had no experience in examining or copying inscriptions
in situ, had not recognised the fact that an exact facsimile was a
necessary preliminary to the successful restoration of the text. He
had generally accepted the transcripts on trust, and his restorations
had often done violence, either to the evidence of those transcripts,
or to the laws of the Greek language. On the other hand, he had
shown great judgement in deciding questions as to the genuineness
of these documents. The twenty-six inscriptions, which the French
traveller, Michel Fourmont, had professed to have found among
the ruins of Amyclae, had been already suspected in England by
Payne Knight and in France by Boissonade, and were conclusively
proved by Boeckh to be forgeries[2]. In the scientific handling of
inscriptions, he had no precursors worthy of the name, except
Corsini and Chandler; so that he is practically the founder of this
branch of learning. The first systematic work on the subject,
that of Franz[3], is based entirely on Boeckh's labours[4]. In editing
the inscriptions of Greece, Boeckh applied his mathematical and
astronomical knowledge to the investigation of important points of
chronology[5], in which he was aided by Ideler (1766—1846)[6].
His mathematical skill is also shown in his examination of the
weights, the coinage-standards, and the measures of the ancients

[1] p. 94 *supra*. The best account of the long controversy between Hermann
and Boeckh, and their final reconciliation, is in Max Hoffmann's Life of Boeckh
(1901), 48—62.

[2] *C. I. G.* i p. 61 f. While all the inscriptions published, or left ready for
publication, by Fourmont were forgeries, there were hundreds of genuine
inscriptions, transcribed by himself, which he never published. Cp. R. C.
Christie's *Selected Essays*, 86—9; p. 86 *supra*.

[3] *Elementa Epigraphices Graecae*, 1840. Cp. Chabert, *Épigraphie grecque*,
1907.

[4] The inscriptions of Attica have since been edited anew, with large
additions, in the four volumes of the *Corpus Inscr. Atticarum* (1873–95),
followed by the earliest Greek inscriptions (1882), and by those of Sicily and
Italy (1890), N. Greece (1892), and the Greek Islands (1895).

[5] On the lunar cycles of the Greeks, *Kl. Schr.* vi 329 f; on Manetho and
the Dog-star period, *ib.* iii 343.

[6] Author of the *Handbuch* (1825 f) and the *Lehrbuch* (1831) of Chronology,
and of many papers on the history of ancient Astronomy.

(1838), a work that gave the first impulse to all subsequent investigations. His wide and comprehensive view of the various
branches of classical learning was attested in the course of lectures
repeatedly given by him at Berlin and since published by one of
his pupils[1]. His systematic account of the field of learning, as a
whole, is practically founded on that of Wolf, the *details* of whose
system he criticises with some severity. Boeckh's system, however, shows a marked advance on that of Wolf; and other systems
are reviewed by Boeckh himself[2]. Among the many subsequent
schemes are those of Emil Hübner, and of Martin Hertz[3].

The list of his pupils includes not a few distinguished names.
He was keenly interested in the subsequent career of K. O. Müller
at Göttingen, and of Edward Meier at Greifswald and Halle, and
in the later work of Gerhard in Berlin. Among his other pupils
were Göttling and Döderlein, Trendelenburg and Spengel, Droysen
and Preller, Lepsius and Dünker, Otto Jahn and Bonitz, and
Ernst and Georg Curtius[4]. Some of them, such as Trendelenburg
and Spengel, had already been pupils of Hermann, and several of
the foremost of Hermann's pupils, such as Ritschl, Köchly, and
Arnold Schaefer, were among the warmest admirers of Boeckh[5].

---

[1] *Encyklopädie und Methodologie der philologischen Wissenschaften*, ed.
Bratuscheck (1877), 824 pp.; ed. 2 (1886). Cp. Bursian, ii 703-5, and Max
Hoffmann's *Boeckh*, 147—152.

[2] *Encyklopädie* etc. p. 64 f.

[3] Reviewed by Bursian in *Jahresb.* vii (1876) 145, and xi (1877) 36,
respectively.

[4] Max Hoffmann, 79 f. Cp. *Jahrb. f. Philol.* lxxv 238 f.

[5] *ib.* 128 f.—Many of Boeckh's monographs are collected in his *Kleine
Schriften*, 7 vols. (1858–74). On his life and works, cp. R. H. Klausen, in
S. F. Hoffmann's *Lebensbilder berühmter Humanisten*, i (1837) 29 f; B. Stark,
Ueber Boeckh's Bildungsgang in *Vorträge* etc. (1880) 409–, and in *A. D. B.*;
Bursian, ii 687—705; Urlichs, 128[2] f; *Briefwechsel zwischen August Boeckh
und Karl Otfried Mueller* (1883); Ernst Curtius, *Altertum und Gegenwart*, iii
115—155 (1885); and Max Hoffmann, *August Boeckh, Lebensbeschreibung und
Auswahl aus seinem wissenschaftlichen Briefwechsel* [his correspondence with
Welcker, Niebuhr, Thiersch, Schömann, Gerhard, A. Schaefer, Ritschl, A. v.
Humboldt; followed by his Pindaric Ode of 1829], 483 pp. (1901); also
Leutsch, in *Philol. Anz.* 1886, 232 f; S. Reiter, in *Neue Jahrb. f. kl. Alt.* xiii
(1902) 436—458; and Gildersleeve, in *Oscillations and Nutations*, 2—7, and
in *A. J. P.* xxxviii 232.

Hermann and Boeckh, as the great representatives of pure and applied scholarship respectively, are men of whom all the votaries of classical learning may well be proud. At a later point we shall return to Boeckh's devoted pupil and friend, K. O. Müller[1]. Meanwhile we must briefly trace the careers of some of the scholars who belonged to the school of Hermann.

[1] Chap. xxxiv *init*.

CHAPTER XXX.

GRAMMARIANS AND TEXTUAL CRITICS
FROM LOBECK TO RITSCHL.

THE grammatical and critical school of philology is partly represented by two of Hermann's contemporaries, who were not, however, in complete agreement with his views. The works of both were defective in aim and in method; and their authors may be described as independent members of the parliament of scholars.

Gottfried Heinrich Schaefer (1764—1840), the librarian of Leipzig in

G. H. Schaefer 1818–33, was essentially a student, and not a teacher. In three successive editions of Viger, Hermann stated that he had only been able to make a partial use of the *marginalia* placed at his disposal by Schaefer. This statement gave offence to the latter, who in his commentary on Demosthenes retaliated by attacking Reisig and other pupils of Hermann[1]. A man of wide learning, especially in the province of Greek prose, Schaefer buried much of that learning in the works of others[2]. The most important of his own works was the *Apparatus Criticus* to Demosthenes, including excerpts from all the earlier commentators, with valuable additions of his own[3]. His editions (usually accompanied by prolix commentaries of the old Dutch type) included Dionysius of Halicarnassus, *De Compositione Verborum*. His edition of Gregorius Corinthius, and other writers on Greek dialects, was equipped with a valuable *Commentatio Palaeographica* and facsimiles by Bast[4]. He also edited many of the Tauchnitz Classics, with emendations of his own, but there is a marked absence of any definite critical principles or any methodical recension of the text[5].

The same defect is obvious in the productions of an abler critic, Friedrich

Bothe Heinrich Bothe (1770—1855), who held no educational position, but spent his whole life in the mechanical manufacture of classical books. His best work was connected with the Greek and Roman

---

[1] Koechly's *Hermann*, 215 f.

[2] *e.g.* in the London ed. (1815 f) of the Greek *Thesaurus* of H. Stephanus.

[3] 5 vols. (London, 1824–7); vol. vi, *Indices* by E. C. Seiler (1833).

[4] ii p. 397 *supra*.   [5] Bursian, ii 707–9.

drama. He repeatedly edited all the Greek Dramatists, including the fragments, with criticisms on Aristophanes (1808) under the pseudonym of Hotibius
(an approximate anagram of Bothius). His criticisms on the Greek Comic
fragments were published under his own name in the Didot series (1855).
Plautus, Terence and Seneca, were edited by him separately, as well as in a
collected form (1834). In all these works there is a lack of critical method,
but there are many excellent emendations. The same holds good of his
editions of the Homeric Poems, and of Horace and Phaedrus[1].

One of the earliest and most distinguished of the pupils of
Hermann was Christian August Lobeck (1781—
1860), who taught at Wittenberg in 1802–14, and   **Lobeck**
was professor at Königsberg for the remaining 46 years of his
life. Hermann himself[2] has dwelt in glowing terms on the
profound learning that pervades every page of his pupil's edition
of the *Ajax*[3]. The same learning, combined with a singular
faculty for grouping large masses of facts under general laws of
language, is manifest in his second great work, his edition of the
Atticist, *Phrynichus* (1820). A fragment of Herodian is appended
to the latter, and the last 300 pages are mainly devoted to the
laws of word-formation in Greek. Similar subjects are treated
in his *Paralipomena Grammaticae Graecae* (1837) and his
Rhematikon (1846). The terminations of Greek nouns are the
theme of eleven dissertations comprised in the *Prolegomena* to
the *Pathologia Sermonis Graeci* (1843), followed by the two
parts of the *Pathologia* (1843–62). His valuable additions to
Buttmann's Greek Grammar have been already mentioned[4]. All
of these works are marked by a singularly comprehensive knowledge of the whole range of Greek literature, by an acute
perception of real or apparent analogies, and a fine sense of
the life of the language. His clear insight and wide erudition
enable him to deduce definite laws and rules of usage from an
almost overwhelming multitude of details. He holds aloof from
the methods and the results of the Comparative Philology of
his day, but one of the foremost of Comparative Philologists has

---

[1] Bursian, ii 709–11.

[2] *Praef. ad Soph. Aiac.* ed. 4 p. vi, 'cuius in editione nulla pagina est qua
perlecta non doctiorem se factum sentiat qui discere didicerit'.

[3] 1809; ed. 3, 1866.

[4] p. 84 *supra.*

stated that the suggestions modestly put forward by Lobeck 'are always combined with such a wealth of learning, such fine philological discrimination, and such careful regard for tradition, that they contribute much to the comprehension of the principles of Greek Etymology, and, even where his results cannot be accepted, the process of his inquiry is exceedingly valuable'[1].

His interest in the history of Greek religion is exemplified by the anonymous notice of Creuzer's *Dionysus*, in which he makes merry over the mystic meanings which Creuzer sees in the pots and pans of ancient houses and temples[2]; by the similar review of the *Symbolik*, where he attacks the author's passion for 'finding symbols under every stone'[3]; and, above all, by his *Aglaophamus*[4], a masterly work of astounding learning, in which all that is really known as to the Greek mysteries is set forth in instructive contrast to the fanciful speculations of the Symbolists.

Lobeck's wit and humour, as well as his devotion to the old Greek texts, are well exemplified in a short letter to Meineke :—

What is this that I hear, my dear friend? I can hardly believe my ears. Are you *really* wanting to visit Italy? Why Italy, of all parts of the world? Simply to see a few statues with broken noses? NO ! If I cannot visit Niagara, or the Mississippi, or Hekla, I prefer sitting here beside my own warm stove, reading GREEK SCHOLIASTS,—which is, after all, the true end of the life of man[5].

Twenty years later, Hermann, at the age of 70, wrote as follows, when he was endeavouring to induce his old pupil to pay him a visit at Leipzig :—

You talk of your 'old pain in the chest'. Why! *I*, who, as a matter of fact, have a constant cough, and am not unfrequently coughing, day and night, for four weeks together, never stop to inquire whether I have *one* lung or *two*, so long as I can breathe with the lung that I have. You also talk of 'life's setting sun'. Why! that, in the phrase of 'Longinus'[6], would give us the promise of a new *Odyssey* as the counterpart to the *Iliad* of your *Aglaophamus*[7].

---

[1] G. Curtius, *Principles of Gk Etym.* i 14, E. T.

[2] *Jena Allg. Litteratur-Zeitung* (1810), no. 18—20, p. 137 f.

[3] *ib.* 1811, no. 96 f ; cp. 1812, no. 71—73.

[4] *Sive de theologiae mysticae Graecorum causis*, 2 vols., 1392 pp. (1829). Cp. Koechly's *Hermann*, 45, 183.

[5] *Mittheilungen aus Lobecks Briefwechsel*, ed. Friedländer, 67 (1821).

[6] c. 9.

[7] *Br.* p. 121 (1842); *Ausg. Briefe*, ed. Ludwich, p. 317 f. On Lobeck, cp. Lehrs, *Erinnerungen* in *Populäre Aufsätze* (1875[2]) 479 f ; Friedländer's

Among the earliest pupils of Lobeck in his Wittenberg days, were several who did good work on the Greek Epic poets.   Franz Ernst
Heinrich Spitzner (1787—1841) produced an edition of the   **Spitzner**
Iliad with a critical commentary, and a number of excursuses founded on a careful observation of the language and the prosody of the Homeric poems. His *Observationes* include many excellent emendations on Quintus Smyrnaeus[1].

Another pupil of Lobeck, Gregor Wilhelm Nitzsch (1790—1861), was a professor for 25 years at Kiel and, for the last nine years of his   **Nitzsch**
life, at Leipzig.   With the exception of some papers on the
history of Greek religion and on Plato, with an edition of the *Ion*, his work as a scholar was mainly devoted to Homer.   Grammatical exposition is well represented in his explanatory notes to the first twelve books of the *Odyssey* (1826–40); but he is best known as an early and an effective opponent of Wolf's theory on the Homeric question.

While Wolf regards Homer as a primitive bard, who began to weave the web of the Homeric poems, and only carried it down to a certain point, Nitzsch looks upon him as a 'great poetical artist who, coming after the age of the short lays, framed an epic on a larger plan'[2].   Thus Wolf places Homer at the *beginning* of the growth of the poems, Nitzsch nearer to the *end*.   Nitzsch regards the *Iliad* as *mainly* the work of Homer, but this view does not exclude the introduction of minor interpolations and changes at a later date.   The *Odyssey* he considers to be the work of perhaps the same poet, who (he holds) was more original here than in the *Iliad*.   In the course of the controversy Nitzsch observed that some of the 'Cyclic' poems of the seventh and eighth centuries B.C. presupposed our *Iliad* and *Odyssey* in something like their present form, and, further, that the Greek use of writing was probably older than Wolf had assumed[3].

Nitzsch was conscious of a certain obscurity of style, which prevented his views from becoming widely known, but he worked on to the very end at the favourite theme of his life.   On the day of his death, a sultry day in July, when he was about to lecture at noon on the *Odyssey*, he hastened to his house to fetch

---

Mittheilungen etc. (1861); and *Programmen* (1864), i, iii—v ; Lehnerdt's *Auswahl aus Lobeck's akademischen Reden* (1865); *Ausgewählte Briefe* (1802–78) *von und an C. A. Lobeck und K. Lehrs*, ed. Ludwich, 1049 pp. (1894); Bursian, ii 572–5, 711–4.

[1] Bursian, ii 713 f.

[2] Jebb's *Homer*, 121.

[3] (1) *De Historia Homeri, maximeque de scriptorum carminum aetate meletemata* (Hanover, 1830–7), with supplements in Kiel programs 1834–9; (2) *Die Heldensage der Griechen nach ihrer nationalen Geltung* (Kiel, 1841); (3) *Die Sagenpoesie der Griechen kritisch dargestellt* (Braunschweig, 1852); (4) *Beiträge zur Geschichte der epischen Poesie der Griechen* (Leipzig, 1862).

a book that he had forgotten, and died of the sunstroke which befell him on his way back to the lecture-room[1]. A funeral-oration by Overbeck described him as one whose name would be remembered forever in the history of learning by the side of Wolf and Lachmann and Welcker. A strict integrity of character is the leading trait that strikes one in his broad and square-set face as it appears in the portrait prefixed to his life[2].

Among the correspondents of Nitzsch none, perhaps, agreed more completely

Nägelsbach

with his views on Homer than Karl Friedrich Nägelsbach (1806—1859), who, after teaching for 15 years at the *gymnasium* of Nüremberg, spent the last 13 years of his life as a professor at Erlangen. Nitzsch and Nägelsbach had also a common interest in the theology of the Homeric poems[3]. The published works of Nägelsbach include Notes on the first three books of the *Iliad*, omitting the Catalogue of Ships (1834), and two important volumes on *Homeric* and *Posthomeric Theology* (1840-57), besides papers on Aeschylus and a posthumous edition of the *Agamemnon* (1863). The most widely appreciated of his works is that on 'Latin Style', with special regard to the differences of idiom between Latin and German prose[4].

Among the pupils of Lobeck, Spitzner and Nitzsch were even surpassed

Spohn

in ability by Friedrich August Wilhelm Spohn (1792—1824) who, for the last nine years of his brief life, was a teacher in the university of Leipzig. Following in the track of Wolf, he wrote a short paper on the discrepancies in the topography of the Trojan plain, as represented in the *Iliad* (1814), and a commentary supporting the opinion of Aristophanes of Byzantium and of Aristarchus, that the conclusion of the *Odyssey* was a later composition (1816). He also published, with supplementary notes, Morus' edition of the *Panegyricus* of Isocrates, a school-edition of the *Works and Days* of Hesiod, with the critical marks invented by the Alexandrian Grammarians, a monograph on Tibullus, and textual criticisms on Theocritus. He was the first of German scholars to attempt to decipher the hieratic and the demotic writing of the ancient Egyptians[5]. He was proposing to produce works on the ancient Geographers, on the Mythology of the Eastern and Northern

---

[1] F. Lübker, 87.

[2] F. Lübker, *G. W. Nitzsch in seinem Leben und Wirken* (1864), esp. 24 f, 84 f, 89, 105 f, 108—110, 119—123, with bibliography on 188—193; also Volkmann, *Gesch....der Wolfschen Proleg.* 184—190, 204, 216; Bursian, ii 714—716.

[3] Lübker's *Nitzsch*, 105-7, 185-7.

[4] *Lateinische Stilistik*, 1846; ed. 9 (Iwan Müller, with full Index), 1905. Cp. in general Döderlein's *Oeff. Reden*, 1860, 239 f, and Lübker's *Lebensbilder*, 1862; also Bursian, ii 715 f.

[5] Letter to Lobeck in Lobeck's *Briefwechsel*, ed. Friedländer, 74 f, and Ludwich's ed. of *Ausg. Briefe*, 7 f.

nations, and on the literature of the Augustan age, when his life came to an untimely end[1].

The foremost of Lobeck's pupils at Königsberg was Karl Lehrs (1802—1878), who was one of his master's colleagues for the last 29 years of that master's life, **Lehrs** and was himself the head of the Königsberg School for 18 years after. Under Lobeck and Lehrs the School was distinguished by a special interest (1) in the history of grammatical studies among the Greeks from the beginning of the Alexandrian to the end of the Byzantine age, (2) in the study of the language, metre and composition of the Greek Epics, from Homer down to Nonnus and his imitators, and (3) in the investigation of the religious opinions of the Greeks, with special reference to the *ethical* content of the myths, excluding all attempts to interpret those myths by means of the phenomena of *Nature*. Lehrs made his mark in all three lines of research.

In the first, his principal work related to the 'Homeric Studies of Aristarchus'[2]. In the earliest of his *Quaestiones Epicae* (1837) he showed that Wolf had exaggerated the value of the grammarian Apion's services to the text of Homer. His papers on the history of the Greek originals of the terms *philologus*, *grammaticus*, and *criticus*[3], and on the grammarian Asclepiades of Myrlea, were reprinted as an appendix to an improved edition of three minor works of Herodian[4], which paved the way for the great edition of the whole of that grammarian's works by the pupil of Lobeck and Lehrs, August Lentz (1820—1868)[5]. Lastly, in his volume on the *scholia* to Pindar (1873), he arranged the confused mass of the extant *scholia* in certain groups and endeavoured to determine the date of each.

(2) In his *Quaestiones Epicae*[6], after examining the *Works and Days* of Hesiod, he arrives at the conclusion that the original nucleus of the poem is to be found in lines 383—694. In the same work he investigates the linguistic

---

[1] Life by G. Seyffarth, prefixed to Spohn, *De lingua et litteris veterum Aegyptiorum* (1825); Bursian, ii 716-8.

[2] *De Aristarchi Studiis Homericis*, 1833, 1865[2], 1882[3] (506 pp.). In the *Epimetra* to ed. 2 and 3 he deals with the lexicography, grammar and metre of the Homeric poems, and with questions as to the genuineness of single lines or larger portions of the poems. He handles similar questions in the Appendix to his pupil Eduard Kammer's work on the Unity of the Odyssey (1873).

[3] Cp. vol. i 6—11 *supra*.

[4] περὶ μονήρους λέξεως, περὶ Ἰλιακῆς προσῳδίας, περὶ διχρόνων, 1848.

[5] *Herodiani technici reliquiae* (1867-70), with *Indices* by Arthur Ludwich.

[6] 179 f.

and metrical peculiarities of Nonnus, and the characteristic differences between the genuine *Halieutica* of Oppian and the *Cynegetica* erroneously attributed to that author.

(3) In his 'Popular Essays'[1] he maintains that the Greek Mythology is founded on an *ethical* basis, and not on the phenomena of *Nature*, thereby ascribing to the infancy of the Greek race an attitude of mind that is more in keeping with its maturer age. In the same Essays, however, he gives proof of a fine perception of the moral and religious opinions of the Greeks during the time of their highest developement.

His researches on the Greek Grammarians have won a far wider approval than his criticisms on Ovid's *Heroides*, and on Horace, many of whose *Odes* he rejected (1869)[2].

The interest in the Greek epic poets and grammarians is a tradition of the Königsberg School, which has been well maintained by living scholars.

Returning from the line of the descendants of Lobeck to the immediate pupils of Hermann, we note the name of Lobeck's fellow-student and friend, Johann Friedrich August Seidler (1779—1851), who, under Hermann's direct influence, made a brilliant beginning with a work of permanent value on the dochmiac metre (1811-2), and edited three plays of Euripides[3] on the model of Erfurdt's edition of Sophocles. Hermann had so great a respect for his former pupil's ability as to print in the preface to his *Ion* some 16 pages of notes supplied by Seidler.

Seidler

Another pupil of Hermann, Carl Christian Reisig (1792—1829), left Leipzig for Göttingen, served as a serjeant among the Saxon troops that fought Napoleon in 1813–15, and, after studying for two years at Jena, became a professor at Halle in 1820, and, nine years after, died on his way to Venice, at the early age of 37. He was a man of marked ability and energy, and of singularly sound judgement. His general character resembled that of Wolf. At Wolf's university of Halle he lectured mainly on the Greek Drama, as well as on Horace and Tibullus, Demosthenes and Cicero, with Greek and Roman Antiquities, and Greek and Latin Grammar. The importance of his lectures on the last subject may be gathered from the edition afterwards published with valuable supplements by his pupil, Friedrich Haase[4]. Of the three subjects treated in this volume, Etymology, Semasiology, and Syntax, the second owes its origin to Reisig. The work published by himself

Reisig

---

[1] *Populäre Aufsätze*, 1856, 1875[2].

[2] Cp. E. Kammer in *Biogr. Jahrb.* for 1878, 14—28; *Briefe*, ed. Farenheid (1878); *Briefe an M. Haupt* (1892); *Ausgewählte Briefe*, ed. Ludwich (1894); Bursian, ii 718—724; *Kleine Schriften*, with portrait, ed. Ludwich (1902), 582 pp., and Ludwich's *Rede*, 1902, *ib.* 554 f.

[3] *Tro.* 1812; *El.* and *Iph. T.* 1813. Cp. Bursian, ii 725 f.

[4] *Vorlesungen über lat. Sprachwissenschaft* (1839).

was mainly concerned with Aristophanes and Sophocles. A copy of the second Juntine edition of Aristophanes was his constant companion during his campaign against France, and, in the following year, he dedicated to Hermann a series of conjectures on the text, mainly suggested by considerations of metre (1816). His critical edition of the *Clouds* appeared in 1820, while his interest in Sophocles is attested by his very full commentary on the *Oedipus Coloneüs*[1]. Lastly, his emendations on the *Prometheus Vinctus* of Aeschylus were published by Ritschl, who was one of his most devoted pupils at Halle[2].

Much was meanwhile done for the exegesis of Sophocles by Eduard Wunder (1800—1869), who spent the last 43 years of his life at the Saxon school of Grimma. In the interval between his early   **Wunder**
studies on Sophocles and his explanatory edition of 1831–50, he produced an elaborate commentary on Cicero, *pro Plancio* (1830), besides publishing readings from an important MS of Cicero, then at Erfurt and now in Berlin[3]. Wunder's edition of Sophocles appeared in the series edited by Jacobs and Rost at Gotha. In the same series, seven plays of Euripides[4]   **Pflugk**
were edited by August Julius Edmund Pflugk (1803—1839). On the early death of Pflugk at Danzig, four more plays[5] were added to the series by Reinhold Klotz[6].

Hermann's pupil, August Ferdinand Naeke (1788—1838), distinguished himself at Bonn as an able lecturer on some of the principal   **Naeke**
Greek and Latin poets, and on the History of Greek poetry. Singularly fastidious in his taste, he produced only one important work, a collection of the fragments of the epic poet, Choerilus. His edition of the *Dirae* and *Lydia*, which (like Scaliger) he ascribed to Valerius Cato, was posthumously published in 1846. His minor works were collected in two volumes of *Opuscula*, the second of which includes the fragments of Callimachus. His paper on Latin alliteration is only to be found in the *Rheinisches Museum*[7], of which he was an editor for a few years. The outlines of his courses of lectures, still preserved in the library at Bonn, were described by Ritschl as marked by the same devotion to the discovery of truth, and the same calm judgement, as his few published works[8].

One of Naeke's colleagues at Bonn, Karl Friedrich Heinrich (1774—1838), was educated at Gotha and Göttingen, and, after holding a   **Heinrich**
mastership at Breslau, was professor at Kiel in 1804–18, and

---

[1] 3 vols. (1820–23).

[2] Ritschl, *Opusc.* i 378—393; cp. *Kl. Philol. Schr.* v 95 f; Ribbeck's Life of Ritschl, i 34—52; Haase's Preface to the *Vorlesungen*, v f; and Bursian, ii 726.

[3] *Variae Lectiones* (1827).

[4] *Med., Hec., Androm., Heracl., Hel., Alc., Herc. Furens.*

[5] *Phoen., Or., Iph. T., Iph. A.*

[6] p. 125 *infra*.

[7] iii (1829) 324 f.

[8] *ib.* N. F. xxvii 193 f. Bursian, ii 729 f.

at Bonn for the remaining 20 years of his life. At Bonn he lectured with marked success on the Roman satirists, and was even more successful as the director of the classical *Seminar*. While still a student under Heyne at Göttingen, he produced an edition of Musaeus, and three volumes of explanatory notes on the *Aeneid*. He was aided in the latter by Georg Heinrich Noehden (1770—1826), who published a work on Porphyry's *scholia* to Homer, with appendices on the Townley and Eton MSS[1], and for the last fifteen years of his life held an appointment in the library of the British Museum. As a master at Breslau, Heinrich produced not only a treatise on Epimenides, but also an edition of Nepos and of Hesiod's *Shield of Achilles*. These early works had been prepared under the influence of Heyne, the rest were produced under that of Wolf. At Kiel, in 1816, he published, in conjunction with Andreas Wilhelm Cramer (1760—1833), the fragments of Cicero *pro Scauro, pro Tullio,* and *pro Flacco*, recently discovered by Mai in the Ambrosian Library; at Bonn, he edited the speech of Lycurgus against Leocrates (1821) and Cicero, *De Republica* (1823–8). His editions of Juvenal and Persius were posthumously published. His critical notes on the treatise of Frontinus on the Roman Aqueducts were included in Dederich's edition (1841). Heinrich had intended to edit the work in conjunction with the eccentric scholar, Christoph Ludwig Friedrich Schultz (1780—1834), who fancifully regarded the works of Vitruvius and Pomponius Mela as fabrications of the Middle Ages[2].

Among the earliest and most important of the pupils of Hermann was Friedrich Wilhelm Thiersch (1784—1860).

Thiersch

Educated at Schulpforta under Hermann's former tutor, Ilgen, he studied the Greek poets, and acquired an exceptional facility in Greek verse, under Hermann at Leipzig. In 1807 he was drawn to Göttingen by Heyne; two years later he left for Munich, where his success as a school-master led to his being entrusted with the direction of a philological *Seminar* which was incorporated in the Bavarian university on its transfer from Landshut to Munich in 1826[3]. He also lectured on Greek Art, after studying the sculptures in the Louvre and the British Museum (1813–5). These studies were continued in Munich itself on the founding of the *Glyptothek* by the Crown Prince, Ludwig, and were still further extended by half a year's absence in Italy (1822–3). Classical studies were languishing at Munich during the later years of Ast, when they were revived by the energy of Thiersch, who, for 15 years, was ably supported by

---

[1] Göttingen, 1797.   [2] Bursian, ii 731–3.

[3] Papers by the director and his friends (including Döderlein, Spengel, and Halm) were published in the *Acta Philologorum Monacensium*, 1812–29.

Spengel. His jubilee as a Doctor was celebrated in 1858; he retired from active work in the following year, and he died in 1860.

Thiersch took an important part in the organisation of the schools and universities of Bavaria, as the champion of classical education and of intellectual freedom[1]. In 1837, at the celebration of the centenary of Göttingen, he brought into existence an annual congress of the scholars and school-masters of Germany. He also took a warm interest in the cause of Greek independence, and in the organisation of the Greek kingdom under Otho of Bavaria[2]. He was a prolific writer on political and educational questions, and on general literature. His contributions to classical learning fall under three heads :—(1) Greek Grammar; (2) criticism and interpretation of Greek poetry; (3) archaeology, including topography and epigraphy.

(1) His 'Greek Grammar, with special reference to the Homeric dialect' (1812), reached a third edition (1829); his shorter Grammar (1815) was considerably enlarged in its fourth edition (1855)[3]. The Grammar of 1812 led to a controversy on Homeric moods with Hermann[4]. His life-long interest in grammar was further proved by papers on Greek word-formation and on Greek particles[5], preparatory to a proposed edition of the *Agamemnon*. He was also familiar with modern Greek, but his paper on the language of the present inhabitants of N.E. Laconia[6] has since been superseded by more accurate investigations[7].

(2) He was also interested in Hesiod and the early elegiac poets, and in Pindar and Aeschylus. In one of his first papers, he maintained that the poems bearing the name of Hesiod were fragments from various poems of different ages, the relics of an old Boeotian school of epic poetry[8]. He regarded the *Works and Days* as composed by several poets, and also treated it in connexion with the gnomic poetry of Greece[9]. He edited Pindar, with an introduction and explanatory notes, and with a German translation in the

---

[1] Thiersch, *Ueber gelehrte Schulen* (1826–31); cp. Paulsen, ii 418—430[2].

[2] His interest in modern Greece is attested in his work, *De l'état actuel de la Grèce*, 2 vols. (1833).

[3] Cp. Eckstein, *Lat. und Gr Unterricht*, 396.

[4] Thiersch, *Acta phil. Mon.* i 1, 175, 435, 468, and Hermann's *Opusc.* ii 18 f.

[5] Munich Acad., *Denkschriften*, xxvii 379, xxx 307, xxxiii 1.

[6] *ib.* (1835) 511 f.

[7] M. Deffner, *Zakonische Grammatik*, 1881.

[8] *Denkschriften*, iv (1813).

[9] *Acta Phil. Mon.* iii 389, 567.

original metres. He wrote on *lacunae* in Aeschylus and on passages calling for correction by transposition of lines[1], and left behind him, ready for press, a lengthy commentary on the *Agamemnon*.

(3) In archaeology, his earliest work consisted of three papers on the 'Epochs of Greek Art'[2]. They represented a relapse from the sounder views of Winckelmann, and were strongly opposed by K. O. Müller[3], though supported by Thiersch's pupil, Feuerbach (1798—1851). Thiersch's visit to Italy led to his planning a great work on Italy and its inhabitants, and its treasures of art in ancient and modern times, but the only portions that ever appeared were his own account of his tour, and Schorn's description of Ravenna and Loretto (1826). A plan for a similar work on Greece ended in some papers on Paros and Delphi, and on the *Erechtheum*[4]. The collection of Greek vases formed by king Ludwig I prompted a paper showing that the vases found in Etruscan tombs were really Greek and mainly Athenian[5], and also opposing the opinion that they were connected with the Mysteries[6].

Ast

Among the immediate predecessors of Thiersch in the Bavarian university, Georg Anton Friedrich Ast (1778—1841) was a classical professor for the last 36 years of his life, first at Landshut, and next, at the new seat of that university, in Munich. Besides editing the *Characters* of Theophrastus, he had made his mark as an expositor of Plato, had written on Plato's Life and Works, had edited all the Dialogues with a Latin translation, had annotated the *Protagoras*, *Phaedrus*, *Gorgias* and *Phaedo*, and had crowned all this with his celebrated *Index* to Plato (1834–8). In his later years he was somewhat remiss as a lecturer, and it was then that (as we have seen) a new life was breathed into the classical studies of Munich by the energy of the youthful Thiersch. Thiersch was strongly supported in Munich by Leonhard Spengel, who was then a master at the Old Gymnasium, and who worked with Thiersch for 15 years at the university[7]. From 1843 Thiersch had the

[1] *Denkschriften*, xxi (1846).

[2] Era of (1) religious style, ending *c.* 580 B.C.; (2) artistic developement, 580—490 B.C.; (3) perfected style, from Pheidias (500—430) to Hadrian (d. 138 A.D.) and M. Aurelius (d. 180 A.D.). Ed. 2, 1829.

[3] *Kleine deutsche Schriften*, ii 315 f.

[4] *Denkschriften*, xxi (1849) 79; xxvii (1850) 99, 230.

[5] *Abhandlungen* of Munich Acad., iv (1844) 1 f.

[6] Cp., in general, Life by H. W. J. Thiersch (2 vols., 1866); Bibliography in J. Pözl's *Rede* (Munich, 1860); Bursian, ii 733, 738–49.

[7] p. 180 *infra*.

support of the eminent Aristotelian, Carl Prantl (1820–88)[1], and, from 1844, that of Ernst von Lasaulx (1805—1861).

Classical education in Bavaria was also ably promoted by Ludwig Doederlein (1791—1863), who was born at Jena and educated at Schulpforta. His studies, **Doederlein** begun at Munich under Thiersch, were continued at Heidelberg, Erlangen, and Berlin. As a professor at Bern he produced in 1819 a volume of philological papers in conjunction with Bremi[2]. At Erlangen he was professor from 1819, and head-master of the local school from 1819 to 1862. As director of the philological *Seminar*, he had for his colleague, first, Joseph Kopp (1788—1842), a man of vast learning who, on principle, produced nothing; next, the eminent stylist, K. F. Nägelsbach[3], and lastly, the future editor of the Latin Grammarians, Heinrich Keil, who, on Doederlein's death in 1863, continued his work until 1869, when he left for Halle. As a university lecturer, Doederlein was interesting and stimulating, but unduly prone to paradox. As head of the local school, he made his mark by his impressive personality and by his forcible eloquence[4]. He was less happy as a writer of works on Latin Synonyms, and on Greek and Latin Etymology, in which he was apt to be unduly subtle, while his wide learning gave a factitious support to fanciful and eccentric views[5]. The same eccentricity and lack of method are evident in his editions of Homer and the *Oedipus Coloneüs*, and of Theocritus, the *Epistles* and *Satires* of Horace, and Tacitus[6]. Henry Sidgwick, who met him at Brunswick in 1860, describes him as 'a dear old man with such a loving face, and, at the same time, very refined features, expressing the thorough scholar in the Cambridge sense of the word'[7].

Among the other schoolfellows of Thiersch at Schulpforta was Ludolph Dissen (1784—1837), who was also **Dissen** his fellow-student under Heyne at Göttingen.

[1] p. 180 *infra*.

[2] *Philologische Beiträge aus der Schweiz* (1819).

[3] p. 106 *supra*.

[4] *Reden* etc., 1843, 1847, 1860.

[5] *Lat. Synonymen und Etymologien*, 6 vols. (1826–38); *Lat. Synonymik* (1839, 1849[2]); *Lat. Etym.* (1841); *Hom. Glossarium*, 3 vols. (1850–8).

[6] Bursian, ii 749 f, and in *A. D. B.*   [7] *Life*, 59.

Dissen did not actually belong to Hermann's school; he was in fact opposed to Hermann's method of interpreting the Classics; but he was none the less a representative of the grammatical and critical type of classical learning. With the exception of a brief stay at Marburg (1812–3), he resided at Göttingen from 1808 to his death in 1837. At Göttingen he produced his earliest work, that on Greek moods and tenses[1]; at Marburg he published an inaugural discourse on the *Memorabilia* of Xenophon[2]; and, late in life, he wrote a paper on Plato's *Theaetetus*[3]. But his main interest, as a classical scholar, lay in the investigation of the laws of poetical and oratorical composition. As a leading exponent of the artistic and aesthetic interpretation of the Classics, he illustrated his principles in his editions of Pindar (1830)[4] and Tibullus (1835)[5], and of Demosthenes, *De Corona* (1837). The acumen and the powers of observation, which Dissen applies to the study of these works, are worthy of all praise, but his method is unduly artificial and tends to obscure our sense of the living genius of the poet and the orator[6].

A fine sense of the beautiful in poetry and art, combined with
Passow
a thorough knowledge of the classical languages, and a methodical skill in the collection of lexicographical materials, are the main characteristics of Franz Passow (1786—1833). A pupil of Jacobs at Gotha, he attended Hermann's lectures for two years at Leipzig, before studying ancient art at Dresden. After showing special aptitude as a school-master at Weimar and near Danzig, he left for Berlin, where he attended Wolf's lectures at the age of 28. For the last 18 years of his life he was professor at Breslau, where his appointment led to a revival of classical studies at that university. He was warmly supported by that thorough scholar, Karl Ernst Christoph Schneider (1786—1856), who afterwards edited Plato's

---

[1] *Kleine Schriften*, 1 f.   [2] *ib.* 89 f.   [3] *ib.* 151 f.

[4] Criticised by Hermann, *Opusc.* vi (1) 3—69, and Boeckh, *Ges. kl. Schr.* vii 369 f (cp. *Briefwechsel zwischen Boeckh und K. O. Müller*, 289—291). Dissen had already contributed to Boeckh's ed. of 1821 a commentary on the *Nemean* and *Isthmian* Odes.

[5] Criticised by Lachmann, *Kl. Schr.* ii 145 f.

[6] Bursian, ii 751–3. Dissen's *Kleine...Schriften* (1839) include reminiscences by Thiersch, Welcker and K. O. Müller.

Republic and took part in the Didot edition of Plato, besides producing a critical recension of Caesar's *Gallic War*, and claiming for Petrarch the 'Life of Caesar' wrongly ascribed to 'Julius Celsus'. Passow had hitherto been mainly interested in Persius, Musaeus, and Longus; he now devoted himself to the laborious task of producing in 1819–23 a greatly enlarged and improved edition of the Greek lexicon of J. G. Schneider (1750—1822), then one of the senior professors at Breslau. The work was so largely altered that, in the fourth edition, Passow's name alone appeared on the title-page (1831)[1]. Passow contributed to Ersch and Gruber's *Encyclopaedia* articles on Aeschines and on the Latin Anthology, which are reprinted in his 'Miscellaneous Works', with his article on Bast, his essays on Hieronymus Wolf and Henricus Stephanus, and his paper on Philostratus the elder. Next to his lexicographical labours, his most important works were his extensive program on the *Persae* of Aeschylus, and his shorter papers on Sophocles and Aristophanes, and on late Greek authors[2]. He made some preliminary preparations for an edition of Stephanus of Byzantium, which he proposed to produce in conjunction with August Wellauer (1798—1830), the editor of Aeschylus

Wellauer

and of Apollonius Rhodius, and the compiler of the *Lexicon Aeschyleum*. The only Latin texts edited by Passow were Persius and the *Germania* of Tacitus. It may be added that it was at his instance that the Leipzig publisher, B. G. Teubner (1784—1856), began in 1824 his celebrated series of Greek and Latin texts, and, in 1826, the *Jahrbücher für Philologie und Pädagogik*[3].

Among Passow's earliest pupils at Weimar was his life-long friend, Karl Wilhelm Göttling (1793—1869), who, for the last 47 years of his life, was a professor at Jena. He lectured on classical

Göttling

---

[1] It was subsequently made the foundation of a large lexicon prepared by V. C. F. Rost, in conjunction with Friedrich Palm and other scholars (1841–57). Meanwhile, Wilhelm Pape (1807—1854) had added to his Lexicon of 1842 a lexicon of proper names, which, in Benseler's improved edition of 1863–70, became an admirable work of reference, well described as a 'model of compendious learning' (Tozer's *Geography of Greece*, 335 n.). Cp. p. 168 *infra*.

[2] *Opusc. Acad.*

[3] Passow's *Leben und Briefe* (1839); Bursian, ii 753—761.

Οὐκ ἔτι κάλλος οἶον ἀλφεὺ ἔχω.

Dr. Meineke

MEINEKE.

Reduced from Engelbach's lithograph of the presentation portrait by
Oscar Begas.

archaeology as well as classical literature[1] ; and he edited Aristotle's *Politics* and *Economics*, as well as Hesiod.   The help derived from Hermann's severe review of this last was acknowledged in grateful and generous terms in the improved and corrected edition of 1843[2].

Among Göttling's colleagues at Jena was Ferdinand Gotthelf Hand (1786—1851), a many-sided scholar, best known as the author of the unfinished work on Latin particles known as Hand's   **Hand** *Tursellinus*[3], and also of a manual on Latin style.   Göttling's colleague in the next generation was Karl Ludwig Nipperdey (1821—1875),   **Nipperdey** the editor of Caesar, Nepos, and Tacitus, and the author of an important paper on the *Leges Annales* of the Romans[4].

Göttling, the university professor of Jena, was far surpassed, as a scholar, by his contemporary, the Berlin school-   **Meineke** master, August Meineke (1790—1870).   Born in the old Westphalian town of Soest, he was educated under his father at Osterode in the Harz, and afterwards under Ilgen at Schulpforta.   While he was still at school, he wrote scholarly papers on the death of Cato, and of Regulus, and his valedictory dissertation consisted of criticisms on many of the Greek poets[5]. At Leipzig he came under the immediate influence of Hermann. His own influence was no less effective in both of his head-masterships, during his 9 years at Danzig and his 31 years at Berlin, where, as a scholar, he was the peer of the leading professors:—Boeckh and Bekker, Buttmann and Lachmann[6]. Elected a member of the Berlin Academy in 1830, he lectured on Horace and Aeschylus in 1852-3[7].   As an editor of important classical works, he was the first since Bentley to make his mark on the criticism of Menander and Philemon (1823). His 'Critical History of the Greek Comic Poets' appeared as an introduction to his 'Fragments of the Comic Poets', which filled three further volumes (1839-41). In this edition, the fragments of Aristophanes were collected by Meineke's assistant-master and future son-in-law, Theodor Bergk.   The fifth volume was published in two parts

---

[1] A wide range of subjects is covered in his *Abhandlungen* (1851 ; ed. 2, 1863), and his *Opuscula* (1869).

[2] p. xxxii, 'quem ego virum fortissimum lubentissime sequi soleo, habent enim eius arma hoc cum armis illius herois commune, ut etiam medeantur, dum sauciant'; cp. p. 94 n. 9 *supra*.   [3] Four vols. (1829-45); ii 369 *supra*.

[4] *Abhandl. sächs. Ges. d. Wiss.* v.

[5] F. Ranke, *August Meineke*, 20 f.   [6] *ib.* 63.   [7] *ib.* 115.

(1857), including an excellent index by Heinrich Jacobi (1815–66). Meanwhile, a new edition of the Fragments had appeared in two volumes (1847). Meineke's work on Attic Comedy was completed by his text of Aristophanes, with a prefatory *Adnotatio Critica* (1860), and a postscript entitled *Vindiciarum Aristophanearum liber* (1865).

His study of the Alexandrian poets is best represented by his *Analecta Alexandrina* (1843), a collection of monographs on Euphorion, Rhianus, Alexander Aetolus, and Parthenius, and by his third edition of Theocritus, Bion, and Moschus (1856). Less important than these are his Callimachus (1861), his selections from the Greek Anthology (1842), and his edition of the geographical poems of 'Scymnus of Chios', and of Dionysius, son of Calliphron (1846). His study of the geographical poets led him to produce a new recension of Stephanus Byzantius (1849), while his preliminary work for a proposed commentary on that lexicon ended in his publishing a new edition of Strabo, with a pamphlet of *Vindiciae Strabonianae* (1852).

The rest of his works originated mainly in his study of Attic Comedy, namely his text of Athenaeus with the *Analecta Critica*, and his Stobaeus and Alciphron. His editions of Joannes Cinnamus and Nicephorus Bryennius in the *Corpus* of Byzantine historians were works done to order, in which he took little interest. His friendship with Lachmann led to his contributing to Lachmann's *Babrius* a collection of fragments of the Greek choliambic poets, while his position as head-master of a great classical school prompted his editions of the *Antigone* and *Oedipus Coloneüs*, both of them followed by critical monographs. It also prompted his edition of the *Odes* of Horace, in which he applied the rule, simultaneously discovered by himself and Lachmann, that all the Odes of Horace are written in stanzas of four lines (1834)[1]. The preface to the second edition (1854) includes many fine criticisms, which are only marred by the editor's excessive fondness for suspecting the presence of interpolations.

As a keen and vigorous textual critic, not uninspired by a poetic taste, he extended to all the Greek Comic Poets the work which his great prototype, Bentley, had begun in the case of

---

[1] The only exception is the Ode to Censorinus (iv 8).

Philemon and Menander[1]. As a school-master he was a man of remarkable moral force and thoroughly religious spirit. He had a strong physique, a broad brow, prominent cheeks and thin lips. The quiet voice of his ordinary conversation rang out loud and strong, whenever he had occasion, as a master, to use the language of reprimand[2]. His resignation of his mastership in 1856 was commemorated by the painting of his portrait, which was reproduced in lithograph with a line in his own hand-writing:— οὐκ ἔστι κάλλος οἷον ἀλήθει᾽ ἔχει[3]. In the year of his retirement, he excused himself from lecturing in the university by humorously remarking:—'if any one asks why I do not lecture, you have only to tell him that, after teaching for forty-one years, I have at last made up my mind to try and learn something myself'[4].

One of Meineke's assistant-masters from 1827 to 1838 was the eminent Greek Grammarian, Karl Wilhelm Krüger (1796—1874), who was born at a small village in the heart of Pomerania, and was a student at Halle from 1816 to 1820. On resigning his mastership at the age of 42, he devoted himself to the preparation of text-books, published by himself in Berlin and elsewhere, until his death at the little town of Weinheim in the Odenwald, N. of Heidelberg.

Krüger

His Greek Grammar for Schools[5] is divided into two parts, (1) on the Attic, and (2) on the other Dialects, and each of the two parts is divided into Inflexions and Syntax. This arrangement is convenient for educational purposes, but it conveys a false impression as to the historic developement of the language. The rules are, however, stated with clearness and precision, and are illustrated by excellently chosen examples. Krüger declined to recognise in his Grammar any of the results of Comparative Philology, and he even attacked the principles followed in the Greek Grammar of G. Curtius (1852) in a series of polemical writings, the bitterness and violence of which can only be excused by their author's many misfortunes[6].

Grammatical exegesis is the strong point of his editions of Xenophon's *Anabasis*, and of Herodotus, Thucydides, and Arrian. Wider interests are apparent in his critical questions on the Life of Xenophon, his treatise on the *Anabasis*, his edition of the historical work of Dionysius of Halicarnassus, and

---

[1] Cp. Ranke, 119—121.   [2] Ranke, 82 f.

[3] Ranke, 132 ; p. 116 *supra*.

[4] *ib.* 140. On Meineke, cp. *Lebensbild* by Ferdinand Ranke, 175 pp. (1871); also Sauppe's *Erinnerung* (1872); Haupt, *Opusc.* iii 228 f; and Bursian, ii 764–9.

[5] *Griechische Sprachlehre*, Berlin, 1843 ; ed. 5, 1873–9.

[6] Cp. Krüger's pamphlet of 1869, and the epilogue on pp. 193—214 of Part II, vol. ii of his Grammar, ed. 3, 1871.

his later writings on the Life of Thucydides, his supplements to his Latin translation of Fynes Clinton's *Fasti Hellenici*, and his two volumes of Historical and Philological Studies[1].

As a Greek Grammarian, and as an editor of Xenophon, Krüger found an
Kühner
able rival in Raphael Kühner (1802—1878), who was born and educated at Gotha, studied at Göttingen, and was, from 1824 to 1863, a master at the Lyceum of Hanover, where he died 15 years afterwards. His large Greek Grammar in two volumes (1834-5)[2] is a vast repertory of grammatical lore, that has attained a third edition in four volumes under the editorial care of Blass and Gerth (1890—1904). He also produced a Greek Grammar for Schools (1836), and a still more elementary work on the same subject (1837), which has gone through many editions, together with corresponding works on Latin Grammar (1841 etc.). On retiring from his mastership, he published a large Latin Grammar (1877-9), which is a monument of learning and industry. His work as an editor is best represented by his commentary on Cicero's *Tusculan Disputations*[3].

The study of Greek Dialects was advanced by Heinrich Ludolf Ahrens
Ahrens
(1809—1881), a native of Helmstedt, who studied at Göttingen, and, after holding several scholastic appointments, was Director of the Lyceum of Hanover in 1849-79, having Kühner as one of his senior assistants for 14 of those years. Ahrens was still a master at Ilfeld when his great work on the Greek Dialects was being published at Göttingen (1839-43)[4]. He published a Grammar of the Homeric and Attic Dialects[5], an important critical edition of Theocritus, Bion, and Moschus, with many papers[6] in the *Philologus* founded at Göttingen by his fellow-countryman and friend, Friedrich Wilhelm Schneidewin, and continued by Ernst Ludwig von Leutsch. The two scholars last mentioned were also associated in a complete edition of the Greek *Paroemiographi* (1839-51).

Schneidewin (1810-56), who had studied under K. O. Müller
Schneidewin
at Göttingen, was a school-master at Brunswick from 1833 to 1836, and there came under the influence of Adolph Emperius (1806—1841), who edited Dion Chrysostom, and of Hermann's pupil, Ferdinand Bamberger (1809—1855), who was specially interested in the criticism of Aeschylus. Thus, although his academic training was mainly archaeological, he proved his affinity to the critical school of Hermann by the editions of the Greek Lyric Poets, which he

---

[1] W. Pökel, *K. W. Krüger's Lebensabriss*, with portrait and bibliography, 40 pp. (1885); Halm in *A. D. B.*; and Bursian, ii 769—771.

[2] Transl. by W. E. Jelf, 1842-5.   [3] 1829; ed. 5, 1874. Bursian, ii 771 f.

[4] Recast by R. Meister (1882 f).   [5] 1853; ed. 2, 1869.

[6] *Kleine Schriften* (*Zur Sprachwissenschaft*), 1891.

began at Brunswick and continued at Göttingen, where he held a professorship for the last 20 years of his life. At Göttingen he produced his excellent edition of Sophocles, with introductions and brief German notes (1849–54), besides many papers on that poet[1]. He contemplated a similar edition of Aeschylus, but only lived to complete the *Agamemnon* (1856). He produced two editions of Martial (1842 and 1853), and an edition of the speeches of Hypereides *pro Euxenippo* and *pro Lycophrone*, in the same year as Churchill Babington's *editio princeps* (1853)[2].

Schneidewin's colleague, Von Leutsch (1808—1887), edited the fragments of the Cyclic *Thebais* (1830), and produced an outline of lectures (with extracts from the ancient authorities) on Greek Von Leutsch Metre (1841). Almost all his energies were afterwards devoted to editing the *Philologus* and the *Philologischer Anzeiger*, and he did little else, except completing in 1851 the joint edition of the *Paroemiographi*[3].

A new impulse was given to the systematic study of Syntax by one of the last survivors of the school of Wolf, Gottfried Bernhardy (1800—1875), who was born of Bernhardy Jewish parentage at Landsberg an der Warthe, and was educated in Berlin, where he was baptized at the age of sixteen. He studied under Wolf and Boeckh, besides displaying the most assiduous industry in his private work. After holding minor scholastic appointments (for which he was not specially suited), he qualified for a university career in Berlin by producing a learned dissertation on the *Fragments of Eratosthenes*. This was followed by an edition of Dionysius Periegetes. Meanwhile, he had become acquainted with Meineke and Buttmann, Zumpt and Lachmann, and had written in a Hegelian organ published in Berlin some excellent reviews of works such as Hermann's *Opuscula* and Lobeck's *Aglaophamus*. In 1829 he published a volume of some 500 pages on the 'Scientific Syntax of the Greek Language'[4]. Syntax is here regarded in relation to the History of Literature, and the author's characteristic tendency towards the systematic and the encyclopaedic method of treatment receives its earliest

[1] Göttingen *Abhandlungen*, v 159 f, vi 3 f, 229 f; *Philologus*, iv 450 f, 633 f, vi 593 f.   [2] Bursian, ii 774 f.

[3] Bursian, ii 776 ; *Biogr. Jahrb.* 1887, 41—48.

[4] Supplemented in the *Paralipomena*, 1862.

exemplification. In the same year he was appointed to succeed
Reisig at Halle, a position which he held for the remaining
46 years of his life, besides being an efficient librarian for the
last 31 of those years. As Pro-Rector he published in the winter
session of 1841-2 a program on the History of Halle, concluding
with an admirable eulogy on Wolf[1]. The influence of Wolf is
apparent in Bernhardy's conception of classical learning as a
whole, and in the thoroughness with which he explores its several
parts. That of Hegel is no less apparent in the profundity of his
research, and in the obscurity of his style. In 1832 he published
his own System of Classical Learning, in which Grammar is
treated as the *instrument* of that Learning, and Criticism and
Interpretation as its *elements*, while a subordinate place is assigned
to the History of Art, with Numismatics and Epigraphy[2]. This
work was published after his *History of Roman Literature* (1830)[3],
and before his *History of Greek Literature* (1836–45)[4]. In both
of these important works the subject is divided into two parts,
(1) a general account of the historical developement of literature
in chronological order ; and (2) a special account of its several
departments, with biographical and bibliographical details on each
author. This division involves the frequent repetition, in the
special portion, of points already mentioned in the *general* survey;
and, although three volumes are devoted to Greek literature, the
special history of Greek Prose is never reached. Both works,
however, deserve to be remembered with respect, in so far as they
were the first to set a distinctly higher standard of what is meant
by the History of Literature.

Bernhardy's edition of Suïdas (not completed until 1853) was
already in the press when that of Gaisford was published (1834).
It was partly founded on a study of the Paris MS, but owed its
value mainly to the notes, and to the *commentationes* in the
second volume[5]. His principal colleague as a classical professor

----

[1] Volkmann's *Gottfried Bernhardy*, 40, 131.

[2] *Grundlinien zur Encyklopädie der Philologie*, 420 pp. (1832). Volkmann,
77—80.

[3] *Grundriss der römischen Litteratur*, ed. 5, 1872.

[4] *Grundriss der griechischen Litteratur*, ed. 4 in 3 vols. (1876–80) ; ed. 5
of vol. i, 844 pp. (ed. Volkmann, 1892).

[5] Volkmann, 65—68, 92 f.

was M. H. E. Meier, the specialist on Greek Antiquities, and, although their rivalries in the management of the classical *Seminar* put a severe strain on their relations with one another, there was no lack of generosity in Bernhardy's obituary notice of his colleague[1]. It was mainly owing to Bernhardy's efforts that Meier was succeeded by Bergk, who soon, however, became estranged from Bernhardy, and, happily for the latter, left for Bonn in 1869, when he was succeeded at Halle by a more congenial colleague in the person of Heinrich Keil. In the same year a proposal to commemorate Wolf's connexion with Halle bore fruit in the excellent edition of his Minor Works[2], produced by Bernhardy, the last survivor of the great master's immediate pupils.

He had a delicate constitution, but his very early hours, his simple diet, his habit of constantly standing at his desk near an open window, his fondness for swimming, and for walking for an hour or two every day (with his arms thrown behind his back), helped to prolong his years to the age of 75. He was immediately commemorated by a medallion portrait at the place of his birth, and by a generous eulogy on the part of his colleague at Halle, Heinrich Keil[3]. Of his many pupils, few owed more to his guidance and his suggestiveness than Nauck[4]. The best tribute to his memory is the sketch of his career ultimately written by another of his distinguished pupils, Richard Volkmann[5].

Bernhardy's work on Roman Literature found a rival in that of Wilhelm Sigismund Teuffel (1820—1878), who taught at Tübingen during the last 34 years of his comparatively short life. Much of his time was devoted to the continuation of the *Real-Encyclopädie* begun at Stuttgart in 1839 by August Pauly (1796—1845). His work on Roman Literature (1870), the fourth edition of which was revised and supplemented by L. Schwabe (1882) and translated by G. C. W. Warr (1900),

Teuffel

---

[1] Program of 1806, 'On the age of Harpocration'; Volkmann, 96.

[2] F. A. Wolf, *Kleine Schriften*, 1200 pp.

[3] Volkmann, 116, cp. 158, and Ritschl's tribute (in 1872), 109.

[4] *ib.* 150 f.

[5] *Gottfried Bernhardy, zur Erinnerung an sein Leben und Wirken*, 160 pp., with portrait (1887); cp. Eckstein in *A. D. B.*, and Bursian, ii 776—780.

though not characterised by the profundity and the originality of
Bernhardy, excelled in clearness of style and arrangement[1].

Bernhardy's three volumes on Greek Literature were mainly confined to
the poets. An endeavour was afterwards made by Rudolf
Nicolai of Berlin to supply a complete History of Classical
Greek Literature in three volumes[2], followed by a History of Modern Greek
Literature, and of Roman Literature. His History of Greek Literature
was regarded by a competent critic as completely inadequate[3]. That of
Bergk (to which we shall shortly return) extended to four volumes, mainly on
the poets.—While 'Scientific Greek Syntax' had been ably treated by Bernhardy,
Syntax was well represented in the elementary Greek Grammars produced in
South Germany (1856 etc.) by Bäumlein (1797—1865), and in North Germany
(1868) by Aken (1816—1870). The Grammar of the Attic Inscriptions was
successfully handled by Konrad Meisterhans (1858—1894),
Meisterhans
who studied at Zürich under Hug and Blümner, and, after
spending a year in Paris, in the course of which he worked through all the
Greek inscriptions of the Louvre, was appointed to a mastership at Solothurn,
and held that position for the remaining eleven years of his brief life. The
work by which he is best known was suggested by Hug, and was dedicated to
Kaegi[4].

The earliest author of a systematic Latin Grammar, in Germany, was
Konrad Leopold Schneider (1786—1821), who in the last
K. L.
Schneider   three years of his short life produced a large Grammar, which
is, however, confined to Accidence. The only works that he
had found useful were the *Aristarchus* of G. J. Vossius (1635) and the
Institutiones of Thomas Ruddiman (1725–31). The usage of Latin authors
on points of Accidence was afterwards set forth in full detail by Christian
Friedrich Neue (1798—1886), a master at Schulpforta in 1820–31, and a
professor at Dorpat in 1831–61, who spent the last 25 years of his life at
Stuttgart[5].

Syntax is included in the comprehensive Latin Grammar of
Karl Gottlob Zumpt (1792—1849), who studied at
Zumpt
Heidelberg, as well as at the university of his

---

[1] Described by Bernhardy, in pref. to ed. 5 of his own work, as *eine mit
gelehrten Belegen und Studien ausgestattete Chronik*. Teuffel drew up a conspectus of the literature of Plato (1874), with a view to a History of Greek
Literature. His early works included editions of the *Clouds* and *Persae*. The
variety of his interests is indicated by his 'Studies and Characteristics' (1871;
ed. 2, 1889). Cp. *Biogr. Jahrb.* 1878, 2 f.

[2] 1865–7; ed. 2, 1873–8.   [3] Bursian, ii 779.

[4] *Grammatik der attischen Inschriften* 1885; ed. 3, 1900. Schulthess in
Biogr. Jahrb. 1896, 35—44.

[5] *Formenlehre* (1861–6), ed. 3 Wagener, in 4 vols. incl. Index (1888—1905).

native-place, Berlin, where he had 15 years' experience as a
school-master, besides holding a professorship of Roman Literature for the last 22 years of his life. His Latin Grammar of
1818, which was limited to classical prose, passed through many
editions and was translated into English. It held its own in
Germany until it was superseded in 1844 by that of Madvig.
Zumpt also produced a useful Chronology of Ancient History
down to 476 A.D.[1] Roman Antiquities were the main subject
of his lectures in the university, and of his papers in the Academy
of Berlin. He also produced editions of Curtius, the *Verrine
Orations* of Cicero, and the *Institutio Oratoria* of Quintilian[2].

Latin Grammar and Lexicography were the main interests of the many-
sided but somewhat superficial scholar, Reinhold Klotz

R. Klotz

(1807—1870), who studied at Leipzig, where he held a professorship for the last 38 years of his life. His admirable 'Handbook
of Latin Style', which owed its excellence to the author's constant study of
Cicero, was posthumously published by his son. Cicero had been the theme
of his earliest work, the *Quaestiones Tullianae*; he also prepared critical
notes on the *Cato maior* and *Laelius*, and commentaries on all the Speeches
and the *Tusculan Disputations*, with a complete edition of the text (1850–7)[3].
He further edited Terence, with the ancient commentaries, and devoted his
practical experience of agriculture to an edition of the *Georgics*, which he
unfortunately failed to finish. The Greek texts which he edited included
several plays of Euripides[4], the *Somnium* of Lucian, and the works of
Clement of Alexandria. As a textual critic he is extremely conservative;
passages that are clearly corrupt, he attempts to defend by means of highly
artificial explanations, while his own emendations, which he vainly endeavours
to support by palaeographical devices, fail to carry conviction.

His intermediate Latin Dictionary (1853–7) was to have been founded
throughout on the direct study of the Latin Classics, but pressure on the
part of the publishers compelled him to call in the aid of F. Lübker and
E. E. Hudemann. This led to a certain unevenness in the execution, and also
to the introduction of errors arising from unverified references borrowed from
the Dictionary of Freund (1834–45)[5], which is little more than a compilation
from Forcellini. He added much new material in his edition of the work
of Devarius on the Greek particles[6]. He also planned a History of Latin

---

[1] *Annales*, 1829, 1862.

[2] On his supplement to Spalding's ed., see p. 82 *supra*. Cp. A. W. Zumpt,
De Caroli Timothei Zumptii vita et studiis narratio (1851); Bursian, ii 783–5.

[3] Also numerous papers in *Jahrb. f. Philol.*, which he edited in 1831–56.

[4] *Phoen., Or., Iph. T., Iph. A.*

[5] b. (of Jewish parents) 1806, d. 1894 (at Breslau); compiler of *Triennium
Philologicum* etc.   [6] Vol. ii p. 78 *supra*.

LACHMANN.

Reduced from A. Teichel's engraving of the photograph by H. Biow.

Literature on a large scale, but the only part that was published (1846) hardly reached the threshold of the subject[1].

A passing notice is here due to Johann Friedrich Jacob (1792—1854), the Director of the school at Lübeck[2], the editor of the *Aetna*, and of Propertius, as well as the *Epidicus* of Plautus, and the astronomical poem of Manilius. He was also a translator of Terence, and the author of a work on Horace and his friends. Munro describes his edition of the *Aetna* as, 'like his Manilius, sadly wanting in precision and acumen', while 'its prolixity exceeds all bounds of toleration'[3].

J. F. Jacob

Latin lexicography and Latin style were among the interests of Albert Forbiger (1798—1878). His father, Gottlieb Samuel Forbiger (1751—1828), was for 33 years Rector of the Nicolai School at Leipzig. The son, who was for nearly 40 years on the staff of that School, left in 1863 for Dresden, where he spent the remaining 15 years of his life. His early dissertation on Lucretius was followed by an edition of that poet and of Virgil, both of them marked by laborious industry rather than by critical acumen. Meanwhile he had produced a German-Latin Dictionary and a work on Latin Style. He also published a comprehensive work on Ancient Geography[4], a translation of Strabo, and, in extreme old age, a popular work entitled *Hellas und Rom*[5]. The name of Forbiger is familiar to the readers of Lachmann's commentary on Lucretius. In the case of Forbiger in particular, the habitual sternness of Lachmann even 'passes into ferocity'[6]: but (as Munro[7] charitably adds) 'most of his errors, that scholar could hardly avoid in the circumstances in which he was placed'.

Forbiger

Karl Lachmann (1793—1851) was the son of an army-chaplain, who was afterwards appointed preacher at a church in Brunswick, where his son was born and bred. Karl studied for a short time under Hermann at Leipzig, where he was already interested in MSS of the Greek Testament,

Lachmann

---

[1] *Nekrolog* in *Jahrb. f. Philol.* civ (1871) 153 f; Bursian, ii 785–8.

[2] Life by J. Classen (Jena, 1855).

[3] *Aetna*, p. 27. Cp. Bursian, ii 934.

[4] Bursian, ii 1128.   [5] *ib.* 1195. Cp. *Biogr. Jahrb.* 1878, 3 f.

[6] *e.g.* p. 13, Forbigero iniuriam faciat qui eum vel minimam rem per se intellegere postulet ; 14, Forbiger nihil usquam laudabile gessit ; 15, (nostri) mercennariam Forbigeri operam, in qua neque ratio ulla esset neque diligentia, contemnere debebant ; note on i 280, Forbiger, quod absurda tam fortiter concoquere possit, laudari postulat ; i 814, a Forbigero iudicium expectari non potuit ; ii 734, hoc saeculum avaritia librariorum nutrit Forbigeri sordibus ; ii 760, Forbiger quid faceret, nisi contemneret ? ii 795, impudenter respondet ad haec Forbiger ; iii 476, Forbigeri mendacium ; cp. i 922, 996 ; ii 502 ; iii 361, 1088 ; iv 391 ; vi 56 f.

[7] Lucretius, vol. i p. 21[3].

and for six years at Göttingen, where Lachmann and Bunsen joined in founding a Philological Society, with Dissen as president.   Meanwhile, he had taken his degree at Halle on the strength of a dissertation on Tibullus (1811).   In 1815, when he had just completed, but had not published, the first of his two editions of Propertius, he joined the volunteers and marched into France, not forgetting to take with him his favourite copy of Homer.   Napoleon had been defeated at Waterloo before Lachmann crossed the Rhine.   However, the volunteers pressed on, and Lachmann visited Paris twice, saw the treasures of art in the Louvre, and found the triumphal arch of Julius Caesar imbedded in the walls of Rheims[1].   In 1818–24 he was a professor at Königsberg, where the best of his pupils was Lehrs. But Lachmann found himself overshadowed at Königsberg by the fame of Lobeck, and accordingly failed to win that scope for his great abilities which he obtained in 1825 at Berlin, where he was one of the foremost professors for the remaining 26 years of his life.

As a Latin scholar he produced, besides his early edition of Propertius (1816), a second edition of that poet, together with Catullus and Tibullus (1829)[2].   He also edited the poem of Terentianus Maurus, *de litteris, syllabis, et metris*[3], and the Fables of Avianus[4].   Late in life he produced his masterly edition of Lucretius (1850).   His Lucilius was posthumously published in 1876.   Of all these, by far the best known is his Lucretius.   The first serious thought of this undertaking occurred to him on the deck of a steamer between Bamberg and Schweinfürt, during a tour in the autumn of 1845 in the company of Haupt, who warmly supported the proposal[5].   As to the merits of this work, it will be enough to quote the generous eulogy written by another great editor of that poet:—

‘ This illustrious scholar, great in so many departments of philology, sacred, classical and Teutonic, seems to have looked upon Latin poetry as his peculiar province. Lucretius, his greatest work, was the main occupation of the last five years of his life, from the autumn of 1845 to November 1850. Fortunately, he had the full use for many months of the two Leyden MSS. His native sagacity, guided and sharpened by long and varied experience, saw at a glance

---

[1] Hertz, 22—32.   [2] *ib.* 120–2.   [3] *ib.* 126.
[4] *ib.* 138.   [5] *ib.* 139.

their relations to each other and to the original from which they were derived, and made clear the arbitrary way in which the common texts had been constructed. His zeal warming as he advanced, one truth after another revealed itself to him, so that at length he obtained by successive steps a clear insight into the condition in which the poem left the hands of its author in the most essential points....Though his Latin style is eminently clear, lively, and appropriate, yet from his aim never to throw away words, as well as from a mental peculiarity of his, that he only cared to be understood by those whom he thought worthy to understand him, he is often obscure and oracular on a first reading....But, when once fully apprehended, his words are not soon forgotten '[1].

Among his papers on Latin poets, may be mentioned his review of Dissen's *Tibullus*[2]; his chronological, critical, and metrical observations on the *Odes of Horace*[3]; his attempt to distinguish between the genuine and the spurious *Heroides*[4]; and his attribution of the Latin Homer of 'Pindarus Thebanus' to the time of Tiberius[5]. In the department of Latin prose, his name is associated with two editions of Gaius, and with the text of a joint edition of the Roman land-surveyors[6].

In the editing of texts of Greek prose he is represented by his important recension of the Greek Testament finished in 1850, and by an edition of Genesius contributed to the *Corpus* of Byzantine Historians at the request of Niebuhr. His interest in the Greek poets is exemplified in his able review of Hermann's edition of the *Ajax*[7]; a paper on the date and purpose of the *Oedipus Coloneüs*[8]; and two Königsberg programs on the Choral Odes and the Dialogue in Greek Tragedy, contending that the total number of lines assigned to each Chorus and each Dialogue, as well as the total number of the lines assigned to each actor, was divisible by seven,—a contention that has not been generally accepted.

The discovery of a MS of the Fables of Babrius by the Greek Minas in a monastery of Mount Athos, and its somewhat hasty publication by Boissonade in November, 1844, led to Lachmann's producing in the space of four months an excellent edition of the text, to which contributions were made by Meineke, Bekker,

---

[1] Munro's *Lucretius*, i p. 20[3] f.   [2] *Kleinere Schriften*, ii 102.
[3] *Kl. Schr.* ii 77.   [4] *ib.* ii 56.   [5] *ib.* ii 161.
[6] *Gromatici Veteres*; Hertz, 133 f.   [7] *Kl. Schr.* ii 1 f.
[8] *Kl. Schr.* ii 18.

Hermann, and Haupt, the first of whom added an Appendix of the fragments of all the other choliambic poets[1].

Lachmann's study of Wolf's *Prolegomena* led him to apply the principles of that work to the great German epic of the *Niebelungen-noth*, and to show that the latter, which attained its final form early in the thirteenth century, could be resolved into a series of twenty primitive lays[2]. More than twenty years afterwards he applied the same principles to the Homeric poems themselves in two papers presented to the Berlin Academy[3].

'Lachmann dissected the *Iliad* into eighteen separate lays. He leaves it doubtful whether they are to be ascribed to eighteen distinct authors. But at any rate, he maintains, each lay was originally more or less independent of all the rest. His main test is the inconsistency of detail. A primitive poet, he argued, would have a vivid picture before his mind, and would reproduce it with close consistency. He also affirms that many of the lays are utterly distinct in general spirit'[4].

Lachmann was the true founder of a strict and methodical system of textual criticism. He has laid down his principles most clearly in the preface to his edition of the Greek Testament. Here and elsewhere his great example is Bentley[5].

The restoration of an ancient literary work involves a two-fold process, (i) an investigation of the author's personality, and of the original form of the work, and (ii), an exposition of his thoughts and feelings, as well as the circumstances which gave rise to them. The first of these two processes is *Criticism* ; the second, *Interpretation*. Criticism has three stages, (1) the determination of the text as it is handed down in MSS (*recensere*), (2) the correction of corruptions (*emendare*), and (3) the discovery of the original form of the work (*originem detegere*). The original form of a work may be ascertained in two ways, (*a*) by weighing the evidence of the MSS, and (*b*) by correcting their evidence when it is false. It is therefore necessary, in the first place, to ascertain what has been attested by the most credible witnesses ;

---

[1] Hertz, 136 f.

[2] *Kleinere Schriften*, i 1 f (1816) ; Hertz, 128 f.

[3] *Betrachtungen über Homers Ilias* (1837–41) ; reprinted with additions in 1847, 1865, 1874.

[4] Jebb's *Homer*, 118 f ; for criticisms on Lachmann's theory, cp. Friedländer's *Hom. Kritik*, 1853, 17 f ; Bonitz, *Vortrag*, 1860, 47[4] f.

[5] In his *Studien und Kritiken* (1830), 820 f, he admires the *grossartige Weise* of Bentley, *des grössten Kritikers der neueren Zeit*. In his *Lucretius* p. 13, he writes:—'In iuvenilibus Bentleii schediasmatis permulta sunt summo et perfecto artifice dignissima'.

in the second, to form a judgement as to what the writer was in a position to write; and, in the third, to examine his personality, the time when he lived, the circumstances in which, and the means whereby, he produced his work. The first business of the critic, *recensio*, the settlement of the text handed down to us in the best MSS, can (and indeed must) be carried out without the aid of *interpretatio*. On the other hand, the two other stages of the critical process are most closely connected with *interpretatio*; for (1) *emendatio*, or conjectural criticism, and (2) the investigation of the origin of any given work (or the 'higher criticism' as it is called), assume as their foundation an understanding of the work, while, on the other side, a *complete* understanding can only be attained by the aid of the results of a critical examination.

These principles were applied by Lachmann in all his editions of Latin or Greek or German texts. His aim in all was, firstly, the *determination* of the *earliest* form of the text, so far as it could be ascertained with the aid of MSS, or quotations; and, secondly, the *restoration* of the *original* form by means of careful emendation[1].

'The influence of Lachmann on the general course of philological study' was 'probably greater', says Nettleship[2], 'than that of any single man' during the nineteenth century. 'Many scholars who never saw him, and to whom he is only known by his books, have been inspired by the extraordinary impulse which he gave to critical method; Greek, Latin, and German philology have alike felt the touch of the magician.' 'Hardly any work of merit' (says Munro[3]) 'has appeared in Germany since Lachmann's *Lucretius*, in any branch of Latin literature, without bearing on every page the impress of his example'....'His love of merit of all kinds incites in him a zeal to do justice to all the old scholars who have done anything for his author; while his scorn and hatred of boastful ignorance and ignoble sloth compel him to denounce those whom he convicts of these offences'.

'In their activity of mind and body' (says Donaldson[4]), Hermann and Lachmann came nearer to Englishmen than 99 out of 100 Germans; and both of them made more progress in classical composition than any *Gelehrten* of their time'....Both 'were little, wiry, and nimble men, full of spirit and energy—as different as possible from the usual type of German bookworms'.

---

[1] Cp. Haupt, *De Lachmanno Critico*, in Belger's *Haupt*, 43; Bursian, ii 789 f.

[2] *Essays*, i 9.

[3] *Lucretius*, i p. 20[3].

[4] *Scholarship and Learning*, 157 f. Cp. Lachmann, *Kleinere Schriften*, 2 vols. (1876); *Briefe an Moriz Haupt*, ed. Vahlen, 264 pp. (1892); M. Hertz, *Biographie* (1851); J. Grimm, *Rede* (1851), reprinted in Grimm's *Kleinere Schriften*, i 145—162; Haupt, *De Lachmanno Critico*; M. Schmidt, *De C. Lachmanni studiis metricis*, 1880; and Bursian, ii 788—792; also F. Leo (Göttingen, 1893), 18 pp.; Vahlen, *Berlin Akad. Bericht.* 1893, 615 f; Weinhold, *Berl. Akad.* 1894, 37 pp.

In connexion with the Homeric question, the earliest follower
of Lachmann in his theory of lays was Hermann

Köchly   Köchly (1815—1876).   The son of a Leipzig
publisher, he was educated at Grimma under Wunder.   At the
university of Leipzig he was an enthusiastic pupil of Hermann;
he commemorated the centenary of his master's birth by delivering in 1872 an admirable oration in his memory, and by
publishing it in 1874 with a full appendix of authorities.   Three
years of experience as a schoolmaster at Saalfeld, near Meiningen,
were followed by nine at Dresden, where his career was cut short
by the political events of May, 1849, which compelled him to
flee from Saxony[1].   He escaped to Hamburg and Brussels, where
his study of the Greek Tragic poets was resumed in his examination of the problem of the *Prometheus*, and in his other early
work on the *Alcestis*, *Hecuba*, and *Helena*.   He also continued
his critical edition of Quintus Smyrnaeus, and, in three weeks,
he had finished his notes on the last five books, which, in his
busy Dresden days, might have taken three years.   He further
undertook to edit Manetho for the Didot series, in the hope that
it might ultimately lead to a professorship[2].   Meanwhile, he was
actually appointed to fill the place which had remained vacant
at Zürich since the death of Orelli.   He held that position from
1850 to 1864, when he was invited to Heidelberg, to hold a
professorship at that university for the remaining twelve years of
his life.

The structure of the *Iliad* is examined in his seven Zürich
dissertations (1850–9), and in a paper on ' Hector's Ransom '
(1859); that of the *Odyssey* in three Zürich dissertations (1862–3).
The results of his examination of the *Iliad* were embodied in a
practical form in an edition of sixteen lays published at Leipzig
in 1861[3].

Köchly's 'lays' do not, however, correspond to Lachmann's.   'The two
operators take different views of the anatomy'.   A theory of short lays,
' whatever special form it may assume, necessarily excludes the view that any
one poet had a dominant influence on the general plan of the poems '[4].

---

[1] E. Böckel, *Hermann Köchly*, 109—135; Gustav Freytag, *Erinnerungen*,
1887; E. T. 1890.

[2] Böckel, 127—132.   [3] Cp. Böckel, 187 f.

[4] Jebb's *Homer*, 119.

Apart from works on educational policy, most of Köchly's publications were concerned with the post-homeric epics.   He produced a critical edition of Hesiod, in conjunction with his pupil Kinkel, as well as a plain text (1870).   Meanwhile, he had edited Aratus, with Manetho and Maximus, in the Didot series, and had published a separate edition of Manetho, two editions of Quintus Smyrnaeus (1850–3), and lastly, Tryphiodorus and Nonnus.

As early as 1840 he gave a lecture on the *Antigone*, and the performance of that play at Dresden in 1844 led to his delivering his first popular lecture on Greek Tragedy[1].   He gave proof of his critical skill by his emendations (1860–2) on the *Tauric Iphigeneia*, by his edition of that play (1857), and by his paper on the *Birds* of Aristophanes.   In a course of lectures on Schiller, he traced the influence of the Greek and Latin Classics on the poetry of Germany[2].   At Zürich, the exile from Saxony was joined in 1852 by other exiles from that land, by Haupt and Jahn and Mommsen ; and we learn that, in a private reading of *Antony and Cleopatra*, the historian of the Roman republic took the part of Octavius Caesar[3].   Köchly was the heart and soul of similar readings of the *Agamemnon*, the *Antigone*, and the *Bacchae* at Heidelberg[4], and brought about a fine performance of the *Persae* at Mannheim in 1876[5].   At Zürich and at Heidelberg he gave a course of six public lectures on Demosthenes[6], whose speech *De Corona* he translated into German[7], as well as Cicero *pro Sestio* and *pro Milone*[8].   He joined the military expert, Rüstow, in translating Caesar, and he also wrote an Introduction to the *Gallic War* (1857).   In 1863, his work on Caesar was specially recognised by Napoleon III.

While he was a devoted pupil of Hermann, he was led by the advice of Wachsmuth to enlarge the range of his interests by the study of the writings of Boeckh, and he was also attracted to K. O. Müller's ' History of Greek Literature'[9].   In conjunction with Rüstow, he wrote a ' History of Greek Warfare' (1852), and

[1] *Opusc.* ii 148 f.   [2] Böckel, 44.   [3] *ib.* 172.
[4] Böckel, 322.   [5] *ib.* 350, 387.   [6] *ib.* 222.
[7] *ib.* 182; anon. 1856.   [8] *ib.* 325.
[9] *ib.* 41, 177 ; cp. esp. 273 f.

edited the Greek writers on Tactics (1853–5). As President of
the Congress of Scholars and School-masters at Heidelberg in
1865, his influence with the Grand Duke of Baden led to the
military experts being authorised to construct full-sized models of
the *ballista* and *catapulta*[1]; and, at the Congress at Würzburg,
in 1868, he gave practical illustrations of the handling of the
hasta amentata of the ancients[2].

In his proposals for the reform of German secondary education, instead of
vainly attempting to exact a complete command of the Latin language in
speaking and in writing, he preferred to promote a perfect understanding of
the classical texts and a historical grasp of the ancient world[3]. He urged
that the modern languages should be learnt first, that Latin and Greek should
not be begun until the age of fourteen, and that a knowledge of the Greek and
Roman world, in its historic aspect, should be the main object in learning
those languages[4].

The dream of his life was a visit to Greece. That dream was
fulfilled in the autumn of 1876, and in the company of his pupil,
the prince Bernhard von Sachsen-Meiningen. But, unhappily,
his health was already failing ; he fell from his horse on the field
of Marathon, and died at Triest. He was buried at Heidelberg,
where an admirable oration was delivered in his memory[5].

While Köchly was connected with Lachmann in maintaining
that the *Iliad* was formed from a number of primitive lays, there
was a still closer connexion between Lachmann and

Haupt

Haupt (1808—1874). Both of them were inspired
with a keen interest in German as well as Classical Scholarship,
and both of them devoted their main energies to the criticism of
the Latin poets. They were also united by the closest bonds of
friendship, and were successively professors in Berlin. Moritz
Haupt was born at Zittau in Saxony. From his father, a man of
poetic taste and of fiery temper, he inherited a keen and im-
petuous spirit, as well as a vivid interest in poetry. At Leipzig
he was the pupil of Hermann, whose daughter he afterwards

---

[1] Böckel, 241.   [2] *ib.* 319.   [3] *ib.* 50.

[4] *ib.* 94. Cp. Paulsen, ii 469[2] f.

[5] Bernhard Stark, *Vorträge* etc. 427 f ; cp. A. Hug, *Hermann Köchly*
(1878), 43 pp.; Eckstein in Ersch and Gruber ; Bursian, ii 798 ; and esp.
Ernst Böckel, *Hermann Köchly, ein Bild seines Lebens*, with portrait, 426 pp.
(1904).

married. It was by reading Hermann's edition of the *Bacchae*
that he first learnt what was meant by 'really understanding an
ancient author'. He spent seven years at Zittau, tending his aged
father (1830–7), and working at Catullus and Gratius; in 1834
he accompanied his father to Vienna and Berlin, where he first
met his life-long friend, Lachmann[1], and in the same year he
printed his *exempla poësis Latinae medii aevi*[2]. In 1837 he began
his professorial career at Leipzig by the publication of his
Quaestiones Catullianae. In 1850 he was suspended from his
professorship on political grounds, and, although he was acquitted
by a court of justice, he was arbitrarily deprived of his office.
For the last twenty-one years of his life he filled with distinction
the professorship vacated by Lachmann in Berlin.

From 1837 to 1854 his interests as a professor had been
equally divided between old German and Latin poetry, but, for
the last twenty years of his life, the place of the old poets of
Germany was taken by those of Greece. At Leipzig he had been
highly successful as the Director of the Latin Society which
flourished by the side of the Greek Society founded by Hermann,
and his double interest in Classical and German philology led
to his frequently lecturing on the *Germania* of Tacitus. He
also expounded the *Iliad*, with select plays of Aeschylus,
Sophocles, Aristophanes, Plautus and Terence, and Theocritus,
Catullus, Tibullus and Propertius.

His *Quaestiones Catullianae* (1837), a work of special importance in connexion with the textual criticism of Catullus, was
succeeded by his critical edition of the *Halieutica* of Ovid and
the *Cynegetica* of Gratius and Nemesianus, and by his *Observationes Grammaticae*, including a number of fine grammatical and
metrical criticisms on the Roman and the Alexandrian poets.
In 1847 he added a supplement to Lachmann's 'Observations'
on the *Iliad*, and, in 1849 and 1852 respectively, published
Hermann's posthumous editions of Bion and Moschus, and of
Aeschylus. In 1850 he produced his own edition of the Pseudo-
Ovidian *Epicedion Drusi*, and, in 1852, a tastefully printed text
of Horace.

His entry on his professorship at Berlin was marked by his

[1] Belger, *Moritz Haupt*, 17 f.   [2] *ib.* 48.

treatise on the Eclogues of Calpurnius and Nemesianus. He also published a school-edition of the first seven books of Ovid's *Metamorphoses*, and elegant editions of Catullus, Tibullus and Propertius, and of Virgil. His first edition of this last author was anonymous; the second included, among the *Pseudo-Virgiliana*, an improved text of the *Aetna*. In Latin prose, he only edited the *Germania* with brief critical notes. A wide range of interests is covered in his published papers, in the lectures and speeches delivered before the Academies of Leipzig and Berlin, and in an unbroken series of 42 Latin programs, for the corresponding Semesters of all the 21 years from 1854 to 1874 inclusive. He was a frequent contributor to the *Rheinisches Museum* and the *Philologus*, and finally to *Hermes*, which he founded in 1866.

Haupt, like Lachmann, perpetuated in an intense form the polemical spirit of his master, Hermann[1]. Among his main characteristics was his masterly precision as a critic, and his skill in applying his familiarity with the early poetry of Germany and France to the attainment of a profounder knowledge of the poetry, and especially the epic poetry, of Greece and Rome. His energy, his proud self-consciousness, his high ideal of the scholar's aim in learning and in life, the keenness and the remorselessness with which he condemned all that was mean or common, and even all that was merely weak or immature, in fact everything that failed to satisfy his own high ideal, has been commemorated by Bursian[2], who was one of his pupils at Leipzig. His lectures on the *Epistles* of Horace at Berlin, which began with an exposition of the principles to be followed in constituting the text, and included a running fire of criticisms on Orelli, were attended by Nettleship, who then learnt for the first time to appreciate the true greatness of Bentley. One of Haupt's life-long friends was Gustav Freytag. In the *Verlorne Handschrift* the character of Felix Werner is to some extent founded on that of Haupt, who himself suggested part of the plot[3]. Freytag has told us how Haupt, who had a great flow of language in the company of his friends, and could even rise to eloquence in the presence of a congenial audience (as in the case of his famous

---

[1] Belger, 19.   [2] ii 800 f.   [3] Belger, 19, 34 f.

eulogy of Boeckh[1]), had the greatest difficulty in composing anything that would satisfy his own standard as a writer.   All that
he wrote, however, was admirably terse and transparently clear[2].

Haupt's contemporary, Friedrich Haase (1808—1867), was
born and bred at Magdeburg, studied under Reisig
at Halle, and was a school-master at Charlotten-   F. Haase
burg and Schulpforta, where the fact that he was a member of a
political association of German students led to his being condemned in 1835 to six years' imprisonment at Erfurt.   He was
released after a year, and proceeded to Halle.   He afterwards
visited the libraries of Paris, Strassburg, Munich and Vienna,
and, for the last 27 years of his life, was a distinguished professor
at Breslau.

His earliest independent work was a commentary on Xenophon's treatise on the constitution of Sparta (1833).   His interest
in military tactics was exhibited by the illustrations to that work,
and by his study of the MSS of the Greek and Roman tacticians
during his travels abroad[3].   He contributed to the Didot series
an edition of Thucydides, with an excellent Latin translation,
and afterwards published papers on points of textual criticism in
that author[4].   In Latin scholarship his proficiency is proved by the
notes to his edition of the Lectures of his master, Reisig[5], and
by his own Lectures on Semasiology, with an introduction on the
History of Latin Grammar[6].   As a textual critic he is best known
through his editions of Velleius Paterculus, Tacitus, and Seneca.
Separate passages of Greek and Latin authors, and Greek inscriptions, with questions of lexicography and literary history, are
treated in his *Miscellanea Philologica*.   He also paid special

---

[1] Belger, 63 f.

[2] A. Kirchhoff, *Gedächtnissrede* (1875); Gustav Freytag, *Im Neuen Reich*
(1874) 347 f; Haupt, *Opuscula*, 2 vols. 1875–6 (with portrait); C. Belger,
Moritz Haupt als akademischer Lehrer, 340 pp. (1879); Nettleship, *Essays*,
i 1—22; Bursian, ii 800—805.

[3] *De militarium scriptorum...editione* (1847).

[4] *Lucubrationes Thuc.* (1841, 1857).   He also published an important
paper on the *Athenische Stammverfassung* (Breslau Abhandl. 1857), and
articles on *Palaestra, Phalanx, Phrygia* etc. in Ersch and Gruber.

[5] p. 108 *supra*.

[6] *Vorlesungen*, ed. Eckstein and Peter (1874–80).

RITSCHL.

From a lithograph of the drawing by A. Hohneck (1844), published by Henry
and Cohen, Bonn, with autograph and motto, *nil tam difficilest quin quae-
rendo investigari possiet* (Ter. *Haut.* 675).

attention to the History of Classical Learning[1]. His own contributions to that subject included a paper on the *Subscriptiones*
in Latin MSS[2], and a valuable disputation on the philological
studies of the Middle Ages[3]. As a man of frank and straight-
forward character, and full of fresh enthusiasm for high ideals
in public life and in scholarship, he exercised a healthy and a
lasting influence on all who came under his care. In his portrait
the most striking point is his steady gaze, looking upward[4].

The birth of Haase and Haupt was preceded by two years
by that of a still greater scholar, Friedrich Ritschl
(1806—1876). The son of the pastor of a Thurin-   Ritschl
gian village, he was educated at Erfurt and Wittenberg under
Spitzner, and studied for a short time under Hermann at Leipzig,
and for some years under Reisig at Halle. Under the influence
of Reisig, his early interest was directed towards the Greek poets.
That interest bore fruit in his dissertation on the age of Agathon
(1829), and in his articles, in 'Ersch and Gruber', on the Greek
Ode, on Olympus the *aulêtês*, and on the poet Onomacritus.
About the same time he produced an edition of Thomas Magister
(1832), discussed the Greek grammarians Orus and Orion, and
published, with appendices, his essay on the Alexandrian
Libraries (1838). Meanwhile, his four years of university teaching at Halle (1829–33) had been followed by a call to Breslau.
The rest of his life falls into three periods during which he was
professor first at Breslau (1833–9), next at Bonn (1839–65), and
finally at Leipzig (1865–76).

His interest in Plautus was first displayed at Breslau. It was
there that in 1834 he wrote the review of Lindemann's work,
in which he promised a critical edition of his own. In 1835 he
edited the *Bacchides*, and, about the same time, contributed to
the *Rheinisches Museum* a bibliographical survey of the criticism
of Plautus[5]. In 1836–7 he visited Italy and spent several months
of a bitterly cold winter in deciphering the Ambrosian palimpsest

---

[1] F. Salgo (pseudonym), *Vergangenheit und Zukunft der Philologie*
(1835); Bursian, ii 810–2.

[2] Breslau program, 1860.   [3] *id.* 1856.

[4] C. Fickert, Breslau Gymn. progr. 1868; Bursian, ii 805—813.

[5] *Opusc.* ii 1—165.

of Plautus at Milan. He embodied the results in a letter addressed to Hermann, in which that scholar's views on Plautine prosody were amply confirmed[1]. The accuracy of Ritschl's report of the readings of the palimpsest was in vain attacked by Karl Eduard Geppert (1811—1881), who had studied at Leipzig under Hermann and under Boeckh in Berlin, was an adept in music and in recitations from Shakespeare, was interested in the Greek and Roman theatre, and had revived several of the Plautine plays in Berlin, and edited nine of them[2]. The palimpsest has since been deciphered (so far as practicable) by Gustav Löwe and Wilhelm Studemund. Meanwhile, in 1841, Ritschl started a new series of papers on Plautus, which were published with additions in 1845 under the title of *Parerga*, and won for him the name of *sospitator Plauti*. In 1848 he began his edition of Plautus, and, by the end of 1854, had published nine plays[3]. He produced new editions of these nine, and entrusted the preparation of the rest to three of his ablest pupils :—Gustav Löwe, Georg Götz, and Friedrich Schöll. Ritschl's papers on Plautus, and his edition of the text, mark an epoch in the study of that author. The field that had been inadequately cultivated by previous editors, such as Weise, Lindemann, and Bothe, now attracted the attention of eager and well-trained scholars of the new generation. Ritschl himself studied the laws of the ancient Latin language with the aid of the oldest Roman inscriptions, and applied the results to the extension or correction of the views expressed in his *Prolegomena*. Many points of detail were taken up by his friends and pupils, while others attempted to support the traditional text.

Ritschl's Plautine studies led him to investigate the history of the Latin language. His numerous papers on that subject are included in the fourth volume of his collected works. But the most important monument of his labours in this department is his great collection of Ancient Latin Inscriptions[4]. Many points

---

[1] ii 166—201.   [2] *Biogr. Jahrb.* 1884, 134–6.

[3] *Trinummus, Miles, Bacchides* (1849); *Stichus, Pseudolus* (1850); *Menaechmi* (1851); *Mostellaria* (1852); *Persa, Mercator* (1854).

[4] *Priscae latinitatis monumenta epigraphica* (1862); *Supplementa* in *Kleine Schriften*, iv 494—571.

of early Latin Grammar are here illustrated, either in the descriptive letter-press or in the elaborate *indices*. It was followed by
an important paper on the History of the Latin Alphabet[1]. In
the investigation of the laws of the Saturnian verse, Ritschl held
that we should begin, not with the fragments of Livius Andronicus and of Naevius, as recorded by the grammarians, but with
the inscriptions; and he discovered that the fragments of Cato's
Carmen de moribus were written in Saturnian verse[2]. His examination of the early fortunes of the plays of Plautus led him to
inquire into the literary activity of Varro, to set forth the wide
extent of his labours, and to determine the character of his
Disciplinarum Libri, his *Imagines*, and his *Logistorici Libri*[3]. He
also wrote an important paper on the survey of the Roman
Empire under Augustus[4]. Some of his minor papers were
concerned with the modern pronunciation of Latin[5], the recent
History of Classical Philology[6], and the Plautine studies of Veit
Werler (*fl.* 1507–15)[7] and Camerarius[8], with biographical sketches
of Passow and Reisig[9].

The completion of 25 years of successful teaching at Bonn
was celebrated in 1864 by the publication, not only of a volume
of papers by eight of his pupils of that time[10], but also of a
collection of papers contributed by no less than 43 pupils of
former years[11].

While Ritschl is associated mainly with Latin Scholarship,
it must not be forgotten that almost all his early career as an
Academic teacher was connected with Greek[12]. It is to be
regretted that he did not begin his work on Plautus at an earlier
date, and that he was diverted from the completion of his edition
by taking up a number of points incidentally suggested by his
Plautine studies. At Bonn he was a most successful teacher for
26 years. It was at his suggestion that Otto Jahn was invited
to accept a professorship at that university, and it was owing to

---

[1] *Kleine Schriften*, iv 691—726.　　　[2] *ib*. 82 f.　　　[3] *ib*. iii 352—592.
[4] iii 743 f.　　　　　　　　　[5] *ib*. iv 766 f.　　　　[6] *ib*. v 1—18.
[7] *ib*. v 40—92.　　　　　　　　　　　　　　　　　[8] iii 67—119.
[9] v 92—98.　　　　　　[10] *Liber Miscellaneus*.
[11] *Symbola Philologorum Bonnensium* (1864–7), ed. Fleckeisen.
[12] He edited Aesch. *Septem* in 1853.

unfortunate differences between Jahn and himself that he resigned
his professorship and withdrew entirely from Prussia, to spend
the rest of his life at the Saxon university of Leipzig[1].

Foremost among the supporters of Ritschl's views was Alfred Fleckeisen
(1820–99), a native of Wolfenbüttel, who was educated at
Helmstedt, and who studied under Schneidewin at Göttingen.
In his earliest independent work, the *Exercitationes Plautinae* (1842), he was
inspired by the example of Bentley, Reiz, Hermann and Ritschl. From that
time forward he was closely associated with Ritschl, and, on the appearance of
the first volume of the edition of Plautus, welcomed it as supplying in all
important points a firm foundation for the future study of the text[2]. In this
spirit he edited the Teubner text of ten plays, with a full *Epistola Critica*
addressed to Ritschl (1850–1). He also published a text of Terence (1857),
which marked the first important advance since the time of Bentley. Fleckeisen
was for many years Corrector of a School at Dresden, and for 43 years editor
of the *Jahrbücher für Philologie*[3].

Wilhelm Studemund (1843—1889), besides transcribing and publishing
in 1874 the palimpsest of Gaius discovered by Niebuhr at
Verona[4], devoted himself with the most strenuous industry
to the deciphering of the Ambrosian palimpsest of Plautus[5]. He also produced
a large number of papers on Plautine subjects, together with monographs on
points of early Latin Grammar and Prosody prepared by his pupils under his
direction at Strassburg[6]. The conservative side, among editors of Plautus,
was meanwhile represented by Geppert[7] and Moritz Crain, and by the Danish
scholar, Johann Ludwig Ussing. Ritschl's Plautine studies were acutely
criticised by Bergk in a series of reviews and programs[8], and in a special work
on the final D in Latin (1870). His views on the relation of the word-accent
to the verse-accent in Plautus were opposed by an eminent investigator of the
early history of the Latin language, Wilhelm Corssen (1820—
1875), in his work on Latin pronunciation, vocalisation and

Fleckeisen

Studemund

Corssen

---

[1] Curt Wachsmuth in Ritschl's *Kleine Schriften*, iii pp. x—xviii; L. Müller,
Fr. Ritschl, eine wissenschaftliche Biographie (1877; ed. 2, 1878); and esp.
O. Ribbeck, *F. W. Ritschl, ein Beitrag zur Geschichte der Philologie*, 2 vols.
384+591 pp., 1879—81 (with two portraits); cp. Bursian, ii 812—840; Rohde,
Kl. Schr. ii 452—462; Gildersleeve, in *A.J.P.* v 339—355. Bibliography in
Ritschl's *Kleine Schriften*, v 725—756.

[2] *Jahrb. f. Philol.* lx 234 f; lxi 17 f.

[3] *Biogr. Jahrb.* 1900, 125—147; portrait in *Commentationes Fleckeiseni-
anae* (1890).

[4] p. 80 *supra*.

[5] *Apographum*, posthumously published in 1890.

[6] *Studien*, 1873—. Cp. *Biogr. Jahrb.* 1889, 82—103.

[7] p. 140 *supra*.   [8] *Plautina* in *Opusc.* i 3—208.

accentuation (1858–9). Corssen also wrote on the early history of Roman poetry (1846), on the language of the Volsci (1858) and the Etruscans (1874–5), besides papers on Latin Accidence (1863–6) and articles in Kuhn's *Zeitschrift*[1], and in the *Ephemeris Epigraphica* (1874). The dispute between Corssen and Ritschl prompted one of Ritschl's pupils, Friedrich Schöll, to collect and sift all the evidence of the old grammarians on Latin accent, and to inquire into the nature of that accent and the importance of the word-accent in Latin verse (1876). The evidence of the old grammarians had already been discussed at Bonn in 1857 in an important dissertation by another of Ritschl's pupils, Peter Langen (1835—1897), the author of Plautine *Beiträge* (1880) and *Studien* (1886), who was a professor at Münster for the last 27 years of his life[2].

Langen

Among the scholars inspired with the new interest in Plautine studies was Wilhelm Wagner of Hamburg (1843—1880), who edited the *Aulularia*, *Trinummus*, and *Menaechmi*, as well as the whole of Terence, with English notes. Julius Brix (1815—1887), who was born and bred at Görlitz, and studied under Ritschl

W. Wagner
Brix
Lorenz

at Breslau, was in 1838 awarded the prize for an essay on the principles followed in Bentley's *Terence*, and in 1841 produced a dissertation on the prosody of Plautus and Terence. After holding minor scholastic appointments, he was Pro-Rector at Leignitz in 1854–82. At Leignitz he produced several editions of the *Trinummus*, *Captivi*, *Menaechmi* and *Miles Gloriosus*[3]. August Lorenz (b. 1836), who was educated at Copenhagen and ultimately became a school-master in Berlin, edited the *Mostellaria*, *Miles Gloriosus* and *Pseudolus* (1866–76), and wrote many papers and reviews on Plautine subjects. Lastly, Oskar Seyffert (1841—1906), who was educated in Berlin under his namesake, Moritz Seyffert (1809—1872, the editor

O. Seyffert

of Cicero's *Laelius*), and was for forty years on the staff of the Sophien-gymnasium of Berlin, devoted a large part of his energies to the study of Plautus[4]. He saw through the press Studemund's *Apographon* of the Ambrosian palimpsest, enriching it with an important *Index Orthographicus* (1889); and he was ever ready to place his minute and varied learning at the service of other students of his favourite author[5].

---

[1] Vols. x, xvi, xviii.

[2] Editor of Val. Flaccus (p. 194 *infra*); *Biogr. Jahrb.* 1898, 1—13.

[3] *Biogr. Jahrb.* 1887, 63—68.

[4] His works include *Studia Plautina* (1874), and surveys of Plautine literature (1883–94), in Bursian's *Jahresbericht*.

[5] He expanded and improved E. Munk's *History of Latin Literature*; and himself produced a Dictionary of Classical Antiquities (1882), the English edition of which was revised and enlarged by H. Nettleship and J. E. Sandys (1891). See esp. E. A. Sonnenschein, in *Athenaeum*, 4 Aug. 1906, p. 130 f.

CHAPTER XXXI.

EDITORS OF GREEK CLASSICS.

IN turning to the other contemporaries, and the successors, of Ritschl, we shall find it convenient to group them according to the main subject of their studies, beginning with the editors of the Greek Classics.

Karl Wilhelm Dindorf (1802—1883), the eldest son of a

Dindorf

professor of Hebrew at Leipzig, lost his father at the age of ten. Having thus been mainly left to his own resources, he acquired a singular independence of character and a habit of indomitable industry, not unaccompanied by a certain lack of principle and a disregard for social conventions. At the age of fifteen he studied at Leipzig under C. D. Beck and Hermann, supporting himself by correcting proofs for the press. He began his career as an editor by completing in seven volumes (1819–26) the edition of Aristophanes begun in two by Invernizi (1797), and continued in four more by Beck (1809–19). He also produced critical editions of separate plays, reprinting the notes of Hermann, Monk, and Elmsley, together with a complete collection of the Fragments (1829). Meanwhile, he had brought out an edition of Pollux and of Harpocration, and had published, for the first time, certain of the works of the grammarians, Herodian and Philoponus, besides a new edition of Stephanus of Byzantium. For the Teubner series of Greek texts with critical notes, begun in 1824, he edited Homer, Aeschylus, Sophocles, Aristophanes, as well as Aeschines, Isocrates, Demosthenes, and the *Memorabilia* of Xenophon. His brother Ludwig (1805—1871) edited the rest of Xenophon, together with Hesiod, Euripides, and Thucydides.

In the new series of texts begun in 1849, Homer, Aeschylus, Sophocles, and Demosthenes were edited anew by Wilhelm, and Xenophon by Ludwig. All the Greek dramatists were further edited by the former, with notes and *scholia*, for the Clarendon Press (1832–63). The text of the whole was first printed in a single volume in 1830, the well-known *Poëtae Scenici Graeci*, which attained a fifth edition in 1869. The *Lexicon Sophocleum* of 1871 was withdrawn from sale, owing to an unauthorised use of the lexicon of Ellendt (1834 f), a new edition of which was published by Genthe in 1869–72[1]. Dindorf's *Lexicon Aeschyleum*, founded on that of Wellauer (1830), was completed in 1876. His volume on the metres of the dramatists, with a *chronologica scenica*, was a careful and useful work (1842). His editions of Aeschylus and Sophocles were founded on a careful collation of the Laurentian MS by Dübner. He edited, for the Didot series, Sophocles and Aristophanes, with Herodotus, Lucian, and part of Josephus; and, for the Clarendon Press (besides the dramatists), Homer and Demosthenes with the *scholia*; also the *scholia* to Aeschines and Isocrates, the lexicon of Harpocration, and the works of Clement of Alexandria. To the new Tauchnitz series he contributed a text of Lucian. Among the texts prepared by him for other publishers were Athenaeus, Aristides, Themistius, Epiphanius, the *praecepta ad Antiochum* of Athanasius, and the 'Shepherd' of Hermas. The credit of taking part in producing the first edition of this undoubtedly genuine work was unfortunately impaired by his publication of the 'palimpsest of Uranius' on the chronology of the Egyptian kings, which had been fabricated by the discoverer of the genuine Hermas, the notorious Constantine Simonides.

At an early age Dindorf was nominated to 'extraordinary' professorships at Berlin and Leipzig. Failing to be appointed to succeed Beck in 1833, he took up the task of K. B. Hase, as editor of Didot's Paris edition of Stephanus' *Thesaurus Graecitatis*, and the main part of the work, ending with 1864, was done by the brothers Dindorf, who had begun to help as early as 1831. The younger brother, Ludwig, was thrown into the shade by his

---

[1] Cp. Dindorf in *Jahrb. f. cl. Philol.* xcix 103, 105; and Genthe in *Zeitschrift f. Gymn.* xxvi.

elder brother, and, as he never appeared in public, a legend arose
that he did not exist, but was invented by Wilhelm to help to
account for the extraordinary number of editions that appeared
under the name of Dindorf.   Ludwig edited (in addition to the
texts already mentioned[1]) Dion Chrysostom and the Greek
Historians, including Xenophon, Diodorus, Dio Cassius, Polybius,
the *Historici Graeci Minores*, with Zonaras, and the Didot edition
of Pausanias.

Wilhelm Dindorf's industry and thrift made him, in the early
part of his career, a prosperous man, and in 1837 he became
a Director of the Leipzig and Dresden Railway.   But his life
ended in gloom.   In 1871 he had to lament the death of his
younger brother.   A few months later, at the age of 70, he lost
his all by speculations on the stock-exchange, and was even
compelled to part with his library.   But he still worked on,
producing (in 1873–6) his lexicon to Aeschylus, and (in 1875–80)
his complete edition of the *scholia* to the *Iliad*.   His hand-writing
remained clear to the very last, and there was but little failure of
his bodily powers.   After his death, the greatest misfortune that
befell his memory was that even his former friends forgot and
disowned him[2].

The Greek poets were the main theme of study with Dindorf's contemporary, Johann Adam Hartung (1802—1867), who studied
Hartung   at Erlangen and Munich, and was Director of the *gymnasium*
at Erfurt for the last three years of his life.   An over-fondness for conjectural
criticism was his main characteristic as an editor of the texts of the Greek
elegiac, melic, iambic, tragic, and bucolic poets, which he published with
verse-translations, and with critical and explanatory notes.   He also translated
Aristotle's Treatise on Poetry, with notes and excursuses.   In his *Euripides
Restitutus* (1843–5), a work inspired by an unbounded admiration for the poet
whose name it bears, he analyses all the extant plays, and even discusses the
plots of those that have survived in fragments alone.   His earliest works were
on Greek Particles, and on Roman Religion.   The second of these was of far
higher value than his latest work on the Religion and Mythology of the
Greeks.

The Lyric Poets of Greece are associated with the name of
Theodor Bergk (1812—1881).   At his native place,
Bergk   Leipzig, he studied in 1830–5 under Hermann;

---

[1] p. 144 f *supra*.
[2] *Biogr. Jahrb.* 1883, 112—121 ; Bursian, ii 861—870.

four years later, in Berlin, he was assistant-master to Meineke, his future father-in-law; he was afterwards a professor at Marburg and at Freiburg ; then, for twelve years, at Halle (1857–69) ; and, for the last twelve years of his life, at Bonn (1869–81).

Grateful as Bergk was for all that he owed to Hermann, he was not unconscious of the one-sidedness of his master's teaching, and sought to widen his own interests by learning of Boeckh and Welcker and K. O. Müller. While he was still a student, he printed a *Commentatio* on the Fragments of Sophocles. He began his public career by editing the genuine Fragments of Anacreon, and by producing his *Commentationes* on the Old Attic Comedy, a work warmly welcomed by Welcker. Bergk contributed to Meineke's 'Comic Fragments' an edition of the Fragments of Aristophanes, which was followed by several editions of the plays. Meanwhile, he had completed at Marburg, in 1843, the first edition of his *Poëtae Lyrici Graeci*, a work whose merit depends less on any systematic use of the extant MSS than on the felicity of the editor's emendations. In the *Olympian Odes* alone, eleven of these were afterwards confirmed by the MSS. The defects of this work were sharply criticised by Schneidewin in 1844, and improved editions appeared in 1853, 1866, 1878–82. Bergk's paper on the Age of Babrius was first published in the *Classical Journal* of 1845[1]. In 1858 he produced a text of Sophocles, followed by an edition of the *Lexicon Vindobonense* (1859–62). His familiarity with the Epic poetry of Greece is attested not only by the first volume of his 'Greek Literature', but also by several minor works[2]. He is less well known in connexion with his papers on Greek, Latin and Cypriote Inscriptions, on Latin Grammar and the textual criticism of Plautus, and on ancient Prosody, on Greek Mythology and Archaeology, and on the text of the Greek Philosophers and the Alexandrian Poets.

His studies were for a time interrupted by political duties. In 1848 he represented the university of Marburg in the Hessian Parliament, and was one of the delegates to the federal conference

---

[1] *Opusc.* ii 547—569.

[2] *Opusc.* ii 415—444 (Unity of *Il.* i), 409—414 (Tabula Iliaca), and *Emendationes* in Halle Programs of 1859 and 1861.

at Frankfurt. To this period belongs the only portrait of Bergk that was ever painted[1]. In 1852 he accepted a call to Freiburg in Breisgau, where he lived for five years an idyllic life, surrounded by congenial colleagues, and busy with the text of Aristophanes and Sophocles. His subsequent time at Halle was marked by bad health, due in part to over-work. On settling in 1869 at Bonn, a university to which he was attracted by the presence of Otto Jahn, his health improved, and he continued to lecture until 1876. At Bonn he began his 'History of Greek literature' and completed the MS of four volumes in the course of ten years. He also wrote papers on the history and topography of the *Rheinland* in Roman times, and incidentally gave proof of his being an excellent strategist[2]. Though he was able to prepare a fourth edition of his *Poëtae Lyrici*, and to exhibit a singular acumen in the identification of the two Berlin fragments of Aristotle's *Constitution of Athens*[3], he was in failing health for the last five years of his life. The baths of Ragaz in Switzerland, which had proved efficacious in former years, were of no avail in 1881, when his strength finally failed him, and he passed away on the 20th of July.

As a classical teacher, he was thoroughly familiar with the language, literature, and monuments, of Rome as well as Greece. He was characterised by a remarkable breadth of knowledge, and a singular degree of acumen. A severe critic of his own work, he left many of his most elaborate papers unfinished. Opinions, which he deemed unsound in point of scholarship, he was wont to attack with a sharpness which, in the years of failing health, approached the limits of positive rudeness. But, in every controversy, his constant aim was the attainment of the truth ; and in all that he said or wrote, the advancement of classical studies was the joy and the glory of his life[4].

The Greek drama was one of the main interests of Adolf Schöll (1805—
1882), who studied at Tübingen, Göttingen, and Berlin, and
A. Schöll
began his literary career with a dissertation on the origin of

---

[1] Frontispiece of *Opusc.* I.

[2] Peppmüller in Bergk's *Opusc.* I lxxxix f.　　　　[3] *Opusc.* II 505—553.

[4] Arnold Schaefer, in *Biogr. Jahrb.* 1881, 105—110 ; also Peppmüller in Bergk's *Opuscula*, 718 + 813 pp. (1884-6), II xiii—xcv ; Bursian, ii 829, 872-5.

the drama (1828). He afterwards owed much to the influence of K. O. Müller, whom he accompanied on the fatal journey to Greece. Meanwhile, he had produced important papers on tragic tetralogies[1], and had translated Sophocles and Herodotus with the highest degree of literary skill, besides writing a monograph on the ' Life and Work of Sophocles ' (1842)[2]. In the same year he was appointed professor of Archaeology at Halle, leaving in the following year for the directorship of the Art Museum at Weimar, where he died nearly forty years later[3].

The subject-matter of Homer was the principal theme of the classical studies of Eduard Buchholz (1825—1887), who was educated under B. R. Abeken at Osnabrück, studied under K. F. Hermann **Buchholz** and Schneidewin at Göttingen, and ended his scholastic career at the Joachimsthal *gymnasium* in Berlin (1872–81). His German plays on classical subjects are less widely known than his comprehensive and instructive work :—*Die Homerischen Realien*[4].

The text of the Greek tragic poets is associated with the name of August Nauck (1822—1892). The son of a village-pastor in NE Thuringia, he was educated **Nauck** at Schulpforta, studied at Halle (mainly under Bernhardy) in 1841–6, and, after holding scholastic appointments in Berlin, was in 1859 elected a Member of the Academy of St Petersburg, where he was also professor of Greek Literature in 1869–83. His first important work was an edition of the Fragments of Aristophanes of Byzantium (1848), suggested by Bernhardy. His text of Euripides (1854) was followed by an excellent edition of the Fragments of the Greek Tragic Poets (1856), the design for which had occurred to him during his study of the *scholia* in connexion with his edition of Aristophanes of Byzantium. He was busy with the Fragments while he was still an assistant-master to Meineke, and it may be assumed that the editor of the ' Comic Fragments ' was interested in his assistant's work in a similar domain. This undertaking made it necessary for him to traverse the whole range of Greek literature. He thus found traces of the Aeschylean simile of the ' struck eagle '[5], not in Aristophanes alone, but also in Philo, Dionysius of Halicarnassus,

---

[1] *Beiträge zur Gesch. der attischen Tragiker* (1839), i.

[2] Also on Shakespeare and Sophocles in *Jahrb. der deutschen Shakespeare-Gesellschaft* (1865).

[3] *Biogr. Jahrb.* 1882, 63—99.

[4] 3 vols. (1871—85). *Biogr. Jahrb.* 1887, 48 f. [5] Frag. 139.

Athenaeus, Aristides, Galen, and Eustathius. A line, which violated Porson's rule as to the final cretic[1], had been quoted from the *Canones* of either 'Ion' or 'Ioannes'; it had been rashly ascribed to Ion by Heyne; but it was more judiciously assigned by Nauck to Joannes Damascenus, and was subsequently found in that grammarian's works[2]. Another of Meineke's assistant-masters was Adolf Kirchhoff. Kirchhoff and Nauck were simultaneously preparing editions of the text of Euripides. Nauck placed at Kirchhoff's disposal his own collection of quotations from Euripides, while Kirchhoff, both before and after his visit to the Italian libraries in 1853, kept Nauck informed of points that were likely to interest him as an editor. The second edition of Nauck's Euripides included *Prolegomena* on the life, style, and genius of the poet, in which the subject is tersely and succinctly treated, while the original authorities are added in the notes. Like Porson and Elmsley[3], for both of whom he had a high admiration, he was specially strong in his knowledge of metre.

In 1859, on the proposal of Stephani, he was elected a Member of the Academy of St Petersburg, and in that year, and again in 1862, he laid before that Academy the two instalments of his 'Euripidean Studies'[4]. Most of his subsequent work, apart from editions published in Germany, appeared in the Transactions of the Russian Academy, and unfortunately attracted little notice in the land of his birth[5].

From 1856 onwards he was repeatedly engaged in the critical study of Sophocles. Every few years he produced a new revision of Schneidewin's school-editions of the several plays. His own edition of the text (1867) was severely reviewed by Bergk, while he himself was no less severe in his review of the 'Comic Fragments' of Kock. He was less strong in the 'recension' of the text as a whole than in the details of its 'emendation'. In one of his papers he drew attention to the fact that his own conjectures had repeatedly been confirmed by the MSS[6].

---

[1] σειραῖς ἀφύκτοις ὃν διαρθροῖ δακτύλοις.

[2] *T. G. F.* p. xiii.   [3] *Mélanges Gr. Rom.* iv 61, 308 f.

[4] *Mémoires*, Sér. VII, i no. 12, and v no. 6.

[5] *Mélanges Gréco-Romains*, six vols.

[6] *ib.* iii 35, iv 217, 233, 453.

In his edition of the *Odyssey* (1874) and the *Iliad* (1877), the text of Aristarchus is generally retained, resolved forms of diphthongs only introduced where necessary, and conjectures added below the text.   To ascertain his actual views as to the textual criticism of Homer, we have to consult his *Kritische Bemerkungen*[1].   He there avows that the aim of the Homeric critic is to bring the text as near as possible to the *original* form[2], with the aid of Analogy and Comparative Philology.

While his first decade at St Petersburg had been mainly devoted to Sophocles, and his second to Homer, the third was assigned to Porphyry and his circle.   Here again, the first impulse had come from Bernhardy.   In 1846 he had spent three months collating Porphyry MSS at Munich.   On his return to Halle he collected many of the fragments, but, on reaching the Byzantine writers, he left his original task unfinished.   At St Petersburg, however, with the aid of his colleague, Chwolson, he became acquainted with the Arabic authorities on Porphyry's philosophy. In 1860 he produced Teubner texts of three of Porphyry's tracts, namely the Life of Pythagoras, the treatise On Abstinence, and the Letter to Marcella.   Here (as elsewhere) he did more for 'emendation' than for 'recension'.   Indeed, it was shown in 1871 that the Munich MS, which he had followed, was only an ordinary copy of the Bodleian MS[3].   His examination of the Laurentian MS of Iamblichus' 'Life of Pythagoras' in 1879 resulted in an edition of that work (1884), followed by a second edition of the *Porphyrii Opuscula Selecta* (1886).

The main achievement of his life was his final edition of the Fragments of the Greek Tragic Poets.   The first edition had appeared in 1856.   The publication in 1862 of the first part of the second collection of *Volumina Herculanensia*, including many passages quoted from the poets by Philodemus, led to a long and friendly correspondence with its able editor, Professor Gomperz of Vienna.   The loan of a Vienna MS enabled him to publish the *Etymologicum Vindobonense* in 1867, and, three years afterwards, a Vatican MS of that lexicon revealed the name of its author,

---

[1] 1861, 1863, 1867, and esp. 1871.

[2] *Mél. Gr. Rom.* iii 209; see esp. *Biogr. Jahrb.* 1893, 44 f.

[3] Val. Rose, in *Hermes*, v 362 f.

Andreas Lopadiotes[1]. The final edition of the Tragic Fragments appeared in 1889, and the complete Index in 1892. The aged editor had lately lost the sight of one eye and his memory had begun to fail him; yet he was eagerly planning fresh works for the future, when his life came to an end[2].

A critical edition of Pindar was produced in 1864 by Tycho Mommsen (1819—1900), a younger brother of the historian. After studying in 1838–43 at Kiel, which was then a Danish university, he visited Greece and Italy in 1846, and, in 1846–7, collated MSS of Pindar in Rome and Florence. Further collations were made in 1861. The results appeared in his edition of 1864; he also edited a large part of the *scholia* (1861–7). He was Rector of the school at Oldenburg from 1856, and Director of the *gymnasium* at Frankfurt from 1864 to the end of his life. The greatest work of his closing years was an investigation of the usage of the prepositions σύν and μετά in Greek literature beginning with the poets (1874–9) and ending with the writers of prose[3].

Numerous papers on Pindar were produced by Eduard Lübbert (1830—1889), a professor at Giessen in 1865–74, and at Bonn from 1881 to his death. The series began with a Halle program of 1853 and ended with the end of his life[4].

A brief and suggestive Commentary on Pindar was prepared by Friedrich Mezger (1832—1893), a son of the Rector of the *gymnasium* of St Anna at Augsburg, who studied at Erlangen and Leipzig, and, after teaching under his father for eight years at Augsburg and undertaking similar work for eight years at Hof, returned to his father's school in 1871, and there taught for the remaining three years of his life, and for seventeen years after. The fruit of many years of study appeared in his Commentary of 1880, a work intended for those who desired to study the poet for his own sake, without being distracted by the divergent views of his interpreters, with which Mezger himself was perfectly familiar, his own library including some 300 works on the subject. It may be added that he was led to his well-known theory of catch-words in Pindar by the practice of learning each ode by heart before commenting on it[5].

Boeckh's lectures on Pindar at Berlin were attended by Moriz Schmidt (1823—1888), who had already studied under Haase at the university of his native place, Breslau. For the last thirty-

---

[1] Stein's larger ed. of Herod. I lxxv f; Krumbacher, § 238[2] (first half of cent. xiv).

[2] Iwan Müller in *Biogr. Jahrb.* 1893, 1—65 (with complete bibliography); cp. Bursian, ii 870–2.

[3] *Beiträge zu der Lehre von den griechischen Präpositionen* (1886–95), 847 pp. Cp. *Biogr. Jahrb.* 1904, 103—117.

[4] *Biogr. Jahrb.* 1891, 135—171, with list of papers on 169—171.

[5] *Biogr. Jahrb.* 1894, 78—86.

one years of his life he was a professor at Jena. He began his career with a
treatise on the dithyramb and the remains of the dithyrambic poets (1845).
He afterwards collected the fragments of Didymus (1854), and produced as
his *opus magnum* the edition of Hesychius in five volumes, with *Quaestiones
Hesychianae* in the second half of volume IV, and elaborate *Indices* in volume V
(1858–68). He subsequently published in a single volume (1864) the nucleus
of Hesychius, in the form of a restoration of the epitome of the lexicon of
Pamphilus, which Schmidt regarded as identical with the small lexicon of
Diogenianus[1]. He also produced papers on the inscriptions of Lycia (1867–76)
and collected those of Cyprus (1876); edited the fables of Hyginus and the
Ars Poëtica of Horace, the *Poetic* of Aristotle (with a translation), and the
first Book of the *Politics*, besides discussing the Pseudo-Xenophontean treatise
on the Constitution of Athens. In his works on Pindar (1869, 1882) and
Horace (1872), and his editions of the *Oedipus Tyrannus* and the *Antigone*
(1871–80), he showed a special aptitude for conjectural emendation. His
discussion of the metres of Pindar, and of the Tragic Choruses, was founded
on a careful study of Aristoxenus, a translation of whose treatise on rhythm
was placed by Schmidt at the disposal of Westphal. He endeavoured with
very doubtful success to solve the difficulties in the choral metres of Pindar
and Sophocles (1870) by the aid of the modern theory of music. Maturer
work in this field is to be found in his papers on the Choruses of the *Ajax*
and on the structure of Pindar's *Strophae*. He did much for the text of
Aeschylus, and gave proof of an artistic and tasteful style in his excellent
translations of the *Oedipus Tyrannus* and of Pindar's *Olympian Odes*[2].

Homer and Pindar formed a principal part of the wide
province of Greek literature which was illustrated
by the life-long labours of Wilhelm Christ (1831—
W. Christ
1906). Born near Wiesbaden, he studied at Munich and Berlin ;
was a pupil of Karl Halm at Hadamar and Munich, and of
Thiersch, Spengel, Boeckh, Bopp, and Trendelenburg at Munich
and Berlin ; and, for more than half a century, was one of the
praeceptores Bavariae, first as a master at the Max-Gymnasium
and for the remaining forty-five years as a professor in the
university of Munich. Under the influence of Halm, he became
interested in the textual criticism of Cicero, *De Divinatione*, and
De Fato. Under that of Boeckh, he ultimately edited a text of
Pindar, followed by a commentary (1896). Under that of Spengel
and Trendelenburg, he produced a text of Aristotle's *Poetic* and
Metaphysics[3]. As a former pupil of Bopp, he lectured in alternate

---

[1] See index to vol. i *s.v.*

[2] *Biogr. Jahrb.* 1889, 83—130 ; Bursian, ii 875–7.

[3] *Beiträge* in Munich *S. Ber.* 1886, 406—423.

years on Comparative Grammar. He also repeatedly undertook subjects that would otherwise have been unrepresented in the list. His lectures on Homer resulted in his text of the *Iliad* (1884)[1]; those on the *Odes* of Horace, in his Studies on Rhythm and Metre, and on the chronology of the poems in general; those on Demosthenes, in his paper on the edition by Atticus (1882); and those on the *Germania* of Tacitus, in his Studies on Ancient Geography, a subject which he constantly kept in view during his travels in Greece and the Troad. His comprehensive hand-book of Greek Literature has passed through several editions[2]. He was one of the most versatile of scholars. He was capable of examining in archaeology, and of lecturing on ancient philosophy, besides taking an interest in astronomy. His services on the Bavarian Board of Education were recognised by his receiving, among many public distinctions, that of the 'Star of Bavaria'. Even in the last few months of his long life, he had large audiences attending his lectures on the Greek Theatre. He was a loyal and generous colleague; a man of noble nature, and of cheerful temper; one who found his chief happiness in his work, and in his home[3].

The *Supplices* and *Persae* of Aeschylus were edited by Johannes Oberdick
Oberdick (1835—1903), who studied at Münster and Bonn, and at Breslau, where he received an honorary degree in 1874. His principal scholastic appointment was that of Director of the Catholic *gymnasium* of Glatz. He was interested in Latin Orthography[4], and was a corresponding Member of the *Academia Virgiliana* of Mantua[5].

An edition of the *Electra* of Sophocles (1896) was one of the
Kaibel finest of the works produced by Georg Kaibel (1849—1901), who was born and bred at Lübeck, and studied under Ernst Curtius and Sauppe at Göttingen, and under Jahn and Usener and Bücheler at Bonn. He was a student of the Archaeological Institute in Rome in 1873–4, and visited Italy for his health in the winter of 1877–8. In 1878 he published his *Epigrammata Graeca ex lapidibus conlecta*, a work

---

[1] Also in papers on 'repetitions' and 'contradictions' in the *Iliad*; Munich *S. Ber.* 1880–1. On the substance of his *Prolegomena*, cp. Jebb's *Homer*, 126 f.

[2] Ed. 1889; ed. 4, 1905, 996 pp. (with appendix of 43 portraits).

[3] E. W(ölfflin), in *Beilage zur Allgemeine Zeitung*, 11 Feb. 1906, 269 f.

[4] *Studien* in 4 parts (1879–94).   [5] *Biogr. Jahrb.* 1904, 10—14.

containing some 1200 epigrams extending in date over ten centuries. From 1879 to 1886 he was successively professor at Breslau, Rostock, and Greifswald; then, for ten years, at Strassburg, and for the last five years of his life at Göttingen. His principal works, beside the edition of the *Electra*, were his critical text of Athenaeus (1886–90), his collections of the Greek Inscriptions of Italy and Sicily and the West of Europe (1890), the edition of Aristotle's *Constitution of Athens*, in which he was associated with his life-long friend, Wilamowitz (1891), and his independent work on the 'Style and Text' of the treatise (1893). He had only published the first part of his proposed edition of the 'Fragments of the Greek Comic Poets' (1889), when his brief life came to an end[1].

A critical edition of Euripides was begun by Rudolf Prinz (1847—1890), who studied mainly at Bonn, under Otto Jahn, Arnold Schaefer, and Usener. After spending eight months in Paris   **Prinz** examining the MSS of Sophocles and Euripides, he published the *Medea* and *Alcestis* (1878–9). In 1880 he was at work in the Vatican and Laurentian Libraries, and came to the conclusion that the Laurentian MS of Sophocles was in the position of *princeps*, rather than that of *pater* or *avus*, in relation to the other MSS; but his proposed edition of Sophocles never appeared. Work in the cold Italian libraries inflicted permanent injury on his health, and even prevented him from having sufficient energy to make full use of his own collations. In 1882 he left his appointment in the library of Breslau to superintend that of Münster; in the following year he published the *Hecuba*; in 1888 he became librarian at Königsberg, where he suffered from strange mental delusions, and left for a private asylum, where he died[2].

Apart from the complete editions of the text of Aristophanes by Bekker, Dindorf, Bergk, and Meineke, there were many editions of separate plays[3]. Critical editions of five[4] were produced by Adolf von Velsen   **Velsen** (1832—1900), who studied at Bonn, and was for many years a school-master at Saarbrücken. On the failure of his health, his collections were handed over to Zacher with a view to the continuation of the work. Four of the plays[5] had meanwhile been edited with German notes by Theodor Kock (1820—1891), who had studied at Breslau, Halle, and Berlin, and, after holding several scholastic appointments, was   **Kock** Director of a *gymnasium* in Berlin (1860–82), and then settled for the rest of his life at Weimar. He wrote several German dramas on classical themes;

---

[1] *Biogr. Jahrb.* 1904, 15—71.   [2] *Biogr. Jahrb.* 1891, 22—32.

[3] E.g. *Thesm. Ran.* ed. F. V. Fritzsche (1838—45).

[4] *Eq. Thesm. Ran. Plut. Eccl.* (1869–83).

[5] *Nub. Eq. Ran. Av.* (1852–64).

was keenly interested in modern music and ancient art, and paid nine visits to Italy, and two to Greece. He attained a high degree of excellence in translating the whole of Goethe's *Iphigenie* into Greek Iambic verse (1861). His latest work, the 'Comic Fragments' (1880–8), was intended to serve as a new edition of Meineke's *Editio minor*, but a higher standard was expected in 1880 than that which had sufficed thirty-three years before. The new editor attempted to trace lost fragments of Greek Comedy in the prose of Lucian and other late Sophists, and also elsewhere. He even found a fragment of a 'comic tetrameter' in a passage which he failed to identify as part of the sublime language of St Paul[1].

The value of Aristophanes as a historical authority was submitted to a careful and discriminating examination by Hermann Müller-Strübing (1812—1893), who studied in Berlin, and, owing to the part which he played in political movements among the students of Germany, was condemned to death in 1835. His sentence was commuted to imprisonment; and, on his subsequent release, he spent the last forty-one years of his life in London. His constant researches in the British Museum led to his discovery of an excellent MS of Vitruvius, and, in conjunction with Valentin Rose, he published a critical text, which is still the standard edition (1867). His polemical work on 'Aristophanes and historical criticism' was published in 1873[2]. He here enlarges on the unintelligent and uncritical use of Greek Comedy as evidence for the political history of Athens. In his subsequent publications he paid more and more attention to the historic criticism of Thucydides, investigating the dates at which the different parts of the history were composed, and discovering difficulties in his account of the siege of Plataea and the affairs of Corcyra[3]. Among the best of his papers were those on the Pseudo-Xenophontean treatise on the Constitution of Athens (1880), and on the legends as to the death of Pheidias (1882)[4].

The text of the Greek Bucolic Poets was edited by Christoph Ziegler (1814—1888), who was educated under Moser at Ulm. He studied under Hermann at Leipzig, where he was the first student from Württemberg, who chose 'philology' as his sole profession; he also studied at Tübingen under Walz. His interest in archaeology and in the

---

[1] 2 Tim. iv 6, ἐγὼ γὰρ ἤδη σπένδομαι κτλ. (Kock, iii 543 fr. 768; *Classical Rev.* iii 25). On Kock's life, cp. *Biogr. Jahrb.* 1902, 44—49 (with full bibliography).

[2] Bursian's *Jahresb.* ii 1001–57, 1360 f.

[3] *Kritik des Thukydides Textes* (1879); *Thuk. Forschungen* (1881); *Das erste Jahr des pel. Krieges* (1883); *Belagerung von Plataia* (1885); *Die Korkyräischen Händel* (1886); *Verfassung von Athen* (1893). The last four in *Neue Jahrb. f. Phil.* 1883–93.

[4] His treatment of Thucydides is ably criticised by Adolf Bauer, *Thuk. und H. Müller-Strübing, Ein Beitrag zur Gesch. der philologischen Methode* (Nördlingen, 1887). Life and bibliography in *Biogr. Jahrb.* 1897, 88—105.

MSS of Theocritus led to his paying four visits to Italy. After the first of these (1841–2) he published the earliest of his critical editions (1844). During his second visit in 1864 he discovered in the Ambrosian Library what is now known as Idyll xxx. Two further editions followed in 1867–79. He also edited the Ambrosian *scholia*, as well as Theognis, Bion and Moschus, with four school-editions of the *Iphigeneia in Tauris*. Lastly, he produced an excellent series of illustrations of Roman topography[1]. He was a school-master at Stuttgart for thirty-one years (1845–76), led a frugal and a happy life, left his library to his school and devoted the rest of his resources to founding stipends for poor students at Stuttgart and Ulm[2].

The text of the Bucolic Poets was ably edited in 1855–9 by H. L. Ahrens (1809—1881), the learned explorer of the Greek dialects[3].

Theocritus was fully expounded by Adolph Theodor Hermann Fritzsche (1818—1878), a pupil of Hermann, and a professor at Giessen and Leipzig. Of his two editions, the first had German notes[4]; the second, a very elaborate Latin commentary[5]. He also expounded the *Satires* of Horace (1875), and edited in the early part of his career the eighth and ninth books of the *Nicomachean*, and the whole of the *Eudemian Ethics* (1847–51)[6].

Ahrens

A. T. H. Fritzsche

Two editions of Apollonius Rhodius were published in 1852–4 by Rudolf Merkel (1811—1885), who is even better known as an editor of Ovid[7]. Callimachus was elaborately edited in 1870–73 by Otto Schneider (1815—1880), who studied under Schömann at Greifswald, and under Boeckh and Lachmann in Berlin, where his closest friends were Merkel and Hertz. His earliest work was on the sources of the *scholia* to Aristophanes (1838), and he afterwards proposed many emendations of the text[8]. Meanwhile, he had published his *Nicandrea* (1856), the two volumes of his index to Sillig's *Pliny* (1857), and his school-edition of selections from Isocrates (1859–60). From 1842 to 1869 he was a school-master at Gotha, where the present writer remembers visiting him after he had retired from scholastic work. Eminent as a scholar, he was also excellent as a teacher, and frank and straight-forward as a man[9].

O. Schneider

The theory of Greek Rhythm and Metre was ably treated by Rudolph Westphal and August Rossbach. Westphal (1826—1892), who studied at Marburg, became a 'privat-docent' at Tübingen, and an 'extraordinary' professor at Breslau (1858–62), and, after living

Westphal

---

[1] 1873–7; school-ed., 1882.

[2] *Biogr. Jahrb.* 1888, 47—52.

[3] Cp. p. 120 *supra*.

[4] 1857; ed. 2, 1869.   [5] 1865–9.

[6] *Biogr. Jahrb.* 1878, 1.

[7] p. 193 *infra*.

[8] *Philol.*, and Fleckeisen's *Jahrb.* (1876–80).

[9] *Biogr. Jahrb.* 1880, 8 f.

at Halle and Jena, and spending six years in Russia, passed the rest of his life at Leipzig, and at Bückeburg, the place of his birth[1].

Rossbach

Rossbach (1823—1898) studied under Hermann at Leipzig and under Bergk at Marburg, where he made the acquaintance of Westphal, and married his sister. He taught at Tübingen (1852–6), and was professor at Breslau for the last forty-two years of his life. He is there commemorated by a portrait-bust as the founder of the archaeological museum. His independent works included a Teubner text of Catullus and Tibullus, and Researches on Roman Marriage (1853), illustrated (in 1871) by sculptured monuments [2].

In the study of Greek metre, Rossbach went back to the original authority, Aristoxenus, and, in conjunction with Westphal, formed a plan for a joint work on (1) *Rhythmik*; (2) *Metrik*; (3) *Harmonik*, *Organik*, and *Orchestik*. Rossbach's volume on *Rhythmik* (1854) was the first to set forth the ancient system of Rhythm, with constant reference to Pindar and the Greek tragic poets. Their joint work on *Metrik* (1856) marked a great advance, and was well received by Boeckh, and by Bergk and Lehrs, and even by the strictest adherents of Hermann. This was followed by Westphal's *Harmonik* and *Melopöie* (1863), his 'General Greek *Metrik*', his revision of Rossbach's *Rhythmik*, and his edition of 'Plutarch', *De Musica* (1865).

After ten years of associated work, Westphal had meanwhile parted from Rossbach. Westphal afterwards produced a Teubner text of Hephaestion with the *scholia* (1866), and an edition of Aristoxenus (1883–93). His treatise on Greek Music (1883) was followed in 1885–7 by a third edition of Rossbach and Westphal's joint work, under the new title of 'The Theory of the Musical Arts of the Greeks'. The work has been widely recognised as a masterpiece which marks an epoch in the study of the subject.

The first edition of Rossbach and Westphal's *Metrik* formed the foundation of the work of J. H. Heinrich Schmidt (born in 1830) 'on the artistic forms of Greek poetry, and their significance'. The choral lyrics of Aeschylus and Pindar are included in the first volume (1868); those of Sophocles and Aristophanes, in the second (1869); and those of Euripides, in the third (1871), while the fourth volume (1872) states the author's views on Prosody and on musical Rhythm, in which he ignores the ancient writers on the theory of Rhythm and Metre, and trusts solely to the evidence of the extant remains of choral lyric poetry [3].

J. H. H. Schmidt

---

[1] *Biogr. Jahrb.* 1895, 40—90; Bursian, ii 981 f. His earliest independent works were papers on the law of the final syllable in Gothic (1852), and on the form of the oldest Latin poetry. His 'Latin Verbal Flexions' (1872), and 'Comparative Grammar' (1873), were largely founded on the labours of others.

[2] *Biogr. Jahrb.* 1900, 75—85; Bursian, ii 984 f.

[3] Bursian, ii 990 f. His introduction to the Rhythmic and Metric of the Classical languages was translated by Prof. J. W. White (1877–9). He is also the author of four large volumes on Greek *Synonymik* (1876–86). Cp. *A. J. P.* vii 406 f. It has been ascertained that he is still living, and that, amid the

The musical instruments and the musical theories of the Greeks were specially investigated by Karl von Jan (1836—1899), who studied at Erlangen, Göttingen, and Berlin.   In Berlin he von Jan was led by Gerhard to examine the stringed instruments of the Greeks.   He next turned his attention to the study of the texts, and took part in the controversies excited by the publications of Westphal.   The discovery of the Delphic hymn gave the final impulse to the publication of the work of his life:—his edition of the *Scriptores Musici Graeci* (1895)[1].

Passing from scholars concerned mainly with Greek poetry to the special students of prose, we note that the Life of Herodotus was the theme of an interesting Dahlmann work[2] by Friedrich Christoph Dahlmann (1786—1860), who studied at Copenhagen, Halle, and Dresden, and was professor at Kiel, and at Göttingen from 1829 to 1837.   In the latter year, Dahlmann and the brothers Grimm, and Gervinus, were among the seven professors who were dismissed for protesting against the violation of the constitution by the king of Hanover[3].   He subsequently lived at Leipzig and Jena, and passed the last eighteen years of his life as a professor at Bonn[4].

Among the editors of Thucydides a place of honour must be assigned to Ernst Friedrich Poppo (1794—1866), who studied at Leipzig, and was Director of the Poppo *gymnasium* at Frankfurt on the Oder from 1817 to 1863.   His larger edition, in eleven volumes, appeared in 1821–38; his smaller, in four, was first published in 1843–51.

Johannes Classen (1806—1891), who was born at Hamburg and studied at Leipzig and Bonn, was for twenty years a master at Lübeck, for eleven Director of Classen the *gymnasium* at Frankfurt on the Main, and from 1864 head of the school of his native place, where he died at the age of 85. His earliest work, *De Grammaticae Graecae Primordiis* (1829), was followed, many years later, by his excellent edition of

active occupations of a hale old age, he has applied his metrical principles to the newly discovered *nomos* of Timotheus and to the odes of Bacchylides. On the recent history of the study of Greek and Roman *Metrik* in Germany, see Radermacher in *Jahresb.* cxxiv 1—11.

[1] *Biogr. Jahrb.* 1900, 104—124.

[2] *Herodot. Aus seinem Buche sein Leben* (1824); E. T. 1845.

[3] Cp. Boeckh and K. O. Müller's *Briefwechsel*, 402.

[4] G. Beseler in *Unsere Zeit*, vi 68—78; A. Springer (Leipzig, 1870).

Thucydides with German notes, first published in 1862–78. At
the age of 70 he wrote an interesting monograph in memory of
Niebuhr, in whose house he had lived as a private tutor before
beginning his scholastic career[1].

A critical text of Xenophon[2] was produced in 1869–76 by
Karl Schenkl (1827—1900), who studied at Vienna
K. Schenkl   and, after holding a mastership at Prag, was appointed to professorships at Innsbruck (1858), Graz (1863), and
Vienna (1875). His other works included a Greek-German
(1858[1]) and German-Greek school-lexicon (1866[1]), and editions of
Valerius Flaccus (1871) and Ausonius (1883). With Benndorf
and others, he took part in editing the *Imagines* of the Philostrati; in conjunction with W. von Hartel, he founded the
Wiener Studien; he was general editor of a useful series of Greek
and Latin texts published in Prague and Vienna; and, late in life
(like Bonitz in his day), he was publicly honoured as the *Praeceptor Austriae*[3].

The *Oeconomicus, Agesilaus, Hieron, Hellenica, Memorabilia, Cyropaedeia*
and *Anabasis* were all edited between 1841 and 1875 by
Breitenbach   Ludwig Breitenbach (1813—1885), who was born at Erfurt,
educated at Schulpforta, studied under Bernhardy at Halle, and was from
1840 to 1860 a master, mainly at Wittenberg. He was ultimately compelled
to resign that position owing to extreme deafness. His favourite authors were
Xenophon and Goethe[4].

The *Anabasis* has often been edited separately. An improved text was
produced in 1878 by Arnold Hug (1832—1895), who studied
Hug   under Köchly at Zürich, and under Welcker and Ritschl at
Bonn, was a master at Winterthur from 1856 and professor at Zürich from
1869 to 1886, when he was laid aside by paralysis for the remaining nine
years of his life. He collected some of his popular lectures on Demosthenes
etc. in his *Studien* (1881); he also produced a critical text of Aeneas Poliorceticus (1874), while his explanatory commentary on Plato's *Symposium* (1876)[5]
attained a second edition in 1884. He was prevented by illness from
completing his careful revision of the *Staatsalterthümer* of K. F. Hermann[6].

---

[1] Life in *A. D. B.*, and in *Biogr. Jahrb.* 1905, 19—33.

[2] *Anabasis* and *Libri Socratici*.

[3] Cp. Wurzbach, *Biogr. Lex.*, and esp. Karl Ziwsa in *Österreich. Mittel-
schule*, 15 pp., and Edmund Hauler in *Zeitsch. f. österreich. Gymnasien*, 1900,
xii, 14 pp.; also *Deutscher Nekrolog*, v 352–8.

[4] *Biogr. Jahrb.* 1886, 292–6.

[5] Also expounded in 1875–6 by G. F. Rettig (1803—1897).

[6] *Biogr. Jahrb.* 1896, 95—104.

The text of Plato had been published by Bekker in 1816–23. A useful edition in ten volumes, with Latin notes, was produced between 1827 and 1860 by Gottfried **Stallbaum** Stallbaum (1793—1861), who had been educated at Leipzig, and spent the last forty-one years of his life at that place, having been appointed Rector of the *Thomas-Schule* in 1835, and extra-ordinary professor in the university in 1840.

Meanwhile an excellent edition of the text was produced at Zürich by Baiter, Orelli, and Winckelmann (1839– 42). Of these Johann Caspar Orelli (1787—1849), **Orelli** the younger cousin of Johann Conrad Orelli (1770—1820)[1], was educated at Zürich, where he was inspired with an interest in the Classics by his cousin, and by an older scholar, Johann Jacob Hottinger (1750—1819). As chaplain and schoolmaster in the reformed community at Bergamo, Orelli produced a new edition of Rosmini's *Vittorino da Feltre* (1812); as a master at Chur, an improved text of Isocrates, *De Permutatione*, together with an edition of Isaeus, *De Meneclidis hereditate*, by his elder cousin, Conrad, and notes on Xenophon's *Symposium* by that cousin's son, the younger Conrad (1814). As master and professor at Zürich, he prepared an important critical text of the whole of Cicero (1826–38), the second edition of which was completed by Baiter and Halm (1846–62). Of his many other works the best known are his annotated editions of Horace (1837–8) and of Tacitus (1846–8).

Orelli's principal partner in the edition of Plato, and his successor in that of Cicero, was Johann Georg Baiter (1801—1877), who was born at Zürich, **Baiter** studied at Munich, Göttingen, and Königsberg, and from 1833 was one of the principal masters at the *gymnasium*, and extra-ordinary professor at the university of Zürich. He was not only associated with Orelli as an editor of Cicero and Plato, but also with Sauppe in their joint edition of the *Oratores Attici*.

The third of the partners in the edition of Plato was August Wilhelm Winckelmann, who was born in Dresden (1810), and began his career by editing the *Euthy-* **A. W. Winckelmann** *demus* of Plato, and the fragments of Antisthenes.

---

[1] Editor of the *Opuscula Graecorum veterum sententiosa et moralia*, 1819–21.

He was on the staff of the school and university of Zürich from
1834 to 1845, when he returned to his native place.   The edition
of Plato, in which he was concerned, was founded on the Paris
MS and the Bodleian MS, and marked a decided advance on that
of Bekker.

The text of Plato was afterwards edited in 1851–6 by Karl
Friedrich Hermann (1804—1855), who studied at
Heidelberg and Leipzig, and was professor at Marburg in 1832–42, and for the remaining thirteen
years of his life at Göttingen.   His interest in Plato is well
represented by the only volume of his 'History and System of
the Platonic philosophy' (1839), and in his 'Collected Papers'
(1849).   He led the way in forming a true estimate of the value
of the MSS and the *scholia* of Persius[1] and Juvenal[2].   The points
of difference between Hermann and Jahn on the *scholia*, and the
over-fondness for quotations displayed by both scholars, were
pleasantly satirised by Haupt[3].   A still wider reputation was
won by Hermann's Manuals of Public, Religious, and Private
Antiquities, originally published in 1831–52, with a concise text,
full quotations from the ancient authorities, and references to the
modern literature.   He also wrote monographs on Laconian
Antiquities (1841), on Greek legislation (1849) and penalties
(1855), and many programs on points of Attic law[4].   The range
and depth of his learning were most remarkable; the general
purport of his teaching on the history of classical civilisation is
preserved in a work published by his pupil Gustav Schmidt[5].

K. F. Her-
mann

Plato was the central theme of the extensive studies of Christian Cron
(1813—1892) for the last thirty-five years of his life.   Born at
Munich, he held scholastic appointments at Erlangen (1838–
53) and Augsburg (1853–85).   He produced successful school-editions of
Plato's *Apology and Crito* (1857), and *Laches* (1860); also a treatise on the
Gorgias (1870) and a paper on the *Euthydemus* (1892)[6].   In
the course of a far briefer life, Julius Deuschle (1828—1861),

Cron

Deuschle

---

[1] *Lectiones*, 1842 ; *Analecta*, 1846 ; text, 1854.

[2] *De codd.* 1847 ; *Schol.* 1849 ; *Vindiciae*, and text, 1854.

[3] Belger's *Haupt*, 61 f.   [4] Bursian, ii 1162 n.

[5] *Culturgeschichte der Griechen u. Römer* (1857–8).   Cp. Bursian, ii
1161–3.

[6] *S.-Ber. Munich Acad.*

who was on the staff of a *gymnasium* in Berlin, wrote able dissertations on Plato's *Cratylus*[1], and the Platonic Myths[2], and edited the *Gorgias* and *Protagoras* (1859-61).

The Attic Orators formed a large part of the theme of the elaborate 'History of Eloquence in Greece and Rome' published in 1833-5 by Anton Westermann (1806–1869), who, with the **Westermann** exception of his schooldays at Freiberg in Saxony, spent the whole of his life in Leipzig, where he was a full professor from 1834 to 1865. Though not a brilliant, or even a stimulating, teacher, he was always clear and thorough. His four papers on questions connected with the history and criticism of Demosthenes[3] and on the documents quoted in the *Meidias*[4] and other speeches[5], were followed by his well-known edition of Select Speeches[6]. He also edited a text of Lysias, Plutarch's *Solon*, the Philostrati and Callistratus, and the Greek *Paradoxographi*, *Mythographi*, and *Biographi*[7].

Baiter's colleague as editor of the *Oratores Attici*, Hermann Sauppe (1809–1893), was born near Dresden, and studied under Hermann at Leipzig (1827–33). On **Sauppe** Hermann's recommendation, he obtained an appointment at Zürich, where he spent twelve years as a master at the newly organised cantonal school, besides being from 1837-8 public librarian, and 'extraordinary' professor. He was subsequently director of the *gymnasium* at Weimar (1845-56), and classical professor for many years at Göttingen (1856-93).

It was at Zürich that he was associated with Baiter in the comprehensive edition of the Attic Orators in two large quarto volumes (1839-50), the first containing the text founded on the best MSS, and the second the *scholia*, with Sauppe's edition of the Fragments, and a full Index of Names. Sauppe celebrated Hermann's Jubilee in 1841 by sending him an *Epistola Critica* of 152 pages of print, with many criticisms on the text of the Orators and of Plato[8]. He had already been associated with Baiter in an edition of the Speech of Lycurgus against Leocrates

[1] *Platon's Sprachphilosophie* (Marburg, 1852).

[2] Esp. that in the *Phaedrus* (Hanau, 1854).

[3] *Quaestiones Demosthenicae*, 1830-7.

[4] *De litis instrumentis* (1844).

[5] *Untersuchung über die...Urkunden* (1850).

[6] *Olynthiacs* and *Philippics*, *De Pace* and *Chers.*; *De Cor.*, *Lept.*; *Aristocr.*, *Con.*, *Eubul.* (1850-1, etc.).

[7] Bursian, ii 890-3.

[8] Reprinted in *Ausgewählte Schriften*, pp. 80—177.

(1834), and of the Fragments of that orator, and, in the interval between the first and second volume of the *Oratores Attici*, they brought out a translation of the second edition of Leake's *Athens* (1844).

Sauppe's independent work included an edition of the *First Philippic* and *Olynthiacs* of Demosthenes with Latin notes, and a German edition of Plato's *Protagoras*; an edition of Philodemus, περὶ κακιῶν, and an admirable discussion of the authorities followed by Plutarch in his *Life of Pericles*; also a long series of papers on Greek inscriptions and antiquities, on Lucretius, Cicero, and Florus, and other Latin authors, together with a large number of festal discourses on classical subjects, and funeral orations on classical scholars, mainly delivered at Göttingen[1]. He was the first to improve the text of Lysias, Isocrates, and Demosthenes, by closely following the best MS of each. His most striking features were the clearness of his style and the simplicity of his character. This simplicity was, however, combined with a profound knowledge of human nature, and both alike had a strong influence on all who were brought into contact with him in the course of a long and strenuous life[2].

The Speech of Lycurgus against Leocrates was edited by Fr. Osann,

Maetzner G. Pinzger and W. A. Blume, and the fragments by Gustav Kiessling. Antiphon and Dinarchus, as well as Lycurgus, were edited in 1836–42 with critical and explanatory notes by Eduard Maetzner, who was born at Rostock (1805), and, after studying at Greifswald and Heidelberg, was a school-master at Bromberg in 1831–5, and in 1838 became Director of the first high-school for girls in Berlin. His later work was mainly connected with English and French Grammar.

Andocides was edited in 1834 by Karl Christian Schiller (1811—1873), who

K. C. Schiller (like Maetzner) was born at Rostock; he edited Andocides immediately after the close of his university career at Leipzig.

A text of Lysias was first produced in 1852 by Karl Friedrich Scheibe

Scheibe Bremi (1814—1869), Rector of a *gymnasium* at Dresden. Select Orations of Lysias, Isocrates, Demosthenes and the whole of Aeschines, had been edited in 1823–34 by Johann Heinrich

---

[1] Cp. *Ausgewählte Schriften* (1896), 862 pp.

[2] His library now belongs to the Columbia Univ., New York. His portrait is prefixed to the *Ausg. Schr.* Cp. Bursian, ii 849, 858–60; Wilamowitz, in *Gött. Gelehrt. Nachr.* 1894, 36—49; and Lothholz in *N. Jahrb.* 1894, 299—304.

Bremi (1772—1837), a native of Zürich, who was educated at his native place by Hottinger, and afterwards studied at Halle under F. A. Wolf. He republished Wolf's edition of the *Leptines* in 1831. In the early part of his career he edited Nepos (1796) and Suetonius (1800), and, from that date to 1829, was a professor at Zürich[1].

Select Orations of Lysias were admirably edited with German notes by Rudolph Rauchenstein (1798—1879), who began his classical studies under Doederlein at Bern, and continued them under **Rauchenstein** Passow at Breslau, where he produced a prize-dissertation on the order of the *Olynthiacs* (1819)[2]. In 1822-66 he was Master (and for many years Rector) of the cantonal school at Aarau, and continued to take an active interest in the school to the end of his long life. He edited Selections from Lysias (1848, etc.) and Isocrates (1849, etc.)[3]. He also published papers on Pindar[4], and on the *Agamemnon* and *Eumenides*[5], and on the *Alcestis* and *Iphigeneia in Tauris*[6].

Selections from Lysias, with long and elaborate German notes, were subsequently published in 1866-71 by Hermann Frohberger (1836—1874), who studied at Leipzig and was a school-**Frohberger** master for the rest of his short life.

An able and comprehensive edition of Isaeus was published in 1831 by Georg Friedrich Schömann (1793— **Schömann** 1879), a scholar of Swedish descent, the son of an advocate and notary at Stralsund. After studying at Greifswald and Jena, he was for seven years a school-master at Greifswald, and for fifty-eight a teacher in the university, being professor of Eloquence for the last fifty-two years of his life. He was Rector of the university on four occasions, including the commemoration of its fourth centenary in 1856, when he discharged his duties with the highest distinction. As a student at Jena, he had owed little to the teaching of Eichstädt, whose superficially elegant Latinity formed a striking contrast to the pithy and eminently original and yet thoroughly classical style of Schömann. His own love of concrete facts attracted him to the difficult and almost unexplored province of the constitutional system and

[1] Bursian, ii 749 n. 2.

[2] Published with Preface by Passow and Observations on the Philippics by Bremi (1822); also abridged and revised in Bremi's *Dem. Orat. Selectae* (1829).

[3] *Paneg.* and *Areop.*

[4] *Einleitung*, 1843; *Commentationes*, 1844-5.

[5] 1855-8.

[6] 1847-60. Cp. *Biogr. Jahrb.* 1879, 1—2.

legal procedure of Athens. His early Latin treatise, *De Comitiis Atheniensium* (1819), was published two years after Boeckh's *Public Economy of Athens*, and was dedicated to Boeckh, under whose influence it was written. Meanwhile, in 1820, Boeckh's favourite pupil, Moritz Hermann Eduard Meier, was invited to Greifswald. In the same year Schömann produced his treatise *De sortitione judicum apud Athenienses*, and, in 1823, was nominated to an extraordinary professorship. In 1824 Meier and Schömann published their joint work on Attic Procedure[1]. Meier left for Halle in 1825, while Schömann remained and became a full professor in 1827 and librarian in 1844. His interest in Attic law led to his producing his translation (1830) and his annotated edition of Isaeus (1831), while his equal interest in Greek constitutions prompted him to edit Plutarch's *Agis* and *Cleomenes* (1839). In the previous year he had produced his systematic Latin work on the Public Antiquities of Greece[2], followed in 1855 by his German 'Handbook' on the same subject[3]. In 1854 he published his able critique on Grote's treatment of the Constitutional History of Athens[4].

Partly under the influence of R. H. Klausen (1807—1840), the author of the *Theologumena Aeschylea* (1829), Schömann became interested in ancient Religion. He was thus led to produce an edition, and a German translation, of the *Prometheus Vinctus*, with an original German play on the theme of *Prometheus Solutus* (1844); to translate and expound the *Eumenides* (1845), to comment on Cicero, *De Natura Deorum* (1850 etc.) and on the *Theogony* of Hesiod, besides editing the whole of the text (1868).

Similarly, the influence of Otto Jahn, his colleague in 1842–7, may be traced in his papers on classical archaeology in 1843–7[5]. In his public lectures he devoted much attention to Greek and

---

[1] *Der attische Process*, 1824; ed. Lipsius, 1883–7.

[2] *Antiquitates juris publici Graecorum*, 1838.

[3] *Handbuch der griechischen Alterthümer*, 1855–9 (E. T. vol. i, 1880); ed. 4 Lipsius, 1897—1902.

[4] E. T. by Bernard Bosanquet, 1878.

[5] *Ueber die Schönheit* (1843); *Winckelmann* and *Die Genien* (1845); *Hera* (1847).

Latin Syntax, and in 1864 wrote a paper on the teaching of the old Greek Grammarians as to the Article[1], and a treatise on the points of permanent value in the ancient views as to the Parts of Speech[2]. In 1827–68 he produced a long series of university programs, collected in the four volumes of his *Opuscula* (1856–71), including papers on his special departments of study, and also on the poems of Theognis, and on 'the silence of Homer'[3].

In the preface to his 'Greek Antiquities' he states that his aim was never to leave his readers in any doubt as to what he regarded as certainly true, or as only probable. His Latin prose has been already noticed; his German style is regarded as in the highest degree plain, popular, and perspicuous. His polemical writings supply examples of every variety of tone. He is respectful towards Grote, conversationally familiar towards K. J. Caesar, humorously ironical with G. W. Nitzsch (whose merits he fully recognises), and unsparing in the severity with which he exposes the 'ignorance' of Bake.

He was a born teacher, but he preferred lecturing to small classes of thoroughly industrious and attentive students. Among his many distinctions he received that of the Prussian 'Order of Merit' in 1864. With the exception of three half-years as a student at Jena, he spent the whole of his academic life in a small but not undistinguished university in the extreme North of Germany, where he found himself able to concentrate his powers on those studies in which he was a recognised master. He had a certain hardness of manner, which made people shy of him, but they soon found themselves reconciled to it by his strict sense of justice, and he was not without traits of distinct good-will. Though he loved a life of retirement, he was always cheerful in really congenial company. In his latter days, he was almost the sole survivor of the great age in which the foundations of modern scholarship were laid under the influence of Wolf[4].

---

[1] *Jahrb. f. Philol. Suppl.* v.

[2] *Die Lehre von den Redetheilen nach den Alten.*

[3] iii 1—29. For his views on the Homeric question cp. his review of G. W. Nitzsch in *Jahrb. f. Phil.* lxix (1854), 1 f, 129 f.

[4] F. S(usemihl) in *Biogr. Jahrb.* 1879, 7—16.

Schömann's collaborator in the *Attische Process*, M. H. E. Meier (1796—

Meier   1855), who was professor at Halle for the last twenty years of
his life, produced many programs, mainly on Andocides and
Theophrastus, which were afterwards collected in his *Opuscula* (1861–3).

Isocrates was studied with the minutest care by Gustav Eduard

Benseler   Benseler (1806—1868), who was born and bred in
the Saxon town of Freiberg, to which he returned
after studying at Leipzig under Hermann in 1825–31. At Freiberg he was a school-master from 1831 to 1849, when his public
career was interrupted for five years by his imprisonment on
political grounds in the castle of Ostenstein at Zwickau. For
the remaining fourteen years of his life he lived in retirement at
Leipzig.

In 1829 he began a translation of Isocrates, which did not
extend beyond the fourth volume (1831). His other early works
were his editions of the *Areopagiticus* and *Evagoras* (1832–4),
followed by his careful and comprehensive treatise of 557 pages
on *Hiatus* in the Greek Prose of (1) the Attic Orators, and (2) the
Historians (1844). While he was still in prison, his critical text
of Isocrates was in course of publication in the Teubner series[1].
It was during the same interval of seclusion that he prepared his
text and translation of selections from Isocrates (1854–5). This
was followed by a text and translation of Aeschines in three parts
(1855–60), and of Demosthenes in ten (1856–61), of which five at
least were by Benseler. His Greek and German School-lexicon
was published in 1859, and his excellent edition of Pape's lexicon
of Greek proper names in 1863–70. He was also one of the
editors of the fifth edition of the Greek lexicon of Passow[2].

While critical editions of the whole of Demosthenes had been

Voemel   produced by Bekker, Dindorf, and Baiter and
Sauppe, the text and the Latin translation were
edited in Didot's series in 1843–5 by Johann Theodor Voemel
(1791—1868), who afterwards published editions of the Public
Orations in 1856, and the *De Corona* and *De Falsa Legatione* in
1862, with full and elaborate *apparatus criticus*. Voemel had
studied at Heidelberg. After holding minor scholastic appoint-

---

[1] Vol. i (1856), vol. ii (1851).

[2] Cp. Bursian, ii 903, and p. 115, n. 1 *supra*.

ments at Wertheim and Hanau, he passed the last fifty years of his life at Frankfurt, where he was Rector of the *gymnasium* for more than thirty years (1822–53). The two most elaborate of his Demosthenic editions were produced after he had retired from that office.

Editions of the speech against *Androtion* (1832) and of the *Olynthiacs* (1834) were produced by Karl Hermann Funkhaenel (1808–74), for many years Director of the school at Eisenach, and the Funkhaenel author of numerous critical papers on Demosthenes. The speech against *Aristocrates* was elaborately edited in 1845 by Ernst (Christian) Wilhelm Weber (1796—1865), for forty years on the staff of E. W. Weber the *gymnasium* at Weimar.

Select Speeches were edited with German notes by Westermann[1] in 1850–2, and by Carl Rehdantz (1818—1879), whose edition of the 'Twelve Philippics' (1860) was superseded by that of the Rehdantz 'Nine' (1865). Born at Landsberg an der Warthe, east of Berlin, he was educated for six years at the principal *gymnasium* of that city, and for three at the university. He was himself a master at the above *gymnasium* from 1840 to 1851, and at Halberstadt until 1858. In 1859 he visited Italy in connexion with his study of Demosthenes. He was successively Rector of the schools at Magdeburg, Rudolstadt, and Kreutzburg in Upper Silesia; and he transformed the last two of these into classical schools in accordance with the Prussian requirements. Even his illness during the last year of his life did not prevent his continuing to take the work of his highest class. He was an admirable teacher, and had a special genius for interesting his pupils and inspiring them with lofty ideals. His earliest work, on the Lives of Iphicrates, Chabrias and Timotheus (1845), appeals to scholars rather than to school-boys, for whom he subsequently produced an excellent edition of the *Anabasis* (with a critical appendix). The thoroughness of his study of the Attic Orators is attested, not only by his editions of the Public Speeches of Demosthenes, but also by that of the speech of Lycurgus, and by numerous papers in the *Jahrbücher für Philologie*[2].

The *Philippics* of Demosthenes and the speeches of Aeschines were edited by Friedrich Franke (1805—1871), Rector of St Afra's at Meissen for the last twenty-six years of his life. An elaborate Franke critical edition of Aeschines was produced in 1865 by Ferdinand Schultz Schultz (b. 1829), afterwards Director of the *gymnasium* at Charlottenburg.

The Life and Times of Demosthenes were elucidated in 1856–8 in an admirable historical work by Arnold Schaefer (1819—1883), who was educated at Bre- A. Schaefer men, where he selected the *De Corona* as the theme of his

---

[1] p. 163 *supra.*   [2] *Biogr. Jahrb.* 1879, 2—4.

valedictory discourse. At Leipzig, he studied mainly under Hermann and Haupt, as well as Klotz and Wachsmuth, while among his contemporaries at that university, and his life-long correspondents, were Max Müller and Hercher. During his tenure of a mastership at Dresden, he produced a treatise on the Pseudo-Plutarchean 'Lives of the Ten Orators'. At Dresden he saw much of Georg Curtius, and of Köchly, until the latter became more and more perilously interested in politics. Though less advanced than his friend, Schaefer published many articles on the critical events of 1848–9. In 1847 he produced the first edition of his frequently reprinted 'Chronological Tables'. In 1851 he was placed on the staff of the school at Grimma, and, in that pleasant and quiet little Saxon town, found time for a large amount of scholarly work[1]. It was there that he produced the first two volumes of his work on 'The Age of Demosthenes' (1856), followed by a third and final volume two years later. From Grimma he often went over to see his friends at Dresden, and it was there that he first met the future Lord Goschen, in whose home he was stimulated to a new interest in English literature, and especially in the Histories of Thirlwall and of Grote.

In 1858 he entered on office as ordinary professor of History at Greifswald. In his published papers he discussed the Spartan Ephors, and the period between the Persian and Peloponnesian Wars; and, in connexion with his lectures, put forth an Outline of the original Authorities on Greek History ending with Polybius (1867), to which a second part, on the Roman Empire down to Justinian, was added in 1881. This outline is justly recognised as a most valuable introduction to the study of Ancient History.

In 1865 he was appointed professor of History at Bonn, devoting most of his time to lecturing, with admirable lucidity of style and attractiveness of manner, on Ancient History down to the end of the Western Empire. In the address which he delivered as Rector in 1871, he traced the influence of the study of the ancient world on the critical study of History, in and after the days of Niebuhr.

His History of the Seven Years' War, founded on the Prussian Archives and on those in the British Museum, and inspired by a

[1] *Das anmutige stille Grimma* (Pref. to *Dem. u. s. Zeit*).

warm admiration of Frederick the Great and of William Pitt, was begun in 1867 and completed in 1874. In October of that year he started on a tour in Greece, Asia Minor, Syria and Egypt, taking Rome on his return in the following spring. His love of teaching led him to decline the honour of being Director of the Public Archives. In the spring of 1879 he visited Sicily and Rome; in 1880, Olympia and Athens; in 1881, Spain and Algiers. A severe attack of rheumatism during his return compelled him in the autumn to resort to Gastein, Baden, and the Isle of Wight. In November, 1882, the completion of the 25th year of his professorship was celebrated by the publication of a volume of historical papers by nineteen of his former pupils. In 1883, after spending some weeks at San Sebastian, he returned with renewed strength to prepare the second edition of his historical work on Demosthenes. On November 19th, he lectured in the forenoon, attended a meeting of the Faculty in the evening, entertained some of his pupils at his house, was attacked by a sudden stroke of paralysis at midnight, and passed away by a painless death at an early hour of the following morning. He was remarkable for the depth and extent of his attainments, for his gift of lucid exposition, for the perfect harmony of his being, and the nobility of his character[1].

Many chronological points connected with the life and times of Demosthenes had already been minutely investigated[2] by a pupil of Niebuhr living in Berlin,—Karl Georg Böhnecke, who subsequently **Böhnecke** criticised[3] Schaefer's results. He maintained the genuineness of all the documents quoted in the Attic Orators, and only too often devoted his undoubted acumen and his wide reading to the elaborate support of untenable opinions[4].

Hypereides was discussed in three papers of 1837–46 by F. Gustav Kiessling (1809–84). The *editio princeps* of the Speech against Demosthenes (1850), and those For Lycophron and Euxenippus (1853), published in England by Churchill Babington, gave a new impulse **F. G. Kiessling** to the study of that long-lost orator. Of the literature thus produced in Germany it may suffice to mention Schneidewin's edition of the *Lycophron* and

---

[1] J. Asbach in *Bi r. Jahrb.* 1883, 32—40, and *Zur Erinnerung* (with portrait) 1895, 80 pp.; cp. Bursian, ii 913.

[2] *Forschungen* (1843).

[3] *Dem., Lykurgos, Hypereides, und ihr Zeitalter* (1864).

[4] Bursian, ii 914.

Euxenippus (1853), and Westermann's 'Index Verborum' to all three speeches (1859–64).

The History of Attic Eloquence was made the theme of an admirable historic survey by Friedrich Blass (1843

F. Blass

—1907). Born at Osnabrück and educated at the local *gymnasium* under B. R. Abeken (the author of *Cicero in seinen Briefen*), he studied at Göttingen under Sauppe, and at Bonn under Ritschl and Otto Jahn. After holding scholastic appointments in various parts of Germany, he distinguished himself as a classical professor at Kiel in 1876–92, and at Halle for the remaining fifteen years of his life.

A dissertation on the rhetorical treatises of Dionysius of Halicarnassus, written for his degree at Bonn in 1863, was the germ of his earliest substantial work, that on the history of Greek oratory from the age of Alexander to that of Augustus (1865). This was followed by the greatest of his works, the four volumes of *Die Attische Beredsamkeit* (1868–80), which attained a second edition in 1887–98. For the Teubner series he edited texts of all the Attic Orators except Lysias and Isaeus; he repeatedly revised Rehdantz' *Philippics*, and produced a school edition of the *De Corona*, and of eight of Plutarch's *Lives*. His critical texts of the Ἀθηναίων πολιτεία (1892) and of Bacchylides (1898) passed through several editions. His treatise on the pronunciation of Ancient Greek[1] and his Grammar of New Testament Greek were translated into English; and he produced a carefully revised edition of the first half of Kühner's *Greek Grammar*, and critical editions of the two works of St Luke, besides writing on the 'Philology of the Gospels' and the 'Criticism of the New Testament'. In the interval between his two works on the Rhythm of Greek Prose[2], he published a sober and sensible treatise on Interpolations in the *Odyssey* (1904), in which the Peisistratean edition of the Homeric poems is frankly denounced as 'an absurd legend'. His latest works were his commentaries on the *Choëphoroe* (1906) and the *Eumenides* (1907).

He held that the rhythm of artistic prose (in Latin as well as in Greek) depended on the symmetrical correspondence between the clauses *within* the period, and not solely on the metrical value of the last few syllables of the sentence; and he applied this principle to the text of the Ἀθηναίων πολιτεία, as well as to that of Demosthenes. In the latter he assigned a perhaps exaggerated importance to the evidence derived from citations and imitations, and also to the law of composition, whereby Demosthenes, so far as possible,

---

[1] 1870 etc.; E. T. of ed. 3 by W. J. Purton (Cambridge, 1890).

[2] (1) *Rhythmen der Attischen Kunstprosa* (1901); (2) *Die Rhythmen der Asianischen und Römischen Kunstprosa* (1905), noticed by J. E. Sandys in *Cl. Rev.* xxi (1907), 85 f.

avoids the juxtaposition of three or more short syllables[1]. His published
works frequently brought him into friendly relations with English scholars.
In 1879 he was the guest of the editor of the *editio princeps* of Hypereides,
Churchill Babington; in that year, and again, many years later, he visited
Cambridge, while, in London and Oxford, and in Dublin (where he received
an honorary degree in 1892), he repeatedly gave proof of his remarkable skill
in deciphering and identifying the fragments of Greek *papyri* and in restoring
the *lacunae* in the Ἀθηναίων πολιτεία and in Bacchylides. One of the most
modest and most unselfish of men, he was ever ready to place the results of his
learning and of his acumen at the service of others[2].

From the scholars who studied the Attic Orators we turn to
the exponents of Greek philosophy. Histories of
Greek and Roman Philosophy (1835–66), and of
Brandis
the influence of Greek Philosophy under the Roman Empire
(1862–4), were published by Christian August Brandis (1790—
1867), who was born at Hildesheim, studied at Kiel and Göttingen, was privat-docent at Copenhagen in 1813, secretary to the
Prussian Embassy in Rome in 1816, and (with the exception of
two years at the court of king Otho in Greece, 1837-8) professor
at Bonn from 1821 to his death in 1867. His earlier works
included a treatise on the Eleatic philosophers (1813), and an
edition of the *Metaphysics* of Aristotle and Theophrastus, with the
ancient *scholia* (1823–37). He afterwards edited the *scholia* for
the Berlin Aristotle[3].

Eduard Zeller, who was born in Württemberg in 1814, and
studied at Tübingen and Berlin, was successively
professor at Bern, Marburg, and Heidelberg (1862–
Zeller
72), and since that date at Berlin. The first edition of his well-
known History of Greek Philosophy in three large octavo volumes
(1844–52) was begun while he was a privat-docent in Theology at
Tübingen, and was finished while he was professor of Philosophy
at Marburg.

---

[1] Cp. Demosthenes, *First Phil. and Olynthiacs*, ed. Sandys, pp. lxxii–iv.

[2] J. E. Sandys in *Cl. Rev.* xxi (1907), 75 f; cp. J. P. M(ahaffy) in *Athenaeum*, 16 March, 1907. Complete bibliography in preparation by H. Reinhold of Halle.

[3] E. Curtius in Göttingen *Nachrichten*, 1867, 552; Trendelenburg's *Vortrag*,
Berlin Acad., 1868. His portrait is included in the monument in memory of
the Emperor Friedrich III at Köln.

The History of Greek and Roman Philosophy *ex fontium locis contexta* was first published with notes in 1838 by
Ritter
and
Preller Heinrich Ritter (1791—1869) and Ludwig Preller (1809—1861)[1]. The work was begun while both were still at Kiel, and was published when Ritter was already professor at Göttingen, and Preller was leaving for Dorpat, where he stayed for a year only, previous to his appointment at Jena. For the last fourteen years of his life, he was librarian at the neighbouring Court of Weimar. Preller's earlier works included the Fragments of the traveller Polemon (1838). He is well known as the author of standard works on Greek and Roman Mythology (1854–8)[2].

Adolf Trendelenburg (1802—1872), who was born and bred at Eutin, studied at Kiel, Leipzig, and Berlin, where
Trendelenburg he became a full professor in 1837. His earliest work, on Plato's doctrine of ideas and numbers, as illustrated from Aristotle (1826), was followed by his edition of the *De Anima*, his treatise on the *Categories* (1833), and his Elements of Aristotelian Logic (1826)[3]. His 'Historical contributions to Philosophy' were published in three volumes in 1846–7, and his minor works in two (1871)[4]. Franz Biese, a school-
Biese
Schwegler
Waitz master at Putbus, produced in 1834–42 the two volumes of his comprehensive work on the Philosophy of Aristotle; Albert Schwegler (1819—1857), professor at Tübingen, edited the *Metaphysics* in 1847–8, and also made his mark by his History of Rome (1853–8), and his History of Greek Philosophy (1859)[5]; while Theodor Waitz (1821—1864), who was born at Gotha, and studied at Leipzig and Jena, and taught at Marburg for the last twenty years of his life, produced an excellent edition of the *Organon* (1844–5). The *Ethics* were edited in 1820 by the versatile Karl Zell (1793—1873) and in 1878 by G. Ramsauer.

The able Aristotelian, Hermann Bonitz (1814—1888), was

---

[1] Ed. 7, 1888.

[2] Ed. 4, Carl Robert, 1887–94; *Ausgewählte Aufsätze*, 1864. Stichling, *Gedächtnissrede*, 1863.   [3] Ed. 8, 1878.

[4] Bonitz, *Zur Erinnerung*, Berlin Abhandlung, 1872; Bratuschek (with photograph), 1872; Prantl, *Gedächtnissrede*, 1873.

[5] Teuffel, *Studien* (1871), no. 24.

educated under Ilgen at Schulpforta, and studied at Leipzig under Hermann and Hartenstein, and in Berlin under Boeckh and Lachmann. For thirteen years **Bonitz** he was a schoolmaster at Dresden, Berlin, and Stettin; for eighteen a professor in Vienna (1849–67), after which he returned to Berlin as Director of the School 'am Grauen Kloster'.

At Hartenstein's first course of lectures at Leipzig, only three students appeared, and it was solely owing to a fourth presenting himself in the person of young Bonitz, that the course was given at all. This event had an important effect on the future career of that student; for it was through Hartenstein's giving the Austrian minister, Exner, in 1842, a letter of introduction to Bonitz,—his only acquaintance in Berlin, that the latter ultimately accepted an invitation to hold office in Vienna, and to reform the educational system of Austria.

In his earliest work, the 'two Platonic disputations' of 1837[1], he gave proof of independence of view, by maintaining that Plato's opinions were not always consistent. He returned to Plato in his 'Platonic Studies' of 1858–60[2]. Schleiermacher's attempt to deduce a comprehensive scheme of Plato's teaching from the dialogues as a whole was attacked by K. F. Hermann and by Bonitz, who laid stress on the gradual growth and developement of the philosopher's opinions.

After thirteen years of scholastic work in Germany, he accepted in 1849 an invitation to fill the Chair of Classical Philology in Vienna, and to aid in the reorganisation of the schools and universities of Austria. In 1854 his scheme came into force, and the consequent recognition of Natural Science, as an educational instrument by the side of Classics, was the work of a classical scholar. As professor, he lectured on Sophocles, and on Greek Public Antiquities, as well as on Plato and Aristotle. The lectures were well attended, and the students crowded to his house for advice and guidance on all manner of subjects. His popular lecture on the origin of the Homeric poems is described as an excellent specimen of his manner of teaching[3]. His suggestions

---

[1] (1) *De Platonis idea boni*; (2) *De animae mundanae apud Platonem elementis.*

[2] Ed. 2, 1875; ed. 3, 1886.

[3] 1860; ed. 5, 1881.

on Thucydides (1854) were nearly all of them accepted in Krüger's second edition. In those on Sophocles (1856–7) he aimed at restricting the extent to which Schneidewin had seen 'tragic irony' in the plays of that poet.

Meanwhile his studies on Plato were being continued, those on Aristotle were attaining their ultimate maturity, and his vast *Index Aristotelicus* slowly approaching completion. After 1866, when Austria came into conflict with Prussia, Bonitz left the land of his adoption for the land of his birth. He accepted the Directorship of an important school in Berlin; and it was there that, in 1870, he completed his *Index Aristotelicus*, a work justly eulogised by Haupt in Berlin[1] and by Vahlen in Vienna[2]. It marked for Bonitz the close of a long series of labours connected with Aristotle. Those labours had begun with his critical observations on the *Metaphysics* (1842), *Magna Moralia* and *Eudemian Ethics* (1844), and had been continued in his edition of the commentary of Alexander of Aphrodisias on the *Metaphysics* (1847), and in his own commentary (1848–9). His work on Aristotle, interrupted for a time by his transfer to Vienna, bore its ripest fruits in the five parts of his 'Aristotelian Studies' (1862–7), which had been preceded by his treatise on the *Categories* (1853). His dream of a new edition of the text of Aristotle remained unfulfilled owing to the pressure of official duties at Berlin. He was undoubtedly one of the greatest scholars of his age. He was in fact a perfect master of that province of classical learning, which includes Greek philology and Greek philosophy[3].

Jacob Bernays (1824—1881), the son of a Jewish Rabbi, was born and bred at Hamburg, and studied at Bonn in 1844–8 under Ritschl and Brandis. After spending thirteen years at Breslau as a classical professor in a Jewish seminary, and as a teacher in the university (1853–66), he returned to Bonn, where he was university librarian and 'extraordinary' professor for the remaining fifteen years of his life.

Bernays

During the earlier of the two periods of his life at Bonn, he

---

[1] *Opusc.* iii 268.   [2] *Zeitschr. f. d. österr. Gymn.* 1872, 532.
[3] Gomperz in *Biogr. Jahrb.* 1888, 53—100 (with bibliography, 91—100); cp. Karl Schenkl's *Rede* (1888); Bellermann's *Vortrag*, and von Hartel's *Vortrag* (1889); Paulsen, ii 475 f, 563 f, 574 f; Bursian, ii 923 f.

obtained the degree of Doctor by producing the first part of his important work on Heraclitus (1848)[1]. He had already written a prize essay on Lucretius (1846), and, as a 'privat-docent', he lectured on that poet and on the introduction of Greek philosophy into Rome, and, subsequently, on the literature of the Epicureans and Stoics. His lectures on the Speeches in Thucydides included a survey of Greek History and Greek Rhetoric, and there were similar surveys in his lectures on Cicero's *Letters* and Aristotle's *Politics*. In 1852 he published an excellent text of Lucretius.

After leaving Bonn for Breslau, he produced his classic work on Scaliger[2], his paper assigning the authorship of the *Phocylidea* to a Jew of Alexandria[3], and his celebrated treatise on 'Aristotle's lost discussion of the effects of Tragedy' (1857)[4]. In the latter he maintained that, by κάθαρσις, Aristotle meant, not a *purification*, but a *purgation* of the emotions of fear and of pity. His reputation was greatly enhanced by this treatise and by the controversy that ensued[5].

Meanwhile in 1852 he had been invited to England by Bunsen, who was eager for aid in his Biblical researches. The result of this visit was an *epistola critica* containing a new instalment of his Heracleitean studies[6]. It was at this time that he gained the friendship of Max Müller and of Mark Pattison. To Max Müller he dedicated his work on the Chronicles of Sulpicius Severus, published in 1861 as a contribution to Classical and Biblical study[7]; to Pattison, his important treatise on the Dialogues of Aristotle in relation to his other works (1863)[8]. His subsequent work on Theophrastus' treatise *On Piety* (1866) is described by himself as 'a contribution to the history of religion', with critical and explanatory remarks on Porphyry's treatise *On Abstinence*[9].

---

[1] Cp. *Rhein. Mus.* 1849.   [2] 1855; Gomperz, *Essays, etc.*, 117 f.

[3] 1856; *Ges. Abh.* i 192—261.

[4] Reprinted in *Zwei Abhandlungen* (1880).

[5] Bernays had been anticipated by Weil (1847). Spengel's attempt of 1858 to support Lessing's interpretation was refuted by Bernays. See also Gomperz, *l.c.*, 118—122.

[6] Appendix to part iii of Bunsen's *Analecta Antenicaena* (1854); cp. *Rhein. Mus.* 1853.

[7] Gomperz, *Essays, etc.*, 115-7.   [8] Gomperz, *l.c.*, 123 f.

[9] περὶ ἀποχῆς ἐμψύχων.

Imbedded in Porphyry he identified important fragments of the lost work of Theophrastus, besides analysing the treatise, and adding instructive comments on the most varied points of ancient philosophy and on the history of religion and literature. The work was dedicated to the Berlin Academy.

On his return to Bonn (1866), in addition to his earlier courses of lectures, he discoursed on the Pre-Socratic Philosophy, on Suetonius' *Life of Augustus*, and on the History of Philology from the sixteenth to the nineteenth centuries[1]. It was these last lectures, and those on Plato, that proved the most popular; those on Aristotle were less well attended, owing to the high standard of work exacted by the lecturer. During the same period he published his treatise 'on the Heracleitean Letters', a contribution to the literature of philosophy and of the history of religion[2]; and a translation of the first three Books of Aristotle's *Politics*, with more than a hundred suggestions for the correction of the text, as well as explanatory comments intended for the general public (1872). In 1876 he presented to the Berlin Academy the text of the Pseudo-Platonic treatise 'on the indestructibility of the world', the order of which he had restored by detecting in 1863 that certain pages had been misplaced. This was followed by a brief and interesting pamphlet protesting against Lucian's unfair treatment of the Cynics (1879)[3]. In the following year he republished his two papers on Aristotle's 'Theory of the Drama'; and shortly before his death, he completed a work on 'Phocion and his recent critics' (1881)[4]. Meanwhile he had produced a large number of articles on Heracleitus and Aristotle, and on Lucretius, Horace, and Cicero. His published works give proof of a wide range of interests, and a rare combination of great critical acumen and profound philosophic insight. Towards the end of his brief life he was contemplating extensive monographs on Gibbon, on the Prophet Jeremiah, and on Erasmus; a new edition of his 'Scaliger', and a comprehensive statement of his

[1] He published articles on Politian and Georgius Valla, on Scaliger, and on the *Correspondence* of Bentley (*Biogr. Jahrb.* 1881, 80).

[2] 1869; cp. Gomperz, *Essays, etc.*, 111–3.   [3] *ib.* 113–5.

[4] *ib.* 124. Criticised by Gomperz, in *Wiener Studien*, iv, *Die Akademie und ihr vermeintlicher Philomacedonismus*.

views on all the writings of Aristotle. It was at his instance that the Berlin Academy began the publication of the Greek commentators on Aristotle; he was also eager for the publication of the works of the Neo-Platonists, and for the preparation of a lexicon of Greek philosophy. In German literature his favourite authors were Lessing and Goethe. As a strict Jew, he saw nothing of general society, but he had a high capacity for friendship, and a wide circle of scholarly correspondents. He died in the faith of his fathers and was buried in the cemetery of his community at Bonn, after bequeathing to the university library a complete collection of his works, including all his *Scaligerana*[1].

The Jew and the Greek were united in the person of Bernays, who was at once a strictly orthodox Jew, and a devoted adherent of Hellenic culture[2]. To Bernays 'Philology' was always the handmaid of History, and History the servant of practical life. Like his great exemplar, Scaliger, he never published lists of emendations, or programs on microscopic points, preferring to deal with each successive theme of his choice as a complete and historic whole[3].

Gustav Teichmüller (1832—1888), who was born at Brunswick, studied under Trendelenburg and others at Berlin. After holding a scholastic appointment for four years at St Petersburg, he **Teichmüller** was a professor at Göttingen and Basel, and, for the last seventeen years of his life, at Dorpat. Up to the age of forty, his work had been mainly limited to investigations of the Aristotelian philosophy on the lines of Trendelenburg. In this spirit he had already published the first two volumes of his 'Aristotelian Researches'[4]. His call to Dorpat was the beginning of a new departure marked by the third volume[5]. In his subsequent 'Studies' he traced the history of philosophical conceptions from Thales to Plato and Aristotle, and dealt with the influence of the Greek philosophers on the Fathers, and finally on Spinoza, Kant, and Hegel[6]. The study of Plato now took a more prominent place in his interests, he came into controversy with Zeller and others, and was led to investigate the Chronology of the Platonic Dialogues (1879), and the 'Literary Feuds of the Fourth Century B.C.' (1881–4). He regarded the

---

[1] Schaarschmidt, in *Biogr. Jahrb.* 1882, 65—83 ; cp. Bücheler, in *Rhein. Mus.* xxxvi 479 f, Bursian, ii 845 n., and Gomperz, *Essays etc.*, 106—125.

[2] Gomperz, *l.c.*, 109.   [3] *ib.* 108 f.

[4] *Poetik* (1867), *Kunst* (1869).

[5] *Gesch. des Begriffs der Parusie* (1873).

[6] *Studien zur Gesch. der Begriffe*, 1874 ; 1876-9.

Dialogues as a series of manifestos, the date of which was to be determined by polemical references to Xenophon, Lysias, and Isocrates, as well as Aristophanes and even Aristotle himself. The first of the two volumes on this theme was unfavourably reviewed by Susemihl and by Blass[1].

The eminent Aristotelian, Leonhard Spengel (1803—1880),

Spengel

who was educated under Thiersch at Munich, studied under Hermann at Leipzig, and Boeckh and Bekker in Berlin, and was on the staff of the ' old *gymnasium* ' in Munich until 1835, when he became a professor in the university. After an interval (1841-7), during which he held a professorship at Heidelberg, he returned to Munich, where he occupied a similar position for the last thirty-three years of his life. His early edition of Varro, *De Lingua Latina* (1826), was followed by a survey of the history of Greek Rhetoric down to the time of Aristotle[2]. In the year of his temporary departure from Munich, he delivered an academic address ' on the study of Rhetoric among the Ancients' (1841), and in that of his return, he edited the *Rhetorica ad Alexandrum* (1847), which (like Victorius) he assigned to Anaximenes. He also published a text of the *Rhetores Graeci* (1853-6), and an important edition of Aristotle's *Rhetoric* with the old Latin translation and with a full commentary (1867). In the Transactions of the Munich Academy he traced the indications of rhetorical artifice in the Public Speeches of Demosthenes[3], and also criticised the *Poetic*, the *Ethics*, *Politics*, *Oeconomics*, and *Physics* of Aristotle[4].

His younger contemporary, Carl Prantl (1820—1888), a pupil

Prantl

of Thiersch and Spengel in Munich, studied for a time in Berlin. He was on the staff of the university of Munich from 1843 to the end of his life, having been full professor of Philology from 1859, and of Philosophy from 1864. His first publication was a dissertation on Aristotle's *Historia*

[1] Bursian's *Jahresb.* xxx 1 and 234. *Biogr. Jahrb.* 1888, 7—17.

[2] Συναγωγὴ τεχνῶν, sive artium scriptores ab initiis usque ad editos Aristotelis de rhetorica libros, 1828, 230 pp.,—still a leading authority on this subject.

[3] *Abhandl.* ix (1) (2), and x (1).

[4] A. Spengel in *Biogr. Jahrb.* 1880, 35—59; W. v. Christ, *Gedächtnissrede*, Munich Acad. (1881); Bursian, ii 736, 915, 924; Thurot, *Rev. de Philol.* v 181—190.

Animalium (1843). His early career was embittered by bigoted attacks on his philosophical opinions; and at the age of thirty-three his objections to a 'confessional philosophy' led to his finding himself forbidden to lecture on philosophical subjects. Instead of discoursing (as heretofore) on Logic and the History of Philosophy, he was only allowed to deal with the safer topics of the Greek Tragic Poets (1852), and the 'Encyclopaedia of Philology' (1855). In 1864, however, he was expressly appointed professor of Philosophy, and thenceforth he was neither attacked nor otherwise hindered in respect to the subjects of his lectures. His principal course on Logic and the general survey of Philosophy was attended by more than 200 students from all Faculties.

Meanwhile, he had devoted his enforced leisure to beginning the main work of his life:—the four volumes of his celebrated 'History of the Study of Logic in the West' (1855–70), beginning with Aristotle and ending with the year 1534. He also published a Survey of Greek and Roman Philosophy[1], and translations of Plato's *Phaedo, Phaedrus, Symposium, Republic,* and *Apology,* and of Aristotle's *De coloribus, Physics,* and *De Caelo* etc., besides Greek texts of those treatises. But his interests were far from being confined to Philosophy and Philology; he was a *Polyhistor* in the best sense of the term. His published works include university history, and biography, and a long series of reviews[2].

Franz Susemihl (1826—1901), who was born in Mecklenburg, and studied at Leipzig and Berlin, settled in 1850 at Greifswald, where he was full professor of Classi- Susemihl
cal Philology from 1863 to the date of his death. Besides writing an important work on the developement of Plato's philosophy[3], he contributed to the Classical Journals many papers on Plato and Aristotle. He is still better known through his edition and translation of Aristotle's *Poetic*[4], and his three editions of the *Politics,* (1) the critical edition with the old Latin translation of William of Moerbeke (1872), (2) the Greek and German edition

---

[1] 1854; new ed. 1863.

[2] Bibliography in *Almanach* of the Munich Academy, 1888, continued in Christ's *Gedächtnissrede*, 45—48. Cp. K. Meiser in *Biog. Jahrb.* 1889, 1—14.

[3] *Die genetische Entwickelung der Platonischen Philosophie* (1855–60).

[4] 1865; ed. 2, 1879.

with explanatory notes (1879)[1], and (3) the Teubner text of 1882. The main results of the seven parts of his *Quaestiones Criticae* on the *Politics* (1867–74) were summed up in a pamphlet of 128 pages published in 1886[2], showing that there were many *lacunae* in the text, and that the transposition of clauses and paragraphs was often necessary. He also produced a Teubner text of the *Ethics* (1887), in which, in common with other critics, he proposed many transpositions, especially in the fifth Book. Lastly, towards the end of his life, he published a full and minute History of Greek Literature in the Alexandrian Age (1891–2).

The historical and political purport of the *Politics* was the theme of an important work published in 1870–5 Oncken by Wilhelm Oncken (1838—1905)[3], who studied at his native place, Heidelberg, and at Göttingen ; and, after spending eight years as a teacher at Heidelberg, was professor of History at Giessen for the last thirty-five years of his life. He was a member of the German Imperial Parliament in 1874–6, and organised an important series of historical works, to which he contributed three volumes on Modern History. His paper on the Revival of Greek Literature in Italy forms an interesting page in the History of Scholarship[4].

Aristotle, *De Anima*, was edited in 1862 by Adolph Torstrik, who was a master in the Bremen *gymnasium* until Torstrik his death in 1877. The Fragments of the lost Heitz Rose works were carefully collected and elaborately discussed by Emil Heitz (1825—1890) who was a professor at the university of his native place, Strassburg[5]; and by Valentin Rose, who studied at Bonn as well as in Berlin, the place of his birth (1825), and has been on the staff of the Royal Library in Berlin since 1855[6].

---

[1] Books I—V have been edited in English with introduction, analysis, and commentary by Susemihl and R. D. Hicks (1894).

[2] Extract from *Jahrb. f. cl. Philol.* Suppl. xv.

[3] *Die Staatslehre des Ar. in historisch-politischen Umrissen*, preceded by *Isocrates u. Athen* (1862), and *Hellas u. Athen* (1865-6).

[4] *Verhandlungen der* xxiii *Philologenversammlung*, 1865.

[5] *Die verlorenen Schriften des Ar.* (1865).

[6] *De Aristotelis librorum ordine et auctoritate* (1854) ; *Aristoteles pseudepi-*

Friedrich Ueberweg (1826—1871) studied at Göttingen and Berlin, began his professorial career at Bonn, and was professor at Königsberg from 1862 to the end Ueberweg of his life. He was the author of a prize dissertation on the genuineness and the chronology of the Platonic writings[1], and an editor and translator of Aristotle's *Poetic* (1875). Ancient Philosophy is the theme of the first volume of his valuable *Grundriss* of the History of Philosophy (1862–6),—a volume, which, in its eighth edition, has been revised by Heinze (1894).

The Greek Rhetoricians were edited by Ernst Christian Walz (1802—1857), who was educated at Tübingen, where he was appointed 'extraordinary' and 'or- Walz dinary' professor in 1832 and 1836 respectively. The former date marks the beginning and the latter the end of the nine volumes of his *Rhetores Graeci*, a series including many works then printed for the first time. He also wrote archaeological and mythological articles for Pauly's Encyclopaedia, and, in 1838-9, was joint editor of Pausanias with Heinrich Christian Schubart (1800—1885), who afterwards produced the Teubner text of 1852–4. Schubart, who was born at Marburg and studied at Heidelberg, travelled in Italy and Sicily, Schubart and was for 47 years librarian at Cassel[2]. Spengel's edition of the most important of the *Rhetores Graeci*, and his other works on ancient Rhetoric, have been already mentioned[3].

A systematic conspectus of Greek and Roman Rhetoric[4] was produced by Richard Volkmann (1832—1892), who studied under Bernhardy at Halle, and, after hold- Volkmann ing minor scholastic appointments, was Director of the *gymnasium* at Jauer from 1865 to his death. Besides editing Plutarch's treatise on Music, he wrote an interesting monograph on its author, as the precursor of Neo-Platonism. Two of his main interests were the study of Neo-Platonism and of Epic Poetry.

---

graphus (1863); *Aristotelis qui ferebantur librorum fragmenta*, printed 1867, published in vol. v of Berlin Ar. (1870), and in Teubner text (1886).

[1] Wien, 1861.

[2] *Biogr. Jahrb.* 1885, 89—95. [3] p. 180 *supra*.

[4] 1872-4; ed. 2, 1885; also a summary in Iwan Müller's *Handbuch* ii, ed. 2, 637—676.

The former is represented in his admirable work on Synesius of Cyrene, and his Teubner text of Plotinus; the latter, in his early dissertation on Nicander, his papers on Ancient Oracles in hexameter verse (1853–8), his *Commentationes Epicae*, and his critical survey of the influence of Wolf's *Prolegomena* (1874)[1].

The Religion, Philosophy, and Rhetoric of the Greeks were only a part of the wide field of learning traversed by Hermann Usener (1834—1905), who studied at Heidelberg, Munich, Göttingen, and Bonn, where he was professor for the last thirty-nine years of his life. The breadth of his erudition is attested by writings on the most varied themes, beginning with Homer[2], and even including Byzantine Astronomy[3], and the *scholia* on Horace and Lucan. Among his works were the *Quaestiones Anaximeneae* (1856), and the *Analecta Theophrastea* (1858). In the latter year, in conjunction with his friend, F. Bücheler, and five other scholars in Bonn, he produced an improved edition of the *Annals* of Granius Licinianus. He published editions of the *scholia* on Aristotle by Alexander of Aphrodisias and Syrianus, and of the rhetorical works of Dionysius of Halicarnassus, viz. (1) the treatise *De Imitatione*, and (2) a critical text of the whole, in conjunction with Radermacher. His *Epicurea* is a critical collection of all the ancient authorities on Epicurus, with an elaborate introduction and excellent *indices*[4]. He also wrote on the text of Plato[5], and on the history of Greek and Roman Grammar[6]; on ancient Greek metre[7], and on Greek cycles[8]; on the names of the gods[9], on the mythology of the old Greek epic[10], on the History of Religion[11], and on the legends of

---

[1] *Geschichte und Kritik der Wolfschen Prolegomena zu Homer*, 364 pp. 1874. Cp. *Biogr. Jahrb.* 1892, 81—103.

[2] *De Iliadis carmine quodam Phocaico* (1875).

[3] *Ad historiam astronomiae symbola* (1876); *De Stephano Alex.* (1880).

[4] Leipzig, 1887.

[5] *Unser Platotext*, in *Göttingen Nachr.* 1892, 25—50, 181—215.

[6] *Ein altes Lehrgebäude der Philologie*, in *S.-Ber.* of Munich Acad. 1892, 582—648.

[7] *Altgriechischer Versbau* (1887).

[8] *Gr. Oktaëteris* in *Rhein. Mus.* xxxiv 388 f.

[9] *Gr. Götternamen*, 1896.

[10] *Gr. Epos*, in *S. Ber.* Vienna Acad. 1897.

[11] See (*inter alia*) *Comm. in honorem Mommseni* (1877), *Sinflutsagen* (1899),

certain Saints[1]. His *Anecdoton Holderi* (1877) threw light on Cassiodorus and Boëthius, and the Roman chronology is illustrated by his edition of the *laterculi imperatorum Romanorum Graeci*. Some of the ablest scholars of Germany passed through his *Seminar*, and the high ideal kept in view in his life and in his works has been eloquently set forth by his colleague, Bücheler[2].

Polybius was edited in 1867–72 by Friedrich Otto Hultsch (1833—1906), who was born and bred in Dresden, where he was appointed Rector of his old school, after studying in Leipzig. His high   **Hultsch** mathematical ability was exemplified in his careful editions of Heron and Pappus (1876–8), and in his important work on Greek and Roman Metrology[3].

The text of the 'Roman Archaeology' of Dionysius of Halicarnassus was edited in 1860–70 by Adolph Kiessling (1837—1893), who studied at Bonn, and   **A. Kiessling** was a professor at Greifswald and at Strassburg. He produced several valuable papers on Plautus and Horace[4], and was associated with Rudolph Schöll in the joint edition of the commentary of Asconius on Five Speeches of Cicero (1875).

Lucian was edited in 1822–31 by Johann Gottlieb Lehmann (1782—1837), Director of the *gymnasium* at Luckau, and in 1836–41, and   **Lehmann** 1852–3, by Karl Gottfried Jacobitz (1807—1875), while   **Jacobitz** F. V. Fritzsche (1806—1887[5], editor of the *Thesmopho-*   **F. V. Fritzsche** *riazusae* and *Ranae* of Aristophanes) produced, in 1860–82,   **Sommerbrodt** three volumes of an elaborate critical edition, and Julius Wilhelm Sommerbrodt (1813—1903) edited selections with excellent German notes and published the readings of the Venice MSS, besides writing valuable papers on the Antiquities of the Greek Theatre[6]. His critical edition of Lucian was completed in 1899.

The text of the Greek Novelists[7] was edited by a Member of the Berlin Academy, Rudolph Hercher (1821—1878), who also edited   **Hercher** the Greek *Epistolographi*, with the minor works of Arrian,

---

Dreiheit (1903), and *Weihnachtsfest* (1889); and cp. *Archiv f. Religionswissenschaft*, 1905.   [1] S. Pelagia, S. Marina, S. Theodosius.

[2] *Neue Jahrb. f. kl. Alt.* 1905, 737—742 (with portrait); also Wendland in *Preuss. Jahrb.* 1905, 373 f; Dieterich, in *Archiv f. Religionswiss.* 1906, i—xi ; E. Schwartz, *Rede* (Berlin, 1906); Otto Kern, *Rede* (Rostock, 1906), 8—10; Usener's *Vorträge und Aufsätze*, 1907.

[3] 1862; ed. 2, 1882; F. Rudio's *Nachruf* at Basel *Philologen-Versammlung*, Sept. 1907.

[4] Bursian, ii 848, n. 1.   [5] *Biogr. Jahrb.* 1887, 99—101.

[6] 1876, *Scenica Collecta*.   [7] *Erotici Scriptores Graeci*, 1858-9.

Aelian, Aeneas Poliorceticus, and Apollodorus. Hercher was one of the founders of *Hermes*[1].

The History of the Greek Novel was admirably written in 1876 by Erwin Rohde (1845—1898), who was educated at Jena and Hamburg, and was a devoted admirer of the teaching of Ritschl at Bonn and Leipzig. At Leipzig, he and his friend, Nietzsche, combined an enthusiasm for riding with an intense interest in classical learning, and they scandalised the more normal students by coming in riding-costume to the classical lectures. Both alike were sworn foes of every form of pedantry. When the friends parted in 1867, Rohde went to complete his studies under Ritschl's future biographer, Ribbeck.

His literary career began with a paper on the *Lucius* of Lucian. It was continued by a dissertation on the authorities of Pollux on the Greek Theatre, by his History of the Greek Novel[2], a brilliant and masterly work (which was partly supplemented by a lecture at Rostock in the same year), and by his sketch of the later Sophists and of their connexion with Asianism[3]. He lectured with great success at Jena (1876) on Ancient Rhetoric, and at Tübingen (1878) on Greek Philosophy.

Next to the History of the Greek Novel, he attacked the problems connected with the growth of the ancient history of Greek literature. He proved that in the biographies preserved by Suïdas the term γέγονε must refer to the date when an author *flourished*, and not to the date of his birth[4]. His subsequent studies on the Chronology of Greek literary history[5] were models of their kind, and led to important results.

During his brief tenure of a professorship at Leipzig in 1886 he gave a course of lectures on Homer, and, in the same year, he was invited to Heidelberg. The third of his three main interests as a scholar, his interest in Greek Religion, was first displayed in his lecture on the Eleusinian Mysteries (1880). Its culminating point was reached in his *Psyche* (1891–4)[6], the most important work on the subject that had appeared since Lobeck's *Aglaophamus*, and far more popular in its method of treatment, and in its style. His main thesis was that the cult of souls was the most primitive stage of religious worship throughout the world, and that there was no reason for excepting the Greeks from this general rule. The apparent inconsistency of this cult with the Homeric theology was solved by an analysis of the earliest epics, showing in Homer, and still more in Hesiod, the existence of rudimentary survivals of a more ancient cult. The religion of the old Epics was thus put in a new light; and the Homeric theology stood out against the dark background of an earlier type of religion. Rohde's interest in the life of Creuzer, one of his predecessors at Heidelberg, was partly inspired by his own study of the history

---

[1] *Biogr. Jahrb.* 1878, 9 f.

[2] *Der griechische Roman und seine Vorläufer*, 1876; ed. 2, 1900.

[3] *Rhein. Mus.* xli (1886) 170 f.

[4] 1878–9; *Rhein. Mus.* xxxiii 161 f, 638; xxxiv 620.

[5] *ib.* xxxvi 380 f, 524 f.   [6] Ed. 2, 1897.

of religion, and led to his publishing a work which was a contribution to the History of Romance rather than to the History of Scholarship[1]. He lived to produce in 1897 a second edition of his *Psyche*, in which many additions were made to the notes. He died at the age of 53. The three stages of his literary life had been marked by the study of three historic problems connected with (1) the Greek Novel, (2) the Chronology of Greek Literature, and (3) Greek Religion. His treatment of all three was marked by thoroughness of research, and clearness of exposition[2].

The medical literature of Greece was criticised and expounded by Karl Gottlob Kühn (1754—1840) and Friedrich Reinhold Dietz (1804—1836), professors at Leipzig and Königsberg respec- **Kühn** tively. Kühn's edition of the Greek medical writers, published **Dietz** in 1821–30, extends to twenty-six volumes, including a Latin translation, with critical and exegetical commentary and indices. Galen alone fills twenty volumes, and the rest are devoted to Hippocrates, Aretaeus, and Dioscorides, this last being edited by Kurt Sprengel (1766—1833), professor of Medicine at Halle. Dietz, after editing 'Hippocrates on epilepsy' (1827), collated many medical MSS in foreign libraries, but did not live to make use of more than a small part of his collations, which are now preserved in the library at Königsberg. Another short-lived scholar, who was also an adept in Natural Science, was Julius Ludwig Ideler (1809—1842), who wrote on Greek and Roman Meteorology (1832), and edited Aristotle's *Me-* **Ideler** *teorologica* (1834–6), and the *Physici et Medici Graeci minores*[3].

---

[1] *Friedrich Creuzer u. Karoline v. Günderode* (1896).

[2] W. Schmid in *Biogr. Jahrb.* 1899, 87—114 (with bibliography); and biographical Essay by O. Crusius, 296 pp., with portrait (1902); also E. Weber in *Deutscher Nekrolog*, vi (1904) 450—465. *Kleine Schriften* in 2 vols., ed. Fr. Schöll, 1901.

[3] Bursian, ii 931 f.

CHAPTER XXXII.

EDITORS OF LATIN CLASSICS.

THE study of the Latin poets has already been represented by Lachmann, Haupt, and Ritschl[1]. Ritschl was
Ribbeck succeeded at Leipzig by one of the earliest of his
pupils, Otto Ribbeck (1827—1898), who studied in Berlin and
Bonn, and, on returning from a tour in Italy, held scholastic
appointments in Germany. After filling professorships at Bern
and Basel (1856–62), he was successively professor at Kiel
(1862–72), Heidelberg (1872–7), and Leipzig (1877–98).

His work was mainly limited to the history and the criticism
of the earlier Latin poets. He published an important collection
of the Fragments of the Latin Dramatists[2], as well as an edition
of the *Miles Gloriosus*, a work on Roman Tragedy in the age of
the Republic[3], and a valuable History of Roman Poetry in three
volumes[4]. He also published a comprehensive critical edition
of Virgil, in five volumes[5], as well as a smaller edition of the
text. His work on Virgil had been preceded by his text of
Juvenal[6], and was succeeded by his *Epistles* and *Ars Poëtica* of
Horace, in both of which he evinced an inordinate suspicion
of textual interpolations. His numerous minor papers included
an important treatise on Latin Particles (1869).

His study of the Latin dramatists led him to their Greek
originals. He accordingly published a lecture on the Middle
and the New Attic Comedy (1857), discussed Greek and Roman
Comedy in his *Alazon*, a work including his German rendering
of the *Miles Gloriosus* (1882), and wrote on the early cult of

---

[1] Chap. xxx. [2] 1852–5; ed. 2, 1871–3; ed. 3, 1897–8.
[3] 1875. [4] 1892, 1894².
[5] 1859–68, abridged ed. 1895.
[6] 1859. Cp. *Der echte und der unechte Juvenal* (1865).

Dionysus in Attica (1869). The story of his life has been partly told by the publication of his Letters, while his own Life of Ritschl is itself a monument of learning, enthusiasm, and good taste[1].

Lucian Müller (1836—1898) was educated at Berlin under Meineke, Moritz Seyffert, and Giesebrecht, and studied at the university of Berlin under Boeckh and Haupt, and at Halle under Bernhardy. After living for five years in Holland (mainly at Leyden), and for three at Bonn, he was appointed professor of Latin Literature at St Petersburg, where he worked for the remaining twenty-seven years of his life.

Lucian Müller

While he was still a student in Berlin, he produced a dissertation on the Latin abridgement of Homer bearing the name of Pindarus Thebanus. In 1861 he published his treatise *De re metrica*, on the prosody of all the Latin poets except Plautus and Terence, an original work of wide learning, which was only marred by a bitterly polemical spirit. A compendium of the same appeared in 1878, together with a summary of Latin orthography and prosody, followed by a text-book of Greek and Latin Metres[2]. His critical acumen was attested in his editions of Lucilius (1872) and Phaedrus, and in the Teubner texts of Horace, and of Catullus, Tibullus, and Propertius. In his edition of Horace he adhered closely to the MSS, while he admitted some of the best modern emendations, and assumed the existence of interpolations. He also edited the *Odes* and *Epodes* with German notes, and produced a text of Namatianus and Porfyrius, as well as papers on the Latin Grammarians, on the Tragedies of Seneca, and on the Latin Anthology. His edition of Lucilius was followed by a sketch of the life and work of that poet, ending with a restoration of a number of scenes from his *Satires* (1876). In 1884 he wrote a work on Ennius, and published the remains of Ennius, and the fragments of

---

[1] *Otto Ribbeck, Ein Bild seines Lebens aus seinen Briefen* (1846–98, mainly to relations and friends, including six to Ritschl), 352 pp. with two portraits by Paul Heyse (1901); *Reden und Vorträge*, 1899; cp. Bursian, ii 723, 840f; *Deutsche Rundschau* (Dec. 1898, W. Dilthey), (Feb. 1902, A. Hausrath).

[2] 1880; ed. 2, 1885; transl. into French, Italian, Dutch, and English.

Naevius' epic on the Punic War. In the following year he edited the fragments of the plays of Livius Andronicus and of Naevius, and published a work on the 'Saturnian Verse'. The fragments of the old Roman poets led him to Nonius, and he accordingly produced in 1888 an edition of that grammarian and lexicographer, extending over 1127 pages, the index alone filling 55. This led him to write a treatise on Pacuvius and Accius (1889 f), followed by two works of general interest on the artistic and the popular poetry of the Romans (1890). After that date he prepared three important works: (1) an enlarged edition of his *De re metrica* (1894); (2) an annotated edition of the *Satires* and *Epistles* of Horace for the use of scholars (1891–3); and (3) a similar edition of the *Odes* and *Epodes*, posthumously published in 1900. His 'Life of Horace' had appeared in 1880.

As a child, he had lost the sight of one of his eyes, and was very short-sighted ; as a boy, he repeatedly read through Zumpt's larger Latin Grammar and made himself the best Latinist in his school. During his brief experience as a school-master, he proved an ineffective disciplinarian ; his head-master, in the hope of improving the discipline of the boys, solemnly told them that they 'did not deserve to be taught by so learned a master', and repeated this remark to Müller, who replied, 'Yes ! that is exactly what I have told them myself'. He held that, for a great scholar, it was essential that he should have, not only wide learning and clear judgement, but also a strong power of concentration on a definite field of labour. It was this that led to his own success in the province of Latin poetry. But he was far from neglecting Greek, for he also held that, without Greek, a fruitful study of Latin was impossible. He was a skilful writer of Latin verse, and insisted on the practice of verse composition as a valuable aid towards the appreciation of the Latin poets. He was impressed with this fact during the preparation of his 'History of Classical Philology in the Netherlands' (1865), and he returned to the point in his biographical sketch of the life of Ritschl (1877–8), in the course of which he urged that it was, on the whole, more important for an eminent classical professor to train first-rate school-masters than to turn out classical specialists[1].

[1] *Biogr. Jahrb.* 1899, 63 –86 ; cp. Bursian, ii 934–6.

One of Lucian Müller's rivals as an editor of Latin poets was his former pupil at Bonn, Emil Baehrens (1848—1888). He owed much, not only to the teaching of L. Müller, but also to that of Jahn **Baehrens** and Usener; he afterwards studied for a year under Ritschl at Leipzig. In 1872 he visited the Italian libraries, remaining six months in Rome. In 1873 he settled for a time as 'privat-docent' at Jena, but in the next year he was already working in the libraries of Louvain, Brussels, and Paris, and, in 1875, in those of Paris, London, and Oxford. In 1877 he was appointed professor of Latin at Groningen, and, being unfamiliar with Dutch, delivered in Latin an inaugural address on the History of Scholarship from the Revival of Learning. He was professor at Groningen for the remaining eleven years of his life.

He began his literary career with a dissertation at Jena, on the Satire ascribed to Sulpicia. This was followed by his *Analecta Catulliana*, and his editions of the *Panegyrici Latini* and Valerius Flaccus; his text of and commentary on Catullus (1876—1885); and his editions of the *Silvae* of Statius, and of Tibullus. In 1878 he produced his *Miscellanea Critica*, a little-known volume of 200 pages including emendations on Q. Cicero, Propertius, Horace's *Ars Poëtica*, and the *Agricola* of Tacitus. His principal work was his edition of the *Poëtae Latini Minores* in five volumes (1879—1883). In the laborious preparation of this work he examined more than 1000 MSS. It was supplemented by his *Fragmenta Poëtarum Romanorum* (1886). Meanwhile, he was editing Propertius, and the *Dialogus* of Tacitus, proposing as many as 125 conjectures in the 42 chapters of that work, and, lastly, a text of his favourite Classic, the *Octavius* of Minucius Felix. The mere titles of all that he produced in the last eighteen years of his life would fill four and a half pages of print.

He was a most industrious scholar, and an excellent teacher, especially in the case of the more diligent students; and he did much to improve the pronunciation of Latin in Holland. But many of his works were marred by over-haste. He saw one of the principal MSS of Catullus for the first time in March, and the other in May, and completed his edition of the text in September. Similarly, the Commentary, for which he had long been making collections, was prepared for the press in less than eleven months. Among his other defects were an exaggerated self-assertion, and an unduly polemical spirit. He excluded himself from society, and accordingly did not know how to 'give and take'. In his Commentary on Catullus, as well as in his criticisms of the Roman renderings of Aratus, he very seldom quotes from the Alexandrian poets,—an omission which has been attributed to a very superficial knowledge of Greek[1].

For the textual criticism of Terence a firm foundation was laid in 1870 by the critical edition prepared by Franz Umpfenbach (1835—1885), who, after studying at his **Umpfenbach** native place, Giessen, and also at Göttingen under K. F. Hermann,

---

[1] Halbertsma in *Biogr. Jahrb.* 1890, 7—46; cp. Bursian, ii 936-8.

at Bonn under Ritschl, and in Berlin under Boeckh, spent
two years in Italy collating the MSS of Terence (1863–5). He
began by publishing all the *scholia* of the Bembine MS, during
his five years' stay in Munich[1].

The expenses of his seven years' preparation for his edition
made it necessary for him to take school-work for three years at
Frankfurt, followed by eleven years of similar work at Mainz.
A man of good breeding and good manners, he found his later
years clouded by his failure to obtain any university appointment,
and by his increasing deafness. In the end his brain was
touched, and his powers of speech failed him[2].

Tibullus is the poet specially associated with the name
of Eduard Hiller (1844—1891), who was educated
under Classen at Frankfurt, and studied under Ritschl
Hiller
and Jahn at Bonn, and under Sauppe and E. Curtius at Göttingen.
He was a 'privat-docent' at Bonn (1869–74), and a professor
at Greifswald (1874–6) and Halle (1876–91). His early work
was connected with the Greek Grammarians, and Eratosthenes;
he also prepared a new edition of Fritzsche's *Theocritus* and of
Bergk's *Poetae Lyrici*, as well as an *Anthologia Lyrica*. He
edited Tibullus in the Teubner texts, and in Dr Postgate's *Corpus
Poëtarum Latinorum* (1890)[3].

Among the successors of Haupt and Ribbeck, as editors of Virgil, mention
may here be made of Philipp Wagner (1794—1873) who
P. Wagner
brought out a new edition of Heyne's Virgil, followed by a
brief commentary. A commentary, followed by a critical text, was published
by Theodor Ladewig (1812—1878). An excellent Latin com-
Ladewig
Gossrau
mentary on the *Aeneid* alone was first produced in 1846 by
Gottfried Wilhelm Gossrau (1810—1888), who was educated
at Schulpforta, studied at Halle, and was a teacher at Quedlinburg from 1835
to 1875. One of the best of his other works was his *Lateinische Sprachlehre*[4].

The editors of the text of Horace fall into three groups,
characterised as (1) conservatives, (2) more or less
Keller
and Holder
moderate liberals, and (3) radicals. The first group
is represented by Otto Keller (b. 1838), now professor at Prag, and by Alfred Holder (b. 1840), librarian at

[1] *Hermes*, ii 337—402.   [2] *Biogr. Jahrb.* 1886, 1—10.

[3] *Biogr. Jahrb.* 1891, 83—113.

[4] 1869; ed. 2, 1880. *Biogr. Jahrb.* 1888, 107—118.

Karlsruhe, in their joint edition of 1864–9[1]. The second, by
Meineke, Haupt, and Lucian Müller; the third, by
Lehrs and Otto Ribbeck, and by Gustav Linker   Meineke
(1827—1881), formerly professor at Prag, in his   Lehrs
edition of 1856.   Among commentaries on Horace may be
mentioned that in Latin by Wilhelm Dillenburger[2]; and those in
German, on the *Odes* and *Epodes* by K. Nauck and H. Schütz; on
the *Satires* and *Epistles* by G. T. A. Krüger (1793—1874), and
A. T. H. Fritzsche.   In 1854 f a bulky edition of the *Satires* was
produced by Karl Kirchner (1787—1855), Rector of Schulpforta.
The early quotations from Horace were industriously collected
in the *Analecta* of Martin Hertz[3].

The textual criticism of Ovid was promoted not only by
Alexander Riese (b. 1840)[4], Otto Korn (1842—1883)[5], and
Hermann Peter (b. 1837)[6], but also by Rudolf
Merkel (1811—1885), who produced at his own   Merkel
university of Halle his earliest work, the *Quaestiones Ovidianae
Criticae*.   He had proposed to qualify for an academic career in
that university, but the part he played in certain political dis-
turbances led to his being imprisoned in Berlin.   In prison he
went through a severe course of study, borrowed MSS from
Leyden and Gotha, and worked through the letters of the Dutch
scholars and the materials left by N. Heinsius, with a view to the
preparation of an edition of Ovid.   On his release (which was
apparently due to the absence of sufficient proof of his guilt), he
remained in Berlin and there produced his edition of the *Tristia*
(1837).   He was afterwards a school-master at Schleusingen and
elsewhere.   In 1841 he published the *Fasti*, probably his most
important work (including information as to the Calendars and
the Religious Antiquities of Rome, with the fragments of Varro
on that subject); followed, in 1852–4, by his two editions of
Apollonius Rhodius.   In 1863 he visited Italy, and his 'transcript'

---

[1] *Ed. minor* 1878; cp. Keller, in *Rhein. Mus.* xix 211 f, and *Epilegomena*
(1879 f).   In this ed. the *Codices Blandinii* of Cruquius are regarded as of
minor importance; cp. Schanz, *Röm. Litt.* § 263.

[2] 1844; ed. 6, 1875.   [3] 1876–80.   Bursian, ii 943 f.

[4] Ed. 1871–4.

[5] Ed. of Sauppe's *Met.* i—vii, and ed. of viii—xiv (1876).

[6] Ed. *Fasti* (1874; ed. 2, 1879).

of the Laurentian MS of Aeschylus was afterwards printed by the
Clarendon Press (1871). Meanwhile he had produced two papers
on Aeschylus (1867–8), and an edition of the *Persae*. He held
a mastership at Quedlinburg until 1879, when he removed to
Dresden, where he spent his time in the study of Aeschylus and
Archaeology. He edited the *Metamorphoses* in 1874. Many of
his conjectural emendations are excellent[1].

Among the imitators of Virgil, Valerius Flaccus was edited, not only by
Georg Thilo and by Emil Baehrens, but also by Karl Schenkl (1871); an
explanatory edition was the latest work of Peter Langen (1896–7). The
ancient *scholia* to Lucan were published by H. Usener from MSS at Bern
(1869), and the text was edited by C. Hosius (1892); the MSS of Silius Italicus
were carefully discussed by Hermann Blass[2]; the textual criticism of the
Thebais and *Achilleis* of Statius was advanced by Otto Müller and Philipp
Kohlmann; the *Achilleis* was edited by Alfred Klotz, and the *Silvae* by Klotz
(1900) and, with a commentary, by Fr. Vollmer (1898).

Persius was edited in 1843 and 1851 by Otto Jahn, and Juvenal in
1851, and both (together with the Satire of Sulpicia) in 1868; Martial, by
Schneidewin (1842–53), and Friedländer (1886); and Claudian, by Ludwig
Jeep (1876–9), and Theodor Birt (1892).

The *Mosella* of Ausonius was edited in 1845 by Eduard Böcking (1802–
1870), who was born at Trarbach on the Mosel, and was pro-
Böcking   fessor of Law at Bonn from 1835 to his death; it has since
Peiper   been edited by Hosius (1894). The text of the whole was
revised in 1886 by Rudolf Peiper, and in 1883 by Karl Schenkl of Vienna.
Peiper (1834—1898) studied at the university of Breslau, and, from 1861 to his
death, was a master in the local *gymnasium*, but his real interest lay in
scholarly research. One of his ambitions was to produce a *Corpus* of the
mediaeval Latin poets. He collected evidence as to the study of Plautus and
Terence[3], and of Catullus[4], and wrote an important paper on 'profane
comedy'[5], in the Middle Ages. In addition to his Ausonius, he edited the
tragedies of Seneca, as well as Boëthius and the Heptateuch of the Gallic poet,
Cyprian. His mediaeval texts included Waltharius, Walter of Châtillon, and
the *Carmina Burana*, but the first of these was superseded by the editions of
W. Meyer, A. Holder, and P. Winterfeld. In 1883, when he received an
honorary degree from the university of Breslau, he was described as 'de
litterarum per extrema pereuntis antiquitatis saecula studiis augendis ac pro-
pagandis bene meritus'[6].

[1] Georges in *Biogr. Jahrb.* 1885, 100–2.
[2] *Jahrb. f. Philol.* Suppl. viii 159.
[3] *Rhein. Mus.* xxxii 516—537.
[4] *Beiträge*, 1875.   [5] *Archiv für Lit.* v 493—542.
[6] Traube in *Biogr. Jahrb.* 1901, 14—27.

In the *Monumenta Germaniae Historica* the third volume of the *Poëtae Latini aevi Carolini*[1] was ably edited in 1886–96 by Ludwig Traube (1861—1907). Born in Berlin, he was connected, for practically the whole of his academic career, with the university of Munich, where a call to Giessen in 1902 led to his being specially retained as professor of the Latin Philology of the Middle Ages. He was an eager and able pioneer in an obscure and intricate region of classical learning, and by his independent research he acquired a profound knowledge of mediaeval palaeography, and of the history of the survival of the Latin Classics[2]. In connexion with the literature of the early Middle Ages, he edited the Orations of Cassiodorus[3], and elaborately investigated the successive changes in the text of the Rule of St Benedict[4]. It is deeply to be regretted that most of the memorials of his erudition have to be sought in academic and periodical publications[5], and that he never produced the comprehensive History of the Latin Literature of the Middle Ages, which was once announced under his name. But his work as a teacher is perpetuated by his pupils, some of whom have contributed to the important series of *Quellen und Untersuchungen*[6] which he instituted only three years before his lamented death[7].

From verse we turn to prose. An edition of Cicero in eleven volumes (1850–7) is the best known work of Reinhold Klotz (1807—1870), professor at Leipzig from 1832 to his death; while a widely popular edition in a single folio volume[8] had been produced some thirty years previously by Karl Friedrich August Nobbe (1791—1878) who studied under C. D. Beck and Hermann at Leipzig, where he was for fifty years Rector of the *Nicolai-Schule*.

A far higher fame as an editor of Cicero was won by Karl Felix Halm (1809—1882), who was born and bred in Munich, and studied at the university of his

Marginal notes: Traube; R. Klotz / Nobbe; Halm

[1] Cp. *Karolingische Dichtungen untersucht*, 161 pp., Berlin, 1888; also *O Roma nobilis*, in *Abhandl.* of the Munich Acad. XIX ii, 1891, 299—395.

[2] *E.g. Ueberlieferungsgeschichte*, in *S. Ber. ib.* 1891, Heft 3; on Suetonius, in *Neues Archiv*, 1902, 266 f; on Ammianus, in *Mél. Boissier*, 1903.

[3] *Mon. Germ. Hist.* 1894.   [4] *Abhandl.* of Munich Acad. 1898.

[5] *E.g.* on *Perrona Scottorum*, in *S. Ber. ib.* Dec. 1900; and on Sedulius of Liége, in *Abhandl.* 1891; also *Varia libamenta critica*, Munich, 1883–91.

[6] *E.g.* E. K. Rand, *Johannes Scottus*; S. Hellmann, *Sedulius Scottus*.

[7] Cp. *Ludwig Traube zum Gedächtnis* (Seven Funeral Orations, Munich, 21 May, 1907, with portrait); P. Marc and W. Riezler in *Beilage zur Allgemeine Zeitung, ib.* 22 May, p. 223; and W. M. Lindsay in *Cl. Rev.* xxi 188; bibliography by P. Lehmann.

[8] Also in 10 small Tauchnitz vols. *Biogr. Jahrb.* 1878, 29.

native place.   After fifteen years' experience as a school-master at
Munich, Speyer, and Hadamar, he was in 1849 appointed Rector
of the newly founded *gymnasium* at Munich, and in 1856 director
of the public library and professor in the university.   During
forty-eight years of active life, he did much towards extending
an interest in Classics among his pupils.   His editorial labours
were mainly limited to the field of Latin prose.

His early papers on the orator Lycurgus, and on Aeschylus,
his elementary work on Greek Syntax, his Greek Reader, and his
Lectiones Stobenses, were followed by editions of Cicero, *pro Sulla*
and *pro Sestio* (1845) and *in Vatinium* (1848).   On the death of
Orelli in 1849, he joined Baiter in completing the second edition
of the whole of Cicero[1].   Meanwhile, he had begun the preparation
of the first edition of seven Select Speeches with German notes
(1850–66), followed by a text of eighteen (1868).   He also
published a critical edition of the *Rhetores Latini Minores* and
of the *Institutio Oratoria* of Quintilian.   He further edited
Tacitus and Florus, Valerius Maximus, Cornelius Nepos and
Velleius Paterculus.   In connexion with the Vienna *Corpus* of
the Latin Fathers, he examined the Swiss MSS, and himself edited
Sulpicius Severus, Minucius Felix, and Julius Firmicus Maternus.
To the *Monumenta Germaniae Historica* he contributed an edition
of Salvianus and of Victor Vitensis.

His previous work on Greek authors was resumed in his Aesop,
and in his papers on the *Rhetoric* of Anaximenes and the minor
works of Plutarch.   To the History of Scholarship he contributed
many biographies of German scholars[2].   As librarian, he organised
the preparation of the great Catalogue of MSS, and himself took
part in the Catalogue of the Latin MSS.

His early career had been a noble example of triumphing over
difficulties.   The son of an art dealer, he lost his father as an
infant, and had only passed through the lower divisions of his
school, when he was sternly compelled by his step-father to enter
a grocer's shop, where he had to work from six in the morning till
nine in the evening, and could only read his favourite Classics in
the dead of night.   He was only released from this drudgery on

---

[1] Speeches, 1854–6 ; Philosophical Works, 1861.

[2] *A. D. B.* (1875 f).

promising that, as soon as he had completed his education at school, he would maintain himself.   It was during the two quiet years at Hadamar (1847–9) that he had the leisure for preparing his edition of the speeches and philosophical works of Cicero.   It was not until he had reached the age of 70, that he resigned his professorship[1].

The criticism of Latin authors, as well as Latin Inscriptions, Roman Antiquities and Roman History, formed part of the wide field of learning traversed by Theodor Mommsen (1817—1903).   Born in the province of Schleswig and educated at Altona, he studied law and philology at Kiel, travelled in Italy and France from 1845 to 1847, and was appointed 'extraordinary' professor of Law at Leipzig in 1848.   The part that he played in the political movements of the time led to his being exiled from Saxony in 1850.   Together with Jahn and Haupt, he left for Zürich, where he held a professorship for an interval of two years (1852–4).   On his return to Germany, the four years of his professorship at Breslau (1854–8) were followed by his call to Berlin, where he was professor of Ancient History and a member of the Academy for the remaining forty-five years of his life.

In the field of Latin literature, Mommsen did much for the study of manuscript evidence.   He transcribed the palimpsest of part of Livy discovered by Mai at Verona, and edited Books III—VI with the readings of other important MSS[2].   In conjunction with Studemund, he contributed to the textual criticism of the third decade in the *Analecta Liviana* of 1873.   His edition of Solinus had meanwhile appeared in 1864[3].   Those of Cassiodorus[4], Iordanes[5], and the *Chronica Minora*[6], were contributed to the *Monumenta Germaniae Historica*.   He produced important papers on Cluvius Rufus as an authority for the early part of the *Histories* of Tacitus[7], on the Life of the Younger Pliny[8] (with the historical index to Keil's larger edition), and

Theodor Mommsen

---

[1] Bursian, ii 949—952, and in *Biogr. Jahrb.* 1882, 1—6; bibliography in Wölfflin's *Gedächtnissrede*, 1883, 33 f.

[2] Berlin Acad. 1868.   [3] Ed. 2, 1895.

[4] *Chron.* 1861; *Varia*, 1894.   [5] 1882.   [6] 1891—1898.

[7] *Hermes*, iv 295 f.   [8] *ib.* iii 31—139 (*Hist. Schrift.* i 366—468).

on the chronology of the Letters of Fronto[1], besides many
contributions to the Transactions of the Academies of Saxony
and of Berlin[2]. His important works connected with Latin
Inscriptions and Antiquities and History will be mentioned on a
later page[3].

The Commentary of Asconius on Five Speeches of Cicero was edited in
1875 by Adolph Kiessling[4], in conjunction with Rudolf Schöll
R. Schöll (1844—1893, son of Adolf Schöll of Weimar), who studied
at Göttingen and Bonn, and held professorships at Greifswald, Jena, Strassburg,
and Munich. He was specially interested in the Public Law of Athens and
of Rome. His earliest work was a Dissertation on the Laws of the XII Tables.
His edition of the *Novellae*, begun in 1880, was completed by W. Kroll (1895).
To the volume in honour of Mommsen he contributed a paper on certain
extraordinary magistracies at Athens, and other papers on the Public Antiquities
of Athens were among his later works. At the time of his death he had made
extensive preparations for a new edition of Phrynichus[5].

The textual criticism of Cicero's Letters 'Ad Familiares' was much advanced by the critical edition published in 1893 by Ludwig
Mendelssohn Mendelssohn (1852—1896), who studied under Sauppe and
C. Wachsmuth at Göttingen and under Ritschl at Leipzig. His early work
was connected with the literary chronology of Eratosthenes, and the Roman
decrees quoted by Josephus. After qualifying as a teacher in Leipzig, he
visited Italy with a view to collating MSS of Cicero's Letters and of Appian
and Aristeas. His edition of Appian was the first to mark a real advance on
that of Schweighäuser; he also edited Herodian and Zosimus. His edition of
the Letter of Aristeas, a document of importance in connexion with the
history of the Septuagint, was completed by Wendland; and the materials he
had collected on the subject of the Sibylline Oracles were handed over to
Harnack. His most successful work was his edition of Cicero's Letters, in
which a new weight was assigned to the evidence of MSS other than the
Medicean. The last twenty years of his life were spent at the Russian university of Dorpat. The decline of German influence in that university cast a
gloom over his later years, and he was hoping to transfer his home to Jena,
when he met his end in the waters of the Embach at the early age of 44[6].

For the textual criticism of the Latin historians and
grammarians much was done by Martin Hertz
Hertz (1818—1895), who was born in Hamburg, and
educated in Berlin. After studying under Welcker at Bonn, he

---

[1] *ib.* viii 198 f.   [2] Bursian, ii 952–4.

[3] p. 235.   [4] p. 185 *supra*.

[5] *Biogr. Jahrb.* 1897, 9—40.

[6] Goetz in *Biogr. Jahrb.* 1898, 49—60.

returned to Berlin, and worked under Boeckh and Lachmann. He was a 'privat-docent' in that university in 1845, went abroad to examine MSS for his editions of Gellius, Priscian, and the scholia to Germanicus, until 1847; and was professor at Greifswald from 1855, and at Breslau from 1858 to his death, thirty-seven years later.

He produced the standard edition of Priscian in 1855–9; he also edited a text of Gellius, prior to his great critical edition of 1883–5. Meanwhile he had edited Livy. He also wrote papers on the grammarians, Sinnius Capito and Nigidius Figulus, and on the annalist, Lucius Cincius, and his namesake, besides delivering popular lectures on 'Writers and the Public in Rome', and on 'Renaissance and Rococo in Latin Literature', a subject suggested by his study of Gellius.

After completing his edition of that author and collecting his *Opuscula Gelliana* (1886), he returned to the literature of the golden age. He had contributed to the criticism of Cicero, *pro Sestio*, had traced reminiscences of Sallust[1] (and of Gellius[2]) in the pages of Ammianus Marcellinus, and (in his *Analecta*) had followed the traces of the study of Horace down to the sixth century. In 1892 he edited Horace with short critical notes, including much that was not to be found elsewhere. Georges dedicated the seventh edition of his Latin lexicon to Hertz, who had contributed to its pages. From 1858, when the proposal for a *Thesaurus* of the Latin language was first made at Vienna, Hertz never left the scheme out of sight, but it was not until he was president of the Congress at Görlitz, that he publicly proposed that such a work should be undertaken by the German Academies. A conference followed in 1890, and in the following year Hertz drew up the report[3].

His interest in archaeology at Greifswald may be traced to the influence of Welcker; his lectures on the general scheme of classical learning[4] to that of Boeckh. Similarly his interest in the Roman historians was due to Niebuhr, and that in the

---

[1] 1874. [2] *Opusc. Gelliana.*

[3] *Berichte* of Berlin Acad. 1891, 671—684.

[4] Cp. his paper *Zur Encyclopädie der Philologie* in the Mommsen *Comm.* 507—517 (1877).

Latin grammarians to Lachmann. His biography of Lachmann is a masterpiece of its kind (1851); he also wrote several articles on Boeckh, and gave an excellent lecture on the early humanist, Eobanus Hessus. His work was marked by minute and conscientious accuracy; and, in his own person, he was characterised by a strong sense of justice towards others, and an exemplary mildness of manner, even towards his opponents. He will be remembered as the erudite editor of Priscian and of Gellius, and as the unwearied promoter of the scheme for the *Thesaurus Linguae Latinae*[1].

Sallust was edited in a cumbersome form in 1823-31 by F. D. Gerlach (1793—1876), professor and librarian at Basel, who also **Editors of Sallust** edited Nonius in 1842 in conjunction with his colleague, Karl L. Roth (1811—1860). The historian's diction was specially studied in the editions of J. F. Kritz, a school-master at Erfurt (1798—1869), and E. W. Fabri (1796—1845). In that produced by K. H. Frotscher, the head-master of Freiberg (1796—1876), the text was taken from Kortte and the notes from Havercamp. The MSS were discussed by K. L. Roth, and a critical edition published in 1859 by R. Dietsch (1814—1875), head-master of Grimma.

A critical edition of greater importance was produced in 1866 (ed. 2, 1876) **Jordan** by Henri Jordan (1833—1886), a professor at Königsberg, who had been a pupil of Haupt in Berlin and of Ritschl at Bonn, and was a friend and ally of Mommsen, and a son-in-law of Droysen. He also edited the historical and oratorical works of the elder Cato, with 109 pages of *Prolegomena* (1860). He visited Rome for the first time in 1861, and produced several valuable works on Roman topography (1871—86), and on the ancient religion of Rome, as well as critical contributions to the history of the Latin language (1879). In 1864 he published a critical edition of the *Scriptores Historiae Augustae*, the first that had appeared in Germany for 76 years[2]. The joint editor of this work was Franz **Eyssenhardt** Eyssenhardt (1838—1901), who (like Jordan) had been born in Berlin and had studied under Boeckh and Haupt. In 1866-71 Eyssenhardt edited Martianus Capella, Phaedrus, Macrobius, Apuleius, the *Historia Miscella*, and Ammianus Marcellinus. After completing these editions, he devoted much of his time to studies in the history of civilisation. He had a remarkably ready pen. Two of his popular lectures were on Homeric poetry, and on Hadrian and Florus. He also wrote a biographical Essay of 286 pages

---

[1] *Biogr. Jahrb.* 1900, 42—70; cp. Bursian, ii 955 f; *Thes.* I p. iii, 'causae ancipiti ac situ quodam pressae sua contentione et commendatione favorem conciliavit'.

[2] *Biogr. Jahrb.* 1886, 227—249 (with bibliography).

on Niebuhr. He spoke seven languages fluently, and travelled widely, especially delighting in his visits to Italy, but also extending his journeys as far as Scotland, while he kept up a constant correspondence with Lucian Müller in St Petersburg[1].

Commentaries on Caesar (1847), Nepos (1849), and Tacitus (1852), were published by Karl Ludwig Nipperdey (1821—1875), who was a professor at Jena in 1855; an acute critic, who had a fine taste in Latin prose, and gave proof of his familiarity with Roman Antiquities by his treatise on the *Leges Annales*[2].

    Nipperdey
    Kraner
    Doberenz

Caesar, *De Bello Gallico*, and *De Bello Civili*, were edited with German notes by Friedrich Kraner (1812—1863), Rector at Leipzig, and by Albert Doberenz (1811—1878), Director of the *gymnasium* at Hildburghausen.

Materials for the textual criticism of Livy were supplied in 1839-46 by the editions of Books I—X, XXI—XXIII, and XXX by K. F. S. Alschefski (1805—1852). A higher critical faculty was displayed in the complete edition of J. G. Kreyssig (1779—1854), a master at the Saxon School of Meissen.

    Alschefski
    Kreyssig
    Weissenborn
    Kuhnast

The best commentary with German notes was that first published in 1850-1 by Wilhelm Weissenborn (1803—1878), for more than forty-three years a master at Eisenach[3]. The Syntax of Livy was laboriously set forth in 1871 by Ludwig Kuhnast (1813—1872), a school-master at Marienwerder.

Tacitus was edited, not only by Orelli, Halm, and Nipperdey, but also, in and after 1834-6, by Franz Ritter (1803—1875), for many years professor in Bonn, who produced editions of Horace (1856-7) and of Aristotle's treatise on Poetry (1839). The *Annals* and *Agricola* were edited in 1868-9 with German

    Ritter
    Dräger
    Heraeus

notes by A. A. Dräger (1820—1895), who studied at Leipzig, and was Director of the *gymnasium* at Aurich. He was also the author of a useful work on the 'Syntax and Style of Tacitus', followed by a comprehensive volume on the 'Historical Syntax of the Latin language'[4]. Among good editions with German notes may be mentioned that of the *Histories* by Karl Heraeus (1818—1891), who studied at Marburg and Göttingen, and was for the last thirty-four years of his life a master at the Westphalian Gymnasium of Hamm[5]; the *Dialogus* by G. Andresen; the *Agricola* by F. K. Wex (1801—1865), F. Kritz, and Karl Peter. Critical texts of the *Agricola* were produced by K. L. Urlichs, and of the *Dialogus* by Adolf Michaelis. The *Germania* was edited by Müllenhoff, Schweizer-Sidler, A. Baumstark, and A. Holder. The *Lexicon Taciteum* (1830) of W. Boetticher (d. 1850) has been superseded by the exhaustive work of A. Gerber of Glückstadt and A. Greef of Göttingen (1903).—Of the other historians, Curtius was

---

[1] *Biogr. Jahrb.* 1902, 100—127 (with bibliography). Cp. Bursian, ii 958 f.
[2] *Abhandl.* of Saxon Acad. v. Cp. Bursian, ii 762.
[3] *Biogr. Jahrb.* 1878, 33—38.   [4] *Biogr. Jahrb.* 1896, 92-4.
[5] *ib.* 1891, 114—121.

edited by E. Hedicke and Th. Vogel; Justin by Jeep; and Eutropius by
W. Hartel and Hans Droysen[1]. The more important works on Cicero and
Quintilian have been already mentioned[2].

Among the above-mentioned editors of the *Germania* of Tacitus a place of
special honour is due to Heinrich Schweizer-Sidler (1815—

Schweizer-
Sidler

1894), who studied at Zürich and Berlin. For forty of the
more than fifty years of his work at Zürich, he taught at the
local school as well as at the university. He had studied Sanskrit under Bopp,
and he was frequently visited by Muir and by Henry Nettleship. His Latin
Grammar of 1869 was recast in 1888, and attained a wide recognition. His
study of German Antiquities led him to lecture on the *Germania*, which he
repeatedly edited with German notes. He also prepared an elaborate revision
of Orelli's edition of the treatise[3].

The discovery and collation of the Bamberg MS of the elder Pliny in 1852,
by Ludwig von Jan (1807—1869), then master at Schweinfurt and ultimately
Rector at Erlangen, had an important influence on Sillig's edition of 1853–5.

Urlichs

The criticism and explanation of Pliny were afterwards promoted by Karl Ludwig von Urlichs (1813—1889), a native of
Osnabrück, who was educated at Aachen, and studied under Welcker at Bonn
(1829–34). After spending five years in Rome, as tutor in Bunsen's house,
and doing much for the study of Roman topography[4], he returned to Bonn in
1840, remaining there until his call to Greifswald in 1847. In the same year
he visited the British Museum, and there discovered an important *anecdoton* on
the literary activity of Varro[5]; was in the Prussian Parliament from 1849 to
1852, and professor at Würzburg from 1855 to his death, thirty-four years
later.

From 1847 to 1855 he was mainly occupied with Pliny and the History of
Ancient Art. This work bore fruit in his *Vindiciae Plinianae* (1853–66), his
Chrestomathia Pliniana (1857) and his conspectus of the authorities for the
books of Pliny on the History of Art (1878)[6]. The text of Pliny was edited
in 1860–73 by D. Detlefsen; and von Jan's edition of 1854–65 has been
edited anew by C. Mayhoff in 1875–1906.

The best editions of the text of the younger Pliny were those produced in

Keil

1853 and 1870 by Heinrich Keil (1822—1894), who studied
at Göttingen and Bonn, and spent two years in Italy (1844–6),
taught at Halle (1847–55) and Berlin (1855–9), and was appointed professor in
1859 at Erlangen and 1869 at Halle, where he resided for the remaining
twenty-five years of his life. His earliest work was his critique on Propertius

---

[1] Bursian, ii 964 f.   [2] p. 195 f.

[3] *Biogr. Jahrb.* 1898, 96—122.

[4] He took part in the *Beschreibung,* and published the *codex urbis Romae
topographicus* (1871), etc.

[5] Ritschl's *Opusc.* iii 421 f.

[6] Wecklein in *Biogr. Jahrb.* 1892, 1—15, and H. L. Urlichs in Pref. to
Iwan Müller's *Handbuch,* i (1891).

(1843), followed by his texts of 1850 and 1867. During his stay in Italy, and in France (1851), he collated many MSS for his friends and for himself; he supplied Merkel with the *scholia* to Apollonius Rhodius, and O. Schneider with those on Nicander, and his collations, though less extensive than those of Bekker, were more accurate. At Halle he edited the Commentary of Probus on the *Eclogues* and *Georgics*. His vast edition of the *Grammatici Latini* was published in 1857–80, five of the seven volumes being edited by himself, and the two volumes of Priscian by Hertz. Of his other works the most important were his elaborate editions of the agricultural works of Cato and Varro (1884–94), with Teubner texts of both (1889 and 1895)[1].

Vitruvius was edited, in 1867, by Valentin Rose and Hermann Müller-Strübing[2] on the basis of the MS of the ninth century collated by the latter in the British Museum. An Index was produced in 1876 by Nohl.

Among modern Latin lexicographers a place of honour must be reserved for Karl Ernst Georges (1806—1895), who spent nearly the whole of his life at Gotha. It was originally intended that he should succeed his father as chief-glazier to the local Court, and he was even removed from school for that purpose; but, at his earnest entreaty, he was allowed to continue under the tuition of Doering and Wuestemann, and the grammarian and lexicographer, V. C. F. Rost. Being in delicate health, he was sent for a change of air to Nordhausen, where he received much encouragement from the lexicographer, Kraft. He afterwards studied at Göttingen and Leipzig, where he helped in revising a new edition of Scheller. His German-Latin lexicon was completed in 1833[3] and accepted at Jena in lieu of a dissertation for his degree. In 1839–56 he was one of the higher masters at Gotha, but a weakness of eyesight, and a desire for further leisure, led to his retiring on a pension, and devoting all his time to his lexicographical labours.

Georges

The series of excellent Latin-German lexicons had been begun by that of Scheller (1783). On the death of Luenemann in 1830, the preparation of a new edition of Scheller was taken over by Georges, whose name appears on the title-page of the edition of 1837. Of the seventh edition in two volumes, filling 6,088 columns, 15,000 copies were printed in and after 1879. This work was confessedly founded on those of Gesner, Forcellini, and Scheller, as well as on his own extensive collections. It was warmly eulogised by Wölfflin, the editor of the *Archiv* and the organiser of the new *Thesaurus*; and, on the completion of 60 years of lexicographical labour in 1888, the indomitable veteran was congratulated by English scholars in the following terms:—

> 'Id scilicet laudamus in Lexico tuo Latino, multo labore et adversa interdum valetudine condito, quod artem ita adhibuisti criticam, ut inter omnia huiusmodi opera linguae Latinae studiosis sit utilissimum'[4].

---

[1] *Biogr. Jahrb.* 1896, 49—80.   [2] p. 156 *supra*.

[3] Ed. 7, 1882.

[4] Doubtless written by H. Nettleship.

Georges also began a *Thesaurus*, continued by Mühlmann down to the letter K. In his later years, when his sight began to fail, he prepared a useful lexicon of Latin Word-forms (1890). By 1891 six editions of his small Latin-German and German-Latin *Handwörterbuch*, and five of the corresponding *Schulwörterbuch*, had been published. His German-Latin lexicon was the foundation of the English-Latin work of Riddle and Arnold. He was a constant correspondent of scholars in England, as well as France and Germany, and liberally placed his stores of learning at the service of others. His little world was his library, enriched with a complete set of the *Corpus Inscriptionum Latinarum* presented by the publishers, and adorned with portraits of his fellow-labourers in the field of Latin lexicography. His small and neat round hand resembled that of Fr. Jacobs. Even bodily pain never prevented him from going quietly on with his life-long work. It was only in his biographical notice of Wuestemann and in a Latin *Gnomologia* that he deserted the domain of Latin lexicography[1].

In connexion with Latin lexicography, two names may here be added.

Paucker
Rönsch
Karl von Paucker (1820—1883) was the author of the *Addenda lexicis Latinis*, begun in 1872. After studying at Dorpat and Berlin, he returned to the former university as professor in 1861. Towards the close of his life he began to collect his scattered lexicographical papers in a comprehensive volume of *Supplementa*, which was unfortunately left unfinished[2]. His *Vorarbeiten* for the history of the Latin language were, however, published soon after his death by Hermann Rönsch (1821—1888), the learned author of *Itala und Vulgata*[3].

---

[1] R. Ehwald in *Biogr. Jahrb.* 1896, 143—150; Wölfflin's *Archiv*, 1895, 623 f; G. Schneider in *Ill. Zeitung*, 1897, 139 f. In 1880 he gratefully accepted Prof. Mayor's dedication of his ed. of Book iii of Pliny's Letters, *seni indefesso, Latinae linguae lexicographorum quotquot hodie vivunt Nestori*.

[2] Rönsch in *Biogr. Jahrb.* 1883, 93—96.

[3] 1869; ed. 2, 1875; *ib.* 1889, 159—174.

FRANZ BOPP.

From the frontispiece of the Life by Lefmann (Reimer, Berlin, 1891).

[*To face p.* 205 *of Vol. III.*

CHAPTER XXXIII.

COMPARATIVE PHILOLOGISTS.

THE founder of the comparative study of language in Germany was Franz Bopp (1791—1867). Born at Mainz, and educated at Aschaffenburg, he lived in Paris from 1812 to 1815, studying Arabic and Persian under Silvestre de Sacy, and teaching himself Sanskrit with the help of the Grammars of Carey (1806) and Wilkins (1808), and the translation of the *Bhagavadgîta* by the latter, and that of the *Râmâyana* by the former. In the university of Berlin he was an 'extraordinary professor' in 1821, and full professor for the last forty-two years of his life[1]. From the publication of his earliest work on the comparison of the conjugational system of Sanskrit with that of Greek, Latin, Persian, and German (1816) to the very end of his career, he was engaged in the unremitting endeavour to explain the origin of the grammatical forms of the Indo-Germanic languages. This was the main object of his 'Comparative Grammar' (1833). But his endeavours were regarded with indifference or distrust by the leading scholars and grammarians, such as Hermann[2] and Lobeck[3]. The method and the results of comparative philology were also attacked, with more wit than wisdom, by the Greek archaeologist, Ludwig Ross[4]. This lack of appreciation was not so much due to any limitation of vision on the part of the scholars of the day, or to an excess of conservatism, or a contempt for their contemporaries. It was mainly prompted by the uncertain and tentative methods of the earlier pioneers, by their imperfect knowledge of the languages with which they

Bopp

---

[1] Lefmann, *F. B., sein Leben u. seine Wissenschaft* (Berlin, 1891–6).

[2] Pref. to *Acta Soc. Graecae*, quoted in vol. i p. 12 n. 5.

[3] Pref. to *Pathol.* p. vii ; but even Lobeck would have been ready to study Comparative Philology, had life been long enough for the purpose (*Paralip.* 127).

[4] *Italiker und Graeken* (1858 f.).

were concerned, and by their indifference to the rules of classical
syntax. This distrust has, however, passed away. Its departure
is due to the labours of those who have taken up the science
created by Bopp, supported by Jacob Grimm[1], and developed
by Pott[2] and Kuhn[3] and Schleicher[4] and others, and who have
applied its method to Greek and Latin, and have thereby laid a
sure foundation for the new fabric of the Etymology of those
languages[5].

Foremost among these was Theodor Benfey (1809—1881), whose
father, a Jewish merchant in the kingdom of Hanover,
Benfey   taught him the Talmud and aroused in him an interest
for language. It was at Frankfurt that the son prepared a translation of Terence, and also (under the influence of Poley) devoted
himself to the study of Sanskrit. In 1817 he settled at Göttingen,
and, with the exception of a year at Munich (1827–8), he there
abode for the remaining sixty-four years of his life. In 1848 he
left his ancestral faith for that of Christianity, and was in the same
year appointed to a poorly paid 'extraordinary' professorship; it
was only for his last nineteen years that he was a full professor.

In the introduction to his 'lexicon of Greek roots', which
was the first scientific treatment of Greek Etymology (1839–42),
he drew up a scheme for a series of works treating of Greek
Grammar in the light of Comparative Philology, but this scheme
was never carried out. Its author devoted most of his subsequent
career to the study of Sanskrit Grammar, and to researches in
the Vedas. He, however, published many articles on subjects
connected with Greek and Latin Grammar in the Transactions
of the Göttingen Academy, and in his quarterly review, *Orient
und Occident* (1862–6). His principal works were an edition of
the *Sâmaveda* (1848), a complete Sanskrit Grammar (1852), the

---

[1] 'German Grammar', 1819[1]–22[2]. On Rask and Verner, see chap. xxxviii.

[2] 'Etymological Investigations', 1833–6.

[3] On Adalbert Kuhn (1812—1881), cp. *Biogr. Jahrb.* 1881, 48—63.

[4] p. 209 *infra*. Cp., in general, P. Giles, *Manual of Comparative Philology* (1895) §§ 39—44.

[5] Bursian, ii 971 f. Cp. Delbrück, *Einleitung in das Sprachstudium*,
cap. i; Benfey, *Gesch. der Sprachwissenschaft*, 370–9, 470—515; and Thomsen's *Sprogvidenskabens Historie* (Copenhagen, 1902); a brief sketch in J. M.
Edmonds' *Comparative Philology* (Cambridge, 1906), 189—200.

Pantschatantra (1859), and the History of the study of language and of oriental philology in Germany (1869)[1].

Benfey's pupil, Leo Meyer (b. 1830), on his appointment as professor of Comparative Philology at Dorpat in 1865, had just completed the second volume of his Comparative Grammar of Greek and Latin[2], dealing only with the doctrine of sounds and the formation of words.   Meanwhile, he had published a brief comparison between the Greek and Latin declensions (1852).   His Grammar remained unfinished, but he investigated the Greek aorist (1879), and published a number of minor papers on the diction of Homer[3].   He has since resided as an honorary professor at Göttingen.

L. Meyer

The recognition of the comparative method among Greek and Latin scholars and school-masters was mainly due to Georg Curtius (1820—1885), the younger brother of the historian of Greece.   Born and bred at Lübeck, he studied at Bonn and Berlin, and, after spending four years as a master at Dresden, and three as a 'privat-docent' in Berlin, he was professor for five years at Prag, for eight at Kiel, and, for the remaining twenty-four years of his life, at Leipzig.   In his inaugural lecture at this university he stated that it was his purpose, as professor, to bring Classical Philology and the Science of Language into closer relation with each other[4].   His zeal and success in carrying out this purpose were attested, not only by his own works, but also by the ten volumes of 'Studies' on Greek and Latin Grammar produced by his pupils (1868–78), by the papers connected with the Science of Language published in his honour in 1874, and by the five volumes of 'Leipzig Studies', edited by himself and three other professors in 1878–82.   The principal works produced by himself were his 'Greek Grammar for Schools' (1852), his 'Principles of Greek Etymology' (1858–62), and his treatise on the 'Greek Verb' (1873–6).   The first of these was published at Prag, while Curtius was a professor in

G. Curtius

[1] Bezzenberger in *Biogr. Jahrb.* 1882, 103—107; Delbrück, 36; Bursian, ii 973.

[2] 2 vols., 1861–5; ed. 2 of vol. i, in two parts, 1270 pp., 1882–4; Benfey, 591.   [3] Bursian, ii 975 f.

[4] *Philologie und Sprachwissenschaft*, 1861 (also in *Kl. Schr.* i); cp. *Die Sprachvergleichung in ihrem Verhältniss zur cl. Philologie* (1848[2]), E. T. Oxford, 1851.

that university. It was primarily intended for use in the Austrian schools, then in course of reorganisation under the guidance of Bonitz, and, notwithstanding the bitter and violent opposition of K. W. Krüger[1], it was widely accepted in the schools of Germany[2]. It was followed by a volume of 'Elucidations' for the use of teachers[3]. His early work on 'Greek and Latin Tenses and Moods in the light of Comparative Grammar' (1846) was the precursor of his important work on the 'Greek Verb'[4]. His 'Principles of Greek Etymology' reached a fifth edition in 1879[5]. The first Book contains an introductory statement on the principles, and the main questions, of Greek Etymology; the second deals with the *regular* representation of Indo-Germanic sounds in Greek, exemplified by a conspectus of words or groups of words arranged according to their sounds; and the third investigates the *irregular* or sporadic changes[6]. 'Curtius was not a student of language, availing himself of the aid of Latin and Greek to attack the general questions of linguistics, but a classical scholar studying the languages of Greece and Rome in the light of comparative philology'[7].

The leading representative of the study of language in its
psychological aspect was H. Steinthal (1823—1899),

Steinthal   who studied in Berlin (1843–7) and Paris (1852–5), and was professor of the Science of Language in Berlin from 1863 to his death. He wrote on the origin of language[8], the classification of languages[9], the developement of writing; also a work on grammar, logic, and psychology, their principles and their mutual relations (1855), which was expanded in his Intro-duction to the Psychology of the Science of Language (1871); and lastly, a History of the Science of Language among the Greeks and Romans, with special reference to Logic[10].

---

[1] p. 119 *supra*.   [2] Ed. 12 (Gerth); E. T. 1867.

[3] 1863 ; E. T. 1870.   [4] E. T., Wilkins and England, 1880.

[5] E. T., Wilkins and England, 1875–6 ; ed. 2, 1886.

[6] Bursian, ii 975–8 ; cp. Angermann in Bezzenberger's *Beiträge*, x ; E. Curtius in vol. i of his brother's *Kleine Schriften* ; and Windisch in *Biogr. Jahrb.* 1886, 75—128 ; also Delbrück, 39 f.

[7] Wilkins in *Class. Rev.* i 263.

[8] 1851 ; ed. 3, 1877.

[9] 1850 ; ed. 2, 1860 ; cp. Benfey, 787 f.

[10] 1863 ; ed. 2, 1890–1 ; cp. Bursian, ii 980.

August Schleicher (1821—1868), who was born at Meiningen and educated at Coburg, studied Theology at Leipzig and Tübingen, and Philology under Ritschl **Schleicher** at Bonn. In 1845 he became 'privat-docent' at Bonn, in 1850 extraordinary professor in Prag, and in 1857 honorary professor at Jena, where he died in 1868. In his 'Compendium of the Comparative Grammar of the Indo-Germanic languages'[1], he stated the results of all the recent investigations on the vocal changes in a series of 'laws of sound'[2]. 'With all his wide linguistic attainments', he was not a classical scholar, either in the first or even in the second place. 'He was at heart a Darwinian botanist, who handled language as if it were the subject-matter of natural and not of historical science'[3].

The series of Indo-Germanic Grammars, published by Breitkopf and Härtel in Leipzig, included a volume on the physiology of sound by Eduard Sievers (1876)[4], an Introduction to the history and method of the comparative study of language by Delbrück (1880), and a Greek Grammar (1880) by Gustav Meyer (1850—1900)[5]. A Latin Grammar has been produced by Sommer (Heidelberg).

'The *physiology* of sound does not suffice to enable us to attain a clear conception of the work of man in the province of speech....We need a science that takes **The New Grammarians** cognizance of the *psychic* factors, which enter into the innumerable movements and changes of sound, and also into all the workings of analogy'. Such is part of the programme of the New Grammarians, as it is unfolded by its most active representatives Hermann Osthoff of Heidelberg, and Karl Brugmann of Leipzig[6]. The outline of such a science had been already drawn in Steinthal's Essay on assimilation and attraction in their psychological aspects[7]. Other representatives of the New School are August Leskien[8] of Leipzig and Hermann Paul[9] of Munich.

---

[1] 1861 ; ed. 2, 1866; E. T.

[2] Bursian, ii 978 f; Benfey, 587 f; Lefmann's *Skizze* (1870); Delbrück, 41–56.

[3] Wilkins, in *Cl. Rev.* i 263.　　[4] Ed. 4, 1893 (*Grundzüge der Phonetik*).

[5] *Biogr. Jahrb.* 1902, 1—6.

[6] Osthoff and Brugmann, pref. to *Morphol. Untersuchungen*, i (1878).

[7] *Zeitschr. für Völkerpsychologie*, i 93 f.

[8] *Decl. im Slavisch-Litauischen u. Germanischen* (1876).

[9] *Principien der Sprachgeschichte* (1880 etc.).

The principles of this school are (1) that all changes of sound, so far as they are mechanical, are under the operation of laws that admit of *no exception*, and (2) that the principle of *analogy*, which plays an important part in the life of modern languages, must be unreservedly recognised as having been at work from the very earliest times.

The first of these principles has been opposed by the later followers of Benfey, especially in the periodical edited by A. Bezzenberger of Königsberg[1].—One of the representatives of the New School, August Fick, formerly professor at Breslau, and the author of a 'Comparative Dictionary of the Indo-Germanic languages'[2], produced an excellent work on the formation of Greek names of persons (1894), showing that originally all names of persons among the Indo-Germanic peoples were compound words formed from two roots, and that from these compound words names including a single root were formed either from the first or the second of the two elements. The names thus resulting were *Kosen-namen*, or 'names of endearment'[3]. The principles of the New School are set forth in H. Paul's 'Principles of the History of Language'[4], and far more fully in Karl Brugmann's '*Grundriss* of the Comparative Grammar of the Indo-Germanic Languages'[5]. An estimate of the movement has been given in the above-mentioned 'Introduction' by B. Delbrück, the author of a 'Comparative Syntax of the Indo-Germanic Languages' (1893 f).

Fick

Among the workers in this field who have already passed away was Ludwig Lange (1825—1885), professor at Leipzig from 1871[6]. Twenty years previously he had given a lecture at Göttingen, in which he had insisted on the importance of the *historic* method of investigation, and had illustrated it by the use of the prepositions in Sanskrit and Greek[7].

L. Lange

[1] *Beiträge zur Kunde der indogerm. Sprachen.*

[2] 1870–2; ed. 3, 1874–6; ed. 4, 1891 f.   [3] Bursian, ii 999.

[4] Eng. adaptation by H. A. Strong, 1888. See also Paul's *Grundriss*, i (1891 etc.).

[5] 1886 f (E. T. 1888 f); ed. 2, 1897 f; 'Short Comparative Grammar', 1904.

[6] *Biogr. Jahrb.* 1886, 31—61.

[7] Bursian, ii 1001.

The first to attempt to set forth the history of sounds in Latin, in the light of the new science of language, was Albert Agathon Benary (1807—1860)[1]. Abundant **Benary** materials for the historic grammar of the Latin language were subsequently supplied by the researches of Ritschl, Mommsen and others, on Plautus, on the early Roman inscriptions, and on the remains of the old Italic languages. These materials were applied with considerable acumen and independence, and with constant regard to the results of the comparative study of language, in the investigation of the changes of the Latin consonants and vowels by Wilhelm Corssen (1820— **Corssen** 1875). Born at Bremen, he studied in Berlin (1840–4), and was a master at Schulpforta (1846–66), living afterwards in Berlin, and, from 1870, in Rome. His principal work was on the 'Pronunciation, Vocalisation, and Accentuation of the Latin language'[2], a work dealing with the orthography, pronunciation, and prosody of Latin in connexion with the old Italic dialects, and in the light of comparative philology[3]. It was partly supplemented by the work on the vocalisation of vulgar Latin published in 1866–8 by Hugo Schuchardt (b. 1842), formerly professor at Graz.

The general results of Comparative Philology were incorporated in Kühner's larger Latin Grammar, and, more systematically, by Heinrich Schweizer-Sidler[4], in his outline of the elements and forms of Latin for schools (1869), and by Alois Vaniček (1825— 1883)[5], formerly professor at Prag, in his elementary Latin Grammar (1873), and his Etymological Dictionary of the Latin language (1874), followed by his Greek and Latin Etymological Dictionary (1877). A Comparative Dictionary of Latin, Greek, Sanskrit, and German, published at Vienna in 1873 by Sebastian Zehetmayr, was expanded in 1879 into a comprehensive etymological Dictionary of all the Indo-Germanic languages[6]. A Greek Etymological Dictionary has since been published by Prellwitz[7].

---

[1] *Die römische Lautlehre, sprachvergleichend dargestellt* (Berlin, 1837).

[2] 1858–9; ed. 2, 1868—70. For his other works, see p. 142 f *supra*.

[3] On Corssen, cp. Ascoli's *Kritische Studien*, p. ix (Delbrück, 41).

[4] p. 202 *supra*.   [5] *Biogr. Jahrb.* 1884, 56 f.

[6] Bursian, ii 1003–6.   [7] Göttingen, ed. 2, 1905.

KARL OTFRIED MÜLLER.

Reduced from a drawing by Ternite lithographed by Wildt.

CHAPTER XXXIV.

ARCHAEOLOGISTS AND HISTORIANS.

Down to the time of Winckelmann and Heyne the investigation of the political, social, religious, and artistic life of the ancients had occupied a subordinate position in comparison with the study of the Greek and Latin languages. The new impulse then given had been carried forward by Niebuhr[1] and by Boeckh[2], while, among their immediate successors, the most brilliant and versatile, and the most widely influential, was Karl Otfried[3] Müller (1797—1840). Born at the Silesian town of Brieg, he studied at Breslau, where the perusal of Niebuhr's 'History of Rome' prompted him to concentrate his energies on historical subjects. In Berlin, under the influence of Boeckh (1816–7), he acquired a new interest in the history of Greece, and it was to Boeckh that he owed the earliest successes of his literary and academic career. He began by publishing a monograph on the ancient and modern history of Aegina[4]. Part of this work was on the Aeginetan Marbles, which had been discovered in 1811[5], and had recently been purchased (in 1812) by Ludwig, the Crown Prince of Bavaria. At that time Müller's sole authority for these works was a description by the sculptor, J. M. Wagner, with criticisms on the style by F. W. J. Schelling

Karl Otfried Müller

[1] p. 77 f *supra*. [2] p. 95 f *supra*.

[3] His original name was simply Karl. To distinguish himself from the many Karl Müllers, he added the name of Gottfried, which, on Buttman's advice, he changed to Otfried in 1817 (after the publication of his first work). The form Ottfried is incorrect.

[4] *Aeginetarum liber; scripsit Carolus Mueller, Silesius* (1817).

[5] By Cockerell and Foster, in conjunction with Haller von Hallerstein, and Linckh. Cp. Michaelis, *Die archäologischen Entdeckungen* (1906), 31 f.

(1817). It was not until his appointment to a Chair of Classical
Alterthumswissenschaft at Göttingen in the summer of 1819 that
he was able to study some of the actual remains of ancient art at
Dresden. At Göttingen in 1820 he gave a course of lectures
on Archaeology and the History of Art; two years later he
enlarged his knowledge by visiting the collections in Paris and
London, and he continued lecturing on the above subjects with
ever increasing success until the end of the summer-term of 1839.
In September of that year he left for Italy and Greece, and on
the first day of August, 1840, he died at Athens of a fever
contracted while he was copying the inscriptions on the wall
of the *Peribolos* at Delphi. A marble monument marks the spot
where he was buried on the hill of Colonos.

At Göttingen he lectured repeatedly on Mythology and the History of
Religion, on Greek Antiquities, Latin Literature, and Comparative Grammar,
and also on Classical authors, such as Pindar, Aeschylus, Herodotus,
Thucydides, Tacitus, Persius and Juvenal. His early work on Aegina was
followed, three years later, by that on 'Orchomenos and the Minyae'[1]; in
1824, by the two volumes of the 'Dorians'[2]; in the next year, by his
'Prolegomena to a scientific Mythology'[3]; and, in 1828, by his 'Etruscans'[4].

Five years later, he published his edition of the *Eumenides*, with a German
rendering and with two Dissertations, (1) on the representation of the play,
(2) on its purport and composition[5]. In the preface to this work, he was
prompted by Hermann's attack on Dissen's Pindar[6] to describe Hermann as
'the distinguished scholar, who has long been promising us an edition of
Aeschylus, and who is ready to attack all who write on that poet before
proving that he possesses a clear conception of the connexion of thought
and the plan of a single play, or indeed of any work of ancient poetry'[7].
While Müller poured contempt on the professional scholars of the day, he
added that another race of men had already arisen, men who were asking the
old world deeper questions than could be answered by any mere *Noten-
gelehrsamkeit*. Hermann naturally protested, pointing out that Müller's
attitude was 'mistaken' as well as 'presumptuous'. This review, severe as it
was, did not prevent the just recognition of Müller's *Eumenides* as a distinctly
useful edition. The editor had set special store by his translation, and the
accuracy of that portion of the work was not contested by his great opponent,
while the first of the two dissertations certainly threw new light on the Greek
theatre and led to further research on that subject.

---

[1] 1844[2].   [2] E. T. 1830.   [3] E. T., Leitch.
[4] 1877 ed. Deecke.   [5] E. T. ed. 2, 1853.
[6] *Opusc.* vi. 3—69.
[7] *ib.* vi (2) 12 ; Müller and Donaldson's *Gr. Lit.* i xxiv ; Bursian, ii 675.

In the same year as the first edition of the *Eumenides*, Müller published a critical edition of Varro, *De Lingua Latina* (1833). He had been drawn in this direction by his Etruscan studies. Following in the lines laid down by Spengel, he introduced many corrections into the text, but he left much to be done by his successors, and Spengel himself returned to the work of his youth and prepared a new edition, which was published by his son. Müller also emended and annotated the remains of Festus, together with the epitome of the same by Paulus (1839, 1868[2]).

An invitation from the London Society for the Diffusion of Useful Knowledge led to his undertaking a 'History of Greek Literature', which he began in 1836, but left unfinished on his departure for Greece. The first twenty-two chapters were translated by George Cornewall Lewis, to whose suggestion the work was due, and the rest by Dr Donaldson in 1840, when the greater part of the work was published. The work was subsequently completed by Donaldson, who wrote chapters 38—60 for the edition published in three volumes in 1858[1]. The original author's aim was to show 'how those illustrious compositions, which we still justly admire as the *classical* writings of the Greeks, naturally sprang from the taste and the genius of the Greek races and the constitution of civil and domestic society as established among them'[2].

Müller had naturally been led to study the archaeology of art by the duties of his professorship. In this domain he produced a considerable number of separate treatises, as well as a comprehensive conspectus of the whole field. The former included his papers on the Delphic tripod, the cult and temple of Athena Polias, and the life and works of Pheidias. The latter is embodied in his well-known 'Handbook of the Archaeology of Art'[3]. Illustrations to this work were supplied in Müller's *Denkmäler* (1832), continued by his pupil, Friedrich Wieseler. Müller also wrote on Hesiod's *Shield of Heracles*, the Apollo of Kanachos, the date of the temple at Bassae, the vases of Vulci, the topography of Antioch, the frieze of the temple of Theseus, and the fortifications of Athens[4]. His account of the Museums of Athens was the only part of the results of his visit to Greece that was published by his fellow-traveller, Adolph Schöll (1843).

'As a classical scholar, we are inclined (says Donaldson) to prefer K. O. Müller, on the whole, to all the German philologers of the nineteenth century. He had not Niebuhr's grasp of original combination, he was hardly equal to his teacher, Böckh, in some branches of Greek...antiquities; he was inferior to Hermann in Greek verbal criticism; he was not a comparative philologer, like Grimm and Bopp and A. W. Schlegel, nor a collector of facts and forms like Lobeck. But in all the distinctive characteristics of these

---

[1] Müller's German text was published, from the rough drafts, by his younger brother in 1841; ed. 4 (E. Heitz), 1882–4.

[2] i 1 ed. Donaldson (1858).

[3] 1830; ed. 3 (Welcker) 1848; ed. 4, 1878; E. T., Leitch, 1850.

[4] *Kleine deutsche Schriften*, vol. ii, 1848.

eminent men, he approached them more nearly than most of his contemporaries, and he had some qualifications to which none of them attained.
In liveliness of fancy, in power of style, in elegance of taste, in artistic
knowledge, he far surpassed most, if not all, of them '[1].

While K. O. Müller, even in his study of ancient mythology
Welcker   and art, mainly followed the *historical* method of
research, the *poetic and artistic* side of the old
Greek world had won the interest of his predecessor at Göttingen,
Friedrich Gottlieb Welcker (1784—1868), who was born thirteen
years before him, and survived him by no less than twenty-eight[2].
The son of a country-clergyman in Hesse, he worked by himself
at Giessen, where he afterwards lectured, first on theological
subjects, and next on Plato's *Symposium*, and the *Prometheus*.
In 1806–8 he visited Italy, holding a tutorship in Rome in the
family of Wilhelm von Humboldt. In Rome he came under
the influence of the able Danish archaeologist, Zoëga, subsequently writing his life, and translating and publishing his works[3].
In 1809 he became a professor at Giessen; in 1814, a volunteer
in the war against Napoleon; in 1816, a professor at Göttingen,
and in 1819 at Bonn, where he was also librarian and director
of the Museum of ancient Art, the earliest institution of the
kind. At Bonn he continued to live for nearly fifty years, the
last seven of which were spent in retirement owing to failing
eyesight. During his long tenure of office in that university, he
spent two years travelling in Greece[4], Asia Minor, Italy and
Sicily.

His lectures at Bonn covered a wide range, including Greek and Latin
poets, Greek mythology, and the history of ancient art. His audience was
profoundly impressed by his noble personality, and by a fulness of thought,
which was not accompanied by any remarkable richness or clearness of
language[5].

---

[1] *On the Life and Writings of K. O. Müller*, p. xxxi, in *Hist. of the Lit.
of ancient Greece*, I xv—xxxi (with portrait); cp. *Lebensbild* by K. F. Ranke
(Berlin, Gymn. Progr., 1870): *Erinnerungen* by E. Müller, and F. Lücke;
Briefwechsel with Boeckh (Teubner, 1883); and Bursian, ii 1007—1028; also
K. Hildebrand in Fr. transl. of *Gk Lit.*, 1865, 17 f; E. Curtius, *Alt. u.
Gegenwart*, ii[2] 247 f; Hertz, Breslau, 1884; K. Dilthey, Göttingen, 1898.

[2] On Müller and Welcker, cp. Michaelis, *Die arch. Entd.*, 253.

[3] Chap. xxxviii *infra* (Denmark).   [4] *Tagebuch* (1865).

[5] Classen, quoted by Kekulé, 174 f.

His general aim was to realise and to represent the old Greek world under the three aspects of Religion, Poetry, and Art. His researches in Greek mythology were embodied in the three volumes of his *Griechische Götterlehre* (1857–62). This was supplemented by his edition of Hesiod's *Theogony*, with general introductory essays on Hesiod, and a special dissertation on the *Theogony*.

In the earlier part of his career he had been attracted by the Greek lyric poets and Aristophanes. He translated the *Clouds* and the *Frogs*, with explanatory notes; wrote a paper on Epicharmus[1], and several on Pindar[2]; collected the fragments of Alcman and Hipponax, Erinna and Corinna; and repeatedly defended the character of Sappho[3]. In an edition of Theognis, he arranged the poems according to his own views, adding critical and explanatory notes and full prolegomena. He also published a *Sylloge* of Greek Epigrams, and criticised Hermann's proposals for restoring the text. His works on the tragic poets began with a treatise on the Aeschylean trilogy of Prometheus, which was attacked by Hermann, and defended by Welcker in a treatise on the Aeschylean trilogy in general. The most extensive of his works on the drama was that on the 'Greek Tragedies in relation to the Epic Cycle'[4]. As a preliminary to this he had produced a work on the Epic Cycle itself[5]. In the department of Greek prose authors, he supplied Fr. Jacobs with archaeological notes on the Philostrati and Callistratus; he also wrote papers on Prodicus[6], and on the rhetorician Aristides[7].

His main strength as an archaeologist lay less in the *history* of art than in its *interpretation*. At Göttingen, the greater part of the single volume of the *Zeitschrift* on the history and interpretation of art was written by Welcker alone (1818); and at Bonn, he published an explanatory catalogue of the Museum of Casts[8]. He was a member of the 'Roman Institute for Archaeological Correspondence' from its foundation in 1829, and frequently contributed to its publications, and to other archaeological periodicals. The most important of his papers were collected in the five parts of his *Alte Denkmäler* (1849–64), which had been partly preceded by the five volumes of his *Kleine Schriften* (1844–67)[9].

While Welcker's interests traversed the literary as well as the artistic sides of the old Greek world, a narrower field was covered by his friend and fellow-labourer,   Gerhard

---

[1] *Kleine Schriften*, i 271—356.   [2] ii 169—214, v 252 f.
[3] i 110—125, and esp. ii 80—114; cp. iv 68, v 228—242. For papers on other lyric poets, cp. i 89, 126; ii 215, 356.
[4] 3 vols, 1839–41.   [5] 1835; ed. 2, 1865 (part ii, 1849, ed. 2, 1882).
[6] *Kl. Schr.* ii 393—541.   [7] iii 89—156.
[8] 1827; ed. 2, 1841.
[9] Bursian, ii 1028—1046; cp. Life by Kekulé, with portrait (1880); Correspondence with Boeckh, in Max Hoffmann's *Boeckh*, 152—208; also Wilamowitz in *Eur. Her.* i[1] 239 f.

Eduard Gerhard (1795—1867), who regarded archaeology as 'that part of the general science of the old classical world which is founded on the knowledge of monuments', and claimed for it an independent place by the side of 'philology' in the narrower sense of that term. Born at Posen, he studied at Breslau and Berlin, but was compelled by weakness of sight to abandon the work of teaching that he had begun at Breslau and at the place of his birth. He visited Italy in 1819–20 and 1822–6, and again in 1828–32, and in 1833 and 1836. In 1837 he became director of the Archaeological Museum in Berlin, and was a full professor from 1844 to his death in 1867.

It was his first visit to Italy that inspired him with his earliest enthusiasm for ancient art, and during his long residence in that land he became familiar with archaeologists of other nations, such as Bröndsted (1780—1842), the representative of Denmark, and Stackelberg (1787—1834), the Esthonian nobleman, who was then preparing his two great works on the Temple of Bassae (1826), and on the Graves of the Greeks (1837). Stackelberg had fallen under the spell of Creuzer's *Symbolik*, and it was owing to the influence of Stackelberg that Gerhard was led to believe that the works of art found in ancient tombs were connected with the cult and the mysteries of Dionysus.

In 1823 Gerhard was joined by Theodor Panofka (1801—1858), who entered the university of Berlin in 1819, and, after promoting the interests of the international Archaeological Institute in Rome and in Paris, returned to Berlin, where he became a Member of the Academy, and, for the last fifteen years of his life, an 'extraordinary' professor. A man of wide but rather confused learning, he had an undue fondness for discovering mythological explanations of works of ancient art[1], for finding traces of allegory in the most unimportant objects, and for indulging his fancy in matters of etymology, as well as in the interpretation of works of art or handicraft[2].

Panofka

The influence of Panofka is apparent in Gerhard's *Venus Proserpina*, in his *Roms antike Bildwerke*[3], his *Prodromus* to the mythological interpretation of art, and his *Hyperboreische-römische Studien*. His views were not materially altered in his Berlin[4] papers, or in the two volumes of his 'Greek Mythology' (1854–5).

---

[1] *Verlegene Mythen* (1840) ; cp. Bursian, ii 1049 n. 3.

[2] Among his more valuable works are his *Res Samiorum* (1822), his *Bilderatlas antiken Lebens* (1843), his *Griechinnen und Griechen nach Antiken* (1844), and his descriptions of the terra-cottas in Berlin and Naples, and in private collections elsewhere.

[3] In Platner and Bunsen's *Beschreibung der Stadt Rom*, i 277—334.

[4] *Gesammelte Akad. Abhandlungen* (with 4to vol. of Plates), 1866–8.

Gerhard had a remarkable aptitude for classifying ancient monuments, a marvellous memory for all the known representatives of each class, and an ample store of illustrative classical learning. Even his weakness of eyesight did not interfere with a rapid apprehension of the salient points, and the general style, of any work of ancient art. This is exemplified in his descriptive catalogue of the Vatican Museum, and in his unfinished account of the works of ancient art in Naples. Apart from his catalogues of the collections in Berlin, his best-known works were his four volumes on Greek vase-paintings[1], his descriptions of Etruscan mirrors[2], and his numerous papers on the mythology and cult of the Greeks[3].

During his third stay in Rome (1828–32), Gerhard, in conjunction with Bunsen and Kestner, took in hand the foundation of the 'International Institute for Archaeological Correspondence'. Gerhard, Kestner, Fea, and Thorwaldsen met at Bunsen's official residence, the Palazzo Caffarelli on the Capitol, on the anniversary of the birth of Winckelmann, the 9th of December, to draw up a scheme for the new Institute, which was to be founded in 1829, on April 21, the traditional date of the founding of Rome. Its publications subsequently included a monthly *Bulletino,* annual volumes of *Annali* and *Monumenti,* and, in and after 1872, the *Ephemeris Epigraphica.*

The success of the Institute in Rome was largely due to the ability of its secretaries. Bunsen was general secretary in 1829–38, and was aided, at first, by Gerhard and Panofka, and (on Gerhard's departure) by Ambrosch, and by the chaplain of the legation, H. Abeken, and the Danish scholar, O. Kellermann (1805—1838). The last of these was the first to propound a great scheme for a critical collection of Latin inscriptions.

When Gerhard returned to Rome in 1833, he was accompanied by an able amanuensis, August Emil Braun (1809—1856), who was born at Gotha, and had studied classical archaeology in Göttingen, Munich, Dresden, and Paris, and who acted as secretary of the Institute until his death. Braun was an authority in matters of archaeology, but in later years he developed an inordinate repugnance to the use of ancient literature in illustration of the remains of ancient art[4].

Braun

As secretary, Braun was associated with the celebrated Egyptologist, Richard Lepsius, and with Wilhelm Abeken (1813—1843), the author of a work on the early inhabitants of ancient Italy, and Wilhelm Henzen (1816—1887), Welcker's pupil and fellow-traveller in Greece, who afterwards (under the influence of Mommsen) devoted most of his energy to the *Corpus Inscriptionum Latinarum*[5].

---

[1] *Auserlesene Gr. Vasenbilder* (1840–58).   [2] 4 parts (1843–68).

[3] Life by Otto Jahn in Gerhard's *Abhandlungen,* ii 1—122; cp. Urlichs in *A. D. B.,* and Bursian, ii 1046—1066.

[4] His chief works were *Antike Marmorwerke* (1844); *XII Basreliefs* (1845); *Gr. Götterlehre* (1854); *Vorschule der Kunstmythologie* (1854). Cp. (A. Michaelis), *Gesch. des deutschen Archäol. Inst.* 53 f, 101 f, 112 f, 125 f.

[5] *Biogr. Jahrb.* 1888, 135—160.

Gerhard's biographer was the able and scholarly archaeologist, Otto Jahn (1813—1869), who studied at Kiel, Leipzig, and Berlin; was a 'privat-docent' at Kiel in 1839, professor at Greifswald in 1842–7, and at Leipzig from 1847 to 1851, when he was dismissed on political grounds and found a city of refuge in Zürich. For the last fourteen years of his life he was professor at Bonn, and, in 1869, he died at Göttingen.

Jahn

An adept in music, he found his chief interest in classical scholarship, and in the scholarly study of classical archaeology. Under the influence of Nitzsch at Kiel, and Lachmann in Berlin, he became an eager student of the Greek and Latin poets. His earliest interest in archaeology was aroused by his visits to Paris in 1837 and Rome in 1838, when he came under the influence of Emil Braun. Greek vases were the theme of a large number of his papers; he also wrote an introduction to their study in his Description of the Collection in the Munich *Pinakothek* (1854). Shortly after his return from Italy, he began his career as an academic teacher. That career was only interrupted by his political activity at Kiel in 1848, by the enforced leisure of 1851–5, and by the illness that immediately preceded his death.

His well-equipped series of text-books for university lectures included the Story of Cupid and Psyche from Apuleius, the Description of the Athenian Acropolis in Pausanias[1], the *Electra* of Sophocles, the *Symposium* of Plato, and the treatise on the Sublime[2]. All except the last were embellished with illustrations from works of ancient art. His annotated school-editions included the *Brutus* and the *Orator* of Cicero[3]. His critical recensions comprised Persius (1843) and Juvenal (1851), followed by a new edition of both (1868); also Florus, and Censorinus, and the *Periochae* of Livy, together with Julius Obsequens. One of the best of his papers was that on the *Subscriptiones* at the end of MSS of the Classics[4].

His work in archaeology, apart from the Introduction to Greek Vases already mentioned, includes a large number of masterly monographs. The subjects of the earlier group included Telephus and Troilus, the paintings of Polygnotus, 'Pentheus and the Maenads', 'Paris and Oenone', with discourses on Ancient Tragedy and Goethe's *Iphigenie*, on Welcker and Winckelmann, and on Hellenic Art, as well as an essay on the Palladium[5], and the collected papers entitled *Archäologische Aufsätze* and *Beiträge* (1845–7).

At Leipzig he published numerous papers in the transactions of the local Academy, including one on the art-criticisms of the elder Pliny[6], and on

[1] 1860; ed. 2 (Michaelis) 1880; ed. 3, 1901.

[2] 1867; ed. 3 (Vahlen), 1905.

[3] 1849–51; ed. 3, 1865–9; ed. 4 of *Brutus*, 1877.

[4] *Sächs. Berichte*, iii (1851) 337 f.   [5] *Philologus*, i 55 f.

[6] *Sächs. Berichte*, ii 105 f.

scenes from Greek poets on Greek vases[1].   He also contributed to the publications of the learned societies of Munich, Vienna, Zürich, Bonn, and Rome.

His lectures at Bonn were lucid and unadorned in style, and while the
salient points were brought into clear relief, there was a perfect mastery of all
the details.   He lavished his resources on the collection of a splendid library,
which enabled him to acquire a minute familiarity with the remotest corners of
ancient life, a familiarity exemplified not only in his learned commentary on
Persius, but also in his elaborate paper on the ancient superstition of the
' evil eye '[2].

It was at Bonn that he delivered his two discourses on the general position
of Classical Studies in Germany (1859–62)[3].   Even in his years of failing health
he produced much of the work that appears in his ' Popular Essays ' (1868).
His latest work, that on the Greek inscribed reliefs of mythological and
historical scenes, was edited after his death by his distinguished nephew and
pupil, Adolf Michaelis[4].

A new life was given to the Archaeological Institute by
Henzen, and by Heinrich Brunn (1822—1894), a
pupil of Welcker and Ritschl at Bonn, where he

Brunn

submitted for his degree a dissertation on the sources of Pliny's
chapters on the History of Art (1843).   He resided in Rome
from that date to 1853, the year of the publication of the first
volume of his well-known ' History of the Greek Artists '[5].   After
a brief interval at Bonn, he lived once more in Rome from 1856
to 1865, when he became professor at Munich, holding that
position with conspicuous ability for nearly thirty years.

Many of his published papers were preparatory to a comprehensive
' History of Greek and Roman Art ', the early portions of which were printed
in 1893–7.   A volume of Essays entitled *Griechische Götterideale* was
published by himself (1893) ; his minor works have since been collected in
three volumes[6] ; and a series of fine reproductions of ' Monuments of Greek
and Roman Sculpture ', begun in his life-time, has been continued since his
death.   His style as a teacher was marked by simplicity and clearness, by
enthusiasm for his subject, and by a complete absence of rhetorical adornment.
Not content with giving results, he also pointed out the strictly scientific

---

[1]   *Abhandl.* iii 697 f.

[2]   *Sächs. Berichte*, vii (1855) 28—110.

[3]   Winckelmann, Hermann, and Ludwig Ross are admirably treated in his
Biographische Aufsätze (ed. 2, 1866).

[4]   *Bilderchroniken* (1873).   Cp. Michaelis in *A. D. B.*, and *Arch. Entd.*
254 ; also Bursian, ii 1070–80, esp. the quotations on p. 1075 ; Vahlen, 1870,
24 pp.; Mommsen, in *Reden und Aufsätze*, 458 f.

[5]   1853–9 ; ed. 2, 1889.   [6]   1898—1905–6, with portraits.

method by which they had been attained[1]. Among his numerous discoveries may be mentioned his recognition of the so-called 'Leucothea' of the Munich *Glyptothek* as the 'Eirene and Plutus' of Cephisodotus[2]; and his identification of a series of scattered works of sculpture (all belonging to a Roman find of 1514) as the remnants of the four groups of figures set up by Attalus I on the Acropolis of Athens to commemorate the battles of the Pergamenes against the Galatians, of the Athenians against the Persians and the Amazons, and of the Gods against the Giants[3]. The relations between the literature and the art of Greece are exemplified in his paper on the indications of artistic inspiration in Greek idyllic poetry[4]. The discovery in modern times of many works of ancient art unrecognised by Pliny or Pausanias has led to a more independent study of Greek sculpture for its own sake, and to a closer attention to the *analysis of artistic style*. The pioneer in this new movement was Heinrich Brunn[5].

Brunn's successor as secretary at Rome was Wolfgang Helbig
Helbig (b. 1839), a pupil of Jahn and Ritschl, who is best known as the author of two volumes on the wall-paintings of Pompeii, proving that nearly all of them were repro-ductions of Hellenistic works (1868–73), and also of a volume in which the Homeric poems are illustrated by the remains of ancient art (1884). His guide to the Roman Museums was published in 1891.

Immediately after the Institute had become an Imperial insti-tution, a branch was opened at Athens (1874). The first secretary at Athens was Otto Lüders, a pupil of Welcker, and author of
Die dionysischen Künstler (1873)[6]. He was suc-
Köhler ceeded by Ulrich Köhler (1838—1903), for many years editor of the *Mittheilungen* and of several volumes of the *Corpus Inscriptionum Atticarum*[7].

[1] G. Körte, in *Berl. Philol. Woch.* 1899, 885 f. At Bonn, in 1843, Brunn had maintained that 'he would rather err *with* method, than hit upon truth *without*'.

[2] 1867; *Kl. Schr.* ii 328—340; cp. Michaelis, *Arch. Entd.* (1906) 267.

[3] 1870; *Kl. Schr.* ii 411—430; cp. E. A. Gardner, *Gk Sculpture*, 457—460.

[4] 1879; *Kl. Schr.* iii 217—228.

[5] Cp. Michaelis, *Arch. Entd.* (1906) 260 f. On Brunn, cp. A. Emerson in *Amer. Journ. of Archaeology*, ix (1894) 360—371 (with two portraits); on his pupils, cp. Bursian, ii 1088.

[6] See, in general, (A. Michaelis), *Gesch. des deutschen archäol. Instituts*, 1829–79.

[7] *Deutscher Nekrolog*, 1905; *Biogr. Jahrb.* 1906, 12—29 (with bibliography). On Dittenberger (d. 1906) and Furtwängler (d. 1907) see *Addenda*.

Among the representatives of the 'statistical' type of archaeologists, who (like Gerhard) aimed at collecting all the extant remains of ancient art and interpreting them in the light of literary and   **Wieseler** artistic evidence, a foremost place must be assigned to Friedrich Wieseler (1811—1892). After studying at Göttingen and Berlin, it was at the former university that he passed through all the successive stages of a professorial career extending over three and fifty years. In his earliest works he discussed the text and the plot of several Greek plays[1], besides writing on the *Thymele*, and publishing an illustrated folio volume on the Greek and Roman Theatre (1851). He produced numerous papers on archaeology, and on mythology in art[2]. He is best known for his continuation of Müller's *Denkmäler*[3].

Another archaeologist of the same general type was Ludolf Stephani (1816—1887), who studied at Leipzig under Hermann and W. A. Becker, and published in 1843 the topographical and   **Stephani** epigraphical results of his tour in Northern Greece. In 1846 he was called to the university of Dorpat, where he continued the study of Greek inscriptions; and, in 1850, was made a Member of the St Petersburg Academy, and Keeper of the coins and other antiquities in the Hermitage. To the publications of the Academy he contributed a number of exhaustive monographs[4]. He also prepared, on a scale of unprecedented magnificence, the reports on the archaeological exploration of the Crimea[5], and the twenty volumes of the *Comptes-rendus* of the Imperial Archaeological Commission, together with the descriptive catalogue of the vases in the Hermitage, and of the antiques in the palace at Pawlowsk[6].

Among those who contributed to the study and appreciation of Greek architecture were Karl Friedrich Schinkel (1781—1841), a practical architect, whose design for the erection of a royal   **Architects** palace on the platform of the Athenian Acropolis was happily never carried out; Leo von Klenze (1784—1864), the author of a work on the temple of Zeus at Agrigentum (1821); Gottfried Semper (1803—1879), the author of an important volume on architectural style[7]; and Karl Boetticher (1806—1889), the author of the *Tektonik der Hellenen*[8]. Johann Heinrich Strack (1805—1880) wrote a monograph on the ancient Greek Theatre (1843), and brought about the complete excavation of the Theatre of Dionysus at Athens (1862)[9]. Richard Bohn (1849—1898) was among the architects employed in the exploration of Olympia and Pergamon[10].

---

[1] *Eum.* (1839), *P. V.* and *Aves* (1843) etc.   [2] Bursian, ii 1092 note.

[3] *Biogr. Jahrb.* 1900, 9—41 (with bibliography).

[4] *Der ausruhende Herakles* (1854); *Nimbus und Strahlenkranz* (1859) etc.

[5] *Antiquités du Bosphore Cimmérien* (1854); also *Antiquités de la Scythie* (1866, 1873).

[6] *Biogr. Jahrb.* 1886, 258—263; Bursian, ii 1092-5.

[7] 1860-3; ed. 2, 1878-9; *Biogr. Jahrb.* 1879, 49—83; Bursian, ii 1107 f.

[8] 1843-52; ed. 2, 1873-81; *Biogr. Jahrb.* 1890, 71—81.

[9] *Biogr. Jahrb.* 1885, 96—100.   [10] Conze in *A. D. B.* xlvii 81.

Archaeological research in many lands was promoted by the excavations
Schliemann   initiated by Heinrich Schliemann (1822—1890). The son
of a German pastor, he had often heard his father tell the
story of the Trojan war, and, at the age of eight, he resolved on excavating
the site of Troy. At the age of fourteen, as a grocer's apprentice, he heard a
miller's man, who had known better days, recite a hundred lines of Homer,
and he then prayed that he might some day have the happiness of learning
Greek. At the age of twenty-five, he founded an indigo business at
St Petersburg, and by the age of thirty-six had acquired a sufficient fortune to
be able to devote himself entirely to archaeology. He had then been studying
Greek for two years, not having dared to do so before, for fear of falling under
the spell of Homer and neglecting his business. In his earliest work, that on
'Ithaca, Peloponnesus, and Troy' (1869), he inferred from Pausanias[1] that the
graves of the Atreidae at Mycenae must be sought *inside* the wall of the
citadel, and he supported the opinion that the site of Troy was on the hill of
Hissarlik. The hill was excavated in 1870–73, and the results published in
1874–5. His exploration of Mycenae (1874–6) was fully described in 1877.
Resuming his work at 'Troy' (1878–9), he published his results in *Ilios*
(1880). After excavating the 'treasury of Minyas' at Orchomenos (1880–1),
he returned to Troy, and published *Troja* (1884). An imperfect exploration
of the 'mound of Marathon' was followed by successful work at Tiryns (1885).
In the island of Cythera he discovered the ancient temple of the Uranian
Aphrodite (1888), and on that of Sphacteria the old fortifications mentioned
by Thucydides[2].

He had a palatial house at Athens inscribed with the words ΙΛΙΟΥ ΜΕΛΑ-
ΘΡΟΝ ; the floor was adorned with mosaics representing vases and urns from
'Troy'; along the walls ran painted friezes with epic landscapes, and Homeric
quotations. The porter's name was Bellerophon, the footman's Telamon, and
Schliemann himself would be generally engaged in reading some Greek
Classic. He had married a Greek wife, who was as enthusiastic as himself in
the exploration of Mycenae; he called his daughter Andromache, and his son
Agamemnon. When the archaeological world was looking forward to his
proposed exploration of Crete, he died suddenly in Naples. He was buried at
Athens in the Greek cemetery south of the Ilissus. His desire that his body
should there rest in the land of his adoption was carried out by Dörpfeld, who
had taken a leading part in the excavations at Tiryns, and who afterwards
published an important work summing up the results of the exploration of Troy,
which was finally completed by Dörpfeld alone[3].

---

[1] ii 16, 4.

[2] iv 31, 2.

[3] *Troja und Ilion* (1902). Cp. in general, Schuchardt, *Schliemanns
Ausgrabungen* (1890), E.T. (with biography); also Bursian, ii 1113–9; Joseph
(Berlin, 1902[2]); Brunn, *Kl. Schr.* iii 279—282; and Michaelis, *Arch. Entd.*
182 f.

All the provinces of archaeological research,—the history of archaeology, the history and interpretation of ancient art, as well as mythology, antiquities and historical topography, were traversed in the professorial teaching, and in the published works, of Karl Bernard Stark (1824—1879). After studying under Göttling, Hermann, and Boeckh, and travelling in Italy, he settled at Jena in 1848, and, in 1855, was called to Heidelberg, where he held a professorship for the last twenty-four years of his life.   Meanwhile, he had produced his first important work, that on Gaza and the Philistine coast (1852), followed by his monograph on Niobe (1863). He spent his latest years in preparing a comprehensive Handbook to the Archaeology of Art, and the first part, including the general survey of the subject, and the history of its study, was posthumously published in 1880.   His Lectures and Essays on Archaeology and on the History of Art were published in the same year[1].

Another short-lived archaeologist, Karl Friederichs (1831—1871), was the author of a full description of the Berlin Museum of Casts (1868; ed. 2, 1885), and of works on Praxiteles and the Philostrati.

An important history of ancient sculpture[2] was published by Joannes Overbeck (1826—1895), a native of Antwerp, who was educated at Hamburg and who studied at Bonn, and was professor of Classical Archaeology at Leipzig from 1858 to his death.   All the Greek and Latin texts on ancient art are conveniently collected in his *Schriftquellen* (1848).   Mythology in art is the sphere of his great series of illustrations connected with the heroes of the Theban and the Trojan Cycle (1853), and with the gods of Greece (1871 f)[3].   His standard work on Pompeii (1856), written before he had visited the place, was afterwards repeatedly enlarged and improved.

Conrad Bursian (1830—1883), who has done due honour to archaeology in connexion with the history of classical philology, received his early education under Stallbaum at Leipzig, where he continued his studies under Haupt

---

[1] *Biogr. Jahrb.* 1879, 40—45 ; Bursian, ii 1100-2.
[2] 1857 f ; ed. 4, 1894.   [3] Bursian, ii 1105.

and Jahn. He also worked for a short time in Berlin under Boeckh. After travelling in Greece (1852–5), he held professorships of Classics and Archaeology at Leipzig, Tübingen, Zürich, and Jena, and for the last nine years of his life was a professor at Munich.

Apart from papers on Greek geography and archaeology, his early works included an edition of the elder Seneca (1856). It was at Tübingen that he completed the first volume of his important 'Geography of Greece' (1867), reserving the second for publication in three parts in 1868–72. Its completion was delayed by his comprehensive monograph on Greek Art in 'Ersch and Gruber'. His interest in Greek Geography was further shown in his editions of several of the minor Greek Geographers. In 1877 he founded an important periodical for the annual survey of the progress of classical learning[1]. He spent his last ten years on the crowning work of his life, his 'History of Classical Philology in Germany'[2].

Otto Benndorf (1838—1907), who studied at Erlangen and (under Jahn) at Bonn, was successively professor of archaeology at Zürich, Prag, and Vienna, where he was placed at the head of the Austrian Archaeological Institute on its foundation in 1898. He began his brilliant career by producing at Bonn in 1865 a well-known dissertation on the Epigrams of the Greek Anthology relating to works of art. In conjunction with R. Schoene he described the ancient sculptures of the Lateran Museum (1867); he also published a work on Greek and Sicilian vases (1869 f), and a monograph on the metopes of Selinus (1873). He was associated with Conze and Hauser in the second Austrian expedition to Samothrace (1875), with Petersen in the exploration of the *heroön* of Giölbaschi near Myra in Lycia (1881 f), and with Heberdey and Wilberg in the excavations at Ephesus (1896)[3].

Another pupil of Jahn, Friedrich Matz (1843—1874), began his brief career with a paper in which he took up a position between that of Karl Friederichs, who had attacked, and Heinrich

---

[1] *Jahresbericht über die Fortschritte der classischen Alterthumswissenschaft.*

[2] 1271 pp. (1883); *Biogr. Jahrb.* 1883, 1—11.

[3] Cp. Bursian, ii 1085, and Michaelis, *Arch. Entd.* 98 f, 158 f, 164 f; *Forschungen in Ephesos*, vol. i (Vienna, 1907).

Brunn, who had defended the authenticity of the pictorial descriptions of the two Philostrati (1867).

Among the earliest of the Germans who took part in the topographical exploration of Greek lands were Friedrich Thiersch[1], and Ludwig Ross (1806 —1859), the explorer of the Greek Islands (1840–52) and the author of a work on the Attic Demes (1852)[2]. **Geographers**

Peter Wilhelm Forchhammer (1801—1894), who was educated at Lübeck and studied at Kiel, travelled in Italy, Greece and Asia Minor from 1830 to 1836, and was a professor at Kiel for the remaining fifty-eight years of his life. The observations made during his earlier Greek travels appeared in his *Hellenika* (1837). During his second tour of 1838–40, he visited the Troad with the English naval officer, T. A. B. Spratt, whose map was published with Forchhammer's 'Observations on the topography of Troy' (1843–50). He also wrote on the topography of Athens (1841), and, nearly forty years afterwards, on the finds at Mycenae. In his numerous mythological papers he contended that Mythology had its origin in natural phenomena, especially in those connected with water. **Forchhammer**

In the earliest of his archaeological publications he rightly maintained, against Boeckh, that cases of homicide were not removed from the jurisdiction of the Areopagus by the reforms of Ephialtes ; and, in his work on 'Socrates and the Athenians', he paradoxically represented Socrates as a revolutionist and the Athenians as prompted by their reverence for the law in condemning him to death[3]. After Kiel had been incorporated with Prussia, Forchhammer became a Member of Parliament. He lived to be more than ninety, and was a keen student of mythology and of art to the very end. His abiding interest in the old Greek world was proved by his discussions of school-reform in 1882, and his paper on 'mind and matter' in 1889[4].

A life of far shorter duration was the lot of another native of Northern Europe, Heinrich Ulrichs (1807—1843), who was born at Bremen, and, during his stay in Greece, explored Delphi and Thebes and the intervening district, as well as the harbours of Athens. He was professor of Latin at Athens in 1834, and died there nine years later[5]. **H. Ulrichs**

The whole of the *Orbis Veteribus Notus* was traversed in the course of the life-long labours of Heinrich Kiepert (1818—1899). In his native city of Berlin he attended the lectures of Boeckh and of Karl Ritter, began his travels in Asia Minor in 1841, was appointed Director of the Geographical Institute at Weimar in 1845, and, after returning to Berlin in 1852, was successively elected a Member of the Academy (1855), 'extraordinary' professor (1859) and 'ordinary' professor of Geography **Kiepert**

---

[1] p. 111 *supra*.   [2] Jahn, *Biogr. Aufs.* 133—164.   [3] p. 74 *supra*.

[4] *Biogr. Jahrb.* 1897, 41—63 (with bibliography).

[5] Life in vol. ii of his *Reisen und Forschungen* (1840–63), ed. Passow.

(1874). He gave lectures in all these capacities. Apart from many separate maps of the highest degree of excellence, the publications by which he is best known are his comprehensive and lucid text-book of Ancient Geography (1878), his *Atlas Antiquus* (1859) and his *Atlas von Hellas* (1872). His *Atlas Antiquus* has attained a twelfth edition, and the publication of his *Formae Orbis Antiqui* has been continued since his death[1].

In Greek topography a wide field was covered by the comprehensive work of Bursian[2], and also by the
Historians:
E. Curtius varied labours of Ernst Curtius (1814—1896).
Born and bred at Lübeck, where his father was
the *Bürgermeister* of that ancient Hanseatic town, he had no
sooner come to the end of his *Lehrjahre* at Bonn and Göttingen
and Berlin than he began his four years of *Wanderjahre* in Greece
(1836–40). His travels and researches bore fruit in an admirable
work on the *Peloponnesos* (1851–2). Meanwhile, he had taken
his degree at Halle, and had begun his distinguished career in
Berlin (1843). He was a professor at Göttingen from 1856 to
1868, when he returned to Berlin, and was one of the ornaments
of that university for the remaining twenty-eight years of his life.

His History of Greece was published in 1857–67[3], while he was still at Göttingen. It has justly been regarded as a brilliant achievement. The author's travels had enabled him to give a vivid impression of the geographical characteristics of the country. The narrative was lucid and interesting, and literature and art found due recognition in its pages[4].

A lecture on Olympia, delivered in 1844 in the presence of the King of Prussia, led to his being appointed tutor to the Crown Prince Friedrich, whom he accompanied to the university of Bonn, and whom he inspired with an interest in ancient and modern art. He was thus enabled in after years to secure high patronage for the exploration of Olympia[5], the successful completion of which was largely due to his influence. His study was adorned with a copy of the *Nike* of Paeonius, the first-fruits of the rich harvest of the Olympian plain. His own marble bust, the gift of his admirers, was also there, and a *replica* of the same was appropriately placed in the Museum at Olympia. His light hair, his sparkling eyes, and the clear-cut profile of his

---

[1] Autobiography in *Globus*, 1899, no. 19.

[2] p. 226 *supra*.   [3] Ed. 6, 1888; E. T. by A. W. Ward, 1868–73.

[4] His theory that the mainland of Greece was colonised by the Ionians of Asia Minor, long before Asia Minor was colonised by a returning wave of colonists from Greece, was first proposed in a paper of 1855, *Die Ionier vor der ionischen Wanderung*, energetically opposed in A. von Gutschmid's *Beiträge* of 1858.

[5] 1875—1881; *Ergebnisse*, 1881–97.

face, as well as his charm of manner, made him a singularly attractive personality. He had a strong physique and enjoyed excellent health. At the age of eighty, he once stood for an hour, delivering without note an admirable discourse on the hereditary priests of Olympia. In his old age, however, his failing eyesight compelled him to submit to several operations for cataract.

Apart from his early work on the *Peloponnesos*, and the 'History' of his maturer years, we have the fruit of his old age in a comprehensive and well-ordered 'History of the City of Athens' (1891)[1]. His occasional discourses on ancient and modern topics have been collected in the three volumes entitled *Alterthum und Gegenwart* (1875–89), and his more learned papers in two volumes published in 1894. A special interest attaches to the articles which he wrote in memory of Colonel Leake, as well as of Boeckh, K. O. Müller, and his younger brother, Georg Curtius[2]. His bust has been already mentioned ; his portrait was painted in oils by Koner for the National Gallery in Berlin, and also by Reinhold Lipsius[3].

The first volume of *Die Stadt Athen im Alterthum* (1874–90) was dedicated to Curtius by Curt Wachsmuth (1837—1905), professor at Marburg, Göttingen, Heidelberg and Leipzig, who in 1884 C. Wachsmuth published the first two volumes of an important edition of the *Anthologium* of Stobaeus, followed in 1895 by his excellent Introduction to the study of ancient history[4].

The exploration of Olympia during the first two seasons (1875–7) was entrusted to Gustav Hirschfeld (1847—1895), who had studied in Berlin under Curtius, whom he accompanied on a G. Hirschfeld tour in Asia Minor, besides working at archaeology during his own travels in Italy and Greece. In 1877–8 he was at work on the Greek Inscriptions of the British Museum, his edition of which was published in 1893. He took a prominent part in the discussions as to the authority of Pausanias[5], and as to the date of the foundation of Naucratis and the antiquity of the early Greek inscriptions[6].

---

[1] The *Sieben Karten zur Topographie von Athen* (1868) were followed by Curtius and Kaupert's *Atlas von Athen* (1876) and *Karten von Attika* (1881–94), and by Milchhöfer's *Uebersichtskarte von Attika* (1903).

[2] *Alterthum und Gegenwart*, vols. ii, iii.

[3] Gurlitt, in *Biogr. Jahrb.* 1901, 113—144; cp. *Ein Lebensbild in Briefen* (1903); also Bursian, ii 1129 f, 1146 f; Broicher, in *Preuss. Jahrb.*, 1896, 582—603; Kekulé's *Rede*, 1896; Keep, in *A.J.P.* xix 121—137; T. Hodgkin, in *Proc. Brit. Acad.* ii (Feb. 1905), 24 pp.; and (A. W. Ward) *Edin. Review*, 1904 (1) 403—431; A. Michaelis, in *Deutscher Nekrolog*, (1897) 56—88.

[4] F. Marx, in *Deutscher Nekrolog*, (1907) 42 f.

[5] *Arch. Zeitung*, 1882, 97—130 ; *Jahrb. f. kl. Philol.* 1883, 769 f.

[6] *Academy*, 9 July, 20 Aug. 1887 ; 4 Jan. 1890; *Rhein. Mus.* XLII (1887) 209 f; *Rev. des études grecques*, 1890, 221 f. Cp. *Biogr. Jahrb.* 1898, 65—90 (with bibliography).

Hirschfeld was the first to urge the importance of the excavation of Pergamon ; but it was owing to the energy of Alexander Conze, who had left

Humann   Vienna for Berlin in 1877, that the explorations begun in
1869 by Karl Humann (1839—1896) were successfully con-
tinued in 1878 by that eager excavator and his colleagues. The exploration
of the acropolis and its precincts, completed in 1886, has disclosed a new
chapter in the history of Greek Sculpture and of Greek Architecture[1].

The erudite historian, Max Duncker (1811—1886), was born in Berlin, and

Duncker   studied philosophy at Bonn under Brandis, and history under
Loebell. He began his literary career with a Latin disserta-
tion on the various methods of treating history (1834). The part that he
played in a political movement among the students at Bonn led to his being
condemned to imprisonment for a term of six years, reduced by the royal
favour to six months, which he spent in strenuous study. During his
eighteen years at Halle, he passed from the early history of the Germans to
that of the Indo-Germanic peoples, publishing in 1852–7 the four volumes of
the first edition of his *Geschichte des Alterthums*. The work was ultimately
expanded into nine volumes, but its concluding portion, the History of Greece,
goes no further than the age of Pericles.

His political opinions led to his resigning his position at Halle; and, after
two years at Tübingen (1857–59), he left for Berlin, where his interest in
politics was unabated. For seven years (1867–74) he was the 'general director'
of the Prussian archives, and he subsequently published several important
papers on Greek history. Imprisoned in his early career for the crime of
being in advance of his times, he lived to see his Pan-Germanic opinions
approved by Prussia, to be the recognised exponent of modern history at the
military academy of Berlin, and even to become the official historiographer of
the house of Brandenburg. His tomb in Berlin lies between those of the two
historians, Nitzsch and Droysen[2].

Gustav Droysen (1808—1884) studied in Berlin, where he remained until

Droysen   1840. In 1840 he became professor of History at Kiel, in
1851 his political opinions compelled him to leave for Jena; in
1859 he was called to Berlin, where he held a professorship for the rest of his
life. In the early part of his career he was keenly interested in the Greek
poets, publishing a translation of Aeschylus[3], and (in 1835) a free and vigorous
rendering of Aristophanes, which attained the honour of a third edition. His
earliest historical work, that on Alexander the Great (1833), was followed by
his well-known history of the successors of Alexander (1836–42). In their
second edition, these works were fused into the three volumes of the 'History
of Hellenism' (1877–8). Besides important works on modern history, he
published papers on the Athenian generals, on the trial for the mutilation

---

[1] Cp. Michaelis, *Arch. Entd.* 140–8, 305, and i 153[2] n. 3 *supra*. On
Humann, see Conze, in *Deutscher Nekrolog*, 1897, 369—377.

[2] *Biogr. Jahrb.* 1886, 147—174.   [3] 1884[4].

of the Hermae, and on the coinage of Athens and of Dionysius I. He was a born teacher, and continued to lecture with unabated spirit for more than half a century[1].

The whole range of Greek history has been covered by the meritorious labours of Gustav Hertzberg (b. 1826), who in 1851 began his long career at Halle. The first volume of his History of ***Hertzberg*** Greece (1832) ended with the invasion by Roger of Sicily, while the third and fourth told the story of the Greek Revolution. His outline of Greek History down to the beginning of the Middle Ages appeared in Ersch and Gruber. He has also written three volumes on Greece under the Romans (1866–75), and four on the period beginning with Justinian and ending with the present day (1876–9)[2]. In part of his labours he has had the advantage of being preceded by Carl Hopf, the author of an important History of Greece from the beginning of the Middle Ages to the year 1821[3].

The able historian of Sicily and Greece, Adolf Holm (1830—1900), was, like Ernst Curtius, born at Lübeck. Educated at the local school under Fr. Jacob and Classen, he was hardly seventeen ***Holm*** when he entered Leipzig, where he studied under Hermann and Haupt and Otto Jahn. From Leipzig he went to Berlin, where he studied under Boeckh, Lachmann, Curtius, Ranke, and Ritter. His work under Trendelenburg resulted in his producing a prize-dissertation on the ethical principles of the *Politics* of Aristotle.

His first appointment was a mastership in French at his old school at Lübeck; he accordingly studied the language strenuously in Paris, but he made a far greater impression on his pupils when he took them through the sixth Book of Thucydides a year or so before the publication of the first volume of his own 'History of Sicily'. In 1857 he carried out his long-cherished plan for visiting Rome and Naples.

In 1863 he paid a second visit to Paris, this time with a view to studying the Duc de Luynes' collection of the coins of Sicily and Magna Graecia. In 1866 he was busy with the topography of Sicily, while his former pupil, Schubring, who had lived at Messina, became one of his colleagues at Lübeck. The year 1870 saw the result of the labour of fifteen years in the publication of the first volume of his 'History of Sicily'. In the winter he paid his first visit to the island, and it was noticed that he actually knew his way about the country even better than the local guides. The second volume (1874) brought the history down to the eve of the first Punic War. In 1876–7 he spent the winter in Sicily. His Florentine friend, Amari, had meanwhile become Minister of Education, and, owing to this fact, Holm found himself invited, at the age of 46, to be professor of History at Palermo. The

---

[1] Max Duncker, in *Biogr. Jahrb.* 1884, 110—118; Giesebrecht, *Münch. Akad.* 1885, 208—219; *Kleine Schriften,* 1893 (including his paper on the spuriousness of the documents in the *De Corona*).

[2] Bursian, ii 1148.   [3] In Ersch and Gruber, vols. 85, 86.

offer was accepted, and the six years of his professorship (1877–83) mark the zenith of his career. In 1882 he visited England to examine the Greek coins in the British Museum, and this visit led to a closer study of English history and to a better appreciation of the merits of Grote. In 1883 he produced, in conjunction with Cavallari, a great archaeological work on the topography of Syracuse. In 1883–96 he held a professorship at Naples, spending most of his time on his 'History of Greece', which he finally brought down to the Battle of Actium[1]. His historical work in general gives proof of the influence of Ranke and Classen, while his artistic skill as a writer reflects the teaching of Fr. Jacob. He has himself said, in one of his reviews :—'even works of learning ought to be works of art ; unhappily they seldom are'. Freeman has spoken of 'the sound judgement of Holm' as a historian of Sicily, and an English review of his History of Greece justly commends its 'conciseness', its 'sound scholarship', and its 'conscientious impartiality'. In the spring of 1897 he left Italy for Freiburg in Baden, where, at the close of the year, he wrote the preface to the third and last volume of his 'History of Sicily', published four and twenty years after the second. It includes no less than 200 pages (with plates) on the coinage alone, and it gives us an instructive comparison between Cicero's accusation of Verres and the modern impeachment of Warren Hastings, a comparison doubtless inspired by Holm's visit to England. Towards the end of his life in the South he gave a new proof that he had not forgotten his first home in the distant North. A monograph on Lübeck, with more than 100 plates, was his latest work. He is one of the sanest of historians, and he is never dull[2].

The Public Antiquities of Greece were the theme of the learned labours of Wilhelm Wachsmuth (1784—1866), whose work of four

W. Wachsmuth

volumes (1820–30) was conveniently reduced to two in the second edition (1844)[3]. Born at Hildesheim, he studied at Halle, where he began his career as a university teacher before holding professorships at Kiel (1820–25) and Leipzig (1825–66)[4]. The same field was traversed (as we have already seen) by Schömann[5], and by K. F. Hermann[6].

A labourer in a similar province of study, Adolf Philippi (b. 1843), studied mainly at Göttingen under Curtius and Sauppe, at whose

Philippi

instance he worked at Attic law in connexion with the Attic orators. His papers on the latter (1866–7) were followed by his 'Contributions to the history of the Attic law of citizenship' (1870), and treatises on the Attic law of agreements (*de syngraphis*, 1871), and on the 'Areopagus and the Ephetae' (1874). In that year he became a professor at Giessen. He studied the Greek lexicographers for ten years in preparation for a proposed edition of

---

[1] 4 vols., 1886–94 ; E.T. (with *Index*) 1894–8.

[2] F. von Duhn, in *Biogr. Jahrb.* 1901, 50—112.

[3] *Hellenische Alterthumskunde.*

[4] Autobiography in *Nieder-Sächsischen Geschichten.*

[5] p. 165 *supra.*   [6] p. 162 *supra.*

Pollux. About 1893 he resigned his professorship. His interest in art and archaeology led to his residing in Dresden, where he wrote his autobiography[1].

An excellent Handbook of Greek Constitutional Antiquities was published in 1881–5[2] by Gustav Gilbert (1843—1899), the son of a Hanoverian pastor, who was educated at Hildesheim, and studied at Göttingen, Leipzig, and Berlin. It was probably at Sauppe's recommendation that, in 1871, he was appointed to a mastership under Marquardt at the *gymnasium* of Gotha, and he held that position to the end of his life. Some of his earliest works related to the primitive constitutional history of Sparta and Athens. These were followed by his 'Contributions to the internal history of Athens during the Peloponnesian war' (1877). It was the success of this work that led to his being invited by its publisher (Teubner) to prepare the 'Handbook' which was the principal literary achievement of his life. It supplies a clear outline of the subject with the original authorities, and references to the modern literature, at the foot of each page. The second edition of the volume on Sparta and Athens (1893) includes an excellent monograph on the Ἀθηναίων πολιτεία[3]. Of his later publications the most valuable is that on 'the history of the developement of Greek law and legal procedure' (1896). His favourite authors were Homer, Horace, and Goethe; and his character has been aptly summed up by a life-long friend in the words :—*er war ein Ehrenmann, treu wie Gold, frei und edel gesinnt*[4].

The study of Roman History in the critical spirit of Niebuhr was continued by Albert Schwegler (1819—1857), professor at Tübingen, the three volumes of whose History ended with the Licinian Rogations; and by Karl Peter (1808—1893), for many years Rector of Schulpforta, who brought his History down to the death of Marcus Aurelius[5]. He is well known as the author of the 'Chronological Tables of Greek and Roman History'[6]. In 1838 he edited Cicero's *Orator*, in conjunction with Christian Gottlob Weller (1810—1884), a pupil of Hermann, who was for many years a master at Meiningen[7] : this was followed by Peter's edition of the *Brutus* (1839). Towards the close of his life, while he was honorary professor at Jena, he produced two editions of the *Agricola* of Tacitus (1876–7)[8].

Gilbert

Schwegler
Peter

Of those who have treated a limited period, we may here notice Wilhelm Drumann (1786—1861), professor at Königsberg, who produced in 1834–44 a history of the transition from the Republic to the Empire, dealing with Pompey and Caesar, and handling Cicero with singular severity. The history of Rome

Drumann
Hoeck
Ihne

---

[1] *Biogr. Jahrb.* 1895, 156—176.   [2] Ed. 2, 1893 ; E. T. of vol. i, 1895.

[3] This volume was translated into English (1895) by E. J. Brooks and T. Nicklin (with a prefatory note by J. E. Sandys).

[4] Dr R. Ehwald, in Gotha program, March, 1899, 24—27, with list of his contributions to *Philol.* and *Jahrb. f. kl. Philol.*   [5] 1853–69 etc.

[6] 1835–41 etc. ; E. T. of the *Greek Tables* (Cambridge, 1882).

[7] *Biogr. Jahrb.* 1884, 64.   [8] *ib.* 1895, 110—151.

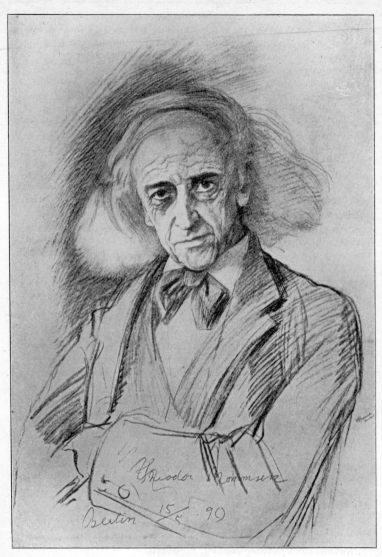

THEODOR MOMMSEN.

From the original drawing by Sir William Richmond (1890), now in the
possession of Prof. Ulrich von Wilamowitz-Moellendorff.

from the decline of the Republic to the age of Constantine was treated in three volumes (1841–50) by Karl Hoeck (1799—1864), professor at Marburg. Wilhelm Ihne (1821—1902), professor at Heidelberg, published in 1868–90 a History in eight volumes[1] founded on a critical study of the authorities, and avowedly written for the general public rather than for specialists. The eighth volume ends with the battle of Actium.

A far wider range of historical and antiquarian research was traversed in the memorable career of Theodor Mommsen (1817—1903), the outline of whose life has been traced on a previous page, in connexion with his work on Latin texts[2]. He had begun by making his mark in the study of Roman Law. At Kiel, in 1843, he had produced his two earliest works:—(1) his dissertation on the law *de scribis et viatoribus*, and (2) his pamphlet on the Roman *Collegia* and *Sodalicia*. In the following year, he published a treatise on the Roman 'tribe' in its administrative relations. Having thus given proof of his legal learning, he next produced his two linguistic works, his 'Oscan Studies' (1845–6), and his 'Dialects of lower Italy' (1850). During his absence in Italy (1845–7) he had studied inscriptions with the aid of Borghesi and Henzen, and he now began a series of papers on that subject in the Transactions of the Leipzig Academy, besides preparing his 'Inscriptions of the Kingdom of Naples' (1852). In that work he showed a consummate skill in applying the results of epigraphical research to the elucidation of the constitutional history and the law of the Italian communities. He also presented to the Leipzig Academy a valuable treatise on Roman Coinage[3], which, in its expanded form, became an authoritative history of that subject[4].

Such were the preliminary studies that paved the way for his 'Roman History', a work in three volumes (1854–6)[5], ending with the battle of Thapsus. It was a history, not of Rome alone, but also of Italy, from the earliest immigrations to the end of the Roman Republic. The plan of the series unfortunately pre-

---

[1] Ed. 2 of vols. i, ii, 1893–6; vols. vii, viii, mainly by A. W. Zumpt. Eng. ed. 1871–82, five vols.

[2] p. 197 *supra.*   [3] *Sächs. Abhandl.*, ii (1850) 221—427.

[4] 1860; Fr. T. 1865–75.

[5] Ed. 9, 1903–4; E. T. 1862, new ed. 1894–5.

cluded the quotation of authorities, and points of detail were
attacked by Karl Wilhelm Nitzsch (1818—1880), professor of
History in Berlin[1], by Karl Peter[2], and by Ludwig Lange (1825
—1885)[3], professor at Leipzig, and author of the three volumes
of an elaborate work on Roman Constitutional Antiquities
(1856–71). Mommsen's critics desired to revert to the view of
Roman History that had been held before the time of Niebuhr,
and to accept the tradition of the Roman annalists, and of the
other writers who uncritically transcribed, or rhetorically adorned,
the work of their predecessors. Mommsen afterwards took up
the History of Rome at a later point, by publishing a work on
the Roman rule of the Provinces from Caesar to Diocletian[4].
In connexion with his Roman History he had meanwhile produced a work on Roman Chronology[5], his aim being to justify
certain of his own opinions, and incidentally to refute those of his
brother, August[6]. The controversy excited by this work served to
stimulate a renewed activity in the field of chronological investigation. One of the leading explorers of that field was G. F. Unger,
professor at Würzburg, whose papers appeared in the 'Philologus',
and in the Transactions of the Berlin Academy.

Many of Mommsen's papers on Roman history and chronology
and public antiquities, and on the criticism of historical authorities, were collected in the two volumes of his 'Roman Researches'[7]. While the absence of quotations from authorities
was one of the characteristics of the widely popular 'History of
Rome', students and specialists found an abundance of learned
details in the work on 'Roman Public Law'[8], which takes the
place of the corresponding portion of the Handbook of Roman
Antiquities begun by W. A. Becker and continued by Joachim
Marquardt (1812—1882), the Director of the *gymnasium* at
Gotha, who had studied under Boeckh and Schleiermacher at

---

[1] *Jahrb. f. kl. Philol.* lxxiii 716 f, lxxvi 409 f; *Die römische Annalistik* (1873).

[2] *Studien* (1863); p. 233 *supra*.   [3] *Biogr. Jahrb.* 1886, 31—61.

[4] 1885 (with 8 maps); ed. 5, 1894; E. T. 1886.   [5] 1858; ed. 2, 1859.

[6] b. 1821; author of *Römische Daten* (1856), articles in *Rhein. Mus.* xii,
xiii, *Philol.* xii, *N. Jahrb.* Suppl. 1856-9; *Gr. Heortologie* (1864); *Gr.
Chronologie* (1883).

[7] *Römische Forschungen* (1863-79).

[8] *Römisches Staatsrecht*, 1871-88; Fr. T. 1887-96; *Abriss*, 1893.

Berlin, and under Hermann at Leipzig. The revision of this Handbook by Marquardt and Mommsen made it practically a new work[1].

The early preparations for a *Corpus Inscriptionum Latinarum* are associated with the name of August Wilhelm Zumpt (1815— 1877), who aimed at little more than extracting and rearranging the inscriptions that had been already published. His papers on inscriptions[2] brought him into frequent conflict with Mommsen, who laid his own scheme before the Academy in 1847[3]. This scheme, which ensured a strictly scientific exploration of the whole field, was approved, and its execution was entrusted to Mommsen, whose great powers of work and capacity for organisation ensured its complete success[4]. An excellent selection of inscriptions was published in 1873 by G. H. C. Wilmanns (1845—1878), whose early death prevented his completing his work on the inscriptions collected in Tunis and Algiers (1873-6).

Mommsen's edition of the *Digest* (1868-70) formed the larger part of the subsequent edition of the *Corpus iuris civilis* (1872 etc.)[5]. He also edited the *Monumentum Ancyranum*[6], the Edict of Diocletian (1893), and the *Codex Theodosianus* (1904-5)[7]. Some of his texts of Latin authors have been already mentioned[8]. A volume of his Speeches and Essays was published in 1905; the series of his Collected Writings, beginning with three volumes on Roman Law (1905-7), already includes the first of the volumes on Roman History (1906).

Mommsen was the greatest of German scholars since the time of Boeckh. Beginning with Roman jurisprudence, he applied to

[1] Vols. i—iii were prepared by Mommsen ; iv—vi (on Roman administration) and vii (on private life) by Marquardt.

[2] Collected in *Comm. Epigraphicae*, 1850-4.

[3] Reprinted in Harnack's 'History of the Berlin Academy', ii (1900) 522 f.

[4] The volumes containing the early Latin (i), oriental (iii), and central and southern Italian (ix, x) inscriptions were edited by Mommsen ; the inscr. of Spain (ii) and Britain (vii) by Hübner ; those of S. Gaul by O. Hirschfeld ; of Pompeii etc. (iv) by Zangemeister ; of N. Italy (xi) and Rome (vi) by Bormann, Henzen and Huelsen.

[5] Including *Institutiones*, ed. P. Krüger.

[6] 1865 ; ed. 3, 1883 ; Fr. T., 1885.

[7] In conjunction with P. M. Meyer.   [8] p. 197 *supra.*

the investigation of Roman History the strict intellectual training
that he had derived from the study of Roman Law. Equally
skilful in negative criticism, and in the art of the historic reconstruction of the past, he brought to bear on the science of history
a singular mastery of the science of language. He combined
breadth of learning with a lucid and a lively style, and vast
powers of work with a genius for scientific organisation[1].

Latin Epigraphy and Archaeology were the special province
of Emil Hübner (1834—1901), who was the son
of an accomplished artist at Düsseldorf. After his
early education at Dresden, he studied at Berlin and Bonn,
and travelled in Italy, Spain, and England. Meanwhile he had
settled in Berlin (1859), where he was appointed to an 'extraordinary' professorship in 1863, and was a full professor for the
last thirty-one years of his life. His travels in Spain resulted
in his volumes on the 'ancient works of art at Madrid', on the
Inscriptions of Spain[2], and on the 'Monumenta linguae Ibericae'.
His travels in England were undertaken with a view to the
Latin Inscriptions of that country[3]. In recognition of this work
in particular he received an honorary degree at Cambridge in
1883, and, to the end of his life, he had a most friendly regard
for England. He was for many years an editor of *Hermes*
(1866–81), and of the *Archäologische Zeitung* (1868–72). Among
his most useful works were his elaborate and comprehensive
Outlines of the History of Roman Literature[4], of Latin[5] and

Hübner

---

[1] Bibliography in Zangemeister, *T. M. als Schriftsteller* (1887), completed
by E. Jacobs, 188 pp. (1905). Biographical notices by Bardt (1903);
K. J. Neumann in *Hist. Zeitschr.* 1904, 193—238; E. Schwartz in *Gött.
Nachr.*, 1904; Gomperz, *Essays*, 133—143; Harnack, *Rede* (1903); Huelsen,
in *Mitt. deutsch. archäol. Inst.* xviii 193—238; C. Wachsmuth, in *Sächs.
Gesell. d. Wiss.* 1903, 153—173; L. M. Hartmann, in *Biogr. Jahrb. u.
Deutscher Nekrolog*, ix (1906) 441—515. Portrait in *Ges. Schr.* i, and two in
Reden. The portrait by Ludwig Knaus represents the historian in his study,
with a bust of Julius Caesar; the drawing by Sir William Richmond is reproduced on p. 234; a characteristic photograph, taken by Mr Dew-Smith, is
published by Messrs Heffer, Cambridge. The Cambridge Address *Germaniae
suae novo Varroni* (written by Prof. Mayor) is printed in *Literature*, 18 Dec.
1897.

[2] *C. I. L.* vol. ii.   [3] *C. I. L.* vol. vii.
[4] 1869 etc., ed. Mayor, 1875.   [5] Ed. 1876 etc.

Greek[1] Grammar, and of the History of Classical Philology[2], including an excellent bibliography, which has often been of service in the preparation of the present work[3].

The History of Rome in the Middle Ages was written by Ferdinand Gregorovius (1821—1891), who was born on the eastern borders of Prussia. He once said that he should never have written on mediaeval Rome, if he had not spent his boyhood in a mediaeval palace of the German knights. It was on a day in 1855, as he stood on the Ponte Sant' Angelo, looking across the Tiber at the former Mausoleum of Hadrian, that he was first inspired with the design of writing the History of Rome in the Middle Ages. He had already written on Hadrian (1851), and was to return to this theme at a later date (1884). The publication of the eight volumes of his History of Mediaeval Rome extended from 1859 to 1872[4], and was followed by that of his two volumes on Mediaeval Athens (1889). Rome was his head-quarters from 1852 to 1874, and the remaining seventeen years of his life were spent in Munich. On leaving Rome he wrote:—"I can say with Flavius Blondus: 'I brought into being that which was not already there; I threw light on eleven dark centuries of the city, and gave the Romans the History of their own Middle Ages'". In 1876 the Senate of the new capital of Italy enrolled him as an honorary 'citizen of Rome', and, when he publicly declined all congratulations on completing his seventieth year in Munich, he signed his name with no other title than *Civis Romanus*[5]. The interest of the historical works already mentioned, as well as that of the five volumes of his *Wanderjahre in Italien*, his *Capri* and *Korfu*, his poem of Pompeii (*Euphorion*) and his 'Graves of the Popes', is enhanced by the charm and the clearness of his style.

Passing from mediaeval Rome to prehistoric Greece, we may assign a foremost place among modern works on Greek Mythology to the classic treatise[6] of Ludwig

Gregorovius

Preller

---

[1] Ed. 1883. [2] 1876; ed. 2, 1889.

[3] See esp. Gildersleeve, in *A. J. P.* xxii 113.

[4] Ed. 5, 1903; E. T. by A. Hamilton.

[5] *Biogr. Jahrb.* 1892, 106—113.

[6] 1854; ed. 4, with excellent Indices, by Carl Robert, 1887-94.

Preller[1]. Preller, like Heyne and Welcker, regarded the oldest and the most important of the Greek myths as myths of Nature, as representations of 'the elementary powers and processes of Nature, the sunshine and lightning, the falling rain and the flowing river, and the growth and ripening of vegetation'[2]. His Roman Mythology, a work of less note, appeared in 1858.

Comparative Mythology, in connexion with Comparative Philology, was well represented by Adalbert Kuhn (1812—1881), Rector of one of the schools in Berlin[3]. Comparative Ethnology was the dominant interest in the mythological works of J. W. E. Mannhardt (1831—1880), who laid the foundation for the future fabric of a Mythology of the Germanic nations by a complete collection of the folklore of tillage and harvest in his great work on forest and field-cults[4]. Ancient Mythology, which is little noticed in the first part of this work, holds a prominent place in the second, where the primitive cults are explained in the light of the traditions of Northern Europe[5].

We have lingered long in the lands united by the common tie of the German language, but we have seen far less of Austria and of German Switzerland than of Northern and Southern Germany. No part of those lands has been so prolific in classical scholars as the protestant North. It is true that the birthplace of Boeckh was in Baden, but the principal scene of his learned labours was Berlin. Classical education was reorganised in Bavaria by Thiersch, in Austria by Bonitz, both of them North Germans born beside the same stream in Saxony. German Switzerland has been represented partly by Baiter and Orelli; Austria by Karl Schenkl and the cosmopolitan Otto Benndorf. Theodor Gomperz and Wilhelm von Hartel are happily still living. From our survey of 'Germany,' in the widest sense of the word, we now turn to the latest fortunes of the land which was the earliest home of the Revival of Learning.

---

[1] p. 174 *supra*.

[2] *Gr. Myth.* p. 1; cp. Bursian, ii 1196—7; Block in *Jahresb.* vol. 124, 429 f.

[3] Bursian, ii 1200—2.   [4] *Wald- und Feldkulte*, 1875—7.

[5] *Biogr. Jahrb.* 1881, 1—6.

CHAPTER XXXV.

ITALY IN THE NINETEENTH CENTURY.

EARLY in the nineteenth century one of the foremost scholars in Italy was the learned Jesuit, Angelo Mai (1782—

Mai

1854). Born in the province of Bergamo, he became Librarian of the Ambrosian and Vatican Libraries, and was raised to the dignity of a Cardinal in 1838.

As Librarian in Milan (1811-9), he published, from MSS formerly at Bobbio, fragments of six Speeches of Cicero[1], the correspondence of M. Aurelius and Fronto, portions of eight Speeches of Symmachus, fragments of the *Vidularia* of Plautus, as well as *scholia* and pictorial illustrations from the Ambrosian MS of Terence (1814-5). His publications from Greek MSS included a large addition to the Speech of Isaeus *De hereditate Cleonymi*, a hitherto unknown portion of the *Roman Antiquities* of Dionysius of Halicarnassus (1816), and an ancient fragment of the *Iliad* (with illustrations) as well as *scholia* on the *Odyssey* (1819); he also took part in an edition of the newly discovered Armenian version of the Eusebian Chronicle (1818). In Rome he published from a Vatican palimpsest large portions of Cicero's lost treatise *De Republica* (1822), collected the remains of the prae-Justinian Civil Law (1823), and summed up his wonderful work as an editor of hitherto unknown texts by producing from the MSS of the Vatican three great series, of ten volumes each, the *Scriptorum veterum nova collectio* (1825-38), the *Classici auctores* (1828-38) and the *Spicilegium Romanum* (1839-44). After an interval of eight years the *Spicilegium* was followed by the *Patrum nova collectio* of the last two years of his life (1852-4)[2].

Cardinal Mai died at the age of 72. The age of 85 was attained by an able but less productive worker in the same field, Victor Amadeo Peyron (1785—1870),

Peyron

formerly a professor at Turin. His best-known work is an edition of new fragments of the Speeches *pro Scauro, pro Tullio* and *In Clodium*, and of the remains of the *pro Milone*, from the Turin

---

[1] *Pro Scauro, Tullio, Flacco, in Clodium et Curionem, de aere alieno Milonis,* and *de rege Alexandrino* (1814; ed. 2, 1817).

[2] Life etc. by B. Prina (Bergamo, 1882); G. Poletto (Siena, 1887).

S. III.   16

and Milan MSS formerly at Bobbio, together with an inventory
of the Bobbian MSS made in 1461 (1824). He also published
fragments of Empedocles and Parmenides (1810), a commentary
on the treatise on prosody by Theodosius of Alexandria (1817)
with a new fragment of the latter (1820), and an account of the
Greek *papyri* at Vienna (1824) and Turin (1826–7)[1].

Beyond the bounds of Italy the Turin professor, Tommaso

Vallauri

Vallauri (1805—1897), was best known as the opponent of the principles maintained by Ritschl in the
textual criticism of Plautus. His edition of four of the plays[2]
was followed by a critical text of the whole (1873). Ritschl's
discovery that the true name of the poet was T. Maccius Plautus[3]
was opposed in 1868 by Vallauri, who adhered to the traditional
name of M. Accius Plautus. He also wrote a critical history of
Latin literature (1849), and edited a large number of school-texts
of Latin Classics[4].

Comparative Philology has been well represented by Pezzi

Pezzi

and Ascoli. Domenico Pezzi was professor of the
Comparative History of the Classical and Romance
Languages at Turin (1844—1906). His principal work, *La lingua
greca antica* (1888), begins with a historical sketch of the study
of Greek, followed by a systematic account (1) of the phonology

Ascoli

and morphology of the language, and (2) of the
Greek dialects[5]. Graziadio Ascoli (1829—1907),
who was appointed professor of Comparative Philology in Milan
in 1860, was the founder of the 'Archivio Glottologico Italiano'
(1873). His lectures on Comparative Phonology and his Critical
Studies have been translated into German, and his edition of the
'Codice Irlandese' of the Ambrosian Library (1878) is an important aid to the study of Celtic[6].

---

[1] Sclopis, in *Atti di accad. di Torino*, 1870, 778—807.

[2] *Aul., Miles, Trin., Men.* (1853–9).

[3] *Parerga*, 9—43; Ribbeck's *Ritschl*, ii 100.

[4] Autobiography (1878); Bursian, ii 824 n. 1, 1239.

[5] *Cl. Rev.* iii 209 f. His earlier work, *Glottologia Aria Recentissima*
(1877; E. T. by E. S. Roberts, 1879), practically ends with Ascoli's discovery
of the 'velar' gutturals (1870).

[6] A. de Gubernatis, *Dict. Internat., s.v.*; *Athenæum*, 2 Feb. 1907, p. 136;
Rivista di Fil. 1907, no. 2; Bursian's *Jahresb.* lvi 168 f; Giles, *Comp. Phil.* §41.

The study of Greek has for obvious reasons been less prominent in Italy than that of Latin. Plato has,
however, been translated by the Italian statesman, Bonghi
Ruggero Bonghi (1828—1895), who is also known as the author
of a History of Rome[1], and of a work on Roman Festivals[2].

Among Latin scholars, a place of honour is due to Vincenzo
De-Vit (1810—1892), who was educated at the
Seminary of Padua, was Canon of Rovigo and De-Vit
Librarian of the local Academy (1844–9), became a member of
the Institute of Charity founded by Rosmini at Stresa (1849–61),
and, after a year in Florence, spent the rest of his life mainly in
Rome. His revised and enlarged edition of Forcellini, begun
before 1857, was completed in 1879. This was supplemented by
his *Onomasticon*, extending from A to O (1869–92). His earliest
work was on the Fragments of Varro (1843); he also collected
the Inscriptions of the region of Adria (1853), and wrote lexicographical articles on Latin inscriptions, besides discussing the
Britons and the Bretons[3], and the inscriptions and the historic
associations of the Lago Maggiore and the Valley of the Ossola.
It was in the College of the Rosminists at Domodossola that he
spent the last few months of a life consecrated to the duties of a
priest and a scholar[4].

Forcellini has also been edited anew in 1864–90 by Fr. Corradini (1820—1888). This edition, founded to a considerable extent on the work of Reinhold Klotz[5], Corradini
was completed by Perin, who (like Corradini and De-Vit,
and Forcellini himself) was an *alumnus* of the Seminary of
Padua.

Among other Latin scholars may be mentioned Giovanni
Battista Gandino (1827—1905), professor of Latin
at Bologna, who (apart from a number of successful Gandino
school-books) published studies on ancient Latin (1878), contri-

---

[1] Vol. 2, 1888; Lectures on Ancient History, 1879.

[2] *Le Feste Romane*, 1891; Germ. T., [1891].

[3] *Opere*, vol. x (ed. 1889).

[4] Ermanno Ferrero, in *Biogr. Jahrb.* 1899, 26—30.

[5] Cp. Georges, in Bursian's *Jahresb.* ii 1456, iii 170, and *Philol. Anz.* iii
446 f.

buted valuable articles to the *Rivista di Filologia*[1], and produced an excellent work on Latin style (1895)[2].

No account of Classical Scholarship in Italy would be complete without the name of the Italian Senator, Comparetti Domenico Comparetti, who was born in Rome (1835) and became professor of Greek at Pisa and Florence. He produced a critical text of Hypereides, *pro Euxenippo*, and of the *Funeral Oration* (1861–4). He is widely known as the author of the standard work on 'Virgil in the Middle Ages'[3]. He subsequently produced an important edition of the 'Laws of Gortyn' (1893), and a text and translation of Procopius. Among his numerous papers may be mentioned those on the *papyri* of the Villa of the Pisos at Herculaneum[4]. He was the founder of the 'Museo Italiano d' antichità classica' (1884 f).

Classical Archaeology has been studied in Italy with ever increasing success. In the first half of the century Archaeologists one of the foremost authorities on ancient archi- Canina tecture was Luigi Canina (1795—1856), who studied in Turin and, in 1818, left for Rome, where he produced in 1844 the second edition of his classic work in twelve volumes, entitled *L' architettura antica*[5]. He wrote besides on the exploration of Tusculum and Veii, and on the topography of Rome. Rome was also the scene of the archaeological work of Guattani (d. 1830) and Fea (d. 1836), the representatives of Italy among the founders of the Archaeological Institute in 1829. But the Italian interest in archaeology was far from being confined to Rome. In the first half of the century there was no country in Europe that could vie with Italy in the number and the variety of the separate Academies for the study of local archaeology. That study assumed divergent forms in Naples, Rome, Florence, Turin,. Modena and Venice, while the most distinguished archaeologist in all Italy, Bartolommeo Borghesi (1781—1860), whose Borghesi archaeological correspondence covered every part of the peninsula, spent the last thirty-nine years of his life in

---

[1] v 101—160 (Gen. in *-as*) ; vi 453—473 (termination of the comparative).

[2] A. de Gubernatis, *Dict. s. v.*   [3] 1873 ; ed. 2, 1896 (E. T. 1895).

[4] A. de Gubernatis, *s. v.*; esp. in Comparetti and De Petra's *Villa Ercolanese*, folio (1883).

[5] 'Luigi Caninas phantasievollen Arbeiten' (Michaelis, *Arch. Entd.* 217).

the smallest of the Italian States, as citizen and podestà of the still-independent Republic of San Marino. His activity was mainly devoted to the study of coins and inscriptions. He produced two volumes on the new fragments of the *Fasti Consulares* (1818–20), and his collected works filled nine volumes (Paris, 1862–84)[1]. The *Corpus Inscriptionum Latinarum* owed much to his friendly aid. The study of coins was long represented at Modena by Don Celestino Cavedoni (1795—1865), the author of 'Observations on the coins of the Roman *gentes*' (1829–31)[2].

Cavedoni

In Naples Francesco Maria Avellino (1788—1850) was professor of Greek, and (in and after 1839) director of the Museo Borbonico. He wrote on the *aes grave* of the Museo Kircheriano, and the inscriptions of Pompeii, and contributed largely to the *Bullettino Archeologico Napolitano*, which was founded by himself, and continued to the end (1861) by Minervini (1825—1895)[3]. Naples was the birth-place of the learned Jesuit, Raffaele Garrucci (1812—1885), who published the first edition of his *Graffiti di Pompéi* shortly before the thirty years of his residence in Rome. He prepared a *Sylloge* of Inscriptions of the Roman Republic (1875–7, 1881); his latest work, that on the 'Coins of Ancient Italy', was published in Rome in the year of his death. The antiquities of Etruria were fruitfully studied by Ariodante Fabretti (1816—1894), professor of Archaeology and director of the Museum at Turin, the author of a *Corpus* of ancient Italian inscriptions (1867–78). Meanwhile, the antiquities of Sicily had been set forth in five folio volumes in 1834–42 by the Duca di Serradifalco with the aid of Saverio Cavallari[4], the able archaeologist who was associated with Holm in the great *topographia archeologica di Siracusa*[5].

Avellino

Garrucci

A. Fabretti

Serradifalco
Cavallari

---

[1] Noël des Vergers on *Marc Aurèle* (Paris, 1860) ; Henzen, in Fleckeisen's *Jahrb.* lxxxi 569—575.

[2] *Notizie*, Modena, 1867.

[3] *Biogr. Jahrb.* 1900, 18—20.

[4] 1809—1898 ; L. Sampolo, in *Bullettino* of Palermo Acad. (1899) 41 f.

[5] Palermo, 1883 ; Germ. ed. B. Lupus (Strassburg, 1887).

The political union of Italy, begun in 1860 and completed in
1870, had an important effect on the organisation of
Fiorelli   archaeological research. On the expulsion of the
Bourbons from Naples in 1860, Giuseppe Fiorelli (1824—1896) was
placed at the head of the great local Museum, and superintended
the systematic excavation of Pompeii (1860–75) until he was called
to Rome to become Director General of Museums and Excavations.
The municipality of Rome had established an archaeological commission in 1872, and soon began the publication of a monthly
Bullettino. At Bologna an important Museum was founded for
the preservation of prehistoric, Etruscan, and other antiquities,
and an Etruscan Museum was also founded in Florence. The
revived interest in archaeology extended to the utmost limits of
Italy, and antiquarian periodicals were published in many places,
extending from Turin in the North to Palermo in the South[1].
But the centre of archaeological interest has remained in Rome.
1890 is the date of the discovery of the inscription commemorating
the *ludi saeculares* and including the statement : *carmen composuit
Q. Horatius Flaccus*[2]. Since the end of 1898 the excavations in
the Roman Forum have comprised the discovery of the site of
the 'Lacus Curtius', the base of the colossal statue of Domitian
described in the *Silvae* of Statius, the pavement on which the
body of Caesar was burnt, the legendary tomb of Romulus, and
the earliest of all Latin inscriptions.

Latin inscriptions were among the most important of the antiquarian interests of Luigi Bruzza and Giovanni Battista de Rossi.
Bruzza   Bruzza (1812—1883) was a Barnabite monk, who
taught Latin and Greek in Piedmont and in Naples,
and first made his mark as an antiquarian at Vercelli. Called
to Rome by his Order in 1867, he incidentally produced an
important monograph on the inscriptions on the marble blocks of
the recently discovered *Emporium* on the Tiber (1870), and also a
complete collection of the Roman inscriptions of Vercelli (1874),
a work that won the highest praise from Mommsen[3], while the
grateful citizens of Vercelli called their local Museum by the
name of Bruzza and struck a gold medal in his honour. He was
president of the Roman Society for the cultivation of Christian

---

[1] Cp. Stark, 301–4.   [2] *C. I. L.* vi 4 (2) p. 3242.   [3] *ib.* v 736.

archaeology; and it was while he was superintending the excavation of the crypt of St Hippolytus that he met with an accident which ultimately proved fatal. On his death, his services to the cause of archaeology were warmly eulogised by de Rossi[1].

Giovanni Battista de Rossi (1822—1894) was great in many branches of archaeology and especially great in Latin epigraphy. One of his most important achievements in that department was the publication of all the early collections of Roman inscriptions[2]. He took part in collecting the inscriptions of Rome for vol. vi of the *Corpus*. He also did much for the study of Roman topography, including the ancient lists of the Regions of the City. In 1849 his methodical investigations resulted in the discovery of the fragmentary inscription which led to his identification of the cemetery of San Callisto[3]. He is justly regarded as the founder of the recent study of Christian Archaeology in Rome[4], but De Rossi himself had a special reverence for the memory of 'the true Columbus' of the Catacombs, Antonio Bosio (1575—1629), the learned and industrious author of a far earlier *Roma Sotterranea* (1632).

De Rossi

Late in the eighteenth century, Don José Nicolás de Azara (1731—1804), a friend of Winckelmann and Mengs, returned to Spain from Rome with a valuable collection of ancient busts, now in the Royal Gallery of Sculpture, Madrid[5]. Hübner's visit in 1860–1 aroused in Spain and Portugal a new interest in Latin inscriptions and in works of ancient art[6]. But the study of Greek has long been at a low ebb, and the modern literature of the subject is mainly limited to translations[7].

Spain and Portugal

---

[1] *Biogr. Jahrb.* 1884, 121–4; and F. X. Kraus, *Essays*, ii (1901), 31—39.

[2] *Sylloge Einsidlensis* etc. in *Inscr. Christianae*, vol. ii, pars 1 (1888), and in *C. I. L.* vi *init.* (1876–85).

[3] *Inscr. Christianae* (1857–88); *Roma Sotterranea* (1864–77).

[4] *Biogr. Jahrb.* 1900, 1—17; Baumgarten, *De Rossi* (Köln, 1892); Kraus, *Essays*, i (1896) 307—324.

[5] Hübner, *Die antiken Bildwerke in Madrid* (1862), 19 f.

[6] Stark, 305; Bursian, ii 1241.

[7] Apraiz, *Apuntes para una historia de los estudios helénicos en España*, 190 pp. (1876), *ad finem*, reprinted from *Revista de España*, vols. xli—xlvii (cp. Ch. Graux, in *Revue Critique*, 12 août, 1876).

CHAPTER XXXVI.

FRANCE IN THE NINETEENTH CENTURY.

THE literary life of the industrious scholar, Jean Baptiste

Gail

Gail (1755—1829), is equally divided between the eighteenth and the nineteenth centuries. During the eighteenth, his published works were connected with Lucian and Theocritus, Anacreon and the Greek Anthology, and the

BOISSONADE.

From a cast of the Medallion by David d'Angers.

authors included in the fourteen volumes of his *Scriptores Graeci*;
during the nineteenth, with Homer, Thucydides, and Herodotus.
He also edited the speech of Demosthenes, *De Rhodiorum
Libertate*, and was the author of certain *Observations grammaticales
au célèbre M. Hermann* (1816).   Appointed professor of Greek
at the Collège de France in 1792, and *Conservateur* of the
Paris Library in 1814, he edited during the next fourteen years
of his life a classical periodical called *Le Philologue*.   His
numerous publications attained only a moderate degree of excellence, their main value depending on their collations from Paris
MSS[1].   His contemporary, Simon Chardon de la
Rochette (1753—1814), Inspector of the Paris   Chardon
Libraries, published a notice of the Greek *scholia*   de la Rochette
on Plato (1801) and three volumes of *Mélanges* on criticism and
philology (1812)[2].

A far higher reputation attaches to the name of Jean François
Boissonade de Fontarabie (1774—1857), who suc-
ceeded Larcher as professor of Greek in the uni-   Boissonade
versity of Paris (1813), and Gail as professor at the Collège de
France (1828).   He began his classical career by editing the
Heroicus of Philostratus (1806).   In the course of nine years
(1823—32), he produced the twenty-four volumes of his annotated
series of Greek poets.   A greater novelty characterises his publication of the first edition of the Greek translation of Ovid's *Metamorphoses* by Maximus Planudes (1822), the *editio princeps* of Babrius
(1844)[3], the five volumes of his *Anecdota Graeca*, and his *Anecdota
Nova*.   The larger part of his editorial work was connected with
the later writers of Greek prose, *e.g.* the Letters of Aristaenetus
(1822), and Philostratus (1842); and, in his prefaces to such
writers, he was fond of modestly saying that the mediocrity of
their genius was suited to the mediocrity of his own ability.   But
he also published an Aristophanes (1832), and spent many years

---

[1] Cp. Dacier in *Mém. de l'Acad. des Inscr.* ix 22 ; and Bähr, in Ersch and
Gruber.

[2] He was a friend of Koraës, whose Letters to Rochette were published in
1873-7; cp. Thereianos, *Koraës*, i 176 f, and *passim*; also preface to Didot ed.
of *Anth. Pal.* i ix.

[3] p. 129 *supra*.

over a proposed commentary on the Greek Anthology. He contributed largely to the new edition of the Greek *Thesaurus*, and among his correspondents abroad were Wolf and Wyttenbach, and the Greek lexicographer, Edmund Henry Barker. It is said that the whole of his first lecture at the Collège de France was devoted to the exposition of the first three words of Plato's *Ion*[1]; and his love of detail led him to spend half-an-hour on the elucidation of the term *adamas*. In his lectures he also gave proof of his being a fluent translator, but he only once began his course with a general introduction on the life and works of the author whom he proposed to expound. The exception was in the case of Plutarch (1813). He seldom lectured on any author so late as Plutarch, while he seldom edited any author so early. It is to be remembered to his honour that, but for his editorial aid, many of the minor Greek authors might still have been buried in oblivion[2].

An edition of Longus was produced in 1810 by Paul Louis
Courier Courier (1773—1825), the brilliant writer and officer of artillery, who translated the *Hipparchicus* and *De re equestri* of Xenophon (1813), and the *Asinus* of Lucian (1818), besides annotating a new edition of Amyot's *Heliodorus* (1822), and leaving notes on the *Memorabilia*, which were posthumously published by Sinner (1842). He completed the translation of Pausanias (1814–23) by his brother-in-law, Étienne Clavier (1762—1817).

We may briefly notice Jean Louis Burnouf[3] (1775—1844),
the author of a celebrated Greek Grammar, and
J. L. Burnouf the translator of Tacitus; and Joseph Naudet (1786—1878), the editor of Oberlin's Tacitus, and of Catullus and Plautus, and the author of works on the
Naudet postal organisation of the Romans, on the Roman *Noblesse*, and on the public administration from Diocletian to Julian. We next reach the notable name of the versatile

[1] τὸν Ἴωνα χαίρειν.

[2] Egger, in *Mém. de litt. anc.* 1862, 1—15; also notices by Le Bas, Naudet, and Saint-Beuve; some of his Letters in the correspondence of P. L. Courier.

[3] Father of Eugène Burnouf (1801–52), the critic of Bopp (1833), and the first decipherer of 'Zend', one of the foremost orientalists of France.

Victor Cousin (1792—1867), who was professor at the Sorbonne in 1815–22 and 1828–30, and Minister of Education in 1840. He is connected with Greek scholarship by his *editio princeps* of Proclus (1820–7), and by his French rendering of the whole of Plato (1821–40)[1]. He threw new light on the less-known works of Abelard, and contributed to the elucidation of the history of the scholastic philosophy.

Cousin

Cousin's contemporary, Henri Joseph Guillaume Patin (1792 —1876), dean of the Faculty of Letters in Paris, and a member of the French Academy, is known as a translator and an exponent of Horace, as the author of a course of lectures on the history of Latin poetry, and a series of studies on the ancient Latin poets[2], and on the Tragic poets of Greece[3], —a work which has been justly characterised as admirable in its learning and in the soundness of its taste[4].

Patin

Latin lexicography is represented by Louis Marius Quicherat (1799—1884), who in 1849 received an appointment in the department of MSS in the Bibliothèque Sainte-Geneviève, rose to be *Conservateur* of that library in 1864, and retired in 1882.

Quicherat

His appointment happily left him sufficient leisure for literary work. For his *Thesaurus Poëticus Linguae Latinae*, first published in 1836, he worked through all the Latin poets, and, in the course of its preparation, he incidentally edited Virgil, Horace, Persius, Phaedrus, the *Metamorphoses* of Ovid, and the *Andria* and *Adelphi* of Terence (1828–32). He also edited Nepos and Curtius, the *Germania* and *Agricola* of Tacitus, and the *Brutus* and *Somnium Scipionis* of Cicero (1829–42). Except in the case of Nepos, the notes to these editions were in Latin, in accordance with the custom that still prevailed in France. His *Thesaurus Poëticus* was followed in 1844 by his Latin and French Dictionary, in which he was aided by A. Daveluy, afterwards Director of the French School at Athens. His Dictionary of Latin Proper Names (1846) included about 19,000 items, while his *Addenda Lexicis Latinis* (1862–80) supplemented the existing lexicons with more than 2000 words. His French and Latin Dictionary of 1858 filled as many as 1600 pages of three columns each, and passed through 26 editions. To his three Dictionaries he

---

[1] *Rev. de l'Instr. Publique*, 1867, 679; Naudet's *Notice* (Paris, 1869); portrait in the *École Normale Supérieure*.

[2] *Études sur la Poésie latine*, 2 vols. 1868–9.

[3] 4 vols. 1841–3; ed. 5, 1879.

[4] Cp. Boissier and Legouvé, *Discours à l'Acad.*, and Caro, *Journal des Savants*, 1876 (Reinach, *Manuel de Philologie*, i 21 n. 11).

devoted thirty years of his life. The same department of learning was represented in his edition of the Latin lexicographer and grammarian, Nonius
(1872). During the next seven years he was engaged on the preparation of a
new issue of his *Thesaurus Poëticus*, in the preface of which he laments the
decline in the interest in Latin verse in France. His minor works were
connected with French and Latin versification, while some of them gave proof
of his special skill in Music. In 1879 he published a collection of 30 of his
articles under the title of *Mélanges de Philologie*. He regarded with suspicion
certain reforms in Latin orthography suggested by Ritschl and his school, but
he was no blind follower of the beaten track. In his own work he always
insisted on going back to the original authorities. While he made his mark
mainly as a Latin lexicographer, and an editor of Latin Classics, it may be
added that he produced editions of some dialogues of Lucian, the *De Corona*
of Demosthenes, the *Ajax* of Sophocles, and the *Iliad* of Homer[1].

An excellent Greek and French lexicon was produced by
his contemporary Charles Alexandre (1797—1870),
who is also known as the editor of the Sibylline
Oracles (1841–56, '69[2])[2]. The eminent French lexicographer,
Maximilien Paul Émile Littré (1801—1881), began
his brilliant and varied career as a student of medicine. In 1839 he was elected a member of the Academy of
Inscriptions. In the same year he commenced his celebrated
edition and translation of Hippocrates, which was completed in
ten volumes in 1861, and laid the foundation of the modern
criticism of this author.

Alexandre

Littré

The popular side of classical literature was represented by Désiré Jean Marie
Napoléon Nisard (1806—1888), professor of Latin Eloquence
at the Collège de France, the author of Studies on the Latin
Poets of the Decadence (including Phaedrus, Seneca, Persius, Statius,
Martial, Juvenal, and Lucan)[3], and on the four great Latin Historians[4], and
also of an ingenious essay on Zoïlus[5]. Personally interested in ancient
literature, he nevertheless had no pretensions to being a scholar, and he was
less of a historian than a literary critic. In his *Notes et Souvenirs*, he frankly
confesses that he had no concern with erudition, which he regarded with
suspicion as an importation from Germany. In his opening lecture at the
École Normale he even warned his audience against that form of learning,
notwithstanding the presence of the Director of the School, Guigniaut, whose
own reputation had been made by his elaborate edition of Creuzer's *Symbolik*.

Désiré Nisard

---

[1] Emil Chatelain in *Biogr. Jahrb.* 1884, 128—133.

[2] Guigniaut, *Acad. des Inscr.* xxix.

[3] 2 vols. 1834, etc.   [4] 1874.   [5] 1880.

Désiré Nisard was the editor of a popular series of French translations from the Latin Classics, while his younger brother, Charles Marie Nisard (1808—1889), contributed to the series a translation of **Charles Nisard** all the elegiac poems of Ovid (except the *Heroides*), as well as Martial, Valerius Flaccus, and Fortunatus[1], with part of Livy and Cicero, and a separate volume of notes on Cicero's *Letters*[2]. The earliest of his works ostensibly connected with the History of Scholarship was the study of the careers of Lipsius, Scaliger, and Casaubon, contained in his *Triumvirat Littéraire au XVI siècle* (1852). In the preface he tells us how his MS of a complete index of persons and places in the Latin Classics, which he kept at his office in the Tuileries, perished in the flames in February, 1848, when the MS of his *Triumvirat Littéraire* happily escaped a similar fate. This work, so far from really being a chapter in the History of Scholarship, is mainly a study of literary manners, teeming with amusing anecdotic details on the lives and the quarrels of the scholars concerned. It is doubtful whether the author ever made any serious attempt to comprehend the chronological researches of Scaliger, the account of which fills a few pages borrowed from Hallam[3]. He deserves credit, however, for making the personages whom he studies live and move before the reader's eyes, and, if he says too little of their works, he is certainly familiar with their foibles[4]. Another work of the same type, bearing the fantastic title of *Les gladiateurs de la république des lettres au XV—XVII siècles* (1860), contains studies on Filelfo, Poggio, Valla, Scioppius, and the elder Scaliger, and also on Fr. Garasse (1585—1631), a Jesuit of Angoulême, who violently attacked the Calvinists, Casaubon and Estienne Pasquier[5]. Here again, as in the *Triumvirat*, he is absorbed in the analysis of polemical pamphlets. Himself the most peaceable of men, he had almost a passionate interest in the literary quarrels of others. In 1876 his election as a member of the Academy of Inscriptions in the place of Didot stimulated him to work on with renewed energy to the age of 80. In the year after his election, he published the correspondence of the Comte de Caylus, the Abbé Barthélemy and P. Mariette, with the Theatine priest, Paciaudi (*c.* 1757–65), a correspondence proving that Paciaudi had a considerable share in the editing of the last five volumes of the *Recueil d'Antiquités* of Caylus[6].

---

[1] His papers on this poet were republished after his death by M. Boysse, with a bibliography on pp. 193—200.

[2] Severely reviewed in the *Philologische Wochenschrift* 1883, 1156.

[3] *Hist. Lit.* i 530[4].

[4] The work is characterised by Bernays, *J. J. Scaliger*, 19, as unworthy of mention from a scholarly point of view, and as having misled an able reviewer into believing that Scaliger was a *très franchement mauvais homme*.

[5] Cp. *Mémoires de Garasse*, ed. Ch. Nisard (1860).

[6] Nisard also wrote on this subject in the *Revue de France*. Cp. Stark, 147-9, and esp. S. Reinach, in *Biogr. Jahrb.* 1889, 153—158.

In contrast to the brothers Nisard, whose principal aim was the popularising of the Classics, their contemporary, Bénigne Emmanuel
Clément Miller (1812—1886), was an unwearied student of
MSS, who found a greater delight in adding new words to the Greek *Thesaurus*
than in setting forth the merits of the masterpieces of the ancient world. In
1834 Miller entered the manuscript department of the Paris Library, and
under the influence of K. B. Hase, who had been in that department 'for
nearly thirty years, he was inspired, not only with a passion for the quest of
new words, but also with a keen interest in the exploration of the later Greek
literature. In the course of his researches he became one of the most expert
palaeographers in Europe. In 1835 he was sent to Italy to examine the *scholia*
on Aristophanes. In 1839 he published an edition of the minor Greek
geographers, Marcianus, Artemidorus, and Isidore of Charax, and in 1841 a
new Greek version of Aesop. For five years (1840–5) he took a leading
interest in the short-lived *Revue de Bibliographie Analytique*. In 1843 he was
sent by Villemain to explore the libraries of Spain; his Catalogue of the Greek
MSS of the Escurial appeared in 1848, and his supplement to Iriarte's
Catalogue of the Madrid MSS in 1884. Among the MSS brought by 'Mynas'
from Mount Athos in 1840, Miller fortunately identified part of the *Phi-
losophumena* of Origen, and edited it for the Clarendon Press (1851).
Meanwhile, he had left the Library in the Rue Richelieu for that of the
'National Assembly', and he was the head of that Library from 1849 to 1880.
In 1855–7 he published the 25,000 lines of the Byzantine poet, Manuel Philes.
After exploring the libraries of Russia, he found among the MSS of the Seraglio
at Constantinople the work of the Byzantine historian, Critobulus of Imbros.
During his subsequent examination of more than 6000 MSS at Mount Athos, he
paid a visit to Thasos, which led to important discoveries connected with
Greek inscriptions and Greek sculptures[1]. In 1868 and 1875 respectively, he
produced his *Mélanges de littérature grecque*, and *de philologie et d'épigraphie*.
In the former he published, among many inedited texts, the *Etymologicum
Florentinum* and the *Et. parvum*, with certain works of Aristophanes of
Byzantium and Didymus of Alexandria. He also published the historical
poems of Theodorus Prodromus (1873), the Greek historians of the Crusades
(1875–81), and the Chronicle of Cyprus (1882). He preferred exploring the
avia loca of Byzantine literature to lingering amid the Classics of the golden
age; and probably no one since the days of Leo Allatius and Du Cange was
more familiar with mediaeval Greek than Emmanuel Miller[2].

In 1867 Miller, in conjunction with Beulé and Brunet de Presle, was one
of the founders of the Association for the encouragement of
Greek studies. Another of the founders was Gustave d'Eichthal
(1804—1886), a Saint-Simonian, who represented philosophy as well as
philology, and who wrote on the doctrine of Socrates, as well as on the study

---

[1] Cp. Michaelis, *Arch. Entd.* 88.
[2] Salomon Reinach in *Biogr. Jahrb.* 1886, 14—23.

of modern Greek. In 1833 he spent nearly two years at Athens, and at that time, as well as thirty years later, advocated the adoption of a purified form of modern Greek as a universal language. In 1874 he wrote in favour of Lechevalier's view that the site of Troy was to be found on the hills above Bunárbashi (1785) and not on Schliemann's mound of Hissarlik, pleading at the close of his article for the sanitation of the plain of Troy and the rebuilding of the 'palace of Priam'[1]. His paper on the religious teaching of Socrates (1880) was translated into modern Greek by Valettas. To Greeks residing in Paris, or passing through it, he was one of the two perpetual *proxeni* of their nation. The other was Émile Egger[2].

Egger (1813—1885) was of Austrian descent. At the early age of twenty, he became a Doctor of Letters on the strength of his two theses on Archytas of Tarentum and on Roman education.   He began his literary career by editing 'Longinus' *On the Sublime*, and Varro *De Lingua Latina* (1837). These followed by the fragments of Festus and of Verrius Flaccus (1839), by a prize essay on the historians of the rule of Augustus (1844), and by an edition of Aristotle's treatise on Poetry[3]. This last was originally appended to his excellent essay on the 'History of Criticism among the Greeks' (1850), which was republished separately after the author's death. His 'elementary notions of comparative grammar' (1852) was the earliest work of its kind in Europe; and, under the title of 'Apollonius Dyscolus' (1854), he published an essay on the history of grammatical theories in antiquity.   He wrote much on Greek *papyri*, and on Greek inscriptions, as well as on the language, history and literature of Greece and Rome.   Many of his papers were collected in his *Mémoires* of ancient literature, and of ancient history and philology (1862-3).   In connexion with the History of Scholarship, he wrote on Polemon the *periegetes*, and on the Duc de Clermont-Tonnerre, while (apart from his admirable essay on the History of Criticism) his most important and most popular work was his 'History of Hellenism in France' (1869).   He was himself one of the first in France to assimilate the strict and scientific methods of German scholarship, and to clothe its results in the lucid and elegant style characteristic of his

> Egger

---

[1] *Annuaire de l'Association*, 1874, 1—58.

[2] Salomon Reinach, in *Biogr. Jahrb.* 1886, 24—29; Queux Saint-Hilaire, in d'Eichthal's collected *Mémoires et Notices* (1864-84), 1887.

[3] 1849; ed. 2, 1874.

countrymen. In the last three years of his life, he was blind, and was compelled to avail himself of the services of a secretary. But he continued in all other respects to have perfect possession of his faculties, and, even in extreme old age, to retain the energy and the vivacity of youth [1].

The versatile scholar, Thomas Henri Martin (1813—1884),

Martin studied natural sciences as well as classical literature at the *École Normale*, where he also attended the lectures of Victor Cousin. His career as a scholar began with a critical analysis of Aristotle's treatise on Poetry [2]. For more than forty years he was an active member of the Faculty of Letters at Rennes.

It was there that he prepared the two volumes of his studies on Plato's *Timaeus* (1841), including the text and explanatory translation, analysis and commentary, and a series of treatises showing a wide knowledge of ancient Music, Astronomy, Cosmography, Physics, Geometry and Anatomy. The work was crowned by the Academy, and, in conjunction with his edition of the Astronomy of Theon of Smyrna (1849), led to his name being widely known abroad.

During his study of the *Timaeus* he formed a plan for a comprehensive history of ancient Astronomy and Natural Science. This prompted the publication of his second great work, the *Philosophie Spiritualiste de la Nature* in two volumes (1849), being an introduction to the ancient history of the physical sciences. The admirable survey of the study of the natural sciences among the Greeks down to 529 A.D. (included in his second volume) led to his election as a corresponding member of the Berlin Academy. He subsequently produced many important monographs on special portions of the subject of this work, *e.g.* on the writings ascribed to Heron of Alexandria, and on Cosmography and Astronomy. Thenceforth, his published works were almost exclusively devoted to the natural sciences, as studied by the ancients, and were very seldom connected with the Greek literature that was the main theme of his public lectures. These lectures, however, suggested his writing papers on the Greek

---

[1] Salomon Reinach, *Biogr. Jahrb.* 1885, 108—111.

[2] Caen, 1836.

Aspirates (1860), and on the trilogy of the *Prometheus*[1]. In his other writings his ideal was that of a Christian philosopher. His work on the Christian doctrine of a future life (1855) passed through three editions[2].—In the next generation the history of Greek science was ably treated by Paul Tannery (1843—1904), the editor of Diophantus[3].

Tannery

A history of medical science was published in 1872 by Charles Victor Daremberg (1817—1872), the translator of Oribasius (1851–76), and of select works of Hippocrates and Galen (1854–6), and the joint editor (with Saglio) of the celebrated Dictionary of Antiquities.

Daremberg

The able Aristotelian, Charles Thurot (1823—1882), was the son of Alexandre Thurot (1786—1847), the translator of one of Heeren's historical works. After passing through the *École Normale*, he was a professor at Pau, Rheims, and Bordeaux, and finally, in 1849, at Besançon, where he formed a life-long friendship with the eminent Greek scholar, Henri Weil. From 1854 to 1861 he was professor of Ancient History at Clermont-Ferrand; from 1861 to 1871, *Maître de Conférences* in Grammar at the *École Normale*; and, for the remaining eleven years of his life, Director of Latin studies at the *École Pratique des Hautes-Études*, as the successor of Gaston Boissier. He succeeded Villemain as a member of the Academy of Inscriptions, and was also a member of the Munich Academy.

Thurot

His scholarly labours were mainly concentrated on the philosophy of Aristotle, and on the history of Grammar. He published valuable papers on Aristotle's *Rhetoric*, *Poetic*, and *Politics*, and on the *Animalium Historia* and the *Meteorologica*[4]. He further distinguished himself by his edition of the commentary of Alexander of Aphrodisias on Aristotle *de sensu et sensibili*[5]. He also supplied an introduction and notes to his uncle's[6] translations of Epictetus and the eighth book of the *Ethics* (1874–81).

As a Latin scholar, he was mainly interested in the History of

---

[1] *Mém. Acad. Inscr.* xxviii (2) 1875.
[2] *Biogr. Jahrb.* 1884, 119—128.   [3] *ib.* 1906, 46—48.
[4] Mainly in *Revue Archéologique*, 1861–70; list in *Biogr. Jahrb.* 1882, 24 f.
[5] *Notices et Extraits*, xxv (2), 1875, pp. 454.
[6] François Thurot (1768—1832), professor at the Collège de France.

Education and in the Grammatical Studies of the Middle Ages.
In his theses for the degree of Doctor, he dealt with the mediaeval
organisation of the university of Paris[1], and with the Grammar
of Alexander de Villa Dei (1850). He also published documents
on the history of the university of Orléans[2], while the results of his
careful examination of some hundred MSS were incorporated in
his valuable collection of materials for a history of the grammatical
doctrines of the Middle Ages[3]. In a controversy with Prantl
he held that the Latin form of a synopsis of Logic by Petrus
Hispanus was the original, while Prantl maintained the originality
of the Greek form of the synopsis by Michael Psellus. Thurot's
opinion has since been confirmed[4]. He was a scholar of wide
outlook; he did much towards making France familiar with the
results of foreign scholarship; he was a great admirer of Madvig,
and, in his lectures, drew special attention to the value of the first
volume of the *Adversaria Critica*[5].

Sophocles was ably edited in 1867 by Edouard Tournier
Tournier (1831—1899); and seven plays of Euripides (1868)
and the principal speeches of Demosthenes (1873-7)
by Henri Weil (b. 1818)[6]; while Aristophanes and the Alexandrian
poets were tastefully studied by A. Couat (d. 1899).

The Latin Classics were the field of labour chosen by Louis
Benoist Eugène Benoist (1831—1887), who, after twelve
years' experience as a teacher at Marseilles, was on
the staff of the Faculty of Letters at Nancy from 1867 to 1871;
and, after a few years at Aix, succeeded Patin as professor in
Paris (1874–87). In 1884 he was elected a member of the
Academy of Inscriptions, but was prevented by ill health from
doing much for the remaining three years of his life.

While he was still at Marseilles, he edited the *Cistellaria* and *Rudens* of
Plautus and the *Andria* of Terence, but his main attention was devoted to

---

[1] Dezobry, Paris, 1850, 232 pp.

[2] *Bibl. de l'École des Chartes*, xxxii (1871) 376—396.

[3] *Notices et Extraits*, xxii (2) 1869, 592 pp.; cp. *Documents* in *Comptes rendus* of the Acad. of Inscr. vi (1870) 241—270.

[4] Stapfer in *Festschr.*, Freiburg in B., 1896, 130-8; *Byz. Zeitschr.* vi 443 f.

[5] *Biogr. Jahrb.* 1882, 23—29, after *Rev. Crit.* 241 f; *Rev. Hist.* 386 f; *Rev. de Philol.* 171-8; *S. Ber. bayer. Akad.* iii 414-6 (all for 1882); Bailly, 1886.

[6] Aeschylus, 1884, 1907[2]; *Études*, 1897-1900; cp. *Mélanges H. Weil*, 1892.

Lucretius and Virgil. His first edition of Virgil appeared in three volumes in 1867–72. His course of lectures in Paris began with a eulogy of his predecessor, Patin, while, in the following year, his studies in Plautus were appropriately combined with an encomium of Ritschl[1]. His larger edition of Virgil was published in 1876–80. With the aid of Lantoine, he published in 1884 an edition of the fifth book of Lucretius, followed by a school-edition in 1886. Meanwhile, he had embarked on an edition of Catullus, for which the translation into French verse was executed in 1878–82, by his celebrated pupil, Eugène Rostand, but this edition was never completed. Besides numerous articles on the authors above mentioned, he wrote on ' Horace in France '[2], but he failed to finish his proposed edition of that poet. In conjunction with his able pupil, O. Riemann, he produced an edition of Livy, XXI—XXV (1881—3), in which Riemann was responsible for the text and notes and the critical and grammatical appendices, while Benoist dealt with the religious, civil, and military institutions. His literary activity extended over a quarter of a century, during which he devoted unsparing toil to the textual criticism and exegesis of the Latin Classics. He was thoroughly familiar with the work of the Latin scholars of Germany, and his editions were distinctly superior to those that had hitherto held the field in France. Among the able Latin scholars that belonged to his school were Riemann, Waltz, Uri, Constans, Gölzer, Plessis, and Causeret[3].

Othon Riemann (1853—1891), as a student of the French School of Athens, spent two years (1874–5) in Italy, collating MSS of Xenophon and Livy. His third year was reserved for the Ionian islands. **Riemann** As a teacher at Nancy, he produced his theses on the language and grammar of Livy and on the text of Xenophon's *Hellenica*, with his archaeological researches on the Ionian islands and the first part of his studies on the evidence of Inscriptions as to the Attic dialect. In Paris, shortly after 1881, he succeeded Thurot as professor of Greek at the *École Normale*. During the latter part of his short life, he published an enlarged edition of his admirable work on Livy, and two editions of his excellent Latin Syntax (1886–90)[4].

During a brief life of thirty years, the highest distinction in palaeography was attained by Charles Graux (1852 —1882), who began his studies in the *Collège* of his **Graux** native town of Verviers. For his sound knowledge of Greek he was indebted to an aged curé, whose learning was only equalled by his modesty. He continued his study of Greek under Tournier in Paris, where he worked at Comparative Grammar under Bréal.

---

[1] *Rev. de Philol.* i 91.

[2] *Rev. politique et litt.* viii (1875) 719 f.

[3] *Biogr. Jahrb.* 1887, 112—117.

[4] Since enlarged in Riemann and Goelzer, *Gram. Comparée du Grec et du Latin*, 2 vols. (1899—1901). *Biogr. Jahrb.* 1891, 133 f.

At the age of 21, he was already editing in a scientific spirit the
Revue de Philologie and the *Revue Critique*.　His proficiency in
Greek Palaeography led to his being repeatedly sent to explore
the MSS of foreign libraries.　In 1879 he published a catalogue
of the Greek MSS of Copenhagen; and, during his journeys in
Spain, he examined the contents of no less than sixty libraries,
while he devoted special attention to the treasures of the Escurial.
He there found the materials for his Essay on the origins of
the department of Greek MSS in the Escurial, which includes a
sketch of the Revival of Learning in Spain[1].　In the Royal
Library of Madrid he discovered a new recension of certain of
Plutarch's *Lives*.　During his stay in Madrid, he was presented to
the King of Spain, and characteristically seized the occasion to
suggest the possibility of lending Spanish MSS to scholars in
France.　To the *Revue de Philologie* he had contributed an important article on ancient Stichometry[2], and he kept this subject
in view during all his researches abroad.　Some of his earliest
works had been connected with the Greek writers on fortifications,
and he had published the treatise of Philon of Byzantium, as well
as a memoir on the walls of Carthage.　He had thus chosen the
application of critical scholarship to the study of ancient history
as his special field of labour.　Early in 1881 he was appointed to
the new office of instructor in Greek History and Antiquities in
the Faculty of Letters in Paris.　Before beginning his course, he
visited Florence, and stayed for a longer time in Rome, where he
aided the officials of the Vatican in dating the Greek MSS which
they were then engaged in cataloguing.　On his return to Paris,
after a brief respite from work, he announced his first lecture,
but, before the date fixed for its delivery, he was carried off by a
sudden illness in the thirtieth year of his age.　His memory was
honoured by the publication of a volume of papers contributed
by seventy-eight of the leading scholars of Europe; and his literary remains were collected in memorial volumes including the
editio princeps of certain of the works of Choricius, an edition
of Plutarch's *Lives of Demosthenes* and *Cicero*, founded on the

---

[1] *Bibl. de l'École des hautes études*, XLVI (1880).

[2] *Rev. de Philol.* 1878, 97—143. (Lydus, περὶ διοσημειῶν, *ib.* 1896,
23—35.)

Madrid MS, a revised text of part of Xenophon's *Oeconomicus*, and the treatise on fortifications by Philon of Byzantium[1].

Some of the French translations of the Latin Classics have been noticed in connexion with the brothers Nisard. Cicero was translated by Joseph Victor Le Clerc (1789—1865)[2], and Sallust by Moncourt. In the department of Greek literature, Homer was translated by Giguet, Thucydides by Zévort, the *Antidosis* of Isocrates by Cartelier, Demosthenes by Stiévenart and by Dareste, Dio Cassius by Gros, and the *Dionysiaca* of Nonnus by the Comte de Marcellus (1795—1861), (who presented to the Louvre the Venus de Milo[3]). Lycophron and the Greek Anthology were rendered by Dehèque (d. 1870), who counted Egger among his pupils; Aeschylus and the *Metaphysics* of Aristotle, as well as M. Aurelius and Plutarch, by Pierron, the author of Histories of Greek and Latin literature (d. 1878)[4].

Translators

Aristotle was expounded, as well as translated, by Barthélemy-Saint-Hilaire (1805—1895), who was professor of Greek and Latin philosophy in 1838, and, during his public career, was principal secretary of the provisional government of 1848. His translation of Aristotle, begun in 1832, was completed in 1891[5].

Barthélemy-Saint-Hilaire

The following critique is from the pen of Lord Acton[6]:—

' He knows Greek thoroughly for working purposes, but not exquisitely as a scholar; and he has done little, on the whole, for his idol Aristotle in the way of consulting the MSS and improving the unsettled text '.... He 'is quite at the top of scholars and philosophers of the second class. Not a discoverer, not an originator, not even clever in the sense common with Frenchmen, not eloquent at all, not vivid or pointed in phrase; sufficient in knowledge, but not abounding, sound, but not supple, accustomed to heavy work in the darkness, unused to effect, to influence, or to applause, unsympathetic and a little isolated, but high-minded, devoted to principle, willing, even enthusiastic, to sacrifice himself, his comfort, his life, his reputation, to public duty or scientific truth.... Not the least of his merits is that, having spent his life on Aristotle, he told me that he thought more highly of Plato; and in his

---

[1] *Textes grecs*, 1886; *Notices bibliogr.* 1884; Graux et Martin, *MSS grecs en Suède* (1889), *Espagne et Portugal* (1893), *Fac-similés* (1891). *Biogr. Jahrb.* 1882, 18—21; portrait, life by Lavisse, and bibliography in *Mélanges Graux*, 1884.

[2] *Notice* by Guigniaut, 1866.   [3] Cp. Michaelis, *Arch. Entd.* 45 f.

[4] See also Egger's *Hellénisme en France*, ii 469—476.

[5] Index of subjects in two vols. (1892). Picot, *Notices Historiques*, i (1907) 107—148.

[6] *Letters*, 1904, 37—39 (27 Sept. 1880).

Introduction to the Ethics he showed the weakness of his hero's attack on Platonism'.

In his edition and translation of the *Politics* (1837), the Books are arranged in the following order :—I, II, III, VII, VIII, IV, VI, V. It was a French translator, Nicolas Oresme (d. 1382), who was the first to place Books VII and VIII immediately after I, II, III, while Saint-Hilaire was the first to place VI before V[1].

The 'physiology' of Aristotle was the subject of a thesis by Charles Waddington (born in 1819), a member of an English family which settled in France in 1780. He lectured on Logic at the Sorbonne (1850–6), but, being opposed as a Protestant, withdrew to Strassburg. On returning in 1864, he lectured on philosophical subjects. He wrote a monograph on Ramus (1855), followed by works on Pyrrhonism (1877), on the authority of Aristotle in the Middle Ages (1877), and on the Philosophy of the Renaissance and its antecedents (1872–3).

C. Waddington

The study of ancient geography was advanced by Charles Athanase Baron Walckenaer (1771—1852), who lived in Scotland during the French Revolution, and was in the service of France from 1816 to 1830. In 1840 he became Secretary of the Academy of Inscriptions. His best-known work is that on the Geography of Gaul[2]. He also edited the Irishman Dicuil's treatise *De mensura orbis terrae* (1807), and wrote on the life and works of Horace[3]. The ancient geography of France was similarly studied with marked success by A. E. E. Desjardins (1823—1886), who also made his mark in Latin Epigraphy, while the diplomatist, Charles Tissot (1828—1884), published an important memoir on Caesar's campaign in Africa (1883). The Roman inscriptions of Algiers were systematically edited by Léon Renier (1809—1885), the author of an able monograph on the siege of Jerusalem by Titus, and the compiler of a large collection of Roman military diplomas[4].

Walckenaer

Desjardins
Tissot
Renier

The historian Prosper Mérimée (1803–70), besides producing two volumes on Catiline, and on the Social War, took part in the preparation of the *Histoire de César* published in 1865–6 by Napoleon III (1808—1873), while Amédée Thierry (1797—1873) wrote on Rufinus, Stilicho, and Eutropius[5], and Brunet de Presle

Mérimée
A. Thierry
De Presle

---

[1] Susemihl-Hicks, *Politics*, p. 16, n. 4.

[2] 3 vols., with atlas, 1839.

[3] Naudet's *Notice*, 1852 ; Saint-Beuve's *Lundis*, vi.

[4] Salomon Reinach in *Biogr. Jahrb.* viii (1885) 103 f; Chatelain in *Rev. de Phil.* x (1886) 1 f.

[5] Also author of *Hist. des Gaulois*, and *Hist. de la Gaule*; notice by G. Lévèque, 1873.

(1809—1875), a specialist in modern Greek, treated of the Greeks in Sicily (1845) and of Greece under Roman rule (1859)[1].

As a member of the French School at Athens, Fustel de Coulanges (1830—1889) published a memoir on the island of Chios[2]. His Latin thesis on the 'Cult of Vesta', written on his return to France (1858), contained the germ of his best-known work, *La Cité Antique* (1864), a work coinciding in many points with Sir Henry Maine's *Ancient Law* (1861). In 1874 he began the publication of his 'History of the Institutions of France', and in the following year became professor of Ancient History at the Sorbonne, where, in all his lectures, he strongly insisted on the study of the original authorities. A proposal to found in his honour a new Chair of Mediaeval History was delayed until Gambetta had been assured in 1879 that the recognition, in the *Cité Antique*, of the important part played by religion did not really imply the author's sympathy with modern 'clericalism'. After spending three years as Director of the *École Normale*, he resumed for the last six years of his life his fruitful labours in the Chair of Mediaeval History at the Sorbonne[3]. His *Gaule Romaine* was posthumously published in 1890.

Among the distinguished representatives of Classical Archaeology in France was Aubin Louis Millin de Grandmaison (1759—1818), author of the *Monuments antiques inédits* (1802–6), and of the *Galérie mythologique* (1811)[4]. Of Italian descent, he learned German in Strassburg, and, for the last twenty-three years of his life, edited a journal that formed a valuable link between the archaeological studies of France and Germany. In the course of his travels he produced one of the fullest descriptions of the Roman remains in the South of France, and his visits to Italy led to the first systematic examination of monuments connected with the *Oresteia* (1817)[5]. He introduced into classical archaeology the terms *monuments antiques* and *antiquité figurée*[6].

A. C. Quatremère de Quincy (1755—1849), in his illustrated volume, *Le Jupiter Olympien* (1814), was the first to enable archaeologists to form a clear conception of the chryselephantine

[1] Queux Saint-Hilaire, in *Assoc. Études grecs*, 1875, 342.

[2] *Archives des missions scientifiques*, vol. v.

[3] Paul Guiraud in *Biogr. Jahrb.* xii (1889) 138—149.

[4] Plates in his *Peintures de vases antiques* (1808–10) and *Pierres gravées inédites* (1817–25) republished by S. Reinach, 1891–5.

[5] Stark, 257 f.   [6] *ib.* 50.

work of the ancients. It was not until he actually saw the sculptures of the Parthenon in 1818 that he fully appreciated their importance[1]. He was the first to recognise the value of 'Carrey's' drawings of those sculptures[2].

An epoch in the study of ancient sculpture was made by Jean Baptiste Comte de Clarac (1777—1847), who, after living in Switzer-
Clarac
land, Germany and Holland, returned to France, and became tutor in the family of king Murat at Naples. He there wrote a report on the discoveries at Pompeii (1813). In 1818 he succeeded Visconti as Conservator of the Louvre. His catalogues of 1820-30 ultimately became a manual of the history of ancient art (1847-9). Under the title of *Musée de sculpture antique et moderne* he published two volumes of outline engravings of the sculptures of the Louvre (1826-30), followed by two further volumes containing more than 2500 copies of the 'Statues of Europe', arranged according to subjects (1852-7), and completed by a volume of reliefs, and another of Egyptian, Greek and Roman Iconography. This vast collection of outlines was the foundation of all subsequent works on ancient sculpture[3].

Raoul Rochette (1783—1854) produced in his *Monumens inédits* (1828) a work of the same title and general aim as that of his contem-
Raoul Rochette
porary, Gerhard. As the successor of Millin at the Louvre he published during twenty-five years a large number of papers on archaeological discoveries. He wrote a critical history of the Greek Colonies, and a work on the antiquities of the Crimea. He was specially interested in the Pergamene artists, and in the sculptured representations of Greek heroes[4]. His views[5] and those of Guigniaut (1794—1876), the learned translator and reviser of Creuzer's *Symbolik*, were keenly criticised by Jean
Letronne
Antoine Letronne (1787—1848), the author of works on ancient geography, including a critical essay on the topography of Syracuse (1812), researches on Dicuil, *de mensura orbis terrae* (1814), and on the Periplus of 'Scylax' (1826) and the fragments of Scymnus and 'Dicaearchus' (1840). He also discussed the fragments of Heron of Alexandria (1851), and wrote masterly papers on ancient astronomy, and on the statue of Memnon[6]. His greater works were connected with Greek and Roman coinage (1817-25), and with the Greek and Latin Inscriptions of Egypt (1842-8)[7].

Philippe Le Bas (1794—1860), who had learnt his Greek from Boissonade, made the acquaintance of Italian and German archaeologists
Le Bas
during his residence in Rome as tutor in the family of queen

---

[1] Letters to Canova.   [2] Stark, 258; vol. ii, p. 299 *supra*.

[3] Stark, 367 f. S. Reinach, *Clarac de Poche* (1897—1904); bust in the Louvre.

[4] Stark, 297; portrait by his daughter engraved by her husband, Luigi Calamatta.

[5] *Peintures antiques inédites* (1836).   [6] *Inscr. de l'Égypte*, ii 325—410.

[7] Longpérier, *Notice*, 1849; Egger, *Mém. de Philol.* 1—14. *Mélanges* (with Walckenaer's *Éloge*), 1860; *Œuvres Choisies*, 1881-5.

Hortense. The two years of his mission to Greece and Asia Minor (1843–4) were devoted to the collection of 450 drawings of ancient monuments, and 5000 inscriptions. Several parts of the *Voyage archéologique en Grèce et en Asie Mineure* were published in 1847–8. After the death of Le Bas, the collection of the inscriptions was greatly enlarged in 1861–2 by W. H. Waddington, who extended the quest to Syria and Cyprus, and by P. Foucart[1]. The results of the exploration of Asia Minor in 1833–7 by Texier (1794—1860) were published in 1849[2].

Texier

The Duc de Luynes (1803—1867), who played an important part in the early history of the Archaeological Institute[3], and generously supported the publication of the two volumes of *Nouvelles Annales* for 1838–9, independently produced by the French section of that Institute in 1840–5, distinguished himself by his admirable works on the exploration of Metapontum (1836), on the coins of the Satraps (1848), and on the coins and inscriptions of Cyprus (1852). He was the liberal patron of archaeological work at home and abroad, but, in all his varied interests, he ever returned to the art of ancient Greece as the 'shrine of beauty'. He lavished his resources on Simart's restoration of the chrysele-phantine statue of Athena Parthenos. He was to France what the Earl of Arundel was to England, and he left all his vast collections of works of ancient art to the Museum in the Paris Library[4].

Duc de Luynes

Charles Lenormant (1816—1881), the discoverer in 1860 of the fine relief of the divinities of Eleusis, was the author of the five volumes of the *Trésor de numismatique et de glyptique*, and of the three of the *Élite des monuments céramographiques*. He also produced a commentary on Plato's *Cratylus* (1861). He died during his travels in Greece, and was buried on the hill of Colonus[5]. His son François (1837—1883) was a versatile explorer in the most varied fields of archaeology, epigraphy, and numismatics. Among his principal publications were his 'archaeological researches at Eleusis' (1862), and his monograph on the sacred 'Eleusinian way' (1864). His earliest important work was his Essay on the Coins of the Ptolemies (1857). Among the most comprehensive of his articles in Daremberg and Saglio's Dictionary were those on the Alphabet, and on Bacchus and Ceres. He produced numerous memoirs on Greek and Latin inscriptions, on works of ancient sculpture, and on numismatics. He took part in preparing seven volumes of masterpieces of ancient art, mainly from the Museum at Naples, and in producing highly popular works on Magna Graecia, and on Apulia, and Lucania. In conjunction with

C. Lenormant

F. Lenormant

---

[1] Stark, 329. Plates published by S. Reinach (1888).

[2] Cp. Michaelis, *Arch. Entd.* 76, 150.

[3] *ib.* 286; Michaelis, *Gesch. d. Inst.*, 44, 63, 85, 95.

[4] E. Vinet, in *L'art et l'archéologie*, 468 f; Stark, 300 f.

[5] *Notices* by Wallon, 1859; and Laboulaye, 1861; portrait in the *Gazette archéologique*, 1885.

Baron de Witte, he founded the *Gazette Archéologique* in 1875; on the death
of Beulé in the previous year he was appointed professor of Archaeology at the
Bibliothèque Nationale, and held that position with the highest distinction for
the remaining nine years of his life[1].

Among archaeologists intermediate in age between the elder and the

Longpérier
Beulé

younger Lenormant were Adrien de Longpérier (1816—1881),
who wrote on the Bronzes of the Louvre (1869) and on the
Coins of the Sassanides (1882), and whose archaeological
papers were collected by Schlumberger[2]; and Charles Ernest Beulé (1826—
1875), who helped to popularise archaeology by his works on the Acropolis
(1854) and the Coinage (1858) of Athens, on the Peloponnesus (1855), and on
the arts at Sparta, on Greek art before Pericles, and on Pheidias. He also
wrote on Augustus (a political pamphlet), and on Tiberius and Titus[3]. The

Laborde

mediaeval topography of Athens was excellently illustrated
by the work of Léon de Laborde on Athens in centuries
XV—XVII (1854). Athens and the Acropolis were the theme of a work by
Émile Burnouf (1877), the second Director of the French School (1821-1907)[4].

Though the Duc de Luynes was one of the warmest friends of the Archae-

The School
of Athens

ological Institute of Rome, the Duc de Blacas its first president, and the learned Guigniaut (the friend of Panofka and
the 'father of the School of France'[5]) one of the earliest
members of the Institute, nevertheless it was not the Institute of Rome that
suggested the foundation of the School of Athens. The germ of the French
School was the Roman Academy of France, the Academy of artists founded
by Colbert in 1666[6]. The School of Athens was founded in 1846; during the
first sixty years of its existence it has had five Directors:—Amedée Daveluy
(1846-67), Émile Burnouf (1867-75), Albert Dumont (1875-78), Paul Foucart
(1878-90) and Théophile Homolle, the present Director; and the story of its
fortunes under these five Directors has been admirably told by Georges
Radet[7]. It has explored and excavated in Asia Minor, in Cyprus, Syria,
North Africa and even in Spain, as well as in Greece, in Thrace and Macedonia, and in the islands of the Aegean. It has lately won fresh laurels at
both of the ancient shrines of Apollo, at Delos and at Delphi. It has also
added much to the learning and to the literature of France. Among the
students entered under Daveluy we find Charles Lévêque[8], Émile Burnouf,

[1] Babelon in *Biogr. Jahrb.* 1884, 151—163; Rayet's *Études*, 405—424.

[2] 1882, with complete bibliography; Rayet's *Études*, 396—404.

[3] Gruyer, in *Gaz. des Beaux Arts*, 1874; portrait in G. Radet's History of
the French School of Athens, opp. p. 274.

[4] Portrait in Radet, p. 153.

[5] Portrait in Radet, opp. p. 108.

[6] Homolle, quoted by Radet, 4.

[7] *L'Histoire et l'Œuvre de l'École Française d'Athènes*, 1901, 492 pp.,
with 133 illustrations, including portraits of all the Directors.

[8] *La Science du Beau* (1861).

Jules Girard, Beulé, Edmond About, Fustel de Coulanges, Heuzey, Georges Perrot, Paul Foucart, Wescher, Decharme, and Albert Dumont. [Among those entered under Émile Burnouf:—Rayet, Collignon, Homolle, and Riemann; under Albert Dumont:—Paul Girard, Jules Martha, Bernard Haussoullier, and Edmond Pottier; and under Paul Foucart:—Hauvette, Salomon Reinach, Monceaux, Pierre Paris, Diehl, Radet, Deschamps[1], Fougères, Lechat, and Victor Bérard. Many of these names are widely known, there are none of them that are not φωνάεντα συνετοῖσιν, and there is abundance of promise and more than promise among their successors, the pupils of Théophile Homolle. Most of the names represent various departments of classical archaeology, but the study of Greek literature is also represented by É. Burnouf, J. Girard, Perrot, Decharme, and Hauvette, and the linguistic side of classical learning by the careful treatment of Attic usage in the epigraphic works of Foucart, Riemann and S. Reinach, and by Homolle's preliminary paper on the primitive dialect of Delphi. Greek texts were edited by Wescher; while Riemann collated the Ambrosian MS of Xenophon's *Hellenica* and examined the *scholia* on Demosthenes and Aeschines in the monastic library of Patmos[2]. Part of the recent progress of excavation and discovery in the Hellenic world has been traced by S. Reinach[3], and the documentary history of the French exploration of the East in the seventeenth and eighteenth centuries has been published by H. Omont[4]. The French School of Athens published its results first in the *Archives des missions scientifiques et littéraires*, and next in a *Bulletin* begun in 1868 and transformed into the well-known *Bulletin de correspondance hellénique* in 1879. The French School of Rome is the younger sister of the School of Athens. When (by the Versailles decree of 1871) the Archaeological Institute of Rome was placed under the control of the Berlin Academy and thus ceased tȯ be 'international', a French School of Rome became a necessity, and it was accordingly founded in 1873. Its work is partly represented in the *Bibliothèque* of the Schools of Athens and Rome (which includes De Nolhac's volumes on Petrarch and Humanism, and on the Library of Fulvio Orsini); its special organ is *Mélanges d'archéologie et d'histoire*; and its present Director is Mgr Duchesne.

The study of epigraphy and numismatics was ably represented by William Henry Waddington (1826—1894), a cousin of Charles Waddington[5]. He was born at the family *château* near Dreux, was educated in Paris and at Rugby, rowed in the university-boat at Cambridge, and was a Chancellor's Medallist and second in the first class of the Classical Tripos of that university in 1849. His early travels in Greece and Asia Minor resulted in his *Voyage en Asie Mineure au*

W. H. Waddington

---

[1] *La Grèce d'aujourd'hui* (1892) etc.

[2] Details in Radet, 397, and, in general, 379—414.

[3] *Chroniques d'Orient*, 2 vols., 1891–6.

[4] *Missions archéologiques*, 2 vols. 4to, xvi + 1237 pp. (1903).

[5] p. 262 *supra*.

point de vue numismatique (1853)[1]. This was followed by his *Mélanges de numismatique et de philologie* (1862–7), his edition of the Edict of Diocletian (1864), the Greek and Latin Inscriptions in his continuation of Le Bas' *Voyage archéologique* (1868), his 'Greek and Latin Inscriptions of Syria' (1870) and his '*Fasti* of the Asiatic provinces of the Roman Empire (ed. 2, 1872)[2]. He was elected a member of the Chamber of Deputies in 1871, and of the Senate in 1876, was Minister of Public Instruction in 1876–7, and Ambassador of France to England in 1883–93. As a Member of the Academy of Inscriptions in Paris (1865) and of the Academy of Sciences in Berlin, and an Honorary Doctor of the University of Cambridge (1884), he was an archaeologist who conferred distinction on the land of his ancestors as well as on the land of his adoption. 'His manly loyalty to France lost nothing by the discipline of Rugby and Cambridge, and he adorned public life without ceasing to deserve well of archaeology'[3]. It is nevertheless true that he would have served that science still better, had he withdrawn from public life two-and-twenty years before his death. He might thus have lived to complete and publish his long-expected work on the Coinage of Asia Minor[4], a work founded on the studies of a life-time and illustrated by an unrivalled collection consisting entirely of coins that were either very rare or absolutely unique[5]. His political popularity was probably at its height in 1877–9, when he was Minister of Foreign Affairs and Plenipotentiary of France at the Congress of Berlin (June, 1878). It was to Waddington that Greece then owed the promise of a rectification of her frontiers. Early in 1880, on ceasing to be responsible for foreign affairs, he paid his first visit to Rome, where Salomon Reinach met him in the Lateran Museum. Waddington had at that moment an immense reputation as a philhellene, and Reinach suggested a tour in Greece. 'On vous recevra' (he added) 'sous des arcs de triomphe.' 'Mais précisément' (replied Waddington) 'je n'aime pas les arcs de triomphe.' A more sober form of gratitude would doubtless have been preferred by that calm and dispassionate politician and archaeologist who, in all his writings, seldom, if ever, allowed himself to lapse into a rhetorical phrase. Attracted mainly towards the solution of difficult problems of chronology, he

---

[1] *Revue numismatique*, 1851–3.

[2] All these works (except the *Mélanges*) originally formed part of his continuation of 'Le Bas.' He also wrote on the chronology of the life of the rhetorician Aristides (*Mém. Acad. Inscr.* 1867), and on the coinage of Isauria and Lycaonia (*Rev. num.* 1883) and the inscriptions of Tarsus (*B. C. H.* 1883).

[3] Jebb in *J. H. S.* xiv p. vii.

[4] In course of completion by Babelon and Theodore Reinach, for publication by the Academy of Inscriptions.

[5] Purchased for the *Cabinet de Médailles* in 1897 (Babelon's *Inventaire Sommaire*, 1898; Waddington, Babelon, Th. Reinach, *Recueil de Monnaies d'Asie Mineure*, 1904–7).

regarded the sciences of epigraphy and numismatics solely as handmaids to history or (if we must deny ourselves that phrase in such a context) solely as aids to the attainment of historic truth[1].

Among important works on Numismatics may be mentioned the well-known *Description de médailles antiques grecques et romaines* (1806 f) by Mionnet (1770—1842), the consular and imperial Roman coins of Cohen (ed. 2, 1881); and the Byzantine coins (1838) of De Saulcy (1807—1880), the oriental traveller and archaeologist[2].

Mionnet

Our survey of the classical archaeologists of France cannot close without some record of the brief but brilliant career of Olivier Rayet (1847—1887). At the *École Normale* he came under the inspiring influence of his future father-in-law, Ernest Desjardins, whose lectures on Ancient History and Geography were varied with vivid reminiscences of eminent archaeologists, such as Mariette and Borghesi. Rome and Paestum and Selinus were among the land-marks of the memorable journey of 1869 that led Rayet to the School of Athens. At Athens he began the fruitful studies which resulted in his papers on the Cerameicus. There too he obtained for the Louvre, and for his own collection, some of the finest of the early examples of the Tanagra figurines, a branch of ancient art in which he soon became a recognised expert. He regarded these graceful figures as having no mythological or symbolic significance; they were placed in the tombs (he held) simply as substitutes for the victims sacrificed in primitive times as companions to the spirits of the dead[3]. In 1872-3 he was engaged in excavating the theatre of Miletus and the temple of Didyma, and in the discovery of important sculptures and inscriptions on both sites[4]. Early in 1874, on his return to Paris, he began his lectures on Greek inscriptions and terra-cottas, and on the topography of Athens; these were followed by further lectures on the history of ancient art; and ten years after his return he succeeded F. Lenormant as professor of archaeology at the *Bibliothèque Nationale*. In February 1887 he died at the age of less than forty, after two years of ill health due to a malady probably contracted during the exploration of Miletus. The only work which he lived to complete was his series of *Monuments de l'art antique* (1884). His important *Histoire de la Céramique grecque* was completed by Collignon (1888), and the same year saw the publication of an interesting collection of his more popular papers[5].

Rayet

For the ten years that preceded his last illness he held a unique position

---

[1] Cp. S. Reinach, in *Biogr. Jahr.* 1897, 1—8.

[2] He also wrote on *César dans les Gaules* (1860); cp. *Revue Celtique*, 1880; Froehner, 1881; Schlumberger, 1881 (with bibliography).

[3] *Études d'archéologie et d'art*, 1888, 320 f.

[4] *ib.* 99 f. The work was resumed by Haussoullier in 1895-6 (*Études sur l'histoire de Milet*, 1902).

[5] *Études d'archéologie et d'art*, with portrait, and biographical notice by Salomon Reinach.

among the archaeologists of France, as a man whose taste and judgement were respected by experts and artists, and also by collectors of works of ancient art. He did not pretend to any profound learning in the domain of mythology, but he had a fine sense of style. On his return from Olympia he wrote two admirable articles on the newly discovered pediments of the temple of Zeus and on the German excavations in general[1]. With an eager patriotism he elsewhere urged that Paris should not be allowed to fall behind Berlin or London in the organisation of its Museums of Ancient Art. It may be added that his articles on this theme were written at the instance of Gambetta, for whom he had an unbounded admiration; and, after his hero's death, it was not without emotion that he reproduced and described in his *Monuments de l'art antique* the exquisite figurine presented to that eminent politician by the gratitude of the Greeks of Epirus[2].

During the nineteenth century in France classical learning had no darker days than those of the First Empire. Bon-Joseph Dacier regretfully reports to Napoleon I:—'La Philologie, qui est la base de toute bonne littérature et sur laquelle repose la certitude de l'histoire, ne trouve presque plus personne pour la cultiver'[3]. The first Napoleon studied Caesar for his own purposes[4], and the third followed his example[5]. Under the Restoration, Latin was recognised anew in 1821 as the proper medium of instruction in philosophy, but this recognition was withdrawn after the Revolution of July, 1830[6]. A literary reaction, however, ensued, a reaction connected with the notable names of Abel François Villemain and Victor Cousin. The latter, who had studied philosophy and educational organisation in Germany, and had written *inter alia* on Aristotle's *Metaphysics*, was Minister of Public Instruction in 1840[7]. Villemain (1790—1870), the Minister of 1839, had been appointed professor of French Eloquence at the Sorbonne, had translated Cicero's *Letters* and *De Republica*, had published a romance on

Villemain

---

[1] Reprinted in *Études*, 42—85.

[2] S. Reinach, in *Biogr. Jahrb.* 1887, 35—41, and esp. in his ed. of *Études* (1888), pp. i—xvi.

[3] *Rapport sur les progrès de l'histoire et de la littérature ancienne*, 1789—1808 (Paris, 1810).

[4] *Précis des guerres de César*, ed. Marchand, 260 pp. (1830).

[5] *Hist. de Jules César* (1865-6).

[6] Gréard, *Éducation et Instruction* (*Enseignement Secondaire*), ii c. ix, x.

[7] p. 251 *supra*.

the Greeks of the fifteenth century[1], and a popular treatise on Roman Polytheism[2]. He is a representative of the rhetorical side of classical scholarship. Like Guizot and Cousin (both of whom had been Ministers of Public Instruction as well as professors), Villemain gave brilliant courses of lectures, which, although delivered from the professorial chair, were addressed to the general public, there being hardly any regular students or duly organised schools of learning[3].

A more solid type of erudition was represented by the Minister of 1875, Henri Alexandre Wallon (1812—1905)[4], for many years 'perpetual secretary' of the Academy of Inscriptions, who, besides not a few important contributions to historical or theological literature, had in the early part of his career produced a learned history of ancient slavery[5]. His able contemporary, Jean Victor Duruy (1811—1894), the author of a Historical Geography of the Roman Republic and the Roman Empire (1838) and of well-known Histories of Rome[6] and Greece[7], crowned his many services as Minister by the establishment of the *École pratique des hautes études* in 1866. The date has been recognised as marking a renaissance of classical studies in France[8]. It is also the date of the foundation of the *Revue Critique*, which, as the organ of a sound and sober type of scholarship, dealt a final death-blow to the 'pale imitators of Villemain'. The characteristic of this renaissance has been described by the author of the *Manuel de Philologie* as an alliance between the French qualities of clearness and method, and the solid learning of other nations[9].

Wallon

Duruy

---

[1] *Lascaris*, 1825. [2] *Nouveaux Mélanges*, 1827.

[3] L. Liard, *Les Universités Françaises* (Report of 1897).

[4] Portrait in *Comptes rendus* of Acad. of Inscr. 1906.

[5] 1847; ed. 2, 1879 (Perrot in *Rev. Arch.* 1879, 260 f).

[6] Six vols. (1876–79); ill. ed. in eight vols. (1878–86); E. T. ed. Mahaffy, 1883 f.

[7] 1861; two vols. 1883; ill. ed. three vols. 1887–9; E. T. ed. Mahaffy, 1892.

[8] S. Reinach, *Manuel de Philologie*, i 13. In 1877 the *Revue de Philologie* was founded, and Cobet writes to Tournier in that year, expressing his delight, *renata esse et tam laeta florere in Gallia severa literarum veterum studia* (*Rev. de Philol.* ii 189).

[9] S. Reinach, *l. c.*

Among German scholars who settled in France may be mentioned Karl
Benedict Hase (1780—1864), who, after studying at Jena and
K. B. Hase
Helmstedt, left in 1801 for Paris, where he held an appoint-
ment in the Library, besides being a professor of Modern Greek and of
Palaeography (1816), and of Comparative Grammar (1852). He wrote the
Prolegomena to the *editio princeps* of Lydus, *de magistratibus Romanis*, and
edited Lydus *de ostentis*, etc., as well as Julius Obsequens, Valerius Maximus,
and Suetonius. He contributed many papers to the *Notices et Extraits* of the
MSS of the Paris Library. In the study of palaeography his most famous pupil
was Charles Graux[1]. Hase took part in the first volume only of the new
edition of the Greek *Thesaurus* projected by Didot[2].

One of Didot's most active supporters in the series of the Classics that
bears his name was Johann Friedrich Dübner (1802—1867),
Dübner
who had studied at Göttingen, and was invited to Paris in
1832 to take part in the new edition of the *Thesaurus*. He was the editor of
many volumes in Didot's series, being sole editor of Menander and Philemon,
Polybius, Plutarch's *Moralia*, and the *Characters* of Theophrastus, with Marcus
Aurelius, Epictetus, Arrian etc., Himerius, Porphyry, and the *scholia* to
Aristophanes, and joint editor of Strabo, the Tragic Fragments, the minor
Epic Poets, and the *scholia* to Theocritus, Nicander and Oppian[3]. He
completed in two volumes the edition of the Greek Anthology for which
preparations had been made by Boissonade, and a third volume, containing
the Epigrams quoted by ancient authors or preserved in inscriptions, was
edited (1850) by Ed. Cougny (1818—1889), who was led by
Cougny
Egger to the study of ancient rhetoric and edited in 1863 four
Progymnasmata from a MS discovered by himself at Bourges. He also
printed Brunck's correspondence with interesting details on his *Analecta*, and
a sketch of his career[4]. During the last fifteen years of his life he was engaged
on the edition of the Greek Epigrams above-mentioned, and also on a
collection of the Greek writers on the geography and history of Gaul, a work
that owed much to the encouragement of Egger[5].

Dübner was naturally the medium of communication between the publisher
and Dübner's countrymen. Thus it was through Dübner that Köchly made
his proposal to edit Manetho, and was informed that the usual *honorarium*
was 1200 francs for a volume of 40 sheets ; but half this sum was usually paid
in books of nominally equivalent value published by Didot[6]. Apart from the
ordinary Greek Classics, the series included Strabo, edited by Dübner and
Carl Müller, the editor of the *Geographi Graeci Minores* and the fragments of

---

[1] p. 259 *supra*.

[2] Guigniaut, *Notice*, 1867.

[3] Bursian, ii 868 f.

[4] *Annuaire Assoc. Études grecs*, ix 106, viii 447, x 142.

[5] S. Reinach, in *Biogr. Jahrb.* 1889, 149—152.

[6] Böckel's *Hermann Köchly*, 131.

the Greek historians. The fragments of the philosophers were edited by Mullach[1].

The Didot series derived its name from Ambroise Firmin Didot (1790—1876), the celebrated printer and publisher, whose ancestors were associated with the book-trade from 1713. Didot was **Didot** himself a translator of Thucydides (ed. 2, 1875), and the author of an essay on Anacreon, and of works on Musurus and Aldus Manutius (1875), and on Henri Estienne (1824), the author of the Greek *Thesaurus*. With the aid of the brothers Dindorf, this great work was published anew by the 'modern Estienne' (1831–65)[2]. .

Colmar in Alsace was the birthplace of Victor Henry (1850—1907), a pupil of Abel Bergaigne, and a lecturer at **V. Henry** Douai and Lille, and at the Sorbonne, where he was professor of Comparative Philology for the last twelve years of his life. His treatise on Analogy in Greek (1883) was followed by his *Esquisses Morphologiques* (1882-9); and his Comparative Grammars of Greek and Latin[3], and of English and German, were translated into English. His other works deal with the psychology of language, and with Sanskrit literature. He was a man of wide and varied culture, and his interest in language extended from the dialect of his Alsatian birthplace to that of the Aleutian islands that link the North of Asia to the North of America[4].

Our survey of classical scholarship in France may here be followed by the briefest mention of a representative **Bétant** of French Switzerland, a professor at Geneva,— E. A. Bétant (1803—1871). His French translation of Thucydides was published in Paris (1863). He had already produced a lexicon to Thucydides in French (1836) and in Latin (1843-7), and editions of the *Nubes* and *Plutus*. He closed his career in 1871 by giving to the world of scholars the *editio princeps* of Boëthius *De Consolatione*, as rendered into Greek by the Byzantine monk, Maximus Planudes[5].

[1] Cp., in general, Egger's *Hellénisme en France*, ii 459—463.

[2] Nine folio vols.; cp. Egger, *l.c.*, ii 451; on Didot, cp. *Assoc. Études gr.* 1876, 225.

[3] 1887, 1893[3]; E. T. 1890.

[4] Cp. Gubernatis, *Dict. Int.* 1905, and *Athenaeum*, 16 Feb. 1907.

[5] Cherbulioz-Bourrit, *Notice nécrologique*, Gen. 1873.

COBET.

Reproduced from a copy of the presentation portrait drawn
by J. H. Hoffmeister and lithographed by Spamer; p. 282 *infra*.

CHAPTER XXXVII.

THE NETHERLANDS IN THE NINETEENTH CENTURY.

(i) HOLLAND.

WE have seen in a previous chapter that Wyttenbach was professor for twenty-eight years (1771—1799) at Amsterdam, and for seventeen (1799—1816) at Leyden[1]. Among his pupils at Amsterdam was Mahne; he was followed to Leyden by van Lennep; while his later pupils, at Leyden alone, included Bake and van Heusde.

Pupils of Wyttenbach

The earliest of these favourite pupils, Willem Leonardus Mahne (1772—1852), had a special admiration for his master. To Wyttenbach he dedicated the first-fruits

Mahne

of his learning, his dissertation on the peripatetic philosopher, Aristoxenus (1793). After holding appointments at several of the Latin schools of Holland, he became a professor at Ghent in 1816, publishing in that year a dialogue on the study of classical literature. Like many of his countrymen, he lost his appointment owing to the Belgian revolution, but he found a home at Leyden as a professor in 1831. In his inaugural discourse he pleaded for a wider study of the History of Greek and Latin literature, which had hitherto been confined to the learning of a few names and dates in connexion with the general History of Greece and Rome[2]; but he was prevented by ill health from carrying his reform into practice. Nevertheless he did useful work in connexion with the History of Scholarship. His Life of Wyttenbach (1823—35) was indeed unequal to Ruhnken's eulogy of Hemsterhuys, but he did good service by publishing selections from Wytten-

---

[1] ii 461 *supra*.　　　　　　[2] p. 12 (L. Müller, 13 n.).

bach's letters (1826–30), as well as the correspondence of Ruhnken with Valckenaer and Wyttenbach (1832) and with other scholars (1834)[1].

Wyttenbach's pupil at Leyden, as well as Amsterdam, David Jacobus van Lennep (1774—1853), was professor of Eloquence at Amsterdam from 1799 to his death.

D. J. van Lennep

He produced two editions of Ovid's *Heroides*; he also edited Terentianus Maurus and Hesiod[2].

The third of Wyttenbach's pupils, Philipp Willem van Heusde (1778—1839), who was born and bred at Rotterdam, and studied at Amsterdam and at Leyden, became professor at Utrecht in 1804, and died during a Swiss tour in 1839.

P. W. van Heusde

He was an exception to the rule that Wyttenbach's pupils were repro-ductions of Wyttenbach on a smaller scale, and confined themselves to the study of Greek Philosophy and Cicero. A wide range of interest was displayed in his *Specimen Criticum in Platonem* (1803). But the expectations of further work in the field of pure scholarship, raised by that treatise[3], were not fulfilled by his *Initia philosophiae Platonicae*[4]. Here, and in a Dutch work on Socrates published during the same period, he insisted on the educa-tional importance of the Socratic dialectic, and on the permanent value of the Platonic philosophy. He was in fact more interested in philosophy than in scholarship, and his lectures lacked the foundation of a sound grammatical knowledge[5]. Among his pupils, Karsten showed a more decided interest in scholarship, while his two sons, and De Geer and Hulleman, were mainly concerned with writing monographs, either on Greek Philosophy or on the History of Roman Literature[6].

His younger contemporary, Petrus Hofman-Peerlkamp (1786 —1865), belonged to a family of French refugees named Perlechamp. He studied at his birth-place, Groningen, and also at Leyden. After holding scholastic appoint-ments at Haarlem and elsewhere, he returned to Leyden as

Peerlkamp

---

[1] Also *Suppl. ad Ep. R. et W., itemque alia...anecdota* (1847).

[2] Life by his son, ed. 4, Amst. 1862.

[3] Wyttenbach, on p. xxxiii of the *epistola*, prefixed to the *Specimen*, heralded his pupil as the future *sospitator Platonis*. Cp. Bake, *Scholica Hypomnemata*, iii 20—26.

[4] 1827–36; ed. 2, 1842.

[5] This is emphasised by his pupil and successor, Karsten. Cp. Francken's Life of Karsten (L. Müller, 104).

[6] L. Müller, 103–5; N. C. Kist (Leyden, 1839); Rovers (Utrecht, 1841).

professor from 1822 to 1848, when he retired, and was succeeded by Cobet.

At Groningen, Peerlkamp had been a pupil of Ruardi (1746—1815), who had inherited Schrader's taste for Latin versification. Under the influence of Ruardi, Peerlkamp imitated Cornelius Nepos, and Cicero, respectively, in his 'Lives' and 'Letters' of distinguished Dutchmen (1806–8); and, forty years later, he found his model for a biographical composition in the *Agricola* of Tacitus. But Ruardi had also learned Greek under Valckenaer and Ruhnken; Peerlkamp was thus led to produce in 1806 a critical paper on Xenophon Ephesius, followed by an edition in 1818. This edition gave no indication of the editor's future line as a critic. In the same year the Brussels Academy offered a prize for the best account of the lives and works of the Latin poets of the Netherlands[1], and thus prompted the ultimate production of Peerlkamp's work *de vita, doctrina et facultate Nederlandorum qui carmina latina composuerunt* (1838[2]). Meanwhile he had begun to give proof of a keen interest in Horace. In his preface to Osterdyk's Dutch translation of the *Odes* and *Epodes* (1819), he states that he had himself collected materials for an edition, adding that all the difficulties could be removed by a careful interpretation of the text. Thus far, there was no indication of the bold line that he was to take in his edition of 1834. At Leyden, his critical spirit had been awakened by scholars such as Bake and Geel, and the orientalist, Hamaker. The first result of this influence is to be seen in his edition of the *Agricola* of Tacitus (1827–63), which includes a few happy emendations, and gives the earliest proof of the editor's wide reading in Latin. This was followed by his celebrated edition of the *Odes* of Horace (1834), which gave rise to a considerable controversy.

It even formed a school, represented in Sweden by Ljungborg, and in Germany by Lehrs and Gruppe, while it was regarded with sympathy by Hermann and Meineke. On the other hand, Orelli[2] said of its editor: 'Horatium ex Horatio ipso expulit'; Madvig denounced his 'pravitas et libido', and described him as 'inaniter et proterve ludens'[3]; while Munro characterised him 'as a man of real learning in his way and of much reading in the later Latin poets', but 'hardly less wild (than Gruppe) in his mode of dealing with the odes of Horace and the *Aeneid*'. 'Some of his comments' (he adds) 'such as those on *Carm.* iii 29, 5—12, are enough to make anyone blush who feels that a philologer should be something more than a pedant at his desk ignorant of men and things. Near the beginning of the *Aeneid* he rejects a passage closely imitated by Ovid'[4].

---

[1] Meaning from 1815 to 1830 the *Royaume des Pays-Bas*, and including Belgium as well as Holland.

[2] Cp. ed. 2, p. 29; L. Müller in *Jahrb. f. Philol.* 1863, 176—184.

[3] *Adv. Crit.* ii 50; cp. Boissier, *Rev. de Philol.* 1878, and L. Müller, 113–5.

[4] King and Munro's *Horace*, xviii.

Peerlkamp's edition of the *Odes* was followed nine years later by that of Virgil's *Aeneid*. These two works are regarded as his claim to an abiding reputation as a Latin scholar. On the other hand, his reconstruction of the *Ars Poëtica* is infelicitous[1], and hardly one of his conjectures on the *Satires*[2] can be accepted, though his wide reading in the Latin poets has enabled him to contribute much towards the interpretation of the text. The posthumous publication of his edition of the 'Queen of Elegies'[3] did not add to his reputation. In Peerlkamp a hypercritical spirit was combined with undoubted learning and acumen, and his editions of Horace had at least the merit of adding a new stimulus to the study of that poet[4].

Peerlkamp's work on the Latin poets of the 'Netherlands', first published
    Hoeufft   in 1822, was preceded in 1819 by the work to which a silver
            medal had been awarded in the same competition:—The
Parnasus Latino-Belgicus[5] of Jacob Henrik Hoeufft (1756—1843). The Latin poets of the 'Netherlands' are there commemorated in terse epigrams followed by precise biographical and bibliographical details. The author had already collected the Latin poems of Van Santen, and had published his own *Pericula Poëtica* and *Pericula Critica.* His name is still remembered in connexion with modern Latin verse. By bequeathing to the Royal Institute of Amsterdam a sum of money, now held by the Royal Academy of that city, he founded prizes for original Latin poems on any subject, which are open to scholars of any nationality[6].

Janus Bake (1787—1864) studied under Wyttenbach at
    Bake   Leyden (1804–10), where he was successively
            'extraordinary' and 'ordinary' professor of Greek and Roman literature. In 1810 he edited the fragments of Poseidonius, in 1815 delivered an inaugural discourse on the merits of Euripides and the other tragic poets, and in 1817 showed a higher degree of originality in his second inaugural

---

[1] 1845; Bernhardy, *Röm. Litt.* 606[5].   [2] 1863.

[3] Prop. iv. 11.

[4] L. Müller, 110—117; presentation portrait lithographed in 1842.

[5] Amsterdam and Breda, 1819 (cp. L. Müller, 176 n[2], and Van der Aa, *s.v.*).

[6] The prize is a large gold medal of the value of 400 florins; it was won in 1899 by the *Pater ad Filium* of J. J. Hartman, professor of Latin at Leyden; silver medals were awarded to four Italian competitors who were highly commended; and all the five successful poems were published in one volume by J. Muller of Amsterdam (*Cl. Rev.* xiii 461). The prize was won more than once by Giovanni Pascoli, professor of Latin at Messina. The poems are sent before the first of January to the Registrar of the *Philologisch-Historische Afdeeling* of the Royal Academy of Sciences, Amsterdam; the *other* conditions are correctly given in *Cl. Rev.* xiv 241.

discourse, in which he declared his adhesion to the critical school of Ruhnken and Valckenaer[1].

This new departure was due to his deeper study of the characteristics of the two critics just mentioned, and also to his intercourse with two English adherents of the school of Porson, namely, Dobree and Gaisford, both of whom visited Leyden in 1815-6[2]. He was specially interested in the Attic Orators as authorities on Athenian antiquities, and in Cicero, as a master of style. His own ideal of the orator's style was so high that he held that the Catilinarian Orations[3], and the speeches *pro Archia*[4] and *pro Marcello*, were unworthy of Cicero[5]. He also held that the secret of Cicero's style was lost after his death, and that the writers of the silver age were of no value for the higher criticism of his works[6]. Lastly, in one of his discourses, he insisted that there were actually certain defects in Cicero's style, and that he was not the best model for the orators of modern times[7]. In the higher criticism of Cicero he was less happy than in the textual emendations of that author included in his *Scholica Hypomnemata*, and in his edition of the *De Legibus* (1842), which is superior in this respect to his latest work, his edition of the *De Oratore* (1863). In his commentaries on Cicero, his models were mainly Muretus and Ernesti. He regarded with suspicion the method pursued by critics like Madvig in distinguishing between interpolated and uninterpolated and intermediate MSS; in reconstructing the archetype; and in setting aside the conjectures due to the age of the humanists. Except in showing more regard for ancient MSS and in reducing the mass of various readings, he differs little from the Dutch scholars of the seventeenth and eighteenth centuries. In his study of the Attic Orators, he did good service in elucidating points of Attic law. He also set his face against the indiscriminate admiration of the Athenian democracy which had prevailed since the time of Niebuhr[8]. He edited for the Clarendon Press the *Rhetoric* of Apsines and Longinus (1849), his only edition of a Greek work[9].

Bake's pupil, Rinkes[10], following in his master's footsteps, maintained in 1856 the spuriousness of the first (as well as the other three) of the Catilinarian orations. This had been maintained before their time, but the audacity of the declaration that the oft-quoted

Rinkes

---

[1] *De custodia veteris doctrinae et elegantiae, praecipuo grammatici officio.*

[2] Bake, *Scholica Hypomnemata*, vol. ii, pp. iii—viii.

[3] *ib.* v 1—115 (mainly against Madvig).

[4] *Praef. de emend. Oratore*, 27.   [5] Bakhuizen, 21.

[6] Cp. Bake's *De Or.* (1863) x—xiv.

[7] *De temperanda admiratione eloquentiae Tullianae*, in *Schol. Hyp.* i 1—33.

[8] L. Müller, 96, 105—109.

[9] Cobet, *Allocutio ad Joh. Bakium munere Academico decedentem* (1857); Bakhuizen van den Brink, *Rede* (1865).

[10] 1829—1865.

Quousque tandem was written, not by Cicero, but by some unknown orator of the first century, aroused a perfect storm in Holland. An early·death unhappily prevented Rinkes' undoubted acumen from reaching full maturity[5].

Suringar   Of Bake's other pupils, Suringar (1805—1895) produced a useful *Historia critica Scholiastarum latinorum* (1829-35), and gave proof of his inherited interest in Cicero in the two volumes of his ' Life and Annals of Cicero' (1854). Another pupil, Groen van Prinsterer, was the author of the *Prosopographia Platonica*.

Jacob Geel (1789—1862), who was born and bred at Amster-
Geel   dam, was Librarian and honorary Professor at Leyden for the last twenty-nine years of his life. Before his appointment as Head-Librarian, he edited Theocritus (1820) and wrote the *Historia Critica Sophistarum* (1823), the earliest detailed work on that subject in modern times. After 1833, he produced an excellent edition of the *Phoenissae* of Euripides (1846), in which he defended the opinions of Valckenaer, and gave proof of his acumen and learning, and also of his affinity with the English adherents of Porson[1].

The critical school of Greek scholars that gathered round Bake and Geel at Leyden included Hamaker (1789—1835)[2], Hecker (1820—1865), W. A. Hirschig (b. 1814), editor of the *Scriptores Erotici Graeci* (1856), and his brother, R. B. Hirschig (b. 1812), editor of Plato's *Gorgias* (1873).

A short life fell to the lot of Geel's archaeological contemporary Caspar
Reuvens   Jacob Christian Reuvens (1793—1835), who, after studying at Leyden and Paris, and professing Greek and Latin for three years at Harderwyk, was appointed extraordinary professor of classical archaeology at Leyden, where he was full professor for the last nine years of his life. At that time classical archaeology was not a popular subject in Holland, and his lectures were scantily attended, but his papers in classical periodicals made him well known abroad. He supported the opinions of Quatremère de Quincy as to the true orientation of the Parthenon, and contributed to Thorbecke's *Commentatio* (1821) an appendix on the monuments of art that adorned the Library founded by Asinius Pollio. He died in the summer vacation of 1835, shortly after visiting the monuments of Greek Art in the British Museum. In his *Collectanea Litteraria* he published conjectures on Attius, Diomedes, Lucilius, and Lydus, with a brief paper on Greek pronunciation. Some of his conjectures are good, but the work as a whole gives proof of a decline in the study of old Latin in Holland since the

---

[1] Cp. L. Müller, 97. Cobet's letters to Geel (1840-5) in *Brieven van Cobet aan Geel* (Leiden, 1891).

[2] Bake, *Schol. Hyp.* i 37—48.

days of Fr. Dousa and of G. J. Vossius[1]. In archaeology Reuvens had a most able successor in the person of the excellent archaeologist and epigraphist, L. J. F. Janssen (1806—1869), the
unwearied explorer of many a primaeval grave-mound, the discoverer of Roman as well as Germanic remains in the Netherlands, who published illustrated descriptions of the principal monuments of art in the Museum at Leyden, and repeatedly urged the excavation of Katwyk, between Leyden and the sea[2].

Janssen

The History of Greek Civilisation, a work in eight volumes, written in French (1833–42), was the main achievement of Pieter van Limbourg-Brouwer (1796—1847),
Doctor of Philosophy and Medicine, and professor
at Groningen. His early writings on philosophical subjects were followed by papers on the poetry of Pindar, Aeschylus, Sophocles, and Euripides. During the publication of his principal work, he incidentally attacked Forchhammer's opinion as to the cause of the condemnation of Socrates[3]. He closed his career with a memoir on the allegorical interpretation of Greek mythology.

Limbourg-
Brouwer

Van Heusde's lack of sound scholarship, as we have already seen[4], was noted with regret in the inaugural address
of his pupil and successor Simon Karsten (1802—
1864), who was professor at Utrecht for the last twenty-four years of his life. He had previously collected the fragments of Xenophanes, Parmenides, and Empedocles (1825–38), and had prepared a Dutch treatise on 'Palingenesis', which was not published until 1846. In the same year he wrote on Sophoclean trilogies. His principal contribution to scholarship was an edition of the *Agamemnon* (1855), including many original conjectures. The 'wise and weighty words' in which he expresses his general principles are quoted with approval in Kennedy's second edition[5], where the English editor adopts as his motto the phrase of the Dutch critic:—'principium et fundamentum critices est iusta interpretatio'[6]. Karsten's work on Horace (1861) was translated

Karsten

---

[1] Latin life by Leemans in Pref. to Catalogue of Reuvens' Library; Bake's *Schol. Hyp.* i 33—36 ; L. Müller, 230.

[2] Du Rieu in the Dutch *Spectator*, 1869, 366 f, 376 f; Stark, 295; Report of recent excavations in *Mededeelingen* of Leyden Museum, 1907, 23 f.

[3] p. 227 *supra*. [4] p. 276 *supra*, n. 5.

[5] Ed. 1882, pp. xxiv—xxvi. [6] p. xxviii.

into German.   His abiding interest in Greek philosophy was
shown in the posthumous edition of the Commentary of Simplicius
on the fourth book of Aristotle *De Caelo*.   Among his pupils were
his biographer, Francken, and his son H. T. Karsten, the author
of a dissertation on Plato's *Letters* (1864)[1].

Cornelius Marinus Francken (1820—1900), a pupil of Karsten, and professor at Groningen and Utrecht, was the author of the *Com-*
mentationes Lysiacae (1865).   His productions as a professor
of Latin included a Dutch edition of the *Aulularia* (1877).   In 1891 he
resigned his professorship, and nine years afterwards, at the age of 80,
published his *Varroniana* in the pages of *Mnemosyne*[2].

Johannes Cornelius Gerardus Boot (1811—1901), who was born and bred
at Arnheim, and studied at Leyden, was Rector at Leeuwarden
(1839–51) and professor at Amsterdam (1851—1881).   He
delivered an inaugural discourse *De perpetua philologiae dignitate*, and distinguished himself mainly by his admirable commentary on Cicero's *Letters to*
Atticus[3].   An excellent monograph on Atticus was produced in 1838 by
Jan Gerard Hulleman (1815—1862)[4].

The greatest of the modern Greek scholars of the Netherlands,
Carolus Gabriel Cobet (1813—1889), was born in
Paris.   He was the son of a Dutchman in the
French public service, who had married a Frenchwoman, Marie
Bertranet.   One of his Dutch biographers protests against the
frequent remark that it was from his French mother that Cobet
derived his brilliant wit and his keen acumen[5].   When he was
only six weeks of age, he was taken to Holland.   He was educated
at the Hague, under an admirable head-master, Kappeyne van
de Coppello, whom he always remembered with gratitude.   On
entering the university of Leyden, he was already familiar with
the whole range of the ancient classics, but his father was then
proposing that he should follow a theological career, and his
distinction as a scholar remained unrecognised until the publication of his *Prosopographia Xenophontea* (1836).   This was a prize-
dissertation, produced when its author was only twenty-three,
but its high promise aroused among the foremost scholars of

Francken

Boot

Cobet

---

[1] Cp. L. Müller, 104.

[2] xxviii (1900) 281—297, 395, 422—435.   *Life* by J. van der Vliet
(Amsterdam Acad., 10 March, 1902).

[3] 1865–6; ed. 2.   [4] Cobet, *in memoriam H.*, 1862.

[5] J. J. Hartman in *Biogr. Jahrb.* 1889, 53.

Holland the expectation that its author would rival the fame of a Ruhnken or a Valckenaer. Four years later, he produced his critical observations on the fragments of the Comic Poet, Plato[1]. Shortly afterwards, on the proposal of Geel, he received an honorary degree at Leyden[2], and was sent by the Royal Institute of Amsterdam on a mission to the Italian libraries. The ostensible object was the examination of the MSS of Simplicius, but the real aim was to give this remarkably promising scholar the opportunity of gaining a wide acquaintance with Greek MSS in general. His term of absence was extended to five years in all[3], and by the end of that time he had become an experienced and accomplished palaeographer. He had also incidentally won the friendship of a congenial English scholar, Badham.

On his return, he was appointed to an ' extraordinary ' professorship at Leyden, and delivered an inaugural address which is one of the landmarks of his career (1846)[4]. As has been well said, we here have ' Cobet himself—strong, masculine writing, a style clear and bracing....Every sentence has its work to do, and there is a moral force behind it all, an intense enthusiasm for truth, a quality that marks the whole of Cobet's critical work'[5]. He succeeded Peerlkamp as full professor in 1848. In 1850–1 he presented to the Royal Institute three important *Commentationes Philologicae*, which are less widely known than many of his papers[6]. These were followed by his best-known works, the *Variae Lectiones* (1854)[7] and the *Novae Lectiones* (1858), and,

---

[1] Amst. 1840.

[2] The *ordinary* degree involved a knowledge of Roman law, which Cobet declined to study.

[3] Cp. *Brieven van Cobet aan Geel uit Parijs en Italië*, Nov. 1840—Juli, 1845 (Leiden, 1891).

[4] *Oratio de arte interpretandi grammatices et critices fundamentis innixa*, 36 pp. + 123 pp. of notes, 1847. In 1846 he had contributed *Scholia Antiqua* to Geel's ed. of Eur. *Phoenissae*.

[5] W. G. Rutherford, in *Cl. Rev.* iii 472.

[6] (1) *De emendandae ratione grammaticae Graecae discernendo orationem artificialem ab oratione populari*; (2) *De sinceritate Graeci sermonis post Aristotelem...depravata*; (3) *De auctoritate et usu grammaticorum veterum in explicandis scriptoribus Graecis*. Printed at Amst. 1853.

[7] 399 pp.; ed. 2, + *Supplementum* (399—400) + *Epimetrum* (401—681), 1873.

twenty years later, by others of the same general type, the *Miscellanea Critica* (1876) mainly on Homer and Demosthenes, the *Collectanea Critica* (1878), and the critical and palaeographical observations on the 'Roman Antiquities' of Dionysius of Halicarnassus (1877). An inaugural lecture on the study of Roman antiquities, including some of his own reminiscences of Rome, was published in 1853, and he also printed six professorial discourses in 1852—1860[1]. He reluctantly edited Diogenes Laërtius for Didot, without any prolegomena (1850). He also published critical remarks on the newly recovered work of Philostratus, περὶ γυμναστικῆς (1859), as well as a text of two speeches of Hypereides (1858–77), and school-editions of Xenophon's *Anabasis* and *Hellenica* (1859–62) and of Lysias (1863)[2]. He was long the mainstay of the classical periodical *Mnemosyne*[3], which derived a new life from his vigorous contributions, while, in conjunction with his friend and pupil, K. S. Kontos of Athens, he edited three volumes of the λόγιος Ἑρμῆς, written entirely in Greek, and including Cobet's corrections of Clemens Alexandrinus (1866–7).

While Cobet shared with his fellow-countrymen their aptitude for conjectural criticism, he rose superior to them in the strict severity of his scientific method. With Cobet, the *ars grammatica* (or the intimate knowledge of the language, and its historical developement, attained in the course of constant reading) was combined with an intelligent use of the best MSS, as the preliminary condition for the *ars critica*, *i.e.* the detection and the correction of corruptions of the text. On these principles he proposed in the pages of *Mnemosyne*, and of his *Variae* and *Novae Lectiones*, a large number of emendations on Greek authors.

[1] *Allocutio ad commilitones* (1852, '53, '56); *Praefatio lectionum de Historia Vetere* (1853–4); *Protrepticus* (1854) and *Adhortatio* (1860) *ad Studia Humanitatis*. Also *Or. rectoralis de monumentis literarum veterum suo pretio aestimandis* (1864).

[2] He took part in preparing an Attic Greek Reader (1856), and a text of the Greek Testament (1860). The only Latin author he edited was Cornelius Nepos (1893[3]).

[3] Founded in 1852; the editors of 1852–62 were E. J. Kiehl (1827—1873), professor in Deventer, Groningen and Middelburg, E. Mehler (b. 1826), Naber, Bake and Cobet. The new series was started in 1872.

The merits and the defects of his method are there made manifest. His marvellous familiarity with Greek, his wide reading, the skill derived from the study of many MSS during his Italian *Wanderjahre*, enabled him to detect the source of a corruption, and to divine the appropriate remedy. On the other hand, his excessive confidence in the rules founded on observations made in the course of his reading, is open to criticism. No sooner has he ascertained what he regards as a fixed rule of Greek usage, than he remorselessly emends all the exceptions. But it cannot be questioned that he supplies the student of textual criticism with golden rules for his instruction, and the advanced scholar with rich stores of interesting and stimulating information[1]. With Cobet the study of institutions is subordinate to the study of language, and the study of Latin less prominent than that of Greek. But his Latin style is admirable, and his singular mastery of fluent and lucid Latinity could not have been attained without long and laborious study of the language[2]. He was one of the very few scholars who were capable of making an extemporaneous speech in really good Latin. At the celebration of the tercentenary of Leyden in 1875, when Cobet and Madvig confronted each other, the delegates of all the universities of Europe looked on in awe at the prospect of the two thunder-clouds closing in conflict. But they soon found themselves admiring the prompt dexterity of the great Greek scholar, as he caught up the phrases used by several of the previous speakers; the generous and spirited language in which he addressed Madvig:—*pugnabimus tecum, contendemus tecum, eoque vehementius contendemus, quo te vehementius admiramur*; and, lastly, the calm exordium of the great Latinist's reply:—*post Cobetum Latine loqui vereor*[3]. In 1884, at the age of 70, Cobet became *emeritus*, and placed on the screens of his university the notice, which was read by at least one passing traveller:—*Carolus Gabriel Cobet, propter aetatem immunis, commilitonum studia quantum poterit adjuvabit*. On the death of Cobet it fell to the

---

[1] Urlichs, 112[2]; cp. L. Müller, 78, 117—122.

[2] His Latinity is criticised in a letter purporting to come from Ruhnken (*Ex Orco, Datum Saturnalibus*), which Cobet publishes in *Mnemosyne*, 1877, 113—128, with his own reply.

[3] I owe this reminiscence to Professor Mayor, cp. *Cl. Rev.* i 124.

lot of the present writer to send to Leyden an unofficial letter of condolence signed by more than 70 of the scholars of Cambridge[1], and to receive on their behalf a kindly reply which formed a new link in the long tradition of scholarly sympathy between the Netherlands and England.

Cobet was sometimes charged with neglecting or ignoring the work of his predecessors[2]. He was attacked by Gomperz in 1878[3]. In the next number of *Mnemosyne*[4] he replied with a paper on Philodemus, praising the edition produced by Gomperz, adding his own elucidations of points that had been left obscure, and ending with the apt quotation from Menander :—

$$\H{\eta}\delta\iota o\nu\ o\mathring{v}\delta\grave{\epsilon}\nu\ o\mathring{v}\delta\grave{\epsilon}\ \mu o\nu\sigma\iota\kappa\acute{\omega}\tau\epsilon\rho o\nu$$
$$\H{\epsilon}\sigma\tau'\ \grave{\eta}\ \delta\acute{v}\nu\alpha\sigma\theta\alpha\iota\ \lambda o\iota\delta o\rho o\acute{v}\mu\epsilon\nu o\nu\ \phi\acute{\epsilon}\rho\epsilon\iota\nu.$$

In the same year he was attacked by the Greek editor of Plutarch's *Moralia*, Gregorius Bernardakis, who accused him of appropriating proposals already made by Koraës. In his defence he showed himself less concerned for his personal fame than for the credit of his accuser[5]. His discussion of Stein's estimate of the MSS of Herodotus is a delightful example of kindly and genial criticism, in the course of which he vividly treats the MSS under examination as though each was endued with a living personality[6]. Reiske was more highly appreciated by Cobet than by the Germans of his own day. He had a high regard for the Dindorfs, for Bergk, Meineke and Lehrs, and for the best points in the work of Nauck. He was ever eager in confessing his debt to 'the three great Richards', Bentley, Dawes, and Porson, and the later representatives of the Porsonian school, Elmsley and Dobree. The influence of the English school was at work among his teachers, and he had freed himself from that of the German school by the time of his return from Italy. It was through Cobet that the traditional English method, which was in danger of being forgotten in England itself, became dominant in Holland

---

[1] Reprinted in *Cl. Rev.* iii 474.

[2] Cp. L. Müller, 117 f.

[3] *Die Bruchstücke der griechischen Tragiker und Cobets neueste Manier.*

[4] vi (1878) 373—381 etc.

[5] *Mnemosyne*, 1878, 49—54.

[6] *ib.* 1882, 400—413, with Stein's reply in Bursian's *Jahresb.* xxx 186.

and attained a still wider range. It would be difficult to compare Cobet with any other scholar than Scaliger or Bentley. He himself regards Scaliger as an 'almost perfect critic'[1], while he resembles Bentley in his 'high-handed, hard-hitting criticism', and in his 'consciousness of power'[2].

In contrast to the genial and expansive Cobet, a calmer and more reserved type of character is represented by his colleague, William Georg Pluygers (1812–1880), who, in 1862, succeeded Hulleman as professor of Latin. In his inaugural oration he refers in fitting terms to his predecessor, and also to Bake and Cobet. In middle life he had been interested in the Alexandrian editors of Homer (1847), and he subsequently contributed to the textual criticism of Cicero and Tacitus. He was much appreciated at Leyden as a learned and original lecturer on Horace and Lucretius[3].

Pluygers

Samuel Adrianus Naber (born 1828), who studied at Leyden and was professor of Greek at Amsterdam until 1898, is best known as the editor of the lexicon of Photius (1864–5). Naber was present at Cobet's celebrated inaugural lecture of 1846, and he has lived to publish in the pages of *Mnemosyne*, sixty years later, an almost complete bibliography of his master's writings.

Naber

Among the other pupils of Cobet, we may here mention Tjalling Halbertsma (1829—1894), who studied under Bake, Geel, and Cobet at Leyden, and, after examining MSS in France, Spain, and Italy, was appointed Rector at Haarlem in 1864, and professor of Greek at Groningen in 1877. He was far from being a prolific writer, but he contributed papers on Greek and Latin criticism to the pages of *Mnemosyne*, and published *Lectiones Lysiacae* (1868). After his death his *Adversaria Critica* were edited by Herwerden[4].

Halbertsma

His contemporary, Willem Nicolaas du Rieu (1829—1896), was also a pupil of Bake and Cobet, and worked at MSS in France and Italy. His long services to the Library at Leyden were crowned by his appointment as principal Librarian in 1881. He was the originator of the scheme for the complete photographic reproduction of important Greek and Latin MSS, which has been carried out under the auspices of his successor, E. S. G. de Vries[5].

Du Rieu

---

[1] *De arte interpretandi*, 25.

[2] W. G. Rutherford, in *Cl. Rev.* iii 470–4. Cp., in general, J. J. Hartman in *Biogr. Jahrb.* 1889, 53—66; J. J. Cornelissen, *ad Cobeti memoriam*, 1889; H. C. Muller, *in memoriam* (in English), Amst. Ἑλλάς, ΙΙ i 49—54; bibliography by S. A. Naber in *Mnemosyne*, xxxiv (1906) 430—443, xxxv 440.

[3] On this last point cp. K. Kuiper in *Biogr. Jahrb.* 1903, p. 98.

[4] *Biogr. Jahrb.* 1897, 82—87; portrait in *Adv. Crit.*

[5] *ib.* 1899, 31—53; Naber in *Mnemosyne*, xxvi 277—286.

Cobet was the only master who won the allegiance of J. J. Cornelissen
    Cornelissen   (1839–1891), professor of Greek and Latin at Deventer, rector
at Arnheim, and, for the last twelve years of his life, successor
of Pluygers in the Latin Chair at Leyden. The influence of Cobet is manifest
in the severe review of Alexandrian literature, which is the theme of his
inaugural discourse at Deventer (1865), but the rest of his work is mainly that
of a specialist in Latin. It includes a paper attacking the credibility of
Caesar's *Commentarii de Bello Civili* (1864), dissertations on the life of
Juvenal (1868) and the text of Velleius Paterculus (1887), a volume of
Collectanea Critica comprising some 250 conjectures on Cicero and Caesar
(1870), and, lastly, editions of the *Agricola* of Tacitus and the *Octavius* of
Minucius Felix (1881–2). In a Dutch manifesto of his educational principles,
published after four years' experience at Deventer, he urges that the growing
indifference towards classical learning in Holland should be counteracted (as
in Germany) by encouraging the study of history, geography, mythology,
archaeology, and the history of literature, subjects which (as he held) had been
unduly neglected in comparison with grammar and textual criticism[1]. In his
inaugural lecture, delivered ten years later at Leyden, he describes in
admirable Latin the characteristic merits of that *par nobile amicorum*,
J. F. Gronovius and N. Heinsius, and draws a contrast between the way in
which Latin was learnt by the contemporaries of those great scholars, during
the first glow of classical enthusiasm in Holland, and the position which it
holds in modern times, when it is no longer the common property of all
educated persons. 'But' (he continues), 'if our study of Latin has lost in
breadth, it has gained in depth. The evidence of MSS is weighed with a more
judicious care; in the light of comparative philology, grammar receives a more
scientific treatment; our knowledge has been enriched by the recovery of
innumerable inscriptions; an indiscriminating admiration for all the contents
of the Classics has been corrected by the aid of historical and literary criticism.
The various branches of classical learning are now more minutely studied, but
there is a danger lest, in our excessive punctiliousness on minute matters of
detail, we should lose the vital force and vigour of our great ancestors. Latin
has now left the light of public life and has become a cloistral language;
Latin, that once lived and breathed, is regarded by the modern man as inert
and well nigh dead. If any one of those great ancestors were restored to life,
there is grave reason to fear that he would admonish and rebuke us in the
language applied by Gronovius to Graevius:—"nae tu, qui varia et multiplici
doctrina eruditum te iactas, *Grammatice*, non *Latine*, scis"[2].

From a Latin professor of Leyden we finally turn to a Latin professor of
    van der Vliet   Utrecht. The versatile scholar, J. van der Vliet (1847—1902),
studied Latin literature under Pluygers at Leyden, and Greek

---

[1] *De studie der classike oudheid* (in *Tijdspiegel*, 1869).

[2] *Burmanni Oratio in obitum Graevii*, p. 91 (Cornelissen, *Oratio
Inauguralis*, 24); the passages above quoted from the *Oratio* are only a brief
summary of the original; cp. Van Leeuwen, in *Biogr. Jahrb.* 1892, 52—63.

palaeography under Cobet; and the influence of the latter is clearly marked in his *Studia Critica* on Dionysius of Halicarnassus (1874). As a schoolmaster at Haarlem, he had sufficient leisure to become familiar with the language of Java, and with Sanskrit. Ultimately he succeeded Francken at Utrecht (1891), having meanwhile concentrated himself on Latin, especially on that of the Silver Age. In the course of his Latin studies he passed from Seneca and Tacitus to Apuleius, and from Apuleius to Tertullian and Sulpicius Severus. In his interest in Latin there was in fact no lower limit of time. He was familiar with the prose and the verse of the Italian humanists[1]; he discoursed on the results of the Renaissance as exemplified in the Latin poems of the Dutch statesman, Konstantyn Huygens (1596—1687)[2]; he composed an ode of the mediaeval type for the opening of the new university buildings in 1892, and he even imitated the style of Persius in an annotated satire entitled *Vanitas Vanitatum*. In all the minuteness of his statistical statements on points of Latin usage, he never lost his fine sense of the importance of literary form. In a review of a German pamphlet, bristling with references and citations, he remarks:—'I am well aware that (as a reviewer) the ideal scholar ought to have the digestion of an ostrich, which is capable of assimilating the driest and hardest substances in the shortest space of time, but it must not be forgotten that even the reviewer is a human being and that a writer will do no detriment to the cause of learning, if, for the reader's sake, he lends his work some little charm of style'[3]. As a professor of Latin van der Vliet produced critical editions of the *Histories* of Tacitus[4], and of (1) the *Metamorphoses*, and (2) the *Apologia*, *Florida* and *De Deo Socratis*, of Apuleius[5]. For Tacitus he depended mainly on the collations of Meiser; for Apuleius, he minutely examined the MSS during his two visits to Italy, but, however careful he was in recording the results of that examination, he remained, for the most part, true to the precept he had learned from Cobet:—*Codicibus manuscriptis plane nihil fidendum est*[6].

Our survey of the nineteenth century has thus far been limited to the Northern Netherlands. It began with the pupils of Wyttenbach, and it has ended with the pupils of Cobet. During the whole of the century, the staff of classical professors in each university continued to be small; and those professors, besides being responsible for elementary and advanced courses on Latin

---

[1] *Trifolium Latinum* (Beyers, Utrecht, 1893), esp. *Petrarcae Studia Latina*.

[2] *Verhand. v. h. Utrechtsch Genootschap*, 1894.

[3] Review of Stangl's *Tulliana*, in the *Museum* for 1900.

[4] Groningen, 1900.

[5] Leipzig (Teubner), 1897 and 1900.

[6] K. Kuiper in *Biogr. Jahrb.* 1903, 97—115.

and Greek, were compelled to give more or less popular instruction on Greek and Roman History and Antiquities. An interest in ancient Art was hardly represented in the universities except by Reuvens and Janssen, and by Du Rieu, who studied classical archaeology (as well as palaeography) during his repeated visits to Rome. In the published works of the professors, as contrasted with their oral teaching, the dominant note was textual criticism.

As a *Latin* scholar and as the editor of Terence and Horace, Bentley had had little influence on Dutch scholarship. Editions of the Latin Classics, modelled on those of Burman, with a confused mass of prolix variorum notes, remained long in vogue. The acquisitive instinct of Holland seemed to delight in constantly adding to the accumulating pile of erudite annotation. Happily, however, in the latest Dutch edition of Cicero's *Letters to Atticus*[1], the notes are never over-loaded with unnecessary detail, but are always brief and terse and clear; and the same is true of a still more recent edition of Aristophanes[2]. The influence of Bentley, as a *Greek* scholar, had been effectively transmitted through Hemsterhuys to Valckenaer and Ruhnken, and ultimately through Ruhnken to Wyttenbach. But the attention of those scholars had not been concentrated on the Greek authors of the golden age. Lucian, even more than Aristophanes, had been studied by Hemsterhuys, who bestowed on Xenophon of Ephesus the time that he might well have reserved for Xenophon of Athens; the Alexandrian and Hellenistic writers, no less than Herodotus, had been explored by Valckenaer; the researches of Ruhnken ranged over a wide field of literature extending from the Homeric Hymns to Longinus, and from the early Greek Orators to the late Greek Lexicographers[3]; while Wyttenbach, who edited only one dialogue of Plato, devoted the largest part of his life to Plutarch. The time that Hemsterhuys and his followers thus lavished on the 'Graeculi', on late writers like Lucian and other artificial imitators of the genuine Attic authors, was repeatedly lamented by Cobet[4], who

---

[1] Ed. Boot, Amst. 1865 f.   [2] Ed. van Leeuwen, Leyden, 1896 f.

[3] (Ruhnkenius) ecquem sprevit ac fastidivit eorum qui diu post exstinctam Graeciam balbutire Graece rectius quam dicere ac scribere dicantur' (Cobet, *Commentationes Philologicae*, 1853, ii 6).

[4] *e.g. Commentationes, l.c.*

found his main occupation in studying the great originals themselves, and in ascertaining and enforcing a fixed standard of Attic usage.　The love of reducing classical texts to the dead level of a smooth uniformity had already been exemplified by Latin scholars, such as N. Heinsius and Broukhusius[1], who had attempted to assimilate the vigorous and varied style of a Catullus or a Propertius to the monotonous uniformity of an Ovid.　The same love of uniformity was exemplified (as we have seen), in the case of Attic Greek, by Cobet and his immediate followers.　Such a tendency may even perhaps be regarded as a national characteristic of the clear-headed and methodical scholars, who dwell in a land of straight canals rather than winding rivers, a land of level plains varied only by a fringe of sand-dunes, a land saved from devastation by dikes that restrain the free waters of the sea.　But, as we look back over the three-hundred and thirty-three years which have elapsed since the foundation of the first of the universities of the Northern Netherlands, we remember that it was the breaking of those dikes by the orders of William the Silent that brought deliverance to the beleaguered city of Leyden, and that the heroism of its inhabitants was then fitly commemorated by the founding of its far-famed university[2].

Leyden became, in general, the model for the later universities of the Northern Netherlands.　Franeker was thus founded in Friesland, in 1585; Groningen, in the northern province of that name, in 1614; Utrecht in 1636; and Harderwyk, on the south-east shore of the Zuider Zee, in 1648.　The seventeenth century also saw the foundation of an Athenaeum at Deventer and at Amsterdam.　In 1811 Franeker and Harderwyk were suppressed by Napoleon I, who was happily foiled in his attempt to suppress Utrecht.　The Athenaeum of Amsterdam was transformed into a university in 1877.　At the present time the number of students exceeds 1300 at Leyden, 1100 at Utrecht, and 1000 at Amsterdam, while it is less than 500 at Groningen.　Leyden and Utrecht have long been the principal seats of classical learning.

Dutch universities

---

[1] ii 325, 330, *supra*.　　　　[2] ii 300 *supra*.

(ii) Belgium.

Meanwhile, in the Southern Netherlands, the university of
Louvain had been founded in 1426 at a place
Belgian uni- praised by its founder for the salubrity and the
versities beauty of its situation amid the meadows and vine-
yards of Brabant[1]. Within twenty years of its foundation it began
to resemble the universities of England by its institution of com-
petitive examinations and by its adoption of the collegiate system[2].
The most famous of its Colleges was that for the study of Latin,
Greek and Hebrew, the *Collegium Trilingue*, founded in 1517 by
Busleiden, and fostered during its first decade by Erasmus[3]. This
College was one of the first-fruits of the Revival of Learning in
the Netherlands, while the University, which was opposed to the
principles of the Reformation, was the chief stronghold of the
Catholic cause in and after the sixteenth century.

Some of the leading representatives of learning at Louvain in
the sixteenth century have already been briefly noticed[4]. Lipsius
belongs to Leyden[5] as well as to Louvain, the university of his
youth and his old age, which he proudly describes as the 'Belgian
Athens'[6]. During his life-time, the Northern Netherlands re-
volted against the power of Spain, and a struggle that began in
1568 did not end until the independence of the 'United Provinces'
was formally and finally recognised by the Peace of Westphalia
(1648). The Southern Provinces remained subject to Spain until
1714, when they passed under the power of Austria. Eighty years
later, after a single year of independence (1790), they fell for
twenty years under the power of France (1794—1814). The
university of Louvain, which was closed for a time under the
Austrian emperor Joseph II, was suppressed by the French in
1797. When the united kingdom of the Southern and Northern
Netherlands had been brought into existence in 1815 by the
Congress of Vienna, king William I founded in 1816–7 the two
new universities of Ghent and Liége, and, in the same year, placed

---

1 Baron de Reiffenberg's *Mémoires*, 1829, p. 19 n.
2 Hamilton's *Discussions*, 406 f, 645—650; Rashdall, II i 259—263.
3 ii 212 *supra*.   4 ii 215 f *supra*.   5 ii 301 *supra*.
6 *Lovanium*, Lib. iii, cap. 1, Salvete Athenae nostrae, Athenae Belgicae.

at Louvain a *Collège philosophique*, making attendance at that College compulsory on all future inmates of the episcopal Seminaries. The resentment thus aroused among the clergy contributed towards the revolution of 1830, which dissolved the union between the North and the South and led to the foundation of the separate kingdom of Belgium. The universities did not emerge from the crisis without serious mutilation. Late in 1830 Liége lost its Faculty of Philosophy; Ghent retained only those of Law and Medicine; the Faculties of Science and Law disappeared at Louvain, but that of Law was partially restored soon afterwards. The general aim of all this was the institution of a single central university, which, it is assumed, would have been located at Louvain. The proposal for a central university was lost in 1834 by five votes; thereupon the universities of Ghent and Liége were retained and reorganised, and that of Louvain suppressed. In November, 1834, a 'free' university was founded in Brussels. In the same month the Belgian bishops founded at Malines a catholic university which was transferred to Louvain in the following year[1].

Brussels is the seat of an Academy of Science and Letters, founded during the Austrian rule, under the auspices of the empress Maria Theresa, in 1772. This Academy was suppressed during the French occupation in 1794, was re-established in 1816, and began a fresh lease of life in 1832. In the sequel we shall notice a few of the more prominent representatives of classical learning in the nineteenth century, confining ourselves almost exclusively to members of the Brussels Academy. With the exception of Baron de Witte, all of those whom we propose to mention were professors at one or other of the Belgian universities.

While textual criticism is a prominent characteristic of Dutch scholarship, the study of classical archaeology and of constitutional antiquities has been admirably re-presented among natives of Belgium. The cosmopolitan archaeologist, Jean Baron de Witte (1808—1889), was born in Antwerp. At the age of thirteen he was taken to Paris, where he soon gave promise of his life-long interest in art and archaeology. He travelled extensively in Europe and the East (1838–42). During

De Witte

---

[1] Cp. in general, the *Introduction* to Prof. A. Le Roy's *L'Université de Liége* (1867), xxxi, xliii—xlvii.

his travels he became a full Member of the International Archaeological Institute in Rome; after his return to Paris, where he
resided for the rest of his life, he was elected à Corresponding
Member of the Academy of Inscriptions, a Foreign Member of
that body in 1864, and in 1887 an honorary Foreign Member of
the Antiquarian Society of France (1887). Meanwhile, ever since
1851, he had been a full Member of the Royal Academy of his
native land. As an archaeologist, he was profoundly influenced
by Panofka, whom he aided in editing the Paris volumes of the
Annali of the Archaeological Institute (1832–4). He published
catalogues of several archaeological collections, and was a constant
contributor to the leading archaeological periodicals. For many
years he was one of the editors of the *Gazette archéologique* and
of the *Revue Numismatique*. His colleague in the former was
François Lenormant, whose father, Charles Lenormant, had been
one of his companions during his visit to Greece, Smyrna, and Constantinople, and was associated with him in the most important of
his works. This was the well-known *Élite des monuments ceramo-
graphiques*, in four quarto volumes with four further volumes of
no less than 455 plates (1844–61), being only part of the materials
for a complete representation of the social and religious life of the
ancient world. De Witte also published elaborately illustrated
researches on the Roman Emperors who had held sway in Gaul
during the third century (1868)[1].

For nearly forty years De Witte counted among his correspondents the able representative of classical archaeology
in Belgium, J. E. G. Roulez (1806—1878). Born
in Brabant, he studied under Creuzer's pupil,
G. J. Bekker, at Louvain, and, after winning the prize at Ghent
for his essay on Carneades, and at Louvain for that on Heracleides
Ponticus, continued his studies at Heidelberg under Creuzer, in
Berlin under Boeckh, and at Göttingen under Dissen and
K. O. Müller. His interest in mythology was due to Creuzer;
and, a year after his return to his native land, he dedicated to
Creuzer the textual criticisms on Themistius, which he presented

Ghent:
Roulez

---

[1] *Biogr. Jahrb.* 1892, 118 f; A. Michaelis, *Gesch. der deutschen arch. Inst.*
44, 57 f, 62; Stark, 296, 367; *Bibliographie Académique*, 15 pp. (Bruxelles,
1886).

for his Doctor's degree at Louvain. In 1832 he became a professor of Greek History and Ancient Geography at the Athenaeum
of Ghent, and in 1834 he published at Leipzig the *Novae Historiae*
of Ptolemaeus Hephaestion. While the university of Ghent was
partly in abeyance, he was an active member of the *Faculté
libre de philosophie et lettres*. When the university was fully
restored in 1835, he was appointed to a professorship, and continued to lecture until 1863 on Greek and Roman literature, on
Art and Archaeology, and on ancient and modern Law. He had
repeatedly discharged the duties of rector with conspicuous
success, and, for the next ten years of his life, he was the official
supervisor[1] of the university, which ultimately acquired his valuable
library. In the controversies as to the primitive inhabitants of
Belgium he played a good-tempered and a dignified part; he also
explored the Roman roads and the other antiquities of the country.
The principal papers which he presented to the Brussels Academy
were collected in the seven books of his *Mélanges* (1838–54). His
masterpiece was a fine volume on select vases from the Leyden
Museum, published in Ghent with twenty coloured plates (1854).
His archaeological studies had been fruitfully pursued during his
single visit to Italy in 1839; he repeatedly published vase-paintings
from the Pizzati collection then in Florence, but since dispersed;
he was a frequent contributor to the *Annali* of the Archaeological
Institute in Rome, and to the *Gazette archéologique* of France. As
an archaeologist, he was even better known abroad than in his
native land. At Rome, in 1877, when M. Gevaert, the eminent
Belgian authority on ancient music, asked Fiorelli to explain the
musical instruments in a bas-relief of an Archigallus in the Capitoline Museum[2], Fiorelli replied with all his Neapolitan vivacity:—
'When you return to Belgium, ask Roulez, he knows more about
that class of monuments than any man in Europe'[3].

Among the contemporaries of Roulez at Ghent was Joseph
Gantrelle (1809—1893), a native of Echternach,
who was educated at the Athenaeum of Luxem-

Gantrelle

---

[1] Administrateur-inspecteur.   [2] Millin, *Galer. myth.* lxxxii 15*.
[3] See esp. De Witte in *Annuaire* of Brussels Acad. 1879, 167—203, with
portrait and bibliography; also A. Wagener, in *Rev. de l'instruction publique*,
Gand, xxi (1878) 140 f; and *Biogr. Jahrb.* 1878, 4 f; Stark, 296.

burg. He studied at Ghent under Mahne (the biographer of Wyttenbach), who left for Leyden soon after Belgium had seceded from Holland. After holding scholastic appointments in Brussels and at Hasselt, Gantrelle was appointed in 1837 to a professorship at Ghent, where he became professor of Latin rhetoric in 1851–4, inspector of intermediate education 1854–64, and professor once more from 1864 to the end of his career in 1892. He had been naturalised as a Belgian in 1839, and in the same year had published a valuable memoir on the early historical relations between the Southern Netherlands and England[1], and a Latin Grammar, which marked a new departure in the schools of Belgium[2], and was highly esteemed by Eckstein in Germany and by Benoist and Thurot in France. His classical publications were mainly connected with Tacitus. He published in Paris a study of that historian's 'Grammar and Style'[3], as well as contributions to the criticism and interpretation of his works[4], with highly appreciated editions of the *Agricola* (1874), *Germania* (1877) and *Histories* (1881). He characterised the *Agricola* as an *éloge historique*[5], and the same was the general character of his own 'panegyrical biography' of Ratherius, bishop of Verona and Liége[6]. To the publications of the Brussels Academy he contributed three papers, on the following subjects:—(1) the order of words in a Latin sentence: (2) the Suevi on the banks of the Scheldt; and (3) the rules and method of criticism, in connexion with the controversy raised by the previous paper[7]. He steadily resisted the attacks directed against a classical education; in conjunction with Wagener he started in 1874 a 'society for the promotion of philological and historical studies', and, late in life, he anonymously assigned to the Brussels Academy the sum of 45,000 francs for the foundation of a biennial prize for the encouragement of 'classical philology'. In his immediate circle, though he was loyal and devoted to his personal friends, he was not universally popular; he was recognised

---

[1] *Nouvelles Archives historiques*, 1839.

[2] Repeatedly revised and improved; ed. 12, 1889.

[3] 1874, 1882[2].　　　　　　　　　　[4] 1875; partly translated into German.

[5] *Revue de l'Instruction publique*, 1878; and *Neue Jahrb.* 1881.

[6] *Nouvelles Archives historiques*, 1837, written in accidental ignorance of the great work of the brothers Ballerini (Verona, 1765).

[7] *Bulletins*, Sér. 3, vi 611, xi 190, xiii 344.

as a man of undoubted learning, but of uncertain temper; his
leading characteristic was a passionate and indomitable energy;
labor improbus was in fact the law of his life[1].

The *Revue de l'Instruction publique en Belgique* gave scope to
a large part of the editorial energy of Gantrelle and
his colleague, Wagener. Auguste Wagener (1829—   Wagener
1896) was born and bred at Roeremonde in Limburg, east of
the present boundaries of Belgium. He studied for two years at
Bonn under Lassen, Welcker and Ritschl, and for one year at
Liége; he also spent six months in Paris, where he became
acquainted with Littré, Egger, Daremberg and Renan, before
beginning his lectures on Moral Philosophy at Ghent (1851). The
bishop soon detected and publicly denounced 'five dangerous
errors' in his teaching; the lecturer replied with moderation and
dignity, but shortly afterwards he was happily sent on an archaeological mission to Greece and Asia Minor, and, on his return,
was appointed to lecture on the safe subjects of the Latin language
and ancient literature (1854). He became a full professor in 1862,
and, after the resignation of Roulez in 1864, lectured on Roman
Antiquities, and, subsequently, on constitutional history. For
thirteen years he was superintendent of public instruction at
Ghent, and in 1878, when the liberal party came into power,
became general supervisor of the university, thus attaining the
distinction of being afterwards described by the rector, in the
familiar English phrase, as 'the right man in the right place'. In
1882–6 he was Member of Parliament for Ghent, and had charge
of the budget for public instruction. After resuming his duties
as professor, he lectured on Greek Epigraphy and on Roman
Constitutional History, resigned office in 1895 and died in the
following year.

Wagener and Gantrelle, though differing widely in character, were united
in their devotion to classical studies. They were associated as editors of
Tacitus, and also as editors of the Belgian *Revue*. But, while Gantrelle was
interested in the grammatical side of Classics, Wagener had a distinct taste for
archaeology and history. As a scholar Wagener ranged himself under the
banner of Boeckh and K. O. Müller. He did not read the Classics with a

---

[1] A. Wagener, in *Annuaire* of Brussels Acad. 1896, 45—114, with portrait
and bibliography.

view to constantly detecting the errors of the copyist, and the few corrections that he proposed were founded on solid proof of their absolute necessity. In his public career, he proved himself a born orator and an admirable lecturer; he assimilated all that was best in the French and German types of scholarship, while he remained true to the best traditions of his own country. Shortly before his death, when his friends and former pupils assembled to do honour to his past services, he unconsciously portrayed his own character in his *novissima verba*. He said that 'he had found the law of his life in the precept γνῶθι σεαυτόν; he was conscious of his own limitations; he had played an unobtrusive part, had made some small discoveries but had not thrown a new light on whole provinces of ancient learning; in the world of public and social life, he had not opened out any new paths, and he would not be remembered as a parliamentary orator; the kind sympathy expressed by his friends and pupils on that day was perhaps inspired by the fact that he had always walked consistently in the same path, the path of duty'. The classical authors that he mainly studied were Antiphon[1] and Plutarch[2], Cicero[3] and Tacitus. He wrote a remarkable article on the textual criticism of the *Dialogus de oratoribus*[4]; produced an excellent edition of the first book of the *Annals* (Paris, 1878), and easily refuted Hochart's paradoxical ascription of the *Annals* and *Histories* to the authorship of Poggio[5]. The influence of Ritschl is apparent in his Bonn dissertation on the *Origines* of Cato (1849), that of Lassen in his memoir on the apologues of India and of Greece[6]. His visit to Asia Minor led to his discovery and elucidation of a metrological monument in N.W. Phrygia[7], and to his publication of fifteen other inscriptions[8], followed by one connected with the corporations of artisans, which he had himself copied at Hierapolis[9]. His merits were not overlooked by the Academy of Brussels, but he was elected a correspondent of the Archaeological Institute at Rome (1863), before attaining a similar distinction in his own land (1871). After his election as a full member, he gave a lecture on the political opinions of Plutarch and Tacitus[10], and on liberty of conscience at Athens[11]. He was

---

[1] *Revue de l'Instruction Publique*, xii 149—157, xiii 88—113.

[2] *De EI in Delphis*, *ib.* xi 162 f, xxxii 171 f.

[3] Esp. in his repeated revisions of his father's *Pro Milone*, with the commentary of Asconius, where, in c. 29, *luco* (for *lecto*) *Libitinae* is due to Wagener.

[4] *Revue*, xx 257—284.

[5] *ib.* xxxiii 141 f, xxxviii 149 f.

[6] Brussels Acad. *Mémoires des savants étrangers*, 4°, xxv (1853).

[7] (At Ouchak *i.e.* Ushak) *Mém.* xxvii, 1855.

[8] *ib.* xxx, 1859.

[9] *Revue*, xi (1869) 1—14.

[10] *Bulletins*, Sér. 2, 1876, xli 1109.

[11] *ib.* Sér. 3, 1884, vii 574.

also an expert in Music. The question whether 'harmony' was known in ancient Music had been repeatedly asked since the days of the Renaissance; it had recently been answered in the negative by Fr. Fétis, and in the affirmative by J. H. Vincent. Wagener took the affirmative side in a memoir[1] that inspired François Auguste Gevaert with a desire to extend his knowledge of the subject. When Gevaert embarked on his memorable work on the 'History and Theory of Ancient Music'[2], he obtained the collaboration of Wagener on points connected with the revision and the interpretation of the ancient texts. Wagener was associated with Gevaert and Vollgraff in an edition of the *Musical Problems* of Aristotle, two parts of which were published by Wagener's survivors in 1900 and in 1901. Gevaert, who was born in 1828, and owed his early training to Ghent, is a practical musician and composer of a very high order, and is also known as the accomplished and versatile historian of ancient Music. Since 1871 he has been director of the Royal *Conservatoire* of Music in Brussels[3].

Gantrelle and Wagener had been preceded as editors of the *Revue* by Louis Chrétien Roersch (1831—1891). Born at Maestricht, the capital of the Dutch district of Limburg, he was educated at the local Athenaeum

Liége:
Roersch

before beginning his studies at Louvain. Owing to the large number of new appointments created by a law of 1850, he soon obtained a place on the staff of the Athenaeum of Bruges. He was then only twenty, and so youthful was his appearance that, on the prize-day, when he was seen descending the steps of the Hôtel de Ville empty-handed, the boys in the street called out:—'Look at that idle dog! he has not carried off a single prize!'. At Bruges he remained for fifteen years. Meanwhile, in 1855, he had contributed to the *Revue Pédagogique* an elaborate notice of J. L. Burnouf's Greek Grammar. This periodical had been started in 1852 at Mons; it was transferred in 1858 to Bruges, where under the new title of *Revue de l'instruction publique* it was edited by Roersch and his colleague Feys, whose sister he married. When Gantrelle and Wagener became editors, it was transferred to Ghent, but the name of Roersch was retained even after he had been compelled in 1868 to resign the immediate direction owing

---

[1] *Sur la symphonie des anciens*, in *Mém. des sav. étrang.* xxxi, 1861.

[2] Henzel, Paris, 1875—1881; cp. Bursian's *Jahresb.* xliv 15—19; also *La Mélopée Antique* (1895), *ib.* lxxxiv 285, 514.

[3] On Gevaert, cp. Grove's *Dictionary of Music and Musicians*, ed. 1906; on Wagener, *Annuaire* of Brussels Acad. 1898, 155—204.

to the pressure of his new duties at Liége.   In 1865 he had been
appointed at the *École Normale* to an important lectureship, which,
in 1872, was combined with a classical professorship in the university.   He was convinced that the study of the old classical
world was an indispensable means towards the progress of modern
civilisation[1]; but he gave a wide interpretation to that study.   At
Louvain, he had combined with it the study of Sanskrit, while, at
Liége, he gave proof of his interest in Germanic (and especially in
Flemish) and even in Semitic philology.   He delighted in studying
the Old Testament in the original Hebrew and in passing his
evenings in reading the Coran with the aid of the professor of
Arabic, and Homer, Virgil or Dante in the company of the
professor of Criminal Law.   Late in life he was rector of the
university and for three years discharged the duties of that office
with complete success during a transitional time of extraordinary
difficulty.   On resigning in October, 1891, he delivered a discourse
on the early constitution of Athens, in connexion with the recently
recovered treatise of Aristotle ; twelve days later, he was listening
to the classical cantata of *Andromeda*, and, only three days afterwards, he died.

As a classical scholar, he had devoted special attention to the
Latinity of Cornelius Nepos[2].   For the text, he had collated
four MSS, and in particular the Louvain MS from the adjacent
abbey of Parc.   In 1861 he produced an excellent school-edition
(ed. 2, 1884), followed by similar editions of Caesar, *De Bello
Gallico* (1864), and Cicero, *pro Archia et pro rege Deiotaro* (1867).
In 1885 he published, in conjunction with Paul Thomas of Ghent,
an excellent Greek Grammar, which was warmly welcomed by the
learned Societies of Belgium.   For the national encyclopaedia
entitled Van Bemmel's *Patria Belgica*[3] he condensed into the
brief compass of 26 pages a 'History of Philology in Belgium',
which is described by his biographer as 'a difficult task involving
long and laborious research', and as 'undoubtedly the most

---

[1] *Discours Rectoral* of 1889, and Van Bemmel's *Patria Belgica*, iii 432 (cp.
P. Willems, *Notice*, 526 f).

[2] *Revue*, 1858, 1861 f.

[3] iii (1875) 407—432.

important of his works'[1].   To the *Biographie Nationale* he contributed, during the last ten years of his life, more than twenty
notices of modern Latin poets or scholars who were natives of the
Southern Netherlands, the most prominent of these being Gruter,
D. Heinsius and Lipsius.   In 1888, he accompanied his future
biographer, Pierre Willems, on a pilgrimage to the house in which
Lipsius was born, only to discover that the great scholar's books
and furniture, after remaining safe for three centuries, had unfortunately been sold by auction at a recent date.   Thirty years
previously, he had published two letters from Kuster to Bentley
and Hemsterhuys, which he had discovered in the National
Library of France[2].   His studies and his published articles ranged
over a wide field, while his administrative duties left him little
leisure for any work on an extensive scale.   But he was fully
capable of producing works of far larger compass, any one of
which might have ensured him a permanent place in the history
of the scholarship of his country[3].

We may here add a brief notice of one or two of the early German
professors in the Belgian universities.   In 1817 the govern-   **Fuss**
ment of the united kingdoms of Holland and Belgium found
it necessary to invite scholars of German nationality to fill certain of the
professorships in the newly constituted universities of Louvain, Ghent and
Liége.   Among these was J. D. Fuss (1782—1860), who had been educated
by the Jesuits in his native town of Düren in Rhenish Prussia.   He had afterwards studied at Würzburg under Schelling and at Halle under F. A. Wolf;
he had also made the acquaintance of W. von Schlegel and Madame de Stael,
by whose advice he had studied for some years in Paris.   He had there
translated into Latin the treatise of Ioannes Lydus on the Roman magistrates,
as his own share of Hase's *editio princeps* (1812).   In 1815 he was appointed
by the Prussian Government to a classical mastership in the *gymnasium* of
Cologne; and, two years later, was called to the professorship of ancient
literature and Roman antiquities at Liége.   Among his best works was a
Latin manual of Roman Antiquities (1820), the third edition of which was
translated into English at Oxford in 1840.   His Jesuit training had made him

---

[1] P. Willems in *Annuaire* of Brussels Acad. 1893, with summary on
pp. 532–6.

[2] *Revue*, 1858, 318 f, 368 (incl. a letter to Bignon).

[3] P. Willems, in *Annuaire*, 1893, 515—542, with portrait, and conspectus
of passages in Greek and Latin authors discussed, 543 f; also complete
bibliography by A. Roersch, *ib.* 545—565.

a skilful composer of Latin verse. In the course of an excellent Latin ode on the foundation of the University of Liége, he thus refers to Louvain, as well as Liége and Ghent :—

> ' Priscum en refulget Lovanii decus,
> Binaeque Belgis, astra velut nova,
> Surgunt sorores : en Camoenae
> Auspiciis rediere laetis '[1].

He was also an adept in writing accentual rhyming Latin verse of the mediaeval type. A good example of this is the rendering of Schiller's *Lied von der Glocke*[2], included in his original and translated *Carmina Latina*[3]. In 1830, when the Dutch professors were expelled from the Belgian universities, Fuss, who was threatened with expulsion, protested that he was not a Dutchman but a German ; the plea was allowed, but he soon found the whole of the Faculty to which he belonged suppressed by the government. Nothing daunted, he continued to teach as a member of a *Faculté libre*, and, five years later, was reinstated, as professor of Roman antiquities only. He had a better command of Latin than of any other language, and he consoled himself for the fact that he was no longer a professor of Latin literature by writing volumes of Latin verse and by enlarging the range of his private reading. He was rector of the university in 1844–5, and, on laying down his office, delivered a discourse on the permanent importance of modern Latin. Later in life he became a diligent student of Dante, though he took no interest in the mediaeval scholasticism of the *Divina Commedia*[4].

The counterpart of Fuss at Liége was G. J. Bekker (1792—1837) at

G. J. Bekker Louvain. As a pupil of Creuzer at Heidelberg, he prepared a dissertation on Philostratus' Life of Apollonius, which was published in 1818. In the previous year he had been called to Louvain as professor of ancient literature. Within a year he acquired a perfect knowledge of Flemish as well as of French ; and, as the envoy of Louvain at the commemoration of the fifth jubilee of Leyden, he gave proof of his perfect command of Dutch. He had a genuine admiration for the great Dutch scholars, especially for Wyttenbach. On the suppression of the university of Louvain in 1834, he left for Liége, where he was rector of the university for the next academical year, and died not long after. At Louvain he had produced little besides an edition of the *Odyssey* and of Isocrates *ad Demonicum* ; but he was a man of no small merit, and he derives a reflected fame from his pupils, Baguet and Roulez[5].

---

[1] Reprinted in Le Roy's *Liége*, 56 f.

[2] Extract, *ib.* 323.   [3] 1822 ; ed. 2, 1845–6.

[4] Life and bibliography in Le Roy's *Liége*, 314—331.

[5] Baron de Reiffenberg, in *Annuaire*, 1838 ; Le Roy's *Liége*, 70—77 ; portrait in *Iconographie des Universités*. His biographer, the singularly versatile Baron de Reiffenberg (1795—1850), published excerpts from the elder Pliny (1820), a paper on Lipsius in the *Mém. couronnés* of the Brussels

The former of these, François Baguet (1801—1867), belonged to a thoroughly catholic family in the south of Brabant. On leaving school at the age of 16, he found the universities of **Baguet** Ghent and Liége just coming into being and that of Louvain in course of reconstruction. He was accordingly compelled to wait for a year before entering Louvain, where he studied Greek and Latin under G. J. Bekker. He published in 1822 in a quarto volume of nearly 400 pages an elaborate prize-essay on Chrysippus, and obtained his Doctor's degree on the strength of an edition of the eighth book of Dion Chrysostom (1823). When he was offered a lectureship in Greek and Latin in the newly constituted *Collège Philosophique* of Louvain, he declined the offer, but, as soon as a catholic university was established at Malines, he was appointed classical professor and secretary of that body and retained these posts on its transfer to Louvain. Though he was familiar with Flemish and Dutch (as well as with French) he never took the trouble to learn German, and consequently found himself at a constant disadvantage as a classical scholar. His papers on intermediate education (1842–62) were published in the *Revue Catholique* and in the *Bulletins* of the Brussels Academy, which included in its *Mémoires* of 1849 his only extensive production, a notice of the life and works of the Jesuit scholar, André Schott, the correspondent of Casaubon. In Baguet, the man was worth even more than the scholar. He was remarkable for his thoroughness, his devotion to duty, and his resolute self-effacement. The motto of his life was *ama nesciri*[1]. We next turn to a name of far greater note.

Félix Nève (1816—1893), a native of Ath in Hainaut, was educated beyond the borders of his native land at Lille, where he gave early proof of being a skilful **Nève** versifier in Latin as well as in French. Like Namèche, the future historian of Belgium, he was one of the first to enter Louvain on its reconstitution as a catholic university in 1835. In addition to his ordinary classical studies, he there attended Arendt's lectures on oriental literature, and, after learning a little Sanskrit, continued that study under Lassen at Bonn, Windischmann in Munich, and Eugène Burnouf in Paris, where he also studied Hebrew, Syriac, and Persian. He was appointed professor of ancient literature and oriental languages at Louvain in 1841, and became a full professor twelve years later. For ten successive years he lectured on ancient philosophy, and, for thirty-six in all, on Greek and

Acad., iii (1821), *Archives philologiques* (1825–6), and five *Mémoires* (1824–34) on the early history of the university of Louvain. Cp. *Annuaire*, 1852, and Le Roy's *Liége*, 170—198.

[1] Roulez, in *Annuaire* of Brussels Acad. 1870, 103—123, with bibliography.

Latin literature, though all the while his main interests lay in the
direction of oriental studies.   From time to time he lectured on
Sanskrit; and among those who attended these lectures were men
of no less mark than Roersch and Willems.   Of his published
works by far the greatest part related to oriental languages,
especially Sanskrit, Armenian and Syriac.   But, in 1846–55, his
interest in these languages incidentally led to his writing a series
of notices of the Belgian orientalists; and these in their turn
formed the prelude to his important memoir on the *Collegium
Trilingue* at Louvain[1].   In the course of this history of the
College from 1517 to 1797, he surveyed the study of the learned
languages at Louvain during the sixteenth, seventeenth and
eighteenth centuries.   The merit of the work was recognised by
the award of the gold medal of the Brussels Academy.   Thirty-
four years later, in the evening of a long life, the author returned
to the same theme in a work of wider scope and more highly
finished form[2].

In this work he collected and revised and supplemented all his scattered
notices of the minor humanists of the Southern Netherlands.   But this was
not all.   After a suggestive Introduction, in the course of which he urges that
the Renaissance had only accidental points of contact with the Reformation,
he devotes nearly a hundred admirable pages to Erasmus, with special
reference to his life at Louvain.   He next dilates on Jerome Busleiden and
Sir Thomas More, and on the theologian, Martin Dorpius (1485—1525), the
defender of humanistic studies, who lectured on Plautus and wrote amusing
prologues for performances of the *Aulularia* and the *Miles Gloriosus*; on
Adrien Barlandus (1487—1539), a commentator on Terence (1530); on
Jacques Ceratinus de Horn (d. 1530), the compiler of a Greek and Latin
dictionary dedicated to Erasmus; on the Greek scholar and magistrate,
François de Craneveldt (d. 1564), the friend of Erasmus and More, and the
translator of the work of Procopius on the buildings of Justinian; and lastly
on Guy Morillon (d. 1548), the diligent student of Livy and Suetonius, and
the secretary of Charles V.   Nothing is here said of such well-known scholars
of the sixteenth century as Vivès and Lipsius, but we have a comprehensive
monograph on Clenardus[3].   The seventeenth century is represented by Jean

---

[1] 1856; cp. ii 212 n. 2, *supra*.

[2] *La Renaissance et l'essor de l'érudition ancienne en Belgique*, 439 pp.,
Louvain, 1890.

[3] pp. 224—274. Cp. Chauvin and Roersch in *Mémoires couronnés* of the
Brussels Acad. LX (1900 f), no. 5, 203 pp., and ii 158 *supra*.

Baptiste Grammaye (1579—1635), the author of a work on the alphabets of the sixteen best-known languages[1]; by Petrus Castellanus (1585—1632), professor of Greek at Louvain, and author of lives of famous physicians, also of a treatise on the festivals of Greece, and another on the viands of the ancient world, afterwards incorporated in the *Thesaurus*[2] of Gronovius. The last two chapters deal with Andreas Catullus (1586—1667), the author of a Latin play on the origin of the sciences, under the title of *Prometheus* (1613), and Valerius Andreas, the compiler of a geographical and biographical dictionary of Belgium (1623), and of the earliest history of the university of Louvain (1635)[3].

While Félix Nève was an orientalist who became incidentally interested in the scholarship of the Southern Netherlands, we have in the person of Jean Joseph Thonissen (1816—1891) an eminent jurist and politician who included in the long series of his historical and legal writings a luminous work on Criminal Law in primitive Greece and at Athens. Born at Hasselt, the capital of Limbourg, and educated at his native place and at Rolduc, he studied at Liége and (for two years) in Paris. For 36 years professor of Criminal Law at Louvain and for 27 Member for Hasselt, he was presented with his bust in marble by his constituents in 1873 and by his friends and pupils seven years later. In 1884–7 he was Home Secretary and Minister of Public Instruction. The rumour of his death in 1888 led to the premature publication of generous tributes to his great services as a liberal catholic, as a statesman, and as the author of a highly appreciated commentary on the constitution of Belgium. His study of modern socialism was preceded by an examination of the Laws of Crete, Sparta and Rome, as well as the institutions of Pythagoras and the *Republic* of Plato[4]. His papers on the criminal law of India, Egypt, and Judaea[5], and his two large volumes on the same subject (1869), were succeeded by his work on the Criminal Law of Legendary Greece and on that of Athens under the democracy, the evidence as to the former being directly

Thonissen

---

[1] *Specimen litterarum et linguarum*, Ath (1622).

[2] ix 351—404.

[3] On the life of Nève, cp. T. J. Lamy in *Annuaire* of the Brussels Acad. 1894, 90 pp., with portrait and bibliography.

[4] Esp. in *Le socialisme depuis l'antiquité jusqu'à*...1852, 2 vols. (Louvain, 1852).

[5] Collected in his *Mélanges*, 1873.

derived from Homer and Hesiod. For Athenian Law he relies on the Attic orators and other ancient texts.

He begins with a brief review of the sources of our information. In the second book, he deals with the different kinds of penalties; in the third, he classifies the offences against the state, against the person etc; in the fourth, after some general considerations, he examines Plato's and Aristotle's opinions on punishments. He closes with reflexions on the general character of the Athenian system of penalties, its merits and its defects[1].

Even before the publication of the second of his four volumes on the History of Belgium under Leopold I (1855–8), his merits were recognised by the Royal Academy of Brussels, and one of his most permanent services to that body was his comprehensive survey and methodical analysis of several hundreds of papers presented to the Section of Letters (under the head of epigraphy, linguistics, ancient and mediaeval literature etc.) during the first century of its existence[2].

While the Criminal Law of Athens was one of the many subjects that attracted the attention of Thonissen, the Political Institutions of Rome were the principal theme of the life-long labours of Pierre Willems (1840—1898). Born and bred at Maestricht, and educated at Louvain, he received the distinction of a government grant, which enabled him to study for two years in foreign universities (1862–3). In Paris he worked at oriental languages under Oppert, Greek under Egger, and Latin literature under Patin[3]. He continued to study oriental languages in Berlin, and completed his *Wanderjahre* by visiting the university of Utrecht, and by working at Greek under Cobet at Leyden. During his absence abroad he paid hardly any attention to the Institutions of Rome, nor did he ever attend any lectures on that subject at Louvain. On his return he was appointed to a professorship which he held for the remaining 33 years of his life. For the last 25 of those years he was also secretary of the university.

P. Willems

[1] *Le Droit pénal de la République athénienne, précédé d'une étude sur le droit criminel de la Grèce légendaire*, 490 pp., 1875.

[2] *Rapport Séculaire sur les travaux de la Classe des lettres*, 1772—1872, 304 pp. Cp. T. J. Lamy in the *Annuaire* for 1892, 106 pp., with portrait and bibliography.

[3] *Revue Belge*, xv (1863) 492.

He is best known as the author of standard works on the Political Institutions of ancient Rome. In 1870 he published his comprehensive treatise on 'Roman Antiquities'[1], which in all subsequent editions bore the title of *Le droit public romain*[2]. The author aims at combining the didactic method of W. A. Becker and the historic method of L. Lange, and at avoiding the drawbacks of both. He displays an intimate knowledge of the original authorities and the best modern treatises on the subject; and he constantly insists on drawing a sharp distinction between facts and hypotheses. His treatment of a somewhat dry subject is characterised by a remarkable clearness of style. It is the first complete work of the kind that has been written in French. It passed through six editions, and was ultimately translated into Russian by command of the Russian Minister of Public Instruction.

An even higher degree of success attended the publication of his great work on the Senate under the Roman Republic[3]. His fundamental principle is that the Senate remained an exclusively patrician body until about 400 B.C. It is on this basis that he grounds his description of the composition (and the attributes) of the Senate down to the *plebiscitum Ovinium* (*c.* 338—312 B.C.), which required the censors to choose the persons best qualified for the Senate without distinction between patricians and plebeians. Finally, he brings his subject down to the end of the Roman Republic. The work was carefully discussed[4], and elaborately reviewed[5] in Germany and elsewhere. As many as twenty-seven reviews are enumerated in the preface to the second edition (1885) of the first volume; and Mommsen, who is not lavish of citations from the works of other investigators, makes an exception in the case of Willems[6]. The author's single aim was the attainment of

---

[1] *Les antiquités romaines envisagées au point de vue des institutions politiques*, 332 pp. (Louvain, 1870).

[2] *Jusqu'à Constantin* in ed. 1872, '74; *jusqu'à Justinien* in ed. 1880, '83, '88 (nearly 700 pp.).

[3] *Le Sénat de la république romaine;* i (*La composition*), ii (*Les attributions du Sénat*), iii (*Registres*), 1878—1885; 638 (724^2) + 784 + 115 pp.

[4] L. Lange, *De plebiscitis Ovinio et Atinio disputatio*, Lips. 1878, 52 pp.

[5] *e.g.* by Hermann Schiller in Bursian's *Jahresb.* xix (1879) 411—427.

[6] Pref. to *Römisches Staatsrecht*, III ii (1888) p. vi. It has been noticed

historic truth.   He made a point of studying all the original
authorities, and of never consulting any modern writers until he
had formed his own opinion.   One of the most striking features of
the work is the elaborate biographical register of the members of
the Senate in 179 and in 55 B.C.   The author afterwards began a
work on the equestrian and senatorial orders under the Empire,
and his register of the Senate of 65 A.D. has been published by
his son[1]. His work was highly esteemed in other lands, in France,
England and Italy, no less than in Germany, but he never visited
Rome, nor indeed any part of Italy.   Among his minor works the
most widely interesting is the public lecture in which he gives a
detailed and vivid description of the municipal elections at
Pompeii[2].   Such slighter efforts were, however, quite exceptional;
he generally preferred concentrating himself on an *opus magnum*,
such as his work on the Senate and on the *Droit public romain*[3],
and even his minor publications had usually some connexion with
his larger undertakings.   At Louvain, in 1874, he founded among
the members of his class a *Societas Philologa*, the first of its kind
in Belgium ; and one of its earliest members was Charles Michel,
now a professor at Liége and editor of the compact and comprehensive *Recueil d'Inscriptions Grecques* (1900).   Willems was also
the founder and first organiser of the Classical Quarterly called
the *Musée Belge* (1897).   In his own works he showed in general
a greater affinity with the German and Dutch than with the French
type of classical learning[4].   He was more interested in the pursuit
of positive facts than in the elegant literary analysis of the Classics.
His courses of lectures dealt with a considerable variety of classical
authors, together with Latin inscriptions.   They also included a
general outline of the whole province of 'classical philology', which

that, in the third edition of vol. 1, Mommsen is apt to emphasise points of
difference, while he appears to have modified some of his opinions in the light
of those of Willems.

[1] 140 pp., Louvain, 1902 (extract from *Musée Belge*, vols. iv—vi).

[2] *Les élections municipales à Pompéi*, with tables and notes, 142 pp. (1886),
extract from the *Bulletins* of the Brussels Acad., Sér. 3, xii (1886) 51 f.

[3] He also collected a large mass of materials for a comprehensive work on
Flemish dialects.

[4] *In medio virtus* is his own motto in *Revue Belge*, xv (1863) 508 f.

he defined as 'the science of the civilisation of Greece and Rome'[1]. He was profoundly impressed with the importance of maintaining classical studies in intermediate and in higher education. He was also interested in the earlier fortunes and the later progress of those studies, he regretted the absence of a complete history of the humanists of Louvain, and he was devoted to the memory of men like Nève and Roersch, who had made important contributions towards such a history. In all the breadth and solidity and accuracy of his own attainments he gave proof of his possession of that genius which consists in an infinite capacity for taking pains[2], thus adding a new glory to the Chair that had been filled three centuries before by a man of more brilliant literary talent, but of less stability of character, the greatest Latin scholar of the Southern Netherlands, Justus Lipsius[3].

[1] *Lettres chrétiennes*, Paris (1882) 453.

[2] 'La génie n'est qu'une grande aptitude à la patience' (Buffon); Carlyle's *Frederick*, i 415, ed. 1870.

[3] On the life and works of Pierre Willems, cp. esp. Victor Brants in the *Annuaire* of the Brussels Acad. 1899, 60 pp., with portrait and bibliography; also Lamy in *Bulletins* of Brussels Acad. (1898) 297, and Waltzing in *Musée Belge*, 1898.

NΠNEYMATI KAI AΛHΘEIA

MADVIG.

From a photograph reproduced in the *Opuscula Academica* (ed. 1887) and in the *Nordisk Tidskrift*, Ser. II, vol. viii; p. 319 *infra*.

CHAPTER XXXVIII.

SCANDINAVIA.

DENMARK, Norway and Sweden, the three constituent portions of the ancient Scandinavia, formed a single kingdom from 1397 to 1523, that is, from the accession of queen Margaret, the Semiramis of the North, to the proclamation of Gustavus Vasa as king of Sweden. Copenhagen, the capital of Denmark in and after 1443, became the seat of a university founded in 1479 by Christian I under the sanction of Sixtus IV (1475). The statutes which it received from the archbishop of Lund were modelled on those of Cologne. Sweden (as already implied) became a separate kingdom in 1523; from 1523 to 1560 Gustavus Vasa was king of Sweden, and Frederic I and Christian III successively kings of Denmark and Norway, and in 1527–36 protestantism was established in all three countries. In 1539 the university of Copenhagen, which had collapsed during a time of civil and religious commotion, was refounded by Christian III on the model of the protestant university of Wittenberg. It was destroyed in the great fire of 1728, and rebuilt and reorganised in 1732 under Christian VI, who was also the patron of the 'Society of Sciences'[1] founded in 1742. The university was finally reorganised in 1788[2]. Nearly three centuries before the foundation of that university, the Latin secretary of the archbishop of Lund, and the earliest authority for the tragic story of Hamlet, was known by the name of Saxo Grammaticus[3], and we shall see in the sequel that the preparation of text-books of Latin Grammar

[1] Det Kongelige Danske Videnskabernes Selskab. Cp. p. 314 infra.
[2] Cp. Matzen's Retshistorie (1879); Rashdall, ii 291 f; and Minerva, II.
[3] His elegantly written Danorum Regum Heroumque Historia (c. 1200) was first published by the Danish man of letters, C. Pedersen (Paris, 1514).

was a prominent part of the work of scholars in Denmark from
the days of Jersin and Bang, Ancherson and Baden, down to those
of Madvig.

Our list of scholars begins with Thomas Bang (1600—1661),
who, after spending three years abroad in the study
of Latin, Hebrew and Theology at Franeker and
Wittenberg, became professor of Hebrew, librarian, and professor
of Theology in the university of Copenhagen. An orientalist by
profession, he was a layman in Latin, but he was convinced of the
supreme importance of maintaining that language in the schools of
Denmark. As a Latin scholar, he is best known for having revised
at the royal command the Latin Grammar (1623) of J. D. Jersin,
rector of the school at Sorö and ultimately bishop of Ribe.
Bang's *praecepta minora* and *majora* of 1636–40 were followed in
the latter year by his principal grammatical work, the *Observationes
Philologicae*, in two volumes of more than 700 pages each. He
also published a Latin primer under the attractive title of *Aurora
Latinitatis* (1638). Oriental languages are the main theme of two
of his other works:—the *Coelum orientis et prisci mundi* (1657),
and the *Exercitationes litterariae antiquitatis* (1638–48)[1]. In the
latter he starts from Pliny's phrase, *aeternus litterarum usus*[2], and
discourses at large on the 'book of Enoch' and the language of
the angels. In accordance with the general belief of his time, he
holds that all languages (as well as all alphabets) have their source
in Hebrew[3].

Bang's contemporary, Johan Lauremberg (*c.* 1588—1658),
professor of Latin Poetry at Rostock, left Germany
for Denmark in 1623, and was mathematical master
at Sorö for the remaining 22 years of his life. His edition of
the *Sphaera* of Proclus (1611), his Latin *Antiquarius*, or vocabulary of archaic and antiquarian words and phrases (1624), and his
collection of maps of ancient Greece[4], are now of little note in

Bang

Lauremberg

---

[1] Reprinted at Cracow, *Exercitationes…de ortu et progressu litterarum*, 1691.

[2] vii 193.

[3] Professor M. C. Gertz, in Bricka's *Dansk Biografisk Lexikon* (1887—
1904). Prof. Gertz has also written on most of the scholars mentioned below;
all these articles have been carefully consulted.

[4] Ed. Pufendorf, 1660.

comparison with the literary interest of his Danish and Latin Satires[1].

In the same century Oluf Borch, or Olaus Borrichius (1629—1690), after studying medicine at Copenhagen, travelled in Holland, England, France and Italy, and, on his return in 1666, became professor in the university, and physician to the king. He was one of the most versatile of men. He lectured on philology, as well as on medicine, botany and chemistry, besides filling (late in life) the office of librarian. In philology his earliest work was a compendious guide to Latin versification, quaintly named *Parnassus in nuce* (1654). His *dissertatio de lexicis Latinis et Graecis* (1660) was followed by his principal work in this line of study:—the *Cogitationes de variis linguae Latinae aetatibus* (1675). This was supplemented by his *Analecta*, and by his dissertation *De studio purae Latinitatis*. The historical side of scholarship is represented by his notable *Conspectus* of the principal Latin authors, and by his ' Academic dissertations' on the Greek and Latin poets, and on the topography of Rome and the oracles of the ancients[2]. The science of language is exemplified in his *Dissertatio de causis diversitatis linguarum* (1675).

Oluf Borch

Language, in his view, was originally given to man by God, and there was the closest correspondence between the original words, as images of things, and the things themselves. Man had also received the gift of an aptitude for inventing new words, on which common custom impressed certain meanings ; hence the further developement of languages. After the building of the tower of Babel, there was a confusion of tongues. The primitive language was preserved completely among the Hebrews, and only partially among other nations. Hence in all languages there were some words which were related to Hebrew, but these languages had diverged in different directions. This was due to a variety of causes, such as diversities of climate and of modes of living, which affected the organs of speech. In the conception of language which is here presented, *onomatopoeia* plays an important part.

---

[1] Ed. Lappenberg, Stuttgart, 1861 (Bursian, i 320); cp. L. Daae, *Om Humanisten og Satirikeren, Johan Lauremberg*, Chr. 1884. His Satires were not without influence on that versatile man of genius, Holberg (1684—1754), the Molière of Denmark, who, in his Comedies, owed much to Plautus. One of those Comedies, *Niels Klims' subterranean journey*, was actually written in Latin (1741).

[2] 1676–87 ; ed. 2, 1714–5.

In the rest of Borch's views there is much that is obscure, and, as a whole, they are out of date; but they are not devoid of interest, while they have the advantage of being clothed in an attractive form[1].

In the first half of the next century Hans Gram (1685—1748)

Gram

was appointed professor of Greek (1714), as well as historiographer, librarian and archivist of Copenhagen (1730 f). We still possess the rectorial oration in which he dilated on the literary history of Denmark and Norway down to the foundation of the university[2]. It was in his time that the university was rebuilt and reopened, and it was owing to his influence that the 'Society of Sciences' was founded in 1742. He was specially interested in Greek science and in Greek history. He wrote on the 'Egyptian origin of geometry', and published observations on Archytas and Aratus. He carefully studied the works of Xenophon and the *scholia* on Thucydides, and edited the *Characters* of Theophrastus. He also published a brief history of Greek literature, and he is the reputed author of a Latin-Danish and Danish-Latin Dictionary, called the *Nucleus Latinitatis*, which remained in use until it was superseded by the work of Jacob Baden. Gram never left his native land, but he counted Fabricius, Havercamp and Duker among his correspondents abroad. It was once the fashion to describe him as 'the greatest man in Denmark', but he never produced any *magnum opus*. He buried his extensive learning in a considerable number of minor lucubrations, and he was only too apt to lose himself in mazes of minute detail. Nevertheless he did good service to his country by the organisation of learning and by the critical examination of its ancient history[3].

Gram's contemporary Christian Falster (1690—1752) was in-

Falster

terested in Greek and Roman literature and criticism. He produced at Flensborg his supplement to Latin lexicons (1717) and a comprehensive introduction to the study of Latin literature entitled *Quaestiones Romanae* (1718). At Ribe he prepared his notes on Gellius[4]. When the com-

[1] Gertz, in Bricka.

[2] 1745; *Altes und Neues aus Dännemark*, i (1768) 439—518.

[3] Cp. Harless, *Vitae Philol.*, iii 146—156; *Nouvelle Biographie Générale*, *s.v.*; and esp. Gertz, in Bricka.

[4] *Vigilia prima noctium Ripensium* (1721).

mentary was completed, it was calculated that it would fill three folio volumes. It was impossible to find a publisher, and the author accordingly bequeathed his MS, with all his other books, to the library of the university of Copenhagen. Meanwhile, his friend, Hans Gram, 'on hearing that the *Noctes Ripenses* had been doomed to eternal darkness'[1], prevailed on the author to allow some small portions of these *Noctes* to see the light of day[2]. His *Memoriae Obscurae*, largely derived from Gellius, and published at Hamburg in 1722, is practically a supplement to the *Bibliotheca Latina* of the great Hamburg scholar, Fabricius. In his *Cogitationes Variae Philologicae* (1715) he regards classical literature as a handmaid to theology and protests against the opinion that the 'pagan' Classics should be avoided by the Christian student. Among the classical *desiderata* of his time, he here mentions a history of Greek literature and adds an outline of a future work on the subject. He also discusses the essential points in an ideal edition and incidentally denounces the Dutch fashion of accumulating a mass of 'various readings'[3].

He recurs to the same theme in a work originally described by himself as *Sermones*, to which his Dutch publisher adroitly gave the more attractive title of *Amoenitates Philologicae*[4]. It is written in a style that is eminently readable without being perfectly pure. One of the chapters describes the author's conversation with a youth of high promise who found his chief delight in reading the lives of great scholars and was inspired with the ambition of following in their steps[5]. Another conversation, on the scholar's religion, ends with the author's description of himself as a 'Christian philosopher':—'studeo, non tam ut doctior quam ut melior evadam'[6]. This is the most celebrated of his works, but, notwithstanding its title, the largest part of it has no connexion with 'philology'. Its writer is also known as a Danish satirist, as

[1] *Amoenitates Philologicae*, iii 214.

[2] Printed *ib.* at end of vols. ii and iii.

[3] P. 11, *cogit.* iii, v.

[4] iii 7, Amst. 1729–32, 3 vols., with vignette. In the dedicatory preface to vol. i Hans Gram is apostrophised as *amplissime* and *nobilissime Gram*.

[5] i 11 f.

[6] i 43 f.

a commentator on the fourteenth satire of Juvenal, and as the author of a Danish rendering of Ovid's *Tristia*[1].

Later in the same century Jacob Baden (1735—1804), who began his studies at Copenhagen and continued them at Göttingen and Leipzig, held scholastic appointments at Altona and at Helsingör (Elsinore), and was professor of 'eloquence' at Copenhagen for the last 24 years of his life. His portrait was engraved by Lahde[2] and his bust modelled by Thorwaldsen. A compendious Latin Grammar produced in 1751 by the Danish schoolmaster, Sören Ancherson (1698—1781), was the authorised text-book for use in all the schools of Denmark and Norway, and it held its ground until the author's death, thirty years later. In the very next year it was superseded by Baden's Grammar, just as Baden's was ultimately superseded in 1846 by that of Madvig. Baden was also the compiler of standard Latin-Danish and Danish-Latin Dictionaries (1786-8), the former of these being founded on Gesner. He produced creditable editions of Phaedrus, Virgil and Horace, and translations of Xenophon's *Cyropaedeia*, and of Horace, Suetonius, Tacitus and Quintilian (x, xi). He was far less successful as the author of a Greek Grammar and Chrestomathy.

His son, Torkil Baden (1765—1849), studied at Göttingen and acquired an interest in art during his travels in Italy. He was a professor at Kiel in Holstein (then part of Denmark) and (in 1804-23) at Copenhagen. His published works (such as his dissertation on Philostratus) were partly inspired by his interest in ancient art. He 'had read nearly all the Greek and Latin Classics', but the result of all this reading is inadequately represented in his edition of the *Tragedies* of Seneca[3]. His edition of his grandfather's *Roma Danica* brought him into feud with other scholars. He was more fortunate in his new and improved edition of his father's Dictionaries (1815-31).

Intermediate in date between the two Badens is Rasmus

J. Baden

T. Baden

----

[1] Cp. Thaarup, in *Christian Falsters Satirer* (1840); Bursian, i 367–9; and Gertz, in Bricka.

[2] Lahde og Nyerup, *Portraite*, iii (1806).

[3] Leipzig, 1819-21.

Nyerup (1756—1829), the learned librarian of Copenhagen, who, besides producing numerous works connected with Scandinavian literature, was the first to publish the contents of eight *Glossaria antiqua Latino-Theotisca*[1]. The fifth of these is ultimately derived from the important Latin and Anglo-Saxon glossary preserved in a Leyden MS of the eighth century, which formerly belonged to Isaac Vossius and was probably once at St Gallen[2].

Nyerup

One of Nyerup's less productive contemporaries is Niels Iversen Schow (1754—1830), the professor of Copenhagen, who studied MSS in Rome and Venice, edited the Homeric Allegories of Heracleides Ponticus (1782) and Joannes Lydus *De Mensibus* (1794), and began editions of Stobaeus and Photius, which unfortunately remained unfinished. In bygone years he had studied at Göttingen under Heyne; he had thus acquired an interest in archaeology, and he had produced a handbook of the subject; but his early promise remained unfulfilled. He is far less distinguished than the able and versatile archaeologist and historian, Friedrich Münter (1761—1830), who had also studied under Heyne and ultimately became bishop of Seeland. His younger contemporary Birgerus (Börge) Thorlacius (1775—1829), professor at Copenhagen for the last twenty-six years of his life, edited Hesiod's *Works and Days*, the Speech of Lycurgus against Leocrates, and Cornelius Nepos, besides discussing the *Republic* of Cicero, and producing a considerable series of *Opuscula* (1806–22). His editions of Greek texts were mere reprints from those of foreign scholars. He was a man of wide but superficial learning; ineffective as a Latin professor, he did good service as one of the revisers of the Danish translation of the Greek Testament. The briefest mention must suffice for S. N. J. Bloch (1772—1862), rector of the school at Roeskilde, a compiler of elementary text-books and an editor of Select Speeches of Cicero, who advocated a reform in the

Schow
Münter
Thorlacius
Bloch

---

[1] (Nyerup), *Symbolae ad literaturam Teutonicam antiquiorem*, Hauniae, 1787, pp. 174—410.

[2] *The Leiden Latin–Anglo-Saxon Glossary*, ed. J. H. Hessels, Cambridge Univ. Press, 1906, pp. xiii—xvi.

pronunciation of Greek, and thus came into conflict with Matthiae in Germany, and with Henrichsen in Denmark (1826). It was from a paper on the Latin Imperative (1825) by Niels Bygom Krarup (1792—1842), a teacher at Christianshavn, that Zumpt derived the name of the 'future imperative'. Among natives of Iceland may be mentioned Gudmundur Magnússon (1741—1798), an editor of Terence (1780), and Paul Arnesen (1776—1851), who was educated at Helsingör, held a mastership at Christiania, and finally taught Greek and Latin at Copenhagen. His Greek and Danish dictionary was the first of its kind in Denmark (1830), and was followed by his new Latin dictionary (1845–8).

Krarup

Magnússon
Arnesen

Meanwhile archaeology was represented by Johann Georg Zoëga (1755—1809), who studied at Göttingen and repeatedly visited Italy in and after 1780. He joined the Church of Rome in 1783 and died in Rome in 1809. His earliest work, that on the imperatorial coins of Egypt, was followed by his important folio 'on the origin and use of obelisks' (1797), by his 'Coptic MSS of the Museum Borgianum', and his 'ancient Roman bas-reliefs'[1]. He was commemorated by a medallion executed by his friend Thorwaldsen. Another Danish archaeologist, Peter Oluf Bröndsted (1780—1842), after studying at Copenhagen, worked at archaeology in Paris and in Italy, and in 1810–4 travelled in Greece with Haller and Stackelberg, Cockerell and Foster. Bröndsted's own share in this eventful tour is partly recorded in the two volumes of his travels (1820–30). Meanwhile, he had returned to Copenhagen in 1814, to leave it in 1820 for a tour among the Ionian Islands and in Italy[2]. He visited England in 1824 and 1831, and was professor of Philology and Archaeology for the last ten years of his life. His paper on 'Panathenaic vases' was published by the Royal Society of Literature (1832), and his 'Bronzes of Siris' by the Dilettanti Society (1836). As professor he was succeeded in 1842 by F. C. Petersen (1786—1859), who held this position for the remaining 17 years of his life. His 'Introduction to Archaeology' (1825), which includes a full account of Winckelmann, was translated into German[3]. He also published a handbook to Greek literature, besides com-

Zoëga

Bröndsted

F. C. Petersen

[1] *Abhandlungen* (1817), *Leben*, etc., Welcker (1819); Stark, 245–9; Michaelis, *Arch. Entd.* 13 f.

[2] Stark, 260–2.

[3] 1829, 353 pp. (12 on the history of the study of ancient art, followed by 62 on Winckelmann); 'ein auch heute durch kein anderes ersetztes Buch' (Stark, 52, 58).

ments on Libanius and an excellent paper on the jurisdiction of the Ephetae (1854).   During the student-days of Henrichsen, Elberling and Madvig, Petersen was the only thoroughly efficient lecturer on the classical side of the university.   It was owing to the inadequacy of the other lecturers that these three students (with two of their companions) formed a philological society of their own, which had an important influence on their early career[1]. The fourth of the Danish archaeologists, Olaus Kellermann   Kellermann (1805—1837), began to reside in Rome in 1831 and gave proof of high promise in Latin Epigraphy[2].   Lastly, the Danish expedition to the island of Rhodes, in 1902-4, led to the discovery of inscriptions which determine the date and birthplace of the sculptor Boëthus to be Chalcedon in the Hellenistic age, and prove that the group of Laocoön may be approximately placed at the beginning of the rule of Augustus[3].

The foremost representative of scholarship in Denmark was Johan Nicolai Madvig (1804—1886), the son of a   Madvig subordinate legal official on the Danish island of Bornholm, off the Swedish coast, from which his great-grandfather had migrated to Danish territory.   His name was derived from a fishing-village in the South of Sweden that once belonged to Denmark.   At the early age of eleven, he began copying legal documents for his father, and he always retained a keen interest in law.   After his father's death he was educated at Frederiksborg in Nordseeland under Bendtsen, in whose memory he delivered a public eulogy in 1831, but he was mainly self-taught. After studying at Copenhagen (1820-5), he was appointed professor of Latin (1829) and held that position for more than half a century.   In and after 1848 he was a member of the Danish Diet, Inspector of all the Schools of Denmark, and for three years Minister of Education.   He was President of the Council from 1856 to 1863, and continued to take part in politics until he reached the age of seventy.   At the fourth centenary of the university of Copenhagen (the commemoration of which was, for political reasons, confined to the Scandinavian nations), he discharged his duties as rector in the most admirable manner. Throughout the whole of his long life of more than 80 years, he

---

[1] Gertz on Petersen and Henrichsen, in Bricka.

[2] *Vigilum Romanorum latercula* (1835); O. Jahn, *Spec. Epigr.*, 1841, pp. v—xv; Jörgensen, in Bricka.

[3] Michaelis, *Arch. Entd.* 168 f; p. 28 n. 1 *supra*.

was never seriously ill, and his mental powers remained unimpaired to the very end.

His best work was that devoted to the study of the Latin language and to the textual criticism of Cicero and Livy. In 1825, in conjunction with four young scholars of Copenhagen, he edited a volume of Garatoni's notes on the *Speeches* of Cicero. The dissertation for his degree consisted of emendations of Cicero, *De Legibus* and *Academica* (1826), followed by a treatise on Asconius (1827), an *Epistola Critica* on the last two of the Verrine Orations (1828), and criticisms on *Select Speeches* (1830), and the *Cato Maior* and *Laelius* (1835). His duties as professor involved the preparation of the Latin programs of the university, afterwards published in his *Opuscula Academica* (1834–42)[1]. In the first of these *Opuscula*, a paper originally published in 1829, he proved that certain alleged orthographical fragments of 'Apuleius', which had imposed on Mai and Osann, were forgeries of the fifteenth century[2]. He attained a European reputation by his masterly edition of Cicero, *De Finibus* (1839)[3], one of those standard works which instruct and stimulate the student not only by the knowledge they impart but also by the way in which they impart it[4]. His *Latin Grammar* (1841), followed by a volume of 'Observations' (1844), was translated into all the languages of Europe. 'The great merits of the book are its clearness, and grasp of the subject, within the limits which the writer set himself; its power of analysis, and its command of classical usage'[5]. Meanwhile, he was pursuing those wider studies of the text of the Greek as well as the Latin Classics, which bore fruit in his *Adversaria Critica*. In 1846 he produced his *Greek Syntax*[6], and, in the same year, a tour in Germany gave him the opportunity of making the acquaintance of Schneidewin, and also of Boeckh, with whom he had a close affinity. He was on friendly terms with Halm, and the sixth volume of Baiter and Kayser's *Cicero* was dedicated by Baiter to Madvig,— *Tullianorum criticorum principi*.

---

[1] Ed. 2, 1887.   [2] Nettleship, ii 5—7.   [3] Ed. 3, 1876.
[4] Bursian, ii 946 ; cp. Nettleship, ii 7—10.
[5] Nettleship, ii 10 f.
[6] Followed by *Bemerkungen* in *Philologus*, Suppl. 1848.

When he resumed his professorship in 1851, on ceasing to be Minister of Education, his study of Roman Constitutional History led to his devoting his main attention to Livy. He produced his well-known *Emendationes Livianae* in 1860[1], and his edition of the text, in conjunction with Ussing, in 1861–6[2]. On the completion of his Livy, he made a lengthy tour in Switzerland, Italy and France, and, in 1869, saw still more of Italy. In 1871–3 he published the two volumes of his *Adversaria Critica*, with an admirable introduction on the general principles of textual criticism, illustrated by examples. After producing a German edition of his minor philological writings (1875), he began to suffer from increasing weakness of sight, but did not resign the duties of his professorship until five years later. Meanwhile, he brought out new editions of his works, including several volumes of his Livy, a German translation of his *Greek Syntax*, a selection from Cicero's *Speeches*, and nearly completed a new edition of his *Opuscula Academica* (1887). He had also returned to the study of the text of Cicero, had produced in 1884 an Appendix to his *Adversaria*, and an important work in two volumes on the Constitution and Administration of the Roman State (1881–2)[3]. Finally, when the eyesight of the unwearied veteran began to grow dim, he dictated his Memoirs from the days of his childhood down to 1884.

From the outset of his career as a scholar, his special field had been verbal criticism. A rational method of estimating the value of MSS, and applying the results, had lately come into vogue; MSS were no longer to be counted, but to be weighed in comparison with the original archetype. This method was extended by Madvig, and was carried through with remarkable clearness and precision[4]. In the preface to the *De Finibus* there is a characteristic passage in which he compares the textual critic to a judge whose duty it is to elicit the truth from the conflict of evidence[5].

---

[1] Enlarged ed. 1877.
[2] Cp. Nettleship, ii 11—14.
[3] Cp. Nettleship, ii 16—19.
[4] Cp. his preface to the 12 Orations of Cic., reprinted in his *Opusc.*
[5] Transl. in Nettleship, ii 8.

He had a remarkable aptitude for conjectural emendation. In Cicero, *pro Caelio*, no less than six of his corrections were subsequently confirmed by the MS formerly in the abbey of St Victor[1]. But his conjectures were not all of equal value; he was certainly less successful with the text of Plato than with that of Cicero; and he himself regretted that he was not more familiar with the style of the Greek Tragic Poets. *Quam vellem poëtas Graecos et praesertim Atticos non attigisset*, was Cobet's saying of Madvig; Munro would have extended the remark to the Roman poets[2]; and Ritschl had occasion to attack him for the metrical mistake of changing *mūtasse* into *nătasse* in a passage of Ovid[3].

Verbal criticism he regarded, however, as a means to an end, and that end was the vivid realisation and the perfect presentation of the civilisation of Greece and Rome, whether in literature, or in public or private life. A lecture of 1881 gives proof of the breadth of his interest in the study of language[4], but he cared little for the minor details of Comparative Philology. The subject-matter of the Latin Classics was less largely represented in his published works than in his professorial lectures. In his paper on Asconius, he followed Niebuhr in maintaining the spuriousness of part of the commentary. The earliest of his papers on the Institutions of Rome were those on the *Equites*, the Colonies, and the *tribuni aerarii*[5].

'His familiarity with ante- and post-classical Latin was by no means on a par with his mastery of Ciceronian and Livian style. Nor does he display that nice sense of usage which makes the study of J. F. Gronovius, Ruhnken, Heindorf, Cobet, so instructive. Robust common sense, revolting against impossibilities in thought and expression, a clear perception of what the context requires, a close adherence to the *ductus litterarum* seem to me.' (says Professor Mayor) 'his great merits as a critic'[6].

'Whatever faults may be found in his work,...it has always' (adds Professor Nettleship) 'the characteristic of a sound humanity. The whole man is there: it is not a fragment of a mind, or a half-grown mind, which we see active

---

[1] A. C. Clark, *Anecd. Oxon.* x, xxxi f.

[2] *Journal of Philol.* vi 78.

[3] *Met.* iv 46 ; *Opusc. Philol.* iii (cp. Nettleship, ii 15).

[4] *Was ist Sprachwissenschaft?*

[5] All reprinted in *Opusc.*   [6] *Cl. Rev.* i 124.

before us'. He has 'a certain simplicity and wholesome independence', and he was 'uninfluenced by any definite philological tradition'[1]. 'Clear, sound, and independent judgement, formed always on first-hand study, is one of Madvig's greatest characteristics'[2]. 'He never lost sight of the real position and value of classical philology.... It is not in the literary enjoyment afforded by the Greek and Latin writers, nor in the gymnastic training given to the mind by mastering their grammar, that he places their educational value; but in the fact that they offer the necessary and the only means of obtaining a first-hand view of the Graeco-Roman world, and therefore of the fore-time of European civilization'[3]. 'He was always impressing on the students that the ultimate and highest aim of their studies was to gain a sure insight into history, a clear and living idea of the life of the Greek and Roman world'[4].

All the classical scholars of modern Denmark were trained by Madvig during the half century of his tenure of the Latin Professorship. His general character was marked by a hatred of empty talk and exaggerated phrases, a strong sense of justice and an unswerving integrity. He had a singular grace and ease of manner[5]. In carrying out, however, the principle of his favourite motto, 'speaking the truth in love', he often appeared to emphasise the first part of that motto even more than the second. One of his pupils has aptly applied to his master the language once applied by the latter to the Father of History:—

'quem ob argumenti amplitudinem ingeniique candorem et suavitatem veneramur et diligimus'[6].

The jubilee volume of *Opuscula* presented to Madvig in 1876 by some of his former pupils included papers by R. Christensen (1843—1876), the student of Greek history and archaeology[7], criticisms on Aristotle's *Rhetoric* and *Poetic* by Ussing[8], emendations of Plautus by Sophus Bugge of Christiania[9], and of other Latin authors by Whitte, the translator of Terence[10], translations from Hesiod by C. P. Christensen Schmidt[10], and, lastly, emenda-

---

[1] Nettleship's *Essays*, ii 4 f.   [2] *ib.* 19.

[3] *Kleine Schriften*, 285 f (Nettleship, 20).

[4] Gertz, *ib.* 21 f.   [5] *Cl. Rev.* i 124.

[6] J. L. Heiberg, in *Biogr. Jahrb.* 1886, 202—221; cp. M. C. Gertz in *Berlin. Phil. Woch.* 5 and 12 Feb. 1887, and esp. in Bricka's *Dansk Biografisk Lexicon*; John Mayor in *Cl. Rev.* i 123 f; Nettleship's *Essays*, ii 1—23.

[7] Life in *Tidskrift*, Ser. II iii 279.

[8] p. 325 *infra*.   [9] p. 331 *infra*.

[10] p. 328 *infra*.

tions of Quintilian by M. Cl. Gertz, and remarks on early mediaeval Latin by V. Thomsen, both of whom are still professors at
Copenhagen.

Among Danish editions of Cicero, which had the advantage
of contributions from Madvig, were Rudolf Henrichsen's *De
Oratore* (1830), P. H. Tregder's *Tusculan Disputations* (1841),
and G. F. W. Lund's *De Officiis* (1848). The first of these,

Henrichsen   Henrichsen (1800—1871), was one of the students
associated with Madvig and Elberling in their joint
edition of Garatoni[1]. He was afterwards a schoolmaster at Sorö
and Odense, and was specially interested in the *Anthologia
Palatina*, and in Byzantine and modern Greek; but his principal
work was the above-mentioned *De Oratore*, in which he was

Elberling   further aided by Elberling. Carl Wilhelm Elberling
(1800—1870), the rector of a school in Copenhagen,
produced a useful edition of Plato's *Apology* and *Crito*; he also
studied the Greek lexicographers, and contributed to the London
edition of the Greek *Thesaurus* of H. Stephanus.

Bojesen   E. F. C. Bojesen (1803—1864), whose Copenhagen
dissertations on Greek Music and on Aristotle's *Problems* acquired some celebrity in Germany, was ultimately rector of Sorö.
He edited Sallust; his Handbook of Roman Antiquities (1839),
mainly founded on Madvig's lectures, and his similar work on
Greek Antiquities[2], were translated into German and other languages. His later papers on Aristotle's *Politics*[3], and his translation of *Ethics* viii and ix[4], attained a considerable popularity.

Wesenberg   A. S. Wesenberg (1804—1876), who was a pupil
and afterwards a master at Viborg, owes his repu-
tation to his critical edition of Cicero's *Letters*[5], which was preceded and succeeded by the publication of 'Emendations' on the
text. He also published *Emendatiunculae Livianae* in modest
imitation of Madvig's *Emendationes*. The editor of the *Tusculan

Tregder   Disputations*, P. H. Tregder (1815—1887), rector
of Aalborg, wrote a Danish history of Greek art, a
handbook of Greek and Latin literature (twice translated into

---

[1] p. 320 *supra*.   [2] E. T. 1848.
[3] Sorö progr. 1844 f, 1851 f.   [4] 1858.
[5] Teubner text, Leipzig, 1872-3.

German), a handbook of Greek Mythology, and a distinctly meritorious Greek Grammar (1844). Lastly, G. F.

W. Lund (1820—1891), who began his scholastic career at Christianshavn and Copenhagen and ended it at Aalborg and Aarhus, was 'adjunct' to the cathedral-school of Nykjöbing during the intermediate time when he was editing the *Cato Major* and *Laelius* as well as the *De Officiis* of Cicero, and the *Philippics* and *De Corona* of Demosthenes.

The scholar associated with Madvig in his edition of the text of Livy was Johan Louis Ussing (1820—1905).

As a student at Copenhagen, Ussing was not attracted by Bröndsted to the study of classical archaeology, for Bröndsted was then lecturing on classical philology. He was far more distinctively a pupil of Madvig, who inspired him with a keenly critical temper, without succeeding in interesting him either in Roman Institutions or in Latin Syntax. Madvig, in fact, recommended Ussing to devote himself to archaeology, and introduced him to the art-critic Höyen, who prompted him to study Greek vases, and thus led to his writing the dissertation *de nominibus vasorum Graecorum* (1844).

After travelling for two years in Italy and Greece[1], he lectured on the topography and monuments of Athens, and was appointed Reader in Philology and Archaeology in 1847, the date of his publication of certain Greek inscriptions. Madvig's absence on public service led to Ussing's taking a larger share in the philological lectures, and he became a full professor three years later. While he was associated with Madvig in his edition of Livy, his own masterpiece was his annotated edition of Plautus (1875–87). In that work his sobriety as a textual critic is suggestive of the influence of Madvig. He published critical observations on Aristotle's *Rhetoric* and *Poetic*[2]; and a commentary on the *Characters* of Theophrastus, and on Philodemus *De Vitiis* (1868). His

---

[1] Cp. *Rejsebilleder fra Syden*, 1847; the 'Thessalian tour' and the paper on the Parthenon are included in *Gr. Reisen und Studien*, 1857. His later reminiscences are entitled *Fra en Rejse* (1873), *Fra Hellas og Lilleasien* (1883), and *Nedre-Ægypten* (1889).

[2] *Opuscula ad Madvigium missa*, 221 f.

brief sketch of Greek and Roman Education[1], and his manual of *Metrik*[2] (1893), were translated into German. One of his papers (1896), in which he proposed a new date for Vitruvius, was translated into English[3]. He was the founder of the Museum of Classical Archaeology at Copenhagen, and bequeathed to the Museum his collection of archaeological books. Even in extreme old age he was one of the keenest and most eager of workers, and we are assured by the author of a tribute to his memory that the expression of weariness prominent in his portrait at Copenhagen is untrue to his real character[4].

One of the ablest and most promising of the pupils of Madvig, H. F. F. Nutzhorn (1834—1866), began his brief career by publishing valuable papers on Greek mythology, and on the history of Greek literature, and the lost Epics of the Trojan Cycle[5]. As a candidate for the degree of Doctor, he discussed the origin of the Homeric poems, and his treatise on that subject was published in Danish in 1863. He soon began to lecture with remarkable success on Aristophanes; and, with a view to his further studies, he paid two visits to Italy, late in 1863 and in 1865. On the second of these visits he collated the Venice MSS of Aristophanes, and was looking forward to visiting Greece for the purpose of studying its modern language and literature, when, at the early age of thirty-one, he died of typhoid fever in February, 1866[6]. A German translation of his treatise on the Homeric poems, which had been contemplated while he was still living, was successfully completed

Nutzhorn

[1] 1863–5; Germ. trans. 1874, 1885[2].

[2] New ed. 1895.

[3] Refuted by Krohn, *Berl. Philol. Woch.* 1897, 773; cp. Schanz § 355, p. 350; and M. H. Morgan, in *Harvard Studies*, xvii·(1906) 9; also Degering, in *Rhein. Mus.* 1902, and *Berl. Phil. Woch.* 1907, nos. 43—49. In 1894 Ussing dealt with the 'developement of the Greek column', and in 1897 with the 'history and monuments of Pergamos' (Germ. trans. 1899).

[4] J. L. Heiberg, *Danske Videnskabernes Selskab* (Copenhagen), 3 Nov., 1905, 71—75; cp. E. Trojel in *Nordisk Tidsskrift*, Ser. III, xiii 92—96, with portrait and bibliography; and Sam Wide in *Berl. Phil. Woch.* 1898, 878 f; also biographical sketch and bibliography by Drachmann in *Biogr. Jahrb.* 1907, 125—151, partly founded on Ussing's autobiography (1906).

[5] *Tidskrift*, Ser. I, ii—vii.

[6] Cp. Gertz, in Bricka.

three years after his death, when it was published with a preface
by Madvig[1]. Wolf's views had been criticised by Madvig in his
lectures on Greek literature, and it was these lectures that had
impelled his pupil to take up the question. Madvig, while
admitting the importance of Wolf's famous *Prolegomena* as a
stimulating work, which had justified its existence by destroying
a 'far too naïve tradition,' himself describes it as lacking in
perspicuity, as illogical and inconclusive, and as having turned
the criticism of Homer on to a wrong track[2].

Nutzhorn compares the consequent condition of Homeric criticism to "a
pathless wilderness in which the 'guiding star' might possibly prove a mere
will o' the wisp"[3]. Dividing his own work into two parts, 'historical evidence',
and 'internal criteria', he deals with the former under four heads :—(1) the
evidence on the text; (2) the story about Peisistratus; (3) the Homeridae;
and (4) the contrast between the earlier ἀοιδοί and the later ῥαψῳδοί. He
shows (1) that the known variations of reading do not point to more than
one ancient redaction ; (2) that the evidence as to Peisistratus is late, conflicting, and, in general, unsatisfactory, while Wolf's inference, that the *Iliad*
and *Odyssey* did not exist in a complete form before the time of Peisistratus,
is disproved by 'Homeric reminiscences' in poets as early as Hesiod, Archilochus, Alcman and Hipponax, and by scenes from the *Iliad* on the chest
of Cypselus. (3) Modern criticism is not justified (he urges) in regarding the
Chian clan of the Homeridae as rhapsodes; this chapter is less satisfactory
than the rest of the work. (4) The contrast between the leisurely bards
of the olden age, who sang successive portions of lengthy epic poems at the
courts of chieftains, and the rhapsodes of a later time, who hurriedly rehearsed
selected passages amid the excitement of a popular festival, suggests that
the former is the mode of recitation for which epic poetry was originally
intended, and shows that, in form as well as substance, the Homeric poems
are the creation of a pre-historic age. The rhapsodes were 'an uncongenial
and even destructive element', but the mischief done by them was counteracted
by statesmen like Solon[4], and by the more extended use of writing in Greece.

In the second part Nutzhorn criticises the various attempts that had been
made to resolve the *Iliad* into short lays, and contends that the small
discrepancies, which had been noticed by modern critics with the printed

---

[1] *Die Entstehungsweise der Homerischen Gedichte; Untersuchungen über
die Berechtigung der auflösenden Homerkritik* (Teubner, Leipzig, 1869, 268
pp.).

[2] p. vii.

[3] p. 4; cp. Blass, *Interpolationen in der Odyssee*, 1 'ein Sumpf..., auf dem
die Irrlichter flackerten '.

[4] i 19 *supra*.

page before them, would have passed unobserved by the original audience, and did not suffice to prove a difference of authorship. He also discusses Grote's *Achilleid*, pointing out that the lengthy portions of the *Iliad*, which do not belong to the *Achilleid*, may be regarded as episodes characteristic of the earliest epic poetry, and as serving to help the original audience to realise the long absence of Achilles from the field of battle.

The author is perhaps unduly violent in his invective against the views then prevalent in Northern Germany, and political differences between Denmark and Prussia appear to give a keener edge to his controversial temper. But the permanent value of his work is hardly impaired by the patriotic spirit which makes it (for our present purpose) a characteristic product of the scholarship of Denmark[1].

From the classical scholars we may now turn to four of the Danish translators of the Classics:—(1) the learned lady, Birgitte Thott (1610—1662), who translated Seneca (1658), and Epictetus and Cebes (1661); (2) the Danish poet, C. F. E.

Translators   Wilster (1797—1840), whose renderings of Homer and of eight plays of Euripides are among the classics of his country; (3) the scholar and schoolmaster, H. K. Whitte (1810—1894), who translated Terence into Danish verse; and (4) C. P. C. Schmidt (1832—1895), who continued Wilster's translation of Euripides, and also published excellent renderings of Hesiod[2], Heliodorus and Apollonius Rhodius[3]. Meanwhile, in Iceland, Sveinbjörn Egilsson (1791—1852) had produced, in verse as well as prose, a magnificent translation of the whole of Homer, revealing in his vigorous poetic rendering of the *Odyssey* in particular[4] a perfect consciousness of the kinship between the spirited style of the old Greek Epic and that of the Northern Sagas. His marvellous command of the poetic resources of the old Norse language is also fully proved by his important *Lexicon poëticum antiquae linguae Septentrionalis* (1860)[5].

In conclusion we must briefly mention two Comparative Phi-

---

[1] See esp. D. B. Monro's discriminating notice in the *Academy*, i 26 f.

[2] *Opuscula ad...Madvigium...missa* (1876), 279—293.

[3] Life in *Tidsskrift*, Ser. III, iv 94; papers on Greek Syntax, *ib.* Ser. II (1874-93).

[4] Ed. 1854; *Iliad* in prose, Reykjavik, 1855; *Ljóðmæli, ib.* 1856 (Latin poems on pp. 247—292; Greek, 293).

[5] Late in the previous century an edition of Terence (1780) had been produced in Iceland by Gudmundur Magnússon (1741—1798); p. 318 *supra*.

lologists, Rasmus Kristian Rask (1787—1832) and Karl Adolf
Verner (1846—1896). Rask studied Icelandic in
Copenhagen in 1807 and subsequently visited Iceland. His 'Investigations on the origin of the old
Northern or Icelandic language' were completed in 1814, but
the work was not published until four years later. Meanwhile he
was enabled to extend his knowledge of European and Asiatic
languages by going abroad for six years (1816–22). The first
third of this time was spent in Stockholm, the next in Finland,
Russia and Persia, and the third in India. It was during this
memorable tour that he was the first of European scholars to
acquire a grammatical knowledge of 'Zend'. In 1825 he became
professor of the history of Asiatic literature at Copenhagen, and,
late in life, attained the goal of his ambition in a professorship of
oriental languages. But he was already in failing health, and
died soon after at the early age of 45 [1].

The point of interest in Rask is his partial anticipation of a
law laid down by Jakob Grimm. Rask, in his work on Icelandic
and other languages, gave proof of his having already partially
discovered the law underlying the relations between the mute
consonants (more especially the dentals) in Gothic, Scandinavian,
and German. The work (published in 1818) did not come to
the knowledge of Grimm until the eve of the publication of the
first edition of his *Deutsche Grammatik* (1819)[2]; he immediately
recognised its importance, and this recognition left its traces on
his second edition (1822)[3]. It was here that he fully and scien-
tifically enunciated the law as to the consonantal relations between
(1) Sanskrit, Greek and Latin; (2) High German and (3) Low
German (including English), which in England has always been
known as 'Grimm's law'[4]. But the law has its exceptions. The
discovery that these exceptions were due to the original accentuation of the Indo-Germanic languages was made by Verner. The

---

[1] Life by N. M. Petersen in Rask's and in Petersen's *Afhandlinger*; and
by V. Thomsen, in Bricka; cp. Max Müller's *Lectures*, i 185, 231[5].

[2] Pref. p. xviii (quoted by R. von Raumer, 508).

[3] R. von Raumer's *Gesch. der Germ. Philol.* (1870) 470—486, 507—515;
H. Paul's *Grundriss* (ed. 1901) 80—83; cp. Giles' *Manual*, § 39.

[4] Giles, § 99.

son of a Saxon father and a Danish mother, he was born and
bred in Denmark, was absent, for six years only,

Verner

as a librarian at Halle, and on his return in 1883
became, for the last sixteen years of his life, lecturer and ultimately
'extraordinary' professor of Slavonic languages at his own university
of Copenhagen[1].   He was not a classical scholar ; he never wrote
on anything but comparative philology, phonetics, and Russian
literature, and, except at his matriculation, never passed a classical examination.   Even in his special province of Comparative
Philology he only published three papers, but the name of the
author of 'Verner's law' will probably be perpetually remembered
in the history of the science of language[2].   The discovery of
'Grimm's law' had been partially anticipated by a Dane ; and it
was another native of Denmark who happily explained its apparent
exceptions.

So long as Norway was united to Denmark, Copenhagen was

Norway :
university of
Christiania

the university frequented by students from both
countries, except so far as they resorted to seats
of learning in foreign lands[3].   The desire of the
Norwegians for a university of their own, first openly expressed in
1661, remained unsatisfied until 1811, when the university of
Christiania was founded by Frederick VI[4].   Three years later,
Norway was separated from Denmark and was united with
Sweden,—a union recognised by the Congress of Vienna in 1815
and peacefully dissolved in 1905, when the throne of Norway was
accepted by a prince of Denmark.

In 1814 the separation of Norway from Denmark gave a new
impulse to an independent Norwegian literature ; but the literature

[1] Life by M. Vibæk (with three portraits) in Verner's *Afhandlinger og
Breve* (Cop. 1893).   Cp. V. Thomsen, in Bricka.

[2] The law was first propounded in Kuhn's *Zeitschrift*, xxiii (1877) 97—130,
Eine Ausnahme der ersten Lautverschiebung (reprinted in the *Afhandlinger*,
with two other papers, and with reviews and letters, and phonometric investigations).   Cp. H. Paul's *Grundriss* (1901) 126 f, 369, 386—506 ; King and
Cookson's *Introduction* (1890) 83 f ; and Giles, §§ 42, 104.

[3] *e.g.* Cologne, Prague and Rostock (cp. L. Daae, *Nordiske Studerende*,
Chr. 1875, 1885).

[4] *Minerva*, II.

of Norway has proved to be more independent than its scholarship. As we shall see in the immediate sequel, the foremost
representative of classical and comparative philology in Christiania
owed much to his training in Copenhagen and Berlin. But, in
more than one point, his work is marked by a distinct independence.

'Verner's law', propounded (as we have seen) by a native of
Denmark[1], was further investigated by a native of
Norway.   The   investigator   was   Sophus   Bugge   **Bugge**
(1833—1907). At the age of seventeen, while he was still a
student in Christiania, he produced a paper on consonantal
changes in the Norwegian dialects[2]; and he was barely twenty
when he began to contribute to Kuhn's *Zeitschrift*[3]. His high
promise in the science of language was recognised by his receiving
a royal grant which enabled him to spend two years at the
universities of Copenhagen and Berlin (1858–60). In Copenhagen he studied Latin under Madvig, and Sanskrit under
Westergaard; in Berlin, Sanskrit under Weber and Bopp, and
Germanic philology under Haupt.   In 1864 the offer of a
professorship of Old Norse at the Swedish university of Lund
expedited his appointment to a professorship of Comparative
Philology in Christiania, a position which he held for the more
than forty remaining years of his life. His numerous distinctions
included honorary degrees at the fourth centenary of Upsala
(1877), and at the third of Edinburgh (1884). His reputation
mainly rests on his researches into the languages and literatures
and mythology of Scandinavia, on his works relating to the
ancient Italic dialects, and on his acute (though perhaps unduly
bold) emendations of the text of Plautus[4]. In 1873 he edited the
Mostellaria[5], and, two years later, the play was performed in

---

[1] p. 330 *supra*.

[2] Gubernatis, *Dict. Int.* 1888 *s.v.*

[3] ii 382–7 (on Oscan).

[4] *Tidskrift for Filologi*, I vi (1865–6) 1–20, vii 1—58; *Philologus*,
xxx 636, xxxi 247-62; *Neue Jahrb.* cvii (1873) 401–19; *Opusc. ad Madvigium*,
153—192.

[5] Reviewed by Lorenz in *Philol. Anzeiger* vii 215-9 (on Lorenz, cp.
Ussing's *Suum cuique* in *Tidskrift*, I viii (1868 f) 204—212).

honour of the jubilee of one of the professors of Christiania[1]. The
papers which he published in German included etymological
contributions to Curtius' *Studien*[2], and studies on ' Verner's law '[3],
and on the old Italic dialects[4]; he also aided Whitley Stokes in
his 'Old Breton Glosses '. In his 'Studies on the origin of the
old Northern legends of gods and heroes' he aroused considerable
controversy by maintaining that the Scandinavian mythology was
partly derived from Greek and Latin, and Jewish and Christian,
sources, and by further suggesting that this element was imported
in the age of the Vikings by Northmen who had visited the
British Islands[5]. From Scandinavian mythology he suddenly
turned to the study of runic inscriptions, and to the investigation
of the Etruscan language[6], the origin of which he endeavoured to
elucidate by means of two inscriptions of Lemnos[7]. By all these
vigorous incursions into several important provinces of learning
he gave signal proof of being a most versatile representative of
Scandinavian scholarship[8].

During the Revival of Learning it was the school of Law at
Perugia which supplied the link between certain
scholars of Sweden and the Italian humanists.
Conrad Rogge, a Swede of Westphalian origin, who
had graduated at Leipzig in 1449, resumed his studies by spending
five years (1455–60) at Perugia[9]. He there transcribed for himself

Sweden:
Rogge

[1] L. C. M. Aubert (born in 1807), professor of Latin; a writer on Terence,
and on Latin *Verbal flexion* (1875).

[2] iv (1871) 203 f, 325—354.

[3] Paul and Braune's *Beiträge* (Halle), xii (1887) 399—430; xiii (1888) 167—
186, 311—332.

[4] Christiania, 1878; and Kuhn's *Zeitschrift*, xxii 385—466.

[5] Chr. 1881; Germ. Trans., Munich, 1881–2; criticised by G. Stephens
(London, 1883), and others; cp. *A. J. P.* iii 80, and further literature in
Halvorsen's *Norsk Forfatter-Lexikon* (1885—1901), i 513 f.

[6] Deecke's *Etr. Forschungen*, iv (1883); Bezzenberger's *Beiträge* xi (1886);
Etr. und Armenisch, Chr. 1890.

[7] Chr. 1886 (Bursian's *Jahresb.* lxxxvii 112).

[8] Bibliography in Halvorsen's *Lexikon*, and in *Upsala Jubelfest*, 1877,
p. 353.

[9] Similarly Birgerus Magni, the future bishop of Vesterås, had graduated at
Leipzig (1438) and Perugia (1448); Annerstedt, *Upsala Universitets Historia*,
i (1877) 21.

a speech of Demosthenes and several of the works of Cicero, besides two of the recent orations of the Italian humanist, Aeneas Sylvius Piccolomini.   During his stay in Italy he purchased a fine MS of Lactantius, 'the Christian Cicero', and, on the blank pages at the end, preserved a copy of the brief and unimportant Latin speech delivered by himself in 1460, with a view to his receiving the Doctor's degree.   As the first of the long series of Latin orations written by natives of Sweden, it has a peculiar interest; it is clearly founded on classical models, it is rich in rhetorical phrases, but it has hardly any other merit[1].   Before returning to Sweden, Rogge visited Florence, and stayed for two months at Siena, where Aeneas Sylvius was then residing.   From 1479 to his death in 1501 he was bishop of Strengnäs, where his MS of Lactantius is still preserved[2].   He deserves to be remembered as the earliest of the humanists of Sweden[3].

The spirit of the Revival was still more strongly represented by the brothers Johannes and Olaus Magni.   The elder of these, Johannes Magni (1488—1544), had studied at the Catholic universities of Louvain and Cologne ; and his character was doubtless fully formed when, at the age of 32, he was sent to Rome as the envoy of Sweden, and received a degree in Theology at Perugia[4].   The influence of Italian humanism is nevertheless clearly visible in the correctness of his Latinity and in his inordinate passion for fame.   In 1523 he was sent as Legate to Sweden by Adrian VI (his former preceptor at Louvain).   He was soon elected archbishop of Upsala, but in 1526 was compelled to go into exile, living first at Danzig and finally in Rome.   As the last of the Catholic archbishops of Sweden, he wrote a Latin history of all his predecessors, and also a history of 'all the kings of the Goths and Swedes'.   The latter, with its infinite series of fabulous princes, is

The brothers Magni

---

[1] Printed in Benzelius, *Monum. eccles.* (1709) 106; cp. Henrik Schück, in Schück and Warburg's *Illustrerad Svensk Litteraturhistoria*, i (1896) 167.

[2] Aminson, *Bibl. Templi Cath. Strengensis, Praef.* iv, and *Suppl.*

[3] *Svenskt Biografiskt Lexikon* (Upsala, 1835 f), N. F. (1883) *s.v.* For lives of all the natives of Sweden mentioned in this chapter, cp. the above *Lexikon*, 33 vols., and Linder's *Nordisk Familjebok*, 18 vols., Stockholm, 1876—94.

[4] *Life* by Olaus Magnus in *Script. Rer. Suec.* iii (2), 1876, p. 74, 'accepto in theologia magisterio' during his residence at the 'gymnasium Perusinum'.

a still more uncritical performance than the elaborately written and curiously illustrated 'history of the northern nations', which was published in Rome in 1555 by his younger brother, 'Olaus Magnus' (1490—1557)[1].

Meanwhile, not long before the birth of the brothers Magni, the university of Upsala had come into being. In accordance with a solemn decree of the Swedish clergy, the university was formally founded by archbishop Ulfsson in 1477. In that year, Sixtus IV sanctioned the institution of a *studium generale* in Sweden, on the model of Bologna; the actual pattern adopted was probably that of Cologne or Rostock, while the archbishop and the regent of the realm conceded to the new seat of learning the royal privileges of Paris[2]. Hitherto the Swedes had studied mainly in Paris, Prague, Erfurt, Leipzig, Rostock or Greifswald[3]. Even after 1477, they resorted to the last three universities[4], and, early in the next century, to the Protestant university of Wittenberg or the Catholic university of Cologne[5]. The university of Upsala, founded during the regency of Sten Sture (1470—1503), was splendidly endowed by Gustavus Adolphus (1611-32), who, in 1630, followed up his conquest of Livonia by founding the university of Dorpat. Ten years later, during the minority of his daughter, Christina, a university was founded for Finland at Åbo, there to remain until the town was destroyed by fire in 1827 and the university transferred to Helsingfors.

University of Upsala

Dorpat and Åbo

The first Swede who certainly studied Greek was the turbulent archbishop, Gustaf Trolle (*c.* 1485—1535), who, as a student at Cologne in 1512, was instructed in the *Erotemata* of Chrysoloras. His own copy of that catechism of Greek Grammar, dated 1507, passed with the books of the younger Benzelius into the library at Linköping. On the blank leaf next to the preface, Trolle wrote a short Latin life of Chrysoloras, preceded by the items given below :—firstly, his own

Greek in Sweden: Trolle

---

[1] Schück, 167–9.   [2] Annerstedt, i 23 f; Rashdall, ii 290 f.

[3] Annerstedt, i 5—14.

[4] Stiernhielm (p. 338 *infra*) graduated at Greifswald, which subsequently belonged to Sweden from 1648 to 1815.

[5] Annerstedt, i 15, 44.

name written in the capital letters of the newly acquired language, and next, the name of his instructor, and the date on which he began his study of Greek.

ΤΡΟΛΛΕ

Peculiaris ifta Grece Litterature inftitutio a Johanne Cefario Juliacenfi[1] *in Colonienfi Achademia pridie Kalend. Majas Anni duodecimi fupra < dicto > feculo profpero Hercule feliciter aufpicata*[2].

In the same age Laurentius Andreae, or Lars Andersson (1482—1552), archdeacon of Upsala and chancellor of Gustavus Vasa, gives proof of an independent knowledge of the Greek text in his Swedish version of the New Testament founded on Luther's translation and published at Stockholm in 1526[3]. The same holds good of the Swedish Bible produced in 1541, and partly revised in 1543-9, by the brothers Olaus and Laurentius Petri, or Olof and Lars Petersson, both of whom had studied Greek under Melanchthon at Wittenberg[4]. Laurentius Petri (1499—1573) was archbishop of Upsala from 1531 to his death in 1573. His son-in-law, Laurentius Petri Gothus (1529—1579), who similarly studied Greek at Wittenberg, prefixed to his Latin elegiac poem of 1559 a Greek epigram of his own composition[5]. In 1566 he was appointed by Erik XIV to teach Greek at the university (which had meanwhile passed through a period of decline), and in 1573-9 he was the successor of his father-in-law as archbishop of Upsala.

(marginal notes: Laurentius Andreae; Olaus and Laurentius Petri; Laurentius Petri Gothus)

In 1580, under the catholic king, Johan III, the university was closed, and the professors imprisoned; but the king was not uninterested in Greek, for he instructed Erik, bishop of Åbo, to translate the Swedish liturgy into Greek and to present it to the patriarch of Constantinople[6]. In 1584 the first item in a collection of *Carmina* congratulating Christian Barthold of Viborg on

---

[1] Of Juliers or Jülich, near Cologne (1460—1551). Cp. Jöcher, *s.v.*

[2] E. M. Fant, *Historiola Litteraturae Graecae in Suecia* (ad ann. 1700), in 14 parts forming two vols. with Suppl., Upsala, 1775—1786, i 9.

[3] Fant, i 13; Colophon in Schück, 177.

[4] Fant, i 15 f.   [5] *ib.* i 19.

[6] *ib.* i 20.

receiving a degree from Johann Possel (1528—1591), the Greek
professor at Rostock, was a set of 24 Greek hexameters contributed by Olaus Martini, archbishop of
Upsala,—one of the first Greek poems produced in Sweden[1].
In the same year, Jacob Erik, Greek professor at
Upsala, published an edition of Isocrates *ad Demonicum*[2].

Olaus Martini

Jacob Erik

In 1604–13 professorships in Mathematics and Hebrew were
held by Johan Rudbeck (1581—1646), the future
bishop of Vesterås, who studied Greek at Wittenberg, and required his pupils always to speak either Latin or
Greek[3]. In a synod which he held at Reval in 1627, the less
learned clergy listened in amazement while his secretaries dis-
puted in Greek with Gabriel Holsten of Vesterås (1598—1649),
who, like Rudbeck, had learnt his Greek at Wittenberg[4]. In
1621 a professorship of Greek was instituted at Upsala by Gustavus Adolphus, the Chair being filled in 1622 by Laurentius
Matthiae, and in 1624—40[5] by Johannes Stalenus,
who held disputations in Greek and produced
fifteen sets of verses in that language[6].

J. Rudbeck

Stalenus

The 'Constitutions' of 1626 required the professor to teach the Grammar
of Clenardus or Gvalperius[7], and to illustrate it in a 'Socratic' manner from
the Greek Testament and the Fathers, and from Homer, Euripides, Pindar,
Theocritus, Sophocles and Gregory Nazianzen, at 7 o'clock in the morning.
At 3 P.M. the professor of Poetry was to give instruction in the art of writing
verses in accordance with the precepts of Aristotle, or any other approved
author, with examples from the Greek poets and from Virgil, Horace,
Buchanan, Ovid etc.[8] In the *Collegium Regium*, founded at Stockholm in
1625 by the celebrated statesman Johan Skytte, the study of Latin and Greek

---

[1] Quoted by Fant, i 21—25, who in the note adds a list of 50 sets of
Greek verses by other Swedes, not mentioned elsewhere in his work, with
50 more on pp. 117 f.

[2] Fant, i 25 f.

[3] Fant, i 41; Annerstedt, i 116 f, 122 f; portrait in Schück, 193.

[4] Fant, i 53.   [5] Annerstedt, i 194, 248.

[6] Fant, i 64, ii 107.

[7] 'Otho Gualtperius' of Wittenberg (1546—1624).

[8] Lundstedt, *Bidrag till kännedomen om Grekiska Språkets Studium vid de
Svenska Läroverken från äldsta till närvarande tid* (Stockholm, 1875, 84 pp.),
18, with many other details as to the teaching of Greek in schools.

is enjoined, *quia ut Latina sine Graeca recte non intelligitur, sic ne Graeca sine Latina explicari quidem et tradi potest*[1]. Greek is to be studied, not merely in the Grammar, but also in some *libellus succi plenus*. The authors specially named are Demosthenes, Isocrates, and Homer[2].

The study of Greek rose to a higher level under a pupil of Stalenus named Henricus Ausius (1603—1659), a man of such high reputation in his day that no foreigner (we are informed) visited Upsala without calling upon him. He was professor of Greek in 1641–6, and his inaugural oration *de necessitate Graecarum litterarum* led to his being recognised as the *stator*, or true founder, of the study of Greek in Sweden. He published five disputations and fifteen epigrams in that language[3]. He was a many-sided man, being also proficient in Law and Natural Science.

Ausius

In Sweden the Reformation of 1527 was followed by a pale reflexion of the Italian Renaissance. Even the distant North awoke to a new admiration for the unapproachable perfection of the ancient Latin poets, and endeavoured to realise the literary associations of the Augustan age. Every princeling was eager to play the part of an Augustus or a Maecenas, and looked for a new Virgil to sing his praises. The demand soon created the supply. By the orders of 1571 and 1611, the boys in the highest class of the public schools were required to write a set of Latin verses once a week. The model for these verses was Virgil, just as Cicero was naturally the model for prose; and, even in the case of versifiers of maturer years, the poem which was a perfect cento of Virgilian phraseology was invariably deemed the best. This type of artificial composition was introduced by a German humanist, Henricus Mollerus, Hessus (*fl.* 1557–9), who was summoned to Sweden by Gustavus Vasa to celebrate her ancient kings[4]. The first Swede to win repute as a Latin poet was Laurentius Petri Gothus, who was followed by Ericus Jacobi, by the prolific versifier Sylvester Johannis Phrygius,

Latin verse

H. Mollerus

Laurentius Petri Gothus

---

[1] Lundstedt, 27 f.   [2] *ib.* 28.

[3] Fant, i 78—81, ii 108, Annerstedt, i 408 f.

[4] He was one of the tutors of the younger sons of Gustavus Vasa ; cp. Gestrin, *De Statu Rei Litt. in Suecia*, i (1785) 9 (ap. Fant, ii 2) ; and Schück, 219.

and by Laurentius Fornelius (1606—1673), the compiler of an art

Fornelius   of poetry, the *Poëtica Tripartita* (1643), whose own
verses (we are assured) could not be distinguished
from those of Virgil, for the simple reason that they were exclusively written *phrasibus Virgilianis*[1]. The only importance of this
kind of 'poetry' lies in the fact that it taught the Swedes to
appreciate for the first time the significance of form, not only in
Latin, but also in their own language[2]. A few hexameters were
written in Swedish by the royal librarian, Buraeus (1568—1652)[3],

**Buraeus and
Stiernhielm**   the tutor of Gustavus Adolphus. Buraeus was also
the tutor of Stiernhielm, the 'father of Swedish
poetry' (1598—1672), who, by his greatest poem,
the didactic allegory on the Choice of Hercules, made the classical
hexameter one of the national metres of Sweden[4]. Stiernhielm
was at once poet and geometer, philosopher and philologist. As
a philologist he held the patriotic view that almost all languages
were descended from Old Norse[5].

A sounder and more scientific study of the Classics was

Loccenius   represented by his contemporary, Johannes Loccenius (1598—1677), a native of Holstein, one of
the three foreigners who were offered professorial Chairs at
Upsala in the reign of Gustavus Adolphus. The Chair accepted
by Loccenius in 1625 was that of History; he was afterwards
extraordinary professor of Political Philosophy, and (in the reign
of queen Christina) professor of Law, librarian, and historiographer. He was the first librarian of Upsala who constructed
and printed a catalogue, the first foreign scholar who made
his permanent abode in Sweden. His Curtius went through
twenty editions, only one of which, however, was printed in the
North[6]. His other works were connected with the history and
geography, the law and antiquities, of his adopted country[7].

---

[1] L. O. Wallius to Joh. Skytte, 1632 (Fant, i 66 note *v*).

[2] Schück, 219 f.   [3] *ib.* 248 f (portrait facing 256).

[4] *ib.* 248, 258 f, 321—330 (portrait facing 322).

[5] *Origines vocabulorum in linguis paene omnibus ex lingua Svetica veteri*,
Upsala, *s.a.*

[6] Stockholm, 1637; Nepos, *ib.* 1638.

[7] Schück, 261 f (with portrait); and Annerstedt, i 209 f, 336; further details
in the Swedish biographical dictionaries.

Queen Christina (1626—1689), the daughter and successor of Gustavus Adolphus, is connected with the history of scholarship by her wide and varied attainments and also by her patronage of learning during the ten years of her reign (1644–54) and the thirty-five years of her exile (1654–89).   At the age of ten she wrote a Latin letter to her tutor with the solemn promise *posthac velle loqui Latine cum nostro Praeceptore*[1].   In Latin her favourite author was Tacitus. At fourteen she knew all the languages and all the sciences and accomplishments her instructors could teach her[2].   At eighteen she could read Thucydides and Polybius in Greek; in 1649 she reminded Descartes how much he owed to Plato[3]; in 1652 Naudé wrote to Gassendi:—*elle a tout vû, elle a tout lû, elle sait tout*[4].   Educated far in advance of her subjects, she made a spirited attempt to 'engraft foreign learning on the Scandinavian stock'[5].   In pursuit of this aim she turned to the Netherlands and France, to Northern Germany and to the free imperial city of Strassburg, which, owing to its neutral position, remained unmolested as a seat of learning, while Germany at large was suffering from the Thirty Years' War (1618–48).   The Peace of Westphalia, largely due to her own efforts, left her at liberty to carry out her plan.

Grotius, her envoy in France, had already visited her court on the occasion of his recall, but he had soon withdrawn, to die on his homeward journey (1645)[6].   Isaac Vossius, who obeyed her summons in 1649, besides acquiring on her behalf the library of Alexander Petavius of Paris[7], sold her his own father's library, reserving to himself its superintendence, and subsequently appropriating part of its contents[8]. Nicholas Heinsius, a man of far nobler character, who arrived in the same year, was sent to Italy in 1651 to purchase books and MSS on her behalf[9], and, after her abdication, returned twice as his country's envoy.   Of two distinguished natives of France, who had recently resided in the Netherlands, Descartes 'found an honourable asylum and a premature death' at her court[10], while Salmasius left Leyden late in life to spend a single year under the patronage of Christina, who, in recognition of his pedantry, as well as his learning, once described him as *omnium fatuorum doctissimum*[11], and, by her supposed preference for Milton, in his great controversy with Salmasius, won from the author of the 'Second Defence of the English People' the splendid encomium beginning with the words :—*Tě*

---

[1] J. Arckenholtz, *Hist. Merkwürdigkeiten*, iv 264.

[2] J. Arckenholtz, *Mémoires*; French ed., iii 53.

[3] Arck. *Mém.* i 344 f; cp. Fant, i 89 f.

[4] Arck. ii *Append.* 39.   [5] Pattison, i 247.

[6] Cp. Arck. i 77—81 ; ii 317 *supra*.   [7] Arck. i 268, 270.

[8] Heinsius and Vossius, in Burman's *Sylloge*, iii 333, 683 ; Arck. i 272.

[9] *Ib.* i 278—288, and Heinsius to Christina, in Burman's *Sylloge*, v 734—774.   The MSS included Dioscorides and Pollux.

[10] Hallam, ii 461[4]; Arck. i 223—231.   [11] Arck. i 236.

vero magnanimam, Augusta, te tutam undique divina plane virtute ac sapientia munitam[1].   Marcus Meibom (1630—1710), the
Meibom
Naudé author of a treatise on ancient music, came from Denmark, and Gabriel Naudé (1600—1653), a Frenchman, who had lived long in Rome, was now her librarian in the North.   He had written on the art of dancing, and when, to amuse the queen, her French physician compelled Naudé to dance to the singing of Meibom, the scene which ensued led to the student of ancient music being banished from the court[2].   Samuel
Bochart
and Huet Bochart, the geographer and orientalist, arrived from Caen, bringing with him the youthful Huet, who spent his time in transcribing a MS of Origen in the royal library, and soon returned to Normandy[3].   Hermann Conring, who had vigorously refuted the
Conring
Comenius Papal Bull condemning the Peace of Westphalia, received a pension as Councillor of Sweden, and went back to his learned labours at Helmstädt, where he eloquently maintained the cause of Sweden against Poland[4], and gained a high reputation as the earliest historian of jurisprudence in Germany[5].   Comenius, who had published his *janua linguarum reserata* in 1631, was invited to reform the schools of Sweden in 1638, but declined on the ground that he had already been invited to reform the schools of England, and his subsequent visit in 1642 had no permanent result[6].   Strassburg sent no less than three of the representatives
Freinsheim of her flourishing school of Roman history.   The first of these, Freinsheim, the editor of Florus and Curtius, whose Latin panegyric on Gustavus Adolphus (1632) led to his invitation to Sweden ten years later, remained for nine years as librarian and historiographer, delivered at least twenty-three Latin orations[7], lauded Christina in prose, apostrophised her in verse as the *unicum septem columen trionum*[8], and ultimately returned to a more genial clime to complete his restoration of the lost decades of Livy[9].

Boekler Freinsheim's fellow-pupil, Boekler, was made professor of Eloquence at Upsala in 1649 and historiographer in the following year; but the favours granted him made him unpopular with the Swedish professors, nor was he more successful with the students.   Once, in 1650, during a lecture on Tacitus, he unfortunately observed that 'he would say more, if the *plumbea capita* of the Swedes could comprehend it,' whereupon he was soundly beaten by the students outside the lecture-room, and found himself compelled to return to his native land, but not without golden consolations on the part of Christina, as well as the perpetual title of historio-

---

[1] Milton's *Prose Works*, iv 281 Mitford.

[2] Arck. i 241.

[3] Huet, *Comment. de rebus suis*, 107 ; Arck. i 251 f; cp. ii 292 f *supra*.

[4] Arck. i 297, 375.

[5] O. Stobbe, Berlin, 1870 ; cp. ii 368 *supra*.

[6] Arck. i 291 f.   [7] Ed. 1655.

[8] Arck. i 290.   [9] ii 367 *supra*.

grapher of Sweden, which he fully justified by writing the history of the war with Denmark[1]. Boekler had been accompanied by his pupil, Scheffer (1621—1679), who, while the rest were only Scheffer birds of passage, made Sweden his permanent abode. During the remaining 31 years of his life he was at first professor of Eloquence and Political Philosophy, and afterwards librarian and professor of International Law at Upsala. He published treatises on Latin style and on Roman antiquities, together with editions of Phaedrus and Aphthonius, and of writers on tactics (Arrian and Mauricius), which gave proof of an aptitude for textual criticism, though the library of Upsala afforded him few opportunities for the study of ancient MSS. His own Greek MSS were ultimately purchased for the Library[2]. In a far higher sense than Loccenius of Holstein (whose daughter he married), or than his own countryman, Freinsheim, he was the true founder of classical philology in Sweden. His work in Sweden was in fact the principal permanent result of Christina's patronage of learning in the North[3].

Having long resolved on leaving the Lutheran communion, Christina found herself constrained to resign the throne in 1654. The daughter of the great champion of the protestant cause in Europe joined the Church of Rome at Innspruck, rode into Rome in the garb of an Amazon, received the rite of confirmation from Alexander VII, and, in compliment to the Pope and in avowal of her favourite hero, assumed the name of Christina Alexandra. The rest of her life was mainly spent in Rome, varied with visits to Paris where she attended a meeting of the Academy, and where Ménage once bored her by presenting to the impatient Amazon an inordinate number of 'men of merit'[4]. In Rome she took up her abode at the Farnese palace, though this was not her only place of residence. As in the North, she surrounded herself with savants. She enlarged her choice collections of manuscripts and of works of art[5]. She permitted Spanheim to reproduce her coins and medals in his work on Numismatics, and to dedicate Spanheim that work to herself in gratitude for her aid and her inspiration[6]. Many of the coins were also published by Havercamp[7] and the gems engraved by Bartoli[8]. Early in 1656, she formed an Academy whose members met once a week at her palace[9]. The first rule of literary style laid down for her Academy shortly before 1680 was the avoidance of false ornament, and the

---

[1] Arck. i 295 f.　　　[2] O. Celsius, *Bibl. Ups. Hist.* (1745) 49.

[3] Cp. Arck. i 294; Fant, i 123—133; Schück 262 f (with portrait, 264); and ii 368 *supra*.

[4] *Menagiana*, iv 24[3]; Arck. i 555.

[5] Catteau-Calleville, ii 291 f; Grauert, ii 323 f.

[6] 'Conscriptus hic liber non solum tuo nutu sed gazae tuae opibus instructus.'

[7] *Numophylacium Christinae* (1742); Arck. ii 83, 324 f.

[8] *Museum Odescalcum*, Rome, 1747—51.

[9] Arck. i 501 f, Jan. 1656.

imitation of the models followed in the ages of Augustus and of Leo X[1]. She was also recognised as the virtual founder of the quaint Academy of the Arcadians[2]. In 1668 she had some passing hopes of receiving the crown of Poland, but the self-exiled queen of Sweden was never really happier than when she was breathing the atmosphere of Rome. Thirty-five years after her abdication she died and was buried in the Basilica of St Peter's. In 1690 her MSS, which had been catalogued by Montfaucon[3], were purchased for the Vatican by Alexander VIII, who caused a medal to be struck in commemoration of the event[4]. Her collection of gems, medals, statues and pictures was bought by Don Livio Odescalchi, the nephew of Innocent XI. Many of the works of sculpture were removed to Spain, and one of these is well known as 'the group of San Ildefonso'[5]. The Vienna Cameo of Ptolemy Philadelphus and Arsinoe, and Correggio's picture of 'Mercury teaching Cupid to read in the presence of Venus,' now in the National Gallery of England, once belonged to the virgin queen Christina, while the Royal Library of Stockholm still possesses seventeen of her marble busts of famous men of old, including Homer, Demosthenes and Zeno[6].

The minority of Charles XI, the son of Christina's martial successor, Charles X, was marked by two events connected with the history of learning. The first of these was the foundation of the university of Lund (1668) in the district of Scania in South Sweden, which had ceased to belong to Denmark in 1658[7]. The second was the institution of the *Collegium Antiquitatum* for the study of the languages, legends, laws, ecclesiastical history, and antiquities of Sweden (1667). Its

University
of Lund

Collegium
Antiquitatum

---

[1] Arck. iv 28 (p. 41 of Germ. ed.), § 28.   [2] Arck. ii 137 f.

[3] 2111 MSS in *Bibliotheca Bibl.* 14—97; about 1900 was the number which passed into the Vatican; cp. *Dudikii Iter Romanum* (Vienna, 1855), *Codices msc. Graeci Reginae Sueciae*...ed. H. Stevenson sen., including Plutarch's *Moralia* and Strabo and a few other classical MSS (1888), and Mantheyer in *Mélanges d'archéologie et d'histoire*, xvii—xix, also Narducci's *Bibl. Alexandrina* (1877).

[4] Copied in Arck. ii 322.

[5] Hübner, *Ant. Bild. in Madrid*, 12 f, 73-9; Friederichs-Wolters, *Ant. Bild.* no. 1665.

[6] Fant, i 96. Cp., in general, J. Arckenholtz, *Mémoires concernant Christine*..., 4 vols. 4° (Amst. and Leipzig, 1751–70), the French ed. of the same author's *Hist. Merkwürdigkeiten* (1751–60); Catteau-Calleville's *Histoire*, 2 vols. (Paris, 1815): Ranke's *Popes of Rome*, Book viii § 9; Grauert's *Christina und ihr Hof* (Bonn, 1837–42); Pattison's *Essays*, i 246—255; F. W. Bain's *Christina* (1890), and the authorities quoted in most of these works.

[7] Weibull and Tegnér, *Lunds Universitets Historia*, 1868.

founder was Count Magnus Gabriel de la Gardie; Stiernhielm
was its first president, while its earliest members included classical
scholars, such as Loccenius and Scheffer, whom we have already
noticed, and Verelius and Normann, to whom we shall shortly
return. In the autograph list of their undertakings (1670)[1], Stiernhielm proposes to write on the origin and affinities of languages[2],
while Loccenius announces that he is already engaged on a Latin
translation of the laws of Sweden. In 1684 the Collegium was
transferred to Stockholm, and, in 1692, merged into a department
of the State.

At the time when Christina was gathering scholars around her
in the North, an excellent Latinist of Dorpat and
Upsala, Olof Verelius (1618—1682), was travelling   Verelius
abroad and delivering Latin orations in Paris on the Coronation
of Christina, and at Leyden on the Peace of Westphalia. He was
afterwards professor of History, and of Swedish Antiquities. His
Latin *Opuscula* were deemed worthy of publication
in 1730[3]. The tutors of Charles XI included   Figrelius
Edmund Figrelius (1622—1675), professor of His-   (Gripenhielm)
tory, and subsequently librarian and chancellor to his royal
pupil. Figrelius was a capable composer of Latin verse, and
was the author of eighteen learned dissertations in Latin prose,
while his treatise *De statuis illustrium Romanorum* (1666) makes
him an exception to the rule that the Swedish successors of the
German scholars patronised by Christina mainly confined themselves to attempting the composition of Ciceronian prose or
Virgilian verse[4]. Among these typical Swedish
humanists was Johan Columbus (1640—1684), who   J. Columbus
married a daughter of Scheffer. Columbus was professor of
Latin poetry at Upsala. He corresponded with N. Heinsius[5] on the
text of Valerius Flaccus, and was one of the best of the Latin poets
of Sweden[6]. He gave proof of an interest in Greek by translating

---

[1] Facsimile in Schück, facing p. 284.   [2] p. 338, n. 5 *supra.*

[3] Portrait in Schück, 265.

[4] Schück, 306; ennobled under the name of Gripenhielm.

[5] Burman's *Sylloge,* v 163—187.

[6] 'Omnium...suavissimus', says Ihre in his *Dissert. De Poëtis,* p. 27. His
contemporary, A. Nordenhielm (1633—1694), professor of Eloquence at Upsala (1672), was a master of Latin style.

and annotating 'an uncertain Greek writer's' Homeric allegories
on the wanderings of Ulysses (1678)[1]. Lastly, he wrote Swedish
verse and had a wide knowledge of modern languages[2]. An
interest in Latin and Swedish literature was also
combined in the person of Petrus Lagerlöf (1648—
1699), who, at the age of 20, distinguished himself as a Latin poet
and orator, and after travelling on the continent and in England,
was professor successively of Logic, Poetry, and Eloquence at
Upsala, and finally historiographer of Sweden. In his Latin
'Introduction to Swedish poetry' he opposed Stiernhielm's adoption of the Latin hexameter as the metre of vernacular verse[3].
His Latin 'orations, programs and poems' were published in
1780, nearly a century after his death. The Latin
orators of the age included Johan Upmark and Lars
Norrman. Upmark (1664—1743), the master of a
dignified type of Academic Latinity, whose gravest and most
solemn orations were not unfrequently enlivened with flashes of
wit[4], was ennobled under the name of Rosenadler, and ended his
days as an honorary Secretary of State. Norrman
(1651—1703) was professor of Oriental Languages
and Greek at Lund (1682) and of Greek at Upsala (1686), and
was ultimately archbishop of Upsala, and bishop of Göteborg.
During the third of his tours abroad he examined all the MSS of
Vossius and Scaliger at Leyden, collected a large number of
books, and, on his return, was appointed librarian at Upsala.
From a MS of *c.* 1350, brought from Constantinople in 1658 by
the diplomatist, K. B. Rålamb, he published two orations of
Aristides[5] (1687-8) and the *editio princeps* of the encomium of
Thomas Magister on Gregory Nazianzen, with four other speeches
and eight letters (1693). The same MS contained 154 *Letters* of

Lagerlöf (left margin)

*Upmark
(Rosenadler)* (left margin)

Norrman (left margin)

---

[1] Reprinted L. B. 1745, as Porphyrius, *De erroribus Ulixis*, but really
written by Nicephorus Gregoras (Creuzer, *Deutsche Schr.*, v ii 162). It had
already been printed by Conrad Gesner, 1542.

[2] Cp. Fant, ii 13—16.   [3] Cp. Schück, 334 f.

[4] Lundvall, in Linder, *s.v.*

[5] *Or.* 50, *De ineptiis Sophistarum* (1687); *Or.* 52, *Ad Achillem*, with the
Aldine *Ars Rhetorica* (1687). Norrman was not at first aware that *Or.* 52 had
already been edited by Camerarius (1535) and translated, with the rest of the
orations, by Canter (1566).

Libanius[1], originally collected by Lacapenus, and afterwards edited, mainly from other MSS, by J. C. Wolf[2]. Norrman wrote Greek as well as Latin verses, and produced no less than 72 academic dissertations. Olaus Rudbeck the elder (1630—1702), the celebrated anatomist, botanist, and antiquarian, the 'zealous patriot', who regarded Sweden as the veritable land of the Hyperboreans and the true prototype of Plato's Atlantis[3], had so high an admiration of Norrman's Latin prose that, if the occasion were to arise, he was prepared to say of him : *Ciceronem vidimus, audivimus, amisimus*, but it so happened that Norrman survived his earlier contemporary by a single year. Many of Norrman's books were purchased for the Upsala Library[4]. His *Orationes panegyricae, parentales, et programmata* were collected in 1738, and his *Addenda* to the Greek Thesaurus of Stephanus published by J. H. Schröder in 1830. His services to scholarship have been recounted at considerable length by Fant, who describes him as *multiplici eruditione celebrem* and as *Graecae litteraturae in Suecia peritissimum*[5].

Norrman was doubtless a scholar of wide attainments, but, with his contemporaries even more than with himself, the main interest lay in the imitation of ancient models of style. Like the early Italian humanists, they regarded the old classical world less as a vast empire of learning, every part of which was to be systematically subjected to historical research, than as a realm of beauty, rich with varied treasures which were to be enjoyed, and replete with perfect patterns of art and literature which were to be faithfully reproduced[6].

In editing classical authors the scholars of Sweden were hampered by the absence of MSS. Gustavus Adolphus had enriched the Library of Upsala with the spoils of Würzburg, and, after his death, Christina had added those of Olmütz and of Prague. Among these last was the *Codex Argenteus*, Ulphilas'

---

[1] Cp. R. Förster, *De Libanii libris MSS Upsaliensibus et Lincopiensibus*, Rostock, 1877.

[2] Amst. 1738 (preface); cp. O. Celsius, *Bibl. Ups. Hist.* (1745) 123—132, and *Anonymi* (*sc.* A. Norrelii) *Stricturae* (1746), 48—60.

[3] *Atlantica* (1679); Gibbon, i 217 Bury ; Schück, 268—282 (with portrait).

[4] Celsius, 48.   [5] *Historiola*, ii 53—76.

[6] Cp. Schück, 306 f.

Gothic translation of the Greek Gospels, formerly in the Abbey of Werden near Cologne, a MS which was sent by Königsmark to Christina, and, after passing into the hands of Isaac Vossius, was purchased by Count Magnus de la Gardie and presented to the Upsala Library[1]. Of the 66 MSS which the Count gave to that library in 1669[2], it is the only one of supreme importance. By the removal of Christina's collection scholars in the North were deprived of the best opportunity of consulting or editing classical MSS in their own country[3]. The ancient classics were entirely unrepresented in the few Greek or Latin MSS included among the hundred given to Upsala in 1705 by the great traveller and diplomatist, Johan Gabriel **Sparwenfeldt** Sparwenfeldt[4] (1655—1727), who spent five years in visiting all the great libraries of Europe (including that of the Vatican), and in diligently noting down his observations and in transcribing MSS. As a diplomatist, he afterwards studied Slavonic and other languages for three years in Russia and the adjoining parts of Asia; and, finally, he was sent abroad for a second period of five years to search in Southern Europe and in Northern Africa for every vestige of the 'Goths and Vandals', who, even down to the present day, are named among the subjects of the king of Sweden[5]. Late in life, Sparwenfeldt, a descendant of an ancient Danish king, and a man of majestic presence[6], was Master of Ceremonies at the Court of Sweden. He spoke and wrote fourteen languages, and in the evening of his days, when he had retired to his ancestral estates, he kept up an extensive correspondence with the foremost scholars of Europe. But, from the beginning to the end of his brilliant career, his main interest lay far

---

[1] Arckenholtz, i 307 f.   [2] Celsius, *Bibl. Ups.* 76—115.

[3] On Upsala MSS, cp. P. F. Aurivillius, *Notitia Codicum* (Latin), 1806–13; (Greek), 1806; Graux, *Notices*, ed. A. Martin, Paris, 1889; MS of Livy, J. H. Schröder, Ups. 1831–2, and A. T. Bromann, *ib.* 1855; of Tibullus, J. Bergman, *ib.* 1889; and of Libanius, Förster, Rostock, 1877. See also Annerstedt, in *Upsala Festskrift*, 1894, ii 41—66 *passim*, and in *Bibliographe moderne*, 1898, 407—436.

[4] (E. Benzelius), *Catalogus Centuriae Librorum* (Ups. 1706); cp. Celsius, *Bibl. Ups.* 50—57.

[5] A confusion due to the fact that medieval writers applied the name of the Teutonic Vandals to the Slavonic Wends (Bury on Gibbon, iv 296).

[6] Portrait in Schück, 293.

less in classical than in oriental and Slavonic literature. However, in 1721 he prepared for the press a Swedish translation of Epictetus, and, among the rarer works which he presented to the Upsala Library in the following year, was his own Russian translation of Epictetus and Cebes[1].

All the scholars above mentioned, beginning with Stiernhielm and ending with Sparwenfeldt, belong to the seventeenth century, in which Sweden was one of the greatest powers in Europe. In the next age learning was well represented by Erik Benzelius the younger (1675—1743), who, like *Benzelius* Sparwenfeldt (his senior by twenty years), spent three years abroad, collecting MSS and making the acquaintance of men of mark (1697—1700). He returned to Upsala with a goodly store of Greek and Latin MSS, and was promptly appointed librarian. In and after 1726 he was bishop of Göteborg and of Linköping; he was archbishop of Upsala for the last year of his life[2].

In 1708 he produced an edition of the *Characters* of Theophrastus, the only original element being the emendations proposed here and there in the index[3]. In one of the Selden MSS in the Bodleian he detected the fourth book of 'Special Laws' of Philo; he afterwards collected considerable materials for an edition of that author, and handed all of them over to Thomas Mangey, canon of Durham, whose edition appeared in two large folio volumes in 1742, with a very inadequate acknowledgement of the generous aid he had obtained from Benzelius[4]. In contrast with this conduct, we find J. C. Wolf, the editor of the *Letters* of Libanius (1738), warmly thanking Benzelius for the loan of two of his own MSS, which were among the fifteen subsequently purchased from his former library by the *gymnasium* of Linköping[5].

In 1710, in a year remarkable for the ravages of fire and sword and pestilence, he founded the first of the learned societies of Scandinavia. It was known as the *Collegium Curiosorum.* In

---

[1] Fant, *Suppl.* 14.   [2] Schück and Warburg, ii (1897) 21, with portrait.

[3] Cp. J. F. Fischer, ed. 1763, *Praef.* (Fant, ii 96 f).

[4] *Praef.* p. xvii. The discovery made by Benzelius is ignored in vol. ii 335.

[5] Fant, ii 98—104.

1716 it produced its first publication, under the fanciful title of *Daedalus hyperboreus*; in 1719 it was transformed into the *Societas literaria Sueciae*; in 1728 (after its founder had become a bishop) it was definitely placed under royal patronage, with archaeology and linguistics as part of its province, and finally (in the year of its founder's promotion to the archbishopric of Upsala) received the permanent designation of the *Societas Regia Scientiarum Upsaliensis*[1]. Benzelius was one of the first members of the Swedish Academy of Sciences, founded by Linnaeus and others at Stockholm in 1739.

O. Plantin

A brief survey of the early history of the study of Greek in Sweden was published at Wittenberg in 1736 under the title of *Hellas sub Arcto*[2]. Its author, Olaus Plantin, then residing in Germany, was born in 1701 on the little island of Hernösand, where he afterwards superintended the local school. He is the last of the long series of Greek scholars of Sweden enumerated in a more elaborate work on the same subject, the *Historiola* completed in 1786 by the erudite Swedish historian and archaeologist, E. M. Fant (1754—1817)[3]. Not

Fant

a few of these scholars were in the habit of writing original Greek compositions, either in prose or in elegiac or hexameter verse, but they very rarely produced any editions of Greek authors, and such authors as they happened to edit were seldom of special importance. Only the most prominent scholars have been selected for the briefest mention in the previous pages, but all of them deserve credit for continuing to tend and cultivate in that northern clime the exotic plant of Greek learning, which had flourished for a while in the Adonis-garden of queen Christina.

Fant does not profess to trace the fortunes of Greek beyond the year 1700. In contrast with his detailed notice of the thirteen professors of Greek before that date, he only records the names of the six who were subsequently called to that Chair, beginning with

---

[1] *Minerva*, II.

[2] *Seu Vindemiola Litteraria, qua merita Svecorum in linguam Graecam...* *exponuntur*, 84 pp.

[3] p. 335 n. 2 *supra*. The author is best known as editor of the *Scriptores rerum Suecicarum Medii Aevi*, posthumously published in 1818 f.

Olaus Celsius (1703) and ending with Johannes Flodērus (1762), under whose auspices he began the work. We must here be content with noting that Olaus Celsius the elder (1670—1756), the *polyhistor* who filled the Greek Chair for some twelve years only, is less well known as a professor of Greek than as the author of the *Hierobotanicon* and the earliest patron of Linnaeus, and that Flodērus (1721—1789) was also an able Latin orator, who took a prominent part in no less than 108 Latin disputations, and left behind him a large number of *Opuscula oratoria et poëtica*, posthumously published in 1791.

Flodērus

The above professors belong to Upsala. At Lund, the Chair of Greek and of Oriental Languages was filled in 1780 by the Syriac and Latin scholar, M. Norberg (1747—1826), and that of Latin in 1789 by J. Lundblad (1753—1820), an able writer of Latin verse. The same chair was held in 1826 by his pupil, A. O. Lindfors (1781—1841), the author of a successful Handbook of Roman Antiquities and a Swedish-Latin Dictionary.

Norberg
Lundblad
Lindfors

Lund was also the university of a versatile professor of Greek, who is far better known in the history of Swedish literature than in that of classical scholarship. Esaias Tegnér (1782—1846), the son of a pastor whose parents were peasants, graduated at Lund in 1802, was lecturer in Greek in 1810, and professor from 1812 to 1824, and finally bishop of Wexiö for the remaining twenty-two years of his life. He is famous as the most popular of Swedish poets,— the author, not only of the modern version of the *Frithiofsaga*, but also of the dithyrambic war-song which made him in 1808 the Tyrtaeus of Sweden. Many of his early poems were written in the little room at Lund which was then the study of the professor of Greek, and is still a place of pilgrimage for the votaries of Swedish literature[1]. It may be added that, in two of his letters, he expresses his strong approval of Latin verse composition as an indispensable part of a classical education[2].

Tegnér

----

[1] Schück and Warburg, ii 674—719, with several portraits, etc.

[2] *Efterlemnade Skrifter*, i (*Bref*) 362, 376, Letters to the accomplished diplomatist, Von Brinkman (1764—1847), on his admirable *Elegia ad Tranerum*. Tegnér considers Tranér superior to Lundblad in poetic fancy but inferior in his command of the Latin language.

Greek scholarship is more distinctively represented by Karl
Vilhelm Linder (1825—1882), professor at Lund
Linder   (1859–69), who produced a critical edition of
Hyperides, *pro Euxenippo* (1856), and a treatise on the arrangement of the topics in Antiphon and Andocides (1859). He
published a commentary of Psellus on Plato's opinions as to the
origin of the soul[1], and an extract from an Upsala MS on Plato's
theory of ideas[2]. In conjunction with K. A. Walberg, he produced a Swedish-Greek lexicon (1862). He also published papers
on the Greek Theatre and on Greek Synonyms, and on the longest
of the elegiac poems of Solon[3]. Finally, he was the author of a
collection of original Latin poems. The latest of these was a
Carmen Saeculare in elegiac metre, written in commemoration of
the second centenary of the university of Lund (1868)[4]. For the
rest of his life he devoted himself to theological studies as dean of
the cathedral churches of Vesterås and Linköping. As professor
he was succeeded by Walberg, his fellow-labourer
Walberg   in lexicography[5]. Walberg was, in turn, succeeded
Cavallin   in 1875 by Christian Cavallin (1831—1890), who
edited the *Philoctetes* and the *Iphigeneia in Tauris*, and produced
a Greek Syntax, as well as a Latin-Swedish and Swedish-Latin
Dictionary (1871–6).

Meanwhile, at Upsala, Greek was represented by J. Spongberg
(1800—1888), the Greek professor of 1853–74, and
Spongberg   author of a Swedish translation of the *Ajax*, and by
Aulin
Löfstedt   Lars Axel Aulin (1820—1869), a lecturer on Greek
Knös   at Upsala and a schoolmaster in Stockholm, who
not only published a translation of Krüger's Greek Grammar and
various text-books on Homer, Herodotus and Xenophon, but also
wrote on the style of Callimachus (1856). Einar Löfstedt (1831
—1889), who had studied in Germany in 1869, succeeded Spongberg as professor in 1874, and worked at archaeology in Italy,
Greece, and Asia Minor in 1876–7. His published works
included a highly successful Greek Grammar[6], and an outline of

---

[1] Ups. 1854; published by Vincent in *Not. et Extr.* xvi (1847), 2, 316 f.

[2] *Philologus*, 1860, 523 f.

[3] *Philologus*, 1858. He had already translated it into Latin verse.

[4] *Lunds...Secularfest*, 26—30; bibliography in *Upsala Jubelfest* (1877) 303.

[5] 1827 –1874. Cavallin, in *Tidskrift*, Ser. II ii 73.   [6] 1868; 1885[3].

lectures on Greek 'philological criticism' (1871). Admirable as a teacher, he is gratefully remembered by his former pupils, four of whom are now professors in the university[1]. His younger contemporary, O. V. Knös (1838—1907), appointed Greek lecturer in 1872 and 1880, is best known for his papers on the *digamma* (1872-8).

In the early part of the same century, at Upsala, Olof Kol- modin the younger (1766—1838), who, as professor of political philosophy, included the Roman histo- rians in his province, published translations of large portions of Livy and Tacitus[2]. Towards the end of Kolmodin's life, the Chair of Latin was held by Adolf Törneros (1794— 1839), a Ciceronian scholar, who began his career by supplementing the current lexicons of Greek and ended it by leaving behind him materials for completing a Swedish-Latin lexicon, edited by Ljungberg in 1843. Among the subsequent professors of Latin, we may mention P. J. Petersson (1816—1874), the orator and poet, who translated Stagnelius' 'Vladimir the Great' into Latin hexa- meters (1840-2), and Tibullus into Swedish verse (1860). He held the professorship in 1859-74. His successor from 1875 to 1879 was F. W. Häggström (1827—1893), who had studied in Germany, France and Italy, and had produced a successful edi- tion of Caesar's *Gallic War*. His contemporary, Anders Frigell (1802—1898), 'extraordinary' pro- fessor of Latin, besides editing Caesar and the *Odes* of Horace, paid special attention to the textual criticism of Livy[3], insisting on the importance of taking note of the readings of other MSS besides the Medicean. He also translated and expounded the *Tabula* of Cebes (1878). Not many years later, J. P. Lagergren (born in 1842), rector of the school at Jönköping in 1889, produced a comprehensive treatise on the life and style of the younger Pliny (1872), while C. E. Sandström (1845—1888), lecturer on Latin (1872), pub-

Kolmodin

Törneros

Petersson
Häggström

Frigell

Lagergren
Sandström

---

[1] O. A. Danielsson, P. Persson, K. J. Johansson, S. Wide.

[2] His contemporary, J. V. Tranér (1770—1835), titular professor of Latin in 1815, gave proof of high ability as a Latin poet and also as a translator from Ovid, and from Homer, Sappho and Anacreon.

[3] *Collatio Codicum*, lib. i—iii (1878); *Epilegomena ad lib. i et xxi* (1881); *Prolegomena ad lib. xxii—xxiii* (1883-5). Bursian, *Jahresb.* 80, 149—152.

lished a dissertation on Seneca's *Tragedies*, followed by emendations of Propertius, Lucan and Valerius Flaccus, and critical
studies on Statius (1878)[1].

The prosperity of the university of Upsala under the rule of
the late king Oscar II has been fully set forth in the comprehensive *Festskrift* of 1897, commemorating the completion of the
first 25 years of his beneficent reign, and including an important monograph on the history of the university, with a detailed
description of all its departments, an account of the classical
Seminar, and a complete list of publications.

The above survey of the careers of scholars in Scandinavia
has incidentally shown that not a few of the foremost of their
number have derived considerable benefit from studying in foreign
universities, and from travelling (or residing) in Italy and Greece.
It is the lands last mentioned that have naturally supplied the best
training to her archaeologists, from the time of Zoëga down to the
present day. Again, an intimate knowledge of the Scandinavian
languages has been the starting-point from which men like Rask
and Verner and Sophus Bugge have attained a notable position
among the Comparative Philologists of Europe; and, lastly, in
the province of the language and institutions of ancient Rome,
any country might well be proud of a Latin scholar like Madvig.

Norway is no longer politically united with either Denmark or
Sweden; but, although the ancient Scandinavia has been parted
into three separate kingdoms, friendly relations have been maintained in the domain of scholarship by means of a classical
periodical common to all three countries[2], by philological con-
gresses held in a regular order of rotation[3], and also by a common
interest in the Greek and Latin languages and in classical
archaeology. Among the scholars of the three countries, all
these three elements of union have combined in forming a 'three-
fold cord' that 'is not quickly broken'.

---

[1] For some of the above details as to recent scholars I am indebted to
Prof. Sam Wide; for others to the Swedish biographical dictionaries, and to
Aksel Andersson's 'Bio-bibliografi' in the *Upsala Festskrift* of 1897, vol. iii.

[2] *Tidskrift for Filologi*, begun in 1863, and continued ever since, with
slight changes of title.

[3] *Nordiska filologmöten*, Copenhagen, 1876, '92; Christiania, 1881, '98;
Stockholm, 1886, and Upsala, 1902.

CHAPTER XXXIX.

GREECE AND RUSSIA.

HOWEVER deep may be the debt that Europe owes to Italy for the part she played in the Revival of Learning, the debt of Italy to Greece is deeper still. To a large extent the very learning that was then revived in Italy had its ultimate or immediate origin in Greece. In the age of the Revival Italy became the heir of the renewed interest in the Greek Classics represented in Constantinople about 1150 by Eustathius and about 1300 by Planūdēs and Moschópūlus; and, even before the Eastern Empire fell beneath the tyranny of the Turk, the old Greek learning had gained a new lease of life by its transfer to a land that was ready and even eager to receive it.

Greece

We have already noted the names and recorded the services of the most prominent of the Greek scholars who fled to Italy, whether before or after the fall of Constantinople[1]. Little is known of those who remained in the East; much more, of those who left it. Not a few of these came from the lands that were free from the Turkish yoke, and, in particular, from Crete and the Ionian Islands. Crete, which for four and a half centuries belonged to Venice (1204—1650), became one of the strongholds of Hellenism[2], and Venice was naturally the immediate destination of the scholars who left this island for the West. Among the earlier Cretan immigrants was Georgius Trapezuntius[3]; among those of later date were Marcus Mūsūrus, Zacharias Callierges[4] and Nicolaos Blastós. The *Etymologicum Magnum* of 1499, the first book produced in Venice

Crete

---

[1] ii 59—80 *supra.*

[2] Thereianos, *Koraës* (1890), i 18: Bikelas, *Dialexeis* (1893), 104 f.

[3] ii 63 *supra.*   [4] ii 79 f.

23

by Callierges under the supervision of Musurus, was printed at
the expense of the patriotic Blastós, who is described by Musurus
as 'full of the Hellenic spirit'. The Greek press of Callierges
was in fact a Cretan workshop; Cretans cast the types, Cretans
printed and corrected the proofs, and Cretans were the publishers[1].
Even when the press was removed to Rome in 1515–7, it continued, under the promptings of Lascaris, to do good service to
Greek scholarship by printing the *scholia* to Pindar and Theocritus, and the *eclogae* of Thomas Magister and Phrynichus[2]. It
was a Cretan, Demetrius Dūkas, who aided Aldus in editing the
Rhetores Graeci, and the *Moralia* of Plutarch; a Cretan, Arsenios,
who published the *scholia* to Euripides[3]; while the same island
supplied the West with its most noted calligraphers[4]. Crete,
again, was the native land of Franciscus Portus (1511—1581),
professor of Greek in Venice and elsewhere, and an industrious
commentator on the Greek Classics[5]. A century later another
Cretan, Franciscus Scūphus, a teacher in Venice, published his
Rhetoric in Vienna (1681)[6]. Crete can also claim Cyril Lucar[7],
who studied in Italy and the Netherlands and England, and was
the patriarch of Alexandria and Constantinople. He it was who
in 1627 received the first printing-press brought to the latter city
from London by Nicodemus Metaxas of Cephalonia[8], and in the
following year presented to Charles I the *codex Alexandrinus*
of the Greek Scriptures. Of the 350 scholars enumerated by
Sathas[9], under the years 1500 to 1700, as many as two-fifths were
natives of Crete or of the Ionian Islands.

---

[1] Musurus in *Etym. Magn.*; cp. Didot, *Alde Manuce*, 550.

[2] Didot, 544—578.　　　　　　　[3] 1544; *ib.* 443.

[4] *ib.* 579—586.

[5] Nicolai, *Geschichte der neugriechischen Literatur* (1876), 41 f; Legrand,
Bibliogr. Hellén. xv, xvi s., ii pp. vii—xx. In the next generation the Cretan
Emmanuel Margūnius (*c.* 1549—1602), after studying at Padua, was for five
years an inmate of a Cretan monastery, and in 1584 was consecrated bishop in
Constantinople. At Padua he produced a meritorious edition of Aristotle *De
Coloribus* (1575); his *Hymni Anacreontici* were published at Augsburg (1601),
and, at the time of his death in Venice, he was proposing to take part in Sir
Henry Savile's *Chrysostom* (viii 114 f). Cp. Legrand, ii pp. xxiii—lxxvii.

[6] Thereianos, i 28.　　　　　　[7] 1572—1638.

[8] Nicolai, 49 f.　　　　　　[9] Νεοελλ. φιλολογία (1453—1821), 1868.

The Ionian Islands belonged to Venice for four centuries (1386—1797). In the fifteenth century Corfu gave birth to Nicólaos Sophianós, a pupil of the Greek school in Rome, where he edited the ancient *scholia* on the *Iliad* and on Sophocles (1517-8). He was the first to produce a Grammar of modern Greek (1534)[1], and to translate Plutarch's treatise on education into the ordinary Greek of the day, which, in a purified form, was regarded by him as the best medium for literature and for instruction in modern Greece[2]. Modern *scholia* on Pindar were written by Aléxandros Phórtios of Corfu[3], while Leonárdos Phórtios wrote a rhyming poem on the soldier's life (Venice, 1531). In 1537 another native of Corfu, Antónios Éparchos, fled to Venice, where he supported himself by teaching Greek. Though he was compelled by poverty to sell most of his MSS, he generously presented as many as thirty to Francis I. A devoted adherent of Greek learning, he pleaded the cause of the Greek Church at the diet of Ratisbon, and also composed a celebrated elegiac poem on the unhappy fate of Hellas[4]. The Corfiote, Níkandros Núkios, visited England in the time of Henry VIII, and described his travels in the style of Arrian[5]. Lastly, Phlangínēs devoted the whole of his fortune to establishing a Greek school in Venice[6], while Venice herself in the seventeenth century made Italian the official language of the Ionian Islands. But the clergy and the people happily remained true to their native tongue[7]. In the previous century Zante had given birth to Nicolaos Lucanos[8], whose paraphrase of the *Iliad* was the first work printed in modern Greek[9], and to Demetrios Zênos, who translated the *Battle of the Frogs and Mice* into a popular form of rhyming verse[10]. We shall see in the sequel that the Ionian

---

[1] Reprinted by Legrand, 1874.

[2] Nicolai, 40, 49 ; Thereianos, i 22 f.

[3] Sakkelion, in *Pandora*, xv 354.

[4] Venice, 1544 (Legrand, *Bibliogr. Hellén. xv, xvi s.*, i 259); Nicolai, 86; Thereianos, i 23—27.

[5] Book ii, ed. J. A. Cramer (Camden Soc.), 1841.

[6] 1664. [7] Bikelas, 106.

[8] Also called Lucanis, cp. Legrand, *l.c.*, i 188 f. [9] Venice, 1526.

[10] *c.* 1539, often reprinted (Legrand, *Bibliogr. Hellén. xv, xvi s.*, i 179 f; Constantinides, *Neo-Hellenica* (1892) 176—185).

Islands (as well as Crete) became the home of the popular type of Greek literature[1].

Chios was subject to Genoa for two centuries (1346—1566).

Chios It was not until twenty years after its conquest by the Turks that its most prominent scholar, Leo Allatius, was born (1586—1669). He was educated in Calabria and in Rome, whither he returned to study medicine after living for some time in obscurity in Chios. In 1622 he was the papal agent for the transfer of the Heidelberg MSS to the Vatican Library, over which he presided for the last eight years of his life. Alienated from Greece by his adhesion to the Latin Church, it was solely for the benefit of the Catholic inhabitants that he founded a school in his native island. He is best known for his valuable services to Byzantine literature and for his patriotic paper, *De patria Homeri* (1640). He holds, in fact, the highest place among the Greek scholars of the middle of the seventeenth century[2]. As a writer of panegyrical poetry he was followed by other Chiotes of less distinction, Antōnios Koraës, who travelled in Italy and dedicated a Pindaric ode to a chancellor of France, and Cōnstantînos Rhodokanákēs, who studied in Oxford and attracted attention by a Greek encomium on Charles II[3]. In the same century England was visited by two other representatives of Greece, the Peloponnesian Christóphoros Angelos, who resided in Cambridge and Oxford in 1608–17, and published at the former university a popular account of the condition of Greece (1619)[4], and Leonárdos Philarâs of Athens, to whom Milton addressed two Latin letters in 1652–4. The first of these contains the sentence which has suggested 'the inspiring motto of the Philhellenic movement'[5]:—

'Quid enim vel fortissimi olim viri vel eloquentissimi gloriosius aut se dignius esse duxerunt quam vel suadendo vel fortiter faciendo ἐλευθέρους καὶ αὐτονόμους ποιεῖσθαι τοὺς Ἕλληνας?' [6]

---

[1] p. 375 *infra*.

[2] Legrand, *Bibliogr. Hellén. xvii s.*, iii 435—471 ; Nicolai, 64 f.

[3] Oxon. 1660, Legrand, *l.c.*, ii 126 f ; Nicolai, 93.

[4] A. Gennadios, in *Pandora* (1851), 815 ; Legrand, *l.c.* i 111 f.

[5] Drakoules, *Neohellenic Language and Literature* (Oxford, 1897), 43.

[6] Cp. [Dem.] 7 § 30 ; *Miltoni Epp.* 1674, 34 f, 39 f ; Legrand *l.c.* iii 407—416.

The first step towards the recovery of Greek independence was a literary revival of the Greek language.   It is difficult to ascertain how far a knowledge of classical Greek was preserved among the common people in the 16th, 17th, and 18th centuries.   We learn, however, that in Constantinople, in 1575, the clergy preferred to preach in the 'old Greek language' (*i.e.* in Byzantine Greek), although this language was intelligible to only two or three in their congregations[1].   At Athens, in 1672, very few besides the three public teachers of theology, philosophy and language understood the old Greek literature[2].   After visiting Crete in 1700, a French traveller (perhaps prematurely) writes that 'in the whole Turkish dominions there are hardly twelve persons thoroughly skilled in the knowledge of the ancient Greek tongue'[3].   At Patmos, in 1801, E. D. Clarke declares that neither the superior of the monastery nor the bursar (who acted as librarian) was able to read[4].   Even in an important centre of Greek learning, the Byzantine authors were sometimes preferred to those of the golden age of Greek literature. In 1813, Cyril VII, patriarch of Constantinople, could not comprehend the preference given to Thucydides and Demosthenes over 'polished writers' such as Synesius and Gregory Nazianzen, and considered the iambic lines of Ptōchopródromos more musical than those of Euripides[5].   It is maintained, however, by Finlay[6] that, during the centuries preceding the Revolution, the parish priests had kept up a competent knowledge of the old Greek language and that any Greek who could read and write had some knowledge of the old Greek literature.   A high degree of learning was certainly represented among the laity, and numerous works were published by Greeks in the classical and the popular forms of the language.   These works were printed in many parts of Europe[7].   Venice in particular long remained an important centre for the printing of modern Greek literature[8].

Classical Greek little known

---

[1] Martin Crusius, 197.   [2] Père Babin, *Relation* (1674), 54 f.

[3] Tournefort, *Voyage*, i 104 (E. T. 1741).

[4] *Travels*, vi 41, ed. 1818.   [5] Thereianos, i 41.   [6] v 283.

[7] See the bibliographical works of Bretós (1854–7), Sathas (1868), and Legrand, *Bibliogr. Hellén. xv, xvi* (1885—1906), *xvii s.* (1894—1903).

[8] Catalogue (1821) of the long established house of Glykys, in Carl Iken's *Leukothea* (1825), ii 139 f.

In 1791 a Greek press was founded in Vienna by Geōrgios Ben-
dótēs of Zante, the compiler of a valuable Greek, Italian and
Romaic lexicon, and the translator of Barthélemy's *Anacharsis*.
After his death in 1795 the press continued to flourish, and it was
here that the important periodical called the *Lógios Hermês* began
its course in 1811[1]. The Greek colony at Vienna was connected
with the *Philómūsos Hetairía*, a literary club founded at Athens
in 1812 which enabled some of the future leaders of the Revolution to acquire a European education[2].

The traditions of Byzantine rather than classical culture were
maintained in the patriarchal school of Constantinople. The patriarch Gennadios (1400—1468),
who held that office for the five years immediately
succeeding the Turkish conquest, was an eager student of law,
theology and philosophy, a translator of some of the works of the
Aristotelian churchman, Thomas Aquinas, and a persecutor of the
paganism and an opponent of the Platonism of Gemistos Plethon[3].
By the side of the ancient patriarchal school restored by the influence of Gennadios, rose the famous Phanariote school of 1661
and that of Kuru-Tschesme founded on the Bosporus in 1803[4].
In 1581, Zygomalâs, the chief secretary of the patriarch, described
Greece in general as destitute of schools, though the inhabitants
had a natural genius for profiting by education; 'but the clouds
of an ever-during calamity suffer not the sun of such blessings to
shine forth, or learning to flourish'[5]. During the interval of little
more than 30 years, while the Morea was subject to Venice (1684
—1718), education was fostered by the Catholic clergy at the
college of Tripolitza[6]. In the early part of that
brief period the Parthenon was destroyed during
the Venetian siege of 1687, but, towards its close, the recovery of
Corinth by the Turks in 1715 was soon followed by the founding

*Schools: Con-
stantinople*

Tripolitza

---

[1] Nicolai, 99.   [2] Finlay, vi 98.

[3] κατὰ τῶν Πλήθωνος ἀποριῶν ἐπ' 'Αριστοτέλει, ed. Mēnâs (Paris, 1858);
ii 61 *supra*. Cp. Gibbon, vii 175 f Bury; Finlay, iii 502, v 137; Krumbacher,
Byz. Litt. 119 f; Nicolai, 25 f. Gentile Bellini's 'Gennadios and Mahomet II',
in frontispiece to Legrand, *Bibliogr. Hellén. xv, xvi s.* iii (1903).

[4] Nicolai, 24, 109.

[5] Martin Crusius, *Turcograecia* (1584), 94.

[6] Finlay, v 212.

of a Greek School at Athens. About the same time schools
established in the previous century began to flourish in Macedonia and Thessaly. In 1723 the third of the
                                                          Ioánnina
three great schools of Ioánnina came into being
in the metropolis of Epirus[1]. Evidence as to the fairly
flourishing condition of the Greek schools is supplied in
1714 by Alexander Helládius, who had visited London and
Oxford and had spent some years in Germany[2]. The year
1758 marks the dissolution of a once important   Athos
academy on Mount Athos, and the foundation of   Mesolonghi
                                                          Dimitzána
another at Mesolonghi[3]. In 1764 the ancient
school in the small Arcadian town of Dimitzána was restored by
the learned Agápios[4]. During the same century, and especially
under the rule of Daniel Kerameus[5], there was a successful school
on the island of Patmos, which supplied teachers to
Chios and Smyrna[6]. In the second half of the   Patmos
                                                          Smyrna
century the 'Evangelical School of Smyrna' had
some famous pupils (including Koraës, the future regenerator of
the Greek language), and, at the 'philological *gymnasium*' in the
same city, the Greek Classics were effectually
studied in 1809–18[7]. There were Greek schools at   Trebizond
                                                          Sinope
Trebizond and Sinope; while, in the Danubian
Principalities, the Hellenic school of Bucharest had assumed the
status of an academy in 1698, and the central
school of Iassi was already well known in 1755[8].   Bucharest
                                                          Iassi
The study of the old Greek language and literature
in the above schools, and especially in those of the Danubian Principalities, was among the causes that led to the Revolution of 1821.

---

[1] Further endowed by the brothers Marutzi in 1742. Cp. Nicolai, 54 f;
and A. R. Rangabé, *Litt. Néo-Hellénique* (1877), i 54.

[2] *Status praesens eccl. orientalis*, dedicated to Peter the Great (Norimb.
1714) 60, 'in gymnasiis quae iam Dei gratia in omnibus Graeciae civitatibus
mediocriter florent'; Nicolai, 55 f.

[3] Nicolai, 110 f.

[4] Cp. Kastórchēs, περὶ τῆς ἐν Δημητσάνῃ σχολῆς (Ath. 1847).

[5] Thereianos, i 80.   [6] Nicolai, 110, n. 125.   [7] Nicolai, 114.

[8] Nicolai, 117 f. On Greek education from 1453 to 1821, see pp. 1—32 of
C. P. Oikonomos, *Die pädagogischen Anschauungen des Adamantios Korais*,
116 pp. (Leipzig, 1908), and the earlier literature there quoted.

In Greece itself, early in the century, 'classic history was studied; classic names were revived; Athenian liberty became a theme of conversation among men; Spartan virtue was spoken of by women; literature was cultivated with enthusiasm as a step to revolution'[1].

Greek education owed not a little to the influence of the Phanariots resident in the *Phanar* or Greek quarter of Constantinople, and in particular to those who attained high positions in the service of the Turks. The interests of the Greeks were advanced by Panagiōtákēs Nicósios, who in 1630 attained the diplomatic dignity of chief interpreter to the Sublime Porte[2].

Mavrocordátos

The same position was ultimately attained by Aléxandros Mavrocordátos (1637—1709), the son of a silk-merchant of Chios and the founder of a highly influential family. He studied medicine in Italy, produced at Bologna a Latin treatise on the circulation of the blood (1664), became physician to the Sultan, and, from 1665 to 1672, presided over the patriarchal school of Constantinople. He looked down with contempt on the popular language of his fellow-countrymen, and formed his own style on the old Greek Classics—without succeeding in assimilating their merits. His text-book of Greek Syntax was deficient in method and in clearness, and failed to supersede the current manuals of Gaza and of Lascaris[3]. After his appointment as principal interpreter to the Porte he obtained permission to found schools in Constantinople and Ioánnina and on the island of Patmos, and presented these schools with texts of the Classics printed in Europe[4]. His example was followed by his son, Nicolas, who was the first Greek subject of Turkey to rise to the position of governor of Wallachia and thus 'to forge a sceptre from his chains'[5]. These officials gave a certain impulse to education among those who aspired to public appointments, but, 'fortunately for the Greeks, other contemporary causes tended to disseminate education from a purer source'[6]. During

---

[1] Finlay, vi 17.   [2] Rangabé, i 45—48.

[3] Thereianos, i 49.

[4] Rizo (Iakōbákēs Rízos Nerūlós, prime minister of Wallachia and Moldavia), *Cours de Littérature Grecque Moderne* (Geneva, 1827), 28; Nicolai, 74; Finlay, v 242.

[5] Rangabé, i 52.   [6] Finlay, v 245.

this time modern Greek literature acquired a higher degree of polish under the influence of the pulpit, the synod, and the various select societies of Constantinople[1].

The second half of the 18th century was marked by a further multiplication of schools and by the translation of European works of science, history, fiction and philosophy. These translations played an important part in the developement of a literary language approximating to the old Greek type.

Among the scholars who applied their knowledge of ancient Greek to giving a literary character to the language of the modern Greeks, the earliest name of note is   *Eugénios Búlgaris* that of Eugénios Búlgaris of Corfu (1716—1806), who was educated at Ioánnina. He studied modern languages and Latin in Italy and elsewhere, and was the first reformer of the traditional ecclesiastical type of Greek education, as director of schools at Ioánnina, Mount Athos and Constantinople. He subsequently spent ten years in Leipzig, writing works in ancient as well as modern Greek (1765–75), and was placed at the head of a school for young Russian noblemen in St Petersburg, where he died after holding for a time the bishopric of Sclavonia and Kherson. His masterpiece in ancient Greek was his rendering of the *Georgics* and *Aeneid* in Homeric verse; ancient Greek was also the language of all his strictly philosophical writings, while modern Greek was the medium used in his more popular works[2].

Modern Greek was still more effectively moulded into a literary form by the far-reaching influence of Ada-   *Koraës* mantios Koraës (1748—1833). A native of Smyrna, where he was aided in his early studies by the chaplain to the Dutch consulate, he spent six years as his father's mercantile agent at Amsterdam (1772–8), returned to Smyrna for four years,

---

[1] Rizo, 29.

[2] James Clyde, *Romaic and Modern Greek compared with one another and with ancient Greek* (Edin. 1855), 45—49; Finlay, *History of Greece*, v 284 Tozer; Iken, ii 7, 105 f; Rizo, 34—37; Nicolai, 123; Goudas, Βίοι Παράλληλοι, ii (1874) 1—40, with portrait; Rangabé, i 63; and esp. Thereianos, *Adamantios Koraës* (1889 f) i 63—76. His industrious and contentious contemporary, Neóphytos Kausokalybítês, produced at Bucharest in 1761 a commentary of 1400 pages on the fourth book of Theodorus Gaza (*ib.* 79 f).

and was allowed by his father to abandon a business career and to enter the medical school of Montpellier, where he distinguished himself as a student of medicine (1782–8). He removed to Paris in 1788, and there devoted himself to literary labours for the remaining forty-five years of his life.

Patriotism and a passion for learning were the two guiding principles of his whole career. One of his earliest works (his 'Emendations on Hippocrates') was printed at Oxford in 1792[1]. His excellent edition of Hippocrates, *de aëre, aquis, locis* (1800), was immediately preceded by the *Characters* of Theophrastus, and succeeded by Longus and Heliodorus. The most important of his literary undertakings, the 'Library of Greek literature', was inspired by a distinctly patriotic motive. Long before the outbreak of the Greek revolution, four brothers of the wealthy house of Zosimades consulted Koraës as to the best means for accelerating the regeneration that had already begun in Greece. Koraës advised the publication of the old Greek Classics with notes in ancient and introductions in modern Greek. Such was the origin of the celebrated 'Greek Library', a series of seventeen volumes edited by Koraës in 1805–26. The *prodromos* (containing Aelian's *Varia Historia*, Heracleides Ponticus, and Nicolaus Damascenus) was followed by two volumes of Isocrates, six volumes of Plutarch's *Lives*, four of Strabo, the *Politics* and *Ethics* of Aristotle, the *Memorabilia* of Xenophon with the *Gorgias* of Plato, and lastly the *Leocrates* of the Attic orator Lycurgus. All these were printed by Didot in an exquisitely neat type specially designed for the series, the whole cost of publication was met by the munificence of the brothers Zosimades, and many copies were gratuitously distributed among deserving Greek students in Hellenic lands. Meanwhile, Koraës was producing a series of 'parerga' in nine volumes, comprising Polyaenus, Aesop, Xenocrates[2] and Galen *De Alimento ex Aquatilibus*, the *Meditations* of Marcus Aurelius, the *Tactics* of 'Onesander'[3], five political treatises of Plutarch, Cebes and Cleanthes with the *Encheiridion* of Epictetus, and the two volumes of Arrian's version of his discourses (1809–27). Homer had already been specially edited for the modern Greeks[4], but Koraës produced an edition of *Iliad* i—iv (1811–20). He also edited Hierocles. He translated Herodotus into modern Greek; his notes on Herodotus were printed by Larcher, those on Thucydides by Levesque, and those on Athenaeus by Schweighäuser; while those on Hesychius were posthumously published (1889). His notes in general, especially those in his 'Greek Library', have met with appreciative recognition on the part of

---

[1] *Musei Oxoniensis...specimina.*

[2] Already published by him in Naples (1794).

[3] Ὀνάσανδρος (Christ, § 665). Appended was a poem of Tyrtaeus, translated into modern Greek by Koraës, and into French by Didot.

[4] By Spyridon Blantes (1765—1830), Ven., with the *scholia* of Didymus (Thereianos, ii 82).

subsequent editors[1]. The five volumes of his *Atakta* (1828–35) were largely concerned with Greek lexicography. In his writings in general he aimed at assimilating the language of literature with the living language of modern Greece, and, even in his most scholarly works, he showed his interest in the idiom of the people, while others, such as Kodrikas and Dukas, abandoned this intermediate position and went to the extreme of ignoring the living language and urging the adoption of an artificial style founded on the grammar and the literature of ancient Greece[2]. His autobiography (1829) was translated into Latin and into French. The latter version is prefixed to his Correspondence, which includes many emendations of the Greek Anthology[3].

He was on friendly terms with scholars in Holland[4]. In 1805 Wyttenbach wrote to Larcher describing Koraës as 'not only a Grecian but a veritable Greek', and in 1807 his Isocrates won him the title of the 'patriarch of Greek philology'[5]. His correspondents in England included Thomas Burgess, afterwards bishop of Salisbury, and Holmes, the editor of the Septuagint. He was an ardent admirer of the United States of America[6]. In the land of his adoption, he was associated with Gosselin and La Porte-du-Theil (and afterwards with Letronne) in a French translation of Strabo (1805–19) begun under the generous patronage of Napoleon. Among his principal friends in Paris were Étienne Clavier, the elder Thurot, and Chardon de la Rochette; he was less intimate with Villoison[7], while, as a scholar, he was highly esteemed by Boissonade[8]. His devotion to his country's cause was a ruling passion to the end of his life. With his latest breath he spoke of the land of his fathers, and on his death-bed, while his failing eyesight rested on a portrait of Demosthenes, he exclaimed:—'*That* was a man'[9]. His epitaph, written by himself, told of his love for the land of his adoption as well as for the land of his birth[10], and his character is thus summed up by the English historian of Modern Greece:—

'Koraës...was the great popular reformer of the Greek system of instruction, the legislator of the modern Greek language, and the most distinguished apostle of religious toleration and national freedom...He was indifferent to wealth, honest and independent, a sincere patriot, and a profound scholar... He passed his life in independent poverty, in order that he might consecrate

---

[1] Thereianos, *passim*.

[2] Krumbacher's *Festrede, Das Problem der neugriechischen Schriftsprache* (1903), 44 f, and Koraës' *Gk Grammar* (posthumously published at Athens, 1888); Sathas (1870), and Beaudouin (1883), quoted by Krumbacher, *l.c.* 195; also the criticisms of Hatzidákis, *La Question de la Langue Écrite Neo-Grecque* (1907), 106.

[3] *Lettres inédites*, 1874–7 (Bursian's *Jahresb.* xi 87 f).

[4] Thereianos, i 103, 105. Cp. J. Gennadios, κρίσεις καὶ σκέψεις, 54–72.

[5] Clyde, 50.

[6] Thereianos, iii 61, τῶν Ἀγγλαμερικανῶν διάπυρος θαυμαστής.

[7] *ib.* i 179 f.   [8] *ib.* i 405 f.

[9] Ἐκεῖνος ἦτο ἄνθρωπος, *ib.* iii 152 f.   [10] *ib.* iii 155.

his whole time, and the undivided strength of his mind, to improve the moral and political feelings of the Greeks. His efforts have not been fruitless. He methodized the literary language of his countrymen, while he infused into their minds principles of true liberty and pure morality '[1].

The intermediate position assumed by Koraës in moulding a literary

Kodrikâs

language for modern Greece found its keenest and most implacable opponent in Panagiōtákēs Kodrikâs (1750—1827), an Athenian of distinguished descent, extraordinary gifts, wide learning and high social standing. He was an adherent of the ultra-classical Greek style that had come down from the Byzantine age and was still retained in the documents issued by the patriarch of Constantinople and other official personages. Before 1802 he was chancellor to the governor of Wallachia; and after that date he was a professor of Greek in Paris, and interpreter to the Ministry of Foreign Affairs. His controversy with Koraës began with a letter to the editors of the *Lógios Hermês* (1816) urging them to resist the reforms proposed by Koraës. As this advice was not followed, he published an anonymous 'Apology for the Greeks in Pisa' (1817), which was promptly repudiated by the Greeks concerned. His final contribution to the controversy was the *Melétē*, dedicated in 1818 to Alexander I, emperor of Russia[2]. In all this bitter controversy the only benefit that incidentally accrued to the cause of learning was an admirable treatise published by Koraës under the pseudonym of Stephanos Pantazês[3].

The opinions of Koraës were, in general, supported by the versatile and

Kúmas

accomplished scholar, Kōnstantînos Kúmas (1777—1836), a native of Larissa, who studied in Vienna, was head of the

---

[1] Finlay, *History of Greece*, v 285 Tozer; cp. Gervinus, ap. Thereianos, iii 155. Βίος (Paris, 1829); Fr. T. 1833; Lat. T. 1834–49; Germ., Sinner-Ott (Zürich, 1837); Boissonade in Michaud's *Biogr. Univ.*; I. Bywater in *J. H. S.* i 305–7; Nicolai, 103 f; Rangabé, i 81—90; Constantinides, 332—362; and esp. D. Thereianos, *Adamantios Koraës*, 3 vols. (Trieste, 1889-90). In France he adopted the name of Coray; Villoison considered that Coraï(s) would have been more correct (*ib.* i 179). Portrait in Goudas, ii 73—108. Posthumous works in 7 vols. (Ath. 1881–9), including materials for a French and Greek lexicon (1881), Grammar of modern Greek (1888), notes and emendations on Hesychius (1889), and 3 vols. of Letters (1885–7). On his Letters, cp. J. Gennadios, κρίσεις καὶ σκέψεις (Trieste, 1903), and on his services to Greek education, C. P. Oikonomos, *Die pädagogischen Anschauungen des Adamantios Korais* (Leipzig, 1908).

[2] The presentation copy now belongs to Mr J. Gennadios.

[3] On the ancient dogma νόμῳ καλόν, νόμῳ κακόν (Leipzig, 1819), Thereianos, ii 348 f and reprint in iii (Appendix v). On Kodrikâs, in general, *ib.* ii 283—352; Nicolai, 130; Rangabé, i 90 f; Hatzidákis, 70 f. His opponent, Daniel Philippídēs, regarded the popular type of Greek as the true medium of litera-

school of Kuru-Tschesme in 1813, joined Stephanos Oekonómos in founding the 'philological *gymnasium*' at Smyrna in 1820, and spent the last 15 years of his life at Trieste. A Greek style resembling that of Koraës was the characteristic of his numerous translations from literary and scientific French and German works. His publications amounted to 45 volumes. He produced a Greek and German lexicon, founded on Riemer (1826), and a Greek Grammar (1833), but his greatest achievement was a universal history, the 12th volume of which included his own autobiography. He is held in high repute for his learning and his patriotism, and also for his remarkable success in the organisation of schools [1].

While Eugenios Búlgaris had done good service as a repre- sentative of the old scholastic type of teaching, a new era was opened by one who combined intellectual eminence with all the intensity of moral force and patriotic enthusiasm. This was none other than Lámpros Phōtiádēs (1750 —1805), a native of Ioánnina, who presided over the Greek school at Bucharest for the last 13 years of his life. He was interested in imitating Anacreon, Sappho and Pindar, but he fore- saw that a reform was needed in the scholastic education of his day, and that Greece had a greater need of progressive patriots than of imitative grammarians. Instead of spending his time on the exclusive explanation of words and phrases, he inspired his pupils with admiration for the lofty thoughts of the old Greek writers. He is credited with having prepared translations from Herodotus, Thucydides, Xenophon, Plutarch and Lucian [2], but he published nothing in person. His two books on the theory of metre [3] and his notes on the text of Synesius and of the Attic orators [4] were printed by his pupils [5]. In his old age he welcomed the reforms proposed by Koraës, and, while he is less prominent than that great scholar, he did signal service to his nation. He is remem- bered mainly as the able instructor of the leading scholars of the

Phōtiádēs

---

ture (cp. Rangabé, i 92 f), and the same is true of Athanásios Psalídas, head of the patriarchal school at Ioánnina in 1797—1820 (Nicolai, 141 n.).

[1] Iken, i 300 f; Goudas, ii 263—288 (with portrait); Nicolai, 125; cp. Hatzidákis, 73, 106 f.

[2] *Lógios Hermês,* 1811.

[3] Ed. Zēnobios Pōp (Vienna, 1803).   [4] Ed. Dukas (*ib.* 1812).

[5] Cp. in general Nicolai, 117; Rangabé, i 78 f; Thereianos, i 82; Con- stantinides, 330 f; and Goudas, ii 254—262 (with portrait; the original belongs to Mr J. Gennadios).

Greek Revolution. Among these, the most conspicuous were Neo-phytos Dukas and Georgios Gennadios, who were united in their devotion to a common master, but in their published works stood in the strongest contrast to each other.

Shortly after the death of Photiades, a war between Turkey and Russia made it necessary to close the school of Bucharest from 1806 to 1810. Neóphytos Dúkas (1760—

Dúkas   1845), a native of Epirus and a devoted pupil of Photiades, had already left for Vienna. In Vienna he pre-pared his Greek Grammar, which he dedicated to his former master (1804); he also edited (in 1803-15) a large number of Greek authors including Thucydides, Arrian, Dion Chrysostom, Maximus Tyrius, the *Bibliotheca* of Apollodorus, Synesius, as well as the Attic orators, Herodian, and Aeschines Socraticus. Most of these editions included translations. In 1815 he became the head of the school at Bucharest. After the war, he established a printing-press at Aegina, and continued to spend all his resources in producing his editions of the Classics. In 1834-45 he devoted himself mainly to editing the poets:—Homer, Euripides and Sophocles (1834-5), Aeschylus and Theocritus (1839), Pindar and Aristophanes (1842-5). In the controversy as to the best literary language for modern Greece, he preferred the old classical style to the *via media* advocated by Koraës[1], who was far superior to him as a scholar and as an editor of Greek texts. Dukas, how-ever, deserves credit for the industry which he displayed in adding more than 70 volumes of Greek authors to the scholastic libraries of his day. His edition of Thucydides in ten volumes alone gives proof of any critical faculty, but there is good reason for stating that the credit for this is undoubtedly due to his teacher Pho-tiades. He continued to teach in Athens to the end of his life, and, when he died, he was lamented as a 'benefactor to the nation'[2].

Constantine Bardaláchos (1775—1830), a coadjutor of Pho-tiades, and afterwards director of the schools at

Bardaláchos   Bucharest, Chios and Odessa, is best known as the author of a Greek Grammar founded on the works of Lennep,

---

[1] Thereianos, ii 271—283.   [2] Cp. Nicolai, 132 f; Rangabé, i 162.

Koraës and Buttmann (1832)[1]. His memory is enshrined in the introduction to the edition of the *Cyropaedeia* published by his colleague at Odessa, Georgios Gennadios.

Geórgios Gennádios (1786—1854), who belonged to the same family as the patriarch of that name[2], was born at Selymbria and was the favourite pupil of Photiades. G. Gennádios
In 1809 he began to study medicine at Leipzig, and, in 1814, returned to Bucharest and was soon assisting Dukas in the management of the school. In 1817 he became the head of the Greek School then founded at Odessa (where he began a series of school-books). Three years later he returned to Bucharest as head of his former school. Then, as ever, he gave proof of being a born teacher; and, in that eventful time, he was also an ardent patriot. The study of Demosthenes and Plutarch had inspired him with the love of liberty, and, under his enthusiastic teaching, his pupils at Bucharest were thoroughly imbued with the spirit of patriotism.

One of those pupils, the brilliant scholar, poet, archaeologist, politician and diplomatist, Aléxandros Rízos Rangabês, has told us how, on a day when his master was expounding some ancient classic, the *Panegyric* of Isocrates or the *Pericles* of Plutarch, being deeply moved by the recital of the ancient glories of Athens, he bade his pupils bar the door and forthwith delivered a glowing discourse on the golden age when Greece was still a teacher of the nations, thus arousing in his audience the keenest enthusiasm for the cause of liberty[3]. Not a few of those pupils were among the five hundred of the Sacred Band, most of whom fell in the first conflict with the foe on the 19th day of June, 1821[4]. Gennadios withdrew for a time to Odessa and was soon afterwards studying theology at Leipzig and Göttingen. The next great event of his life was his patriotic speech beneath the plane-tree in Nauplia, which led to his being called the 'saviour of his country'[5]. He distinguished himself at the battle of Karystos, and at the close of the war in 1828 he declined the rank of general. Early in 1830 he opened the school at Aegina by giving an impressive lesson on the Choice of Hercules, in the presence of Capodistria, who 'made a great show of promoting education', but afterwards forbade the reading of the *Gorgias* of Plato[6]. The first modern library worthy of the name

---

[1] Nicolai, 101. [2] p. 358 *supra*.

[3] *Mémoires* etc., quoted by Xenophon Anastasiades, *Georgios Gennadios*, 18.

[4] Finlay, vi 124, 133.

[5] 1826; *ib.* 387; Anastasiades, 33, 37, 56; J. Gennadios, *G. Gennadios ἐν Ναυπλίῳ* (1905–6).

[6] Anastasiades, 45 f (cp. Finlay, vii 48 f, 62).

in the East was founded by Gennadios at Aegina; on its removal to Athens, it remained under his care until 1848; and, when the 'central school' was transferred to Athens, he presided over it until the day of his death, declining to be nominated one of the first professors when the university was established in 1837,—the year in which he took part in founding the Archaeological Society. He was inspired by the same spirit as his great contemporary, Koraës. While Koraës remained abroad, editing the Greek Classics in a patriotic spirit and arousing the martial ardour of his countrymen by a new edition of his σάλπισμα πολεμιστήριον, Gennadios actually fought in the war. While Koraës was a great writer, Gennadios was a great teacher, and in this respect was the true heir of the traditions of Photiades. It is from his Greek Grammar of 1832 that the modern Greeks have learnt their own ancient language for the last three generations. As an honorary doctor of Leipzig, he was described as *vir de litteris in Graecia instaurandis bene meritus*. His tomb in Athens has been adorned with elegiac verses in ancient and in modern Greek, but he can hardly have a terser tribute to his memory than a single line from the Elegy of Zalacostas[1] that is thus translated in the *Greek Lays and Idylls*:—

'Here the apostle of light and the father of learning is sleeping'[2].

'Father of learning' is a free translation for 'father of teachers'. Of his many pupils the most distinguished was A. R. Rangabês. Some of them, such as Phyntiádēs and Eustratiádēs, took an active part in the work of the Archaeological Society; among the rest were Papasliōtēs (1820—1877) and Mavrophrýdēs (1828—1866), both of whom were thorough scholars and exemplary preceptors. The latter wrote on elegiac poetry and on Lucian, besides publishing mediaeval texts, and preparing a history of the Greek language (1871)[3].

The university of Athens had been preceded by the university of Corfu. Owing to the influence of the French Revolution a literary and political *Hetairía* had been founded in that island in 1802; this was followed by the 'Ionic Academy' of 1808; and, finally, in 1824, the famous philhellene, Frederick North, fifth Earl of

The Ionian Islands: the university of Corfu

---

[1] ὧδε κοιμᾶται πατὴρ διδασκάλων, ἀπόστολος φώτων.

[2] Anastasiades, 107. Cp. Goudas, ii 311—338; Xenophon Anastasiades, *Georgios Gennadios* (with portrait), 111 pp., London, 1901; J. Gennadios, *Georgios Gennadios ἐν Ναυπλίῳ*, 1905-6; Constantinides, 420—432; and L. Sergeant, *Greece in the xixth century* (1897), 355, 370. Of his sons the eldest (Athanasios) is a Greek scholar still living in Athens, whose emendations on the 'Αθηναίων πολιτεία have been mentioned in the preface to my edition of that work, while the second was Greek Minister in London in 1886-91 (cp. *Hellenic Annual* 1880, 243—252).

[3] Rangabé, *Litt.* i 168, 175.

Guilford (1766—1827), who had joined the Greek Church in 1791 and was Governor of the Ionian Islands, founded the 'Ionian Academy', as the first university of modern Greece, a university which lasted to the end of the English occupation in 1864.

The first professor of Greek at Corfu was Kōnstantînos Asópios (c. 1790—1872), who had been educated under Psalídas at Ioánnina, and (with the aid of Lord Guilford) had continued his studies in Göttingen, Berlin, Paris and London. He had taught at Trieste since 1817 and was professor at Corfu in 1824–43, when he accepted a call to Athens. His most important production was an unfinished History of Greek Literature, prefaced by a history of Greek philology (1850). His 'Introduction to Greek Syntax' is a diffuse work of 1000 pages (1841)[1].

Asópios

The first professor of Latin was another protégé of Lord Guilford, Christóphoros Philētâs[2], the author of a Latin Grammar (1827), while the first professor of philosophy was N. S. Píkkolos (1792—1865), who afterwards taught in Paris and Bucharest, and prepared a supplement to the Greek Anthology (Paris, 1853), and editions of Aristotle's *History of Animals* (*ib.* 1863)[3] and of Longus (1866)[4].

Philētâs
Píkkolos

An account of the successive 'Academies' of Corfu and of the scholars contemporary with them[5] was written by Andréas Mūstoxýdēs (1785—1860), a native of the island, who was nearly 40 years of age at the foundation of the university. He published his Italian history of Corfu in 1804 and was historiographer of the Ionian Islands until 1819, besides receiving academic distinctions in France, Germany and Italy. In 1820, a diplomatic position (that of secretary to the Russian envoy at Turin) was assigned him by the Foreign Minister of Russia, Capodistria, who, as President of Greece nine years later, made him Director of Education. After his patron's assassination in 1831, he spent the rest of his life in his native island, where he founded

Mūstoxýdēs

---

[1] Goudas, ii 225—242 (with portrait); Nicolai, 141 f; Rangabé, i 171; Thereianos, Φιλολογικαὶ ὑποτυπώσεις (1885), 116—125.

[2] Thereianos, 258 f.   [3] Nicolai, 142.

[4] Thereianos, *Koraës*, i 378 f, iii 7.

[5] *Pandora*, Z', 288—298.

a philological and historical journal, the *Hellēnomnēmōn*[1]. He
was restored to the position of historiographer, and, at the time of
his death, was at the head of the education department. Early in
his career (in 1812) he dedicated to Koraës the 80 new pages of
Isocrates, *De Permutatione*, which he had discovered in the MSS
of the Ambrosian and Laurentian libraries. In 1816–7, in conjunction with Dēmētrios Schinâs of Constantinople, he published
five small volumes of Ambrosian *Anecdota*, including 'arguments'
to seven of the orations of Isocrates, and the *scholia* of Olympio-
dorus on Plato. Lastly, he contributed to a collection of Italian
translations of Greek historians an excellent translation of Herodotus (1822) and some notes on Polyaenus.

One of the most scholarly members of the 'Ionian Academy'

Oeconomídēs   was a favourite pupil of Asópios named J. N. Oeconomídēs (1812—1884). He was a member of a
wealthy family in Cyprus, which fled from the Turkish dominions
to Trieste in 1821, and two years later to Corfu, where he completed
his education. He taught Greek and Latin in the local *gymnasium*, and, when Sir George Bowen was anxious to introduce into
the curriculum a translation of an English text-book, Oeconomides
pointed out the mistakes in the original and won the goodwill of
the governor. Late in 1857 he became secretary for education,
early in the following year professor in the Ionian Academy,
and, in 1860, minister of education as the successor of Mustoxýdēs.
Towards the end of his life he returned to Trieste, where he died
in obscurity and destitution, 64 years after his first arrival in that
city as a fugitive from Cyprus.

His works have been the theme of a full and interesting monograph by one
of his ablest pupils, who gives a complete analysis of his master's dissertation
on Cleanthes[2], and of his scholarly interpretations of passages in Thucydides
and other Greek Classics, besides dealing fully with his studies on Syntax and
on Synonyms and on Comparative Philology. Oeconomídēs contributed to
Mustoxýdēs' History of Corfu a lengthy monograph on the local inscriptions,
including that on a silver lamp belonging to the treasurer of the Ionian
Islands[3]. He elaborately elucidated two Locrian inscriptions in the same

---

[1] Athens, 1843–53.

[2] *c.* 1845; Thereianos, Φιλολογικαὶ ὑποτυπώσεις, 132—171.

[3] James Woodhouse; *ib.* 259 f; Curt Wachsmuth in *Rhein. Mus.* xviii
(1863) 537—583.

collection, (1) a covenant between Oeanthia and Chaleion on the Corinthian gulf[1], and (2) a law of the Opuntian Locrians regulating their relations with their colonists at Naupactus[2]. He also wrote a comprehensive monograph on the form ἐπιμελόσθων in an Athenian inscription on the settlement of Chalcis[3].

A special aptitude for surveying the history of classical learning and analysing the published works of classical scholars was displayed by Dionýsios Thereianós (*c.* Thereianós 1833—1897) a native of Zante, who was educated at Corfu under Oeconomídēs. His excellent account of the life and writings of that scholar fills the last 269 pages of the Φιλολογικαὶ ὑποτυπώσεις published in 1885 at Trieste, where the author was for many years editor of the *Kleio*[4]. The work includes a short essay on the political and literary developement of the ancient Greeks, and an ample literary and historical dissertation on 'Hellenism'. An admirable retrospect of the modern history of Greek learning from Chrysolōrâs to Photiádes fills the first chapter of the three volumes in which he fully sets forth the varied aspects of the life of Koraës. Some of his hero's minor writings are reprinted in the appendix[5]. It is a work in which the highest degree of learning is expressed in the most pellucid form of modern Greek prose. The eloquence and the accuracy of the author have been justly commended by Constantīnídēs[6].

Leaving the shores of the Adriatic, we turn once more to Athens. When the university was opened in 1837, the *Acharnians* of Aristophanes was the theme of the first lecture, which was given by the professor of Greek, Ludwig Ross[7]. The first professor of Latin was H. N. Ulrich, who had already taught that language in the 'central school' at Aegina and Athens, and had produced a Greek Grammar and Reader. His Latin and Greek lexicon was

---

[1] Λοκρικὴ ἐπιγραφή, Corfu, 1850; Hicks, no. 31 ; Thereianos, 273-7.

[2] Ἐποίκια Λοκρῶν γράμματα; Hicks, no. 63 ; Thereianos, 277—287.

[3] Hicks, no. 28 ; Thereianos, 287—296.

[4] 'A treasury of literary and political information, written in as admirable a style as any modern Greek has yet attained' (L. Sergeant, *Greece in the xixth Century*, 375).

[5] Demetrio Economo, Trieste, 1889. He afterwards published a διάγραμμα Στωικῆς φιλοσοφίας, 1892.

[6] *Neo-Hellenica*, 337.

[7] *Erinnerungen* (Berlin, 1863) ix and x.

published in 1843, the year of revolution that 'put an end to the
government of alien rulers'[1], and even removed foreigners from
the public service. For obvious reasons the study of Latin has
been much neglected in Greece[2], but Latin scholarship has been
well represented by Kastórchēs, Kūmanúdēs, and Basēs. In the
more congenial department of Greek literature, a comprehensive
Homeric dictionary was produced by I. Pantazídês. The Homeric
question has been elaborately discussed by G. Mistriótēs (subsequently a professor of Greek at Athens), who maintains the
unity of the *Iliad* and *Odyssey* and regards Homer as the author
of both[3], and a French treatise on the topography and the strategy
of the *Iliad* was published in Paris in the same year by the Cretan
scholar, M. G. Nicolaḯdēs, while private life in Homer has been
ably treated by K. R. Rangabês (1883)[4]. The criticism of the
Greek dramatists is well represented by the *Antigone*[5]
of Semítelos (1828—1898), who subsequently published numerous emendations on the text of Euripides[6]. The
Jerusalem palimpsest of that poet has been carefully described
by A. Papadópūlos-Kerameus (1891), who has also catalogued a
large part of the numerous MSS in the patriarchal library of Jerusalem, as well as all the MSS and works of art in the ' Evangelical
School' of Smyrna (1877). An excellent edition of the *scholia* in
the Laurentian MS of Sophocles is the principal work of P. N.
Papageórgios of Thessalonica (1888). Treatises on the discourses
of Isocrates and on the *Hellenica* of Xenophon were produced by
A. Kyprianós of Paros (1830—1869). A critical text of the
Moralia of Plutarch[7] was published by G. N. Bernardákēs (1834—1907), a native of Lesbos, who
studied in Germany and, after holding a professorship at Athens,
spent the evening of his life in the island of his birth.

(Margin note: Semítelos)

(Margin note: G. N. Bernar-dákēs)

[1] Finlay, vii 178.   [2] *Berlin. Phil. Woch.* 1884, 961 f.

[3] Leipzig, 1867. The same subject has been discussed by Thereianós,
N. Balettas, and A. Blachos.

[4] N. Balettas, besides writing on the life and works of Homer, has been
associated with Kyprianós in the translation of Müller and Donaldson's *Greek
Literature.*

[5] Athens, 1887 ; cp. *Berl. Phil. Woch.* 1888, p. 1077 f.

[6] Bursian, lxxi 239.

[7] Teubner, 1888–96, 7 vols. with *Epilogus* ; also *De* EI *in Delphis*, 1894.

He had frequent controversies with scholars in Holland, Germany, and his own country. His review of an edition of the *Gorgias* by Mistriótēs (1872) led to a war of words between the editor and the reviewer[1]. His attack on Cobet for 'appropriating' the emendations of Koraës met with a good-tempered and dignified reply[2]. His own rejoinders to the criticisms of Wilamowitz[3] may be found in the prefaces to the second and fourth volumes of his Plutarch, and in his *Epilogus*. Lastly, his controversies with Kōnstantînos Kontós, professor of Greek at Athens[4], have left their mark on many passages of a work published by a pupil of Kontós, named Charitōnídēs[5].

The Cretan, Dēmétrios Bernardákēs, formerly professor of History at Athens, followed the example of Kūma-nū́dēs[6] in combining the cult of literature with that of scholarship.   He was a dramatist and satirist, as well as the author of an excellent Greek Grammar[7].   Another professor of History at Athens, Cōnstantînos Papar-rigópūlos of Constantinople, produced an important work in five large volumes on the History of Greece in classical, Byzantine, and modern times. A French abridgement of this work has been published in a single volume.   Its general aim is to set forth the continuous life of Greek civilisation from the earliest ages to the present day[8]. Among recent books of reference one of the most important is a Lexicon of ancient and modern Greek, the concluding volume of which was published in 1907 by Anéstē Constantinídēs.

D. Bernar-dákēs

Paparrigó-pūlos

Constantīnídēs

Many of the Greek Classics have been translated into modern Greek, but these translations are less and less needed in proportion as the literary language approaches a more classical standard[9]. Among them may be mentioned the version of Plutarch's *Lives* by A. R. Rangabês, who also made the experiment of rendering the first book of the *Odyssey* into accentual hexameters[10]. The versification of ancient

Translations

---

[1] Bursian, xvii 243 f.   [2] p. 286 *supra*.

[3] Göttingen progr. 1889; *Hermes*, xxv (1892) 199 f; *Gött. Gelehrt. Anz.* (1896) 104.

[4] Author of συμμικτὰ κριτικά in *B.C.H.* i—iii, etc.

[5] ποικίλα φιλολογικά, 907 pp. (Ath. 1904).

[6] p. 383 *infra*.   [7] Rangabé, i 164, ii 118.

[8] Rangabé, i 184 f; medallion portrait in L. Sergeant's *Greece*, facing p. 375.   [9] Nicolai, 201 f; Rangabé, i 164 f.

[10] Rangabé, ii 72 ; Constantinides, 113.

Greece was skilfully imitated by A. G. Levkías of Philippopolis, who wrote 2200 hexameters on the coronation of king Otho[1]. Phílippos Iōánnū of Thessaly, professor of philosophy at Athens, translated into classical Greek the *Germania* of Tacitus, with three of Virgil's *Eclogues*, two of the longer poems of Catullus (lxiv and lxvi), and the first five books of Ovid's *Metamorphoses*, besides composing original poems in the old Greek style[2]. The same volume includes his well-known rendering of a Klephtic poem into Homeric hexameters:—

> μῆτερ ἐμὴ τριφίλητ', ὠμόφροσιν οὐκέτι Τούρκοις
> δουλεύειν δύναμαι· τέτρυταί μοι κέαρ ἔνδον[3].

His letter to Bretós on the controversy as to the best literary language for the modern·Greeks is an excellent introduction to the study of that subject[4].

For more than nineteen centuries the Greek nationality had survived subjection to the Romans, the Byzantines, and the Turks; and, for all those

The language of Greek literature

centuries, the Greek language had maintained an unbroken life, but in two divergent forms. The first of these was the language of the higher literature; the second the language of ordinary life and of the popular literature founded on the popular language. At the end of the classical period (about 300 B.C.), the Attic dialect survived all others as the normal type for prose and as the foundation of a universal literary language[5]. Its earliest important representative is Polybius. Since his time the natural developement of the common literary language has been artificially checked at three successive stages:—

(1) in the first four centuries of our era, when Attic Greek was specially cultivated by Dionysius of Halicarnassus and his followers; (2) in the last four centuries of the Byzantine empire, when there was a marked revival of interest in classical Greek; and (3) in the nineteenth century, when the purists gained a predominant position in the prose literature of modern Greece[6].

The spoken language of ordinary life is represented in the Alexandrian age

The language of ordinary life

by the non-literary papyri, and even to some extent in the Egypto-Alexandrian dialect used in the cramped translational style of the Septuagint[7]. It is also represented in the larger part of the Greek Testament[8]; and it has left its mark on the

---

[1] Rangabé, ii 198—206.   [2] Φιλολογικὰ πάρεργα (1865), *ib.* 207 f.

[3] Constantinides, 390.   [4] 1860; Constantinides, 1—16.

[5] Cp. Thumb, *Die gr. Sprache im Zeitalter des Hellenismus* (1901).

[6] Krumbacher's *Festrede*, *Das Problem der neugriechischen Schriftsprache* (1903) 18—21.

[7] Deissmann's *Bible Studies* (E. T. 1901), 66 f, and Giessen *Vortrag*, 1898.

[8] J. H. Moulton's Winer, 1906, Deissmann in *Theol. Rundschau* (1902)

Chronicles of John Malalas (cent. vi) and on that of Theophanes (ix), and on the writings of Constantine Porphyrogenitus (x)[1]. The first important representative of the distinctively popular literature is the great national epic of Digenis Akritas (the earliest elements in which are ascribed to the 11th century)[2]. This popular literature flourished in Crete in the 16th and 17th centuries, its most prominent products being the *Erotokritos* of Vincenzo Cornaro and the *Erophile* of Georgios Chortatzes[3]. It also found representatives in the Ionian Islands in the 16th and in the early 19th century. In the latter the most conspicuous name is that of Solōmós of Zante, who has been succeeded by Balaōrítēs (Valaoritis) of Leukas, and, later still, by I. Polylas (d. 1896), and G. Kalosgūros (d. 1902), the translators of the *Iliad* and the *Prometheus* respectively[4].

The controversy turns mainly on the question whether the literary language should be founded on the language of the people[5] or on the language of the purists. Of the purists a majority have followed in the general lines of the compromise between colloquial and classical Greek advocated by Koraës[6], while some have urged a return to a more strictly classical standard[7]. This apparently interminable controversy is preeminently one that must be settled by the Greeks themselves. They are apt to warn foreign scholars that a stranger must not intermeddle in the fray, but it has its points of interest to every student of the history of classical scholarship, to whatever nation he may belong. Some of these points are indicated in the calm and dispassionate language of an eminent representative of modern Greece, who has a special right to be heard on this subject:—

---

58 f; Thumb, *ib.* 85 f; and Milligan on *Thess.* (1907) 121 f; also Deissmann's *Lectures on Biblical Greek* (1908).

[1] Krumbacher, 26 f, 33 f.　　　[2] *ib.* 35.　　　[3] *ib.* 39.

[4] *ib.* 53 f, and *Byz. Litt.* 787—801 f. For specimens of the popular language of the earlier part of centuries v to xvi, see E. A. Sophocles, *Gk Lex.* 52—56, and, for that of the whole period, M. Constantinides, *Neohellenica* (1892) 60—80, 142 f, 173 f.

[5] J. Polylas, ἡ φιλολογικὴ μας γλῶσσα (Ath. 1892); Psycharis, ῥόδα καὶ μῆλα (Ath. 1902), and Krumbacher's *Festrede* (Munich, 1903) with the literature there quoted.

[6] G. H. Hatzidákis, *La Question de la langue écrite néo-grecque* (Ath. 1907), and earlier works. Many examples of this intermediate style, beginning with the Greek Testament and ending with 1759, are quoted *ib.* 133—159.

[7] S. D. Byzantios (the lexicographer, 1835), P. Sûtsos (poet, and author of the νέα σχολή) and G. Chrysobérgēs, who have been opposed by the moderate purists Asṓpios, D. Bernardákēs, Kontós, and Hatzidákis (*La Question*, 75 f). For a conspectus of the existing forms of modern Greek, cp. Jannaris, *Modern Greek Dictionary* (1895), p. xiii. This scholar has also produced an 'Ancient Greek Lexicon for Modern Greeks', and a 'Historical Greek Grammar' (1897).

'The Greek people were guided in the progressive development of their language by practical and urgent needs. The movement which has made, within the last century, such rapid and giant strides, was not the result of scholastic pedantry or of political fanaticism; it was not imposed or forced; it was not mechanical. It was the result of the spread of education and of the gradual re-civilization of the country. It is a remarkable fact that it preceded political emancipation. The culture of the Greek language and the study of Greek literature have undoubtedly had, at all times and places, and still have, as an immediate result, the awakening of a sense of individual dignity and of national freedom. But that is one of the primary reasons why the study of Greek is advocated the world over as an indispensable adjunct to a liberal education.'[1]

Another important controversy, that on the pronunciation of Greek, must here be very briefly noticed. The earlier stages of this controversy have been duly set forth by Blass[2]. The 'Erasmian' method, dating from 1528, prevails in various forms throughout Europe, and has even been accepted in Russia[2]. This method has been criticised by Theodōros Dēmētrakópūlos[3] and others[4]. The modern Greeks in general hold that their own pronunciation has descended to them by an unbroken tradition from the Greeks of the classical age. This view has, however, been refuted by their foremost living scholar, G. N. Hatzidákis, who has shown that neither the 'Erasmian' nor the modern Greek pronunciation can be identical with any single ancient pronunciation of the language, although he admits that, in many points, and especially with regard to the vowels, the 'Erasmian' method comes theoretically nearer to the truth[5].

Greek pronunciation

The East has retained a comparatively scanty store of its ancient classical manuscripts. During the Revival of Learning, and in particular between 1408 and 1427, scholars such as Guarino, Aurispa and Filelfo transferred not a few important MSS from Constantinople to places of greater security in the West[6]. On the fall of Constantinople, large numbers of Greek MSS are said to have been sold by the Turks[7]; but there is no reason for believing that any were deliberately destroyed, though they may easily have been damaged or lost for want of proper care. In 1574 Martin Crusius wrote to

Greek MSS: Constantinople

---

[1] J. Gennadios, *Preface* to Kolokotronês, ed. Mrs Edmonds, 1892, p. vii.

[2] *Pronunciation of Ancient Greek* (E. T. 1890), 2—6.

[3] βάσανος τῶν περὶ τῆς Ἑλληνικῆς προφορᾶς ἐρασμικῶν ἀποδείξεων.

[4] Cp. J. Gennadios in *Nineteenth Century*, Oct. 1895 and Jan. 1896, and in *Contemporary Review*, March, 1897; and Constantinides, 304 f.

[5] Ἀκαδημεικὰ ἀναγνώσματα (1904), 284 f (Krumbacher, 91).

[6] ii 36 f *supra*.　　　　　　　　[7] i 437 f *supra*.

Stephan Gerlach, chaplain of the German legation, inquiring after
MSS of Aristotle's *Constitutions*, Theophrastus etc., and was
informed in reply that even the more learned Greeks confined
their reading to the Fathers, to the neglect of the old poets and
philosophers, and that any MSS of the Classics which still survived
had doubtless been bought up by the agents of Italy or France[1].
When the library of Michael Cantacuzenus (who had fallen into
disfavour with the Sultan) was sold, a few Greek MSS were bought
by Gerlach[2] and ultimately sent to Germany[3].   In 1543 Soliman
the Magnificent presented a small collection to Diego de Mendoza, the envoy of Charles V[4].   After 1562, under the same
Sultan, another envoy, Busbecq (1522—1592), sent to Vienna
some 240 MSS, including the famous illustrated Dioscorides (v),
which he had bought from a Jew, the son of the physician to the
Sultan[5].   In 1565–75 catalogues of private libraries in Constantinople and Rhaedestos[6] included MSS of Ephorus and Theopompus,
Philemon and Menander, but the authority of these ascriptions is
very doubtful[7].   The collection of MSS in the old *Seraglio*, the
ancient palace of the Sultans, which presumably includes part of
the former library of the Palaeologi, has long been veiled in a
certain degree of mystery.   During the revolution of 1687 the
Paris Library acquired from the Sultan's collection fifteen Greek
MSS of centuries xi—xv, including a Herodotus (xi) and a Plutarch
(xiii)[8].   On the same occasion, 200 other Greek MSS were dispersed, and the representative of France informed the librarian
in Paris that there were no Greek MSS left.   It was almost exclusively Latin MSS from the library of Matthias Corvinus that were
restored to Budapest in 1869 and 1877[9].   During the 19th century several scholars had access to the MSS, including J. D. Carlyle
(1800), Weissenborn (1857)[10], and E. Miller (1864)[11].   To the last

---

[1]   *Turco-Graecia*, 419, 487.   [2] *ib.* 509.

[3]   Krumbacher, *Byz. Litt.* 506[2].

[4]   Graux, *L'Escurial*, 172—182.

[5]   *Ep.* iv (1562) *ad fin.*; *Life and Letters* (ed. Forster and Daniell, 1881),
i 417.

[6]   R. Foerster (Rostock, 1877).   [7] Krumbacher, 509[2].

[8]   Delisle, *Cabinet des MSS*, i (1868) 296 f; list in Nicolai, 58 f.

[9]   Blass in *Hermes*, xxiii (1888) 228.

[10]   *Neue Jahrb.* lxxvi (1857) 201 f.   [11] *Mélanges*, p. iv.

of these we owe the list of Greek MSS reproduced by Blass in the account of his visit in 1887[1]. This list includes paper MSS of the *Iliad* (xiii) and Polybius i—v (xv). Among the six other Greek MSS independently noticed by Blass is a volume on Tactics (xv). One or two of the ecclesiastical MSS may have belonged to the library of the Palaeologi. A Livy mentioned by Miller was not found by Blass. It was in a private collection that the MS of Joannes Lydus (x) was identified by Choiseul-Gouffier in 1785, and it was in the ancient library of the Jerusalem monastery, in the Greek quarter, that the unique MS of the 'Teaching of the Apostles' was discovered in 1873 by Bryennios (ed. 1883)[2].

An important MS of the Constantinian excerpts from Polybius and other historians was discovered in Cyprus in 1631 by the agents of Nicolas Peiresc[3].

Cyprus

In 1650 the library of the patriarch of Jerusalem contained 'more MSS than could be read in a life-time'[4], but it now has little of classical interest except a palimpsest of parts of Euripides[5], fragments from the comic poets, and from the *Bibliotheca* of 'Apollodorus'[6], and some of the letters of the emperor Julian.

Jerusalem

The MSS belonging to the monastery of St John, founded in 1088 on the island of Patmos, have been recorded in three early catalogues dated 1201[7], 1355[8] and 1382. At the earliest of these dates the number was already 330. When Villoison visited the island in 1785, the monks assured him that, twenty years previously, they had burnt from two to three thousand![9] The library was 'in a most neglected state' in 1801, when E. D. Clarke identified and purchased the important MS now known as the Bodleian Plato[10]. Next year, after the monks had become better aware of the value of some of their possessions,

Patmos

---

[1] *Hermes*, xxiii 219 f, 622 f.

[2] The library of the *Syllogos* has been catalogued by A. Papadopulos Kerameus (1892), who has also catalogued the MSS in Jerusalem, Smyrna, Lesbos etc. (Krumbacher, 510[2] f).

[3] i 405 *supra*.　　　　　　　　[4] Nicolai, 62.

[5] p. 372 *supra*.　　　　　　　　[6] *Rhein. Mus.* xlvi (1891) 161 f.

[7] Diehl in *B. Z.* i 488 f.　　　　[8] Mai, *Nova patrum bibl.* vi (2) 537 f.

[9] E. D. Clarke, *Travels*, vi 44 n.

[10] *ib.* 47; and cp. Sakkelion in Δελτίον, ii 427.

an inscription in unmetrical hexameters to the following effect was placed over the door of the library :—

In this place are lying whatever MSS there are of note : more estimable are they to a wise man than gold : guard them, therefore, watchfully, more than your life; for on their account is this monastery now become conspicuous[1].

The library is now 'a spacious and airy room, and the books are arranged in cases along its walls'[2]. Its 735 MSS, including a not very important Diodorus (xi), have been catalogued by I. Sakkelíon[3], who discovered certain *scholia* on Thucydides[4], Demosthenes and Aeschines[5]; and some *scholia* on Pindar in two copies of the *editio princeps*. These last were published by Semitelos; those on the Pythian odes (which correspond to the *scholia* in the Breslau MSS) have been ascribed to Triclinius[6].

On the monastic library of *Megaspēlaion*, near Corinth, we have only to note that some of the many MSS saved from the fire of 1600 were acquired in 1840 for the library of the Sorbonne[7]. The MSS found in different parts of the kingdom of Greece are now preserved in Athens, but only 14 of the 1856 MSS are connected with classical Greek[8].

Megaspēlaion

Athens

The libraries of Mount Athos were successfully explored by Janus Lascaris on behalf of Lorenzo de' Medici[9], and by Nicólaos Sophianós on behalf of Mendoza, the envoy of Charles V[10]. MSS of Homer, Hesiod and the Greek dramatists and orators are mentioned by travellers in the 18th century, and in the first third of the 19th[11]. In and after 1820 many were destroyed. The *codex Athous* of Ptolemy's *Geography*, formerly part of the same volume as the Strabo (xii), has been

Athos

---

[1] Walpole, *ib.* 44 n.   [2] Tozer, *Islands of the Aegean*, 190.

[3] Ath. 1890; cp. Krumbacher, 510[2].

[4] *Revue de Philologie*, i 182 f.

[5] *B. C. H.* i 1—16, 137—155 (Bursian, ix 253).

[6] Bursian, *Jahresb.* v 107.

[7] Th. Zographos, *Heptalóphos* (Ath. 1861) 243 f.

[8] Nos. 1055—68 in Sakkelion's *Catalogue*, 1892.

[9] ii 37 *supra*.   [10] p. 377 *supra*.

[11] J. D. Carlyle in Walpole's *Turkey*, 196, and Hunt, *ib.* 202, 209; E. D. Clarke, viii 19 (ed. 1818); and R. Curzon's *Monasteries of the Levant*, 309, 318 (ed. 5).

published in *facsimile*[1]. In 1880 Spyridon P. Lampros spent four months in cataloguing the MSS, and his work, in its final form, was published by the Cambridge University Press[2]. Among the very few classical MSS there recorded are single plays of Sophocles, Euripides and Aristophanes, and separate speeches of Demosthenes, with parts of Plato and Aristotle. There are also several MSS of portions of the fables of Aesop and of Babrius.

Babrius is the author specially associated with Minōïdēs Mēnâs or 'Mynas' (1790—1860), formerly professor of philosophy and rhetoric at Serrae in Macedonia, who fled to France on the outbreak of the Greek Revolution of 1821. In 1840 he was commissioned by Villemain to search for MSS in the East. In the library of St Laura on Mount Athos he discovered a MS containing 122 fables of Babrius, of which he made a fairly accurate transcript. This transcript was promptly edited by Boissonade (1844) and more accurately by Lachmann and his friends[3]. On a subsequent visit he acquired the original, a parchment MS (x or xi), which was purchased by the British Museum in 1857. In this MS, fable 123 was represented by a single line, but Menas in his transcript added six barbarous lines of his own[4]. The success of this little venture led him to produce 95 more fables, his copy of which was purchased by the Museum in the same year, and edited in 1859 by G. C. Lewis, who was fully conscious of the imperfections of the text but accepted it as genuine[5]. The spuriousness of this second collection was, however, soon detected and exposed by Dübner[6] and Cobet[7]. It was from a genuine MS found by Menas that Boissonade produced in 1848 a new edition of the *Facetiae* of Hierocles and Philagrius. Menas also brought back from Mount Athos a MS of century x including a new collection of *Poliorcetica* and part of the work of a previously unknown but unimportant historian, Aristodemus, once believed to be a forgery[8] but now accepted as genuine[9]. Lastly, he discovered an important MS identified by E. Miller as

Minōïdēs Mēnâs

---

[1] Paris, 1867, with introd. and bibliogr. by V. Langlois.

[2] Two large quarto vols. 1895, 1900. He has since written on the mediaeval and modern Greek copyists and collectors of MSS (Ath. 1902–3).

[3] p. 129 *supra*.

[4] Rutherford's ed., p. lxvii f; cp., in general, *Prolegomena* to ed. by O. Crusius (1896).

[5] This continued to be the view of Bergk and Bernhardy.

[6] *Revue de l'instruction publique en Belgique* (1860) 84.

[7] *Mnem.* ix (1860) 278 f (cp. viii (1859) 339 f). See also Ficus in Rossbach, *Metr.*[3] 808 f.

[8] C. Wachsmuth, in *Rhein. Mus.* xxiii 303 f.

[9] Cp. Schwartz in Pauly-Wissowa.

the lost books iv—x of the 'Refutation of all Heresies', sometimes called (from the title of book i) the *Philosophumena* of Hippolytus[1].

It was also on Mount Athos that, in or before 1851, the lost '*Shepherd* of Hermas' was discovered by Constantine Simonides (1824— 1867). The discoverer made a copy of six leaves, carried off **Constantine Simonides** three others, and submitted the whole to certain scholars at Leipzig, where the author was at once identified by Gersdorf and the work published by Dindorf (1856)[2]. The discoverer described himself as a native of Hydra, who had been educated at Aegina and on his mother's native island of Syme, N.W. of Rhodes. It is beyond the scope of these pages to dwell on his extensive travels and his extraordinary adventures[3]. Suffice it to say that he paid three visits to Mount Athos, in 1839 f, 1848 and 1851 f. On the first of these visits he professed to have discovered a secret store of MSS, including an Anacreon, a Hesiod and a Homer of unprecedented antiquity. In 1848 these MSS were examined at Athens without any unanimous result, and they were afterwards bought in England by Sir Thomas Phillipps[4]. Simonides pretended to have found (among many other MSS) the lost work of Demetrius Magnes 'On authors bearing the same names', and, being unaware that the writer in question lived in the first century B.C.[5], repeatedly quoted it as his authority for matters of later date, such as the life of Nonnus in the fifth, or of Uranius in the fourth century A.D., the 'Egyptian History' of the latter being one of his most flagrant forgeries. In 1862 he even claimed to have written on Mount Athos in 1840, the most ancient MS of the Greek Bible, the *Codex Sinaiticus* discovered by Tischendorf on Mount Sinai in 1844—59, a MS which (curiously enough) ends with the opening chapters of the '*Shepherd* of Hermas'[6]. Many years had then passed since the Greeks themselves had discovered that Simonides was an impostor. Kumanúdes had pronounced against him in 1848; Rangabês had denounced all his MSS as forgeries in

---

[1] p. 254 *supra*. Minoïdes Menas wrote on Greek pronunciation (1824), edited the 'Dialectic' of Galen (1844), and translated into French Aristotle's *Rhetoric* (1837) and Philostratus, *De Gymnastica* (1852). He was the first to print in 1858 the treatise of the patriarch Gennadios against the Platonism of Plethon. He has sometimes been unjustly confounded with Constantine Simonides (as in Christ's *Gr. Litt.* pp. 652, 922[3]).

[2] On these six leaves see Lampros in *Catalogue*, no. 643 and in Dr Armitage Robinson's pamphlet on Hermas (Cambridge, 1888); also Prof. Lake's preface to the *facsimile* (Oxford, 1907).

[3] Cp. C. Stewart's *Memoir*, 78 pp., 1859; and J. A. Farrer's *Literary Forgeries* (1907), 39—66.

[4] *Athenaeum*, 4 Feb. 1857.   [5] i 161 *supra*.

[6] On this claim, cp. Prothero's *Life of Henry Bradshaw*, 92—99; also *Journal of Sacred Literature*, Oct. 1862 (248—253) and Jul. 1863 (478—498), and (on Uranius) Apr. 1856 (234–9).

1851[1], while in 1849 Mustoxýdes, on receiving from him a presentation copy of the '*Symais* of Meletios', acknowledged the gift in a letter of exemplary courtesy, making it perfectly plain that he had detected the fraud[2]. The fact that he was a notorious impostor is almost all that is now generally associated with his name. It is only fair, however, to remember that some of his MSS were genuine and some of his statements were true. The true and the false were, in fact, so strangely intermingled that he might with perfect truth have said of himself in the words of the poet whose 'most ancient' MS he falsely claimed to have discovered:—

> ἴδμεν ψεύδεα πολλὰ λέγειν ἐτύμοισιν ὁμοῖα,
> ἴδμεν δ', εὖτ' ἐθέλωμεν, ἀληθέα μυθήσασθαι[3].

While the old Greek Classics (as edited by Koraës and others) have naturally been studied with enthusiasm in modern Greece, a prominent place has also been taken by the study of archaeology. Kyriakós Pittákes (*c.* 1806—1863),

Pittákes

who in 1836 succeeded Ludwig Ross as Conservator of Antiquities at Athens, had published in 1835 a meritorious work entitled *L'Ancienne Athènes*. He spent most of his energies on editing inscriptions[4]. The interest in archaeology, exhibited in 1837 by the foundation of the Greek Archaeological Society and the ἐφημερὶς ἀρχαιολογική, was revived by the energy of Aléxandros Rísos Rangabês (1810—1892), who

Rangabês

was born at Constantinople, was educated at Odessa, and studied in Munich. At Athens he successively became Minister of Education (1832), professor of Archaeology (1845–56), and Foreign Minister (1856–9). He was afterwards Greek Minister in Washington, Paris and Berlin. As professor, he published his *Antiquités Helléniques* (1842–55) and his *Hellenica* (1853). He excavated part of the Heraeum of Argos (1855)[5], translated Plutarch's *Lives* into modern Greek (1864–6), wrote a history of modern Greek literature (1877), and published no less than fourteen volumes of philological "Ατακτα (1874–6)[6].

---

[1] *Pandora*, 1851 f, and *Litt. Neohellén.* i 188—191.

[2] *Pandora*, i (1851) 263; Constantinides, 376—380.

[3] Hesiod, *Theog.* 27.

[4] Cp. Michaelis, *Arch. Entd.* 49; Rangabé, i 179; Edmond About and S. Reinach quoted by Th. Reinach in *L'Hellénisme*, 1 July 1907.

[5] Michaelis, 121.

[6] Cp. *Litt. Néo-Hellén.* ii 48—104; portrait in *Hellenic Annual* (Lond. 1880) 240.

The Archaeological Society founded amid the ruins of the Parthenon in April, 1837, was, for the first thirty years of its existence, mainly concerned with inscriptions[1]. A valuable collection of Greek epitaphs was published in 1871 by Stephanos Kumanúdēs[2] (1818—1899). It comprised more than 2800 items, it represented the work of six and twenty years, and was printed at the author's own expense. The author, a native of Philoppopolis, was an ideal scholar and an ideal teacher. He had been appointed professor of Latin in 1845, had made his mark as a poet (1851), and, owing to his high character and his many-sided learning, had been appointed instructor to the young king of the Hellenes on his first arrival in Greece. Meanwhile the Society had resumed the excavation of the Dionysiac theatre, vigorously taken in hand by Strack in 1862[3]. The success of Konstantinos Karapános at Dodona (1875 f) prompted the Society to explore the precinct of Asklēpios, S. of the Acropolis (1876), the shrine of Amphiaraüs at Orôpus (1884–7), the sacred sites of Eleusis (1882–91) and Epidaurus (1881–3)[4], and the Heraeum of Samos (1902)[5]. The excavation of the platform of the Acropolis, begun by Stamatákēs in 1884, was completed by his successor Kabbadías[6], the explorer of Epidaurus.

Kumanúdēs

A Hellenic Philological Society was founded in Constantinople, and was supported by Germans such as Mordtmann, Frenchmen such as Dethier, and Englishmen such as Alexander van Millingen[7]. Smyrna, which has for centuries been a place of resort for collectors of antiquities, ending with the numismatist, Borrell, is well known as a centre of Greek culture[8].

A series of mediaeval Greek texts has been edited by Konstantinos Sathas[9]. The History of the study of Byzantine

---

[1] Kastorches, Ἱστορικὴ ἔκθεσις (1837–79), Ath. 1879; Kabbadías, Ἱστορία τῆς Ἀρχαιολογικῆς Ἑταιρείας, 1900; and Th. Reinach, La Grèce retrouvée par les Grecs, in L'Hellénisme for 1 July—1 August, 1907.

[2] p. 373 supra.

[3] Michaelis, 204. The excavation extended over twenty years (1858–78).

[4] ib. 113—120.   [5] ib. 158.

[6] ib. 206.   [7] σύλλογος, 1860 f.

[8] Cp., in general, Stark, 342.

[9] Μεσαιωνικὴ βιβλιοθήκη, i—vi (Ven. 1872 ; Paris, 1874–7) ; Μνημεῖα, i ii

and Modern Greek lies beyond the limits of the present work. An interesting outline of the scope of such a History, with a summary of the extant literature of the subject, has been given by Krumbacher, the scholar who is most competent to fill the *lacuna*[1].

In Russia, the systematic study of the classical languages goes back to the seventeenth century. In the ecclesiastical 'Academy' of Kiev, founded in 1620, Latin was thoroughly studied from 1631 to the end of the century; in fact, it was almost the only medium of instruction, and the use of even a single word of the vernacular language was severely punished[2]. One of the students produced a translation of Thucydides, and of Pliny's *Panegyric*.

Russia

From Kiev the study of the Classics was transmitted to Moscow. The Latin Grammar in use was that of Alvarez[3]. The printing-school, founded at Moscow in 1679, was the first institution involving the study of Greek, that was subsidised by the government. Throughout the eighteenth century, the Slavo-Greco-Latin Academy (founded in 1685) was the principal source of classical learning. The first teachers of note were two brothers of Greek origin, named Likhûdēs, who were natives of Cephalonia. They had taken their doctor's degree at Padua; and, under their tuition, the students acquired a remarkable facility in Latin[4]. The Academy was highly favoured during the reign of Peter the Great (1689—1725).

During the eighteenth century, and the early part of the nineteenth, classical publications were limited to translations. The principal Greek and Latin authors were translated in twenty-six volumes by Martynov (1771—1883). The first quarter of the nineteenth saw the publication of the earliest works on the archaeology of the Northern shore of the Black Sea[5].

(Paris, 1880–1); *Digenis Akritas* (ed. Sathas and E. S. Legrand, 1875); *History of Psellus* (London, 1899). Cp., in general, Bursian, ii 1244–8.

[1] *Festrede*, 186 f.

[2] Boulgakov, *Hist. de l'Académie de Kiev* (Kiev, 1873) 13, 175 f.

[3] ii. 163 *supra*.

[4] Sramenski, *Les écoles ecclésiastiques en Russie avant la réforme de* 1808 (Kazan, 1881), 740.

[5] Mouraviev-Apostol, *Le voyage en Tauride en* 1820 (St Pétersbourg,

At the university of Moscow (founded in 1755) R. T. Timkovski (1785—1820), who had listened with admiration to Heyne's lectures at Göttingen, produced   Moscow:
an edition of Phaedrus, and a Latin thesis on the   Timkovski
Dithyramb (1806), in which he gave proof of his   Kriukov
                                                        Goerz
command of a clear Latin style.   D. L. Kriukov   Ivanov
                                                        Leontiev
(1809—1845), who attended the lectures of Morgenstern, Francke,
and Neue at Dorpat, and of Boeckh in Berlin, published papers
on the age of Quintus Curtius, and on the tragic element in
Tacitus, with an edition of the *Agricola*, and a work on the
original differences in religion between the Roman Patricians and
the Plebeians[1].   K. K. Goerz (1820—1883), one of the earliest
professors of archaeology in Russia, wrote on the Peninsula of
Taman, also on Italy and Sicily, and on the discoveries of
Schliemann.   The admirable Latin scholar, G. A. Ivanov (1826—
1901), besides producing excellent renderings of the masterpieces
of Latin literature, wrote on Cicero and his contemporaries (1878),
and translated Plutarch, *De facie in orbe lunae*, and the 'Harmonic
Introduction' ascribed to Euclid.   Leontiev, who lectured on
Roman Antiquities and Greek Mythology, and published a work
on the worship of Zeus in ancient Greece, founded in 1850 a
periodical called the *Propylaea*, including papers on classical
subjects by Katkov (on Greek philosophy), Kudriavtsev (on
Greek literature and on Tacitus), and Kriukov (on Roman literature and antiquities).

The university of Vilna, founded in 1803, was superseded in
1833 by that of Kiev, which was not placed on the   Kiev
same level as the other universities until 1863–84.

At the university of St Petersburg (founded in 1819),
N. M. Blagoviestschenski (1821—1891), who attended the lectures

1823; German transl. 1825–6; Italian transl. 1833).   J. Stempovski,
Recherches sur la situation des anciennes colonies grecques du Pont-Euxin,
St Pét., 1826).   Both of these scholars published many other works in
Russian and in French.—For the principal works in Greek and Latin scholar-
ship published in Russia, cp. Paul Prozorov, *Index Systématique*, xvi + 374 pp.,
St Pet., 1898; and Naghouievski's *Bibliographie de l'histoire de la littérature
latine en Russie* 1709—1889, 48 pp. (Kazan, 1889).

[1] Posthumously published under the pseudonym of Dr Pellegrino (Leipzig,
1849).

of Hermann, W. A. Becker, and Haupt at Leipzig, and of Creuzer
and Schlosser at Heidelberg, was the earliest notable
professor of Russian birth. His masterpiece was a
work on Horace and his age[1]. He also produced
an annotated translation of Persius, and wrote
papers on Virgil's *Copa*, on Niebuhr's views as
to the relation of the lays of ancient Rome to the early
histories of the city, and on the coincidence between the story
of the *Matrona Ephesia* of Petronius and a popular narrative
of the district of Perm. Karl Joachim Lugebil (1830—1888),
who was of German parentage, studied at St Petersburg, where
he dedicated to the memory of Graefe an able dissertation
De Venere Coliade Genetyllide (1859). Accompanied by his wife,
he travelled in Germany, Italy and Greece. His best-known
works were connected with Athens:—(1) On Ostracism and
(2) On the history of the Athenian Constitution[2]. His Cornelius
Nepos passed through several editions. Among his contributions
to classical periodicals may be mentioned his papers on the
untrustworthiness of the Alexandrian system of accentuation[3].
He was a man of fine character, and an admirable teacher[4].
V. K. Iernstedt (1854—1902), one of the best of Russian Hel-
lenists, produced an excellent edition of Antiphon (1880)[5], which
had been preceded by studies on the minor Attic Orators.
He also published the 'Fragments of Attic comedy acquired by
bishop Porphyrius' (1891), adding largely to the portions of
these fragments that had been deciphered by Tischendorf[6], and
contributing many important criticisms on points of palaeography
and exegesis. The Historico-Philological Institute was founded
at St Petersburg in 1867 with a view to training school-masters
in history, literature, and the classical languages.

St Petersburg :
Blagoviest-
schenski
Lugebil
Iernstedt

At the university of Kazan (founded in 1804), the earliest
writings of D. T. Bieliaev (1846—1901) were
mainly concerned with 'Hiatus in the *Odyssey*',
and with the political and religious opinions of

Kazan :
Bieliaev

---

[1] 1864 ; ed. 2, 1878.

[2] *Jahrb. f. cl. Phil.* Suppl. iv—v (1861–71).

[3] *Rhein. Mus.* 1888.   [4] *Biogr. Jahrb.* 1888, 26—32.

[5] Cobet, in *Mnem.* v 269 f.   [6] Ed. Cobet, 1876.

Euripides (1876). He is best known in connexion with his *Byzantina*, a work including a detailed commentary on the court of Constantine Porphyrogenitus[1].

At the university of Odessa (founded in 1865), L. F. Voevodski (1846—1901) studied Homer, and the primitive Greek mythology. In his earliest work, 'on cannibalism in Greek Mythology', he regarded the myths as inspired, not by a creative imagination, but by the observation of the daily phenomena of nature (1874). His 'introduction to the mythology of the *Odyssey*' (1881) was mainly on 'Solar Monotheism'.

Odessa:
Voevodski

Lastly, at the university of Kharkov (founded 1804), I. I. Kroneberg (1788—1838) was one of the foremost representatives of classical scholarship in Russia during the early part of the 19th century. He was of German origin, but acquired a perfect mastery of the Russian language. His Latin-Russian Dictionary passed through six editions (1819–60). He also published a compendium of Roman Antiquities, and editions of Horace's *Epistola ad Augustum*, Cicero *pro lege Manilia*, and Sallust, and a paper of literary criticism on Persius. His numerous articles on the Classics, as well as on general literature and art, appeared in the periodicals entitled, *Amalthée*, *Brochures*, and *Minerve*, which filled the same place at Kharkov as the *Propylaea* founded by Leontiev at Moscow. He was celebrated for his aphorisms, *e.g.*

Kharkov:
Kroneberg

'Tout livre doit être cosmopolite; mais il y en a qui ne reflètent que la ruelle, où ils sont nés'; 'Tel homme ressemble à un livre, et tel livre ressemble à un homme. La vraie lecture est une lutte. On ne commence souvent à aimer un homme qu'après s'être bien querellé avec lui ; il en est de même pour les livres'[2].

The above survey is mainly limited to scholars of Russian birth, among whom Lugebil and Kroneberg alone were of German parentage. The university of Dorpat, founded in Livonia by Gustavus Adolphus in 1632, was

Dorpat

[1] Cp. *Byz. Zeitschr.* i 345, iii 184.

[2] Almost the whole of the above account of native Russian Scholarship is abridged from a survey of the subject, which Prof. A. Maleyn of St Petersburg has kindly written in French on my behalf, at the request of Prof. Zielinski.

reconstituted by Alexander I in 1802. Four years previously, all Russian subjects had been recalled from the universities of Germany, but Dorpat remained a centre of German influence from 1802 to 1895[1]; thenceforward the Russian language alone was allowed to be used in the lecture-rooms.

The university of Finland, founded by Sweden at Åbo in 1640, was transferred to Helsingfors by Russia in 1827. The professor of Latin in that university, F. W. Gustafsson (b. 1825), has published criticisms on the text of Cicero *De Finibus*, and on that of Apollinaris Sidonius. At Borgo, E. of Helsingfors, a professorship of Classics was assigned in 1837 to the Swedish poet, Runeberg (1804—1877), who was thoroughly familiar with the Greek and Latin poets.

Helsingfors

The earliest of the German scholars, who resided in Russia for a large part of their lives, was Christian Friedrich Matthaei (1744—1811). He had been a pupil of Ernesti at Dresden, and had also studied at Leipzig; he was rector and professor in Moscow (1772–85), and, after spending four years as head of the school at Meissen, and sixteen as professor of Greek at Wittenberg, returned to Moscow for the last six years of his life. He is best known for having discovered at Moscow in 1780 a MS of the Homeric Hymns, including the *Hymn to Demeter* (first published by Ruhnken[2]) and twelve lines of a *Hymn to Dionysus*[3]. Almost all his own work was connected with Byzantine literature.

Germans in Russia:

C. F. Matthaei

One of Hermann's pupils, Christian Friedrich Graefe (1780—1851), who became professor, librarian, and keeper of Antiquities at St Petersburg, studied Meleager and the Bucolic poets, and edited Nonnus (1819–20). He gave

Graefe

---

[1] The long list of Germans appointed to teach classical or cognate subjects at Dorpat begins with K. Morgenstern (1802), C. L. Struve (1805), J. V. Francke (1821), W. F. Clossius (1824), F. K. H. Kruse (1828), C. F. Neue (1831), L. Preller (1838), and E. Osenbrüggen (1843). Among the latest was L. Mendelssohn (1876).

[2] ii 460 *supra*.

[3] Bursian, ii 551 f. Matthaei mutilated certain Greek MSS in Moscow and carried his plunder off to Germany. He was charged with this theft as early as 1789, and the charge has since been confirmed (Oscar von Gebhardt, in *Centralbl. für Bibl.*, 1898).

instruction in Greek to his friend Count Uvarov (1785—1855), the Russian Minister of Education, who wrote in French on the Mysteries of Eleusis and in German on the Poetry of Nonnus and on the Prae-Homeric Age. He uses German in his work on Nonnus because 'the revival of classical learning belongs to the Germans'[1]. He exemplifies the influence of the New Humanism beyond the borders of Germany[2].

Friedrich Vater, son of J. S. Vater, studied at Berlin, where he died (1810—1866). Of his earlier works, the best known is his edition of the *Rhesus* (1837). His **F. Vater** papers on Andocides, begun in Berlin, were continued at Kazan, and he also published at Moscow an edition of the *Iphigenia in Aulis* (1845). During the forties, classical studies in Russia were much influenced by German scholarship, as represented by Boeckh and K. O. Müller on the one hand, and by Ritschl on the other. The last 33 years of the life of Nauck (1822–92), and the greater part of the last 28 years **Nauck L. Müller** of that of Lucian Müller (1836–98), were devoted to the teaching of Greek and Latin respectively at St Petersburg[3].

Jacob Theodor Struve (1816—1886), who studied at Dorpat and Königsberg, taught for twenty years at the university of Kazan, was Greek professor at **J. T. Struve** Odessa (1865–70), and finally, for eight years, director of the *gymnasium* at St Petersburg. He is best known for his criticisms on Quintus Smyrnaeus[4], having been led to study that poet by his uncle, Carl Ludwig Struve, whose *Opuscula Selecta* he edited.

---

[1] Reprinted in his *Études*. Cp. Georg Schmid, *Zur russischen Gelehrten-geschichte*, 99. Count Uvarov's German Essay was dedicated in 1817 to Goethe, who calls him *einen fähigen, talentvollen, geistreich gewandten Mann* (in *Ferneres über deutsche Litteratur*, xxvii 150 Cotta, quoted by Schmid *l.c.*, in *Russ. Revue*, xxv 77—108, 156—167).

[2] For ten years (1836–46) Graefe counted among his colleagues the professor of Latin, T. F. Freytag (1800—1858). Most of the brief memoranda on classical scholars in Russia, printed by Creuzer, *Zur Gesch. der cl. Philol.* (1854), 166—172, were supplied in 1846 by Freytag, who, besides the more obvious names, mentions Groddeck (1762—1824), professor at Vilna, and Karl Hofmann in Moscow, editor of Thucydides, 1840–3.

[3] See pp. 149 f and 189 f *supra*.

[4] Petrop., 1843; Casani, 1860.

At Odessa, he worked at the local Greek inscriptions, publishing the results of his researches in his *Pontische Briefe* (1871)[1].

The study of classical archaeology in Russia dates from the reign of Peter the Great (d. 1725). The Academy of Sciences, founded in 1725, included the name of Theophil Siegfried Bayer (1694—1738) of Königsberg, who applied an accurate knowledge of numismatics to his works on Greek Chronology, the Achaean League, and the Greek rule in Asia, besides writing a monograph on the 'Venus of Cnidos', in connexion with a statue purchased in Rome by Peter the Great in 1718.

Archaeologists Bayer

The conquest of the Crimea in 1783, and of the Northern coast of the Black Sea in 1792, led to those former sites of Greek civilisation being explored by Russia under an organisation whose centre was in St Petersburg. Under Alexander I (1801–25) Classical Philology and Archaeology were definitely recognised in the Academy of Sciences, and the President of the Academy, Count Uvarov, took the keenest interest in the archaeological exploration of the southern parts of Russia. The discoveries in that region were the theme of the letters addressed to the Academy by a pupil of Heyne, Heinrich K. E. Köhler (1765—1838), who devoted most of his time to the study of ancient gems. His collected papers on archaeological topics were edited for the Academy in six volumes by Ludolf Stephani (1850–3). Von Stackelberg (1787—1834), who studied at Göttingen, and spent many years in Dresden and in Greece and Italy in the study of archaeology[2], did not return to Russia until the last year of his life. In the meantime, his German contemporary, Hermann's pupil, Graefe[3], who was elected a member of the Russian Academy in 1820, was working at the Greek inscriptions of the South coast, while Morgenstern of Halle (1770—1852) was awakening an interest in Greek art at Dorpat. The archaeological work begun by Köhler was ably continued by Stephani (1816—1887), who studied at Leipzig, was professor at Dorpat (1846–50), and keeper of the Antiquities of the Hermitage at St Petersburg for the last 37 years of his life. He was the author of many important monographs on the archaeological discoveries in South Russia[4].

H. Köhler

Stackelberg

Stephani

Hungary was among the homes of humanism in the reign of Matthias Corvinus (d. 1490), whose library was scattered on the occasion of the capture of the capital by the Turks in 1526[5].

Hungary

---

[1] *Biogr. Jahrb.* 1886, 11—13.

[2] p. 218 *supra*.   [3] p. 388 *supra*.

[4] p. 223 *supra*.

[5] ii 275 and iii 377 *supra*.

Latin long remained in use as a living language in Hungary[1]; the debates of the Diet were conducted in Latin until 1825[2]; but there was little interest in classical literature until the middle of the nineteenth century, when there was a revival of learning attested by numerous translations of the Classics, as well as the publication of classical text-books.   Among those who aimed at producing works of more permanent value was   Télfy

Ivan Télfy (1816—1898), Greek Professor at Buda-pest, whose Studies on Greek pronunciation (1853) were followed by his *Corpus Juris Attici* (1868), and by his edition of Aeschylus (1876).   On his retirement in 1886, he was succeeded by Eugen Abel (1858—1889), who owed his knowledge of   Abel

English and German to his mother (a native of England), and who added to the French that he had learnt at school the Italian that he acquired at the university.   At Buda-pest he attracted the attention of the restorer of classical learning in Hungary, Emil Thewrewk de Ponor[3].   In 1877 he laid the foundation of his knowledge of palaeography, and of the history of humanism in Hungary, in the study of certain MSS from the library of king Corvinus, which were then restored by the Turks. He was thus led to explore the libraries of Europe in quest of MSS of the Epic poets of Greece and the humanists of Hungary. On his return he succeeded Télfy as professor of Greek, but held that position for three years only, dying at Constantinople on the eve of his examination of the ancient MSS of that city.

In the department of Greek Epic poetry, he produced critical editions of Kolluthos (1880), the Orphic *Lithika* and the *Orphica* (1881–5), the *Homeric Hymns and Epigrams*, and the *Battle of the Frogs and Mice* (1886).   He introduced the digamma into his edition of the *Homeric Hymns*; his Hungarian commentary on the *Odyssey* was preceded by a Homeric Grammar published in 1881, a year before that of Monro.   He also edited two volumes

---

[1] On the language of Latin literature in Hungary, cp. Bartal, *Glossarium mediae et infimae Latinitatis regni Hungariae* (Leipzig, 1901).

[2] In Hungary, Croatia, and Transylvania, 'Latin conversation was last heard in 1848, and then only from Croat lips' (*Cl. Rev.* xxi 227).   Possibly here (as in Italy) colloquial Latin was killed by the revival of learning.

[3] Born 1838; founder of the Budapest Philological Society, and joint-editor of its literary organ, since 1871.

of *scholia* on Pindar (1884–91), and published the Ancient and Mediaeval Lives of Terence (1887). Among his publications connected with the history of humanism in Hungary were his *Analecta* on the Hungarian humanists and the 'learned society of the Danube' (1880), his article on Hungarian universities in the Middle Ages (1881), and his edition of the remains of Isotta Nogarola of Verona (1886). His work in this department is of special importance for the period between the accession of king Corvinus (1464) and the battle of Mohács (1526)[1].

The publications of the Hungarian Academy are in the Magyar language, which is also used in the principal philological journal[2], but a medium of communication with the scholars of Europe is provided by the *Literarische Berichte aus Ungarn* and by the *Ungarische Revue*[3].

[1] *Biogr. Jahresb.* 1890, 47—52; cp. Bursian's *Jahresb.* xv (1878) 130 f.
[2] *Egyetemes philologiai közlöny*, 1871 f.
[3] Bursian, ii 1243.

CHAPTER XL.

ENGLAND IN THE NINETEENTH CENTURY.

DR PARR, who died in 1825, writes thus in his Diary:—

'In the reign of Ptolemy Greece boasted of her Pleiad; England, in my day, may boast of a Decad of literary luminaries, Dr Samuel Butler, Dr Edward Maltby, bishop Blomfield, dean Monk, Mr E. H. Barker, Mr Kidd, Mr Burges, professor Dobree, professor Gaisford, and Dr Elmsley. They are professed critics: but in learning and taste Dr Routh of Oxford is inferior to none'[1].

The last of these, Martin Joseph Routh (1755—1854), died in the hundredth year of his age, after having been President of Magdalen for three and sixty years.
Routh
He edited the *Euthydemus* and *Gorgias* of Plato in 1784, lived to produce the fifth volume of his *Relliquiae Sacrae* in 1848, and, at the age of 92, summed up his long experience in the precept:—'I think, sir, ...you will find it a very good practice *always to verify your references*'[2]. Edward Maltby (1770—1859), of Winchester and of Pembroke, Cambridge, successively bishop of Chichester and of Durham, was the author of a useful
Maltby
Kidd
Lexicon Graecoprosodiacum (1815)[3]. Thomas Kidd (1770—1850), of Trinity, Cambridge, head-master of Lynn, Wymondham and Norwich, edited the philological and critical works of Ruhnken, the 'Tracts' of Porson, and the 'Miscellanea Critica' of Dawes. 'It was amusing', says Maltby, 'to see Kidd in Porson's company; he bowed down before Porson with the veneration due to some being of a superior nature'[4].

[1] *Memoirs*, i 752 n.

[2] Burgon's *Twelve Good Men*, i 73.

[3] Founded on Morell's *Thesaurus* (1762). In supplementing that work Maltby, the pupil of Parr and the friend of Porson, received valuable assistance from both.

[4] Rogers, *Table Talk*, *Porsoniana*, 325.

The Porsonian tradition passed for a time from Cambridge to Oxford in the person of Peter Elmsley (1773— 1825) of Winchester and Christ Church. After spending several years in Edinburgh, he lived in Kent from 1807 to 1816, when he paid his first visit to Italy. For the rest of his life his headquarters were at Oxford. He spent the winter of 1818 in Florence, studying the Laurentian MS of Sophocles. He collated the MS in 1820, and the earliest recognition of its superiority is to be found in the preface to his edition of the *Oedipus Coloneus*[1]. In 1819 he aided Sir Humphry Davy in examining the Herculanean *papyri* in the Museum of Naples. For the last two years of his life he was principal of St Alban Hall and Camden professor of Ancient History at Oxford.

At Edinburgh he edited the text of Thucydides with a Latin translation (1804), and contributed to the *Edinburgh Review* scholarly articles on Heyne's *Iliad*, Schweighäuser's Athenaeus, Blomfield's *Prometheus Vinctus*, and Porson's *Hecuba*[2]. His most important works were his editions of Greek plays, all of them published at Oxford, namely the *Acharnians* of Aristophanes, the *Oedipus Tyrannus* and *Oedipus Coloneus* of Sophocles, and the *Heraclidae*, *Medea*, and *Bacchae* of Euripides. His editions of the *Medea* and *Heraclidae* were reprinted by Burton, with additions from Elmsley's papers. The latter were also the source of the readings of the Laurentian MS printed in the Oxford Sophocles of 1826.

As a scholar whose editorial labours were almost entirely confined to the Greek drama, Elmsley had a close affinity with Porson, who held him in high esteem until he found him appropriating his own emendations without mentioning his name. Porson's property was thus annexed by Elmsley in his review of Schweighäuser's Athenaeus[3], and in his edition of the *Acharnians*[4]. Elmsley attempted to suppress the latter, but found to his dismay that it had already been reprinted at Leipzig[5]. In his *Medea* he observed that an editor's duty consisted in two things :—correcting the author's text, and explaining his meaning ; the former duty had been discharged by Porson, while the latter had been neglected. In all his editions of Greek plays, Elmsley devoted

---

[1] 1823 ; Jebb, in *Pref.* to *Facs.* 20, n. 5, and in *Introd.* to *Text* (1897) xliii f.

[2] Nos. 4, 5, 35, 37 respectively. He reviewed Markland's three plays in the *Quarterly*; Hermann's *Supplices* and *Hercules Furens* in the *Cl. Journal*; and published his own notes on the *Ajax* in the *Museum Criticum*, i 351 f, 469 f.

[3] *Edin. Rev.* no. 5, Oct. 1803; cp. *Quarterly Rev.* v 207.

[4] *Church of England Quarterly Rev.* v 413 f.

[5] Watson's *Life of Porson*, 310 f.

Elmsley

himself mainly to the illustration of the purport of the text, and to the
elucidation of the laws of Attic usage[1]. He had a wide knowledge of modern
history. He was 'an accurate critic, and a profound and elegant scholar',
remarkable for 'the charm of his conversation', and for 'the gentleness and
goodness of his heart'[2]. He was also a man of calm temper and impartial
judgement, while his fondness for light reading was one of the points in which
he resembled Porson[3]. In his illustrative notes he showed himself fully alive
to the value of the work done by his predecessors, such as Brodaeus and
Barnes, Heath and Musgrave[4]. Elsewhere he says of Casaubon's Athenaeus,
'we know of no work, except perhaps Bentley's *Dissertation on Phalaris*, in
which the reader is presented with such a mass of pertinent information'[5].
His merits as a scholar were highly esteemed by Hermann[6], whose edition of
the *Bacchae* was published solely as a supplement to that of Elmsley, *cuius
viri et doctrinam admiror et animi ingenuitatem maximi facio*.

Among the merits of Elmsley was a high appreciation of the
value of the Laurentian MS of Sophocles. His
careful edition of the *scholia* in that MS was brought
Gaisford
out by Thomas Gaisford (1779—1855), who was born only
six years later than Elmsley and survived him by thirty. A
native of Ilford in Wiltshire, he was appointed Regius professor
of Greek at Oxford in 1812, and was dean of Christ Church
for the last twenty-four years of his life. The Gaisford prizes
for Greek verse and prose were founded in his memory.

Early in his career he produced school-editions of the *Alcestis*, *Electra*, and
Andromache, and saw through the press Musgrave's *Hecuba*, *Orestes*, and
Phoenissae, and Markland's *Supplices* and the two *Iphigeneias*. In 1809 he
published the paraphrase of the *Nicomachean Ethics* by Andronicus of
Rhodes, and in the following year first made his mark by the edition of
Hephaestion, which led Hermann to describe its editor as *dignus qui multa
cum laude commemoraretur*[7]. When the professorship of Greek fell vacant in

---

[1] His notes on the *Heraclidae*, *Medea* and *Bacchae*, 'ad scenicorum
linguam usumque quantum attinet' were reprinted in Gretton's *Elmsleiana
Critica*, 1833.

[2] *British Critic*, April, 1827, 281.

[3] *Gentleman's Mag.*, April, 1825, 374–6 (ascribed by Luard to Edward
Copleston, then Provost of Oriel). Luard's bound volume of *Elmsleiana* has
been lent to me by Professor Mayor.

[4] Preface to *Heraclidae*.　　　　[5] *Edin. Rev.* Oct. 1803, 185.

[6] *Opusc.* vi 95.

[7] Ed. (with Proclus, *Chrest.*) 1810 (Leipzig, 1822); and (with Ter.
Maurus) 1856.

THOMAS GAISFORD.

Reproduced (by permission of Messrs Ryman) from the mezzotint by
T. L. Atkinson (1848) of the portrait by H. W. Pickersgill, R.A.,
in the Hall of Christ Church, Oxford.

1812, acting on the judicious advice of Cyril Jackson, then dean of Christ Church, he sent a handsomely bound copy of his *Hephaestion* (with a letter, dictated by the dean) to Lord Grenville, the minister in whose hands the appointment lay; and, shortly afterwards, he was duly appointed to the position which he adorned for the remaining forty-three years of his life[1].

In 1812 he published catalogues of the Greek MSS of D'Orville and of E. D. Clarke, followed by readings from the Bodleian Plato in his *Lectiones Platonicae* (1820). In the latter year he produced a variorum edition of Aristotle's *Rhetoric*, and completed the critical notes and *scholia* to a new edition of Winterton's *Poëtae Minores Graeci*. He also edited the *Florilegium* and the *Eclogae* of Stobaeus, as well as Herodotus, Sophocles, Suïdas (1834–7), the *Etymologicum Magnum* (1848), and Pearson's *Adversaria Hesychiana*, besides editions of the Greek Proverbs, and the Latin writers on metre, with Choeroboscus, several of the works of Eusebius and Theodoret, and the Septuagint. It was in allusion to his Suïdas and his *Etymologicum Magnum* that the future lexicographer, Robert Scott, in his Homeric verses, described Gaisford as δύω δολιχόσκια πάλλων | λεξικὰ δυσβάστακτα[2].

With a view to his editions of the Greek poets, and of Stobaeus and Suïdas, he spent four months at Leyden studying the MSS in the Library, together with the *Adversaria* of Valckenaer. His visit was agreeably remembered by his constant companion, Bake[3]. During this visit one of the professors made some metrical mistake, whereupon Gaisford poured forth in Latin a flood of learning from Hephaestion and other authors, till the Dutch professor held up his hands, and exclaimed :—*O vir magnae profecto sapientiae, si tam in rebus quam in verbis incaluisses*[4]. The learning and industry that he bestowed on the Greek Poets were eulogised by Hermann[5], who, on being visited by an English scholar, after expressing in vigorous language a certain contempt for Scholefield, reverently added :—'But Gaisford I adore'[6]. George Gaisford used to relate how, when he went with his father to call on Dindorf at Leipzig, 'the door was opened by a shabby man, whom they took to be the famulus, but who, on the announcement of Gaisford's name, rushed into his arms and kissed him'[7].

---

[1] H. L. Thompson's *Life of H. G. Liddell*, 139; cp. *Journal of Cl. and Sacred Philology*, ii 343 f, iii 123; W. Tuckwell's *Reminiscences of Oxford*, 129—134.

[2] W. Tuckwell, 266.   [3] *Schol. Hyp.* vol. ii v—vii.

[4] H. L. Thompson's *Life of H. G. Liddell*, 25.

[5] 1831, *Opusc.* vi 98.

[6] The English scholar was George Butler, Head Master of Harrow. I owe this anecdote to his son, the Master of Trinity. In *Opusc.* vi 97 Hermann notices the lack of originality in Scholefield's *Aeschylus* (1828), while he describes the editor of the *Poëtae Minores* as 'der fleissige und gelehrte Gaisford' (*ib.* 98).

[7] W. Tuckwell, 131.

A certain deflexion from the critical Porsonian tradition is exemplified by Samuel Butler (1774—1839), the editor
S. Butler
of Aeschylus.   He was educated at Rugby, and was
on the point of being entered at Christ Church under Cyril
Jackson, when, by the advice of Dr Parr, who had been struck
by a copy of his Latin verses, he became a member of St John's
College, Cambridge.   At Cambridge he won the gold medal for
the Greek and the Latin Ode, and was also Craven Scholar and
Chancellor's Medallist.   A year before his M.A. degree, his
College elected him head-master of Shrewsbury, a position which
he held to the great advantage of the College as well as the
School from 1798 to 1836, when he became bishop of Lichfield
for the last three years of his life.

The Syndics of the Cambridge Press had invited Porson to edit Aeschylus,
with Stanley's text. The offer, which had been declined by Porson, was
accepted by Butler, whose edition filled four quarto volumes (1809–15),
including the Greek *scholia*, and all the notes of Stanley and his predecessors,
with selections from those of subsequent editors, and a synopsis of the 'various
readings'.

It was ably reviewed by C. J. Blomfield[1], who protested against the
'literal reprint of the corrupt text of Stanley's edition', against 'the extreme
deficiency of illustration from Aeschylus himself and his brother tragedians',
and 'the implicit deference' paid to 'the authority' of Hesychius, Suïdas, and
the *Etymologicum Magnum*. He also regretted that the lucubrations of
Turnebus, Muretus, and Beroaldus, and 'their unworthy imitator, Schütz',
filled up 'a space which would have been more advantageously occupied' by
the 'more useful and concise' notes of the critics of the Dutch school,
Hemsterhuys, Valckenaer, Pierson, Koen and Ruhnken; it was 'an indiscriminate coacervation' of all that had been 'expressly written on Aeschylus'. Butler,
in the course of his reply, remarks that 'probably no man ever undertook a
work of this nature with so little assistance. ' Of the many thousand passages'
from ancient authors 'not one has been pointed out to me by any learned
friend '. He honestly confesses to certain mistakes, but 'continually betrays
the jealousy which Parr's circle entertained towards the Porsonians'[2]. Many
years afterwards bishop Blomfield said of Butler, 'he was a really learned as
well as amiable man, but his forte did not lie in verbal criticism'[3]. His

---

[1] *Edin. Rev.*, Oct. 1809, and Jan. 1810; Feb. 1812 (full extracts in
J. E. B. Mayor's ed. of Baker's *Hist. of St John's Coll.* ii 908—921); cp.
Life and Letters of Dr S. Butler (1896), i 22 f, 53—62.

[2] *Letter to the Rev. C. J. Blomfield*, 1810 (J. E. B. Mayor, 911—915).

[3] *ib.* 917.

'Praxis on the Latin prepositions' (1823) held its ground for about twenty-five years, when it was superseded by books of less interest. The only other work that need here be mentioned is his 'Sketch of Modern and Ancient Geography' (1813), which passed through ten editions, together with 'An Atlas of Ancient Geography' (1822, etc.)[1]. In his 'Ancient Geography' he 'endeavoured to make a dry catalogue of names interesting and useful, by the application of history, chronology and poetry', and especially by quoting select passages from the best classical poets[2]. His interest in classic travel is well exemplified in one of his letters to Parr : —

'My journey, though very laborious, and not free from peril, completely succeeded. I visited every spot connected with the most interesting parts of the Roman history—including Mons Sacer, Tibur, Tusculum, and Alba, and, of course, part of the old Appian way. From Cicero's Tusculan Villa I looked down upon that of his neighbour Cato.... I visited the Alban Villa of Domitian,...and the emissary of the Alban Lake, made by Camillus.... At the grotto of Egeria I trod upon a fragment of marble and drank from the stream running once more through its native *tophus*...'[3].

The Porsonian type of scholarship, represented at Oxford by Elmsley, was maintained at Cambridge by Dobree, Monk, and C. J. Blomfield. The first of these, Peter **Dobree** Paul Dobree (1782—1825), was born in Guernsey, and was indebted to the place of his birth for the mastery of French that made him so acceptable during his visit to Leyden in 1815[4]. Meanwhile, he had been elected a Fellow of Trinity and had joined in founding Valpy's *Classical Journal* in 1810, while he was a frequent contributor to Burney's *Monthly Review*. He edited (with many additions of his own and in particular with his own commentary on the *Plutus*) Porson's *Aristophanica* (1820)[5], which was followed by Porson's transcript of the lexicon of Photius (1822). When Monk vacated the Regius Professorship of Greek, Dobree was elected in his place and held that position for the two remaining years of his life. His *Adversaria* on the Greek Poets, Historians, and Orators, were posthumously published in four volumes (1831–3) by his successor, Scholefield[6]. His transcript of the *Lexicon rhetoricum Cantabrigiense* was printed

---

[1] Republished by Dent, without date, 1907.

[2] Mayor, *l.c.* 936.   [3] Parr's *Works*, vii 372 (1822).

[4] Bake's *Schol. Hyp.* ii, ii—v.

[5] Cp. Hermann, *Opusc.* vi 96.

[6] Ed. Wagner in 2 vols. 1874, with the *Observationes Aristophaneae* of 1820.

in 1834, and his 'Miscellaneous Notes on Inscriptions' in the following year.

While Dobree was a follower of Porson in the textual criticism of Aristophanes, he broke new ground as a critic of the Attic Orators, and of Demosthenes and Lysias in particular. In the Praelection that he delivered as candidate for the professorship once held by Porson, he dilated on Porson's merits, and, after expressing the general regret that Porson had mainly confined his attention to the poets, himself discoursed on the Funeral Oration ascribed to Lysias, giving conclusive reasons for supporting Valckenaer's opinion that it was a spurious production. In the person of Dobree, the old alliance between the scholarship of England and the Netherlands received a new ratification that re-called the age of Bentley and of Hemsterhuys.

James Henry Monk (1784—1856), who was educated at

Monk Charterhouse and was Fellow of Trinity, held the professorship of Greek from 1809 to 1823, having in 1822 been appointed dean of Peterborough. He was conse-crated bishop of Gloucester in 1830, and held the bishopric of Gloucester and Bristol from 1836 to his death twenty years later. Following in the footsteps of Porson and Elmsley[1], he edited four plays of Euripides, the *Hippolytus* and the *Alcestis*, while he was still professor, and the two *Iphigeneias*, when he was already a bishop. All four plays were republished in 1858. In conjunction with E. V. Blomfield he edited the two volumes of the *Museum Criticum* (1814, 1826), which was continued under the name of the *Philological Museum* (1832–3). The year of his consecration as bishop was that of the publication of his admirable *Life of Bentley*.

Monk's fellow-editor of Porson's *Adversaria* in 1812 was

C. J. Blomfield Charles James Blomfield (1786—1857), who was educated at Bury St Edmunds, and was a Fellow of Trinity. He edited with notes and glossaries the *Prometheus*, *Septem*, *Persae*, *Agamemnon* and *Choëphoroe* (1810–24), and it may safely be assumed that he would have edited the *Eumenides*, had he not been appointed bishop of Chester in 1824. Four years later he was transferred to the see of London, which he

[1] Cp. Hermann, *Opusc.* vi 96.

held for the remaining nineteen years of his life. Besides the Aeschylean plays above mentioned, he edited Callimachus (1815), and contributed to the *Museum Criticum* (1814–26) editions of the fragments of Sappho[1], Alcaeus, Stesichorus and Sophron. The best characteristic of his edition of Aeschylus was the glossary[2]. He was an active and vigorous contributor to the Classical periodicals of the day[3].

His younger brother, Edward Valentine Blomfield (1788—1816), Scholar of Caius and Fellow of Emmanuel, was an admirable writer of Greek verse, who translated Matthiae's Greek Grammar, and began to prepare a new Greek Lexicon. The former was published after his death by his elder brother[4].

E. V. Blomfield

E. V. Blomfield's contemporary, Edmund Henry Barker (1788—1839), of Trinity, Cambridge, was the author of controversial works on C. J. Blomfield (1812), followed by *Aristarchus Anti-Blomfieldianus* (1820)[5]. In the latter year he produced from a Paris MS the *editio princeps* of Arcadius περὶ τόνων. Besides writing reminiscences of Porson and Parr, and editing text-books, he took an important part in A. J. Valpy's edition (1816–25) of the Greek *Thesaurus* of Stephanus.

E. H. Barker

A very successful edition of the Greek Testament, and an excellent annotated translation of Thucydides (1829), were the principal works of Dr S. T. Bloomfield, of Sidney Sussex College, Cambridge.

S. T. Bloomfield

Richard Valpy (1754—1836), of Pembroke, Oxford, the successful headmaster of Reading (1781—1830), produced many classical school-books in 1809–16, including the well-known Greek *Delectus* (1816, etc.). His younger brother, Edward (1764—1832), of Trinity, Cambridge, head-master of Norwich, edited the Greek Testament; while, of his sons, Abraham John (1787—1854), Fellow of Pembroke, Oxford, was publisher of a classical journal and part-editor of numerous classical texts in 1807–37, including a reprint of the Delphin Classics, 1819–30; and Francis Edward Jackson (1797—1882), of Trinity, Cambridge, produced a 'second' and 'third' Greek *Delectus* and an Etymological Latin Dictionary.

The Valpys

---

[1] Cp. Hermann, *Opusc.* vi 100. Blomfield's recension of Sappho, Alcaeus and Stesichorus was included in vol. iii of the Leipzig edition of Gaisford's *Poëtae Minores Graeci* (1823).

[2] Hermann, *l.c.* 96.

[3] *Memoir* by Luard in *Journal of Cl. and Sacred Philol.* iv (1858) 96—200; and by A. Blomfield, 1864, chaps. i, ii.

[4] *Memoir* in *Museum Criticum*, ii 520–8.

[5] A reply to C. J. Blomfield's brilliant article on Stephens' Greek *Thesaurus* in the *Quarterly Rev.* Jan. 1820; cp. *Memoir* of C. J. Blomfield, 20 f.

C. J. Blomfield was attacked in Valpy's *Classical Journal*[1] by George

Burges

Burges (1786?—1864), formerly of Charterhouse, Fellow of Trinity, who was for many years a private tutor in Cambridge. Blomfield was charged with plagiarising certain emendations from Porson's unpublished papers, and effectively repelled the charge in the *Museum Criticum*[2]. Burges edited several Greek plays[3] and some of the minor dialogues of Plato. His rashness as a textual critic is the theme of several pages in Poppo's Thucydides[4], but a kindlier judgement is passed on him by the Dutch scholar, Bake, who saw much of him at Leyden[5].

In 1825 a contemporary of Blomfield and Burges, James Scholefield,

Scholefield

Fellow of Trinity (1789—1853), was elected over the heads of Julius Charles Hare and Hugh James Rose to the Greek professorship vacated by Monk's successor, Dobree. He did good service to the memory of his predecessors in the Chair by seeing through the press three editions of Porson's Euripides (1826, '29, '50), and two volumes of Dobree's *Adversaria* (1831–3), which were followed by the *Lexicon Rhetoricum Cantabrigiense* and the *Notes on Inscriptions*. His life-long interest in the Greek Testament is partly embodied in his 'Hints for an improved Translation' (1832). In 1828 he had reprinted Bishop Middleton's 'Treatise on the Greek Article'; in the same year he produced his edition of Aeschylus, the earliest English attempt to embrace in a single volume the results of modern criticism on that poet. A second edition (1830) was reviewed in the *Philological Museum* of 1832 by John Wordsworth, who describes the text as mainly a reproduction of the ultra-conservative text of Wellauer. Scholefield was not endued with the acumen of a Bentley or a Porson, but he fully appreciated their skill and readily accepted the results of their able contributions to the criticism of the text. In a separate edition of the *Eumenides* (1843) he commends K. O. Müller for 'rising beyond the school of mere verbal criticism'[6], and he is not held in high esteem by Müller's opponent, Hermann[7]. Dr T. W. Peile, who gratefully acknowledged that he owed to Scholefield 'his first effectual introduction to the gigantic mind of Aeschylus'[8], described his scholarship as 'more exact, perhaps, than elegant, but always sound and solid and practically useful'[9]; while Dr Kennedy was 'accustomed to regard him as a strong,

---

[1] xxii (1820) 204—218; cp. xxiv (1821) 402—424.

[2] No. vii, Nov. 1821, vol. ii 496—509; cp. *Memoir* of C. J. Blomfield, 20.

[3] Eur. *Tro. Phoen.*, Aesch. *Suppl. Eum. P.V.*, Soph. *Phil.* Cp. Hermann, *Opusc.* vi 97. On his additions to the *Bacchae*, see *Appendix* to the present writer's ed. (ed. 1885, etc.).

[4] Pars III, vol. iv (1838) pp. iv—vii.

[5] *Schol. Hyp.* II pp. viii—xii.

[6] W. Selwyn's 'Notice of prof. Scholefield's Lectures and Editions' on pp. 323—339 of *Memoir* by his Widow (1855), 337.

[7] *Scholefieldium nihil moror* was one of his phrases; see also p. 397 *supra*.

[8] *ib.* 328.   [9] *ib.* 359.

sound, Greek scholar, with fair critical acumen, but not endowed with that brilliant imagination, and exquisite taste, which are the scholar's *vis divinior*[1].

Among the ablest of Samuel Butler's pupils at Shrewsbury was Benjamin Hall Kennedy (1804—1889), who entered St John's College, Cambridge, in 1823, was thrice awarded the Porson Prize for Greek Iambic Verse, and ended a brilliant undergraduate career as the 'Senior Classic' of 1827.   After spending two years as a Lecturer at Cambridge, and six as a Master at Harrow, he was in 1836 appointed by his College to succeed Butler as head-master of Shrewsbury, a position which he filled with the highest distinction and success for thirty years.   For the last twenty-two years of his life, he was Regius Professor of Greek in the University of Cambridge (1867–89).   He was elected to an honorary fellowship at St John's, where his portrait by Ouless may be seen in the College Hall, while a marble bust of the great school-master has a place of honour in the College Library.   It bears the following inscription from the pen of Professor Jebb :—

B. H. Kennedy

> Παλλάδι καὶ Φοίβῳ πεφιλημένος ἔξοχον ηὕρου,
>   κοῦρος ἐών, Κάμου πὰρ δονάκεσσι κλέος·
> εἰς δ' ἄνδρας τελέοντά σ' εὔρροος εἶδε Σαβρίνη
>   μᾶλλον ἀεὶ σοφίας ἄνθεα δρεπτόμενον.
> γηραλέον δὲ πάλιν θρέπτειρά σ' ἐδέξατο Γράντη,
>   στέμμα καλὸν πολιὰς θεῖσά σοι ἀμφὶ κόμας.

His best-known works are his 'Latin Primer'[2] and his 'Public School Latin Grammar'[3].   He also published, with translations and notes, the *Agamemnon* of Aeschylus, the *Oedipus Tyrannus* of Sophocles and the *Birds* of Aristophanes, as well as the *Theaetetus* of Plato.   His school-edition of Virgil[4] was followed by an edition of the text.   His name is associated with a large number of admirable renderings in Greek and Latin Verse, as the principal contributor to the *Sabrinae Corolla*, and as the sole author of *Between Whiles*[5].   His extraordinary facility as a Latin poet may be exemplified by the fact that he was even able to

---

[1] *Memoir*, 358.

[2] 1866 (founded on his work of 1843); revised, 1888. Cp. his *Critical Exam. of Dr Donaldson's Latin Grammar* (1852).

[3] 1871.   [4] 1876; ed. 3, 1881.   [5] 1877; ed. 2, 1882.

compose a Latin epigram of twelve lines during the hours of sleep[1]. The secret of his 'unrivalled success' as a head-master is thus revealed by one of his former pupils :—

' The main cause of his success was to be found in the man himself. To him the literature of antiquity was not a dead letter, but a living voice; it animated and stirred and quickened every pulse of his energetic nature; his enthusiasm, like all genuine enthusiasm, was contagious, and the fire of his own zeal communicated itself to everything inflammable that came within its range. It was not the amount he taught that was wonderful, but the manner in which he taught it. He seemed to breathe into every subject he dealt with the breath of life. There was nothing dead, nothing inert, nothing stereotyped about his method; it was the reflection of his own vivacious temperament —eager, brilliant, impulsive, indomitable ; his pupils left him possessed of the true key of knowledge, a genuine and vigorous love of knowledge for its own sake '[2].

Another of his pupils vividly describes his vigorous and dramatic renderings of Demosthenes :—

' He is not merely translating Demosthenes, he *is* Demosthenes speaking *extempore* in English. The voice is modulated in a most expressive manner— description, question, dilemma, invective, sarcasm, all are rendered in their most appropriate tones '[3].

As professor of Greek, he retained much of the head-master's manner, and he was keenly tenacious of the views he had long held as to the exact interpretation of certain passages of Sophocles. The two parts of his *Studia Sophoclea* (1874–84) were devoted to a criticism of the opinions held on these points by Professor Lewis Campbell, and Professor Jebb. In connexion with these controversies it was happily remarked by the former that, in the region of Attic tragedy, 'the shrine of the Muses... is hard by that of Acheloüs, so that you may chance to be swept away by the torrent, if you approach too near. And the *Heroön* of Dr Bentley is not far off '[4]. Professor Jebb's graceful tribute to his predecessor has been quoted on a previous page[5].

[1] *Between Whiles*, 161.

[2] (T. E. Page), in *The Times*, 9 April, 1889.

[3] W. E. Heitland, in *The Eagle*, xv 455. See also J. E. B. Mayor in *Cl. Rev.* iii 226–7, 278—281.

[4] *Journ. of Philol.* v 1.

[5] Kennedy's genuine appreciation of Jebb is recorded in *Between Whiles*, pp. viii, 337.

Dr Kennedy's younger brother, Charles Rann Kennedy (1808—1867), Senior Classic in 1831, was called to the bar, and is best known as the translator of **C. R. Kennedy** Demosthenes. Intermediate in age between the two Kennedys was Thomas Williamson Peile (1806—1882), head-master of Repton, a pupil of Samuel Butler, whom **T. W. Peile** he gratefully remembers in his elaborate editions of the *Agamemnon* and *Choëphoroe* (1839)[1]. Christopher Wordsworth **Wordsworth** (1807—1885), nephew of the poet, son of the Master of Trinity, and Senior Classic in 1832, travelled in Greece and discovered the site of Dodona[2]; he was afterwards head-master of Harrow, archdeacon of Westminster and bishop of Lincoln. As a classical scholar he is well represented by his *Athens and Attica* (1836), by his 'pictorial, descriptive, and historical' work on *Greece* (1839 etc.), and by his edition of Theocritus[3]. Among the contemporaries of the younger Kennedy was Joseph William Blakesley (1808—1885), Fellow and Tutor of Trinity, Vicar of Ware, and Dean of **Blakesley** Lincoln. Breadth of geographic and historic interest, rather than minute scholarship, was the main characteristic of his able edition of Herodotus (1852–4). He is the 'clear-headed friend' of one of the earliest poems of Tennyson[4], who said of him in prose:— 'He ought to be Lord Chancellor, for he is a subtle and powerful reasoner, and an honest man'[5].

In the Cambridge Classical Tripos of 1832 the first place was assigned to Edmund Law Lushington (1811— **Lushington** 1893), of Charterhouse and Trinity. Long after-wards one of the examiners, Dr Kennedy, described his 'papers in every subject' as 'more finished and faultless' than any he

---

[1] Portrait in the Library of Repton School.

[2] *Greece*, p. 247, ed. 1839.

[3] 1844 and 1877. In the first of these two editions he proposed at least two memorable emendations. In Theocritus, xiv 16, he corrected βολβός τις κοχλίας into βολβός, κτείς, κοχλίας ('bulb, scallop, and cockle'), and in St Clement's *Epistle*, c. 6, he skilfully altered γυναῖκες Δαναΐδες καὶ Δίρκαι into γυναῖκες, νεανίδες, παιδίσκαι. Cp. his *Conjectural Emendations*, etc. (1883), 11, 19, with his *Address on Dodona*, *ib.* 33—41.

[4] Mrs Brookfield's *Cambridge 'Apostles'*, 1906, with portrait of Blakesley facing p. 84.   [5] *Memoir* i (1907) 38.

had ever seen[1]. He had the highest reputation as professor of Greek for many years at Glasgow[2], and one of his ablest pupils has recalled his 'certainty of touch' and 'unfailing strength of presentation'[3]. In the epilogue to *In Memoriam*, Tennyson told of his 'wearing all that weight of learning lightly like a flower'; and, late in life, described his Greek rendering of *Crossing the Bar* as one of the finest translations he had ever read[4].

The second place in the same Tripos was awarded to Richard Shilleto (1809—1876), of Repton, Shrewsbury, and Trinity. He soon became famous as a private tutor in Classics. For more than forty years a large majority of those who attained the highest honours in the Classical Tripos were among his pupils. He was a great master of Greek idiom, and his skill, in Latin as well as Greek, is attested by the numerous compositions which have appeared in the *Sabrinae Corolla*, the *Arundines Cami*, and in a special volume of his collected versions (1901). His genius as a writer of original verse was exemplified in fugitive fly-sheets in the style of Aristophanes or Theocritus. His edition of Demosthenes *De Falsa Legatione*, a masterpiece of its kind, was written, printed, and published in the marvellously short interval of five months (1844). His long-expected edition of Thucydides might well have been brought to a successful completion, had it been begun while he was still in the prime of life. As it was, only two books were ever published (1872–80). The beauty of his Greek handwriting was a characteristic that he shared with Richard Porson. On his death-bed his thanks for some grapes from Dr Kennedy's garden were expressed in three Greek lines 'written in his usual hand, clear and fine, though somewhat tremulous from long illness':—

Shilleto

$$νικᾶν ἄπασι τοῖς κριταῖς λέγω σ' ὅτι$$
$$δισσὼ φίλῳ δέδωκας ἕλικε βοτρύων,$$
$$ὦ φιτυποιμὴν σοῦ κελεύοντος δρέπει[5].$$

[1] *Journal of Philol.* vii 164.

[2] 1838–75; inaugural discourse *On the Study of Greek* (1839).

[3] Lewis Campbell, in *Cl. Rev.* vii 476, and *ib.* 425–8. Among his other pupils were W. Y. Sellar (cp. *Cl. Rev.* iv 429, and Mrs Sellar's *Recollections*, 49) and D. B. Monro, whom he inspired with a life-long interest in Homer. In scholarship, his chief admiration was for Hermann and Boeckh (*Cl. Rev.* vii 427).

[4] Quoted in *Memoir*, ii 367 n.　　　　　[5] *Journal of Philol.* vii 163–8.

Shilleto's distinguished contemporary, William Hepworth Thompson (1810—1886), was Regius Professor of Greek from 1853 to 1867, and, for the last twenty years of his life, Master of Trinity. Singularly effective as a professorial lecturer on Euripides[1], Plato[2], and Aristotle, he unhappily published little besides his excellent edition of Archer Butler's *Lectures on the History of Greek Philosophy* (1855), and his admirable commentaries on the *Phaedrus* and *Gorgias* of Plato (1868–71). Of his minor works the most important is a paper 'On the genuineness of the *Sophist* of Plato and on some of its philosophical bearings'[3], in which he indicates the influence of the Eleatic Logic on the developement of Greek Philosophy. Euripides, Aristophanes, and Plato are the main subjects of his other papers[4]. By his published writings and by his personal influence he did much towards widening the range of classical studies in Cambridge, and preventing their being unduly limited to verbal scholarship. 'His dry humour is exemplified in many memorable sayings, but his sensitiveness and kindliness of feeling were certainly far greater than the world in general was aware.... The serene dignity of his noble presence still survives in the portrait by Herkomer in the hall of his College'[5].

Thompson had a high appreciation of that strikingly original and independent scholar, Charles Badham (1813— 1884), whose father, a translator of Juvenal, was a professor of Medicine at Glasgow, and a collector of gems in Rome, while his mother was a cousin of the poet, Thomas Campbell. In early life a pupil of Pestalozzi, he was subsequently educated at Eton, and, after taking his degree at Wadham College,

Thompson (margin)

Badham (margin)

---

[1] His introductory lecture (1857) is printed in *Journ. of Phil.* xi 243 f.

[2] Cp. Introductory Remarks on the *Philebus* (1855), *ib.* xi 1 f.

[3] *Trans. of Cambr. Philos. Soc.* x (1858) 146 f, reprinted in *Journ. of Philol.* viii (1879), 290 f.

[4] *Platonica-Isocratea* in *Journ. of Cl. and Sacred Philol.* iv; *Aristophanica* and *Platonica* in *Journ. of Philol.* iv; *On the Philebus and Euripidea, ib.* xi; *Aristophanes, Nubes,* and *Babriana, ib.* xii.

[5] J. E. Sandys, in *Social England,* vi 304; cp. C. Merivale in *Journ. of Philol.* xv 306–8; H. Jackson, in *Biogr. Jahrb.* 1886, 221–3; J. W. Clark, *Old Friends at Cambridge,* 302—313 (*Sat. Rev.,* 9 Oct., 1886); *Life of H. Sidgwick,* 458.

Oxford, and travelling for seven years in Germany, France and
Italy, proved his affinity with the Cambridge school of scholarship
by becoming a member of Peterhouse. He was ordained, and
proceeded to the degree of D.D., and successively became head-
master of Southampton, Louth and Edgbaston, but his restless
temperament was little suited for such duties. In 1863 he was
classical examiner in the University of London, and, from 1867
to 1884, he won the highest regard by his services to Australian
education as professor of Classics and Logic at the University of
Sydney.

He edited the *Iphigenia in Tauris*, the *Helena*, and the *Ion* of Euripides,
the *Phaedrus* and *Philebus*, the *Euthydemus* and *Laches*, and the *Symposium*
of Plato. He also wrote on Plato's *Epistles*, and contributed papers to the
Rheinisches Museum, and to *Mnemosyne*. Lastly, he published his inaugural
discourse at Sydney under the title of *Adhortatio ad discipulos academiae
Sydneiensis*.

In scholarship he was especially attracted to the school of Porson, and of
Cobet. He received an honorary degree at Leyden in 1860, and then met
Cobet for the first time ; in 1865 he dedicated to Cobet his edition of the
Euthydemus and *Laches* (with a prefatory epistle to the senate of the
university of Leyden); and it was on his deathbed that he dictated his latest
letter to the great Dutch scholar. His corrections of the text of Aristophanes
won the high appreciation of Thompson, whom he visited at Ely in 1857, and
to whom he addressed the prefatory letter prefixed to the *Symposium* (1866).
Among his other friends were F. D. Maurice, and Sir Theodore Martin[1].

One of the foremost candidates for the Greek Professorship
vacated by Thompson in 1867 was Edward Meredith

Cope

Cope (1818—1869), who was educated under
Kennedy at Shrewsbury, and is best known as the author of an
elaborate Introduction to the *Rhetoric* of Aristotle (1867), the
precursor of a comprehensive edition, which was posthumously
published (1877). His translation of the *Gorgias* was printed in
1864; that of the *Phaedo*, after his death. He criticised the views
of Grote on the Sophists in a series of papers in the *Journal of
Classical and Sacred Philology*, but it was to Grote that he
dedicated his Introduction to the *Rhetoric*[2].

---

[1] Lewis Campbell, in *Biogr. Jahrb.* 1884, 92—98.
[2] Biographical Notice by Munro prefixed to Cope's *Rhetoric* (ed.
Sandys).

Among Thompson's ablest contemporaries was John William Donaldson (1811—1861), Fellow of Trinity, and head-master of the School at Bury St Edmund's **Donaldson** (1841–55). In his *New Cratylus*[1] he gave a considerable impulse to the study of Comparative Philology in England; in his *Varronianus*[2] he advanced a theory of the Gothic affinities of the Etruscans. He was the principal author of a work on the *Theatre of the Greeks*; he edited Pindar (1841), the *Antigone* of Sophocles (1848) and a text of Thucydides (1859); he also completed K. O. Müller's *History of Greek Literature* (1858), and wrote an interesting and suggestive work entitled *Classical Scholarship and Classical Learning* (1856). His *Complete Latin Grammar*[3] was enlarged in 1860; his *Greek Grammar* attained a third edition in 1862. A volume in which he contended in 1854 that the lost book of Jasher constituted 'the religious marrow of the Scriptures' produced much excitement in theological circles, and ultimately led to his resigning his position at Bury, and devoting himself to classical work in Cambridge.

A wide variety of interests was represented by Donaldson's younger contemporary Frederick Apthorp Paley **Paley** (1816—1888), of Shrewsbury and St John's. An eager botanist, and an enthusiastic student of ecclesiastical architecture, he was an active member of the Camden Society at Cambridge; he joined the Church of Rome in 1846, returned to Cambridge as a private tutor from 1860 to 1874, was professor at a Catholic College in Kensington (1874–7), and spent the last eleven years of his life at Bournemouth.

He first made his mark by an edition of Aeschylus with Latin notes (1844–51), followed by an English edition (1855, etc.), which is widely recognised as his best work. He also edited Euripides, Hesiod, Theocritus, and the *Iliad*, as well as several plays of Sophocles, with Ovid's *Fasti*, and Propertius. He was associated with the present writer in an edition of 'Select Private Orations of Demosthenes' (1874). His numerous English translations were not marked by any such distinction of style as that which he attained in Latin prose. An incidental remark of Donaldson's on certain resemblances between Quintus Smyrnaeus and the *Iliad* led him to produce a series of papers, maintaining that the Homeric poems in their present form

---

[1] 1839; ed. 3, 1859.   [2] 1844; ed. 3, 1860.
[3] Criticised by B. H. Kennedy (1852).

were not earlier than the age of Alexander, and that it was mainly through oral tradition that they reached the age of Thucydides[1]. He was unfamiliar with German, and his wide and varied learning was the result of his own reading. Some of his best work is to be found in his prefaces. In the preface to his 'Euripides' he protests against the purely textual notes that were the characteristic of the Porsonian school. The notes to his own edition were composed 'with the hope of inducing students to pay no less attention to the mind and feelings than to the language and idioms of their author'[2].

Shrewsbury and St John's were also represented by Paley's contemporary, Thomas Saunders Evans (1816—1889), for many years master at Rugby. His remarkable skill in classical composition was attested by the volume of *Latin and Greek Verse* published in 1893 'as a memorial of an original and highly gifted man, considered by many to have few rivals in his special department of Scholarship'.

T. S. Evans

The same school sent to Cambridge an accomplished scholar in the person of William George Clark (1821—1878), who ably filled the office of Public Orator from 1857 to 1869. He visited Spain, Italy and Greece, and, besides other works of travel, published in his *Peloponnesus* the results of his Greek tour in the company of Thompson. A critical edition of Shakespeare designed in 1860 was successfully completed by Clark and Aldis Wright in 1866. He also designed an edition of Aristophanes.

W. G. Clark

The text of that author had been already illustrated at Cambridge by the varied learning of Thomas Mitchell (1783—1845), Fellow of Sidney, in his translations of 1820-2, and his editions of several plays in 1835-9; and a fine rendering of five of the plays had been produced at Malta between 1830 and 1840 by John Hookham Frere (1769—1846), Fellow of Gonville and Caius College[3].

Mitchell
Frere

---

[1] 'On the late date and the composite character of our Ilias and Odyssey' (1868); 'Pseudo-archaic words and inflexions in the Homeric vocabulary, and their relation to the antiquity of the Homeric poems' (*Journal of Philol.* vi 114 f, 1876); 'Qu. Smyrnaeus and the Homer of the Tragic poets' (1876); 'Homerus Periclis aetate quinam habitus sit quaeritur (1877)'; 'Homeri quae nunc exstant an reliqui cycli carminibus antiquiora jure habita sint' (1878); 'The truth about Homer' (1887).

[2] Vol. i, pp. liv—lviii, ed. 1872.—*The Times*, 10 Dec., 1888; S. S. Lewis in *Biogr. Jahrb.* 1889, 15—17.

[3] *Life and Works*, ed. 2, 1874.

Clark devoted part of 1867 to examining the MSS at Ravenna and Venice, and began a commentary on the *Acharnians*[1], which his failing health compelled him to leave unfinished. Munro, his friend for nearly forty years, thought that 'his was the most accomplished and versatile mind he had ever encountered'; his work was marked by a 'surprising tact and readiness', a 'consummate ease and mastery'[2]. A Fellow of Trinity for the last 34 years of his life, he left his estates to the College, where his name has been commemorated by the establishment of the 'Clark Lectureship in the Literature of England'.

Clark's contemporary, Churchill Babington (1821—1889), Fellow of St John's, and Disney professor of Archaeology from 1865 to 1880, produced in 1851–8 the *editio princeps* of four of the speeches of Hypereides, beginning with the 'Speech against Demosthenes' and ending with the 'Funeral Oration'[3]. Born a year later than Clark and Babington, Hubert Ashton Holden (1822—1896), Fellow of Trinity, and head-master of Ipswich School from 1858 to 1883, edited a text of Aristophanes with an *onomasticon*, and produced elaborate commentaries on the Seventh Book of Thucydides, the *Cyropaedeia*, *Hieron*, and *Oeconomicus* of Xenophon, eight of Plutarch's *Lives*, and the *Pro Plancio*, *Pro Sestio*, and *De Officiis* of Cicero. In his *Foliorum Silvula* he published a collection of passages from English poetry for translation into Greek and Latin, followed by versions of the same by various scholars in the *Folia Silvulae*.

Among the most brilliant of the classical scholars who contributed to the *Folia* was Arthur Holmes (1837—1875), of Shrewsbury and St John's, who edited the *Midias* and the *De Corona* of Demosthenes, and also published a Prelection on 'the Nemeian Odes of Pindar'[4] (1867).

Churchill Babington

H. A. Holden

Holmes

[1] Notes on *Ach.* 1—578 in *Journal of Philology*, viii 177 f, ix 1 f, 23 f.

[2] *ib.* viii 173–5. His 'silvery talk' is noted in the *Life of H. Sidgwick*, 171.

[3] J. E. Sandys in *Cl. Rev.* iii 135, and *Biogr. Jahrb.* 1889, 26 f; and C. C. Babington, in *The Eagle*, xv 362–6.

[4] E. W. Bowling in *The Eagle*, ix 329 f; his graceful rendering of Tibullus, iv 2 (*Sulpicia*), there quoted on p. 334, is reprinted in Postgate's *Selections from Tibullus*, p. xl.

RICHARD CLAVERHOUSE JEBB.

Reproduced (by permission) from a photograph taken by
Messrs Window and Grove, London.

Richard Claverhouse Jebb (1841—1905), of Charterhouse, Fellow of Trinity College, Cambridge, after winning the Porson Prize, and the Porson and Craven Scholarships, took his degree as Senior Classic in 1862. He was elected Public Orator of Cambridge in 1869, was Professor of Greek at Glasgow from 1875 to 1889, and at Cambridge from 1889 to his death. For the last fourteen years of his life he was M.P. for his University, he received honorary degrees from many seats of learning, was knighted in 1900, and in the summer of 1905 attained the crowning distinction of the Order of Merit. In the autumn of that year, his address[1] as president of the educational section was the most impressive incident of the meeting of the British Association in South Africa; and, before the end of the year, he died.

He will long be remembered as the editor of Sophocles (1883–96) and of Bacchylides (1905), and as the author of the 'Attic Orators'[2]. His other works included a translation of Theophrastus, an 'Introduction to Homer', with lectures on Modern Greece, on Greek poetry, and on Humanism in Education[3], monographs on Erasmus and on Bentley, a brief life of Porson[4], and an appreciation of Macaulay. He contributed articles on Greek literature to the *Encyclopaedia Britannica* and to the Cambridge *Companion to Greek Studies*, and papers on Delos and Pindar to the organ of the Hellenic Society, of which he was the honoured President for the last sixteen years of his life. In 1883 he took a leading part in founding the British School at Athens[5]. A humanist in the highest sense of the word, he had 'not only mastered the form of classical literature', but had 'assimilated its spirit, and applied it to the understanding and criticism of modern life'. His 'Attic Orators' revealed to the literary world the fact that one who was 'among the first of living Greek

[1] *University Education and National Life* in *Essays and Addresses* (1907), 624—648.

[2] 1876; ed. 2, 1893.

[3] Reprinted in *Essays and Addresses*, 506—544.

[4] *D. N. B.*

[5] The scheme was propounded by him first in the *Contemporary Review*, Nov. 1878, and next in the *Fortnightly Review*, May, 1883. See also *Life* by Lady Jebb, 211 f, 244 f.

scholars' was himself 'an artist in English prose'[1]. In that work he ably dealt with the life, style, and speeches of the earlier Orators, closing with a chapter on the matured civil eloquence, as exemplified in Demosthenes. In his 'Sophocles' he gave further proof of his being a critical scholar, as well as a cultivated humanist and an accomplished master of English, who, without pretending to be a specialist either in comparative philology or in archaeology, was able to present the results of the current research in those departments in a perfect literary form. It has been justly characterised as 'one of the most finished, comprehensive, and valuable works, in the sphere of literary exposition, which this age or any has produced'[2]. The same qualities were exhibited in his 'Bacchylides', where the defects of the MS left still further scope for restorations worthy of a genuine Greek poet. His powers as a composer of Greek lyric verse had already been proved by his three Pindaric odes, (1) his version of Browning's *Abt Vogler*[3], welcomed as admirable by the author of the original[4]; (2) his rendering of Rann Kennedy's *Reign of Youth*, a rendering characterised as a 'beautiful work of extraordinary genius, learning, and taste'[5]; and (3) his ode on the eighth centenary of the university of Bologna (1888)[6]. To the third of these odes allusion was made by Tennyson in dedicating to its author his classic poem of *Demeter* :—

> 'Fair things are slow to fade away,
> Bear witness you, that yesterday
>   From out the Ghost of Pindar in you
>   Roll'd an Olympian'.

His volume of *Translations* includes not a few fine renderings in Latin as well as Greek verse, while his mastery of a highly felicitous form of Latin prose was exemplified in the speeches delivered by him during his tenure of the office of Public Orator[7].

---

[1] *Quarterly Review*, 1881.

[2] Verrall in *Biogr. Jahrb.* 1906, 77.

[3] *Translations into Greek and Latin Verse*, 1873 ; new ed. 1907.

[4] Browning's *Agamemnon*, pref.

[5] Kennedy's *Between Whiles*, 339, 352—377.

[6] All these three Pindaric odes are printed in the new ed. of the *Translations*, 1907.

[7] *e.g. Camb. Univ. Reporter*, 23 June, 1874, 481–6.

The best English parallel to these was his admirable speech in honour of the members of foreign Academies in the Hall of Peterhouse in May, 1904. He has been aptly described as 'one of the most brilliant scholars and one of the most accomplished men of letters of his time—a great humanist, who, in his combination of wide learning, consummate critical faculty, and exquisite taste, had few equals and perhaps no superiors, among his contemporaries'[1]; and it has been well said that he was unconsciously pourtraying his own gifts when he translated, in his memorable monograph on Bentley, the passage in which that great scholar says that wide reading and erudite knowledge of all Greek and Latin antiquity are not enough for the modern critic of a classical author :—

'A man should have all that at his fingers' ends.... But besides this there is need of the keenest judgment, of sagacity and quickness, of a certain divining tact and inspiration, as was said of Aristarchus—a faculty which can be acquired by no constancy of toil or length of life, but comes solely by the gift of nature and by the happy star'[2].

In 1885 an improved edition of *Sixteen Speeches of Lysias* was dedicated to Professor Jebb by Evelyn Shirley Shuckburgh (1843— 1906), Librarian and late Fellow of Emmanuel, who produced a large number of annotated editions of the Classics, including a historical Commentary on Suetonius' *Augustus*, followed by his own *Life* of that emperor. He was the author of two histories of Rome and two of Greece, and of a number of translations. Foremost among these were his widely appreciated Polybius, and his eminently readable rendering of Cicero's *Letters*. Of the latter he characteristically says in his preface :—' No critic can take away from me the days and nights spent in closer communion with Rome's greatest intellect'. He has justly been described as 'a true lover of literature'[3]. He dedicated his version of Cicero's Essays on Old Age and Friendship to two of his oldest friends :—*senescentibus senescens, amicis*

Shuckburgh

---

[1] *The Times*, 11 Dec. 1905, p. 6.
[2] *The Times*, *u. s.*; cp. S. H. Butcher in *Class. Rev.*, Feb. 1906, 71 f; A. W. Verrall in *Biogr. Jahrb.* 1906, 76—79, and in Appendix (427—487) to Lady Jebb's *Life and Letters of Sir Richard Claverhouse Jebb*, with portrait, 1907. The collected *Essays and Addresses* (1907) have among their subjects Sophocles and Pindar, the age of Pericles and the Speeches of Thucydides, ancient organs of public opinion, and the exploration of Delos, together with Caesar, Lucian, Erasmus and Samuel Johnson, 'Humanism in Education' and other kindred topics.
[3] H. J. in *Cambr. Rev.*, 18 Oct. 1906, 8.

amicus. Though it was not granted him to 'attain the happiness of old age' he possessed in a marked degree the 'genius for friendship', and the gift of an apparently perennial youth[1].

Among those whose loss was lamented by Sir Richard Jebb, in his speech

Warr

as President of the Hellenic Society in June, 1901, were 'Professor George Charles Winter Warr (1845—1901), author of many valuable contributions to classical literature[2], who at the time of his death was engaged on a work designed to render the masterpieces of the

Neil

Attic drama more fully intelligible to English readers; and Mr Robert Alexander Neil (1852—1901), Fellow and Tutor of Pembroke College, Cambridge, University Reader in Sanskrit and a classical scholar of rare learning and acumen'. Elsewhere he said of Neil:— 'The ancient Classics were always to him great works of literature, and a fine literary sense invariably guided his treatment of them'[3]. The sole memorial of his exact and varied scholarship is a posthumous edition of the *Knights* of Aristophanes. The friends who wrote the preface to that work have rightly said of him:—'He was familiar with the work accomplished by scholars, both in the present and the past, on every side of Classical life and thought and language'. 'While there is no part of Classical life or thought, whìch he did not explain and illuminate, he sought parallels, illustration and comment from the whole range of literature'[4]. Neil was bound by many ties to his

J. Adam

devoted friend, James Adam (1860—1907), who, like himself, was a loyal son of Aberdeen and of Cambridge. Adam was born in the same region of Aberdeenshire as the Scottish humanist, Arthur Johnston, and the author well remembers the patriotic pride with which Adam once told him of that poet's graceful lines on the home beside the river Ury, below the ridge of Bennachie:—

'Mille per ambages nitidis argenteus undis
Hic trepidat laetos Vrius inter agros.
Explicat hic seras ingens Bennachius umbras'[5].

At Aberdeen, Adam came under the inspiring influence of Professor Geddes, the editor of the *Phaedo*, 'whose high enthusiasm and encouragement in early

---

[1] J. Adam, *ib.* 6—7.

[2] *The story of Orestes* (1886); *Echoes of Hellas* (1888); *The Greek Epic* (1895); Teuffel's *Roman Lit.* E. T. (1900). Cp. *Athenaeum*, 2 March, 1901. He was for 25 years professor of classical literature at King's College, London. His epitaph in St Saviour's, Liverpool, ends as follows:—'An eager scholar, he was infinitely patient, and gladly gave up his best to the humblest student. His delight was in beauty; he laboured to right wrongs. He had courage to live by the highest revealed to him, and, loving others better than himself, he won great love'.

[3] *Camb. Rev.* Oct. 1901, 22, 38.

[4] See also the admirable tribute to his memory by his friend, J. Adam, in *Camb. Rev.* Oct. 1901, 21 f, 37 f. [5] ii 249 *supra*.

days' were afterwards described by his pupil as the ultimate source of all his knowledge of Plato[1]. At Cambridge, as Scholar of Gonville and Caius, he took his degree with distinction in pure scholarship, in philosophy and in comparative philology, while, as Fellow of Emmanuel, he won a wide appreciation by his enthusiastic and stimulating lectures on the Greek lyric poets, on Plato and Aristotle, and on the post-Aristotelian philosophers. Similarly at Aberdeen in 1904 he aroused the keenest interest by his Gifford Lectures on *The Religious Teachers of Greece*, and the same may be said of his Cambridge lectures of 1906 on the *Hymn of Cleanthes*. For the Cambridge Press he produced excellent editions of Plato's *Apology*, *Crito* and *Euthyphro*. In the *Protagoras* he was associated with his wife, a no less enthusiastic student of Plato. He also prepared a text (1897), and, ultimately, an elaborately annotated edition, of the *Republic* (1902). For this last work, which is his masterpiece as a classical editor, he was compelled to read and digest 'an enormous mass of critical and exegetical literature,' while he contributed to the elucidation of his author much that was distinctly original. It was in the course of the preliminary studies for this work that he wrote his treatise on *The Nuptial Number of Plato* (1891)[2], and an Assyrian scholar, professor Hilprecht of Philadelphia, has since shown that Adam's interpretation agrees with the Babylonian 'perfect number', which Hilprecht had himself discovered to be the fourth power of $(3 \times 4 \times 5)$, *i.e.* 12,960,000[3]. In his lectures on Plato he was apt to be a severe critic of scholars who proposed what he regarded as unwarrantable alterations of the manuscript text. Among his more obvious characteristics in ordinary life were a love of irony and paradox, an alacrity of mind and an archness of manner, and a singular sprightliness of temper, combined with a serious interest in the religious beliefs of the old classical world. In the praelection which he delivered in the Senate House in January, 1906, he made a fragment of Pindar the text of an eloquent and impressive discourse on the ancient doctrine of the immortality of the soul[4]. In the latter part of his too brief life he was attracted to the study of the points of contact between Stoicism and Christianity. Amid his new interests, he laid aside the translation of the *Republic* and the introductory volume, to which he had once been looking forward when he inscribed on the opening page of his completed commentary the pathetic dedication :—' To the memory of Robert Alexander Neil I gratefully and affectionately dedicate this book—εἰς ἐκεῖνον τὸν βίον, ὅταν αὖθις γενόμενοι τοῖς τοιούτοις ἐντύχωμεν λόγοις'[5]. It was also to Neil that

---

[1] Plato, *Rep. Pref.* x.

[2] See also his Commentary on p. 545 (ii 201 f, 264—312).

[3] Sir W. R. Ramsay, in *Aberdeen Free Press*, 31 Aug. 1907.

[4] *Cambridge Praelections*, 27—67 (on Pindar, *frag.* 131), reviewed by Wilamowitz in *Cl. Rev.* xx 445.

[5] *Rep.* 498 c. Cp. obituary notices in *Times*, 3 Sept.; *Athenaeum*, 7 Sept.; P. Giles in *Camb. Rev.* 17 Oct. 1907, and in *Emm. Coll. Mag.* 1908; also the *Memoir* by Mrs Adam prefixed to the *Gifford Lectures*, 1908.

John Strachan (1862—1907), who entered Aberdeen a year later than Adam,
Strachan dedicated the two volumes of the *Thesaurus Palaeohibernicus*
(1901–3). At Cambridge, where he was elected Fellow of
Pembroke, his university distinctions had been almost exactly the same as those
attained by Adam, but his main strength lay in Comparative Philology. He
studied Sanskrit at Göttingen and Cambridge, and at Jena, where he also
worked at Celtic. Elected professor of Greek at Manchester in 1889, he
edited the sixth book of Herodotus with an excellent summary of the Ionic
dialect, and towards the end of his short life was making many discoveries in
mediaeval Welsh and also preparing an extensive work on the Greek language[1].
Mr Gilbert Norwood's volume on 'the Riddle of the *Bacchae*' is dedicated to
the memory of this 'single-hearted scholar'.

In the generation succeeding that of Elmsley and Gaisford,
Liddell Greek scholarship was well represented at Oxford by
and Henry George Liddell (1811—1898) of Charter-
Scott house, Dean of Christ Church, and by Robert Scott
(1811—1887) of Shrewsbury, Master of Balliol and Dean of
Rochester, the joint authors of the standard Greek and English
Lexicon. Founded partly on that of Passow, the first edition
appeared in 1843; the eighth in 1897. It marked a vast advance
on the lexicons of Donnegan, Dunbar, and Giles; it led to an
immediate abandonment of Dindorf's plan for producing a similar
work; and it still, deservedly, holds the field in England[2].

As Master of Balliol, Scott was succeeded in 1870 by Benjamin
Jowett Jowett (1817—1893), who in 1855 had succeeded
Gaisford as professor of Greek. One of his able
biographers[3] has placed in a clear light 'the admixture of
error' in the 'popular prejudice of the scholastic world' that
Jowett, though a professor of Greek, was not an exact scholar, in
the technical sense of the term. He once said, with an ironic
smile, 'I often think with pleasure that, *unworthy as I am*, I have
to do with the greatest literature in the world'. We are told that,
early in his professorial career, he 'read a book of Homer nightly,—
studied Buttmann's *Lexilogus* at breakfast time, went several times
through Pindar and the lyric poets, and carried Herodotus about
with him on railway journeys. As for Aeschylus and Sophocles

---

[1] *Times*, 2 Oct.; *Athenaeum*, 5 Oct.; P. Giles in *Camb. Rev.* 17 Oct.
1907.

[2] H. L. Thompson's *Life of H. G. Liddell* (with portraits), 65—82.

[3] Lewis Campbell, in *Cl. Rev.* vii 473–6.

he had always loved them....At a later time he had always some
author on hand,—Lucian and Plutarch for example,—outside his
immediate studies'.   In the domain of classical learning, the
foremost of his plans was an Oxford edition of the principal
dialogues of Plato.   The *Philebus* was edited in 1860 by Edward
Poste (1821—1902), the *Theaetetus* (1861) and the *Sophistes* and
Politicus (1867) by Professor Lewis Campbell; and the *Apology*
by Riddell (1867)[1].   Jowett's own part in the scheme was a long-
delayed edition of the *Republic* with text, notes, and essays, in
which he was associated with Professor Campbell (1894).   Meanwhile, he had conceived the design of a complete translation of
Plato, which was happily accomplished in 1871.   This was followed
by his translation of Thucydides (1881) and the *Politics* of Aristotle
(1885), both of which were accompanied by a Commentary.   All
these three great works are justly recognised as masterpieces of
English, and his rendering of Plato in particular, with its admirably
written Introductions, has done much towards popularising the
study of Plato in England and elsewhere ; it has, in fact, 'made
Plato an English classic'[2].   When some minor mistake was pointed
out to him, he would look up and say :—'It is not that I do not
know these elementary things; but the effort of making the English
harmonious is so great, that one's mind is insensibly drawn away
from the details of the Greek'[3].   He was sceptical about the value
of epigraphy and archaeology, and of conjectural emendation.

He wrote of the latter :—'the more we think of the follies into which
great scholars have been betrayed by the love of it, the narrower are the
limits which we are disposed to assign to it '[4].

His doubts as to the importance of the study of epigraphy may almost be
forgiven for the sake of the graceful phrases in which those doubts are finally
summed up :—'To be busy on Greek soil, under the light of the blue heaven,
amid the scenes of ancient glory, in reading inscriptions, or putting together
fragments of stone or marble, has a charm of another kind than that which is
to be found in the language of ancient authors.   Yet even to appreciate truly
the value of such remains, it is to the higher study of the mind of Hellas and
of her great men that we must return, finding some little pleasure by the way

---

[1] p. 422 *infra.*

[2] Jebb's *Essays and Addresses* (1907), 534, 615.

[3] *Cl. Rev.* vii 475.

[4] Plato, *Rep.* vol. II p. xiii.

(like that of looking at an autograph) in deciphering the handwriting of her
children amid the dust of her ruins'[1].

Jowett's contemporary, Mark Pattison (1813—1884), Rector of
Lincoln, was deeply read in the History of Scholarship, especially that of the Renaissance in France,
as is proved in part by his *Life of Casaubon*[2] and his *Essays on
Scaliger*[3].

Intermediate in age between Pattison and Jowett was George
Rawlinson (1815—1902), Fellow of Exeter, Camden
professor of Ancient History, and Canon of Canter-
bury, who produced in 1858 a standard translation of Herodotus,
with notes and essays, partly contributed by the translator's brother,
the Assyriologist, Sir Henry Rawlinson, and by the Egyptologist,
Sir Gardner Wilkinson.   George Rawlinson also published—in
1862–71—the successive volumes of his ‘Five Great Monarchies
of the Eastern World’, followed by volumes on the sixth and
seventh Monarchies in 1873–6.   His portrait in the hall of
Trinity represents him transcribing letters for his memoir of his
distinguished brother[4].

Among the contemporaries of George Rawlinson was the
learned physician, William Alexander Greenhill
(1814—1894), of Rugby and Trinity College, Ox-
ford, who contributed to Smith's *Dictionary of Greek and Roman
Biography* a series of important articles on the ancient writers on
medicine.

Comparative Philology was ably represented at Oxford by
Friedrich Max Müller (1823—1900), who studied
under Bopp and Schelling in Berlin and under
Eugène Burnouf in Paris.   He was welcomed in England by
Bunsen, and was invited by the East India Company to edit the
Rigveda (1849–73).   Defeated in 1860 in his candidature for the
Chair of Sanskrit at Oxford, he gave two admirable courses of
Lectures on the Science of Language at the Royal Institution

Pattison

G. Rawlinson

Greenhill

Max Müller

---

[1] *Thucydides*, vol. I p. cii ed. 1900.   Cp. *Life* by Campbell and Abbott
(with portraits), 1897.

[2] 1875 ; ed. 2, 1892.

[3] Reprinted in his *Essays*, 1889.—Cp. *Memoirs* down to 1860, dictated in
1883 ; *Biogr. Jahrb.* 1884, 47 f ; and *Life of H. Sidgwick*, 404.

[4] Notice in *The Times*, 7 Oct. 1902.

(1861–4), which made the general results of the study of Comparative Philology familiar to Englishmen, and led to his appointment to a professorship of that subject at Oxford in 1868. 'Though much in his works and methods may already be superseded, his writings exercised an extraordinarily stimulating influence in many fields'[1]. Comparative Philology was part of the wide province explored by Edward Byles Cowell (1826—1903), of Magdalen Hall, Oxford (1854), president of the **Cowell** Sanskrit College, Calcutta, and afterwards professor of Sanskrit at Cambridge for the last 36 years of his life. Most of his published work consisted of editions and translations of Sanskrit texts. He was also specially interested in botany, as well as in Welsh, Spanish and Italian literature. He was the first to introduce FitzGerald to Omar Khâyyam and to the *Mosella* of Ausonius[2]. One of his own English poems, written late in life, tells 'how "the slumbering student in his heart" had been awakened in his earliest teens, and he had become the blissful owner of a many-volumed Livy and the newly-published *Corpus Poëtarum*'[3].

Henry William Chandler (1828—1889), Fellow of Pembroke, Oxford, produced in 1862 a standard work on 'Greek Accents'. As professor of Moral Philosophy **Chandler** he lectured with great success on Aristotle; he had a remarkable knowledge of the bibliography of the *Ethics*, and left behind him a large collection of Aristotelian literature which has found a permanent home in his former College.

An excellent edition of the *Ethics* with an English commentary and illustrative essays (1857, 1884[4]) was the most important classical work published by Sir Alexander **Grant** Grant, Scholar of Balliol and Fellow of Oriel (1826—1884). His eight years in India as holder of important educational positions in Madras and Bombay were followed by the sixteen years of his distinguished tenure of the principalship of the university of Edinburgh, 'where his intellectual powers, his knowledge of men,

---

[1] *D. N. B.*; cp. *Biogr. Jahrb.* 1902, 7—39.   [2] i 223[2] *supra.*

[3] p. 120 of 'C. W. M.''s delightful sketch in the *Journal of Philology*, xxix 119—125. Cp. *Life* by G. Cowell (with appendix including an outline of the history of Sanskrit studies in England, drawn up for the use of the present writer in his article on English Scholarship in *Social England*, vi 316).

and his dignity and urbanity, made him a striking figure'[1]. The
year of the completion of his 'Story of the University', and of the
commemoration of its tercentenary, was also that of his death.
The series of 'Ancient Classics for English Readers' was the
richer for his admirable volumes on Xenophon and Aristotle.

An edition of the *Ethics* was produced in 1856 by William
Edward Jelf of Christ Church (1811—1875), who is
W. E. Jelf
best known as the translator of Kühner's Greek
Grammar (1842–5, etc.).

In 1855 two annotated editions of the *Politics* were simultaneously published at Oxford, that of J. R. T.
Eaton and
Congreve
Eaton, Fellow of Merton, and that of Richard
Congreve (1818—1899), Fellow of Wadham, who
in the same year founded the positivist community in London,
and by the date of the unaltered second edition of his commentary (1874) had abandoned the study of the Classics for the
practice of medicine. The Greek index of his edition is far fuller
than that of Eaton's, 'several excellent English expressions' are
borrowed from Congreve's notes in Jowett's translation, while
both editors are repeatedly mentioned in the comprehensive work
of Mr W. L. Newman (1887—1902).

An edition of Plato's *Euthydemus* was the latest work produced
in Oxford at the close of a long life by Edwin
Gifford
Hamilton Gifford (1820—1905) of Shrewsbury
School and of St John's College, Cambridge, who is best known
as the learned editor of the *Praeparatio Evangelica* of Eusebius
(1903). The *Apology* of Plato was excellently edited, together
with an admirable 'Digest of Platonic Idioms', by
Riddell
James Riddell (1823—1866) of Shrewsbury and
Balliol, who began an edition of the *Odyssey*, which was continued
by Dr Merry and completed by Monro.

Among Oxford scholars who devoted special study to the Greek
poets was William Linwood (1817—1878) of Christ
Linwood
Church, whose best-known works were a lexicon to
Aeschylus, and an edition of Sophocles with brief Latin notes
(1846). John Conington (1825—1869), in the early
Conington
part of his career, edited the *Agamemnon* (1848)

[1] Mrs Sellar's *Recollections*, 119; 73, 311.

and *Choëphoroe* (1857) of Aeschylus, and afterwards completed the
Spenserian rendering of the *Iliad* by P. S. Worsley
(1835—1866), the translator of the *Odyssey* (1861).   Worsley
Among the most successful of Homeric translations was the
rendering of the *Iliad* in blank verse, published in
1864 by the Earl of Derby (1799—1869). The   Lord Derby
eloquent leader of the opposite party in politics, William Ewart
Gladstone (1809—1898), has described the study
of Homer as a 'palace of enchantment', and has   Gladstone
compared the spells of the enchanter to a 'remedial specific,
which, freshening the understanding by contact with the truth and
strength of nature, should both improve its vigilance against deceit
and danger, and increase its vigour and resolution for the discharge
of duty'[1]. The Homeric poems were the central theme of the life-
long labours of David Binning Monro (1836—1905),
who was educated at Glasgow[2], was a Scholar of   Monro
Brasenose and Balliol, and Provost of Oriel for the last twenty-
three years of his life.   His earliest publication was a Latin prize-
essay on the voyage of the Argonauts (1852), while the latest
memorial of his learning was an edition of the second half of
the *Odyssey* (1901). The Appendices to this valuable edition
extend to more than 200 pages, dealing with the composition of
the *Odyssey*, the relation of the *Odyssey* to the *Iliad*, Homer and
the Cyclic poets, the History of the Homeric poems, the time and
place of Homer, and the Homeric house.   Nineteen years
previously he had dedicated to the memory of James Riddell his
Grammar of the Homeric Dialect (1882), a monument of sound
and solid learning.   The Homeric Question was the theme of his
able articles in the *Quarterly Review* (1868) and the *Encyclopaedia
Britannica* (1880 etc.).   An important contribution to the solution
of a difficult problem was supplied by his *Modes of Greek Music*
(1894).   He has been well described as

'A man of singularly retiring disposition, shy, indeed, and never given to
anything like display.   In general company he spoke little, but always to the

---

[1] *Studies in Homer and the Homeric Age* (3 vols. 1858), iii 616; *Juventus
Mundi* (1869); *Homer* (in 'Literature Primers', 1878).

[2] p. 406, n. 3 *supra*.

point...His sound judgment, his latent humour, and his shrewd aphoristic speech endeared him as few men of his time were endeared to their contemporaries. He was an accomplished scholar who had also the training of the exact sciences...He was an excellent linguist, and, during his term of office as Vice-Chancellor, he was able to address audiences of foreign scholars in French, Italian, German and modern Greek'[1].

The accurate study of the Homeric poems has been materially promoted by the Concordance to the *Iliad* prepared by Guy Lushington **Prendergast and Dunbar** Prendergast (1875), and that to the *Odyssey* and *Homeric Hymns* (1880) by Dr Henry Dunbar, formerly of Gairloch Head (d. 1883), the author of a complete Concordance to Aristophanes (1883). All three works were published by the Oxford Press, while the name of Prendergast has been commemorated by the foundation of a Greek Scholarship at Cambridge.

Among the numerous text-books published by Henry Musgrave Wilkins, **H. M. Wilkins** Fellow of Merton (1823—1887), we may mention his translation of the Speeches of Thucydides (1870) and his school edition of the *Olynthiacs* of Demosthenes.

A joint edition of the 'Orations of Demosthenes and Aeschines *On the Crown*' was produced in 1872 by two able brothers, George **Simcox** Augustus (1841—1905) and William Henry Simcox (1842-3—1889), both Fellows of Queen's College, Oxford. The elder brother was also the author of an interesting 'History of Latin Literature' (1883). A translation of the *Prometheus* has been described as perhaps 'his most effective work'[2].

The Greek drama was the subject of the two published works of Arthur **Haigh** Elam Haigh (1855—1905), Fellow and Tutor of Corpus, whose *Attic Theatre* (1889)[3] and *Tragic Drama of the Greeks* (1896) have been recognised as marked by 'careful study, sound knowledge, and independent judgment'[4].

Greek scholarship had a singularly able and vigorous representative in the person of William Gunion Rutherford **Rutherford** ford (1853—1907), a son of the manse, who was educated at the High School, Glasgow, and was under Lewis Campbell at St Andrews, and under Jowett at Balliol. After taking a first class in Classical Moderations and a second in Natural Science, and hesitating for a while between the careers of a physician, an architect or a soldier, he found his true vocation decided for him by Jowett, who divined that he was 'one of the

---

[1] *The Times*, 23 Aug. 1905. Cp. esp. J. Cook Wilson in *Biogr. Jahrb.* 1906, 30—40; E. T. (with portrait) Oxford, 1907.

[2] *The Times*, 26 Sept. 1905.   [3] Ed. 3, 1907.

[4] A. Sidgwick in *Biogr. Jahrb.* 1906, 80; *The Times*, 23 Dec. 1905.

few men who could really think upon language'. This decision led to his becoming a master at St Paul's in 1877. His six years at that school, under the inspiring influence of Mr F. W. Walker, were followed by eighteen as headmaster of Westminster, while, for part of the remaining six years of his life, he was an examiner in Greek in the university of London.

His earliest work, an *Elementary Accidence* of Attic Greek (1878), briefly embodying some of the results of his researches, has since been incorporated in the admirably lucid *First Greek Grammar* (*Accidence and Syntax*) of 1891. He made his mark mainly by his *New Phrynichus* (1881), which, under the guise of a commentary on the grammatical rules of an Atticist of the second century, was really a comprehensive treatise on the history and on the distinctive characteristics of Attic Greek[1]. It was the work of a loyal, but independent, follower of Cobet. The *New Phrynichus* was soon succeeded by an elaborate edition of Babrius (1883), with a dissertation on the history of the Greek fable, and on points of metre, and many other topics. His Fourth Book of Thucydides (1889) exemplified the theory that the text of that author had been corrupted by the addition of numerous 'adscripts'; but, when all these 'adscripts' had been eliminated, the rest was in general so easy that it became difficult to understand why Dionysius of Halicarnassus found the historian so hard. His recension of Herondas (1892) was a somewhat premature production; his *Lex Rex*, a collection of cognate words in Greek and Latin and English (the title of which was borrowed from a Rutherford of the 17th century), gave proof of an interest in Comparative Philology; while his new rendering of the *Epistle to the Romans* arrested the attention of those who had long acquiesced in the authorised version. The two volumes of the *Scholia Aristophanica* (1896), in which he 'arranged, emended, and translated' the *scholia* to the Ravenna MS, were followed by a third volume of commentary and criticism under the title of 'A chapter in the history of annotation' (1905). This last volume, his latest legacy to the literature of learning, teems with matters of interest to scholars, setting forth *inter alia* the *genesis* of the *scholia* in the class-room of the professional teacher; their connexion with the dramatic recital of the text, and with its use in illustration of certain tabulated lists of figures of speech; the contrast between the scholiast's neglect of textual criticism and the interest in that subject shown by Galen's remarks on the current texts of the old Greek Classics; and, lastly, the significance of the ancient method of catechetical instruction. The author is justified in implying that his work 'has a bearing upon questions of some importance at the present time'; it contains materials for many essays on modern education, which might well have appealed to a wider audience in a work of more popular form[2].

---

[1] Reprint of *Reviews*, 42 pp. (Macmillan, 1881).

[2] Cp. *Cl. Rev.* iv 110 f, xx 115 f, and obituary notice *ib.* xxi 190 f; *Times*, 20 July; and *Athenaeum*, 27 July, 1907; portrait by Seymour Lucas.

In Scotland the study of Greek was combined with that of
Medicine by Francis Adams (1796—1861), the
physician and classical scholar of Banchory on
the Dee, who translated and edited the Greek
medical writers Paulus Aegineta (1844–7), Hippocrates (1849),
and Aretaeus (1856), and, in recognition of the merits of these
works, was made an honorary M.D. of Aberdeen in the year last
mentioned.　He contributed an appendix on the names of Greek
plants and animals to the lexicon compiled in 1831
by George Dunbar (1774—1851), the professor of
Greek in Edinburgh (1807–51), who edited Herodotus (1806–7),
and incidentally attempted to derive Sanskrit from Greek (1827).
As professor of Greek he was the successor of Andrew Dalzel
(1750—1806), the editor of the *Analecta Graeca Minora* and
Majora whom his pupil, Lord Cockburn[1], describes as 'an absolute enthusiast about learning'[2].　Dunbar's younger contemporary,
a son of the bishop of Edinburgh, was at this time professor of
Greek at Glasgow :—Daniel Keyte Sandford (1798
—1838), who, in 1830, was knighted for his eloquent advocacy of the cause of Reform, and in the same year
published his translation of the Greek Grammar of Thiersch.　To
the end of his life he contributed to *Blackwood*[3] many articles on
classical subjects, with translations from the Greek poets ; his

Marginal notes:
Scotland :
Adams

Dunbar

Sandford

---

[1]　Henry Cockburn's *Memorials* (1856), 19 f.

[2]　Among those who learnt their Greek from Dalzel was Sir Walter Scott's
short-lived friend, John Leyden (1775—1811), who translated the martial poems
of Tyrtaeus, with the war-song of Hybrias the Cretan, and Aristotle's Ode to
Virtue.　He went to the East as a surgeon with a view to investigating the
languages and the learning of India.　He had a remarkable gift for the study
of Arabic, Persian, Sanskrit, and other oriental languages.　'I may die in the
attempt' (he writes to a friend), 'but if I die without surpassing Sir William
Jones a hundredfold in oriental learning, never let a tear for me profane the
eye of a Borderer'.　In his eagerness to examine an ill-ventilated library of
Indian MSS, he caught a fever, of which he died in the island of Java.　His brief
career as a student of eastern languages has a close resemblance to that of
Rask.　He left many treatises in MS, as well as translations from Sanskrit,
Persian and Arabic.　His death was lamented in *The Lord of the Isles* (iv 2),
and his life was admirably sketched by Scott in the *Memoir* which has since
been prefixed to his friend's *Poems and Ballads* (ed. 1858).

[3]　See xi 678 for his Letter to Elmsley (Oxford, 1822).

stretch of the literature of Greece was included in a new edition of Potter's *Archaeologia Graeca*; and his 'Extracts from Greek Authors' found a new editor in William Veitch[1].

William Veitch (1794—1885), who was educated at Jedburgh, the capital of his native county, and afterwards attended Dunbar's lectures in Edinburgh, devoted the whole of his life to the duties of a private tutor. His well-known precision led to his being invited to read the proofs of Dunbar's Lexicon, and to do the same service, at the age of eighty, for that of Liddell and Scott. A comprehensive work on the *Greek Verbs*, produced in 1841 by A. N. Carmichael, one of the masters at the Edinburgh Academy[2], was superseded in 1848 by the fuller work of Veitch entitled *Greek Verbs, Irregular and Defective*, afterwards thrice reprinted by the Clarendon Press. It embraces 'all the tenses used by Greek writers, with reference to the passages in which they are found'. It is a matter of regret that, while new references were added in the later editions, the evidence of Inscriptions was never introduced. But it still remains the best book of its kind[3].

Veitch

A vivid contrast to the quiet and retiring scholar just mentioned is presented by the far more prominent personality of John Stuart Blackie (1809—1895), who was educated at Aberdeen and Edinburgh, and at Göttingen and Berlin, and was for eleven years professor of Latin at Aberdeen, and for thirty professor of Greek at Edinburgh (1852–82). He was mainly interested in the Greek poets. He translated the 'lyrical Dramas of Aeschylus' into English verse, and produced more than one edition of his 'Lays and Legends of Ancient Greece'. In 1866 he dedicated to Welcker, Finlay and W. G. Clark his principal classical work, consisting of two volumes of a vigorous and flowing translation of the *Iliad* in a ballad measure of fourteen syllables, followed by a volume of 'philological and archaeological'

Blackie

[1] On the backward state of Greek in the time of Dunbar and Sandford (and A. Alexander of St Andrews), cp. *Westminster Review*, xvi (1832) 90—110, *Greek Literature in Scotland*. On Sandford's distinguished successor, Lushington, see p. 405 *supra*.

[2] *Greek Verbs, their leading formations, defects, and irregularities, ascertained and illustrated by copious and special references to the Classical Authors*.

[3] W. G. Rutherford, in *Biogr. Jahrb.* 1885, 136–9.

notes, and preceded by another of 'Dissertations'. In the course of these he arrives at the conclusion that there is 'a soul of truth in the Wolfian theory, but its operation is to be recognised among the rude materials which Homer used and fused, not among the shapely fragments of the finished work which Pisistratus collected and arranged'[1]. These Dissertations are well worthy of an attentive perusal. In his teaching of Greek he insisted on recognising the rights of Greek accent[2], and, with a view to facilitating the acquisition of the language, published a small volume of *Greek and English Dialogues* (1871). He was little concerned with the details of a purely verbal scholarship, but he took a large and humane view of the abiding value of the poetic literature of Greece[3].

The Homeric question, ably discussed by Blackie, was more minutely studied by an admirable Greek scholar of northern Britain, William Duguid Geddes (1828—1900), professor of Greek at Aberdeen from 1856 to 1885, when he became Principal, while he attained the further distinction of knighthood in 1892. He was the editor of a collection of Greek and Latin verses by members of his university, and he also produced an interesting edition of the *Phaedo* (1863)[4].

Geddes

In his *Problem of the Homeric Poems* (1878) he accepted Grote's definition of the original Achilleid as consisting of *Iliad* i, viii, xi—xxii, and maintained that the rest was composed by a later poet, the author of the *Odyssey*, who 'engrafted on a more ancient poem, the Achilleid, splendid and vigorous saplings of his own, transforming and enlarging it into an Iliad, but an Iliad in which the engrafting is not absolutely complete, where the "sutures" are still visible'. 'The kinship between the *Odyssey* and the 'non-Achillean' books of the *Iliad* is recognised especially (1) in the mode of presenting Odysseus, Hector, Helen, and some other persons; (2) in the aspects of the gods and their worship; (3) in ethical purpose; (4) in local marks of origin,—the traces of an Ionian origin being common to the *Odyssey* with the non-Achillean books of the *Iliad*, and with those alone'. The work 'will always rank as a very able and original contribution to the question'[5].

---

[1] i 259.

[2] *Discourse on Greek Pronunciation, Accent, and Quantity* (1852), and *The Place and Power of Accent in Language* (Royal Soc. of Edin. 1870).

[3] *Times* for 4 March, 1895; *Life* (with portrait) by A. M. Stodart (new ed. 1906); esp. chap. iii (Göttingen), and xiv (Homer).

[4] Cp. R. A. Neil, in *Aurora Borealis Academica*, 32.

[5] Jebb's *Homer*, 125 f.

Among Latin scholars in Scotland we have James Pillans (1778—1864), Rector of the High School, Edin- Pillans burgh, and Professor of Humanity in the University Carson (1820-63), an editor of selections from Tacitus, Curtius, and Livy; and A. R. Carson (1780—1850), who succeeded him as Rector, and produced editions of Tacitus and Phaedrus. Cicero, *pro Cluentio*, and the *Mostellaria* of Plautus were well edited by William Ramsay (1806—1865), professor W. Ramsay of Humanity at Glasgow for the last thirty-four years of his life, and author of an excellent 'Manual of Roman Antiquities' (1851) and of important articles in Dr William Smith's *Dictionaries* (1842–3)[1].

Meanwhile, in England, James Tate (1771—1843) of Sidney Sussex College, Cambridge, Master of Richmond Tate School from 1790 to 1833, gave proof of the enduring influence of Bentley in his *Horatius Restitutus*, a work in which the poems are arranged in chronological order in accordance with Bentley's views.

Late in the life of Bentley, Virgil's *Georgics* had been edited in 1741 by John Martyn (1699—1768), professor of Martyn Botany at Cambridge for the last 36 years of his Keightley life. His edition of the *Georgics* was followed in 1749 by that of the *Bucolics*, and both of them were repeatedly reprinted during the next generation. A special interest attaches to the illustrations representing the plants mentioned by the poet. About a century later, notes on the *Bucolics* and *Georgics* were published in 1846-8 by Thomas Keightley (1789—1872), the author of popular histories of Greece and Rome.

Thomas Hewitt Key (1799—1875), of St John's and Trinity, Cambridge, studied medicine in London and pro- Key fessed pure mathematics in Virginia, but was far better known as professor of Latin (1828–42) and of Comparative Grammar (1842–75) at University College, London. His essays on Terentian Metres and other subjects were published in a collected form in 1844, his 'Philological Essays' in 1868, and his work on the 'origin and development' of language in 1874. His Latin Grammar had already been completed in 1846, while

[1] *e.g.* on *Agricultura, Cicero, Juvenalis, Lucilius, Lucretius.*

his Latin Dictionary was posthumously printed at Cambridge from his unfinished MS in 1888. He was head-master of University College School in 1828–75. In 1833–42 his colleague in that

Malden

office was Henry Malden (1800—1876), Fellow of Trinity, Cambridge, and professor of Greek at University College from 1831 to his death. He was an excellent teacher, but he published hardly anything except an 'Introductory Lecture' (1831), a small volume 'on the origin of universities and academical degrees' (1835), and a paper 'on the number of the chorus in the *Eumenides*' (1872).

Their contemporary, George Long (1800—1879), Fellow of

Long

Trinity, Cambridge, who, as Craven Scholar, was declared equal to Macaulay and Malden, preceded Malden as professor of Greek in 1828–31 and succeeded Key as professor of Latin in 1842–6[1]. He published 'two dissertations on Roman Law' in 1827, edited Cicero's *Orations* in the *Bibliotheca Classica*[2], and produced a school edition of Caesar's *Gallic War*, together with translations of thirteen of Plutarch's *Lives* connected with the Civil Wars of Rome (1844–6), and of the *Meditations* of Marcus Aurelius (1862) and the *Manual* of Epictetus (1877). His work as a historian is mentioned at a later point[3]. He contributed numerous articles on Roman Law and

W. Smith

other subjects to the great series of Dictionaries organised by William Smith (1813—1893), who was educated at University College, and, after holding professorships in London, became classical examiner in the University (1853). Smith's Dictionaries of Greek and Roman Antiquities (1842 etc.)[4], Biography and Mythology (1843 etc.) and Geo-

[1] Like Key, he had begun his career as a professor (of ancient languages) in Virginia (1824–8).

[2] In organising and superintending this series in 1851–8 Long was associated with A. J. Macleane (who edited Horace, Juvenal and Persius). The series included Paley's editions of Aeschylus and Euripides and of Homer's *Iliad* and Hesiod; Blakesley's Herodotus, R. Whiston's Demosthenes, P. Frost's *Annals* of Tacitus, Thompson's *Phaedrus* and *Gorgias*, Blaydes and Paley's Sophocles, and Conington's Virgil.

[3] p. 439 *infra*.

[4] The third edition was revised and enlarged in 1890 under the editorship of W. Wayte (editor of Plato's *Protagoras* and Demosthenes, *Androtion and Timocrates*), and G. E. Marindin, late Fellows of King's College, Cambridge.

graphy (1857), were followed by Dictionaries of the Bible and of Christian Antiquities and Christian Biography. The abridgements of the first two of these are well known to classical students[1]. The Latin and English Dictionary of 1855 etc., founded on Forcellini and Freund, has its counterpart in the English and Latin Dictionary of 1870, compiled with the aid of Theophilus D. Hall, Fellow of University College, London, and other scholars. Smith's series of Latin and Greek textbooks included an excellent School History of Greece (1854 etc.). The notes to his editions of parts of Tacitus and Plato were avowedly borrowed from German sources. Many articles in his Dictionaries were written by his brother, the Rev. Philip Smith (1817—1885), whose most substantial work was an Ancient History in three volumes (1868). William Smith, who was editor of the *Quarterly Review* for the last 26 years of his life and was knighted in 1892, deserves to be remembered as a great organiser of learned literary labour. When he received his honorary degree at Oxford, he was justly described by Lord Salisbury as *vir in litterarum republica potentissimus*.

A 'Dictionary of Roman and Greek Antiquities, with nearly 2000 engravings illustrative of the industrial arts and social life of the Greeks and Romans', was the best-known work of Anthony Rich (1821—1891), honorary Fellow of Gonville and Caius College[2], who also published an illustrated edition of Horace's *Satires* (1870). His Dictionary attained a third edition in 1873, and had meanwhile been translated into French, Italian, and German.

Rich

Editions of the *Menaechmi* and *Aulularia* of Plautus, with Latin notes and glossaries, were published in 1836–9 by James Hildyard, Fellow of Christ's (1809—1887).

Hildyard

A revised text of Horace, with illustrations from ancient gems, selected by the learned archaeologist, C. W. King[3], was produced in 1869 by Hugh Andrew Johnstone

Munro

[1] The 'Classical Dictionary' has long superseded that of Dr John Lempriere (1788 etc.), a native of Jersey, who was educated at Winchester and at Pembroke College, Oxford, and was headmaster of Bolton, Abingdon and Exeter Schools (1765 ?—1824).

[2] Cp. Venn's *Biographical History*, ii 183 (1898).

[3] 1818—1888, Fellow of Trinity, Cambridge, and author of six works on gems in 1860–72.

HUGH ANDREW JOHNSTONE MUNRO.

From a photograph by Sir William Davidson Niven.

Munro (1819—1885), educated at Shrewsbury, Fellow of Trinity, and first professor of Latin in the University of Cambridge. He held the professorship for three years only (1869–72), but, in those years, he gave the first impulse to a reform in the English pro-nunciation of Latin[1].

The reform was independently supported by Mr H. J. Roby in his *Latin Grammar* (1871), and by Mr A. J. Ellis in his *Practical Hints on the Quantitative Pronunciation of Latin* (1874), and was further promoted by the Cambridge Philological Society in a pamphlet on the *Pronunciation of Latin in the Augustan Period* (1886), and by Professors E. V. Arnold and R. S. Conway in the *Restored Pronunciation of Greek and Latin*[2]. The question of Latin in particular was taken up by the Classical Association of Scotland (1904), and by that of England and Wales (1905); a scheme of pronunciation was approved by the Philological Societies of Oxford and Cambridge, dis-cussed by the various Conferences of Head-Masters and Assistant-Masters; sanctioned by the Board of Education (1906), and unanimously recommended by the Special Board for Classics in Cambridge (1907)[3].

In 1864 the fruit of many years of strenuous study appeared in Munro's masterly edition of Lucretius, with critical notes and with a full explanatory commentary, and a vigorous rendering in English prose. Of the editor it has been justly observed, that of Lachmann and Ritschl, 'though a sincere admirer, he was no slavish imitator; but rather an independent discovererin regions which their labours made accessible to other explorers'[4]. His other works include an edition of the *Aetna* of an unknown poet, 'Criticisms and Elucidations of Catullus'[5], and Emendations of the fragments of Lucilius[6]. He was hardly less masterly as a Greek critic. In 1855 he was the first to maintain the Eudemian origin of the fifth book of Aristotle's *Ethics*[7]; and late in life he paid special attention to the text of Euripides[8]. His *Translations*

---

[1] Pamphlet, 1871; Palmer and Munro's *Syllabus*, 1872.

[2] 1895; ed. 3, 1907.

[3] Cp. *Proceedings of Cl. Assoc. of England and Wales*, Jan. 1905, 7—18; Oct. 1906, 44—62; and *The Times*, 2 Apr. 1907 (S. E. Winbolt); 3 Apr. (J. E. Sandys); 6 Apr. (G. G. Ramsay); also Appendix B and C (p. 29) to J. P. Postgate's pamphlet, *How to pronounce Latin*, 1907.

[4] W. H. Thompson in *Journ. of Philol.* xiv 107 f.

[5] 1878; new ed. 1906.

[6] *Journ. of Philol.* vii 292 f, viii 201 f.

[7] *Journal of Cl. and Sacred Philol.* ii 58—81.

[8] *Journ. of Philol.* x 233 f; xi 267 f.

into Latin and Greek Verse[1] are justly held in high repute. Though not, like Kennedy, 'an original Latin poet'[2], he displayed in his Latin verse 'a masculine vigour' that was all his own. He won the admiration of another master of the craft by his version of Gray's 'Elegy,'—*qui stant quasi marmore versus | et similes solido structis adamante columnis*[3]. He was apparently in the enjoyment of vigorous health, when he died at Rome at the age of sixty-five[4].

A standard edition of Cicero, *De Oratore*, was prepared for the Clarendon Press in 1879–92 by Augustus Samuel Wilkins (1843—1905), of St John's College, Cambridge, for thirty-four years professor of Latin at Owens College, Manchester, who also edited Cicero's *Speeches against Catiline* and Horace's *Epistles*, contributed to the ninth edition of the *Encyclopaedia Britannica* the long and important articles on the Greek and Latin languages, and, in conjunction with Mr E. B. England, translated G. Curtius' *Principles of Greek Etymology*, and also his work on the *Greek Verb*. His fine scholarship and his wide literary knowledge gave real value to his editions of classical texts, and he also did good service in introducing to English readers the results of German research. One of his earliest publications was a Prize Essay on *National Education in Greece*. *Education* was the subject of his contribution to the Cambridge *Companion to Greek Studies* (1905); and a sketch of *Roman Education* was his latest work (1905)[5].

The first professor of Latin at Oxford was John Conington (1825—1869), who was educated at Rugby and held the Latin Professorship for the last fifteen years of his short life. He is widely known as the editor of Virgil (1863–71) and of Persius (1872). Besides translating both of these poets into English prose, he rendered into English verse

---

[1] Privately printed, 1884; published (with portrait), 1906.

[2] Thompson, *Journ. of Philol.* xiv. 109.

[3] T. S. Evans, *Latin and Greek Verse*, 25.

[4] W. H. Thompson, *Journ. of Philol.* xiv 107—110; J. D. Duff in *Biogr. Jahrb.* 1885, 111—117, and in preface to Munro's *Translations*, ed. 1906, and to reprint of his Translation of Lucretius, 1908.

[5] J. E. Sandys, in *The Eagle*, xxvii 69—84, and in *Biogr. Jahrb.* 1906, 41—45.

the whole of Horace, and the *Aeneid*. His rendering of Horace was regarded by Munro as 'on the whole perhaps the best and most successful translation of a Classic that exists in the English language', while, in the judgement of the same scholar, his edition of Virgil 'displays a minute diligence, as well as a fine taste, a delicate discrimination, and a mastery of language, which it requires long study properly to appreciate'[1]. His work as a Greek scholar has already been briefly noticed[2]. William Young

Sellar

Sellar (1825—1890), who was educated at the Edinburgh Academy and at the University of Glasgow, and at Balliol, was a Fellow of Oriel, and held the Professorship of Humanity at Edinburgh for the last twenty-seven years of his life[3]. Immediately before his appointment (1863), he produced his 'Roman Poets of the Republic', a masterpiece of literary criticism, which was happily followed in due time by similar works on Virgil (1877), and on 'Horace and the Elegiac Poets' (1892)[4]. The *Annals* of Tacitus were ably edited at Oxford in

Furneaux

1884 by Henry Furneaux (1829—1900), Fellow of Corpus.

Conington's work on Persius was edited by his successor in the Chair of Latin, Henry Nettleship (1839—1893)

Nettleship

of Charterhouse and of Corpus Christi College, Oxford. He attended Haupt's lectures in Berlin and wrote a graphic account of that master's method[5]. After five years as a master at Harrow, and five more as a lecturer at Oxford, he was elected Latin professor in 1878. As Conington's successor, he completed the latter half of his predecessor's edition of the *Aeneid*.

---

[1] *Journal of Philology*, ii 334–6. Cp. *Memoir* by H. J. S. Smith, prefixed to his *Miscellaneous Writings* (1872).

[2] p. 422 *supra*.

[3] He had previously been assistant to Professor W. Ramsay in Glasgow (1851–3) and assistant professor and professor of Greek at St Andrews (1853–63); he had also contributed to the *Oxford Essays* admirable papers on *Lucretius* (1855) and on *The Characteristics of Thucydides* (1857).

[4] With *Memoir* by his nephew and pupil, Andrew Lang. Paper on *The Birth-place of Propertius* in *Cl. Rev.* iv (1890) 393 f, and Obituary Notice by Lewis Campbell, *ib.* 428 f. See also Mrs Sellar's *Recollections and Impressions* (1907).

[5] *Essays*, i 1—22.

In 1875 he planned a great Latin dictionary, but was only able to publish a tenth part of the proposed work, under the title of 'Contributions to Latin Lexicography' (1889)[1]. He was familiar with the ancient Latin grammarians, and especially with the successive epitomes of Verrius Flaccus. One of his latest tasks was the revision of the edition of Nonius, which had been left unfinished by his former pupil J. H. Onions (1852—1889)[2]. Many of his most valuable papers have been collected in the two volumes of his *Essays* (1885–95)[3].

Several editions of prose authors were produced by scholars who are best known as historians. Thus Cicero's *Speeches* and Caesar's *Gallic War* were edited by Long[4], Sallust by Merivale, and the first book of Livy by Seeley.

Among Latin scholars in Ireland we note the name of James
Henry   Henry (1796—1876), the gold medallist of Trinity
College, Dublin, who practised as a physician till 1845, when he published a verse translation of *Aeneid* i and ii. After travelling abroad, he produced in 1853 his 'Notes of a Twelve Years' Voyage of Discovery in the First Six Books of the Aeneis'. His personal knowledge of all the best MSS and editions of Virgil is embodied in the four volumes of his larger work, the *Aeneidea* (1873–89), which includes many original and valuable contributions to the interpretation of the text. Several of Cicero's
Allen   philosophical works were ably edited in Dublin in
1836–56 by Henry Ellis Allen (1808—1874) under the Latinised name of *Henricus Alanus*[5]. Textual criticism was
Palmer   the forte of Arthur Palmer (1841—1897), a scholar
of Canadian birth, who was educated at Cheltenham

---

[1] The English edition of Seyffert's *Dictionary of Classical Antiquities*, begun by Nettleship, was completed by the present writer, who superintended the second half of the work and selected the illustrations for the whole (1891).

[2] *Biogr. Jahrb.* 1889, 67 f.

[3] With *Memoir* (and portrait) in vol. ii; cf. Haverfield in *Biogr. Jahrb.* 1897, 79—81.

[4] p. 430 *supra*, and p. 439 *infra*.

[5] *De Nat. Deor., De Div., De Fato, De Off., Cato maior, Lael., De Finibus*; also notes on Livy, Sallust and Caesar. His originality is lauded in the *Church of England Quarterly Review* (1838–9), iv 101 f, v 420. His excellent MS of Propertius now belongs to his son.

and at Trinity College, Dublin, where he was successively elected
Fellow (1867), Professor of Latin (1880) and Public Orator (1888).
He was specially interested in the criticism of the Latin Elegiac
poets and of Plautus. He edited the *Amphitruo* of Plautus, the
Satires of Horace, and the *Heroides* of Ovid. Many of his
emendations were first published in *Hermathena*. His skill in
emending Greek poets was best exemplified in Bacchylides and in
Aristophanes, whose position in Greek literature was the theme of
his article in the *Quarterly Review* for October, 1884. One who
knew him well avers that his 'published works, though quite
sufficient to be the basis of a high reputation as a scholar and a
man of letters, gave but a pale reflexion of his intellect'[1].

From editors of Greek and Latin Classics we pass to the
historians. Connop Thirlwall (1797—1875) 'was
taught Latin at three years of age, and at four read
Greek with ease and fluency'[2]. At Charterhouse

Historians: Thirlwall

he was the school-fellow of George Grote, and of Julius Charles
Hare. At Cambridge he won the Craven in his first year. After
his election to a Fellowship at Trinity, he visited Rome, where he
saw much of Bunsen, but apparently nothing of Niebuhr, whose
'History' was afterwards translated by Thirlwall and Hare. The
two friends were the founders and editors of the *Philological
Museum* (1831), which included Thirlwall's well-known essay on
the *Irony of Sophocles*. As a lecturer at Trinity, he gave a greater
breadth to the teaching of Classics, but his College career was
cut short by his 'Letter on the Admission of Dissenters to
Academical Degrees', which led to the Master, Dr Wordsworth,
calling on him to resign his office (1834). On the nomination
of Lord Melbourne, he became Rector of Kirby Underdale,
in Yorkshire (1834–40), and Bishop of St David's (1840–74).
Thirlwall produced the first volume of his *History of Greece*
in 1835 and the last in 1844. His work as a historian was
characterised by soundness of scholarship and refinement of style,
by a judicial temper and a fine sense of proportion. Over his
grave are inscribed the words, *cor sapiens et intelligens ad dis-
cernendum judicium.*

---

[1] Tyrrell in *Hermathena*, x 115—121.
[2] From his father's preface to *Primitiae* (1809).

His school-fellow, George Grote (1794—1871), had embarked
on his history as early as 1823, but did not publish
his first volume until 1846, or his last until ten
years later[1]. Though Thirlwall and Grote not unfrequently met,
the former knew so little of his school-fellow's plans, that he was
heard to say, 'Grote is the man who ought to write the History of
Greece'; and, when it appeared, he welcomed it with a generous
enthusiasm[2]. He was afterwards buried beside Grote in Westminster Abbey. As a historian, Grote shows the keenest sympathy
with the Athenian democracy, and even with the Athenian dema-
gogue; but he is an intelligent interpreter of the ancient historians
of Greece, and his opinions on the political and economic condition
of Athens derive fresh weight from his experience as a banker and
as a Member of Parliament. His 'great work, the work of a man
of affairs, has done much more perhaps than any other one book
of the century, to invest his subject with a vivid, an almost
modern interest for a world wider than the academic'[3].

His representation of Athenian constitutional history was critically examined
by Schömann[4], and, in certain points, must now be revised with the aid of
Aristotle's *Constitution of Athens*. A special importance attaches to his
opinions on the ' Homeric Question '; he regards Homer as ' belonging to the
second, not the first, stage in the development of epos,—as the composer of
the large epic, not as the primitive bard of the short lays'; but he holds that
Homer's original *Achilleid* has been converted by a later poet or poets into
our present *Iliad*[5]. One of the most original parts of the *History* is the
celebrated chapter on the Sophists[6].

His great work on Plato was a solid contribution to the intelligent study of that philosopher[7]. Of his proposed sequel on
Aristotle only two volumes were completed[8]. The wide range of
his interests is admiringly acknowledged by his friend, John Stuart

Grote

---

[1] Ed. 6 in 10 vols. 1888.

[2] J. W. Clark, *Old Friends at Cambridge*, 131.

[3] Jebb's *Essays and Addresses*, 533 f.

[4] 1854; E. T. by B. Bosanquet, 1878.

[5] Cp. Jebb's *Homer*, 122-5, and Friedländer, *Die Homerische Kritik von
Wolf bis Grote* (1853), 28.

[6] c. 67; cp. *Quarterly Rev.* no. 175, and Cope in *Journ. of Cl. and Sacred
Philol.* nos. 2, 5, 7, 9 ; also H. Jackson in *Enc. Brit.*, *s.v. Sophists*.

[7] 3 vols. 1865.

[8] 1872.

GEORGE GROTE.

From a reproduction of the portrait by Stewartson (1824)
now in possession of Mr John Murray.

[*To face p.* 438 *of Vol. III.*

Mill, who says of him :—'Scholarship fills but a corner of his mind'[1].

In the *History of Greece*, Grote, as compared with Curtius, stands at a certain disadvantage owing to the fact that he never visited the land whose history he describes.   That land was not left unexplored by William Mure (1799—1860), who was educated at Edinburgh and Bonn, travelled   Mure
in Greece in 1838, and was for nine years a Member of Parliament. His full and sympathetic treatment of Xenophon lends a special value to part of the five volumes of his 'Critical History of the Literature of Ancient Greece' (1850–7).   Historians of Greece and Rome alike are indebted to the chronological researches of Henry Fynes Clinton (1781—1852), of Westminster,   Clinton
and Christ Church, Oxford, Member for Aldborough (1806–26), the learned author of the *Fasti Hellenici* (1824-32), and the *Fasti Romani* (1845-50)[2].   Thomas Arnold   Arnold
(1795—1842), head-master of Rugby and professor of History at Oxford, did much for the historical and geographical elucidation of Thucydides (1830–5), and left behind him a splendid fragment of a *History of Rome* (1838-43), ending with the close of the second Punic War[3].   Arnold's history was written under the influence of Niebuhr.   Twelve years later an 'Inquiry into the Credibility of Early Roman History'[4] was published   G. C. Lewis
by Sir George Cornewall Lewis (1806—1863), of Eton and Christ Church, Oxford, who translated Boeckh's 'Public Economy of Athens', edited Babrius, and wrote on the 'Astronomy of the Ancients'.   The 'History of the Decline   Long
of the Roman Republic' (1864-74), written with special reference to the evidence of ancient authorities, was the last work produced by George Long[5].   The 'History of the Romans under the Empire' was written in 1850-62,   Merivale
at the College living of Lawford, by Charles Merivale

---

[1] Gomperz, *Essays etc.*, 186.—Cp. *Life* (with portrait) by Mrs Grote, and *Minor Works* (with sketch of *Life* by Bain), 1873 ; Lehrs, *Populäre Aufsätze*, 1875 ; Gomperz, *Essays und Erinnerungen*, 1905, 184—196.

[2] Autobiography etc. in *Literary Remains* (1854).

[3] *Life* by A. P. Stanley.

[4] Rev. by Grote, *Minor Works*, 207—236.

[5] p. 430 *supra*.

(1808—1894) of Harrow and St John's, Cambridge, who was dean of Ely for the last twenty-five years of his life. He also wrote a short 'History of the Roman Republic' and was the author of the Boyle Lectures 'On the Conversion of the Roman Empire'. His skill as a writer of Latin verse is exemplified in his fine rendering of Keats' *Hyperion*, which he published on the completion of his History. Seven years later he produced a translation of the *Iliad* in English ballad metre[1].

The comparative study of ancient institutions was successfully pursued by Henry James Sumner Maine (1822—1888), of Pembroke College, Cambridge, for seven years professor of Civil Law at that university, for another seven years legal member of the supreme government of India, in 1869–78 professor of Jurisprudence at Oxford, and for the last eleven years of his life Master of Trinity Hall, Cambridge. In 1887 he was elected professor of International Law. His best-known works are 'Ancient Law' (1861), 'Village Communities' (1871), 'Lectures on the Early History of Institutions' (1875) and 'Dissertations on Early Law and Custom' (1883). It has been well said that 'the impulse given by Maine' to the intelligent study of law 'in England and America can hardly be overrated... At one master-stroke he forged a new and lasting bond between law, history, and anthropology'[2].

The 'Unity of History' was the theme of the memorable Rede Lecture delivered at Cambridge in 1872 by Edward Augustus Freeman (1823—1892), Fellow of Trinity College, Oxford, and Regius Professor of Modern History at Oxford for the last eight years of his life. The lecture included a characteristic protest against the Revival of Learning on the ground that 'it led men to centre their whole powers on an exclusive attention to writings contained in two languages, and for the most part in certain arbitrarily chosen periods of those two languages', while it warmly welcomed 'the discovery of the Comparative method in philology, in mythology', and 'in politics and history', as marking 'a stage in the progress of the human mind at

Maine

Freeman

---

[1] *Autobiography and Letters* (1898); J. E. Sandys, in *The Eagle*, xviii 183—196.

[2] Sir F. Pollock, *Oxford Lectures*, 1890, 158.

least as great and memorable as the revival of Greek and Latin
learning"[1].

Nine years had already passed since Polybius had been fruitfully studied by Freeman in the preparation of the volume in
which he had 'traced the action of the federal principle in the
Achaian league' of B.C. 281—146. A visit to Sicily in 1878,
followed by three long sojourns in the island between 1886 and
1890[2], bore fruit in the single volume on Sicily in the 'Story of the
Nations' (1892), and in the four volumes of the *History of Sicily
from the earliest times* (1891–4) down to the death of Agathocles
in 289 B.C.,—volumes founded on a thorough study of Pindar and
Thucydides and other ancient authorities. The author's essays on
'Homer and the Homeric Age', on the 'Athenian democracy', on
the 'Attic historians', on 'Ancient Greece and mediaeval Italy',
and on 'Mommsen's History of Rome', have been reprinted in
the second and third series of the *Historical Essays* (1873–9)[3].

Three volumes of a 'History of Greece' ending with 403 B.C.
were published in 1888—1900 by Evelyn Abbott
(1843—1901), Fellow and Tutor of Balliol, writer   Abbott
of a popular work on Pericles (1891), editor of *Hellenica* (1880),
and joint-author of the *Life of Jowett*[4]. The teaching of Roman
history at Oxford was greatly advanced by the inspiring influence
of Henry Pelham (1846—1907) of Harrow and of
Trinity, Oxford, Fellow and Tutor of Exeter, who, in   Pelham
1889, became professor of Ancient History and Fellow of Brasenose, and, in 1897, President of the first of his three Colleges.
His small volume of 'Outlines of Roman History' (1890) has been
described as 'the most useful', and 'the most able, sketch of the
subject that has yet been published'. A special value attaches to
his printed articles and lectures on the same theme, though he
did not live to publish his proposed 'History of the Roman
Empire'. In his public teaching he rose far above 'pedagogic
ends of the narrower sort'; 'follower and personal friend of the

[1] *The Unity of History* (1872), 4, 9.

[2] W. R. W. Stephens, *Life and Letters of E. A. Freeman* (1895), ii 146,
297.

[3] *ib.* i 178—185.

[4] *Times*, 6 Sept. 1901.

great Mommsen, he conceived the study of antiquity in its larger
and severer sense'. A loyal friend to the Hellenic Society and
to the British School at Athens, he took a leading part in the
foundation of the British School at Rome (1901), and was one
of the original Fellows of the British Academy (1902)[1].

One of the foremost of the Greek topographers of the nineteenth
century was William Martin Leake (1777—1860),
Leake   who, after serving with his regiment in the West
Indies, and training Turkish troops in Constantinople, travelled
in Asia Minor in 1800, and surveyed Egypt (1801–2) as well as
European Turkey and Greece (1804–7), where he continued to
reside from 1808 to 1810. On retiring from active military service
in 1815, he devoted all his energies to the cause of classical
learning. The commission, which he received from the Foreign
Office in 1804, included an item of special importance in connexion with the topography of Greece. He was there instructed
'to acquire for the British government and nation a more accurate
knowledge than has yet been attained of this important and
interesting country'. His singular activity as a traveller, great
powers of observation, and his vivid realisation of the close
connexion between topography and history, ensured his carrying
out this instruction with complete success. He thus became 'the
founder of the scientific geography of Greece'[2]. His reputation
as a learned and scientific topographer rests on his ' Researches
in Greece' (1814), his 'Topography of Athens and the Demi'
(1821), his 'Journal of a Tour in Asia Minor' (1824), his 'Travels
in Northern Greece' (1835–41), his 'Morea' (1830), and his
'Peloponnesiaca' (1846). His volume on the 'Topography of
Athens' was translated into German by Baiter and Sauppe, and
that on the 'Demi' by Westermann. His work on Athens, which
attained a second edition in 1841, was the earliest scientific
reconstruction of the ancient city with the aid of all the evidence
supplied by Greek literature, inscriptions, and works of art. It
has been rightly recognised by Curtius as a work of permanent
value; it is, in fact, the foundation of all subsequent research on

---

[1] F. Haverfield and " M.", in *Athenaeum*, 16 Feb. 1907, 197.
[2] Michaelis, *Arch. Entd.* 29.

the same subject. His collection of Greek marbles was presented
by himself to the British Museum in 1839, while his library and the
great collection of coins described in his 'Numismata Hellenica'
(1859) were purchased by the University of Cambridge, which has
placed his bust in the vestibule of the Fitzwilliam Museum [1].

In classical geography useful work of a less original character
was done by John Antony Cramer (1793—1848),
Principal of New Inn Hall, and Regius professor   Cramer
of Modern History, Oxford, in his 'Geographical and historical
description' of ancient Italy (1826) and Greece (1828) and Asia
Minor (1832). Of the rest of his works, the *Anecdota Graeca*
from MSS of Oxford (1834-7) and Paris (1839-41) are those that
appeal most directly to scholars.

His anonymous dissertation on Hannibal's passage of the Alps (1820) was
welcomed in the *Edinburgh Review* as 'a scholarlike work of
first-rate ability'. It argues in favour of the Little St Bernard,   W. J. Law
                                                                        Robert Ellis
a view also maintained by Niebuhr and Arnold, by W. J. Law
(1787—1869), of Christ Church, Oxford (in 1855-66), and by Mommsen. The
rival claims of the Little Mont Cenis were ably supported by Robert Ellis,
Fellow of St John's, Cambridge (d. 1885)[2].

Lycia was traversed in 1838 and 1840 by Charles Fellows (1799—1860),
the discoverer of the Xanthian marbles[3], and in 1842 by   Fellows
T. A. B. Spratt (1811—1888) and Edward Forbes (1815—   Spratt
1854).   Crete was visited in 1851-3 by Spratt, who published
his 'Travels and Researches' in 1865. Cyrene was examined in 1860-1 by
R. Murdoch Smith and E. A. Porcher ; the surroundings of   Murdoch
Cyrene explored by George Dennis, the author of the 'Cities   Smith and
and Cemeteries of Etruria'[4]; and the necropolis of Cameiros   Porcher
in Rhodes excavated by Salzmann and Biliotti in 1858 and   Dennis
1865.   Lastly, Nineveh was explored in 1845 by that eminent   Layard
public servant, Sir Austen Henry Layard (1817—1894).

Layard's able contemporary, Charles Thomas Newton (1816—
1894), was educated at Shrewsbury and at Christ
Church, Oxford, where he impressed Ruskin as   Newton
'already notable in his intense and curious way of looking into

---

[1] J. H. Marsden's *Memoir* (1864) ; cp. E. Curtius, *Alterthum und
Gegenwart*, ii 305—322.

[2] *Treatise* (1853) ; *Journ. of Cl. and Sacred Philol.* 1855-6 ; *Ancient
Routes between Italy and Gaul* (1867).

[3] Michaelis, *Arch. Entd.* 77—81.   [4] 1848 ; ed. 3, 1883.

things '[1]. His work in the British Museum began in 1840 and ended with the twenty-four years of his tenure of the office of Keeper of the Department of Greek and Roman Antiquities (1861–85).

In 1846 his attention was arrested at the Museum by some fragments of reliefs from the Castle of the Knights of St John at Budrum, the ancient Halicarnassus. He divined that these reliefs must have once belonged to the great monument erected in memory of Mausolus. In 1852 he was appointed Vice-Consul at Mytilene with a roving commission to search for ancient remains in the neighbouring lands. From Lesbos he visited Chios, Cos and Rhodes, where he was consul in 1853–4, and was quietly superintending the excavations at Calymnos amid all the excitement of the Crimean war. In November, 1855, he made some excavations in the hippodrome of Constantinople, and thus cleared away the ground concealing the base of the column of the three entwined serpents of bronze, which once supported at Delphi the memorial of the victory of Plataea[2]. In 1856 he explored the site of the Mausoleum, and recovered a large part of the noble sculptures that adorned the tomb. From Didyma near Miletus he sent home a number of the seated archaic figures that lined the approach to the temple of Apollo at Branchidae. From Cnidos he brought away the colossal lion, probably set up by Conon in memory of his victory over the Spartan fleet in 394 B.C., as well as a famous statue of the seated Demeter, and an exquisite statuette of Persephone. The record of all these acquisitions is enshrined in his official *History of Discoveries at Halicarnassus, Cnidus, and Branchidae* (1862), and in his popular *Travels and Discoveries in the Levant* (1865).

Meanwhile, he had been appointed Consul at Rome, whence he was recalled two years later to fill the place of Keeper of Greek and Roman Antiquities at the British Museum, an appointment that marked the dawn of a true interest in classical archæology in England. In 1864–74 he obtained special grants of more than £100,000 for purchases in his department, thus acquiring some of the Farnese statues, and the treasures of the Castellani and Pourtalès and Blacas collections. He also encouraged and supported the excavations in Rhodes and Cyprus, at Cyrene and Priene and Ephesus[3]. In 1877 he visited the excavations of Schliemann at Mycenae (and of Ernst Curtius at Olympia), and

---

[1] *Praeterita*, i § 225; cp. ii § 155 f, ed. 1899.

[2] The inscription was afterwards deciphered by Frick, *Jahrb. Cl. Phil.* Suppl. iii (1859) 554; and by Dethier and Mordtmann, Vienna Acad. 1864, 330.

[3] Cp. Stanley Lane Poole, in *National Review*, 1894, 622 f.

satisfied himself of the fact that the finds of Mycenae really belonged to the prehistoric age. In 1880 he collected his papers of 1850–79 in a single volume entitled *Essays in Art and Archaeology*, including his excellent Essay on Greek Inscriptions. Even when he had retired from the office of Keeper in 1885, he continued to edit the great collection of the *Greek Inscriptions of the British Museum*. He received the distinction of knighthood, and of honorary degrees at Oxford and Cambridge. From 1880 to 1888 he was the first holder of the Professorship of Archaeology at University College, London, his lectures, however, were too popular to be really instructive. Competent students, and even experts, learned much from his ordinary conversation. *Er ist ein voller Mann* was the phrase applied to him by one of the ablest of German archaeologists. His keen and refined features were perhaps best represented in the portrait painted at Rome by Severn, a small reproduction of which he once gave to the present writer. His marble bust stands in the noble hall built under his direction for the sculptures he had discovered at the Mausoleum of Halicarnassus. He was among the first to welcome the opening of the museums of classical archaeology at Cambridge and Oxford. At the inaugural ceremony at Cambridge in 1884 the cast of the little figure of Proserpine, which he had himself discovered at Cnidos, reminded him of 'her ἄνοδος from the darkness of Hades into the light of the upper world', and he happily described the occasion as 'the ἄνοδος of archaeology, so long buried in England'[1].

In the study of Greek Architecture an eminent position was attained by Francis Cranmer Penrose (1817—1903) of Winchester School and of Magdalene College, Cambridge, who in three successive years rowed in the university boat, and for the next three years was 'travelling bachelor of the university' (1812–5). As 'travelling bachelor' he studied architecture at Rome and at Athens, where he was led by the theories of Pennethorne to determine the hyperbolic curve of the *entasis* of the columns of the Parthenon. He resumed his measurements

Penrose

---

[1] Percy Gardner, in *Biogr. Jahrb.* 1896, 132—142; and Ernest Gardner, in *Annual of British School at Athens*, i 67—77. See also Sir Richard Jebb, in *J. H. S.* xxiv, p. li.

in the following season under the auspices of the Society of Dilettanti, and the results were published in *The Principles of Athenian Architecture*[1]. He was the honorary architect and the first director of the British School of Archaeology at Athens, where his name is commemorated in the Penrose Memorial Library[2]. An expert in astronomy, he elaborately investigated the orientation of Greek Temples. He was for many years surveyor of the fabric of St Paul's Cathedral, and he was repeatedly consulted by the Greek Government in connexion with the temples of Athens. He was probably the only person who ever stood on the highest point of the pillars of the *Olympieum*, as well as on the summit of the dome of St Paul's. In 1898 he received honorary degrees at Oxford and Cambridge, and, towards the close of a long life, he read a paper on the evolution of the volute in Greek Architecture[3].

Newton's successor at the British Museum, Alexander Stuart Murray (1841—1904), who studied in Glasgow and
A. Murray
in Berlin, is best known as the author of a 'History of Greek Sculpture' (1880–3), and a 'Handbook of Greek Archaeology' (1892); also of Lectures on 'Greek Bronzes' (1898), and on 'The Sculptures of the Parthenon' (1903)[4].

In the field of Roman Archaeology, Robert Burn (1829—1904),
Burn
of Shrewsbury and of Trinity College, Cambridge, produced a comprehensive work on *Rome and the Campagna* (1871), which, at the time of its publication, was 'the best book on the subject in English', and bears ample evidence of careful study of the classical authors and the modern topographical literature[5]. He also published an epitome of this work under the title of *Old Rome* (1880), and a volume of essays on *Roman Literature in relation to Roman Art* (1888). He has

---

[1] 1851, enlarged ed. 1888.

[2] *Annual* x 232—242. Sir Richard Jebb's inscription was printed with the list of Subscribers.

[3] Obituary notice by F. G. P., also in the *Athenaeum*, 1 Feb., the *Builder*, 21 Feb. and (by J. D. Crace) in the *Journal of the Royal Institute of British Architects*, 9 May, 1903 (with reproduction of the portrait by Sargent).

[4] See memoir and bibliography by A. H. Smith, in *Biogr. Jahrb.* 1907, 100–3.

[5] T. Ashby, quoted by Dr Postgate, *Biogr. Jahrb.* 1905, 143.

been well described as 'a man of lovable character—simple, generous, and sincere, with a high sense of duty, and a kindly heart'[1]. His work on *Rome and the Campagna* was succeeded by that of the Oxford bookseller, John Henry Parker (1806—1884), whose *Archaeology of Rome* appeared in 1874-6. The works on 'Ancient Rome in 1885' and 'in 1888', produced by John Henry Middleton (1846—1896) of Exeter College, Oxford, and Slade Professor and Director of the Fitzwilliam Museum, Cambridge, were revised and greatly enlarged in the two volumes of his *Remains of Ancient Rome* (1892).

Parker

The study of classical archaeology has been fostered in England by the foundation of the Society for the Promotion of Hellenic Studies (1879)[2], and by the institution of the British School of Archaeology at Athens (1883 f) and at Rome (1901). The Hellenic Society has taken part in promoting the exploration of Asia Minor, of Naucratis, of Samos and Thasos, Cyprus and Crete. Cyprus and Crete, as well as Melos and Megalopolis and Sparta, have been the scenes of excavations carried out by the School at Athens, while that at Rome, besides entering on researches in Rome itself, has minutely surveyed the classical topography of the Campagna. Early in the nineteenth century the pure scholarship of the Porsonian school was still in the ascendant. At the end of its first quarter, in the fancy of a writer who failed to forecast the future, the 'last rays' of English scholarship 'were seen to linger on the deathbed of Dobree'[3]. But, since that date, much has been done for the accurate study of Greek and Latin literature; the ancient Classics have also been popularised by means of admirable modern renderings of the great master-pieces; the Greek drama has been revived; new periodicals have been founded for promoting and for recording the advance of classical

Classical
archaeology

---

[1] Dr Postgate, *ib.* Cp. *Cambridge Review*, xxv 274.

[2] *An Outline of the History of the Hellenic Society* 1879—1904, by the Hon. Secretary, G. A. Macmillan; *Journal of Hellenic Studies*, begun in 1880-1. Archaeology has been included in the *Classical Review* from the first (1887); papers connected with Greek, Latin, and Hebrew scholarship have been published in the *Journal of Philology* (begun in 1868).

[3] *Church of England Quarterly Review*, v (1839) 145.

research.   Late in 1903 we have seen the birth of the Classical
Association, which aims at 'promoting the development and
maintaining the well-being of classical studies', while a new
interest in the Classics has also been aroused by the triumphant
progress of classical archaeology.

Turning from archaeological exploration to literary discovery,
we may recall the fact that many of the charred rolls
of Greek papyri discovered at Herculaneum in 1752,
including fragments of Epicurus and Philodemus,
were published, not only at Naples in and after 1793, but also
at Oxford in 1824 and 1891[1].   Private and public enterprise has
since recovered a large variety of papyri from the sands of Egypt.
The first of the literary papyri to come to light was the last book
of the *Iliad*, acquired by W. J. Bankes in 1821.   Fragments of
many other portions of the Homeric poems were afterwards
found, and it is an interesting indication of the wide popularity
of those poems that, in all these finds, Homer is regarded as
'inevitable'.   A far keener interest was awakened by the recovery
of lost Classics.   The two parts of a large roll containing three
of the speeches of Hypereides were independently obtained by
Arden and Harris in 1847, and the same orator's *Funeral Oration*,
by Stobart, in 1856.   About 1890 the British Museum acquired
a remarkable series of literary papyri, including part of the
Philippides of Hypereides, the Ἀθηναίων πολιτεία of Aristotle,
and the *Mimes* of Herodas, followed in 1896–7 by the *Odes* of
Bacchylides[2].   Scholars began to realise something of the rapture
which the quest and the recovery of lost Classics had excited in
a Petrarch or a Salutati, or in a Poggio Bracciolini, in the days
of the Revival of Learning.   They awoke to find themselves
living in a new age of *editiones principes*.   Many a 'Theban
fragment', in the form of paeans of Pindar, has since been
discovered during the fifth season of the fruitful excavations on
the site of Oxyrhynchus[3].   Art rather than literature may hope

Marginal note: Literary discoveries

---

[1] Walter Scott, *Fragmenta Herc.*, ed. Nicholson, 1891.

[2] Cp., in general, F. G. Kenyon's *Palaeography of Greek Papyri*, 1899,
3—7, 56—111.

[3] Grenfell and Hunt, in *Report of Egypt Exploration Fund* (1905-6) 10 f,
and in *Oxyrhynchus Papyri*, v (1908) 11—110.

to profit by the renewed exploration of Herculaneum, and it is to the banks of the Nile rather than to the bay of Naples that we may look for the further fulfilment of the poet's fancy :—

> ' O ye, who patiently explore
> The wreck of Herculanean lore,
> What rapture ! could ye seize
> Some Theban fragment, or unroll
> One precious, tender-hearted, scroll
> Of pure Simonides '[1].

---

[1] Wordsworth, *Poems of Sentiment and Reflection* xxvii (Sept. 1819).   The date is significant.   It was in the first two months of that year that Sir Humphry Davy spent a considerable time in endeavouring to unroll the Herculanean papyri in the Naples Museum.   He was fairly well received, but his endeavours were attended with very slight success ; and, in Feb. 1819, ' when the Reverend Peter Elmsley, whose zeal for the promotion of ancient literature brought him to Naples for the purpose of assisting in the under-taking began to examine the fragments unrolled, a jealousy, with regard to his assistance, was immediately manifested ' (p. 204 of Sir Humphry Davy's Report to the Royal Society in *Phil. Trans.* 15 March, 1821, pp. 191—208).

CHAPTER XLI.

THE UNITED STATES OF AMERICA.

LESS than half a century after the discovery of America, the
Italian poet, Marcantonio Flaminio, foretold that,
even in the New World, the Latin poets of Italy
would be studied by those Western nations, 'on
whom the light of dawn arises, when the sky of Italy is wrapped in
darkness',—

*The New
World*

> For, strange to tell, e'en on that far-off shore
> Doth flourish now the love of Latin lore[1].

But, in Flaminio's lines as to this love of Latin in the Western
hemisphere, we discern not so much a statement of fact, as an
intelligent anticipation of future events. We have, indeed, to wait
for three quarters of a century before finding any proof of the
cultivation of Latin literature across the Atlantic.

It so happens that the first considerable work, written (though
not published) in the New World, was connected with the study
of the Latin Classics. In the year 1623, while the Colony of
Virginia was still in an unsettled state, the treasurer of the
Virginia Company, George Sandys (1577—1643),
the youngest son of the archbishop, was engaged on
his poetic translation of the *Metamorphoses* of Ovid[2]. In dedicating
to Charles I the complete work, printed in London in 1626, the
translator describes it as 'sprung from the stock of the ancient
Romans, but bred in the New World, of the rudeness of which it

G. Sandys

---

[1] 'Nam (mirabile dictu) in iis quoque oris | Nunc linguae studium viget
Latinae' (*Carmina*, 123 ed. 1743); written before 1550; ii 120 *supra*.

[2] Stith's *History of Virginia* (1747), 303; Hooper's *Introd.* to *Poetical
Works* of George Sandys, xxvii—xlii.

cannot but participate; especially having wars and tumults to bring it to light, instead of the Muses'. But 'rudeness' cannot justly be predicated of a poem, which was admired by Pope, and was described by Dryden as the work of 'the best versifier of the former age'[1].

A century elapsed before the first Latin poem was printed in America. It is entitled ' *Muscipula* : the Mouse Trap, or the Battle of the Cambrians and the Mice: a Poem by Edward Holdsworth, translated into English by R. Lewis, Annapolis, 1728 '. The translator proudly calls it ' This FIRST ESSAY | of *Latin Poetry*, in *English Dress*, | which MARYLAND hath publish'd from the Press '. The alternative Greek title of the Latin text is Καμβρομυομαχία, and the purpose of the poem is to celebrate the high antiquity of the Cambrians and to show that the Mouse-trap was invented by the Cambrians, and not by the Greeks. The 'first translation of a Greek or Latin Classic printed in America'[2] was a rendering of Epictetus :— ' Epictetus his Morals, done from the Original Greek, and the Words taken from his own Mouth by Arrian. The Second Edition. Philadelphia, printed by S. Keimer, 1729 '. The printer was Benjamin Franklin's master, and in the same year Franklin began business on his own account. Cato's Moral Distichs, Englished in couplets' (by Chief Justice James Logan[3]), printed and sold by B. Franklin, Philadelphia, 1735, may, if ' Cato ' be regarded as a classic, pass for the ' first translation of a Classic which was both made and printed in the British colonies'[4]. A better claim may, however, be urged on behalf of a real Classic, ' Cicero's *Cato Major*, or his Discourse of Old Age : with explanatory notes; printed and sold by B. Franklin, Philadelphia, 1744'[5]. The translator and annotator was James Logan, and Franklin calls it the ' first Translation of a *Classic* in this *Western World*'. Forty years later we have ' The Lyric Works of Horace, translated into English Verse,...by a Native of America', Philadelphia, E. Oswald, 1786. The translator was John Parke (1754—1789), who became a lieutenant-colonel in the army of General Washington, to whom the work is dedicated[6]. It is probably one of the earliest translations published by a native-born American[7].

Incunabula

---

[1] Preface to Dryden's *Fables*.

[2] C. H. Hildeburn, *The Issues of the Press in Pennsylvania* 1685—1784 ; Brinley Catalogue, no. 3396 (Hartford, 1878—97).

[3] Cp. J. G. Wilson and J. Fiske, *Appleton's Cyclopaedia of American Biography* (1886-9), *s.v.*

[4] Brinley Catalogue, no. 3279.   [5] *ib*. nos. 3281-4.

[6] Brinley Catalogue, no. 6910.

[7] In the above paragraph, the bibliographical material (which I have recast and arranged in chronological order) has been kindly supplied by Prof. Wilfred P. Mustard, of Haverford Coll., Pennsylvania, now of Johns Hopkins, Baltimore.

The earliest centre of classical learning in the New World was
Harvard College, founded in 1636, and deriving its
name from John Harvard of Emmanuel (1607—
1638). He bequeathed half of his fortune and the
whole of his library,—his Homer and his Plutarch, his Terence
and his Horace, to the College which the little colony of Puritans
had on November 15, 1637, resolved on founding at Newtown.
On May 2, 1638, four months before the death of John Harvard,
Newtown assumed the name of Cambridge, in memory of the
university with which many of the colonists were connected.

Colleges and Universities

Next, in order of time, was the 'collegiate school of Connecticut', founded at Saybrook in 1701, and transferred to New
Haven in 1716, which in 1718 took the name of 'Yale College'
from its benefactor Elihu Yale. Princeton, founded elsewhere in
1746, was transferred to its present home in 1757. In Philadelphia,
at the instance of Benjamin Franklin, an Academy was founded in
1751, and, forty years later, was merged into the 'University of
Pennsylvania'. In 1754, George II founded in New York an
institution known as King's College until 1787, when its name was
changed into Columbia College, reorganised as a university in
1890. These were the five earliest centres of learning in the
United States. The fifth was soon followed by the Brown
university at Providence, Rhode Island (1764).

Among the universities founded in the nineteenth century
may be mentioned those of Virginia at Charlottesville (1819), of
Michigan at Ann Arbor (1837), of Wisconsin at Madison (1849),
the Cornell university at Ithaca (1865), that of California at
Berkeley (1868), the Johns Hopkins university in Baltimore (1876),
the Leland Stanford at Palo Alto (1891), and, lastly, that of
Chicago (1892)[1]. There are also between 400 and 500 universities
or colleges of varying degrees of importance. Out of all these
there is gradually emerging 'a limited number of true homes of
learning and research', that 'satisfy the somewhat exacting definition of "a place where teaching which puts a man abreast of the
fullest and most exact knowledge of the time is given in a range
of subjects covering all the great departments of intellectual

[1] Cp. *Minerva, passim.*

life"'[1]. The model for the old Colleges was mainly derived from England, that for the modern Universities mainly from Germany.

We may now mention a few of the more prominent classical scholars, with some notice of their published writings, so far as they come within the scope of the present work.

At Boston in 1836 a 'Greek and English Lexicon to the New Testament' was produced by an able scholar, Edward Robinson (1794—1863), a graduate of Hamilton and tutor in Greek and Mathematics, who in December, 1821, went to Andover to see through the press an edition of 'the first Books of the Iliad' with Latin notes selected chiefly from Heyne. His lexicon passed through many editions, and his work on the Geography of Palestine, entitled 'Biblical Researches', was equally successful. In 1826–30 he studied at Halle and also in Berlin, and, for the last twenty-six years of his life, was a professor of Biblical Literature in New York[2].

Early in the century, as we are assured by a highly cultivated native of Boston, George Ticknor (1791—1871), 'a copy of Euripides in the original could not be bought at any bookseller's shop in New England'[3]. In 1815 Ticknor was sent to Göttingen, and, in his admiration for his Greek tutor at that university, he exclaims, with reference to his own countrymen:—'we do not yet know what a Greek scholar is'[4]. At Göttingen he remained until the end of 1816, and 'saw a good deal of Dissen, and also of Wolf, the coryphaeus of German philologists', who was there on a visit[5]. In the course of his travels he subsequently met Schaefer at Leipzig, and Schütz at Halle[6], Thiersch (as well as Goethe) at Weimar, Welcker at Cassel, Voss and Creuzer at Heidelberg, F. Schlegel at Frankfurt, A. W. Schlegel and Humboldt in Paris, Byron in Venice, Sir William Gell in Naples, Bunsen and Niebuhr in Rome, Monk and Dobree at Cambridge[7]. After his four years of study in Germany, France,

---

[1] Bryce, *American Commonwealth*, chap. cv (ii 667, ed. 1895); Papillon, in *Mosely Commission* (1904), 254.

[2] Portrait in Appleton's *Cyclopaedia of American Biography*, 6 vols. (1887–9).

[3] Ticknor's *Life of Prescott*, p. 13, ed. 1904.

[4] G. S. Hillard etc., *Life of Ticknor*, i 73 n.

[5] *ib.* i 105–7.   [6] *ib.* i 108, 112.   [7] *ib. passim.*

Italy, and Spain, he delivered at Harvard, as professor of the French and Spanish Languages and Literatures, an inaugural oration described as the 'utterance of the ripest scholarship America could then boast'[1].

Among Ticknor's fellow-students at Göttingen was his life-long friend, Edward Everett (1794—1865). As a young man of high promise, he had been appointed Eliot professor of Greek at Harvard in 1815, on the understanding that he spent some time studying in Europe before entering on his professorial duties. He remained at Göttingen for two years. Cousin, who met him in Germany, regarded him as one of the best Grecians he ever knew[2]. During his four years in Europe, he travelled in Greece, and, before the outbreak of the Greek War of Independence, he made the acquaintance of Koraës, who held him in the highest esteem[3]. In 1819 he entered on his duties as a professor[4]; and, in that capacity, produced a translation of Buttmann's *Greek Grammar* (1822) and a new edition of Jacobs' *Greek Reader*. He resigned his professorship for a political career in 1826, represented the United States in London in 1841–5, and was Secretary of State in 1852. His reputation mainly rests on the stately eloquence of his orations. In the tenacity of his memory, and in his singular command of a large variety of historic parallels, he resembled Macaulay. In 1819, after his four years in Europe, he expressed the opinion that, in regard to university methods, America had at that date 'nothing to learn from England, but every thing to learn from Germany'. English scholars have been known to accept the remark as being, '*at the period indicated*, absolutely true'[5]. But Everett lived to receive honorary degrees in 1842–3 from Oxford, Cambridge, and Dublin; his speech at Cambridge ended with the respectful greeting *Salve, magna parens*[6]; and he 'practically recognised' a change in the conditions of 1819 when, forty years

Everett

---

[1] Hillard etc., i 320. Portrait in Appleton, *l.c.*

[2] Hayward, in *Quarterly Review*, Dec. 1840.

[3] Thereianos, *Adamantios Koraës*, iii 23.

[4] 'He lectured on Greek literature with the enthusiasm of another Abelard' (Appleton, *l.c.*).

[5] T. W. Higginson, in *Harvard Graduates' Magazine*, Sept. 1897.

[6] Everett's *Orations*, ii 431 (1842).

later, he sent his own son to Cambridge[1]. His son's lectures *On the Cam* have since given to many besides the Boston audience of 1864 a vivid picture of College-life in that University.

Göttingen was also the goal of another Harvard graduate, George Bancroft (1800—1891), who studied under Heeren and translated his master's 'Reflections on the Politics of Ancient Greece' in 1824, after resigning a tutorship in Greek at Harvard. He afterwards represented his country in England and in Germany (1867–74); he is best known as the Historian of the United States (1840–74)[2].

Bancroft

Among the Greek professors at Harvard, Cornelius Conway Felton (1807—1862) held that position from 1834 to 1860, and was President of Harvard for the two remaining years of his life. He annotated Wolf's text of the *Iliad*, with Flaxman's illustrations (1833 etc.), and also edited the *Clouds* and *Birds* of Aristophanes, the *Agamemnon* of Aeschylus, and the *Panegyricus* of Isocrates. In conjunction with professors B. Sears and B. B. Edwards, he produced in 1849 a volume on 'Classical Studies', including selections from the correspondence of several Dutch scholars. During his first visit to Europe (1853–4), he spent five months in Greece, and in 1856 he published his 'Selections from Modern Greek Writers'. His popular lectures on 'Greece, Ancient and Modern', display his keen enthusiasm for the old Greek world. His interest in the comparative study of the Greek and the modern drama is vividly represented in his early review of Woolsey's edition of the *Alcestis* (1836). He was familiar with German literature and with the works of German scholars, but he refers more frequently to Heyne, Mitscherlich, and Wolf than to Hermann[3]. As professor of Greek

Felton

---

[1] T. W. Higginson, in *Atlantic Monthly*, vol. 93 (1904) 8 f. This later fact is (not unnaturally) suppressed in Professor Hohlfeld's Chicago *Festrede* (*Der Einfluss deutscher Universitäten auf Amerika*), 1904, p. 6, where the earlier remark of 1819 is duly emphasised. On Everett, cp. biographical dates in *Quinquennial Catalogue of Harvard University*, 1636—1905, under 1811; the *Enc. Brit.* etc.; portrait in Appleton, *l.c.*

[2] D.C.L. Oxford, 1849; *Harvard Q(uinquennial) C(atalogue)*, under 1817; portrait in Appleton, *l.c.*

[3] E. Sihler (Prof. at New York Univ.), *Klassische Studien und klassischer Unterricht in den Vereinigten Staaten*, three articles in *Neue Jahrbücher*

he was succeeded in 1860 by W. W. Goodwin (b. 1831), the well-known author of the 'Syntax of the Moods and Tenses of the Greek Verb'[1], who held the professorship until 1901.

Felton's exact contemporary, Evangelinus Apostolides Sophocles

E. A.
Sophocles

(1807—1883), who was born at the foot of Mt Pelion, and spent his early youth near the home of Achilles and some of his maturer years at Cairo and on Mt Sinai, emigrated to the New World in 1828. He taught Greek at Yale (1837 f) and for many years at Harvard (1840—1883), where he was appointed professor of Ancient, Byzantine, and Modern Greek in 1860. Of his publications, the most successful was his *Greek Grammar* (1838 etc.), while the most important was his *Greek Lexicon of the Roman and Byzantine Periods*[2]. He bequeathed to Harvard his literary collections and the whole of his private fortune[3].

The Latin professorship at Harvard was held from 1832 to

Beck

1851 by Carl Beck (1798—1866), who had lived in Germany for the first twenty-six years of his life. Like Lieber and Follen, he was one of the 'highly educated Germans,...who were driven from their country by political uproar about 1825'[4]. In 1846, on the eve of a visit to Europe, that 'fine Petronian scholar'[5] declared that 'he had never before had a

Lane

pupil who could write Latin as well as Lane'. The pupil in question, George Martin Lane (1823—1897), took the professor's place for a single term 'with entire success'. In 1847, like Ticknor and Everett and Bancroft, he left for Germany, where he spent four years, attending the lectures of Schneidewin and K. F. Hermann at Göttingen[6], and those of

---

(1902) 508 f. On Felton, cp. *Harvard Q. C.*, under 1827; *Amer. Journ. of Educ.*, March 1861, x 265—296; *Mass. Hist. Soc. Proc.* 1869, x 352—368. Portrait in Appleton, *l.c.*

[1] 1859 etc.; rewritten and enlarged, 1889.   [2] 1870, and 1887.

[3] Cp. *Harvard Q.C.*, hon. degree, 1847; *Biogr. Jahrb.* 1883, p. 98. He was long a valued correspondent of the *Nation* (xi 46). Cp. Allibone, *s.v.*; and Seymour, in *Bulletin*, v (1902), 8 f; portrait at Harvard.

[4] T. W. Higginson, *u. s.*; Ph. D. Tübingen, 1823; hon. LL.D. Harvard, 1865.

[5] 'The MSS of Petronius...described and collated', 1863.

[6] Ph.D. 1851.

Ritschl at Bonn, as well as courses at Berlin and Heidelberg. In the library of his son, Mr Gardiner Martin Lane of Boston, his notes of Ritschl's lectures and his sketch of the professor were seen by the present writer during a visit in 1905. His review of an edition of Plautus in 1853 has been described by his biographer as 'probably the first recognition' in America 'of the results of Ritschl's studies'[1]. He was Latin professor from 1851 to 1894. 'As a teacher', he 'had all that fine literary appreciation which characterizes the English school, combined, however, with the minute and exact knowledge of the Germans'. Among his marked characteristics were a never-failing good nature, great originality of thought, a prodigious memory, and a familiarity with the most varied types of literature[2]. 'His teaching was always clear and incisive'[3]; his 'sparkling wit was ever ready to illuminate dark corners in even the abstrusest departments of learning, and he could make the driest subject interesting by his skilful and original way of presenting it'[4]. The chief work of his life was his excellent *Latin Grammar*, completed and published in 1898 by his former pupil, professor Morris H. Morgan; he generously co-operated in the production of Lewis and Short's *Latin Dictionary*; and it was mainly owing to his pamphlet of 1871 that a reformed pronunciation of Latin was adopted in all the Colleges and Schools of the United States[5].

Among Lane's older friends was John L. Lincoln (1817—1891), who, like Lane, studied for several years in Germany; he was Latin professor in Brown university (1844 f), and produced editions of Horace and of Selections from Livy[6]. Albert Harkness (1822—1907), Greek professor at Brown, whose *Latin Grammar* was published in 1864[7], was a member of the Managing Committee of the American

Lincoln
Harkness

---

[1] Morris H. Morgan, in *Harvard Studies*, ix 9.

[2] *ib.* 7.   [3] Eliot, *ib.* 8.   [4] Goodwin, *ib.* 8.

[5] *ib.* 9. Some misgivings on this pronunciation have found a voice in Bennett and Bristol's *Teaching of Latin and Greek* (1901) 66—80.—*Memoir* (with portrait) by Morris H. Morgan, in *Harvard Studies*, ix 1—12; posthumous papers, *ib.* 13—26; papers by 17 of his pupils, *ib.* vii; cp. *Harvard Q. C.* under 1846; *A. J. P.* xviii 247, 371 f; *Nation*, lxv, 8 July, 1897, 28.

[6] *National Cyclopaedia of American Biography* (N. Y. 1882–), viii 30.

[7] A very widely popular work, revised in 1874, 1881; Harkness also edited Caesar and Sallust etc. (1870-8).

School of Classical Studies at Athens from its foundation to the end of his life[1].

Frieze

Another graduate of Brown, Henry Simmons Frieze (1817—1889), is known as an editor of Virgil and of Quintilian x, xii. As professor of Latin in the university of Michigan for the last 35 years of his life, he gave to his teaching 'the flavour of a noble realism', being 'more desirous that his pupils should be *Romans* than that they should be *Latinists*'[2].

Lane's younger contemporaries at Harvard included Joseph Henry Thayer

Thayer

(1828—1891), the able editor of a *Grammar* (1873) and a *Lexicon* (1886) of the Greek Testament, originally produced by Winer and by Wilke and Grimm respectively[3].

Lane's colleague as professor of Latin was James Bradstreet

Greenough

Greenough (1833—1901), a student of Harvard, who, after following the profession of the Law for nine years in Michigan, was invited to return to Harvard as a tutor in Latin. This appointment led to his becoming assistant professor in 1873, and to his holding one of the two professorships of Latin for nearly twenty years (1883—1901).

Early in his career as a teacher, he eagerly devoted himself to the study of Comparative Philology, and soon made himself acquainted with Sanskrit. He was stimulated by Goodwin's *Greek Moods and Tenses* to attack the corresponding problems in Latin, and the first result was his privately printed *Analysis of the Latin Subjunctive* (1870), in the course of which he maintained that the only meaning which seemed to be common to all uses of the Subjunctive was that of *futurity*. In this *Analysis* he anticipated the method adopted in the following year by Delbrück, in his *Conjunctiv und Optativ*, a work which became a grammatical classic. The results of the *Analysis* were incorporated in J. H. Allen and J. B. Greenough's *Latin Grammar founded on Comparative Grammar* (1872). Delbrück's work was the subject of an appreciative but searching review by Greenough, in which the reviewer declined to accept *will* and *wish* as the distinction between the Subjunctive and the Optative[4], and Delbrück subsequently admitted that the original idea of both might, after all, be that of *futurity* rather than *will*.

Greenough was the first to lecture on Sanskrit and Comparative Philology at Harvard (1872–80), and his services in fostering those studies 'the historian of American learning will not fail to recognise'[5]. He embodied the main

---

[1] *Brown Alumni Monthly*, viii (1907) 31, with portrait outside no. 1; *Cl. Rev.* xxi 189.

[2] *Cl. Rev.* iv 131 f.

[3] *Harvard Q. C.*, under 1850.

[4] *North Amer. Rev.*, vol. 113 (1871), 415–27.

[5] *Harvard Studies*, xiv 10.

results of his studies and discoveries in his contributions to the text-books known as (J. H.) 'Allen and Greenough's Latin Series'. Among these were his independent editions of Horace's *Satires* and *Epistles*, and Livy I, II[1].

He was keenly interested in Etymology, and contributed learned and ingenious notes on that subject to several volumes of the *Harvard Studies in Classical Philology*. His originality in the analysis of linguistic forms is exemplified in his essay on *Latin Stem Formation* in the tenth volume of those *Studies*, a series founded and in part edited by himself. He wrote English and Latin verse with a singular facility and grace, and he was recognised by his friends as distinctly a man of genius[2].

Among those primarily associated with Greenough in the 'Latin Series' were the two sons of the Rev. Joseph Allen of Northborough (1790—1873). The elder of these, the Rev. Joseph Henry Allen, D.D. (1820— J. H. Allen W. F. Allen 1898), besides producing elementary works on Latin, was the joint author of 'Allen and Greenough's' above-mentioned *Latin Grammar* of 1872. He also published a *Manual Latin Grammar* (1868), and a *Latin Reader*, in conjunction with his younger brother, William Francis Allen (1830—1889), a graduate of Harvard, who in 1867 became professor of Ancient Languages and History at Madison, Wisconsin.

Early in his career, W. F. Allen studied at Göttingen and Berlin, and also travelled in Italy and Greece. He was less interested in the linguistic than in the historical side of classical learning; he was the contributor of 'the admirable historical and archaeological notes' in 'Allen and Greenough's Latin Series'; and he produced independent editions of the *Germania*, *Agricola*, and *Annals* of Tacitus. He was remarkable for an extraordinary capacity for work, a singular breadth of sympathy, and a keen interest in the cause of freedom[3].

The first professor of Classical Philology at Harvard was Frederic de Forest Allen (1844—1897), a graduate of Oberlin, who, after holding a professorship of F. D. Allen Greek and Latin for two years at Knoxville, studied under Georg Curtius at Leipzig in 1868—70, taking an active part in the

---

[1] In other editions he was associated with Mr J. H. Allen and with Professors F. D. Allen, Tracy Peck, and Kittredge.

[2] G. L. Kittredge, in *Harvard Studies*, xiv (1903) 1—16, with bibliography and portrait; *Harvard Q. C.*, under 1856.

[3] C. L. Smith, in *Cl. Rev.* iv 426–8; cp. *National Cycl.* vi 160; *Wisconsin Academy*, viii 439; *Essays and Monographs* (with *Memoir*, 1—21, and *Bibliography*, 351—382), Boston, 1890.

Grammatische Gesellschaft and obtaining his degree by a thesis on the dialect of the Locrians[1]. The remarkable impression made at New Haven in 1871 by his paper on the 'Attic Second Declension'[2] led to his appointment as a tutor at Harvard in 1873. He was professor of Ancient Languages at Cincinnati in 1874–9, and, after a busy year at Yale, became professor at Harvard for the remaining seventeen years of his life. In 1885–6 he was in charge of the American School at Athens; in 1891–2 he studied the *scholia* of Plato at Oxford and Paris, with a view to an edition, which he did not live to complete.

One of his earliest works was an excellent edition of the *Medea* (1876); among his more important papers were those on the origin of Homeric verse[3], on classical studies at the university of Leyden[4], on Greek and Latin Inscriptions from Palestine[5], on Greek Versification in Inscriptions[6], and on the Delphian Hymn to Apollo[7]. It was during his time at Cincinnati that he prepared his compact and comprehensive hand-book of *Remnants of Early Latin* (1880), the value of which has been recognised in England and Germany.

In his chosen department of study he was primarily 'an investigator'. 'He had no interest in the Classics as a mere accomplishment, a pleasing ornament of a man of letters. For him classical learning was a real science, a great branch of anthropology, giving insight, when rightly studied, into the mental operations and intellectual and moral growth of ancient peoples'[8]. He produced the music for the performance of the *Phormio* at Harvard in 1894, and it has been said of him by Professor Seymour that 'probably no other American scholar understood ancient Greek music so well as he'. It has also been said by the same writer :—'Never was mind more open than his to the receipt of light from any quarter....His kindly patience, his accuracy, his absolute sanity, and his clearness of exposition made him a remarkable teacher as well as a great scholar'[9].

---

[1] Curtius, *Studien*, iii 205—279 (1870).

[2] *Trans. Amer. Phil. Assoc.* ii 18—34 (1871).

[3] Kuhn's *Zeitschrift*, xxiv 556—592 (1879).

[4] *Proc. Amer. Phil. Assoc.* XIII (1882) xviii f.

[5] *A. J. P.* vi 190—216.

[6] *Bulletin of the School at Athens*, iv 37—204.

[7] *Harvard Studies*, ix 55—60.

[8] *ib.* ix 30 f.

[9] Seymour in *A. J. P.* xviii 375. Cp. *Memoir* by J. B. Greenough in *Harvard Studies*, ix 27—36, with bibliography and portrait, and with post-humous papers, *ib.* 37—60. Cp. *A. J. P.* xviii 247, 372-5 ; *The Nation*, lxv, 19 Aug. 1897, 144.

Latin scholarship at Harvard lost much by the death of Minton Warren (1850—1907), a graduate-student of Sanskrit and the Classics at Yale, who by holding scholastic appointments for three years in the United States, Minton Warren was enabled in 1876–9 to pursue the advanced study of Comparative Philology and other subjects at Leipzig, Bonn and Strassburg, where the bent of the rest of his life was determined by the influence of the school of Ritschl. From 1879 to 1899 he presided over the advanced and graduate instruction in Latin at the Johns Hopkins university; in 1896–7 he was director of the American School in Rome; and in 1899 was appointed Latin professor at Harvard,—a position which he held with the highest distinction for the remaining eight years of his life. His first publication, 'On the enclitic *Ne* in early Latin'[1], was followed by the *editio princeps* of the 'Glossary of St Gallen'[2], while his latest article dealt with the oldest of Latin inscriptions,—that on the '*Stele* in the Roman Forum'[3]. From his College-days in Germany to his death he was mainly occupied in collecting materials for a critical edition of Terence, in which he was latterly associated with Prof. Hauler and Prof. Kauer of Vienna. Of his work as a teacher at Harvard, his colleague Prof. Wright has said:—'No American Latinist can point to a larger number...of able and productive scholars in his own field, who, if not members of his 'school', at least owed to him their inspiration and their method'[4]. 'Active, fond of out-of-door life, vigorous; sunny, serene, witty; appreciative, sympathetic;...he endeared himself to his friends as few men have done in his generation'[5].

Among the most promising scholars of a later generation was Herman Wadsworth Hayley (1867—1899), a graduate of Amherst, who completed his studies at Hayley Harvard, where he served as tutor before receiving an appointment in the Wesleyan university at Middletown, Connecticut. He produced an edition of the *Alcestis* (1898), and a pamphlet on

---

[1] Strassburg, 1879; *A. J. P.* 1881.   [2] Cambridge, U.S.A., 1885.

[3] *A. J. P.* 1907, nos. 111–2.

[4] Cp. *A. J. P.* Dec. 1907, 489; *Harvard Mag.*, Jan. 1908: Prof. Lindsay in *Cl. Rev.* xxii 25 f.

[5] *Harvard Univ. Gaz.* 10 Jan. 1908.

the *Verse of Terence*, besides contributing to Lane's 'Grammar' the chapter on versification. Five of his papers have been published in the *Harvard Studies*[1].

Harvard has taken a leading part in the modern revival of the Attic drama. It was there that in May, 1881, after seven months of preparation, the *Oedipus Tyrannus* was admirably acted in the original Greek. Art and archaeology, as well as scholarship, united in making the presentation perfect in every detail[2]. Since then we have had the memorable performance of the *Agamemnon* by members of the university of Oxford, the impressive and stimulating series of Greek plays at Cambridge, and the singularly interesting representations amid the idyllic surroundings of Bradfield; while, at Harvard itself, the *Oedipus Tyrannus* of 1881 has been succeeded by the *Agamemnon* of 1906.

At Yale the pioneer professors of Classics included James

Kingsley
Thacher

Luce Kingsley (1778—1852), editor of Tacitus and of Cicero, *De Oratore*, and a master of Latin style[3]. He was professor of Latin from 1831 to 1851, when he was succeeded by Thomas A. Thacher (1815—1886), editor

Tyler

of Cicero, *De Officiis*[4]. Thacher's contemporary, William Seymour Tyler (1810—1897), an editor of select portions of Homer, Demosthenes, and Tacitus, was one of the pioneers as professor of Latin and Greek at Amherst[5].

The 'Literary Convention' held at Yale in 1830 marks an epoch in the history of university education in the United States. The avowed aim was to form a genuine university. On this occasion liberal studies were effectively defended in a long and luminous letter from George Bancroft, while among those who took part in the debates were Francis Lieber of Berlin and Boston, who had fought in Greece, and had lived with Niebuhr

---

[1] 'Social and domestic position of women in Aristophanes' (vol. i); *Quaestiones Petronianae* (ii); κότταβος κατακτός (v); *Varia Critica* (vii); Notes on the *Phormio* (xi).

[2] Henry Norman's *Harvard Greek Play* (1882); cp. Jebb's Introd. to *Oed. Tyr.* p. l f.

[3] Woolsey in Allibone, and Appleton.

[4] *National Cycl.* xi 260 with portrait.

[5] *ib.* x 347; Appleton, vi 201; hon. S. T. D., Harvard, 1857.

in Rome, and Woolsey, who had recently returned from his triennium in Europe[1].

The Greek Professorship at Yale was held from 1831 to 1846 by Theodore Dwight Woolsey (1801—1889), a graduate of Yale[2], who had studied for three years in France, as well as in Germany, where he attended the lectures of Welcker, Hermann and Boeckh at Bonn, Leipzig and Berlin respectively.   During his tenure of the professorship, he edited the *Antigone* and *Electra* of Sophocles, as well as the *Alcestis*, the *Prometheus*, and the *Gorgias*.   He had a remarkable influence over his pupils in Greek, and a still wider fame when, in middle life, he became President of Yale, and professor of International Law[3].   As professor of Greek, he had an able successor in James Hadley (1821—1872), who had also a genius for mathematics, and lectured with success on Roman Law.   His best-known work was his *Greek Grammar*[4]. His 'Essays Philological and Critical' (1873) were edited after his death by his distinguished colleague William Dwight Whitney, who generously described him as 'America's best and soundest philologist'[5].

Hadley was succeeded by Lewis Richard Packard (1836—1884), who studied in Berlin, and visited Greece (1857–8) and was a professor of Greek at Yale from 1863 to 1884, when he died of an illness contracted at Athens as director of the American School.   In conjunction with Prof. J. W. White of Harvard, he projected the 'College Series of Greek authors', since edited by Professors White and Seymour. He translated the lecture of Bonitz 'On the Origin of the Homeric Poems', prepared an edition of the *Odyssey*, which remained unpublished, and produced a considerable variety of essays and lectures, which were posthumously collected under the title of

(marginal note: Woolsey)
(marginal note: Hadley)
(marginal note: Packard)

[1] Sihler in *Evening Post*, N.Y., 7 Sept. 1907.

[2] Hon. S. T. D., Harvard, 1847.

[3] Sihler, 509 f; Timothy Dwight, *Memorial Address*, New Haven, 24 June, 1890.

[4] 1860, etc.; revised and largely rewritten by F. D. Allen (1884).

[5] Sihler, 511; Noah Porter, *Memoir*, with bibliography, New Haven, 1873.   Sketch by Whitney in 'Yale College' (1879); National Academy of Sciences, *Biogr. Memoirs*, 1905, v 249—254, with portrait.

'Studies in Greek Thought'. The address which he delivered in 1881 on the 'Morality and Religion of the Greeks' has been well described as 'the expression of the carefully formed opinions of a student of life as well as of books, upon a topic of wide human interest, indicating the true final object of the enlightened student of Philology to be the knowledge of man, and the acquisition of the means for the judgment of conduct and the understanding of history'[1].

W. D. Whitney (1827—1894), a member of a family 'remarkable for scholarly attainments and achievements',
W. D. Whitney
graduated at Williams College at the age of 18, and, in the early part of his career, took the keenest interest in Natural Science. His elder brother had gone to Germany to study mineralogy and geology, but had incidentally attended a course of lectures on Sanskrit at the university of Berlin; and it was in his elder brother's library that W. D. Whitney found the books that enabled him to begin the study of Sanskrit. Late in 1849 he entered Yale, to continue the study of Sanskrit under Edward E. Salisbury, who had been appointed professor of Arabic and Sanskrit in 1841. Whitney and Hadley were Salisbury's first (and last) pupils in Sanskrit, and they were pupils of whom he might well be proud. In 1850 Whitney went to Germany, spending three winter semesters under Weber, Bopp and Lepsius in Berlin, and two summer semesters under Roth in Tübingen. Salisbury's foresight and generosity led to Whitney's being appointed professor of Sanskrit (1854) and of Comparative Philology at Yale. In course of time a graduate school of philology was organised, which, shortly after 1870, included some of the ablest of the future professors in the United States. Whitney revived the American Oriental Society, and presided over the first meeting of the Philological Association in 1869.

His first great work was the publication of the first volume of the Atharva-Veda-Saṁhitā (1855-6), the second volume of which was posthumously published under the editorial care of his former pupil, Professor Lanman. Two other Sanskrit texts were published in 1862–71; and the value of his work was recognised by the award of the Bopp prize in 1870, followed by

---

[1] J. W. White in *Bulletin* of Amer. School, ii (1885) 7–9; cp. Seymour in *Biogr. Jahrb.* 1884, 68—70.

the crowning distinction of the Prussian Order of Merit; but it has been said of him that he loved learning for its own sake and not for its reward of fame. Meanwhile, he had produced his important Sanskrit Grammar[1], and he was one of the four principal collaborators in the St Petersburg dictionary. Among his best-known works were his Lectures on 'Language and the Study of Language' (1867), his 'Oriental and Linguistic Studies' (1872-4), and his volume on the 'Life and Growth of Language' (1875), which was translated into five of the languages of Europe. He was among the very first to draw attention to *analogy* as a force in the growth of language, and also to demur to the ordinary view that Asia was the original home of the Indo-European race[2].

Yale was the university of Martin Kellogg (1828—1903), who in 1859-93 was professor of Latin first at the College and afterwards at the newly founded uni- Kellogg versity of California, of which he was president from 1893 to 1899. He is best known as the editor of an excellent edition of Cicero's *Brutus*[3]. He also published a pamphlet on Latin pronunciation (1864), while among his popular papers may be mentioned 'Gorgias in California' and 'Fine Art in Ancient Literature'[4].

The teaching of Greek at Yale was for 27 years associated with the name of Thomas Day Seymour (1848—1907), who, after graduating at Western Reserve, Seymour spent two years at the universities of Leipzig and Berlin, besides travelling in Italy and Greece. On his return he taught Greek for 8 years at Western Reserve, and held a professorship of Greek at Yale from 1880 to the end of his life. Apart from a useful volume of 'Selected Odes of Pindar' (1882), his published work was mainly concerned with Homer. He produced *inter alia* two editions of *Iliad* i—vi, and (a few months before his death) completed his scholarly and comprehensive work on 'Life in the Homeric Age',—the ripe result of 35 years of Homeric study. His comparatively early death was ascribed to overwork in

[1] Leipzig, 1879; ed. 2, 1889; Suppl. 1885.

[2] Seymour, in *A. J. P.* xv 271—298; and Lanman in Introd. to *Atharva-Veda-Saṁhitā*; *The Nation*, 14 June, 1894; *Journal of Amer. Oriental Soc.* xix (1897) 1.

[3] 1889; J. E. Sandys in *Cl. Rev.* iii 354 f.

[4] *Overland Monthly*, Dec. 1868, and June 1885. For a complete bibliography I am indebted to the Secretary of the President of the University of California.

connexion with this volume, and with the preparations for an important meeting of the American Institute of Archaeology. He was of the highest service to that Institute, and he was also the historian of the first twenty-five years of the School at Athens[1]. Though he never allowed himself to become a mere specialist, he could keep abreast with specialists in many lines. 'One of the most genial and companionable of men'[2], he was endued with a singular charm, and those who (like the present writer) have shared his hospitality at Yale, and have viewed the Homeric scholar's study and lecture-room with their lofty situation and their wide outlook ἐϋδμήτου ἀπὸ πύργου, will ever retain a kindly regard for his memory. His teaching at Yale will always be associated with that lofty tower. Here let us leave him,—

> 'Leave him—still loftier than the world suspects,
>   Living and dying'.

At Columbia College, Charles Anthon (1797—1867), the son of an English army-surgeon[3], became full professor of Languages in 1835.

Anthon

He was the principal classical book-maker of his time; the number of volumes, which he prepared for Harper's firm, amounted to about fifty, including a large edition of Horace (1830), founded mainly on Döring's, and a Classical Dictionary (1841), which resulted from several revisions of Lempriere. He also produced handbooks of Geography, Antiquities, Mythology and Literature, and many editions of the ordinary Greek and Latin authors. The lavish amount of help provided in some of these editions left the student little to do on his own account. For the last thirty years of his life, he is said to have produced one volume *per annum*.

Anthon founded no school, but the best of his pupils was his biographer[4], Henry Drisler (1818—1897). Drisler .

Drisler

held professorial appointments in Columbia College for more than fifty years, and, in his literary work, devoted himself almost exclusively to Greek lexicography, preparing American editions of Liddell and Scott (1851-2) and of Yonge's English-

---

[1] *Bulletin* v (1902).

[2] *Yale Alumni Weekly*, 8 Jan. 1908, 362, 364 f (with portrait of Prof. Seymour in his study); Prof. Goodwin in *The Nation*, and Prof. J. W. White's *Address*; cp. *Classical Philology*, iii (1908) no. 2.

[3] Originally a German physician, who served in the British Army until 1788, and then married a French wife and settled in New York. The son was at first headmaster of the Grammar School attached to the College.

[4] *Discourse*, N. Y. 1868, 40 pp.

Greek Lexicon (1858). The esteem in which he was held is attested by the volume of 'Classical Studies' dedicated to him by nearly twenty of his most prominent pupils[1]. The Greek Club founded by him in 1857 in conjunction with Howard Crosby (1826—1891), not for writing about the Classics, but for reading them, came to an end 40 years later. Drisler has been described by a former member of this club as 'placid and imperturbable, curiously non-perceptive of the aesthetical and historical side of classic letters'; and Crosby as 'charmer of souls, vivacious and earnest'. One of the fruits of this club was Mr Horace White's 'admirable version of Appian'[2].

Tayler Lewis (1802—1877), of Union College near Albany, was professor of Greek at the New York university (1838–49), and then returned to Union College and taught Hebrew as well as Classics for the remaining twenty-eight years of his life. In Classics, his principal work was an elaborate edition of the tenth book of Plato's *Laws*, in which special attention is paid to the philosophical and religious bearings of the subject-matter[3].

T. Lewis

Charlton Thomas Lewis (1834—1904), a graduate of Yale, who was for a few years a professor of Greek at Troy near Albany, produced in 1879 a new and revised edition of the Latin dictionary (1850) of Dr E. A. Andrews (1787—1858), another graduate of Yale, who founded his work on Wilhelm Freund's abridgement (1834 f) of Forcellini. The part including all the words beginning with the letter A (216 pp.) was the work of Charles Lancaster Short (1821–86), professor of Latin in Columbia College, New York (1868 f)[4]. 'Lewis and Short'[5] was recognised by Nettleship as 'a real advance on any previous Latin-English dictionary', without embodying 'much of

C. T. Lewis

---

[1] *Classical Studies in honour of Henry Drisler* (Macmillan, N. Y., 1894). Cp. *Appleton's Cycl.* ii 232.

[2] Sihler in *Evening Post*, **N**. Y. 7 Sept. 1907.

[3] 1845; Sihler, 510; E. N. Potter, *Discourse*, Albany, 1878; portrait in Appleton.

[4] *Harvard Q. C.*, under 1846; *Memoir*, 1892, 39 pp. ; *National Cycl.* vii 7.

[5] 'Harper's Latin Dictionary' (1879) ; also published by Clarendon Press, Oxford (1880).

the results of modern research'[1].   In extenuation of any errors
and defects that have been noticed in this useful dictionary, it
is fair to remember that it was mainly the work of a busy lawyer
in New York, who was only able to devote his early mornings to
the completion of his laborious task[2].

The professorship of Greek Archaeology and Epigraphy in
Columbia College was held in 1889–94 by Augustus

Merriam

Chapman Merriam (1843—1895), who was on the
staff for nearly twenty-seven years. He edited, with notes and
illustrations, 'the Phaeacian episode in the *Odyssey*' (1880), and
was director of the American School at Athens in 1887–8. His
chief enterprise as director was the successful exploration of the
ancient deme of Icaria, the home of Thespis and of the earliest
Attic drama. He was the first scholar in the United States to
devote himself mainly to classical archaeology. It was during his
'sabbatical year' that he died at Athens, early in 1895[3].

New York was the scene of the last six years of the scholarly
life of Mortimer Lamson Earle (1864—1905), in-

Earle

structor in Greek at Barnard College and Bryn Mawr,
and professor of Classical Philology at Columbia in 1899—1905.
He edited the *Alcestis* and *Medea* (1894, 1904) and the *Oedipus
Tyrannus* (1901), while his latest work was an elaborate study of
the composition of the first Book of Thucydides[4]. He spent a
year at the American School in Athens (1887–8), and died of a
fever contracted in Sicily after a summer spent in Dalmatia,
Greece and Crete[5].

Among the Classical Institutions of the United States may be
mentioned the 'American Philological Association',

Classical
periodicals

founded in New York in 1868, which publishes
Proceedings and *Transactions*. The *American Journal
of Philology*, founded at Baltimore in 1880, has been ably edited
ever since by Professor Gildersleeve (b. 1839), whose paper on

---

[1] *Acad.* xvii 199; cp. Mayor, in *Camb. Univ. Reporter*, 28 Oct. 1879; and
Georges, in Bursian's *Jahresb.* xxiii 393–8.

[2] Cp. *National Cycl.* xi 62, with portrait.

[3] Seymour, in *Bulletin*, v 39 ; also *Report* for 1893–4, p. 15 f.

[4] *A. J. P.* 1905, 441 f.

[5] E. D. Perry, in *A. J. P.* 1905, 454–6.

Oscillations and Nutations of Philological Studies is an interesting chapter in the History of Scholarship[1]. The *Harvard Studies in Classical Philology* have been published annually since 1890, and similar volumes have been published from time to time in connexion with Cornell and Columbia and the university of Pennsylvania. Two new periodicals, *The Classical Journal* and *Classical Philology*, were started at Chicago in 1906.

The first American to study in Greece (1851 f) was Henry M. Baird, the author of *Modern Greece* (1856). The brief visits of Felton and others were followed in 1860 by a longer stay on the part of J. C. van Benschoten of the Wesleyan university (d. 1902), the first American to lecture on Pausanias. The Archaeological Institute of America (1879)[2] has founded the American Schools of Classical Studies at Athens (1881) and at Rome (1895), and Papers are published by both[3]. The chief excavations of the

The Schools
at Athens
and Rome

School at Athens have been those of the Argive Heraeum and Corinth ; the School has also excavated the ancient theatres at Thoricus, Sicyon, and Eretria ; has published the Inscriptions of Assos and Tralleis and of other parts of Asia Minor; and, finally, has investigated the Attic deme of Icaria and the grotto of Vari, the remains of the Pnyx and the Theatre of Dionysus, the Erechtheion and the Olympieion, the Metopes of the Parthenon and the Choragic Monument of Lysicrates, and the historic scenes of the battles of Plataea and Salamis[4]. The first director of the School, Professor Goodwin, prepared in 1882–3 an important paper on the *Battle of Salamis*, published in the first volume of the *Papers of the School*[5], and, after the lapse of nearly a quarter of a century, he has 'fought' his battle 'o'er again' in the latest volume of the *Harvard Studies* (1906).

[1] *Johns Hopkins University Circulars*, no. 150, March, 1901, 13 pp. Cp. *A. J. P.* xxviii (1907) 113.

[2] Index to publications 1879–89 by W. S. Merrill (1891). Since 1885 its principal organ has been the *American Journal of Archaeology*.

[3] Conspectus in last three pages of *Bulletin* v.

[4] See Seymour's 'First Twenty Years' of the School, in *Bulletin* v (1902) 7—49, with 'Head of Hera', and 'Theatre at Sicyon'; also retrospect of first twelve years, by J. W. White, in *Bulletin* iv.

[5] See also *Report* in *Bulletin* i (1883).

An increasing sense of the importance of Latin as an essential
element in secondary education has been noticed by those who
are familiar with the recent history of the United States.   The
statistics of the last decade of the nineteenth century show that
'the study of Latin and Greek is advancing by leaps and bounds'.
In 1898, half the scholars in the secondary schools were learning
Latin, and the number then learning Latin was more than three
times, that of those learning Greek nearly twice as many as in
1890[1].   In the American universities, the position of Greek as
an 'elective' or 'optional' subject is regarded with approval by
some eminent authorities[2], and with regret by others[3].   Meanwhile, the School at Athens has had a most salutary effect on the
staff of all the American educational institutions that have contributed to its original existence and to its continued prosperity[4].
Moreover, it is owing in no small measure to the far-reaching
influence of the School, that the voices of the old Hellenic art
and archaeology, the old Hellenic history and literature, voices
no longer 'mute' among the modern Greeks, have found an echo
' further west
Than' their 'sires' "Islands of the Blest"'.

---

[1] Statistics quoted in G. G. Ramsay's Address on *Efficiency in Education*,
Glasgow (1902, ed. 2), 17 f. See *Trans. Amer. Phil. Assoc.* (1899) p. cxvii.

[2] Eliot and Goodwin, in Birkbeck Hill's *Harvard College*, 227 f, 244.

[3] *e.g.* Prof. Seymour, in the letter to L. Dyer, printed in *Cambridge
Review*, 23 Feb. 1905, 216 f. Cp. H. B. Gray in *Reports of Mosely Commission*, London, 1904, 170; also Sihler in *Evening Post*, N.Y. 7 Sept. 1907.

[4] J. W. White, in *Bulletin* iv 8 f; and Seymour, in *Bulletin* v 22 f.

MEDALLION OF THE AMERICAN SCHOOL OF CLASSICAL STUDIES
AT ATHENS (1881).

Panathenaic Vase, with olive-wreath and inscription, παρθένου φίλας φίλοι,
Aesch. *Eum.* 1000.

The Panathenaic vase on the medallion of the American School at Athens marks the close of our survey of the two thousand five hundred years which began *Retrospect* with the recitation of the Homeric poems at the Panathenaic festivals of the age of Solon.   In the course of that survey we have briefly reviewed the history of the *Athenian age* early study of epic, lyric, and dramatic poetry, the rise of rhetoric, and the beginnings of grammar and etymology, in the Athenian age.   From Athens we have turned to Alexandria with its learned librarians, and its scholarly critics *Alexandrian age* of Homer and of other ancient poets.   From Alexandria we have passed to Pergamon, and have taken note of the grammar of the Stoics, and of the influence of Pergamon on the libraries and on the literary studies of Rome.   In the Roman age we have traced, in Latin literature, the influence *Roman age* of the Greek Classics and the Greek critics and grammarians.   In Greek literature, we have surveyed the literary criticism and the verbal scholarship of the first century of the Empire, the literary revival at the close of that century, the grammar and lexicography of the second century, the rhetoric of the second and third, and the rise of Neo-Platonism.   At the end of the first quarter of the fourth century we have seen Constantinople come into being as a new centre of Greek learning, while, in the same century, Demosthenes was being studied in the school of Antioch, and Homer imitated by a poet of Smyrna.   We have witnessed the end of the Roman age in 529 A.D.,—the memorable year in which the school of Athens was closed by Justinian in the East, and the monastery of Monte Cassino founded by St Benedict in the West.

We have since traversed the eight centuries of the Middle Ages.   Beginning with the East, we have noticed *Middle Ages* in detail the important services rendered by Byzantine scholars in the careful preservation and the studious interpretation of the Greek Classics.   Turning to the West, we have seen in the monks of Ireland the fosterers of the Greek language, and the founders of the monasteries of Bobbio and St Gallen.   We have watched the revival of classical learning in the age of Charles the Great; in the middle of the ninth century,

we have marked the keen interest in the Latin Classics displayed
by Servatus Lupus, the abbot of Ferrières, and, near its close, we
have hailed 'our first translator' in the person of king Alfred.   In
the tenth century we have seen learning flourishing anew in the
ancient capital of Aachen, and have elsewhere found in Gerbert of
Aurillac the foremost scholar of his generation.   We have identified
the tenth and the eleventh centuries as the golden age of St Gallen.
We have marked the rise of the age-long conflict between
Realism and Nominalism in the twelfth century, the century in
which the school of Paris was represented by Abelard and that of
Chartres by the preceptors of John of Salisbury.   The thirteenth
century was (we may remember) made memorable by 'the new
Aristotle', by the great schoolmen, Albertus Magnus and Thomas
Aquinas, by translators such as William of Moerbeke, by Roger
Bacon and Duns Scotus and William of Ockham, and finally by
Dante, the date of whose great poem marks the close of the
century, while the date of his death may well be regarded as the
end of the Middle Ages.   Lastly, we have traced the survival of
each of the Latin Classics in the age beginning with the close
of the Roman age in 529 and ending with the death of Dante in
1321.

Our second volume has begun with the Revival of Learning.
In its opening pages we have found in Petrarch
'the first of modern men', and the discoverer of
Cicero's *Letters to Atticus*; in Boccaccio, the first
student of Greek, and in Chrysoloras, the first
public professor of that language in Western
Europe.   We have watched the recovery of the
Latin Classics by Poggio and his contemporaries, and that of the
Greek Classics by Italian travellers in the East and by Greeks
who fled for refuge to Italy, even before the fall of Constantinople.
We have recorded the rise of the study of classical archaeology,
the foundation of the Academies of Florence, Naples, Rome and
Venice, and the publication of the *editiones principes* of the Greek
and Latin Classics by Aldus Manutius, and by other scholarly
printers in Italy.   We have seen the 'golden age' of Leo X
followed, under another Medicean Pope, by the sack of Rome in
1527, an event which marks the close of the Italian Revival of

*Revival of
Learning*

*The Italian
period of
classical
scholarship*

Learning. In the Italian age of scholarship the chief aim (as we have noticed) has been the *imitation* of classical models of style and of life.

An important link between the Revival of Learning in Italy and its diffusion in Europe has been found in the widely extended influence of the cosmopolitan scholar, Erasmus. The sixteenth century in Italy includes the names of Victorius and Robortelli, of Sigonius and Muretus; it is marked by a special interest in Aristotle's treatise *On the Art of Poetry*, and also by the eager study of classical archaeology. Italy has points of contact with Spain in the persons of Antonio of Lebrixa and Agostino of Saragossa, and with Portugal in that of Achilles Statius. Greek learning, as we have seen, was transmitted from Italy to France by Gregorius Tifernas, by John Lascaris and by Jerome Aleander. The French period of classical learning, with its many-sided *erudition*, begins with Budaeus, the inspirer of the foundation of the Collège de France. Budaeus is soon followed by the printer-scholars Robert and Henri Estienne, the authors of the great *Thesauri* of Latin and of Greek. The elder Scaliger, an immigrant from Italy, is succeeded by Lambinus, by the younger and greater Scaliger, and by Casaubon.

In the Netherlands the influence of Erasmus is best seen in his fostering of the *Collegium Trilingue* of Louvain. In the period between 1400 and the foundation of the university of Leyden in 1575, the interests of education are well represented by Vivès, those of Greek scholarship by Canter who died in 1575, and those of Latin by Lipsius, who lived on to 1606. In England the fifteenth century is marked by the visits of Poggio and Aeneas Sylvius, and by the early renaissance which had its source in the Latin teaching of Guarino at Ferrara. In the same century the study of Greek was begun by the Benedictine monk, William of Selling, and was continued by his nephew, Linacre, and by Grocyn, and, in the sixteenth century, by Sir John Cheke and his contemporaries. In Scotland, during the same century, the foremost name in scholar-

Marginal notes: Erasmus — Century XVI, Italy — Spain — Portugal — France — The French period — Netherlands — England

ship was that of Buchanan. The spread of learning in Germany
Germany is associated with the names of Agricola and Reuch-
lin, followed by those of able and industrious preceptors such as Melanchthon and Camerarius and Sturm, and by
erudite editors such as Xylander and Sylburg.

The seventeenth century in Italy has proved to be mainly an
Century XVII, age of archaeologists and of imitators of the Latin
Italy poets. In France its greatest names are Salmasius,
France Du Cange, and Mabillon. In the Netherlands
Netherlands Lipsius was succeeded in 1593 by Scaliger at
Leyden, which was also the principal scene of the labours of
Salmasius. In the period between 1575 and 1700, the natives of
the Netherlands included Gerard Vossius and Meursius, the elder
and the younger Heinsius, with Gronovius, Graevius, and Peri-
zonius. In the seventeenth century in England we
England have had Savile and Gataker and Selden, with the
Cambridge Platonists, and the scholarly poets, Milton and Cowley
and Dryden. Towards its close we have seen the stars of Dodwell
and of Barnes beginning to grow pale before the rising of the sun of
Bentley. In the same century in Germany we have a
Germany link with England and the Netherlands in the name
of Gruter, while erudition was well represented by the *Polyhistor*
of Morhof. A school of Roman history flourished at Strassburg.
Improved text-books are associated with the name of Cellarius,
and we have points of contact with several of the countries of
Europe in the cosmopolitan Spanheim.

The eighteenth century in Italy is marked, in Latin lexico-
Century graphy, by the great name of Forcellini; in Greek
XVIII, chronology, by Corsini, and, in Italian history, by
Italy Muratori. France claims Montfaucon and a long
array of learned archaeologists, while a knowledge of
France the old Greek world was popularised by Barthélemy.
Alsace was the home of able scholars, such as Brunck and
Schweighäuser. The century closes with Villoison, whose publi-
England cation of the Venetian Scholia to the *Iliad* led to
The English the opening of a new era in Homeric controversy.
and Dutch In England, in the first half of the century, our
period greatest name is that of Bentley, and in the second

that of Porson. It is the age of historical and literary, as well as verbal, *criticism*.

In the Netherlands, the native land of the learned Latinists, Burman and Drakenborch, it was under the in- fluence of Bentley that Hemsterhuys attained his mastery of Greek. Hemsterhuys handed on the tradition to Valckenaer and to Ruhnken, who in his turn was succeeded by Wyttenbach. The friendly relations between the English and Dutch scholars of this age have led to the eighteenth century being regarded as the English and Dutch period of scholarship.

Netherlands

Meanwhile, Germany is represented by the learned Fabricius, by the lexicographers Gesner, Scheller and J. G. Schneider, by the Latin scholar Ernesti, and the self-taught Greek scholar Reiske. An intelligent interest in the history and criticism of ancient art is awakened by Winckelmann and Lessing; Herder becomes one of the harbingers of the New Humanism; and a new era in classical learning is opened by Heyne at Göttingen.

Germany

Late in the eighteenth century the Homeric controversy is raised anew by F. A. Wolf, and is carried on with varying fortunes during the whole of the nineteenth century.

The whole of that century belongs to the German period, which is characterised by the systematic or *encyclopaedic* type of classical learning embodied in the term *Alterthumswissenschaft*.

The early part of the century is the age of Wolf's contemporaries, Voss and Jacobs, Humboldt and the Schlegels; of Heeren and Niebuhr, Schleiermacher and Heindorf, Buttmann and Bekker. After the death of Wolf two rival schools of classical learning confront one another in the grammatical and critical school of Hermann, and the historical and antiquarian school of Boeckh. The school and the traditions of Hermann are represented by Lobeck, Passow, Meineke, Lachmann, Lehrs, Spengel, Ritschl, Halm, Sauppe, Nauck, Ribbeck, and Blass. The school of Boeckh, who had been preceded by Niebuhr and had Welcker for his great contemporary, is ably represented by his pupils K. O. Müller and Bernhardy. Among independent scholars with a certain affinity with this school are the archaeologists, Jahn (a pupil of Hermann, as well as of Boeckh), and Brunn and Furtwängler;

Century XIX,

Germany

The German period

the historians, Curtius and Mommsen; the geographers, Kiepert and Bursian; mythologists such as Preller; students of ancient music such as Westphal; investigators of ancient religions such as Usener and Rohde. In the Science of Language the principal names include Bopp and Benfey, Corssen and G. Curtius, Schleicher and Steinthal, and the 'New Grammarians' of the present generation. In France the foremost names have been those of Boissonade and Quicherat, Egger and Thurot, Riemann and Graux, together with a long line of geographers, historians and archaeologists, whose work has been largely inspired by the French School of Athens. Classical archaeology has in fact proved the main strength, and the very salvation of French scholarship. In Holland, the greatest name has been that of Cobet, while Belgium is best represented by Thonissen and Willems, the Scandinavian nations by Madvig, Greece by Koraës, Russia by a group of scholars beginning with Graefe and ending with Iernstedt, and Hungary by Télfy and Abel. In England the beginning and the end of the century have been marked at Cambridge by the names of Porson and Jebb, at Oxford by those of Elmsley and Monro, while the outer world claims the great name of Grote. In the United States of America Latin was well represented by Lane and by others at Harvard, and Greek at Yale by Seymour, whose latest publication dealt with the earliest possible theme of classical study, *Life in the Homeric Age*. The present work began with the study of Homer, and with the study of Homer it ends. The great classical authors live for ever, but they are interpreted anew by the scholars of each succeeding generation. In our own times, the Homeric controversy has proved as immortal as the Homeric poems, which, in the language of an English critic, remain unsurpassed in the poetry of the world:—

> Read *Homer* once, and you can read no more;
> For all Books else appear so mean, so poor,
> Verse will seem Prose; but still persist to read,
> And *Homer* will be all the Books you need[1].

---

[1] John Sheffield, Duke of Buckingham, *An Essay upon Poetry* (1682), *Works*, i 146, ed. 1723.

ADDENDA.

Multum nuper amisimus. Quint. x i 90.

THE veteran historian of Greek philosophy, Eduard Zeller (1814
—1908), a native of Würtemberg, was educated at
the seminary of Maulbronn and at the universities
Zeller
of Tübingen and Berlin. After he had held professorships of
Theology at Bern and at Marburg, the liberality of his opinions
led to his being transferred to the Faculty of Philosophy, and he
filled a professorship in that Faculty for ten years at Heidelberg
(1862–72) and for twenty-two in Berlin (1872–94). Even in his
life-time he received the distinction of a statue outside the Bran-
denburger Thor, the counterpart in Berlin of the *Propylaea* at
Athens. The evening of his days he spent at Stuttgart, the
capital of the land that gave him birth. He is remembered as
the author of the standard work in three volumes on the 'Philosophy of the Greeks'[1], together with an outline of that subject
in a single volume[2]. His principal work was preceded by his
Platonische Studien (1839), and followed by his annotated
translation of Plato's *Symposium*, by his collected *Vorträge* and
Abhandlungen[3], and by a volume on 'Religion and Philosophy
among the Romans' (1866). One of his numerous subsequent
publications on questions connected with the history of Greek
philosophy[4] discusses Dr Henry Jackson's papers on Plato's
earlier and later theory of ideas; and the closing words of the
paper, in which Dr Jackson, in opposition to Bonitz and Zeller,

---

[1] 1844–52; vol. i[5], 1902; ii[4], 1889; iii[4], 1902; E.T. in 6 vols. (1868–
97).   [2] 1883; 1905[7].

[3] 3 vols i, 1865, '75[2]; ii, '77; iii, '84.

[4] *S. Ber.* Berlin Acad. 1887, 197—220 (Bursian lxvii 43); list in Index
to Bursian's *Jahresb.* 1873–95.

maintains that the *Philebus* was later than the *Republic*, may serve as an appropriate conclusion to this brief notice of the historian of Greek philosophy:—

'As I have found myself throughout in antagonism to two great scholars who are honoured wherever Plato is studied, it seems fitting that the last words of this paper should express the admiring gratitude which I feel toward Eduard Zeller and Hermann Bonitz'[1].

Berlin was the life-long home of the classical scholar and **Kirchhoff** epigraphist, Adolf Kirchhoff (1826—1908), who became a member of the Academy in 1860 and a professor five years later.   As a textual critic he is best known as an editor of Aeschylus[2] and Euripides[3] and Plotinus[4], and of the Pseudo-Xenophontic treatise on the constitution of Athens[5]. The *Odyssey* he regarded as the work of three poets:—the authors of (1) the 'Return of Odysseus', and (2) the hero's adventures after his return to Ithaca, whose 'older redaction' of the poem (before 800 B.C.) was completed (about 600) by a third poet, the author of the adventures of Telemachus[6].   He discussed the origin of Hesiod's *Works and Days* in connexion with a critical text of that poem[7].   He also published papers on the date of the history of Herodotus[8], on the text of Thucydides[9] and the documents quoted by the historian[10], and on the redaction of the *De Corona* of Demosthenes[11].   As an eminent epigraphist, he was associated with Aufrecht in an important work on the Umbrian inscriptions (1849–51); he also wrote on the *tabula Bantina* (1853), and edited part of the fourth volume of the *Corpus Inscriptionum Graecarum* (1859), and the whole of the first volume of the *Corpus Inscriptionum Atticarum* (1873).   His 'Studies on the Greek Alphabet' (1863) attained a fourth edition in 1887[12].

---

[1] *Journal of Philology*, x 298 (1881).

[2] 1881 ; list of emendations in Bursian, xxvi 5.

[3] 1855 ; 1867–8.   [4] 1856.   [5] 1874 ; 1881.

[6] *Die Homerische Odyssee* etc., 1859, 1879 (Bursian, xxvi 270—295); *Die Composition der Odyssee*, 1869 ; Jebb's *Homer*, 129—131.

[7] *Hesiodos' Mahnlieder an Perses* (1889).   [8] 1868 ; 1878.

[9] *Hermes*, xii (1877) 368—381.   [10] Berlin, 1895.

[11] Berlin *Abhandl.* (1875) 59–99.

[12] On his work in connexion with the Berlin Academy, see Wilamowitz' *Nachruf* (1908).

Another eminent epigraphist, Wilhelm Dittenberger (1840— 1906), who began his career at Göttingen with a dissertation *De Ephebis Atticis* (1863), was professor **Dittenberger** at Halle for the last thirty-three years of his life. In the *Corpus Inscriptionum Atticarum*, he edited the volume containing the inscriptions of the Roman age (1878—82), and in the *Corpus Inscriptionum Graecarum* part of those of Northern Greece (1892 –7), while his comprehensive *Sylloge* of select inscriptions (1883) attained a second edition in 1898—1901, which was soon followed by his selections from the Greek inscriptions of the East (1903–5). As a boy at Weimar and as a student at Göttingen, he had been under the immediate influence of Sauppe. In the course of his preparation of no less than eleven editions of Kraner's commentary, he incidentally became a specialist on Caesar, *De Bello Gallico*; but he is far better known as an editor of important collections of Greek inscriptions. He regarded their study, not as an end in itself, but as a means for the attainment of a more accurate knowledge of the history and the public life of ancient Greece. He was specially interested in the *Politics*, as well as the *Metaphysics* and *De Anima* of Aristotle, and in the minute study of the style and language of Aristotle and Plato. His paper on the linguistic criteria for determining the chronology of the Platonic dialogues[1] was followed by similar investigations on the part of M. Schanz, C. Ritter, and W. Lutoslawski. His examination of the speeches ascribed to Antiphon led to his rejecting the *Tetralogies* on legal as well as stylistic grounds[2].

Greek Epigraphy was one of the branches of learning ably represented in Austria by Wilhelm von Hartel (1839—1907), who was educated in Prag, and who **Hartel** studied in Vienna[3], where he was appointed to an extraordinary professorship in 1869. He elaborately examined the prosody of the Homeric poems, including the statistics of the observance and the neglect of the *digamma*[4], discussed the text of Theognis

---

[1] *Hermes*, xvi (1881), 321—345.

[2] *Hermes*, xxxi f, xl (1896 f, 1905). See esp. Wissowa in *Biogr. Jahrb.* 1908, 1—52.

[3] Under Bonitz and Vahlen.

[4] *S. Ber.* Vienna Acad. vols. 68, 76, 78 (1871–4). In his earliest papers

and of Phaedrus[1], and summed up his researches on the constitutional customs of Athens in an important series of *Studien* in
1887–8[2]. He published an important Greek papyrus in the
collection acquired by the Archduke Rainer. He also produced
editions of Eutropius and of Cyprian, and was the general editor
of the Vienna series of the Latin Fathers. As Rector of his
university in 1890, he delivered a comprehensive discourse on
the problems and aims of the study of classical philology[3]. In
1896 the completion of his 35th year of service as a professor
was celebrated by the publication of the *Serta Harteliana*, with
his portrait as the frontispiece. During the last five of those
years he was also Director of the *Hofbibliothek*, and, in that
capacity, published a facsimile of the *Tabula Peutingeriana*. He
did much towards promoting the union, not only of the German
Academies, but also of the Academies of Europe; and, towards
the close of his life, he was for five years the Austrian Minister of
Education[4].

Classical archaeology suffered a severe loss by the early death
of Adolf Furtwängler (1853—1907), who had
studied at the universities of Freiburg and Leipzig,
and (under Brunn) in Munich. It was Brunn who impressed him
with the supreme importance of a first-hand knowledge of the
works of ancient art, and thus enabled him to restore the traditions
of Winckelmann. He also owed much to the influence of the
Italian art-critic, Morelli. He took a prominent part in the
excavations at Olympia, and, after a brief stay at Bonn, was
attached in 1884 to the Museum in Berlin, where he held a
professorship until he was called in 1891 to fill the Chair vacated
by Brunn. As an enthusiastic and stimulating lecturer he
attracted students from every quarter of the civilised world. He
had the mastery of an expert in the departments of vases, gems

he had discussed the origin of the *Odyssey* (*Zeitschr. für Oesterr. Gymn.*,
1864–5).

[1] *Wiener Studien*, i (1879), vii (1889).

[2] *Studien über attisches Staatsrecht und Urkundenwesen*; see also *Demos-
thenische Anträge* in Mommsen Comm. (1877), 518–36, and *Dem. Studien* in
S. Ber. of Vienna Acad. 1877–8.

[3] *Ueber Aufgaben und Ziele der kl. Philologie*.

[4] See esp. Engelbrecht in *Biogr. Jahrb.* 1908, 75—107, with bibliography.

and works of sculpture; he was an original discoverer in the domain of numismatics; and a constructor of catalogues that bore the stamp of his own genius. He found in Roman copies the materials for recovering some of the lost master-pieces of Greek sculpture, and, finally, he was admirably successful as an excavator. It was at Munich that he first made his mark as the author of 'Eros in vase-paintings' (1874). In collaboration with Löschcke, he produced two important works on Mycenaean vases. He also published masterly catalogues of the Berlin vases, the antiques in the Sabouroff and Somzée collections, as well as the bronzes of Olympia and the marbles of Munich. His 'Masterpieces of Greek Sculpture' (1893) was promptly translated into English[1]. The modern knowledge of ancient gems rests mainly on the three vast volumes of his great work on the subject (1900). In Greece he explored Aegina, Orchomenos and Amyclae. It was at Amyclae that he caught the germs of the malady which brought him to an early grave. At Aegina, as the result of excavations begun in 1901, he discovered inscriptions which led him to identify the so-called temple of Zeus or Athena as the shrine of Aphaia, a local counterpart of Artemis. He also discovered fresh fragments of the famous pediments, and proposed a completely new arrangement of the figures which they contained[2]. His exploration of Aegina was the theme of his latest work, and it was soon after his last visit to that island that he met his end in Athens, falling on Greek soil as a martyr (like K. O. Müller and Charles Lenormant) to the cause of classical archaeology. He was an eager, and even passionate controversialist; his great discoveries and the results of his stimulating teaching remain, but his fighting days are done:—

'The great, the fierce Achilles fights no more'[3].

Latin scholarship laments the loss of Franz Bücheler (1837—1908), a student of Bonn, who, after holding professorships at Freiburg and Greifswald, was pro-

Bücheler

[1] Ed. E. Sellers (1895).

[2] *Aegina, das Heiligtum der Aphaia*, 1906 ; cp. *Cl. Rev.* xx 327 f.

[3] *The Times*,...Oct. 1907; see esp. Solomon Reinach, in *Gazette des Beaux-Arts, Supplément* 19 Oct., 309 f; also Bulle, in Beilage to *Allgemeine Zeitung*, Munich, 23 Oct.; Percy Gardner, in *Cl. Rev.* xxi 251 f; Studniczka, in *Neue Jahrb.* 1908 (1) 1—6, with portrait.

fessor in his first university for the last 38 years of his life. His editions of Frontinus, *On Aqueducts*, and of the *Pervigilium Veneris*, were followed in 1862 by the first of his critical editions of Petronius, and by his recensions of the *Homeric Hymn to Demeter* and of the remains of Q. Cicero (1869). His brief monograph on the Latin Declensions and Conjugations (1862), expanded by Havet in French (1875), was thence re-edited by Windekinde in German (1879). In 1886 and 1893 he produced the second and third editions of Jahn's Persius, Juvenal and Sulpicia; in 1895 the *Carmina Latina Epigraphica*. He was also a specialist in the dialects of ancient Italy. His scattered researches on the Iguvine inscriptions were collected and completed in his *Umbrica* (1883), and Oscan and Pelignian inscriptions were repeatedly elucidated by his skill. While he was mainly a Latin scholar, Greek was ably represented in the important work on the 'Laws of Gortyn'[1], in which he was associated with Zitelmann (1885), and in his edition of Herondas (1892). He was the devoted friend of his distinguished colleague Usener, in whose memory he delivered a funeral oration in 1906. In the same year, the 'golden jubilee' of his doctorate was celebrated at Bonn, when the scholars of Europe subscribed in his honour more than 8000 marks, about half of which was expended on a bronze bust, while the rest was devoted by Bücheler himself to forming a fund for encouraging scholars of Bonn to take part in the Latin *Thesaurus* and also in the proposed *Thesaurus* of Greek.

Ludwig von Schwabe (1835—1908), who studied at his birthplace, Giessen, and also at Göttingen, held a professorship at the former university, and, after representing classical archaeology for a time at Dorpat, returned to fill the Chair of Classical Philology at Tübingen. He is best known for his work on Catullus,—his *Quaestiones* of 1862, and his edition of 1886 which includes an excellent index. It was in honour of the philological congress at Tübingen that he published

Schwabe

---

[1] *Franz Bücheler's Goldenes Doktorjubiläum*, reprint from *Bonner Zeitung*, 29 Apr. 1906; photograph of bust presented to all subscribers (*c.* 570). See also Usener, in *Bonner Zeitung*, 25 Apr. 1895, and F. Marx, in *Neue Jahrb.* 1908 (1) 358—364, with portrait. Cp. *A. J. P.* xxix 247.

a paper on Musaeus, in which he conclusively proved that the author of *Hero and Leander* was, in metre, prosody, accentuation and phraseology, an imitator of Nonnus (1876). The poem, which the elder Scaliger regarded as the work of the ancient Athenian bard, was thus finally placed among the latest products of Greek literature.

Brilliancy of style, combined with a sympathetic insight into Latin literature and a genuine interest in Roman archaeology, was the leading characteristic of Gaston Boissier (1823—1908). Born amid the memorials of Roman civilisation at Nîmes, he became a classical professor in 1847 at his native place, and ten years later in Paris, where he rose to the distinguished position of professor of Latin literature at the Collège de France (1865), and Member of the French Academy and the Academy of Inscriptions in 1876 and 1886 respectively. His early writings on Attius and Varro (1857–61) were surpassed in fame by those on Cicero's *Letters*, and in particular by that on 'Cicero and his friends' (1865, 1892⁹), with its accurate and life-like portraits of the orator and his great contemporaries. His subsequent works dealt with 'Roman religion from Augustus to the Antonines' and 'the Opposition under the Caesars' (1874–5). His work on Tacitus, with an appendix on Martial (ed. 2, 1904), was exceeded in importance by his admirable volumes entitled *La Fin du Paganisme* (1891). As a felicitous restorer of the old Roman world, he attained the highest degree of success in his *Promenades archéologiques* on Rome and Pompeii (1880), followed by Horace and Virgil (1886), and *L'Afrique Romaine* (1895)[1]. The present writer vividly remembers being part of the large audience at the Collège de France, during one of Boissier's lectures on the Letters of St Augustine, and also being accompanied by the *Nouvelles Promenades* during a solitary ramble near the site of Horace's Sabine farm in the valley of the Digentia.

Greek literature was well represented by Amédée Hauvette (1856—1908), in his early days a skilful writer of original

Boissier

---

[1] Cp. *La Grande Encycl.* s.v.; *Athenaeum*, 13 June, 1908; and Salomon Reinach, in *Revue archéologique*, Mai—Juin. The *Mélanges Boissier* (with a portrait) were published in his honour in 1903.

Latin verse, who entered the School of Athens in 1878, visited
Ionia and Caria, Lesbos and Cos, and took part
in the archaeological exploration of Delos. He
was the first to write a paper on the small copy of the Athena
Parthenos discovered near the Varvakeion[1]. In 1885 he published
his valuable constitutional treatises on the Athenian *Strategi*[2] and
on the King-Archon. The literature of Greece was, however, the
main theme of his lectures in Paris. A second visit to Hellenic
lands was followed by his attractive volume on 'Herodotus, as
the historian of the Medic wars'. He also published learned and
interesting monographs on Simonides, Archilochus, and Callimachus, which can be studied with advantage by the side of the
comprehensive volumes on Greek Literature by the brothers
Croiset[3].

Hauvette

We turn in conclusion to our latest loss in our own land.
Walter George Headlam, of Harrow and of King's
College, Cambridge (1866—1908), gave early
promise of his distinction as a composer of Greek
verse. As Fellow and Lecturer of King's, he devoted not a few
years of his brief life to emending and translating Aeschylus, and
a brilliant passage from this translation was quoted in his memorable praelection of January, 1906. He also collected a large
mass of materials for the illustration of the Mimes of Herondas.
On the death of Sir Richard Jebb, he was entrusted with the
revision and completion of that scholar's edition of the Fragments
of Sophocles. His aptitude for emendation was exercised from
time to time on the text of Greek authors of all ages, whether
writers of prose or of verse[4]. He had a special gift for the
elucidation of Greek lyrical metres, while his volume of verse-
translations from Greek into English, and from English into
Greek, gave signal proof of his exquisite taste as a sympathetic
interpreter and a felicitous imitator of the Greek poets[5]. Only

Walter Headlam

---

[1] *B. C. H.* v 54—63.　　　[2] *Bibl. des Écoles françaises*, no. 41.

[3] S. Reinach in *Rev. Arch.* 1908, 282–4; cp. *Rev. Int. de l'Enseignement*,
170 f, and *Rev. des Études grecques*, 1—12.

[4] *Journal of Philology*, xx 294 f, xxi 75 f, xxiii 260 f, xxvi 233, xxx 290 f;
Class. Rev. xiii 3 f, etc.; *Restorations of Menander* (1908).

[5] *A Book of Greek Verse* (1907); cp. *Meleager* (1900) and contributions to
Cambridge Compositions (1899).

nine days before his death, he had the pleasure of meeting Wilamowitz, who, in the course of his brief visit to Cambridge, said of some of Walter Headlam's Greek verses that, if they had been discovered in an Egyptian papyrus, they would immediately have been recognised by all scholars as true Greek poetry[1]. Many of his happiest renderings were inspired by the poets of the Greek Anthology. In the words of one of those poets, we may say of him, as of few besides, that, so long as he survived the Cambridge composer of the Pindaric ode to Bologna[2], some echoes of the old Greek music could still be heard :—

> ἦν γὰρ ἔτι προτέρων μελέων ὀλίγη τις ἀπορρώξ,
> ἐν σαῖς σωζομένη καὶ φρεσὶ καὶ παλάμαις.

'Some little spark of ancient song,
    Some fragment still
Was left us, lingering in thy soul
    And in thy skill'[3].

---

[1] *The Times*, 22 June, 1908 ; cp. *Athenaeum*, June 27.

[2] p. 414 *supra*.

[3] *A Book of Greek Verse*, 147, from Leontius in *Anth. Pal.* vii (*Epigrammata Sepulcralia*) 571.

INDEX